T0214421

Lecture Notes in Computer Science   **11318**

Commenced Publication in 1973
Founding and Former Series Editors:
Gerhard Goos, Juris Hartmanis, and Jan van Leeuwen

More information about this series at http://www.springer.com/series/7409

Rebecca Rouse · Hartmut Koenitz
Mads Haahr (Eds.)

Interactive Storytelling

11th International Conference
on Interactive Digital Storytelling, ICIDS 2018
Dublin, Ireland, December 5–8, 2018
Proceedings

Springer

Editors
Rebecca Rouse
Rensselaer Polytechnic Institute
Troy, NY, USA

Mads Haahr ⓘ
Trinity College Dublin
Dublin, Ireland

Hartmut Koenitz ⓘ
University of the Arts Utrecht
Utrecht, The Netherlands

ISSN 0302-9743   ISSN 1611-3349   (electronic)
Lecture Notes in Computer Science
ISBN 978-3-030-04027-7   ISBN 978-3-030-04028-4   (eBook)
https://doi.org/10.1007/978-3-030-04028-4

Library of Congress Control Number: 2018960679

LNCS Sublibrary: SL3 – Information Systems and Applications, incl. Internet/Web, and HCI

This Springer imprint is published by the registered company Springer Nature Switzerland AG
The registered company address is: Gewerbestrasse 11, 6330 Cham, Switzerland

Preface

Authoring Our Own Disciplinary Identity as the Interactive Digital Narrative Field Matures

"Who are you?" said the Caterpillar.
This was not an encouraging opening for a conversation.
-Alice's Adventures in Wonderland, by Lewis Carroll

ICIDS is the premier international venue for sharing research and practice in interactive digital narrative (IDN) and related work across industry and academia from intersecting fields such as narrative and literary studies, computational linguistics, artificial intelligence, and procedural generation, and media studies, as well as related research in games, mixed reality, and interactive art and fiction. This volume contains the proceedings of ICIDS 2018 — the 11th International Conference on Interactive Digital Storytelling, held at Trinity College Dublin, Ireland, December 5–8. It collects the contributions to the conference, as full papers, short papers, demos, workshops, and papers of the doctoral consortium. The international art exhibition, a tradition since the beginning of the conference, became formalized in 2013 and now includes a catalogue and accompanying scholarship published as a separate volume.

Entering its second decade, a major development for ICIDS is the inauguration of a professional society to support the further growth of the community and encourage thoughtful and intentional collaborative work around the project of establishing IDN as a discipline. The new society is ARDIN: the Association for Research in Digital Interactive Narrative (http://ardin.online) and has been formally incorporated in Amsterdam, The Netherlands, as a non-profit organization. ARDIN's mission is to support research in IDN across a broad range of forms, including video and computer games, interactive documentaries, interactive fiction, journalistic "interactives," art projects, educational titles, transmedia, virtual reality and augmented reality, and emerging novel forms of IDN we have yet to imagine.

ARDIN provides a home for our interdisciplinary community and for a variety of activities that connect, support, grow, and validate the IDN discipline. The ICIDS conference represents a core activity of the community, and in the future will be complemented by a range of additional services such as an ARDIN newsletter, job posting board, support for local gatherings, additional conferences, publication opportunities, research fellowships, and academic and professional awards. This broad vision represents the ambition of ARDIN, and forms the initial plan for the ongoing project of developing the association, which includes local ARDIN affiliates and SIGs (special interest groups) as possibilities for the future. Modeled on successful organizational structures employed by associations such as DIGRA, ELO, and SASDG, ARDIN will hold regular general meetings at the ICIDS conference, where all business will be discussed in a public, democratic forum.

What can we gain by crafting our own narrative, and intentionally forming ourselves as a discipline? We can gain a common footing, which while debated (debate is inherent within all disciplines, and necessary for disciplinary health) would allow us to develop a shared understanding of our objects of study, of vocabulary and categories and of areas in need of attention. We can also decide what counts in terms of rigor, quality, and expertise in the field, both in theory and practice, and in research that blends both approaches. This also means an opportunity to ensure scholarly recognition for the kinds of activities that find no representation in the evaluation schemes of older disciplines. While we collectively develop our own standards, we should be keenly aware of the fraught history of rigor, as has been discussed by engineering studies scholar Donna Riley. In developing our own standards and values for IDN as a discipline in a deliberate and considered manner, we can push back against the history of rigor as a weapon wielded for exclusion of marginalized voices under the guise of "merit," to develop more inclusive and forward-looking disciplinary practices.

Even as we move toward disciplining, IDN will of course continue to intersect and collaborate with other fields in productive ways. A key advantage will be a new ability to also turn inward, using our own understanding, vocabulary, and canon to both analyze and produce works. In particular, we know that the games lens is not sufficient for understanding IDN, just as the AI lens and literature lens are also lacking as a comprehensive, nuanced understanding of IDN.

Reflecting Janet Murray's inspired call for a "kaleidoscopic" approach to IDN as a discipline, which is articulated in the Foreword to this volume, we likewise suggest a way forward that values the complexity inherent in IDN, both as a possibility for what Murray discuss as "flexibility of mind," as well as the generative possibilities for IDN to represent and address the increasing social and cultural complexity of our world. The current impulse in the IDN community to come together via ARDIN reflects not only the many decades of progress in the field, but also the current cultural moment of profound and dangerous fragmentation, and a deep desire to ameliorate that social fracture with a move toward a unity that recognizes multiplicity and honors difference, while still seeking common understanding.

We intend for ARDIN to support the evolution of the IDN community in a self-conscious, reflective manner, and in particular to preserve the welcoming "big tent" qualities of the community, especially when reaching out to further communities and engaging areas in which we may have had blind spots in the past. For example, it was pointed out at the community roundtable at the close of last year's conference that the group had very little representation from eastern Europe. This year, we started to address this blind spot by connecting to the "Zip-Scene Conference — Analogue and Digital Immersive Environments" organized by Ágnes Karolina Bakk at the Moholy-Nagy University of Art and Design in Budapest. Concretely, this means coordination of dates, call for papers, as well as the presentation of results such as the Best Paper Award from Zip-Scene being shared at ICIDS. We wish for such connections to proliferate.

In collaboration with the ICIDS Steering Committee, we have developed a new review process, implemented for the first time this year. This review process ensured double-blind reviews, with each submission receiving three reviews, provided by Program Committee members, as well as a summarizing meta-review, provided by associate program chairs. To encourage specific, thorough, and constructive reviews, we designed and implemented a new review form and guidelines. We also provided authors with the ability to comment on the reviews as a further check on the fairness and quality of the process. To encourage and recognize quality across all categories of submissions, in addition to the traditional Best Paper Award given to full papers, we have added awards for Best Short Paper, Best Poster, and Best Demo. While the review process continues to evolve, we are encouraged by the many positive comments we received, and we will recognize the hard work of our Program Committee with the Best Reviewer Award, also new this year. We are extremely grateful to the members of the Program Committee, and thank all of them for their dedication and hard work, and in particular the associate chairs for making this new process possible: Marguerite Barry, Mark Bernstein, Maria Engberg, Joshua Fisher, Chris Hales, Charlie Hargood, Sandy Louchart, Lara Martin, Alex Mitchell, Frank Nack, Christian Roth, James Ryan, Marie Laure Ryan, Benjamin Samuel, Mariet Theune, David Thue, and Maurice Suckling.

In addition to implementing this new review process, we also achieved a record number of 119 submissions across all categories this year. Out of the 56 submitted full papers, we selected 20 full papers for inclusion (an acceptance rate of 35%), and from the 29 submitted short papers, we chose 16 short papers for inclusion (an acceptance rate of 55%). In addition, we selected 17 poster submissions, 11 demos, four as workshops, and 11 doctoral consortium contributions. The ICIDS 2018 program featured research from 181 scholars, with affiliations at 66 institutions and 25 countries worldwide.

This year's accepted contributions have been arranged in this volume in eight sections under the parent heading of "Interactive Digital Narrative Studies: Analyses and Practices." Section 1: **The Future of the Discipline** includes papers addressing the current milestone moment in the IDN community in different ways — from the viewpoint of history, looking forward to the future, and even through a satirical lens on IDN and the power of anti-narrative forces in society. Submissions in Section 2: **Theory and Analysis** provide a collection of critical and analytical frameworks and taxonomies for understanding the field at a range of scales, from the discussion of the micro-genre of "storylets" to methods for sharing IDN design knowledge across the community. This section also includes both qualitative and quantitative analyses of IDN user (or reader, player, or interactor) responses and reception, including a range of foci from interpretation to cognition. Sections 3, 4, and 5: **Practices in Games, Virtual Reality, and Theater and Performance**, respectively, present a selection of works squarely situated in the maturing IDN discipline that connect with these adjacent disciplines. Section 6: **Generative and Assistive Tools and Techniques** and Section 7: **Development and Analysis of Authoring Tools** include research on narrative and plot generation, improvisatory computational techniques, conflict detection, and robotic storytelling, as well as novel authoring systems and critical analysis of authoring tools and systems, both at the case-study level and with a broader view across the IDN field at large. Finally, submissions in Section 8: **Impact in Culture and Society** focus on the ways in which IDN research resonates in broader contexts, beyond the academic field or industry. These works discuss research in IDN and ethics, including gaps in participation within the field itself, case studies on IDN at cultural heritage sites and museums, IDN for change, and IDN in current complex contexts such as the global migration crisis. This final section was developed as a new category for the conference this year, in recognition of the advancement of IDN as a discipline with effects in the larger world, and in an attempt to begin to gather scholarship that critically reflects on the entanglement of impacts and roles of the IDN discipline in the wider world.

Looking to the future, the IDN field presents us with many compelling horizons, both in pure research as well as in cultural and social contexts, and across a variety of industry applications. The record number of submissions received at the ICIDS conference this year is also a testimony to the growing interest in the field. ARDIN is poised to further increase the visibility and reach of research in IDN. Building on Janet Murray's powerful metaphor of the kaleidoscope, we invite readers to take this entire volume as "one turn of the kaleidoscope," one instance, one temporary assemblage of the intriguing research in IDN, and an exciting herald of things yet to come.

Image Credits
Mirjam Palosaari Eladhari

October 2018

Rebecca Rouse
Hartmut Koenitz

Organization

General Chair

Mads Haahr   Trinity College Dublin, Ireland

Program Chairs

Hartmut Koenitz   HKU University of the Arts, The Netherlands
Rebecca Rouse   Rensselaer Polytechnic Institute, USA

Local Chairs

Katja Zibrek   Trinity College Dublin, Ireland
Kelly McErlean   Dundalk Institute of Technology, Ireland

Art Chairs

Lissa Holloway-Attaway   University of Skövde, Sweden
Néill O'Dwyer   Trinity College Dublin, Ireland

Demo and Workshop Chairs

James Ryan   University of Calfornia, Santa Cruz, USA
Sandy Louchart   Glasgow School of Art, UK

Doctoral Consortium Chairs

Nuno Jardim Nunes   University of Lisbon, Portugal
Geoff Kauman   Carnegie-Mellon University, USA

Social Media Chair

Diğdem Sezen   Istanbul University, Turkey

Associate Chairs

Marguerite Barry   University College Dublin, Ireland
Mark Bernstein   Eastgate Systems, Inc., USA
Maria Engberg   Malmö University, Sweden
Joshua Fisher   Georgia Institute of Technology, USA
Chris Hales   Liepaja University/Independent, UK
Charlie Hargood   Bournemouth University, UK

Lara Martin   Georgia Institute of Technology, USA
Alex Mitchell   National University of Singapore, Singapore
Frank Nack   University of Amsterdam, The Netherlands
Christian Roth   HKU University of the Arts Utrecht, The Netherlands
Marie-Laure Ryan   Independent Scholar, USA
Benjamin Samuel   University of New Orleans, USA
Maurice Suckling   Rensselaer Polytechnic Institute, USA
Mariet Theune   University of Twente, The Netherlands
David Thue   Reykjavik University, Iceland

Program Committee

Espen Aarseth   IT University of Copenhagen, Denmark
Ruth Aylett   Heriot-Watt University, UK
Julio Bahamon   UNC Charlotte, USA
Alok Baikadi   Pearson, USA
Ágnes Karolina Bakk   Moholy-Nagy University of Art and Design/Sapientia
                               Hungarian University of Transylvania, Hungary
Jonathan Barbara   Saint Martin's Institute of Higher Education, UK
Rafael Bidarra   Delft University of Technology, The Netherlands
Wolfgang Broll   Ilmenau University of Technology, Germany
Luis Emilio Bruni   Aalborg University, Denmark
Daniel Buzzo   University of the West of England, UK
Beth Cardier   Sirius-Beta, USA
Gail Carmichael   Shopify, Canada
Marc Cavazza   University of Greenwich, UK
Fanfan Chen   National Dong Hwa University, Taiwan
Shauna Concannon   University of York, UK
Chris Crawford   Storytron, USA
Brian de Lint   Utrecht University, The Netherlands
Andrea Di Pastena   Utrecht University, The Netherlands
Teun Dubbelman   HKU University of the Arts Utrecht, The Netherlands
Gabriele Ferri   Amsterdam University of Applied Sciences,
                               The Netherlands
Mark Finlayson   Florida International University, USA
Andrew Gordon   University of Southern California, USA
Mads Haahr   Trinity College Dublin, Ireland
Sarah Harmon   UCSC, USA
Lissa Holloway-Attaway   University of Skövde, Sweden
Ichiro Ide   Nagoya University, Japan
Ido Aharon Iurgel   Rhein-Waal Hochschule, Germany
Dennis Jansen   Utrecht University, The Netherlands
Tom Jenkins   Georgia Institute of Technology, USA
Arnav Jhala   University of California, Santa Cruz, USA
Hartmut Koenitz   HKU University of the Arts Utrecht, The Netherlands
Ben Kybartas   McGill University, Canada

James Lester	North Carolina State University, USA
Boyang Li	Liulishuo Silicon Valley AI Lab, USA
Sandy Louchart	Glasgow School of Art, UK
Gonzalo Mendez	Universidad Complutense de Madrid, Spain
Nick Montfort	Massachusetts Institute of Technology, USA
Amanda Moss	Utrecht University, The Netherlands
Bradford Mott	North Carolina State University, USA
Paul Mulholland	The Open University, UK
Eric Murnane	University of Central Florida, USA
John Murray	University of California, Santa Cruz, USA
Mark J. Nelson	Falmouth University, UK
Michael Nitsche	Georgia Institute of Technology, USA
Neil O'Dwyer	Trinity College Dublin, Ireland
Federico Peinado	Universidad Complutense de Madrid, Spain
Andrew Perkis	Norwegian University of Science and Technology, Norway
Christopher Purdy	Georgia Institute of Technology, USA
Justus Robertson	North Carolina State University, USA
Melissa Roemmele	University of Southern California, USA
Remi Ronfard	Inria, France
Rebecca Rouse	Rensselaer Polytechnic Institute, USA
James Ryan	University of California, Santa Cruz, USA
Digdem Sezen	Istanbul University, Turkey
Tonguc Sezen	Rhein-Waal Hochschule, Germany
Yotam Shibolet	Utrecht University, The Netherlands
Emily Short	Freelance, UK
Mei Si	Rensselaer Polytechnic Institute, USA
Davy Smith	University of York, UK
Ulrike Spierling	RheinMain University of Applied Sciences, Germany
Kaoru Sumi	Future University Hakodate, Japan
Nicolas Szilas	TECFA-FPSE, University of Geneva, Switzerland
Emmett Tomai	University of Texas Rio Grande Valley, USA
Mirjam Vosmeer	Hogeschool van Amsterdam, The Netherlands
Eric Walsh	Rensselaer Polytechnic Institute, USA
Noah Wardrip-Fruin	University of California, Santa Cruz, USA
Stephen Ware	University of New Orleans, USA
Nelson Zagalo	University of Aveiro, Portugal

Additional Reviewers

Zev Battad	Rensselaer Polytechnic Institute, USA
Morteza Behrooz	University of California, Santa Cruz, USA
Nicolas Fischöder	Rhein-Waal Hochschule, Germany
Swen Gaudl	Falmouth University, UK

Max Kreminski   University of California, Santa Cruz, USA
Thomas Laubach   Rhein-Waal Hochschule, Germany
George Palamas   Aalborg University, Denmark
Li Zheng   Rensselaer Polytechnic Institute, USA

ICIDS Steering Committee

Luis Emilio Bruni   Aalborg University, Denmark
Gabriele Ferri   Amsterdam University of Applied Sciences,
                           The Netherlands
Andrew Gordon   University of Southern California, USA
Hartmut Koenitz   HKU University of the Arts Utrecht, The Netherlands
Alex Mitchell   National University of Singapore, Singapore
Frank Nack   University of Amsterdam, The Netherlands
Valentina Nisi   Madeira-ITI, University of Madeira, Portugal
Rebecca Rouse   Rensselaer Polytechnic Institute, USA
David Thue   Reykjavik University, Iceland

Contents

Practices in Games

Practices in Virtual Reality

Practices in Theater and Performance

Generative and Assistive Tools and Techniques

Development and Analysis of Authoring Systems

Impacts in Culture and Society

Introduction

Research into Interactive Digital Narrative: A Kaleidoscopic View

Janet H. Murray[✉]

Georgia Tech, Atlanta, GA 30332, USA
jmurray@gatech.edu

Abstract. We are at a milestone moment in the development of the cultural form of Interactive Digital Narrative (IDN), and in the development of the study of IDN as a field of academic research and graduate education. We can date the beginning of the field to the late 1960s with the release of Joseph Weizenbaum's *Eliza* in 1966, and recognize the late 1990s as another turning point when 30 years of diverse development began to coalesce into a recognizable new media practice. For the past 20 years we have seen accelerated growth in theory and practice, but the discourse has been split among contributory fields. With the convening of IDN as the focus of study in its own right, we can address key questions, such as its distinct history, taxonomy, and aesthetics. We can also recognize more clearly our unique challenges in studying a field that is evolving rapidly, and from multiple intersecting genetic strains. We can also articulate and investigate the potential of IDN as an expressive framework for engaging with the most pressing themes of human culture of the 21st century, and as a cognitive scaffold for increasing our individual and collective understanding of complex systems.

Keywords: Interactive Digital Narrative (IDN) · IDN as academic discipline
IDN education · Understanding complex systems

1 Through the Kaleidoscope, and Across the Decades

1.1 Why Kaleidoscopic?

The kaleidoscopic view of the title refers to the many components and potential taxonomies of the artifacts that are the objects of study in this new field. It also refers, more importantly, to the potential of interactive digital narratives (IDNs) to present us with multiform scenarios in which the same events can be understood in multiple contexts and the same starting points can be imagined as giving rise to multiple possible outcomes. More than anything else, it is the possibility of furthering such a multiform, multi-sequential, multi-vocal, narrative practice that makes the recent formation of a dedicated organization for research in IDN, in which theory and practice are closely intertwined, such a promising milestone.

© Springer Nature Switzerland AG 2018
R. Rouse et al. (Eds.): ICIDS 2018, LNCS 11318, pp. 3–17, 2018.
https://doi.org/10.1007/978-3-030-04028-4_1

1.2 This Moment in Temporal Context

Last year at ICIDS 2017 a group of researchers[1] brought forward a proposal for the Association for Research in Digital Interactive Narrative (ARDIN) as a new interdisciplinary/disciplinary home for the study of this emerging cultural form. The proposal was approved and ARDIN exists but now must define itself. Therefore, we are meeting at a generative moment – a moment in which a dispersed population actively explores a common identity, which I expect to involve stressing points of differentiation, from neighboring and overlapping tribes and from one another within this newly affirmed common tribe. I am hoping to add to the creative momentum by framing the promise of this very moment here in Dublin from my own personally situated perspective, using the vantagepoint of career longevity despite lifelong habits of interdisciplinarity to look backwards across five decades of innovation for context, and to apply the insights gained from that view to speculate forward about the future of Digital Interactive Narrative and how it might change from the effects of reframing ICIDS within this new organization. In addition, I will try to recruit you all to collaborate in what I see as the most important common purpose behind such an organization.

I have been a practitioner/theorist of digital media since 1981, when I began designing interactive digital narratives for language learning in an educational computing project funded by the Annenberg Foundation as part of MIT's pioneering Project Athena. This alone would give me a long view of the traditions of IDN, but I also tend to think in relatively deep temporal horizons both personally, through the luck of family longevity which stretches in two generations back to 1881, and from my training in the history of narrative with important milestones extending not just centuries but millennia, starting with Gilgamesh (c 2000 BCE) through the Book of Kells here at this University where we are gathered (9th Century AD) and up through the multi-century development of the English novel, and the century-long plus evolution of storytelling in moving images. Also highly salient to me is the history of the women's movement which I have both studied as a scholar of the English 19th century, and participated in as an American woman of the "baby boomer" generation. This telescopic view of cultural change and aesthetic evolution over long periods of time has turned out to be a fortunate complement to my privileged (though often challenging) situation as a humanist at MIT (from 1971–1999) and then at Georgia Tech (from 1999 to the present), and to the distortion that comes from overvaluing the latest commercial gamble in high tech, billed as a "magic leap" or something similarly suggestive of large profits.

Being able to think of cultural change over long periods of time does not make it easier to predict the pace of change in the adoption of any particular technology (e.g. how long for television to move from analog to digital, or for VR or AR to become a viable consumer product), or much less the success of any particular platform (such as the iPod, the Kindle, or Google Glass), but it has made for some reliable judgments of the long-term direction of change, and of the innovations that, sooner or later, are likely

---

[1] The ICIDS Steering Committee: Luis Emilio Bruni, Gabriele Ferri, Andrew Gordon, Hartmut Koenitz, Alex Mitchell, Frank Nack, Valentina Nisi, Rebecca Rouse, David Thue.

to take root because they serve human need and add to the coherence of the larger medium of all things digital.

From this long-term perspective, the founding of ARDIN in 2018 seems to me like a significant milestone and perhaps even a tipping point, marking a critical mass of human effort around interactive digital narrative and a shared sense of understanding of new possibilities. And whether it turns out to be so or not, it provides a useful opportunity to take stock of the enterprise from this longer term perspective, assuming a kind of metaphorical elevation to pick out a few landmarks ranging across a larger breadth of practice, perhaps, than is visible from the kind of detailed immersion in more immediately relevant practices that we are all called to maintain in order to "keep up" with such a productive area of research and creative practice.

I offer a set of landmarks here as representative, but necessarily arbitrary. Other people or even I myself on another day would choose other specimens. The field is various and every arrangement is partial, but each one contains information that can help us to understand the whole. So I offer this version not as a canon but as one turn of the kaleidoscope.

2   The First Wave

We could indeed start the story of the narrative structures of interactive digital stories with Gilgamesh or the canonical Christian Bible, both of which exist in multiple versions, or with the Talmud, which annotates the Old Testament stories with rabbinical commentary, including interpretations and additional stories, in hypertextual form. Or we could start in the 18th century with *Tristram Shandy,* which interrupts itself and calls attention to its print delivery surface, or the 19th century with *Wuthering Heights* which tells overlapping parts of the same larger story from multiple narrators, or in the 20th Century with Frank Capra's *It's a Wonderful Life* which includes two play-throughs of the protagonist's childhood, or Borges' stories, or the fragmented rule-generated texts of the Oulipo group or from multiple other cultural or media traditions that pre-date computer-based storytelling. Each of these implied genealogies would be a useful spin of the kaleidoscope, assembling artifacts and narrative strategies that speak to one another across media and across time. There are multiple such intersections and genetic strands twining through IDN practice from a rich heritage of sources.

But by dedicating a new research organization to Digital Interactive Narrative we are provided with a very useful demarcation point. We can start with the moment when storytelling begins is interactive and built out of computational bits. We may discover multiple contenders for this moment, but from my perch looking out on the landscape as someone who spent over 25 years at MIT, there is only one candidate. To my mind, digital interactive narrative practice can be traced to 1966 – a little over 50 years ago— when Joseph Weizenbaum's *Eliza* program introduced the first interactive digital character to world [1].

As I have described written elsewhere [2, 3], Eliza succeeds in creating the illusion of a character by virtue of the conversational structure which scripts the interactor into the role of patient to the Eliza, the automated psychotherapist. Weizenbaum did not invent the conversation by trying to recreate an actual therapy interview. He drew on contemporary narrative tropes – the neurotic seeking help and the absurdly "non-directive" therapist who followed the often mocked teachings of Carl Rogers who advocated neutral and echoing responses. It is the interactive equivalent of sketch comedy. *Eliza* was surprisingly effective in creating the illusion of an actual person, causing her creator to have to warn people against accepting the possibility of actual automated therapists [4]. But now we would see her as a weak version of the familiar narrative genre of the chatbot.

This disruptive invention of *Eliza* was followed over the next 25 years by a rich but heavily siloed set of digital narrative communities of practice. Computer science nerds working on mainframes, inspired by dungeons and dragons created *Adventure* [5], which MIT researches expanded with AI techniques to *Zork* [6], which spawned an energized cult of text-adventure games which continues to this day and which sometimes claims the sole right to the descriptor "Interactive Fiction (IF)." One group of such practitioners created a briefly successful story-game company Infocom (1979–1989), whose games introduced technical innovations such as the heartbreaking sacrifice of Floyd the companion robot, which no save-and-replay strategy could prevent (Planetfall [7]), or the second murder that happened at a particular timestep (Deadline [8]) if you did not solve the initial crime by going to the right rooms in the right order. The parser-based stories, based on later authoring systems, were an important entry point for IDN practice of a specialized nature, and its influence can still be seen in the sardonic narrative voice of the "art game" *The Stanley Parable* [9].

In another silo during the first wave of IDN, academics developed hypertext for educational purposes, creating stand-alone systems before Tim Berners-Lee invented the World Wide Web. One of these, *Storyspace* (released 1987) is still maintained by another dedicated company, Eastgate Systems. The aesthetic of Storyspace stories like *Afternoon, A Story* [10] by Michael Joyce (one of the inventors of Storyspace along with Jay David Bolter and John B. Smith) favors associational linking. When we look at the community of practice around Twine today we can place it in a symmetrical kaleidoscopic pattern with the Storyspace community of the late 1980s and early 1990s.

In a more commercial silo, the video game company Sierra On-Line began producing the earliest graphical adventure games starting in 1980 with *Mystery House* [11] and *Wizard and the Princess* [12], the first adventure in their signature, beloved *King's Quest* series. The introduction of graphics into adventure games were greeted at the time by the fan communities around Infocom text adventures and later by hypertext writers in somewhat the same way that the introduction of sound and color were greeted by movie purists. But as Laine Nooney has pointed out, exaggerating these distinctions leads to a distorted history of game development [13]. This is an area where the affirmation of IDN as its own evolving form can provide a useful new perspective, by ignoring questions of "literary" versus "game" pleasures and looking for the development of a repertoire of techniques that support the common pleasures of interactive narrative, and that have been carried forward within story-driven interactive artifacts. Clara Fernandez-Vara's work in tracing the close alignment between story and game mechanics in adventure games provides a useful framework for understanding graphical adventures [14].

During the 1980s and early 1990s, the critical discourse around digital media was as siloed as the different fan communities. Hypertext was embraced by postmodern literary theorists as a subversion of linearity [15]; computer scientists explored formalist approaches to narrative as an extension of the larger effort of creating artificial intelligence by imitating human cognitive processes [16]; Ted Nelson argued for hypertext [17] as an augmentation of human associative thinking, following the example of Vannever Bush [18]; and the pioneering designer-theorist Brenda Laurel applied Aristotle to argue for computer-based interaction as "theater" [19]. In 1992 I taught what I believe was the first university course in interactive narrative (an undergrad/grad course at MIT called *Structure and Interpretation of Non-Linear and Interactive Narrative*, whose name echoed the intro CS course, *Structure and Interpretation of Computer Programming*). Within a few years I was able to teach it using HTML and the new web technologies, but originally the course was based on Apple's desktop application *HyperCard* (1987–1998) (and its clones) as were my own group's interactive video projects of the 1980s and 1990s [20, 21]. *HyperCard* was also the platform for *Myst* [22] a widely successful narrative-driven puzzle game which many saw as a turning point in commercial games as a new media form.

HyperCard, *InForm* (for parser-based fiction), *Storyspace*, and *Director* (which was based on the temporal framework of animation-authoring software and was a forerunner of Flash) are in themselves important milestones to consider in the history of IDN, and part of the context in which we should consider contemporary platform-based groups. Twine practitioners, for example, are often demeaned as unskilled game designers. But when we take the perspective of IDN as a evolving craft developing over multiple decades and highly responsive to the availability of stable authoring and delivery platforms, we can see the Twine community of practice as one of many such groups, which may appear siloed but which over time have collectively produced a rich repertoire of narrative strategies. In addition, game-oriented professional authoring environments like Unity and Unreal, are a rich area for exploration from the perspective of how their affordances constrain and support interactive narrative.

3 A Turning Point in the Late 1990s

3.1 Stories as Simulations

The first 30 years of active IDN development, then, were marked by a diverse and diffuse effort, from isolated Artificial Intelligence projects modeling character and plot to beloved niche gaming traditions like parser-based fiction and adventure games, to educational simulations and experimental interactive videos. Starting around 1997, around the same time that email became a preferred method of communication outside of academic circles, and newspapers were opening their first websites, these separate communities of practice in IDN began to reach critical mass, and books began to appear that were explicitly directed to the active new boundary between games and stories, including my own *Hamlet on the Holodeck: The Future of Narrative in Cyberspace* [2] and Espen Aarseth's *Cybertext* [23]. The Tamagotchi came out the same year, bringing the concept of the interactive character, which had moved from Eliza to chatbots in online multi-player environments, into the mainstream as a bestselling commercial toy. A few years later, Nick Montfort published a definitive history of the parser-based story form [24].

The block-buster success of *The Sims* [25] in 2000 emancipated interactive characters from the confines of adventure conventions and win/lose structure of conventional videogames and transported them into the everyday world, translating the story elements of the bourgeois bildungsroman into interactive procedural form. Moving from inventories of weapons to household appliances meant inventing new conventions of interaction, such as the backrub, and the icon-driven wordless conversation. These innovations should be seen not merely as game mechanics but as part of the growth of conventions for IDN, building on the repetitive feeding and cleaning structure of the *Tamagotchi*. They are not just a refinement of simulation games like *Sim City,* but part of a community of practice that includes works with similar temporal organization of home-and-work, like Molleindustria's "Every Day the Same Dream" [26] which interprets successful bourgeois life of home-commute-job as alienated labor.

Another milestone of the first decade of the 21st century was the commercially and critically successful *BioShock* [27] whose morality-driven multiple endings created a strong sense of dramatic agency in the interactors by making them feel that their decisions had dramatic consequences. Ever since, the creation of morally challenging decisions in narrative-driven games have become an important design strategy that caters to mass audience expectations. Framing IDN as a discipline can motivate scholars to trace this practice backwards and forwards in other digital artifacts, and perhaps to develop a critical vocabulary for describing important distinctions in the structure and expression of the moral physics of interactive narratives.

The open-world games of this period, including the urban gangster mayhem of *Grand Theft Auto3: Liberty City* [28] and the cowboy gunslinger survival challenges of *Red Dead Redemption* [29] would be important objects of study in this regard, for the ambiguous moral physics that evokes pleasure and discomfort from licensing anti-social behavior. They also advance the practice of interactive narrative design by offering the model of an IDN as a fictional landscape with modular genre-driven actions (steal a car, shoot a mountain lion) rather than a series of plot events. In the important critical task of differentiating amongst different manifestations of IDN, open-world games provide important reference points.

Another crucial reference point for such a taxonomy would be *Façade* [30] which announced itself as an "interactive drama." *Façade* is a virtuoso computational object, that generates a story with great variation of individual beats and story structure while maintaining the coherence of each playthrough [31]. It is a crucial milestone in IDN evolution, for what it achieved in its brilliant substitution system of story elements. It is equally important for its failure to create the experience of dramatic agency because of its interaction design which relied upon open input natural language, in mistaken emulation of open world game design. By telling the interactor they could enter anything they pleased in conversation with the two main characters, the designers set the level of expectation for what the system could understand and respond to much too high, making its actual responses, which were the result of great computational complexity but not adequately responsive to the input, seem arbitrary. Among other things to be learned from *Façade,* which remains unmatched in its story generation aspect, is the need for both scripting the computer and scripting the interactor to create the experience of agency.

3.2   The Current Moment

In the second decade of the 21st century where we currently find ourselves, it is harder to see the pattern in the kaleidoscope because the individual pieces are so much larger to us at this close distance. One artifact that looms large to me is no longer playable though it was released in 2014. Emily Short's *Blood and Laurels* [32] was created on an experimental platform called *Versu* that was meant to scaffold AI-enhanced authoring for non-programmers. Short offers a complex narrative structure that is very text-heavy (200,000 words!) and multi-variant, and which invites us to experience its rich story world (a tale of political intrigue in ancient Rome) by playing through all its variants. The achievement of *Blood and Laurels,* which I would rank in importance to that of *Façade* or *The Sims,* though it is not as widely known, is its coherence. The multiplicity of the variations creates the design problem of making sure that the interactor is not confused about where they are in the story, which Short solves by clear parallelism of story beats and a dramatically appropriate division of time steps and story locales – design strategies intrinsic to the diegetic world. She also makes all of the variants the result of the interactor's choices. In addition, Short provides orientation for the interactor at the non-diegetic meta-level with the appropriate use of the game convention of unlocked achievements (Fig. 1).

Fig. 1. Emily Short's *Blood and Laurels* uses the game convention of locked achievements to help the interactor keep track of potential variants, and to excite curiosity about unlocking them

Another important milestone of this period for many people is Anna Antropy's *Dys4* [33] for its use of interaction mechanics associated with games for the narrative purpose of an autobiographical interactive essay. *Dys4ia* is a much simpler artifact, a kind of a memoir focused on the subjective experience of gender non-conformity and of moments in the transition of a trans-gender male-to-female person. Anna Antropy uses retro game conventions to allow the interactor to enact experiences that serve as explicit models (awkwardness in shaving) or abstract metaphors (fitting a Tetris like piece into a non-conforming space) for the situation of being in a body that does not correspond with one's gender identification. Anna Antropy calls this artifact "an autobiographical game" but I would argue that it is better understood as a narrative artifact that uses game mechanics with a striking fluency, making clear that game elements have now passed into general use as a vocabulary for emotional and political expression. Anna Anthropy's easy appropriation of game mechanics to describe a marginalized social experience is of the kind envisioned by Gonzalo Frasca in his 2001 master's thesis "Videogames of the Oppressed" [34] and very similar to the narratives of Tetris players about how that game reflected their frantic state of mind [2]. These ideas were not commonplace at the turn of the century, but twenty years later, abstract game actions are routinely invoked in conversation (e.g. "I feel like I'm playing whack-a-mole!" "This is a real power-up."), and, as *Dys4ia* shows, even in practice, to describe subjective emotional experiences.

Other unmistakable recent milestones that make clear that we are at a new plateau, in the practice of IDN are the celebrated mass market release of *Gone Home* [35], and the whole body of Telltale Games releases (2004–2018), especially the highly successful *The Walking Dead* (2012–18) (initially released 2012 [36], further episodes in the following years). *Gone Home* builds on a tradition begun with *Zork* [6] and elaborated in *Mystery House* [11] from Sierra On-Line, and *Myst* [22] in which a story is revealed through the examination of a space. Telltale's Walking Dead releases provide a model for episodic storytelling, and for creating parallel paths to a canonical story with a shared story world. It also succeeds in structuring moral choices (whom shall I save from the zombies?), and it establishes new conventions for responding to differences in player choices (e.g. "Clementine will remember [you did] that"), while still funneling the plot into the same outcomes.

Although these examples are generally described, and even labelled by their creators, as "games," they cannot be fully understood within that framework. The design challenges they engaged come into clearer focus when they are juxtaposed with one another and contextualized by earlier examples of interactive narrative innovation. They also reward examination as potential sources for future innovation in their refinement, adaptation, and invention of conventions that are not merely "game mechanics" but mechanics of interactions suitable for games but even more suitable for interactive narratives.

4 The Disciplinary Advantage

4.1 Turning the Kaleidoscope

Although the works that may appear particularly salient to me or to other scholars as milestones in IDN may already have been exhaustively analyzed as hypertexts or videogames or feminist/transgender/LGBTQ manifestos, they will reveal new symmetries, across disparate communities of practice when viewed in the new landscape of investigation implied by the founding of a new research organization dedicated to IDN.

When we discuss *Afternoon* or *Myst* or *Gone Home* or *The Walking Dead* in other venues they become part of other discourses – post-modern cultural discourse, legacy media discourse, feminist discourse, or the multiple conversations around game studies. Each of those discourses has its own critical and interpretative vocabulary, and so makes visible different aspects of the same artifact. In game studies in particular, interactive artifacts that prioritize storytelling can be demeaned by a discourse that pits the satisfaction of playing games against the conventional satisfactions of legacy storytelling forms. The popular discourse around games is even more demeaning, dismissing some of the most successful IDNs as "walking simulators." In post-modern contexts interactive fictions are often praised for their disruption of conventional narrative expectations. In other words, IDNs are judged precisely by the elements they have chosen to leave out, and the storytelling itself is often evaluated by unreflected legacy-oriented notions of what a story is.

When we see IDNs as part of older narrative traditions, then the common story patterns are foregrounded – the bildungsroman, the cowboy story. When we see them as contextualized by videogames then the common game patterns are foregrounded, such as acquiring collectables, leveling up, shooting enemies. When we see them through the lens of traditional narratology we are stuck with a notion of story as something that is told (by narrator or camera) rather than enacted by an interactor within a procedural environment. But when we see them as their own tradition we can put our energies into an emerging set of more specific questions, of strategies for creating interactive plot with dramatic compression, procedural characters with readable emotional depths, dramatic segmentation that motivates replay, variation that reinforces immersion, and so on. We can start to recognize canons of critique as well as canons of creativity, and to share vocabulary that will help us to understand better how we can leverage the work that has gone before to foster more expressive creative practices. We have had over 30 years of focused effort in theory and craft and we have convened a global community of practice around this kind of an artifact. We can therefore see the *Eliza, Zork, Mystery House, Myst, The Tamagotchi, The Sims, Façade, BioShock, Dys4ia, Gone Home* and thousands of other interactive digital narratives as part of a diverse but connected community of practice. We can ask evaluative questions appropriate to the aesthetics of digital interactive narrative rather than comparing them to successful games or movies.

The problem of colonization by Games Studies is in itself a sufficient reason for affirming the independence of IDN studies as its own discipline. Interactive Digital Narratives have many features that overlap with videogames, and they are often distributed and labeled as games. But when we establish a discipline around IDN, we are affirming that IDNs are designed and experienced as a distinct, valid, media tradition which deserves its own name and its own focus as a field of study. Creating a professional organization centered on Digital Interactive Narrative takes us out of several tedious and repetitive conversation such as ludology v narratology and games v movies. We turn the kaleidoscope, and see interactive narratives as creating their own patterns, contextualized not by legacy narratives like movies or interactive artifacts like games, but by other digital interactive narratives.

4.2 Aesthetic Vocabulary for IDN

I have written elsewhere [2, 3] about how to create and assess interactive narrative based on an aesthetics rooted in the affordances of the underlying digital medium. But I want to conclude by pointing to a few terms, and to one compelling long-term goal that I see as particularly helpful as an educator and designer [37].

The most important term to evaluate the success of any IDN is "dramatic agency." I have defined agency as

an aesthetic pleasure characteristic of digital environments, which results from the well-formed exploitation of the procedural and participatory properties. When the behavior of the computer is coherent and the results of participation are clear and well motivated, the interactor experiences the pleasure of agency, of making something happen in a dynamically responsive world. The term is meant as a corrective to the inexact use of "interactive" as both a descriptive and an evaluative term.

Dramatic agency is the

experience of **agency** within a procedural and participatory environment that makes use of compelling story elements, such as an adventure game or an interactive narrative. To create dramatic agency the designer must create transparent interaction conventions (like clicking on the image of a garment to put it on the player's avatar) and map them onto actions which suggest rich story possibilities (like donning a magic cloak and suddenly becoming invisible) within clear story stories with dramatically focused episodes (such as, an opportunity to spy on enemy conspirators in a fantasy role playing game).

We can apply this principle to any choice point in an IDN, asking if the interactor has been appropriately motivated by the storyworld to anticipate specific consequences to an action, and whether the interactor has had reason to expect a choice that is not actually provided by the interactive experience. Note that, unlike in a game, an interactor does not have to have the opportunity to find a "winning" or successful choice. The choice does have to be consistent with the moral physics of the story world, so that the consequences, like the "bad" ending of *Myst,* or the inability to prevent the brutal murder of a child in a Telltale *Game of Thrones* [38] episode, makes sense within the fictional universe. Dramatic agency is also unrelated to whether or not we can change the events of the story, since we can experience narrative anticipation and pleasure in a navigational choice, such as from one point of view to another in a story made up of fixed events. The concept of dramatic agency can help us to analyze our own experience as interactors, considering, for example, why abstract presentation of dialog as assembling miniature jigsaw puzzles in *Florence* [39] (Fig. 2), is so satisfying, despite the fact that we have no choice and the narrative never changes.

Fig. 2. In the mobile interactive story Florence (2018) the interactor cannot change the story but they can enact gestures that represent the protagonist's subjective experience. Here she is experiencing making conversation on a first date as a puzzle. As the conversation progresses, the number of puzzle pieces decreases.

A related aesthetic value for a narrative form that affords variation is whether or not it motivates replay and whether the variations are trivial or dramatically meaningful. For example, in *Façade,* we are motivated to try multiple paths in order to find out the secrets of each of the two quarreling partners, secrets that are hinted at but not revealed in other play-throughs. We are also motivated to note the various ways in which the conflict can end, since that comports well with our sense of open possibilities in conflicts with intimate partners, and with our sense of the poignancy of moments in which the way how we behave can bring us closer or farther apart.

In assessing interactive narratives I would suggest that it is useful to avoid the term "non-linear" since it is very hard to design for a negative quality, and in the context of narrative (as against mathematics) it suggests incoherency. Instead I differentiate between legacy formats as "unisequential" and digital formats as potentially "multi-sequential." IDNs may be multisequential whether or not the interactor can play a role in the story world and whether or not they can change the outcome of events, both of which are separate and useful distinctions for which others have proposed useful terms. "Multisequential" is a substitute for "non-linear" that emphases the coherence of all of the paths through a story with variable parts.

"Multiform" is for me a useful way of referring to a story system composed of parameterized elements within a fixed scenario, so that the same overall pattern can produce multiple parallel instantiations. For example, the distinct endings of *Bioshockcl* closely resemble one another but differ in ways that are all the more dramatically powerful because of the underlying parallelism. Emily Short's *Blood and Laurels* makes the most of this sort of well-constructed parallelism, not just for the ending but for multiple episodes of the story.

I bring these terms forward not to insist upon them as prescriptive of practice or critique, but as examples of the kind of vocabulary we need to describe design strategies originating from the desire to tell a story in way that could only be told through interaction and computation.

In addition there are lines of analysis that should be revisited from the perspective of IDN, including authoring systems thought of as specialized for games or hypertext that have served as platforms for storytelling, and artifacts subsumed under "art games" or "interactive videos" or "museum installations" or "location-based games" or "electronic literature" or "augmented reality" that may turn out to have more in common with one other and with commercial narratives when assembled within this context.

4.3 Kaleidoscopic Form

Finally we come to the most promising aspect of reframing IDN as its own cultural form and envisioning the multiple siloed communities of practice as collaborators in a common enterprise: the fostering of more coherent and expressive storytelling.

I have described the process of assembling this new research community as a gathering of its objects of study into new patterns, like beads re-assembled within a kaleidoscope. But the metaphor of the kaleidoscope is also my own vision for the internal structure of each of the IDNs. By moving storytelling from the unisequential genres of print-based novels and conventional films and TV shows to the new digital medium capable of multiform and multisequential genres like procedural scenarios and branching narratives, we open up the possibility of expanding our understanding of the world and our cognitive capacity.

Every external medium, from spoken language to written and printed words to recorded images expands our capacity to share our individual experiences and thoughts, to preserve them over time, and to benefit from our collective understanding by building upon it. Printed books expanded our ability to organize knowledge and to present through fictional and nonfictional narratives sustained descriptions of inter-connected fates and psychological depths. Because of centuries of collective knowledge-creation we now increasingly understand the world as interconnected systems, and we look for the causes of everything from global climate change to specific instances of human suffering in multiple actions by collective and individual actors over time and distance.

IDN offers us a way of representing these interconnected chains of causation in increasingly coherent form, so that we can zoom in and out through time and space and abstraction layers, and across points of view and frameworks of interpretation. Just as print formats have allowed us to create more extensive arguments and refer to them and dispute them with more precision, so digital formats, and particularly interactive digital narratives can allow us to present the same story from multiple points of view and within multiple cultural and social patterns of cause and effect.

Creating such kaleidoscopic story structures even for fantasy worlds and genre fictions with unrealistic characters and events, will be an important component of building such a medium, because it will expand our cognitive capacity, our ability to keep complex systems of cause in effect and contradictory interpretations of the same scenario in mind. It could also foster greater flexibility of mind, by allowing us to see any set of circumstances as a scenario open to recontextualization and change.

I have elsewhere argued for this kaleidoscopic property of digital media in general [37] and for the power of parameterized stories to move us to a point at which we exhaust all the variations and as a result find a revelation of a new, more progressive and inclusive paradigm, to the point of transformation [2, 3]. Looking back at my selection of landmarks over 30 years of IDN practice I see moments that suggest this kind of transformation, in the implicit critique of consumerism in *The Sims*, for example, or the "he said/she said" presentation of a broken marriage in *Façade* or the multivocal presentation of a stressful family life in *Gone Home*.

The concept of kaleidoscopic form could be helpful in reframing critical discourse that is now hampered by the need to describe IDNs in language appropriate to game design. For example, consider Inkle's adaptation of Jules Verne's *Around the World in 80 Days* (1873) in the "interactive fiction game" *80 Days* (Days:2014vm}. One of the authors, Meg Jayanth purposely created situations in which the protagonist, and player's only character, a European valet accompanying the novel's hero Phineas Fogg, would be unable to get a truthful or openly confiding response from someone because they would be seen as a colonial stranger and therefore not to be trusted. This explicitly disappoints the interactor's expectations, but it is an expression of the moral physics of this retelling of the highly colonialist original. Meg Jayanth frames this difference as being purposely "unfair," to the "player," and justifies it on ideological grounds [40]. But if we reframe the artifact as an interactive digital narrative, then "unfairness" can be understood as intentional procedural irony. We can ask whether the moral physics of anticolonialism is communicated well enough by other aspects of the game so that we can understand why a character is refusing to be communicative. And we can think about whether another version of such a story might allow us to switch point of view, so that the European character might not understand the interaction, but the interactor might abandon the whole adventure and choose to see the world through the eyes and goals and frustrations of the local servants rather than the European masters. From an IDN interpretive position, *80 Days* is not a peculiarly unfair "game" with an ideological argument for a different kind of gaming, but a well-formed interactive narrative with a coherent moral physics offering a new narrative mechanic that could be further developed as part of the collective enterprise of establishing the building blocks of kaleidoscopic form.

It is a common complaint against digital technologies, especially in the areas of journalism and social media that the ubiquitous internet is making us more isolated within our separate interpretive bubbles, unable and increasingly unwilling to hear opposing voices. Taking the long-term view, we can see how computational forms could help us address the problem, not by bringing each of us more of the opposite viewpoints, which could intensify antagonisms, but by promoting a more radical perspective on binary oppositions. For example, a kaleidoscopic habit of thinking could help us to reframe the questions that divide us so that the divisions fall in different places, and through greater insight into formulas of repetition it could bring us to the point of exhaustion at which we begin to wonder who is our common enemy and how are they benefitting from these divisions? It could help us identify the metastructures that foster repetitive patterns of social conflict, and to envision a more integrated transformational future. Newspaper and TV News formats and web-based versions of legacy news sources offer platforms for presenting repetitive story structures with a limited cast of characters. A more flexible and multivocal storytelling format could help us create new forms of shared representations that let us agree on common facts, and recognize that these facts can also be understood in multiple schemas of representation, each reflecting their own explicit values.

This is my own most hopeful scenario. My minimal expectation is that the scholarly study of IDN will improve the practice of IDN and make for richer and more complex stories. I invite you all, the audience/readers for this talk, to take similar advantage of this auspicious moment to make your own list of landmark IDNs and to investigate for yourself what common patterns across time and communities of practice such a kaleidoscopic view can provide.

References

1. Weizenbaum, J.: Eliza — a computer program for the study of natural language communication between man and machine. Commun. ACM **9**, 36–45 (1966)
2. Murray, J.H.: Hamlet on the Holodeck: the Future of Narrative in Cyberspace. Free Press, New York (1997)
3. Murray, J.H.: Hamlet on the Holodeck. The Free Press, New York (2016)
4. Weizenbaum, J.: Computer Power and Human Reason. W. H. Freeman & Co., Oxford, England (1976)
5. Crowther, W.: Adventure [Video Game], (1976)
6. Lebling: Zork [Video Game] (1980)
7. Blank, M.: Planetfall [Video Game] (1983)
8. Blank, M.: Deadline (1982)
9. Wreden, D.: The Stanley Parable [Video Game] (2013)
10. Joyce, M.: Afternoon, A Story. Eastgate (1987)
11. Sierra Entertainment: Mystery House (1980)
12. Sierra Entertainment: Wizard and the Princess (1980)
13. Nooney, L.: Let's begin again: sierra on-line and the origins of the graphical adventure game. Am. J. Play. **10**, 71–91 (2017)

14. Fernández-Vara, C.: Shaping player experience in adventure games. In: Extending Experiences. Lapland University Press (2008)
15. Landow, G.P.: Hyper/Text/Theory. Johns Hopkins University Press, Baltimore (1994)
16. Schank, R.C., Abelson, R.P.: Scripts, Plans, Goals, and Understanding: An Inquiry into Human Knowledge Structures. L. Erlbaum Associates, Hillsdale (1977)
17. Nelson, T.H.: Computer Lib/Dream Machines. Tempus Books of Microsoft Press, Redmond (1987)
18. Bush, V.: As we may think. Atl. Mon. **176**, 101–108 (1945)
19. Laurel, B.: Computers As Theatre. Addison-Wesley, Boston (1991)
20. Furstenberg, G., Farman-Farmaian, A.: A la rencontre de Philippe (1993)
21. Furstenberg, G., Murray, J.: Dans un quartier de Paris (1999)
22. Cyan: Myst (1993)
23. Aarseth, E.J.: Cybertext. JHU Press, Baltimore (1997)
24. Montfort, N.: Twisty Little Passages. MIT Press, Cambridge (2005)
25. Wright, W.: The Sims [video game] (2000)
26. Molleindustria: Every Day the Same Dream. http://www.molleindustria.org/everydaythesamedream/everydaythesamedream.html
27. 2K Games: BioShock (2007)
28. DMA Design: Grand Theft Auto 3: Liberty City (2001)
29. Rockstar: Red Dead Redemption (2010)
30. Mateas, M., Stern, A.: Procedural authorship: a case-study of the interactive drama façade. Presented at the digital arts and culture 2007 (2005)
31. Mateas, M.: A preliminary poetics for interactive drama and games. Digit. Creat. **12**, 140–152 (2001)
32. Short, E.: Blood and Laurels (2014)
33. Anthropy, A.: Dys4ia (2012)
34. Frasca, G.: Videogames of the Oppressed (2001). http://www.ludology.org/articles/thesis/FrascaThesisVideogames.pdf
35. The Fullbright Company: Gone Home [Video Game] (2013)
36. Telltale Games: The Walking Dead [Video game] (2012)
37. Murray, J.H.: Inventing the Medium: Principles of Interaction Design as a Cultural Practice. MIT Press, Cambridge (2011)
38. Telltale Games: Game of Thrones (2014)
39. Mountains: Florence (2018)
40. Jayanth, M.: Practice 2015. NYU Game Center, New York City (2015)

The Future of the Discipline

Science Considered Helpful

R. Michael Young$^{(\boxtimes)}$

Entertainment Arts and Engineering Program and School of Computing,
University of Utah, Salt Lake City, UT 84103, USA
young@eae.utah.edu
http://liquidnarrative.cs.utah.edu

Abstract. As the interactive narrative community continues to mature, discussions are beginning in which we debate the relative merits of differing methodologies, discuss priorities around classes of problems and look at epistemological questions that arise from what we perceive as limitations of our work. Horswill's *Science Considered Harmful* initiated a conversation around the role of science in the advancement of knowledge in our field, putting forward the idea that a scientific mindset restricts our ability to progress. In this paper, I respond, arguing that science, and more generally scientific rigor and the kind of results that it produces, are well served by a discourse that makes productive distinctions between such things as science and not science. In particular, I argue that such a thing as a science of narrative exists, that scientific work is an important way to advance our knowledge of computational models of narrative and that scholarly practice around interactive narrative research does not need to be viewed as only scientific or as only artistic/aesthetic.

Keywords: Interactive narrative · Sciences of the artificial
Theoretical foundations · Methodology, research and scholarship

1 Introduction

In 2013, Ian Horswill published a position paper [26] in which he raised concerns around the role of scientific research and, more broadly, a scientific mindset that he thought was having negative effects in the community of scholars that were using a computational lens to study interactive narrative. His purpose, as he stated, was two-fold. First, he wished to initiate a dialog around the nature of the work done by this community, and second, he wanted to advance the idea that a scientific view in this research community was *harmful* to progress. He titled his paper *Science Considered Harmful*.

I consider many of the points that Horswill makes valid. In fact, they are critical for those of us working in this community to consider as we decide upon courses of exploration for our research programs. However, I also consider many of the points he makes along the way incorrect. Further, in justifying his views, he attributes motives and context to researchers in the community that are inaccurate. At points, he advances a false dichotomy in which the community

© Springer Nature Switzerland AG 2018
R. Rouse et al. (Eds.): ICIDS 2018, LNCS 11318, pp. 21–35, 2018.
https://doi.org/10.1007/978-3-030-04028-4_2

is characterized, like a scientific version of Peer Gynt, as scientifically All or Nothing. And he characterizes scientific approaches to research with negative properties that may be characteristics of poor work but not attributable to science or to the processes of scientific inquiry in our field.

Since the publication of Horswill's paper, there has been unfortunately little dialog around the role of a scientific mindset within our community. There has been no published responses engaging the discussion he initiated and called to continue. But this conversation is of great importance to us as a field, both because the alternative methods of scholarship that Horswill promotes should not be marginalized or diminished by advocates of science *and* because a clear understanding of the distinct values of the different methodologies will help us advance all of them.

I find myself, then, in the surprising position of defending science and scientific inquiry in interactive narrative research. In this paper, I try to answer to some of the questions Horswill raised about the nature of a science of interactive narrative, basing my responses on elements of the work in our research community. But I also describe a perspective on the nature of scholarship in the space of computational narrative and the use of the term science when referring to the study of artificial, rather than natural phenomena.

In *Science Considered Harmful*, Horswill asks four questions about scientific work and then describes a contrasting way of doing scholarly work around computational narrative. His phrasing and the discussion he provides around his questions imply, at least in my own mind, that a scientific view is inappropriate when approaching computational narrative. In the rest of this paper, I try to respond to his questions with concrete answers, discuss existing scholarship that I think is relevant to support my answers, provide examples of how the principles that prompt my answers have been applied and then add to Horswill's call for further engagement on these issues.

There are two conventions that I adopted in the formatting of this paper that warrant short discussion. First, I leave out explicit citation to quotes from *Science Considered Harmful*. Throughout the paper, offset text appearing in italics indicates that the content is a quote from this source. Second, I cite a number of examples of the types of scientific work I mention in my discussion. These works are meant as exemplars; space limitations prevent me from citing the often many, many other relevant papers in any given area. I apologize for these obvious omissions.

2   What Would a Science of Narrative Even Mean?

Horswill asks this question at the start of his paper, as the header of his second section. The question's phrasing presupposes that a science of narrative is a concept that lies far from a direct definition. In my view, there is a ready definition of a science of narrative, drawn from ideas at the core of scholarly work within AI, cognitive science, design and other disciplines. This definition builds directly upon Herbert Simon's model of the *sciences of the artificial* [46]. As

Simon says, the task of an empirical science is to discover and verify invariants in the phenomena under study. A science of the artificial is the application of this pursuit to artifacts rather than to natural phenomena. An artifact can be thought of as "a meeting point, an 'interface' in today's terms between an 'inner' environment, the substance and organization of the artifact itself, and an 'outer' environment, the surroundings in which it operates. If the inner environment is appropriate to the outer environment, or vice versa, the artifact will serve its intended purpose." [46, p. 6].

In my model of the science of narrative as a science of the artificial, narratives are the artifacts that stand in relation between inner and outer environments. Inner environments are the story worlds, their characters and events. The narrative as interface is composed of narrative discourse – text, film, chant, game – that abstracts, filters and presents the narrative to the outer environment. And that outer environment, then is composed of the cognitive, affective, social and broader context of readers' narrative interaction and experience. As a science, then, computational narrative works to identify invariants that hold between some or all of the many elements of each of these three components.

The connection that I'm sketching here between Simon's sciences of the artificial and a science of narrative is relatively specific, and may be a view that is not widely held by others, even others who would characterize themselves as doing science. My intent, however, is not to be prescriptive or definitive, but to give one example of what a science of narrative would even mean.

One thing that a science of narrative does *not* mean is what Horswill asserts that it does, that the idea of science is designed to keep certain kinds of work from being done. From his perspective, Horswill feels that a communal orientation towards scientific thinking is acting like a knife to cut away parts of a scholarly community that do not adhere to an overly restrictive set of norms.

To frame what a science of narrative means in examples of existing research programs, let me first frame a broader notion of scholarship around computational narrative. Boyer [5] provides a compelling model of academic scholarship in the large, in which scholarly work is roughly broken into four distinct categories:

- *The scholarship of discovery*, involving original research expanding our knowledge of a given field.
- *The scholarship of integration* involving the processes of knowledge synthesis across disciplines, sub-fields, or time.
- *The scholarship of engagement* involving the application of a scholar's expertise to real-world problems, with results that can be shared with and/or evaluated by peers.
- *The scholarship of teaching and learning* involving the search for innovative teaching and learning processes in a way that affords public sharing, adoption and evaluation by others.

Boyer's model of scholarship is an integrative one; no category is exclusive of the others. As an example of a long-running research program that can be characterized using this model, consider the work done by me and my colleagues in the Liquid Narrative Group (e.g., [11,27,36,42,54,56]). In the work done in our lab, a science of narrative lies mostly in three of Boyer's categories. It falls mainly within Boyer's scholarship of discovery (the conventional model of scientific inquiry you might see in computer science research) as well as within the scholarship of integration (as this work in computational narrative integrates work from computer science, psychology, narrative theory, game design, cinematography, linguistics, and other disciplines). My work involves, to a lesser degree, a scholarship of application, because a smaller portion of the work there involves the construction of artifacts, either tools or narratives, that are built with sharing as the primary purpose. A model that would seem to align more with Horswill's perspective might be distributed in a kind of inverse of their efforts, with scholarship falling more directly in the third category, engagement, and also in the second, with lesser contact with the first, the scholarship of discovery.

I point out Boyer's model to make the point that perspectives on the nature of research (or, as Boyer makes the shift, *scholarship*) need not be dogmatic all-or-nothing categorizations, and that even within a single field, there are modes of scholarship that differ. Scholarship need not be colonial, exclusive or Darwinian. Academic work doesn't need to be forced into a single category to have academic or scholarly value and work in one category doesn't by its nature drive out work in others.

3   What Do We Mean by Narrative?

Horswill points out that narrative is a broad phenomenon, and I agree. He says that the definition of narrative is difficult to come to universal agreement upon, and I also agree. Narrative theorists, critical studies scholars and authors that reflect on the structure of narrative rarely specify the concepts they use with as much precision as do computer scientists, even when they agree on terms and concepts. Because precise definitions are lacking, many computational researchers that work in the area of narrative identify specific, somewhat stand-alone elements of narrative identified by previous scholars, and rely on characterizations of those elements from narrative theory that, while not universally agreed upon, are well-understood and well-situated relative to contrasting formulations.

Horswill implies that advocates of a scientific approach view narrative as a clearly defined natural kind, and because it's not, he finds their work problematic. I'm not familiar with arguments from computational narrative research that claim that there is a single model of narrative that forms a natural kind. Yes, psychologists and other proponents of Fisher's *narrative paradigm* [19] view narrative as a fundamental mode of understanding the world around us [6]. Psychologists have demonstrated empirically that much of the cognitive and neural activity involved in understanding and producing narrative is increasingly well-understood across genres and media [31]. And there are a number of computational narrative researchers that have stated that these results help motivate the relevance of their work. But proposing a model of a narrative phenomenon is a far thing from asserting that the model is the phenomenon's comprehensive and final characterization.

Nevertheless, Horswill argues that thinking about narrative as a natural kind when it is not could be problematic because trying to maintain a science around a concept with multiple disjoint definitions would mean that some methodologies employed in that effort would fail. He says that this would force us either to miss out on some methodologies by centering on one definition or compelling us to use multiple methodologies.

First, the use of multiple methodologies within a single field should not be seen a problem. In fact, a core portion of any scientific progress is the development of new methodologies to seek new answers to old problems, or to seek initial answers to problems that haven't been tackled before. Competing results, drawn from multiple methodologies addressing a common phenomenon, are *valued* for the ability to foster constructive competition between theories needed for a healthy science. Our field is young, but is just starting to see multiple methodologies used to answer core problems (e.g., data-driven [24, 28] versus declarative approaches [57] to knowledge authoring for story domains). For a scientist, this is a positive thing.

But more centrally, Horswill is wrong in his underlying assumption here that we need a completely proscribed definition of a phenomenon to begin to construct knowledge around it. As philosophers of science are quick to point out, we construct our models incrementally, and we know that those models are bound to be lacking because our understanding is almost always partial. Every area of scientific inquiry has started out in ignorance about its core phenomena and proceeded to build knowledge incrementally. We don't have to travel far to see how this approach plays out, as researchers and philosophers in the 1980s debated the nature of intelligence, artificial and natural, in long discussions (see Nilsson's summary of arguments by Dreyfus, Minsky, Penrose, Searle and others in his book *The Quest for Artificial Intelligence* [37, chapter VI]). Today, these arguments are mostly relegated to historical reading, while AI makes rapid advances in both academic and commercial contexts.

Fortunately, scholars interested in bringing scientific approaches to the exploration of narrative do not lack well-articulated (though often formally imprecise) descriptions of narrative's form and function. One methodology that has been adopted is for a researcher to select a single characterization of a narrative phenomenon, provide a computational refinement of the characterization and then use that refinement either generatively or analytically. The resulting output – a novel narrative artifact or the characterization of an existing corpus – is then evaluated and used to measure refinement.

As an example, in work that provides computational models of suspense [10, 38], researchers based their work on an existing characterization of narrative comprehension. The characterization models readers acting as problem-solvers [20] and views suspense as tension arising from a reader's anticipation of the success or failure of a protagonist's plans [15]. Computational work, then, operationalized these existing models, and experimental work with the resulting systems provided further support for the psychological approaches while also posing new questions about the cognitive processes involved.

4   What Do We Mean by Science?

In thinking about Horswill's question, I realize that its a question to which we should give much more consideration. As an initial framing, let me draw from the on-going discussion in the computer science (CS) community about the scientific nature of CS research. In that discussion, Peter J. Denning gives a characterization of scientific fields typically having the following structure [17]:

- they are organized to understand, exploit, and cope with a pervasive phenomenon.
- they encompass natural and artificial processes of the phenomenon.
- they are codified structured body of knowledge.
- they show a commitment to experimental methods for discovery and validation.
- they value reproducibility of results.
- they advance falsifiability of hypotheses and models.
- they have an ability to make reliable predictions, some of which are surprising.

How does the computational narrative work done in our community align with these characteristics? First, I don't think that anyone would argue that narrative is not a pervasive phenomenon. And it should be clear that the work done by the computational narrative community is, to a great extent, a communal effort to understand, exploit and cope with narrative from a computational perspective.

There are clearly many people working to address natural and artificial aspects of narrative, often addressing both at the same time. Psychologists work to understand narrative understanding, from neurological bases [48] to cognitive work around things like inferencing and affective responses to narrative [33,47], memory [41], goal tracking [32], and many others. AI researchers work to characterize artificial aspects, like the structure and form of narrative seen in cinematic lighting [18], character dialog [29] and the structure and form of plot lines [8,21,51]. Even some narrative theorists, who provide an almost analytic-only view on narrative, also develop a formalized and scientific views of narrative [25,43].

The field of interactive digital storytelling is relatively new. Initial steps grew out of the critical mass catalyzed roughly in 1999 at the AAAI Fall Symposium on Narrative Intelligence [34]. The field has continued to codify its knowledge through traditional publication venues that are intentionally broad in scope (e.g., the International Conference on Interactive Digital Storytelling, the Workshop on Computational Models of Narrative), games-focused (e.g., the conference of the Digital Interactive Games Research Association, the Foundations of Digital

Games conference), AI-centric (e.g., IEEE conference on Computational Intelligence in Games, The AAAI conference on AI and Interactive Digital Entertainment, the workshop on Intelligent Narrative Technologies), or others. Within, take an example of planning-based methods to characterize generative models of plot [39], where much of the work from my group has been directed. Just there, there is the creation of planning based methods [57], the identification of limitations to produce intentional planning [42],the identification of efficient algorithms to produce the same plans [23], the extension to characterize conflict in stories [54], the extension to express character personality through choice of actions [3] and most recently extensions to address character belief and mistaken actions [52], with work also here by Porteous [51], Shrivani and his collaborators [44], and interactions between character beliefs and intention management [55].

The field, as Horswill points out, has a strong commitment to experimental work, particularly in evaluation. Work done by psychologists is particularly experimental in both discovery and validation. As one example, Graesser and Franklin's QUEST model of question-answering in the context of stories [22] is a computational cognitive model of narrative – essentially, a model of narrative understanding that uses a computational model (in a broad sense) of narrative knowledge and the processes that make use of it. The QUEST model makes predictions about how people answer questions about stories after reading them, and makes specific predictions about that behavior that have been born out in years of experimental testing. Because those predictions are both specific and shown to be reliable, researchers on the computational side of narrative generation have been able to use them as proxies for effective human comprehension in a wide range of work (e.g., [1,27,42]).

Much of the work on the generation of narrative also relies on experimental methods, typically involving human subjects and characterizations of the efficacy of new algorithms to build narrative artifacts or experiences (e.g., [30,35,58]). Other work uses experimental evaluation, but relies on analytic or statistical means for validation (e.g., [9,53]). The falsifiability of experimental designs is a critical element in the progression of our understanding in the science of narrative. Unexpected or negative results prompt theory revision, and give rise to new experiments to gauge how proposed new models match the interactions of the Simonian tripartite view of narrative. As one example, Christian and Young's work [11] sought to map plan-based narrative structures to cognitive models used to comprehend cinematic presentations of stories. Their work showed support only for certain types of story structures, and this limitation then prompted follow-on work by Cardona-Rivera and his collaborators [7], who sought to better understand Christian and Young's results by performing comparable experiments over a range of varying mappings and cognitive models.

While not an issue pointed to by Horswill, the lack of emphasis on reproducibility appears to me as a scientific weakness of the work done in computational narrative. Because our area is so new, researchers have a rich field of open questions to choose from and no real canon of successful methods to build upon or to challenge. Consequently, the draw to explore a novel method of one's own devising is so great and the value of exploring undiscovered country so high that we're not stopping to do the hard work around reproducability that already lies within our reach (see the work of Tearse *et al.* [50], in the production of *Minstrel Remixed* as a notable counter-example).

As for our science leading towards surprising predictions, surprise is certainly in the eye of the beholder. Is it a surprise that story structures, plan data structures and mental models storylines align to such an extent that the data structures can predict cognitive processing during story comprehension [7,11,27,36,42]? It was not to me, although to some it might be. As another example, narrative psychologist Radvansky has developed a cognitive model of how narrative consumers build mental models of a story world and its unfolding events, called the *event horizon* model [40]. This model makes accurate predictions about, among other things, the way that readers manage their story memories when the current location in a story change during reading. Radvansky predicted that these changes would also be prompted when the readers themselves moved from one location to another. Surprisingly, at least to me, these predictions were verified [41].

5   On the Relation of Cases to Methodology in Computational Narrative

If you can't gather data across all possible designs and users, then the alternative is to look as deeply as possible at designs you do examine; to glean as much as possible from a specific encounter with a specific piece. So art training and theory are traditionally focused on examining specific pieces, specific cases. And as such, it is in some ways closer to the practice found in law and business than in engineering.

Horswill makes an important point about the relationship between artistic and/or critical training and case-oriented methods used in law and business. I disagree with the premise of the paragraph, that if you can't gather data across all possible designs and users, then *the* alternative (emphasis mine) is to examine a small number of instances. But let's take this argument to a not-so-extreme extension. If physicists are not able to gather data across all possible instances of a phenomenon, then Horswill would have them resort only to studying a small number of cases. When the space of a phenomenon includes all of time and space, physical scientists can't come close to this bar. Studying cases is often a great way to conduct exploratory work, and physical scientists working in an area where knowledge is just emerging may do just that. But it's with an eye towards theory formation, which is a key part of the characterization of experimental computer science and its iteration spelled out by Cohen [13] and others. As Cohen and Howe [14] say when describing the role of evaluation in AI research, "For the individual, evaluation can tell us how and why our methods and programs work and, so, tell us how our research should proceed. For the community, evaluation expedites the understanding of available methods and, so, their integration into further research." This is as true for the study of interactive digital storytelling as it is for the field of AI.

> *Although the goal is in some sense to develop a sufficient understanding to be able to invert the mapping, and predict how a hypothetical design might affect a viewers experience, that understanding is nonetheless always partial and contingent, so the actual creation process is iterative, with each iteration forming a case to be examined and used in the formation of the next iteration.*

> *This presents a serious challenge for AI work in support of the arts because computer science is traditionally, and understandably, resistant to work on cases. One cannot generally get a Ph.D. for writing a program; one gets a Ph.D. for developing a general theory that will help others write some class of programs. But I see no alternative but to relax this constraint for AI work that have specifically aesthetic goals. We have to be open to the case because the case is all we have.*

AI work to support the arts is one view of what a science of narrative does: supporting the arts. But a science is geared towards an increased understanding of a phenomenon, rather than a particular engineering approach, which might be an application of that understanding to a problem like creation of art. Framing the scholarship under Boyer's model, Horswill's view seems to be centered here on a scholarship of application, but a science of narrative affords scholarship of discovery and integration as well.

Further, not all computational work on narrative has explicitly aesthetic goals.[1] But the idea that understanding how a hypothetical design might affect a viewer's experience, is precisely what Simon talks about in characterizing design as a science of the artificial [45].

6   Horswill's Conclusion

> *My concern is that we're at risk of letting our methods drive our inquiries rather than letting our inquiries drive our methods. I have on several occasions been told by students at conferences that they would like to make a game or artwork that demonstrates the ideas from their thesis but that that's not science.*
> *That makes me want to shoot myself.*

Those students are correct. Building an artifact is, on its own, not science (or rather, not doing science). There are a lot of things my students wish to do while being students,[2] and some of those, while amazing, intellectually demanding and

---

[1] Of course, one might argue that not all work in the arts has exclusively aesthetic goals (for example, see [4]).

[2] Aside from Fortnite.

capable of yielding insight into research questions, just are not science. That doesn't mean that these activities would be inappropriate, or that they would not lead to increased knowledge about narrative. It means that they would not be direct contributors on their own to the idea of forming hypotheses about the relevant invariants and testing them out computationally. Building an artifact is not anti-science. Building an artifact that demonstrates the range of relationships you're exploring in your research *is* science, just like building a software simulation of a physical phenomenon might be part of a physicist's exploration of a physical science.

> *If we limit ourselves to using only analytics and psychology-style human subjects experiments, we are at best crippling ourselves and at worst deceiving ourselves with a false sense of rigor. In the worst case, we could end up creating (unironically) a kind of interactive narrative version of Komar and Melamid's Peoples Choice series (Wypijewski, 1997) in which they commissioned a market research company to study the characteristics most- and least-wanted in paintings by different demographic groups, then painted the results. Their United States: Most Wanted Painting (1994) is a realist landscape incorporating trees, water, mountains, George Washington, a happy family, and a pair of deer.*

I object to two points Horswill makes here. First, its unclear to me where the rigor applied in the methods themselves falls short. Second, Horwill's suggestion that use of these methods will lead us to overly specific methods that are too narrowly focused seems to fly in the face of the history of analytic and experimental science. Psychologists make heavy use of controlled human-subjects experiments, and they've validated a significant set of principals that apply broadly (rather than learning how to model the 300 freshmen psychology students that participated in any given experiment).

> *I recognize there is Realpolitik to science. We must all make ourselves intelligible and respectable to our departments, Deans, hiring committees, and funders; and that may require us to use methods and metrics we don't always believe in. But that doesn't mean we have to limit ourselves to only using those methods.*

Scholars should never use methods and metrics that they don't believe in. The integrity of a researcher (including their sincere confidence in their work) is critical to the believablity of results on which progress in a field is based. Belief in the outcomes of research, dependent on the methods and metrics employed, is at the core of any researcher's work. There is a hint here in what Horswill is saying that the savvy and successful academic will engage in *Realpolitik*, pitching the science story *in order to* appeal to a tenure process or a funding review. If I do science, and I work in a system where scientific results are rewarded, is it correct to automatically characterize me as *conforming to get ahead* and then damn me because of it? That would effectively damn scientific scholarship across a good portion of the academy. Horswill paints with too broad a brush here.

By implying that academics, especially junior ones, can be forgiven for presenting as scientists in order to play the tenure game, the sympathetic argument admits without examination the notion that all those folks are well-meaning, worthy of our sympathy, but disingenuous.

I do strongly agree with Horswill that my methods do not need to be your methods, and that valid knowledge can be gained by a diverse set of approaches. Horswill's tack, however, is to call for us to use methods and metrics that are not scientific. While adopting this approach might fit for some scholars' work, for communities of researchers in computational narrative that *are* scientific, those methods stand apart. They don't address many of Denning's properties that scientific fields rely upon. As such, they have limited power to advance relevant types of knowledge. Specifically, they are limited in their means of validation for general claims, they are challenged to support reproducibility, they may not advance hypotheses nor contribute to a process where wrong hypotheses can be falsified, and they don't particularly serve to make reliable predictions about narrative phenomena.

7   Let Me Sum up

In the meantime, I look forward to the day I stop hearing the phrase "I'd like to do X, but that's not science."

To pursue science is not to deny art. When your day job is to do science, however, you have to pick your battles.

Further, to privilege either science or art over the other in the broader community of computational media researchers would be unjustifiable, short-sighted and would have all of the negative effects that Horswill is concerned about. But to advance artistic methods to be on par with or to serve as replacements for scientific ones *within the scientific community working on narrative* would significantly constrain the power of the claims we can make and the knowledge that we would gain. One might conclude from Horswill's paper that scientific approaches in our field ignore the art of narrative. This is hardly the case. Scientific work is all about digging into artistic elements of narrative. The artful scientific work done by Swanson and his collaborators on learning photo composition preferences from gameplay [49] is a great example. Out of many others (e.g., [2,12,16]).

Narrative art and narrative science both exist. They are both individuals in their own right, capable of standing apart one from another. But they are also capable of standing together without straining their individual natures. Rather than call for scientific scholars to dial back those properties of their work that bring some of its strongest internal values, I suggest that we form new discussions that stand apart from our artistic or scientific contributions, but that build upon them. As a potential model, consider SIGGRAPH's inclusion of artistic contributions in the conference's Art Papers track and the Art Gallery format that leverage novel computational advances. Other approaches, like the calls for the ICIDS and FDG conferences, make clear that submissions characterizing critical, computation or aesthetic work are appropriate. By creating these and more venues for dialog, we engage scientists and artists in the creation of a shared body of creative knowledge.

I am in agreement with Horswill on many, many things about our common professional endeavor: the beauty of LaTeX, the primacy of emacs, the use of tabs over spaces. More seriously, I agree with him completely about the critical role in society that we all play as scholars and the special character of work around computational media, play and narrative.

Simon's framing of a science of the artificial is particularly useful for those of us working in computational methods for interactive narrative. As we increase our understanding of the invariants in narrative elements – what relations hold between the design of story worlds, their telling and the resulting experiences of our readers, viewers and players – we can leverage that knowledge to build algorithms that themselves create novel types of playable narrative experiences. Scholarship that contributes to the science of narrative need not come only from the scholarship of exploration, but should be welcomed from work that ranges across all four of Boyer's categories (and, potentially, others).

Scholar of computational narrative, do not shy away from science. In many cases, it has been shown to be helpful.

Acknowledgments. This material is based upon work supported in whole or in part with funding from the Laboratory for Analytic Sciences (LAS). Any opinions, findings, conclusions, or recommendations expressed in this material are those of the author and do not necessarily reflect the views of the LAS and/or any agency or entity of the United States Government.

References

1. Amos-Binks, A., Spain, R., Young, R.M.: Subjective experience of intention revision. In: Advances in Cognitive Systems (2018)
2. Argamon, S., Dubnov, S., Jupp, J., et al.: Style and meaning in language, art, music and design. In: Proceedings of the 2004 AAAI Symposium (2004)
3. Bahamón, J.C., Barot, C., Young, R.M.: A goal-based model of personality for planning-based narrative generation. In: AAAI, pp. 4142–4143 (2015)
4. Bay, M.: Transformers 6: The Last Knight. Paramount Pictures, Murphy, Don and DeSanto, Tom and diBonaventura, Lorenzo and Bryce, Ian (2017)
5. Boyer, E.: Scholarship Reconsidered: Priorties of the Professoriate. Carnegie Foundation for the Advancement of Teaching, New York (1990)
6. Bruner, J.: The narrative construction of reality. Crit. Inq. **18**(1), 1–21 (1991)
7. Cardona-Rivera, R.E., Price, T.W., Winer, D., Young, R.M.: Question answering in the context of stories generated by computers. Adv. Cognit. Syst. **4**, 227–246 (2016)
8. Cavazza, M., Charles, F., Mead, S.: Character-based interactive storytelling. IEEE Intell. Syst. **17**(4), 17–24 (2002)
9. Chambers, N., Jurafsky, D.: Unsupervised learning of narrative event chains. In: ACL, vol. 94305, pp. 789–797 (2008)

10. Cheong, Y., Young, R.: A computational model of narrative generation for suspense. In: Working Notes of the AAAI 2006 Workshop on Computational Aesthetics, pp. 8–14 (2006)
11. Christian, D., Young, R.M.: Comparing cognitive and computational models of narrative structure. In: Proceedings of the National Conference on Artificial Intelligence, pp. 385–390. American Association of Artificial Intelligence, AAAI, Menlo Park (2004)
12. Cohen, H.: The further exploits of AARON, painter. Stanf. Hum. Rev. 4(2), 141–158 (1995)
13. Cohen, P.R.: Empirical Methods for Artificial Intelligence, vol. 139. MIT Press, Cambridge (1995)
14. Cohen, P.R., Howe, A.E.: How evaluation guides AI research: the message still counts more than the medium. AI Mag. 9(4), 35 (1988)
15. Comisky, P., Bryant, J.: Factors involved in generating suspense. Hum. Commun. Res. 9(1), 49–58 (1982)
16. Dannenberg, R.B., Raphael, C.: Music score alignment and computer accompaniment. Commun. ACM 49(8), 38–43 (2006)
17. Denning, P.J.: The science in computer science. Commun. ACM 56(5), 35–38 (2013). https://doi.org/10.1145/2447976.2447988
18. El-Nasr, M.S., Horswill, I.: Automating lighting design for interactive entertainment. CIE 2(2), 15–15 (2004)
19. Fisher, W.R.: Human Communication as Narration: Toward a Philosophy of Reason, Value, and Action. University of South Carolina Press (1989)
20. Gerrig, R.: Experiencing Narrative Worlds: On the Psychological Activities of Reading. Yale Univ. Press, New Haven (1993)
21. Gervás, P., Díaz Agudo, B., Peinado, F., Hervás, R.: Story plot generation based on CBR. Knowl. Based Syst. 18(4), 235–242 (2005)
22. Graesser, A.C., Franklin, S.P.: Quest: a cognitive model of question answering. Discourse Process. 13(3), 279–303 (1990)
23. Haslum, P.: Narrative planning: compilations to classical planning. J. Artif. Intell. Res. 44, 383 (2012)
24. Hayton, T., Porteous, J., Ferreira, J.F., Lindsay, A., Read, J.: Storyframer: from input stories to output planning models. In: Proceedings of the Workshop on Knowledge Engineering for Planning and Scheduling (KEPS), at The 27th International Conference on Automated Planning and Scheduling (ICAPS). AAAI (2017)
25. Herman, D.: Storytelling and the Sciences of Mind. MIT Press, Cambridge (2013)
26. Horswill, I.: Science considered harmful. In: Proceedings of AIIDE (2013)
27. Jhala, A., Young, R.M.: Cinematic visual discourse: representation, generation, and evaluation. IEEE Trans. Comput. Intell. Artif. Intell. Games 2, 69–81 (2010)
28. Li, B., Lee-Urban, S., Johnston, G., Riedl, M.: Story generation with crowdsourced plot graphs. In: AAAI (2013)
29. Lin, G.I., Walker, M.A.: All the world's a stage: learning character models from film. In: AIIDE (2011)
30. Lukin, S.M., Reed, L., Walker, M.A.: Generating sentence planning variations for story telling. In: SIGDIAL Conference, pp. 188–197 (2015)
31. Magliano, J.P., Loschky, L.C., Clinton, J., Larson, A.M.: Is reading the same as viewing? An exploration of the similarities and differences between processing text- and visually based narratives. In: Miller, B., Cutting, L., McCardle, P. (eds.) Unraveling the Behavioral, Neurobiological, and Genetic Components of Reading Comprehension, vol. 8, pp. 78–90. Brookes Publishing Co., Baltimore (2017)

32. Magliano, J.P., Taylor, H.A., Kim, H.J.J.: When goals collide: monitoring the goals of multiple characters. Mem. Cogn. **33**(8), 1357–1367 (2005)
33. Magliano, J., Dijkstra, K., Zwaan, R.: Generating predictive inferences while viewing a movie. Discourse Process. **22**(3), 199–224 (1996)
34. Mateas, M., Sengers, P.: Narrative intelligence. In: Papers from the 1999 Fall Symposium. Technical report, AAAI Press, Menlo Park, CA Technical Report FS-99-0 (1999)
35. Mawhorter, P., Mateas, M., Wardrip-Fruin, N.: Generating relaxed, obvious, and dilemma choices with dunyazad. In: AIIDE, pp. 58–64 (2015)
36. Niehaus, J., Young, R.: A method for generating narrative discourse to prompt inferences. In: Workshop on Intelligent Narrative Technologies, vol. 3 (2010)
37. Nilsson, N.J.: The Quest for Artificial Intelligence. Cambridge University Press, Cambridge (2009)
38. O'Neill, B., Riedl, M.: Dramatis: a computational model of suspense. In: AAAI, AAAI 2014, pp. 944–950 (2014). http://dl.acm.org/citation.cfm?id=2893873. 2894021
39. Porteous, J.: Planning technologies for interactive storytelling. In: Nakatsu, R., Rauterberg, M., Ciancarini, P. (eds.) Handbook of Digital Games and Entertainment Technologies. Springer, Singapore (2016). https://doi.org/10.1007/978-981-4560-50-4_71
40. Radvansky, G.A.: Across the event horizon. Curr. Dir. Psychol. Sci. **21**(4), 269–272 (2012). https://doi.org/10.1177/0963721412451274
41. Radvansky, G.A., Copeland, D.E.: Walking through doorways causes forgetting: situation models and experienced space. Mem. Cogn. **34**(5), 1150–1156 (2006)
42. Riedl, M., Young, R.M.: Narrative planning: balancing plot and character. JAIR **39**(1), 217–268 (2010)
43. Ryan, M.L.: Possible Worlds, Artificial Intelligence, and Narrative Theory. Indiana University Press, Bloomington (1991)
44. Shirvani, A., Ware, S.G., Farrell, R.: A possible worlds model of belief for state-space narrative planning. In: Proceedings of the 13th AAAI International Conference on Artificial Intelligence and Interactive Digital Entertainment, pp. 101–107 (2017)
45. Simon, H.A.: The science of design: creating the artificial. Des. Issues **4**(1/2), 67–82 (1988). http://www.jstor.org/stable/1511391
46. Simon, H.A.: The Sciences of the Artificial. MIT Press, Cambridge (1996)
47. Singer, M., Ferreira, F.: Inferring consequences in story comprehansion. J. Verbal Learn. Verbal Behav. **22**, 437–448 (1983)
48. Speer, N.K., Zacks, J.M., Reynolds, J.R.: Human brain activity time-locked to narrative event boundaries. Psychol. Sci. **18**(5), 449–455 (2007)
49. Swanson, R., Escoffery, D., Jhala, A.: Learning visual composition preferences from an annotated corpus generated through gameplay. In: CIG, pp. 363–370. IEEE (2012)
50. Tearse, B., Mateas, M., Wardrip-Fruin, N.: Minstrel remixed: a rational reconstruction. In: Proceedings of the Intelligent Narrative Technologies III Workshop, INT3 2010, pp. 1–7. ACM (2010). https://doi.org/10.1145/1822309.1822321
51. Teutenberg, J., Porteous, J.: Incorporating global and local knowledge in intentional narrative planning. In: Proceedings of the 2015 International Conference on Autonomous Agents and Multiagent Systems, pp. 1539–1546. International Foundation for Autonomous Agents and Multiagent Systems (2015)

52. Thorne, B., Young, R.M.: Generating stories that include failed actions by modeling false character beliefs. Technical report, University of Utah (2017). eAE TR 2017-001
53. Valls-Vargas, J., Zhu, J., Ontanon, S.: Error analysis in an automated narrative information extraction pipeline. IEEE TCAIG **9**, 342 (2016)
54. Ware, S.G., Young, R.M., Harrison, B., Roberts, D.L.: A computational model of narrative conflict at the fabula level. IEEE TCIAIG **6**(3), 271–288 (2014)
55. Young, R.M.: Sketching a generative model of intention management for characters in stories:adding intention management to a belief-driven story planning algorithm. Technical report, University of Utah (2017). eAE TR 2017-002
56. Young, R.M.: Story and discourse: a bipartite model of narrative generation in virtual worlds. Interact. Stud. **8**(2), 177–208 (2010). Social Behaviour and Communication in Biological and Artificial Systems
57. Young, R.M., Riedl, M.O., Branly, M., Jhala, A., Martin, R., Saretto, C.: An architecture for integrating plan-based behavior generation with interactive game environments. J. Game Dev. **1**(1), 51–70 (2004)
58. Yu, H., Riedl, M.O.: Optimizing players expected enjoyment in interactive stories. In: AIIDE, pp. 100–106 (2015)

Thoughts on a Discipline for the Study of Interactive Digital Narratives

Hartmut Koenitz[(⊠)]

HKU University of the Arts Utrecht,
Nieuwekade 1, 3511 RV Utrecht, The Netherlands
hartmut.koenitz@hku.nl

Abstract. This paper presents arguments for the creation of an academic discipline concerned with the analysis and design of interactive digital narratives, akin to game studies. I analyse the status quo as the result of foundational aspects and the effects of the historical development of games studies before identifying a range of problems that have their root cause in the lack of an academic home and the support structures that come with it. In particular, the lack of a legitimizing framework translates into difficulties with academic recognition, reduced opportunities for grants and scholarships, scarcity of academic positions, and discontinuity of research which amounts to academic memory loss. In order to understand where the field stands, I apply three perspectives on requirements for an academic discipline from outside the field and come to the conclusion that while much progress has been made, there are areas in need of further attention, in particular when it comes to formal programs of study. Conversely, I identify the development of degree programs as an area needing particular attention in order to create an academic discipline.

Keywords: Interactive digital storytelling (IDS)
Interactive Digital Narratives (IDN) · Discipline · Research
Education · Pedagogy · Professional academic association

1 Introduction

Research and practice of interactive digital narratives (IDN) have a considerable tradition. James Ryan has recently reminded us that work on earlier computational systems goes back to the 1960s [1], while analytical and critical research on the PhD level dates back at least to Buckles's 1985 thesis [2]. This means we are looking back at more than half a century of practical work and more than three decades of scholarly enquiry. In recent years, work on the topic has proliferated in all related aspects – on computational systems, on analytical approaches, on the design practice and the effect on audiences.

And yet, it is still unclear where this kind of work belongs in the academic landscape. In this paper, I will argue for the creation of a discipline, provisionally named "Interactive Digital Narrative Studies" and will outline reasons for such a move, most importantly continued development, increased impact, and scholarly recognition.

R. Rouse et al. (Eds.): ICIDS 2018, LNCS 11318, pp. 36–49, 2018.
https://doi.org/10.1007/978-3-030-04028-4_3

The next sections serve as a backdrop to contextualize this argument. I will first reflect on fundamental and historical aspects of research in interactive narrative: specifically the interdisciplinary origins and relevant influential historical developments in video games studies, before proceeding identifying a number of pertinent contemporary issues in interactive narrative research. Then, criteria for academic disciplines will be discussed and applied to evaluate the current status of the field against them. On this basis, I will consider the way forward - what acting as a discipline entails, and discuss the creation of a professional association (ARDIN - Association for Research in Digital Interactive Narratives) and its significance for the field. Finally, I will provide an outlook on future developments.

2   Foundational and Historical Aspects

2.1   Interdisciplinarity

From the outset, a range of disciplines are touched by the topic of interactive narrative: literary studies, narratology, communications, digital media studies, computer science, games studies, but also film studies, fine arts, comparative literature, journalism, psychology and performance studies.

Consequently, the seemingly obvious framing for research in IDN is one of 'interdisciplinary' – which in practice also means to not having a proper academic home and instead a problem that stems from being located at the fringes of several disciplines. This state of affairs often manifests as a considerable effort in translating and contextualizing a given scholar's work for an audience of colleagues and department heads who lack in understanding of the particularities of such a situation and instead expect scholarly output to fit into the established framework and evaluation criteria of a traditional discipline, especially in tenure-track positions. One concrete problem in this regard is the lack of an academic journal on the topic. Another problem is in the absence of the specific category of interactive narrative research in grant applications, forms for academic activity reports and many other kinds of academic bureaucracy. The consequences of this situation are potentially severe and can reach from missed grant opportunities to academic misrepresentation to the rejection of tenure.

2.2   Games Studies

Given the difficulties of interdisciplinary research, the sister discipline of Games Studies represents a considerable success story. Seizing the moment in the early 2000s, its proponents managed to install a separate discipline, able to define its subject, scholarly approach and rules for academic recognition.

Unfortunately, for academics in interactive narrative, the success of games studies also comes with a bitter aftertaste, since the strategic argument for this new discipline was one against narrative and especially against interactive narrative. Instead of understanding video games and interactive narratives as complimentary perspectives that both enquire into the changes that occur to earlier forms once they encounter and embrace the interactive digital medium, early 'ludological' perspectives in particular attacked the notion of 'interactive narrative', which they presented as an imperialistic move ("narrativistic colonialism" [3]) to take over the study of games and instead cast them as a way to make games compatible with traditional narrative studies – c.f. Aarseth's claim about a "drive to reform games as 'interactive narratives'" [3]. For the present discussion it is important to note that Aarseth emphasizes the disciplinary aspect of the ludological perspective quite clearly, represented here in its full extent:

> My warnings about narrativism and theoretical colonialism might seem unduly harsh and even militant. Why not let the matter resolve itself, through scholarly, logical dialogue? The reason for this vigilance, however, is based on numbers. The sheer number of students trained in film and literary studies will ensure that the slanted and crude misapplication of "narrative" theory to games will continue and probably overwhelm game scholarship for a long time to come. As long as vast numbers of journals and supervisors from traditional narrative studies continue to sanction dissertations and papers that take the narrativity of games for granted and confuse the story-game hybrids with games in general, good, critical scholarship on games will be out-numbered by incompetence, and this is a problem for all involved. Hopefully this is just a short-lived phase, but it certainly is a phase that we are in right now. As more scholars from other disciplines, such as sociology, linguistics, history, economics, and geography, start to do research on games, perhaps the narrativist camp (and the visualist camp) will realize more of the many differences between games and narratives, and even contribute valuable analyses using (and not abusing) narratology, but until then the narrativist paradigm will but slowly melt [3].

The irony here is that while Aarseth's argument might make sense logically on an abstract level, it fails the test of actual facts. Evidence for the described imperialist movement is nearly non-existent, as the only two pieces of proof presented for such a move are Janet Murray's allegorical interpretation of *Tetris* [4] as a representation of an overwhelming onslaught of tasks in late capitalist society [5] and her assertion that all games are hero stories [6] – again an abstract interpretation. Neither of these statements make any claims to exclusivity, to being the only valid, normative interpretation, which would be a requirement to make them imperialistic. Even more problematic is the fact that the self-selected enemies of the 'ludologists', the so-called "narratologists" (mainly Janet Murray and Henry Jenkins) do in no way represent the alleged imperialistic tendencies they are accused of. Neither of them epitomize "traditional narrative studies" [3] – instead, both of them were instrumental in building departments and programs that foreground the specific aspects of their objects of study in contrast to traditional perspectives (Murray: Digital Media at the Georgia Institute of Technology, Jenkins: Comparative Media Studies at MIT). Indeed, the inventor of the term ludology – Gonzala Frasca – rejected the "narratology" label for both Murry and Jenkins as early as 2003 [7], but his insightful perspective had little if any influence on the pronouncements of his colleagues.

Therefore, the damage was done and its effects have been lasting. Scholarship on narrative aspects of video games became marginalized and academics working on the topic in the context of games still face considerable resistance and lack of recognition. Presently, the topic of narrative is still not represented as a track at any of the major game conferences (DIGRA, FDG, CHIPlay) – despite the fact that many narrative-focused games exist and achieve both critical and commercial success.

Essentially, academics investigating the topic of interactive narrative separately from traditional disciplines were casualties of the so-called narratology vs. debate, not at home with traditional narrative studies, but now also unwelcome in games studies qua their designation as perpetrators of an alleged academic-imperialistic ploy to take over this nascent field.

3 Three Essential Aspects

After the more general remarks of the previous section, I will now focus on three aspects essential to any kind of scholarly work – academic evaluation, continuity of research and formal education. All three aspects are significantly affected by the lack of a disciplinary framework, as I will show.

3.1 Academic Evaluation

The current state of affairs for scholars in the field might best be described as an "academic diaspora" – IDN scholars are found in diverse constellation and under headings such as AI, Communications, Literary Studies, (Digital) Media Studies. Cultural Studies, Psychology, and many more.

The issues that stem from this state of affairs are not questions of mere labeling. They translate into many uphill struggles related to the lack of a coherent framework and published rules on which scholars can build a career. For example, today, shooting movies and taking pictures as part of anthropological research project can count toward tenure, since formal guidelines for the evaluation of such works exist [8, 9], prepared by the Society for Visual Anthropology, a division of the professional organization of the discipline, the American Anthropological Association. Specific guidelines for the evaluation of "digital scholarship" exist even in the discipline of History [10], yet no such guidelines are available for IDN research, while there clearly is an acute need for them. For example, it is unclear at best, how the many pieces of software created by scholars in the IDN space (e.g. authoring tools like Art-E-Fact [11], the authoring part of the IS engine[12], DraMachina [13], Scenejo [14], Bowman/Zócalo [15], Scribe [16], FearNot! authoring tool [17], Wide Ruled [18], Rencontre [19], ASAPS [20] or HypeDyn [21]) can count as academic work. Currently, in many cases, especially outside Computer Science departments and Art departments, by itself, it will amount to nothing. Yet, the associated academic papers are only part of the work. In addition, if we consider the importance of interoperability (cf. [22]), related work, such as Szilas' and et al's proposal for a shared API [23] also needs to be recognized.

The diasporic state does not mean that there are no success stories – they definitely exist, as names like Janet Murray, Ruth Aylett, Mariet Theune, Michael Mateas, R. Michael Young, Nick Montfort, Fox Harrell, Jichen Zhu and many others show; however, behind these success stories are additional struggles due to the inherent conflict between chosen field of research and a "foreign" host department. These struggles should not have been necessary in the first place and often translate into lost productivity and pragmatic compromises necessary for survival within a foreign academic field. It also means, that there is often no time and energy left in the busy academic schedules to develop the field of IDN studies itself.

3.2 Academic (Dis)Continuity

Academic Memory Loss. James Ryan's archeological work [1] has moved the historical yardsticks of the discipline and alerted us to the fact that research on the topic has started earlier than previously assumed. Yet, that such discoveries are possible is also an indication of academic discontinuity – essentially a kind of 'memory loss' that occurs in the absence of institutional memory provided by a discipline. This state of affairs can lead to a wasteful practice of "reinventing the wheel", the recreation of already existing – but forgotten – knowledge that diverts resources away from more pressing issues. In a related perspective, I have earlier pointed out [22] the effective loss of much of the practical work undertaken at MIT's interactive cinema group and consequently argued for an effort in archiving and an emphasis on sustainability for new projects. Yet, this call to action will ultimately fail to make an impact without an associated institutional framework that provides the necessary resources and required acceptance. After all, archives need a location (a digital one would be fine nowadays), staff and financial support.

Furthermore, the problem should be addressed at the inception of current and future projects in terms of sustainability. In this respect, published guidelines to "future-proof" projects could considerably improve the current situation. Yet also in this case, the existence of an institutional framework is of crucial importance for such guidelines to be created, adopted, and further developed.

Dependency on Grants. An additional instance of academic discontinuity is connected to the considerable dependency on grants to enable IDN research. The topic has been used to write a range of successful grant proposals. Some of these grants have been substantial, e.g. the European "Network of Excellence" IRIS (Integrating Research in Interactive Storytelling) [24] that created a considerable amount of publications. Other examples include SNAPS (Schema for Narrative Authoring and Presentation Systems, US National Science Foundation Award IIS-0739497), the multiple US NSF grants to understand improvisational actors as a basis for virtual characters (Grant Numbers IIS #0757567, #320520, and #1036457) or the UK-bases RIDERS (Research in Interactive Drama Environments, Role-play and Storytelling) network[1]. These grants are a sign of academic recognition. and speak of the potential of the topic. Yet, in the absence of a discipline, work on the subject often stops as soon as the respective funded project ends, since the participating researchers are obliged to fulfil the requirements of host departments with research foci in other areas. While the end of grant period is certainly a disruptive event also in established disciplines, a disciplinary framing assures a certain level of continuity, e.g. by way of positions only partially funded through grants, by student research and by providing infrastructure.

---

[1] http://www.riders-project.net.

3.3 Formal Education

To this day, no academic program in IDN studies exists[2], neither with a focus on design nor on analytical aspects. So far, in education the topic is mostly taken up as part of student participation in research projects or within the context of a game design program. A program with a critical/analytical focus is even more elusive.

An analysis of Princeton Review's top listed Game Design programs[3] shows that interactive narrative courses are at best a minor concentration or integrated within the programs. Typically, these programs contain a single course with a title like "Foundations of Interactive Narrative,"[4] or "Intro to Narrative Design."[5] A rare exception is the bachelor program in "Game Writing" at the University of Skövde[6] in Sweden. Some universities teach interactive narrative design in their evening programs as non-degree courses, which indicates interest from working professionals. Examples include a course on "Game Writing" at UCLA[7] and the "Game Writing Academy" at the University of British Columbia.[8]

This state of affairs mark education as an area in need of additional attention by scholars in the field. Developing curricula, training methods and researching pedagogical aspects of IDN should therefore be a priority in the coming years. In addition, student demand for the topic is crucial in creating and maintaining academic programs and in providing job opportunities for scholars in the field.

4 Criteria for Academic Disciplines

The discussion about the disciplinary status of a field of research and the creation of new academic disciplines are both regular occurrences in academia. For example, Philip McKerrow in 1986 argued for a discipline of robotics [25]. He identifies two main requirements for such a proposal: "defining the conceptual basis for the discipline and developing a core curriculum that reflects that basis." McKerrow's main arguments for the discipline include the lack of specific training of undergrads, the division into subfields – and thus "splintering" of available resources – that might otherwise occur, and the danger of being involuntarily co-opted into existing disciplines like manufacturing technology which do not represent the breadth of work done in robotics.

---

[2] The defunct EUCROMA program (European Cross Media Academy), a collaboration between seven European institutions (DADIU (Denmark), the National Film School of Denmark, the University of Abertay Dundee, Cologne Game Lab, The Animation Workshop, the University of Malta and the Moholy-Nagy University of Art and Design), funded by the EU's MEDIA program and realized in 2013 can be seen as a predecessor with its focus on storyworld building.

[3] https://www.princetonreview.com/college-rankings/game-design.

[4] Rochester Institute of Technology, Game Design and Development BS degree.

[5] NYU, Game Design BFA.

[6] http://www.his.se/en/Prospective-student/education/Masters-Studies/Computer-Game-Development/.

[7] http://www.tft.ucla.edu/programs/professional-programs/video-game-writing/.

[8] https://extendedlearning.ubc.ca/programs/game-writing-academy.

A more recent example is in the discussion around gender studies and related fields, which maps well to the present discussion in regards to the question of interdisciplinarity. For example, Eloise Buker examines the question whether "Women's Studies is a discipline or an interdisciplinary activity" [26]. She develops a number of requirements for a discipline:

(1) a shared narrative of identity and community
(2) a common vocabulary and set of concepts
(3) a set of questions that guide inquiry
(4) a set of methods or strategies of interpretation, which construct what counts as evidence.

An important aspect of Buker's paper is her insight that a field can be both a "discipline and an interdisciplinary mode of inquiry" and that such a dual approach can be sustained as a practice that takes both perspectives into account. Furthermore, Buke counters arguments against a discipline of Women's Studies (essentially, that there is no need for a new discipline, as the topic is already covered in other areas) with a comparison to Political Sciences: "Political Science overlaps with history and philosophy as well as anthropology, sociology, psychology, and others." And yet, Political Sciences provides a distinct approach and perspective that would be considerably reduced without a disciplinary home. In regards to staying an interdisciplinary field, Buker points out the cost of doing so, effectively downplaying the specific expertise, body of knowledge and terminology of the scholarly community concerned with the topic. Furthermore, she points out the danger that without a discipline the "hard-earned knowledge and expertise" of the field can never be claimed at its own. Finally, Buker also identifies some potential downsides to creating a discipline, mostly in regards to the potential loss of interdisciplinary discourse and thus suggest to develop strategies to preserve interdisciplinary dialogue through specific administrative structures.

From a more neutral position, without a personal agenda to establish a discipline himself, Armin Krishnan offers six criteria to understand the status of an academic field as either disciplinarity or interdisciplinarity.

(1) disciplines have a particular object of research (e.g. law, society, politics), though the object of research maybe shared with another discipline
(2) disciplines have a body of accumulated specialist knowledge referring to their object of research, which is specific to them and not generally shared with another discipline
(3) disciplines have theories and concepts that can organise the accumulated specialist knowledge effectively
(4) disciplines use specific terminologies or a specific technical language adjusted to their research object
(5) disciplines have developed specific research methods according to their specific research requirements; and maybe most crucially
(6) disciplines must have some institutional manifestation in the form of subjects taught at universities or colleges, respective academic departments and professional associations connected to it [27].

It is important to note that Krishan does not understand his characteristics as requirements that all disciplines need to fulfill, as he points out using English Literature as an example:

[...] English literature has the problem that it lacks both a unifying theoretical paradigm or method *and* a definable stable object of research, but it still passes as an academic discipline.

Yet, crucially, Krishan does see the number of characteristics fulfilled by fields as an indication of recognition and of the field's ability for self-sustained development, as an ability of "reproducing itself and building upon a growing body of own scholarship."

Taken together, the criteria discussed by McKerrow, Buke and Krishan offer a flexible framework to the present discussion. In effect, they are three different lenses through which the situation of the field of IDN research can be analyzed.

5   Disciplinary Characteristics of the IDN Research Field

In the previous section, I have identified three sets of lenses which can be used to evaluate the status of field as a discipline. In applying these lenses, we can have a "reality check" and gain an understanding where the field stands.

McKerrow's two criteria are (1) defining the conceptual basis for the discipline and (2) developing a core curriculum that reflects that basis. In terms of (1) the criterium can be seen as fulfilled, indirectly in the form of the ICIDS conference series (which indicates a shared conceptual understanding amongst its participants). In addition, a concrete conceptual basis is provided in the form of Murray's seminal book *Hamlet on the Holodeck* [5]. However, the existence of different conceptual models is manifest through Aarseth's *Cybertext* [28] (his position before his game studies publications) as well as Cavazza and Young's introduction [29] of the topic in the *Handbook of Digital Games and Entertainment Technologies* – which makes clear that there is not (only) a singular shared conceptual basis. In that sense, the first criteria might be alternatively seen as only partially fulfilled, or an indication of the conceptual richness of the field. McKerrow's second criteria, the definition of core curriculum, is not fulfilled so far and this finding echoes the need for increased educational efforts I identified earlier.

Buker' categories are: (1) a shared narrative of identity and community; (2) a common vocabulary and set of concepts; (3) a set of questions that guide inquiry; (4) a set of methods or strategies of interpretation, which construct what counts as evidence. For (1), a shared narrative of community has emerged through the ICIDS conference (since 2008) and it its predecessors (TIDSE - Technologies for Interactive Digital Storytelling and Entertainment and ICVS - International Conference on Virtual Storytelling) that can be traced back to the early 2000s. A narrative of a shared identity is more difficult to identify, what exists might be more aptly described as a 'topical belonging'. For (2), a common vocabulary and set of concepts exist (e.g. Murray's theoretical framework of affordances and aesthetic qualities as well as terms like *agency* [5, 30–34], *ergodic* [28], *transformation* [5] or *interactor* [5, 35] are shared in the field. For (3), while no 'official' catalogue of research questions in the field exists, some general questions can be inferred from the publications in the field. Broadly, they are as follows: 'How can we theoretically understand the phenomena of IDN?'; 'How can we understand and improve the design of IDN works?'; 'What advanced computational methods (especially applying artificial intelligence) can we develop and use for IDN?'; 'What are IDNs good for, and how can we evaluate their use in different situations?' For (4), Murray's critical vocabulary and the further refinement of her terms by other scholars (see under question 2) as well as the further development of her model [36] and specific empirical methods [37, 38] exist that creates such scholarly evidence.

Next, I will look at Krishnan's categories (reactions under each category):

(1) disciplines have a particular object of research (e.g. law, society, politics), though the object of research maybe shared with another discipline.

For the present discussion, interactive digital narrative is clearly that object

(2) disciplines have a body of accumulated specialist knowledge referring to their object of research, which is specific to them and not generally shared with another discipline.

The accumulated proceedings of ICIDS, together with the INT proceedings can been seen as such knowledge. Additionally, several monographs and edited books fit into this category [5, 28, 36, 39–41].

(3) disciplines have theories and concepts that can organise the accumulated specialist knowledge effectively.

Aarseth's theory of cybertexts [28] and the ergodic as well as Murray's theoretical framework of affordances and aesthetic qualities [5] provide such organizational framings.

(4) disciplines use specific terminologies or a specific technical language adjusted to their research object.

Specific terminologies definitely exist. Terms like *agency* [5, 30–34], *ergodic* [28], *transformation* [5] or *interactor* [5, 35] are understood by scholars in the field in a specific way.

(5) disciplines have developed specific research methods according to their specific research requirements;

Aarseth's understanding of cybertexts [28] and Murray's theoretical framework of affordances and aesthetic qualities [5] and its further expansion as the SPP model [42, 43] provide critical methods. Roth's measurement toolbox [37, 44] is a specific empirical method to understand the user experience of IDN, which has more recently been developed as a method to evaluate design conventions [38, 45].

(6) disciplines must have some institutional manifestation in the form of subjects taught at universities or colleges, respective academic departments and professional associations connected to it.

Courses in interactive digital narrative are taught in many programs as mentioned earlier. Full programs of study or Departments, do not exist (the defunct Eucroma project (see Footnote 3) can serve as starting point for the development of programs of study) and a professional association is in formation.

6 Discussion: Ways to Move Forward

In this section, I will consider ways to move forward from two angles – in regards to approaching current and future research topics as a community and what a professional association can – and cannot – do for the field.

6.1 Approaching Current and Future Research Topics

The question how to identify shared research foci and then act on them as community, is crucial to move the field forward, since many aspects of IDN research (c.f. the broad questions identified in the previous section - 'How can we theoretically understand the phenomena of IDN?'; 'How can we understand and improve the design of IDN works?'; 'What advanced computational methods (especially applying artificial intelligence) can we develop and use for IDN?'; 'What are IDNs good for, and how can we evaluate their use in different situations?') will require the sustained attention of several researchers and research groups for some time to come. Yet, so far, the field as a whole has not been able to organize the discourse in a sustained manner[9], come to decisions and then act on them.

What has happened during the last decade, is that several proposals for overarching research topics and areas of concentration for future research were made. For example, the IRIS project [24] identified authoring as an area of concern, while Andrew Stern argued for a focus on AI [46] and Janet Murray in 2010 identified a need to consider design conventions [47]. Continuing this line of discussion, in 2014, I identified five key areas in need of attention: theoretical models, interoperability of software, sustainable development, a focus on authoring, and the centrality of the user experience [22].

All of these proposals might be considered reasonable by themselves. However, what has been missing is a follow-up in the form of an organized discussion in the community to decide which proposals to support, with what resources and in which form. At present, feedback is provided mostly in the form of the limited discourse of academic peer review and grant submission feedback. Any additional discussion are piecemeal at best. This state of affairs has been a considerable obstacle to the field's progress. What is needed instead is a sustained discussion and continuous discourse which considers the larger context along with longer trajectories. This also means to

---

[9] The group blog Grand Text Auto (by Mary Flanagan, Michael Mateas, Nick Montfort, Scott Rettberg, Andrew Stern, and Noah Wardrip-Fruin) can be seen as a model for how a small group of scholars can organize the discourse amongst them. The blog served in this capacity for a number of years until its demise in 2013. However, the defunct status of this forum (available at https://wayback.archive-it.org/788/*/http://grandtextauto.org/) alerts us to the danger of discontinuity of volunteer efforts without institutional support.

take additional aspects into account, for example the support of young scholars and general research trends. In effect, this would be the behaviour of a discipline.

Thinking and acting as a discipline would therefore mean to create structures and maintain processes that enable sustainable community engagement in helping to decide future focus areas and how to approach them.

6.2 A Professional Association: ARDIN's Role

A professional association can fulfill some of the functions missing at present. Ultimately though, as the example of many established disciplines and their related professional associations show (e.g. MLA and English Literature, ACM and Computer Science, IEEE and Electrical Engineering). Discipline and professional association are both necessary, as they fulfill different functions. In addition, all of the aforementioned organizations represent more than one discipline and can thus been understood as a means to further interdisciplinary discourse.

It is in this respect that the initiative for ARDIN (Association for Research in Digital Interactive Narratives, http://ardin.online) started at ICIDS 2017, and being incorporated at the time of this writing, should be understood. ARDIN can potentially support IDN research in many ways, as an organizational home for conferences, with the publication of a journal, by providing financial support to young scholars, by recognizing work in the field through awards and fellowships, by offering publication opportunities and by providing an institution that through evaluation guidelines and whitepapers validates individual researchers and the field as a whole. ARDIN can also provide a forum for the community to discuss issues and find common ground in order to develop the field further. Finally, the organization can act as a repository and archive for the community.

However, aspects like organizing degree programs, providing positions for scholars, graduating students, promoting scholars and providing the institutional infrastructure are tasks left for an academic discipline.

7 Concluding Remarks

The points presented in this paper – mainly the lack of specific academic evaluation for scholars working on the topic, discontinuity, and lack of formal education, but also the limitations in the community's approach toward current and future research foci – support one overarching argument, that for the creation of Interactive Narrative Studies, an academic discipline concerned with the analysis (both of works and their impact) and design (both of audience-facing works and of underlying computational systems) of IDN. This step would address many challenges for scholars in this field, including hurdles to academic recognition and tenure for individual researchers due to the lack of guidelines backed by an institutional framework, as well as many of the problems holding back the field as a whole (e.g. academic memory loss, lack of a sustained space for community discussions and decisions and the excessive dependency on grants).

The 'reality check' provided by the three lenses on disciplinary status identifies the lack of fully developed academic programs of study as the largest missing piece for the creation of a discipline. The lack of a professional association is being addressed with the formation of ARDIN. Many additional criteria can be seen as already fulfilled, thanks to the existing body of scholarly research as well as the community framework provided by ICIDS.

Thus, the field has already progressed considerably towards becoming a discipline. If this statement seems surprising to some, it shows how much we have become accustomed to an existence within other disciplines. Yet, this situation can – and should be – changed for the reasons outlined throughout this paper. The destination is clear – the establishment of a discipline concerned with the analysis and design of interactive digital narratives. And while the realisation of this vision might take a while, there is no better time to start than now.

References

1. Ryan, J.: Grimes' fairy tales: a 1960s story generator. In: Nunes, N., Oakley, I., Nisi, V. (eds.) ICIDS 2017. LNCS, vol. 10690, pp. 89–103. Springer, Cham (2017). https://doi.org/10.1007/978-3-319-71027-3_8
2. Buckles, M.A.: Interactive Fiction: The Computer Storygame "Adventure" Ph.D. Thesis, University of California, San Diego (1985)
3. Aarseth, E.J.: Genre trouble. In: Wardrip-Fruin, N., Harrigan, P. (eds.) First Person: New Media as Story, Performance, and Game. MIT Press, Cambridge (2004)
4. AcademySoft: Tetris (1984)
5. Murray, J.H.: Hamlet on the Holodeck: The Future of Narrative in Cyberspace. Free Press, New York (1997)
6. Murray, J.H.: From Game-Story to Cyberdrama. http://electronicbookreview.com/thread/firstperson/autodramatic
7. Frasca, G.: Ludologists love stories, too: notes from a debate that never took place. In: DIGRA Conference (2003)
8. AAA Statement on Ethnographic Visual Media. Am. Anthropol. **104**, 305–306 (2002)
9. Society For Visual Anthropology: Guidelines for the evaluation of ethnographic visual media.   http://societyforvisualanthropology.org/guidelines-for-the-evaluation-of-ethnographic-visual-media/
10. DH Working Group: Guidelines for the professional evaluation of digital scholarship by historians.   https://www.historians.org/teaching-and-learning/digital-history-resources/evaluation-of-digital-scholarship-in-history/guidelines-for-the-professional-evaluation-of-digital-scholarship-by-historians
11. Iurgel, I.: From another point of view: art-e-fact. In: Göbel, S., et al. (eds.) TIDSE 2004. LNCS, vol. 3105, pp. 26–35. Springer, Heidelberg (2004). https://doi.org/10.1007/978-3-540-27797-2_4
12. Cavazza, M., Charles, F., Mead, S.J.: Developing re-usable interactive storytelling technologies. In: Jacquart, R. (ed.) Building the Information Society. IIFIP, vol. 156, pp. 39–44. Springer, Boston (2004). https://doi.org/10.1007/978-1-4020-8157-6_6
13. Donikian, S., Portugal, J.-N.: Writing interactive fiction scenarii with DraMachina. In: Göbel, S., et al. (eds.) TIDSE 2004. LNCS, vol. 3105, pp. 101–112. Springer, Heidelberg (2004). https://doi.org/10.1007/978-3-540-27797-2_14

14. Weiss, S., Müller, W., Spierling, U., Steimle, F.: Scenejo – an interactive storytelling platform. In: Subsol, G. (ed.) ICVS 2005. LNCS, vol. 3805, pp. 77–80. Springer, Heidelberg (2005). https://doi.org/10.1007/11590361_9

15. Thomas, J.M., Young, R.M.: Elicitation and application of narrative constraints through mixed-initiative planning. Presented at the International Conference on Automated Planning & Scheduling 2006, Ambleside, UK (2006)

16. Medler, B., Magerko, B.: Scribe: a tool for authoring event driven interactive drama. In: Göbel, S., Malkewitz, R., Iurgel, I. (eds.) TIDSE 2006. LNCS, vol. 4326, pp. 139–150. Springer, Heidelberg (2006). https://doi.org/10.1007/11944577_14

17. Kriegel, M., Aylett, R., Dias, J., Paiva, A.: An authoring tool for an emergent narrative storytelling system. Presented at the AAAI Fall Symposium on Intelligent Narrative Technologies, Arlington (2007)

18. Skorupski, J., Jayapalan, L., Marquez, S., Mateas, M.: Wide ruled: a friendly interface to author-goal based story generation. In: Cavazza, M., Donikian, S. (eds.) ICVS 2007. LNCS, vol. 4871, pp. 26–37. Springer, Heidelberg (2007). https://doi.org/10.1007/978-3-540-77039-8_3

19. Réty, J.-H., Bouchardon, S., Clément, J., Szilas, N., Angé, C.: Rencontre: an experimental tool for digital literature. In: Electronic Literature in Europe, Bergen (2008)

20. Koenitz, H., Chen, K.-J.: Genres, structures and strategies in interactive digital narratives – analyzing a body of works created in ASAPS. In: Oyarzun, D., Peinado, F., Young, R.M., Elizalde, A., Méndez, G. (eds.) ICIDS 2012. LNCS, vol. 7648, pp. 84–95. Springer, Heidelberg (2012). https://doi.org/10.1007/978-3-642-34851-8_8

21. Mitchell, A.: The HypeDyn Procedural Hypertext Fiction Authoring Tool, p. 1 (2016)

22. Koenitz, H.: Five theses for interactive digital narrative. In: Mitchell, A., Fernández-Vara, C., Thue, D. (eds.) ICIDS 2014. LNCS, vol. 8832, pp. 134–139. Springer, Cham (2014). https://doi.org/10.1007/978-3-319-12337-0_13

23. Szilas, N., Boggini, T., Axelrad, M., Petta, P., Rank, S.: Specification of an open architecture for interactive storytelling. In: Si, M., Thue, D., André, E., Lester, J.C., Tanenbaum, J., Zammitto, V. (eds.) ICIDS 2011. LNCS, vol. 7069, pp. 330–333. Springer, Heidelberg (2011). https://doi.org/10.1007/978-3-642-25289-1_41

24. Cavazza, M., et al.: The IRIS network of excellence: integrating research in interactive storytelling. In: Spierling, U., Szilas, N. (eds.) Interactive Storytelling: First Joint International Conference on Interactive Digital Storytelling, pp. 14–19. Springer, Heidelberg (2008). https://doi.org/10.1007/978-3-540-89454-4_3

25. McKerrow, P.J.: Robotics, an academic discipline? Robotics 2, 267–274 (1986)

26. Buker, E.: Is women's studies a disciplinary or an interdisciplinary field of inquiry? NWSA J. 15, 73–93 (2003)

27. Krishnan, A.: What Are Academic Disciplines? ESRC National Centre for Research Methods (2009)

28. Aarseth, E.J.: Cybertext. JHU Press, Baltimore (1997)

29. Cavazza, M., Young, R.M.: Introduction to interactive storytelling. In: Nakatsu, R., Rauterberg, M., Ciancarini, P. (eds.) Handbook of Digital Games and Entertainment Technologies, pp. 377–392. Springer, Singapore (2016). https://doi.org/10.1007/978-981-4560-52-8_55-1

30. Mason, S.: On games and links: extending the vocabulary of agency and immersion in interactive narratives. In: Koenitz, H., Sezen, T.I., Ferri, G., Haahr, M., Sezen, D., Çatak, G. (eds.) ICIDS 2013. LNCS, vol. 8230, pp. 25–34. Springer, Cham (2013). https://doi.org/10.1007/978-3-319-02756-2_3

31. Harrell, D.F., Zhu, J.: Agency play: dimensions of agency for interactive narrative design. Presented at the AAAI Spring Symposium: Intelligent Narrative Technologies (2009)

32. Wardrip-Fruin, N., Mateas, M., Dow, S., Sali, S.: Agency reconsidered. In: Proceedings of DiGRA 2009: Breaking New Ground: Innovation in Games, Play, Practice and Theory (2009)
33. Knoller, N.: Agency and the art of interactive digital storytelling. In: Aylett, R., Lim, M.Y., Louchart, S., Petta, P., Riedl, M. (eds.) ICIDS 2010. LNCS, vol. 6432, pp. 264–267. Springer, Heidelberg (2010). https://doi.org/10.1007/978-3-642-16638-9_38
34. Day, T., Zhu, J.: Agency informing techniques. In: Proceedings of the International Conference on the Foundations of Digital Fames - FDG 2017, New York, New York, USA (2017)
35. Anstey, J., Pape, D.: Scripting the interactor. In: Proceedings of the Fourth Conference on Creativity & Cognition - C&C 2002, New York, New York, USA (2002)
36. Koenitz, H., Ferri, G., Haahr, M., Sezen, D., Sezen, T.I.: Interactive Digital Narrative: History, Theory, and Practice. Routledge, New York (2015)
37. Roth, C., Vorderer, P., Klimmt, C., Vermeulen, I.: Measuring the user experience in narrative-rich games: towards a concept-based assessment for interactive stories. Entertainment Interfaces (2010)
38. Roth, C., Koenitz, H.: Towards creating a body of evidence-based interactive digital narrative design knowledge: approaches and challenges. Presented at AltMM'17, Mountain View, California (2017). https://doi.org/10.1145/3132361.3133942
39. Mateas, M., Sengers, P. (eds.): Narrative Intelligence. John Benjamins Publishing, Amsterdam/Philadelphia (2003)
40. Meadows, M.S.: Pause & Effect. New Riders Press, Indianapolis (2003)
41. Montfort, N.: Twisty Little Passages. MIT Press, Cambridge (2005)
42. Koenitz, H.: Towards a theoretical framework for interactive digital narrative. In: Aylett, R., Lim, M.Y., Louchart, S., Petta, P., Riedl, M. (eds.) ICIDS 2010. LNCS, vol. 6432, pp. 176–185. Springer, Heidelberg (2010). https://doi.org/10.1007/978-3-642-16638-9_22
43. Koenitz, H.: Towards a specific theory of interactive digital narrative. In: Koenitz, H., Ferri, G., Haahr, M., Sezen, D., Sezen, T.I. (eds.) Interactive Digital Narrative, pp. 91–105. Routledge, New York (2015)
44. Roth, C., Vermeulen, I.: Breaching interactive storytelling's implicit agreement: a content analysis of façade user behaviors. In: Koenitz, H., Sezen, T.I., Ferri, G., Haahr, M., Sezen, D., Catak, G. (eds.) ICIDS 2013. LNCS, vol. 8230, pp. 168–173. Springer, Cham (2013). https://doi.org/10.1007/978-3-319-02756-2_20
45. Koenitz, H., Roth, C., Dubbelman, T., Knoller, N.: What is a convention in interactive narrative design? In: Nunes, N., Oakley, I., Nisi, V. (eds.) Interactive Storytelling, pp. 295–298. Springer, Cham (2017). https://doi.org/10.1007/978-3-319-71027-3_29
46. Stern, A.: Embracing the combinatorial explosion: a brief prescription for interactive story R&D. In: Spierling, U., Szilas, N. (eds.) Interactive Storytelling. ICIDS 2008. LNCS, vol. 5334, pp. 1–5. Springer, Heidelberg (2008). https://doi.org/10.1007/978-3-540-89454-4_1
47. Murray, J.H.: Inventing the Medium: Principles of Interaction Design as a Cultural Practice. MIT Press, Cambridge (2012)

A Villain's Guide to Social Media and Interactive Digital Storytelling

Mark Bernstein[1(✉)] and Clare Hooper[2]

[1] Eastgate Systems, Inc., 134 Main St, Watertown, MA 02472, USA
bernstein@eastgate.com
[2] Vancouver, BC, Canada

Abstract. If we have not yet achieved planetary super-villainy on the desktop, it may be feasible to fit it into a suburban office suite. The familiar perils of fiction and deceit can now be augmented by mass customization, allowing powerful malefactors to shape perceived reality to suit their preferences. Social media permit the modern villain to deploy traditional cruelties to great and surprising effect. Interactive digital storytelling lets us exploit weakness and illness for profit and help us normalize wickedness. Because the impact of villainous techniques is radically asymmetric, our fetid plots are difficult and costly to foil.

Keywords: Hypertext · New media · Literature · Fiction · Implementation
History of computing · Politics · Villainy

1 Introduction

Technological innovation has long facilitated villainy at ever greater scale. Technology, moreover, offers many opportunities to cater to the whims and caprice of the individual villain. The vandal hordes of antiquity were proverbially destructive, but they were hordes: they lacked the personal touch. More recent efforts, such as the M. Ming's Gigantic Nitron Ray, D. Vader's Death Star, and A. Goldfinger's thermonuclear attack on international markets, achieved that personal touch only by commanding vast stockpiles of capital.

Previous technological approaches to villainy depended on doomsday machines, zombie apocalypses, thermonuclear devices and the like, as these were the only available technologies that supported large-magnitude calamities. New media permit the modern villain to deploy traditional cruelties at unprecedented scale. We admit that small cruelties and local harms can be just as satisfying as global conquest, mass destruction, or summoning the elder gods. Still, there is satisfaction in numbers, and only by specifying a victim pool of adequate size can we ensure the statistical significance of our results.

The focus of this work is restricted to villainy. We are not concerned here with merely criminal uses of social media and the interactive storytelling, such as money laundering, theft, or embezzlement. Our concerns, as always, are domination of cities, nations, and planets, accumulation of wealth beyond the dreams of avarice, the destruction of dreams and widespread infliction of pain.

© Springer Nature Switzerland AG 2018
R. Rouse et al. (Eds.): ICIDS 2018, LNCS 11318, pp. 50–61, 2018.
https://doi.org/10.1007/978-3-030-04028-4_4

Our central observation is that important new media technologies provide asymmetric advantage to villainy.

2 The Price of Lies

People have mistrusted fiction since Plato. They have sound reason: there is only one truth, and that truth may be obscure and misunderstood. Against truth, we may place any number of lies. We can choose these lies for their clarity, and for the convincing certainty with which we can expound them.

If we do not know which tall tale might best serve our wicked ends, familiar analytical techniques for real-time sentiment analysis and A/B testing can be deployed in real time to track engagement and propagation of our stories [26]. We can know within minutes what messages are most attractive to different audiences. We can transfer resources to those stories that appeal most strongly to our audience; we need not waste time and attention on less efficient stories, even if they happen to be true. Our successes are our own; our failures cost us little.

In the late age of print, extensive philosophical and empirical investigation into the nature of reading and the formation of meaning cast grave doubt on many former certainties. Readers play a crucial role in giving meaning to texts; much of our experience of a text—whether a novel, a painting, or a televised drama—is derived from knowledge we bring to it, and is not to be found within the boundaries of the work itself. Your experience of *Hamlet* is not mine (fortunately!), nor can you experience *Hamlet* today as you did thirty years ago. This postmodern understanding opened important new vistas in theory and criticism, and for a time cast the very idea of truth into doubt. If you and I experience *Hamlet* and *The New York Times* differently, what can be authentic or real? [35].

This brief solipsistic crisis was resolved in academe by the understanding that we had all witnessed the Holocaust, or knew people who had; the implication that even this was subject to doubt raised objections too great to overcome. But that was within the academy: in the lunatic fringes of the right, Holocaust denial and white supremacy were not only acceptable consequences of Theory: they were reasons to embrace Theory. If the arc of history bends toward Justice, perhaps it could be unbent by inventing a different reality, a different history, and a different truth.

There are a million lies in the naked city, and only one truth. Our sanctimonious rivals will fight endlessly among themselves to define and refine that truth, even if the result is adverse to their personal and political interest. While they parse nuance and endure inconvenient truths, we invent our own, numerous truths and test them rigorously for efficacy. What is more, our untruths are more interesting than truth, and so our foul fantasies will be shared and retweeted more frequently than truthful reports [25].

3 Knowing Your Audience

The wise storyteller has always adapted the story to the interests and inclinations of each audience. Homer knew this: when Odysseus found it inconvenient or perilous to be a prince fallen among working people, he reinvented himself as a minor royal from a distant land—an amusing bum worth listening to, surely, but really just another working guy (*Odyssey* 19.172–184) [27].

Where Homer had to guess, we know. Readers of interactive digital stories tell us about themselves as they make choices that allow us to construct adaptive user models [28]. Given the opportunity, readers will unburden themselves to our systems with astonishing frankness: people Googling for information about possible symptoms of venereal disease frequently tell Google about their thoughts of suicide [29]. We need not depend on such trusting volubility, however; we can, for example, discover the household income of Twitter users from their Twitter preferences, even for passive users who seldom or never tweet [30]. We can also identify social media users who are secretive but who have chosen to retain default privacy settings; where researchers see users who might have failed to learn how to change their preference settings, the villain will recognize the familiar scent of people with something to hide and who feebly are striving to emulate those with nothing to fear [31]. We've been seeking out vulnerable marks for generations; now, neural networks can do the scouting for us.

Here again, our advantage is asymmetric. Diogenes endured a long and fruitless search for an honest man because he was looking for a single, rare strength. We look instead for any weakness, and of finding vice there is no end.

4 Disinformation and Discord

What is better than making one's fellow man believe something that is not true? Why, making multitudes believe something that is both preposterous and harmful! Systematically spreading false news has proven to be of enormous value, and those scientists and thinkers who seek to disrupt our despicable designs have few answers as to how they might limit the havoc that we can wreck [42].

Engagement aroused by provocative and targeted lies benefits us. Our opponents are bound to try to discredit our deceptions; their struggles only increase our reach. Discourse generation, machine translation, and assistive writing tools allow minions with limited skills to manage numerous online personae, each of which helps spread our message. A single semi-literate minion can, in favorable circumstances, engage several distinguished professors and authoritative experts. Because many of the bystanders witnessing the argument will undoubtedly resent teachers—who among us has no desire to avenge old classroom wrongs?—our minion sometimes achieve surprising success. Yet even if our minion is vanquished and today's lies are entirely discredited, no harm is done; our minion can go home, drink a beer, enjoy a good cackle with friends, and tomorrow our minion can pick up its new followers, put on a new persona, and try again. The more we engage, the more traffic we receive.

Disinformation promotes discord. We consider discord good in itself, of course, but discord also weakens our opponents while strengthening our other operations.

Our truthiness itself promotes further discord among our enemies, as each invidious invention may provoke a new fissure among our fractious foes.

Disinformation has revived some of our oldest aspirations. The dream of a single vast database that identifies every prominent Jew (as defined by the *Nürnberger Gesetze!*) once seemed lost forever, but Wikipedia now labors daily to make it real. Wikipedia editors—often the same editors—work to render articles about marginal extremists more prominent and palatable, to excuse (and publicize) racist and anti-Semitic memes, and to defame both contemporary and historic figures. Deliberate campaigns to move the Overton window target topics such as the virtues of Wehrmacht heroes or the revived Nordic Nazi Parties; if Sweden and Norway have white supremacists, they argue, perhaps Nazism is worth a second look?

5 Procuring Victims

Social media and networked games generate vast resources of information about the interests, habits, and circumstances of millions of people throughout the world. Much information is, of course, contained in the users' profiles and user-generated content, data they freely make available for our use. Other useful information is implicit in their use of media to keep in touch with friends and family, to discover entertaining Web sites, or to purchase products—including the valueless but costly virtual products we sell in our storyworlds. We can use this vast stream of data to identify those to whom we most profitably might devote our attentions. Where an advertiser looks for a persuadable and remunerative prospect, villains seek a vulnerable and satisfying victim.

It is useful in this connection to distinguish between intrinsic and extrinsic vulnerability. The intrinsically vulnerable target is subject to attack because of their circumstances and context; the friendless are natural victims, of course, but so, too, are those whose friends are largely disjoint from ours. This is readily detected through the social graph [13]. Extrinsic vulnerability occurs when people have secrets: hidden families, complex love affairs, financial strain are all classic indicators, and these, too, may be detectable from social networks alone [3, 31].

We now know it is possible to de-anonymize anonymous social graphs [2] and that private information like religious belief may be inferred from such secular statistics as Wikipedia edit counts [15]. Remember, too, that we are villains; sometimes, the old ways are the best ways, and a simple kidnapping or a short prison term can lead people otherwise hostile to us to help de-anonymize even the most obfuscated data or to give us the most closely guarded password [7, 14, 17].

Machine Learning provides many attractive ways to detect subtle patterns and to defeat attempts at anonymity. We can, for example, predict from the venues at which a young musician has performed whether they eventually will be rewarded by a recording contract [38]. The Good might use this to bet on the Eurovision contest. Villains like us, on the other hand, could use the same method to predict whether young musicians will follow the career trajectory of Jimmy Hendrix, Janis Joplin, Kurt Cobain and Amy Winehouse; armed with that intelligence, what havoc might we not wreak?

6 Finding Minions

Though extortion is fun reliable (and often fun), new media also allow new opportunities for engaging and recruiting individual members of our audience. A single minion, for example, can provide memorable, hand-crafted play experiences in real-time to numerous players [32]. Such specialized performances, of course, are most profitably provided to those who will pay well for them [33], bellwethers who will recruit many additional customers or those whose opinion and favor we most desire to cultivate. We might, for example, seek out proponents of a political party we oppose in order to distract them, frustrate them, or to mislead them into thinking their fellow-travelers are their antagonists [34]. At the same time, our minion can identify prospects to enter our sinister service.

The power of story can itself be a potent tool for minion recruitment. First, we now understand the importance of *projection* in leading people to attribute complex emotional attributes to simple computational agents [22]. If a computational entity speaks to them, many are provisionally inclined to regard it as deserving politeness, sympathy, or consideration. If it offers to help them, many are inclined to experience gratitude. Seeking to assist storyworld entities or longing for their approval, our audience may be induced to emulate the entities' wicked beliefs and aspirations.

Not every member of the audience will be subject to projection. Indeed, the absence of such empathetic emotions might well merit our further attention as indicating a special aptitude for villainous enterprises. We have always sought out such persons in mean streets and dark corners; networked entertainments may let us pre-screen thousands or millions of would-be minions without tying up our costly personnel. Indeed, the *sorting hats* used for new player onboarding can themselves serve this purpose.

If projection is our ally, *transference* is a weapon honed expressly for our service. Large, persistent storyworlds with cooperating player protagonists naturally lead to hierarchical associations based on player skill and experience. Weak and inexperienced players are inducted into the service of their betters and of their guild. Experienced players offer advice and equipment the new player could not easily match, and their orders and directives give purpose and meaning to virtual existence. The devotion of susceptible audience members in these circumstances may extend to vast expenditures, devoted political service, and (apparently) to murder [43]. The gamification of scurrilous politics such as sexual harassment [44] and the promotion of racial violence [45] lets us deploy tools honed for managing multi-player games to benefit ourselves and our often-surprising allies [19].

7 Dismaying Our Enemies

Not only can we use new media for our dark purposes and analyze it for our nefarious ends, but at the same time we can prevent our enemies from enjoying its benefits.

Social media are exquisitely vulnerable to trolls [1]. Good people can sometimes tolerate unjust censure in referee reports or in the pages of an obscure and dusty journal; to be smeared before one's family and closest friends, on the other hand, will try the patience of saints. Helpfully, bystander apathy is the norm online [23].

We must also remember that conventional villainy may be employed with profit on the new media battlefield. Blackmail, for example, can effectively silence even the most influential and experienced Wikipedia opponent. Elaborate and inconvenient security arrangements can be defeated by accosting the target and displaying a weapon. Indeed, speculating about attacking a pet may suffice, not only from fear of losing the services and cost of the target's mangy little dog, but also because the target will understand that if villains knows about Toto, they also know details of the rest of their beloved circle. Crowd-sourced research can uncover surprising insights into an anonymous writer's life [4], and these may be deployed through conventional means among the target's family, employers, and neighbors. Sometimes, we can sit back and enjoy the fun while the asymmetries of public outrages and confusion do our work for us[1].

8 Mining

Because advertising is most profitably directed to those who require the advertised goods, great efforts have been dedicated to anticipating individual needs by mining users' online behavior. Algorithms can sometimes detect desires before they are consciously expressed—for example, we might deduce from her purchasing and browsing behavior that a woman may be pregnant before she (or her family) knows [11]. Might it be possible to identify women who will soon seek to terminate a pregnancy prior to conception? Even accepting a substantial error rate, great mayhem might be achieved at very little cost. Similar mining efforts directed at other behaviors—romantic entanglements, dread diseases—could yield spectacular dividends [8]. Powerful, well-established methods reliably trick people into revealing more than they intend [24]. The online world is our oyster.

Again, we observe a pronounced asymmetry in the villainous effects of data mining. Our opponents must make do with data that they can access freely or that they can purchase. Unlike them, we are free to use stolen data—either information that happens to have been stolen (John Podesta's emails, Vermeer's *The Concert*), or information whose theft, being advantageous to our plans, we commission. Co-occurrence in large, stolen data stores can be a powerful tool in itself; a cluster of healthy, athletic users of watch-based fitness apps who are geolocated in an area that is blank in Google Maps may be a secret military base [12]. Analysis of big data thrives on bigger data: our data will always be bigger than theirs, and we can always buy, borrow, and steal more.

---

[1] http://www.cbc.ca/news/canada/calgary/jeremy-quaile-knightley-dog-death-calgary-1.4602948.

9 Stealing Candy from a Baby

Although we now employ analytical tools that exceed the wildest dreams of our predecessors, it behooves us to remember the simple joys of bygone days. Let us consider, for example, stealing candy from a baby. Nothing could be easier. Yet, through a single act, we reap many benefits.

- The baby is wretched, naturally, and expresses its dismay with appropriate force.
- An infant's cry of distress cannot be ignored: its parents must stop what they were doing, however virtuous and important their plans may have been, to attend to the child.
- Bystanders will be annoyed and distracted, and may cast disparaging glances at the parents who permit such disruption. Discord is sown.
- The infant may have siblings; if so, they may take advantage of parental distraction to engage in roughhousing, casual vandalism, or indoor parkour practice.
- And, you get a lollipop!

The intent of this perfidious pastorale is not to indulge nostalgia for a simpler era, but to observe the powerful asymmetry we can so gainfully employ. To steal candy from a baby is proverbially easy, yet the theft does not merely please the thief and dismay the child; parents, siblings, bystanders, the owners of the candy shop, the paramedics summoned when indoor parkour practice goes awry, all share and multiply our iniquitous impact. Efforts to foil our scheme are disproportionately difficult: for example, handing out free lollipops to passing infants is unlikely to exert an equal effect.

Not only do the asymmetric effects of villainy benefit from network, but our villainy itself benefits the platform. On the internet, wronged innocents wail online, and their cries attract clicks (which improve the platform's stock valuation) and viewers (to whom advertising may be displayed). Crowds that gather at the crime scene are themselves famously vulnerable to villainous exploitation [9], and a modest effort can keep an event like Gamergate or Pizzagate in play for weeks or months. Virtuous peacemakers, in contrast, diminish platform profits.

Analyzing the crowds gathered at these events may yield useful leads for staffing malevolent enterprises. Conventional global villainy once entailed a costly array of mad scientists and renegade warlords. These indispensible personnel were difficult to manage. Armies of minor minions, moreover, required salaries, training, and cool uniforms. Though villains were pioneers in employing the physically challenged [16], those challenges brought expense, inconvenience, and sometimes betrayal [20]. Much recruitment and support can now be automated; indeed, minions often appear at our crime scenes and volunteer for service. Nor should we neglect the former costs of maintaining entire districts to serve as vile dens and wretched hives of scum and villainy. We can now recruit minions in their own basements to support our repellent endeavor. They advance our dark designs without expensive secret bases or inconvenient hidden fortresses.

10 Abusing Agents and Blowing Stuff up

In interactive digital stories and immersive games, computational agents and characters offer intriguing opportunities to corrupt the naïve and mislead the unwary. In the realm of the (notionally) imaginary, even the good may indulge the darker angels of their nature. In *Call Of Duty* or *Dying Light,* accidental judgments and casual slaughter are delightful fun. Better yet, by situating the action as fictive while rendering with the greatest possible sensual fidelity, we may be able to finesse or obscure complex moral choices, making the same choices equally obscure in the mundane world. If we are Prince Hamlet on the holodeck [36], can we marry Ophelia? Might we seduce her? Marriage requires consent: in what sense can a computational construct give consent if the alternative is to rust unused on the shelf? In the theater, Ophelia drowns nightly (and twice on Sunday) but it's not out fault; on the Holodeck, she suffers just for us [37]. By giving permission to ignore these questions in a fictive context, we may in time convince people to overlook them elsewhere [47].

Though deep learning methods have proven surprisingly powerful, neural networks can be fooled From satire to bias, from fantasy news to intentional misrepresentation of the truth, the truth itself has never been so complicated [39]. Fake content can fool seasoned journalists, and neural nets know even less of the world than cub reporters. For example, consider transfer learning, a machine learning techniques, where a 'student' model learns from a centralized 'teacher' dataset. This approach is exquisitely vulnerable when the 'teacher' dataset is publicly available [40] or when the system is available for reverse-engineering or steganographic attack. This promises many an opportunity to the savvy villain.

Recent research extols just how many routes exist for introducing bias into online material. Flavors of bias include algorithmic, data, second-order and interaction bias. Second-order bias is particularly delicious as a 'rich get richer' phenomenon: for example, the top items in ranked lists receive more clicks and thereby increase their rank. Personal recommendation systems may notionally address this, but their use may confine the audience to closed worlds ('filter bubbles'), without exposure to other views and news. What's more, personalization algorithms collect even more user data for us to exploit [41].

11 Related Work

Though early villainy was sometimes conceived at surprising scale (see *Paradise Lost,* or the *Prose Edda*), it was only after J. Moriarty's invention of organized crime that technology could properly be applied to our ends. The early work of Sauron is typical in its acceptance of the limitations of scale, targeting a mere nineteen initial victims: as the nineteen designated targets were the rulers of the known world, the scheme did demonstrate commendable audacity. Computational efforts to summon the elder gods [18], to mock creation [16] or to bring on the end of the universe [6] anticipate the approaches described here.

Preliminary efforts known as Gamergate, though unsuccessful in reforming ethics in game journalism, did succeed in harming a handful of targeted victims while requiring our opponents to expend thousands of hours in order to oppose our handful of amateur villains. The same methods are believed to have been applied to the 2016 US Presidential Election and to the 2016 Brexit vote with surprising success [34].

Villainy is not new, but the asymmetric advantages that new media provide to villainy are arguably without precedent. Propaganda mattered in WW2, but it mattered equally to allies and axis [46]. That the fascists had better graphic design need not lead us to conclude that graphic design is intrinsically fascist, any more than the superiority of Sergei Eisenstein to Leni Riefenstahl can be taken as evidence that Communism is better suited to film theory than Fascism. When the Melians debated the Athenians, both used the same rhetoric to convince the same audience: the situation was essentially symmetric. That is not the case for contemporary new media and digital narrative: through contrivance or (mis)chance, current technology asymmetrically assists villains in our eternal struggle.

12 Conclusion

Much though we deplore the fact, technological progress can benefit the virtuous as well as the evil. What seems striking in this brief and anecdotal survey of new techniques and recent developments are the prominent asymmetries that redound to the benefit of villainy.

- The villain can lie, the good should not. Disinformation is villainous in itself and leads to discord, which is even better.
- The villain can steal, the good must not. Data mining is powerful, but its power increases as more data becomes available. Our neural networks do not care that some of our data is pilfered.
- Disinformation and rumor may be spread by the idle, the unskilled, and the robot. To confound them requires the attention of skilled advocates.
- We can choose the lies that serve us best; our enemies cannot. There are a million lies but only one truth.
- A working minion, stymied, can dust itself off and work on a new meme. A true believer in the same position may experience profound humiliation.
- The villain, on encountering weakness or derangement, asks "how can this benefit me?" The good must ask, "how can I lend my strength or aid to this sufferer?" Encountering the disordered and distressed, the villain profits while the good suffer delay and distraction.
- A single scurrilous word or damaging disclosure can do lasting harm that a thousand well-intentioned and sympathetic notes will not repair.

Our great opportunity thus lies not in mere network effects or our first-mover advantage. Nor (fortunately for us, because true black-hearted villainy is a rare gift) do our asymmetric advantages depend on superior numbers, talent or funding. It is said that the arc of the moral universe is long and it bends toward justice; with the aid of these advantages, we may at long last hammer it flat. Current research efforts have done little to foil these infernal schemes or to reverse our precious asymmetries, but we should remain vigilant lest researchers shift their focus from winning employment with advertising platforms to saving freedom and democracy.

It has always been the case that some people like to inflict pain, but previous technologies—schools of martial arts, for example—have been hedged with the kinds of disciplines, hierarchies and rituals that villains like us dislike. Today's new media are not encumbered with fun-killing folderol. Publishers profit alike from the cruel and the kind, but because villainy attracts crowds, villains accrue unexpected benefits and unlooked-for allies. If we have not yet achieved planetary super-villainy on the desktop, it may be feasible to fit it into a suburban office suite [5].

Acknowledgments. This is a satire. Don't try this at home. The works cited here are not villainous. We thank David E. Millard, Charlie Hargood, Dr. Fionnbar Lenihan and Robert A. Sullivan for helpful conversations on related topics. Of course, none of them are in any way responsible for this villainous paper.

References

1. Ammann, R.: Jorn barger, the newspage network and the emergence of the weblog community. In: Proceedings of the 20th ACM Conference on Hypertext and Hypermedia. HT 2009, pp. 279–288 (2009)
2. Backstrom, L., Dworkin, C., Kleinberg, J.: Wherefore art thou R3579x?: Anonymized social networks, hidden patterns, and structural steganography. Commun. ACM **54**(12), 133–141 (2011)
3. Backstrom, L., Kleinberg, J.: Romantic partnerships and the dispersion of social ties: a network analysis of relationship status on Facebook. In: Proceedings of the 17th ACM Conference on Computer Supported Cooperative Work & Social Computing, CSCW 2014, pp. 831–841 (2014)
4. Johnson, B.: The Short Life of Kaycee Nicole. The Guardian (2001)
5. Chen, A.: The Agency. New York Times Mag. (2015)
6. Clarke, A.C.: The Nine Billion Names of God; the Best Short Stories of Arthur C. Clarke. Harcourt, Brace & World (1967)
7. Derakhshan, H.: Killing the hyperlink, killing the web: the shift from library-internet to television-internet. In: Proceedings of the 27th ACM Conference on Hypertext and Social Media, HT 2016, p. 3 (2016)
8. Dick, P.K.: The Minority Report: and Other Classic Stories. Citadel Press (2016)
9. Dickens, C.: The Adventures of Oliver Twist. Fields, Osgood & Co (1870)
10. Edwards, M., Peersman, C., Rashid, A.: Scamming the scammers: towards automatic detection of persuasion in advance fee frauds. In: Proceedings of the 26th International Conference on World Wide Web Companion, WWW 2017 Companion, pp. 1291–1299 (2017)
11. Hamilton, D.: The thinking machine. In: King, L.R., et al. (eds.) Echoes of Sherlock Holmes: Stories Inspired By The Holmes Canon. Pegasus Books (2016)
12. Hern, A.: Fitness Tracking App Strava Gives Away Location of Secret US Army Bases. The Guardian (2018)
13. Huang, Q., Singh, V.K., Atrey, P.K.: Cyber bullying detection using social and textual analysis. In: Proceedings of the 3rd International Workshop on Socially-Aware Multimedia, SAM 2014, pp. 3–6 (2014)

14. Le Carré, J.: Smiley's People. Knopf (1980)
15. Rizoiu, M.-A., Xie, L., Caetano, T., Cebrian, M.: Evolution of privacy loss. In: Wikipedia Proceedings of the Ninth ACM International Conference on Web Search and Data Mining, WSDM 2016, pp. 215–224 (2016)
16. Shelley, M.W.: Frankenstein, or, the Modern Prometheus. Modern Library (1984)
17. Sofia El Amine, S.B., Saad, S., Tesfa, A., Varin, C.: Infowar in Syria: the web between liberation and repression. Web Science 2012 (2012)
18. Stross, C.: The Jennifer Morgue. Golden Gryphon Press (2006)
19. Mueller, R.S.: Indictment: United States of America vs. Viktor Borisovich Netyksho et al., U. S. District Court for the District of Columbia, 13 July 2018
20. Czege, P.: My Life With Master. Half-Meme Press (2003)
21. Timberg, C., Harwell, D.: We studied thousands of anonymous posts about the Parkland attack—and found a conspiracy in the making. The Washington Post, 28 February 2018
22. Reeves, B., Nass, C.: The Media Equation - How People Treat Computers, Television, and New Media Like Real People and Places. Cambridge University Press, Cambridge (1996)
23. DiFranzo, D., Taylor, S.H., et al.: Upstanding by design: bystander intervention in cyberbullying. In: CHI 18, Montréal, 21–26 April 2018
24. Brignull, H.: Types of Dark Patterns. https://darkpatterns.org/types-of-dark-pattern
25. Vosoughi, S., Roy, D., Aral, S.: The spread of true and false news online. Science, 1146–1151 (2018)
26. Ramachandran, A., Wang, L.: Chaintreau dynamics and prediction of clicks on news from Twitter. In: Sastry, N., Weber, I. (eds.) Proceedings of the 29th on Hypertext and Social Media, HT 2018, pp. 210–214 (2018)
27. Nagy, G.: A Cretan Odyssey, Part 1. Classical Inquiries Studies on the Ancient World from CHS. https://classical-inquiries.chs.harvard.edu/a-cretan-odyssey-part-1/
28. Brusilovsky, P., Millán, E.: User models for adaptive hypermedia and adaptive educational systems. In: Brusilovsky, P., Kobsa, A., Nejdl, W. (eds.) The Adaptive Web. LNCS, vol. 4321, pp. 3–53. Springer, Heidelberg (2007). https://doi.org/10.1007/978-3-540-72079-9_1
29. Stephens-Davidowitz, S.: Everybody Lies: Big Data, New Data, and What the Internet Can Tell Us About Who We Really Are. Dey St., An Imprint of William Morrow, New York (2017)
30. Aletras, N., Chamberlain, B.P.: Predicting Twitter user socioeconomic attributes with network and language information. In: Proceedings of the 29th on Hypertext and Social Media, HT 2018, pp. 20–24 (2018)
31. Khazaei, T., Xiao, L., Mercer, R.E., Khan, A.: Understanding privacy dichotomy in Twitter. In: Proceedings of the 29th on Hypertext and Social Media, HT 2018, pp. 156–164 (2018)
32. Goodman, A.: The Chalk Artist: A Novel. The Dial Press, New York (2017)
33. Soroush, M., Hancock, M., Bohns, V.K.: Self-control in casual games: the relationship between candy crush saga; players' in-app purchases and self-control. In: IEEE Games Media Entertainment, pp. 1–6 (2014)
34. Mazetti, M., Benner, K.: 12 Russian agents indicted in Mueller investigation. The New York Times, 13 July 2018. https://www.nytimes.com/2018/07/13/us/politics/mueller-indictment-russian-intelligence-hacking.html
35. Eagleton, T.: After Theory. Basic Books, New York (2003)
36. Murray, J.: Hamlet on the Holodeck: The Future of Narrative in Cyberspace. The Free Press, New York (1997)
37. Bernstein, M.: As we may hear: our slaves of steel. In: Proceedings of the 29th ACM Conference on Hypertext and Social Media, HT 2018, pp. 242–245 (2018)

38. Arakelyan, S., Morstatter, F., Martin, M., Ferrara, E., Galstyan, A.: Mining and forecasting career trajectories of music artists. In: Proceedings of the 29th ACM Conference on Hypertext and Social Media, HT 2018, pp. 11–19 (2018)
39. Zhao, B.Y.: Insecure machine learning systems and their impact on the web. In: Proceedings of the 29th on Hypertext and Social Media (HT 2018), p. 63. ACM, New York (2018). https://doi.org/10.1145/3209542.3209544
40. Wang, B., Yao, Y., Viswanath, B., Zheng, H., Zhao, B.Y.: With great training comes great vulnerability: practical attacks against transfer learning. In: 27th {USENIX} Security Symposium ({USENIX} Security 18). USENIX Association, August 2018
41. Baeza-Yates, R.: Bias on the web. Commun. ACM **61**(6), 54–61 (2018)
42. Lazer, D.M.J., et al.: The science of fake news. Science **359**(6380), 1094–1096 (2018)
43. McCurry, J.: Japanese blogger stabbed to death after internet abuse seminar. The guardian, 26 June 2018. https://www.theguardian.com/world/2018/jun/26/japanese-blogger-kenichiro-okamoto-stabbed-to-death-after-internet-abuse-seminar
44. Jason, Z.: Game of fear. Boston Mag. (2015). https://www.bostonmagazine.com/news/2015/04/28/gamergate/
45. Feinberg, A.: The alt-right can't disown charlottesville. Wired, 13 August 2017. https://www.wired.com/story/alt-right-charlottesville-reddit-4chan/
46. Orwell, G.: Politics and the English Languages. Horizon **13**(76) (1946)
47. Flanagan, C.: I believe her. The Atlantic Monthly, 17 September 2018. https://www.theatlantic.com/ideas/archive/2018/09/me-too/570520/

Theory and Analysis

Re-Tellings: The Fourth Layer of Narrative as an Instrument for Critique

Mirjam Palosaari Eladhari[✉️] iD

Södertörn University, Alfred Nobels allé 7, 141 89 Huddinge, Sweden
mirjam.palosaari.eladhari@sh.se

Abstract. The fourth layer of narrative in Interactive Narrative Systems (INS), such as games, is the players' re-tellings of the stories they have experienced when playing. The occurrence of re-tellings can be considered as an indicator for a well designed INS and as an instrument of critique - the experiences of play are important and memorable to such a degree to the players that they find them worthy to tell others about. The notion of the fourth layer is added to the structural model of IN Systems having (1) a base architectural layer giving conditions for a (2) second layer of narrative design, while a (3) third layer is the narrative discourse - eg. the unique, session-specific played or traversed sequences of events. In relation to this, the Story Construction model is described.

Keywords: Interactive narrative systems · Storytelling in games
Story construction · Fan fiction

1 Introduction

Each traversal of a story stemming from an interactive narrative system (INS) is unique. Re-tellings of experiences from playing games, and experiencing other types of interactive narratives is occurring in everyday life when we tell each other about the experiences. As games and INS move towards more complexity with the increased use of procedural computational methods for both world building and story generation, re-tellings of game experiences are becoming increasingly important for those who experience them. The more unique experiences an INS affords, the more notes there are to compare in re-tellings - and this activity becomes an enjoyable activity in its own right.

Types of re-tellings span from the simple act of talking about a game in daily conversation to more elaborate efforts, such as the blog series about the Sim characters Alice and Kev [4]. Another type of re-tellings are players' narrations about their avatars lives and experiences, e.g. tellings of their fictive alternate lives in the worlds that we inhabit in games. Some re-tellings become original work of their own in the genre of fan fiction - a large body of emerging work that merits its own field of study [18].

If a player or user finds a game experience or an interactive story interesting enough to tell someone else about, it means that it is was somehow memorable,

© Springer Nature Switzerland AG 2018
R. Rouse et al. (Eds.): ICIDS 2018, LNCS 11318, pp. 65–78, 2018.
https://doi.org/10.1007/978-3-030-04028-4_5

and important enough to tell someone else about. I propose that if re-tellings emerge in the wake of a game or INS these re-tellings can be seen as indicators that the games or INS are successful designs, perhaps even artifacts with a degree of artistic originality and quality.

1.1 Traditions of Narratological Theory

A lot has been written about narrative in interactive media. In the area of games, classification spaces have been offered. Comparisons have presented similarities to other media and differences have been pointed out (e.g. analyses of interactive media from a cultural-studies perspective, including Aarseth [1], Murray [28], Juul [20], Ryan [32]).

Publications by authors with backgrounds in screen writing and film-making often refer to the Hero's Journey [6,38], and to the restorative three-act structure of drama, described by Danzyger and Rush [11].

Prominent traditions of narrative analysis include the structuralist perspective beginning with Propp's morphology of the folk tale [29] and Greimas' actant theory [16], as well as the tradition of hypertext theory [2,23], that is, systems for causal interactive relationships between story elements in multi-linear stories.

It can be contested whether it is a viable way forward when discussing INS to adopt theories about narrative that are constructed as means to understand linear media better, such as novels and movies. A potential benefit of doing so is that the field of interactive narrative systems can make use of well-defined concepts and use them where applicable in the area of INS. The risk with the approach is that the INS area may limit itself conceptually, being boxed into the linear form, and in this conceptual space it may be more difficult to fully appreciate the unique nature of what it means that a narrative is a system of potential stories, and the telling of these stories. A recent promising model that integrates previous work in the field as well as discussing the unique nature INS is the SPP model by Koenitz [22].

1.2 Three Layers of Text Constituting Interactive Narrative Systems

Drawing upon the rich body of work describing and systematizing the nature of interactive narratives and narratives in games, it can be said that there is an overall consensus of dividing narratives into layers, quite often three of them [1,3, 7,8,15,16,19,28,33,40]. I have previously described [12] these three layers as - at the lowest layer, a code, or architectural layer, making up the existence of a world where stories can take place. This first layer spans many genres - from table top games, text-based interactive fiction, single player story driven games to larger game worlds with thousands of simultaneous players. This base architectural layer is the foundation for adding actants with driving forces, making up the deep structure of the potential stories. A second layer is often seen as the narrated content provided by game designers and game writers, while the third layer is the narrative discourse - eg. the unique, session-specific played sequence of events. There are many models, using different terminology to describe these three layers, among them Koenitz [22] who uses the terminology of protostory for the systemic architectural layer, process for the performative instantiation by players/interactors, and product, a played instantiated story. It is because of this general division in three layers that I propose to call the retelling of experiences in games and INS the *fourth* layer.

It has to be noted that any model that is constructed in order to understand a complex reality better is constructed in order to understand them in a certain *way*. By constructing a model, we apply a lens in order to understand a slice of reality better, and to be able to discuss complex constructs using the same language. Doing so, we minimize the inevitable degree of misunderstanding that will occur in any conversation. When mapping Koenitz's SPP model [22] to the model of Story Construction (SC) [12] it is notable that Koenitz's model adopts a lens of gaining deeper understanding when analyzing an *existing* work of INS. The Story Construction model [12] has a different focus, the lens being more adapted to discussing the *creation* of INS and constructing potential stories within them. While the main topic of this paper is the postulation of re-tellings as an important narrative layer whose occurrence can be seen as an indicator of success, a stick of measurement if you will, it is also imperative to present the underpinnings of the occurrence of said layer. Therefore I offer a partial description of the SC model insofar that it may add to the SPP model, limiting the text to the aspects that are necessary for teasing out the authorial issues to take into account from a narratological perspective when creating INS and designing potential stories for them. Further, despite the risk of adopting concepts derived from analysis of linear stories I use some of that terminology in order to make this text more accessible.

2   Fundamental Terms and Concepts

When the word *story* is used in this text it means a fixed temporal sequence of events and the actors that take part in these, that is, the content that a narrative is about.[1] Events in narratives are not necessarily told about in the order in which they have happened. In multi-linear narratives readers or players can often choose when to be told about a certain event, but the order in the sequence of events as such does not change in most cases—only the sequence of experiencing them, or being told about them. A *narrative* is a story the way it

---

[1] The use of the terms story and narrative in this text conforms to Genette's theoretical framework for narrative analysis. Genette's definition of histoire, or in the English translation, story, reads as follows [15, p. 27]: 'I propose [...] to use the word story for the signified or narrative content'. Slomith Rimmon-Kenan uses Genette's definition in her book Narrative Fiction, but accentuates the chronological aspect of the concept: "Story' designates the narrated events, abstracted from their disposition in the text and reconstructed in their chronological order, together with the participants in these events.'.

is told. *Narration*, or the art of story telling, concerns how to tell a story.[2] As players do one thing after another in a world the sequence of events that emerge is what I, in this text, call the character's *discourse*, a concept borrowed from Chatman [8].

In multi-user virtual game worlds (VGWs), being places, there is generally little to no story telling in the design of the world in the traditional sense. The same is true for INSes, and games using procedural generation of narrative elements. Instead, in INSes and VGWs, there are elements that have *narrative potential*, a term used by Laurel [24] and described by Fencott [14] as the integration of agency and narrative. Fencott elaborates on narrative potential in [13] as the 'accumulation of meaningful experience as a result of agency—allows participants to construct their own appropriate narratives. Narrative potential thus arises from agency but is not determined by it.' The term *agency* was defined by Murray in [28, p. 126] as 'the satisfying power to take meaningful action and see the results of our decisions and choices'. Mateas and Stern [25] distinguish between *local agency* where users' actions cause 'immediate, context- specific, meaningful reactions from the system' and *global agency*, where the global shape of the experience of the system may be determined by users' actions.

Virtual worlds as places support the emergence of stories. *Emergence* in this context means the emergence of a higher-layer structure from the interaction of many simpler, lower-level primitives. In this case, emergent narrative can be understood as a system in which lower-level elements interact to result in the emergence of a pattern of events that may be told about in ways conforming to a specific higher-level pattern of narrative structure.

Koster [26] distinguishes between impositional and expressive forms of interactive narrative in VGWs. The impositional form is used in choose-your-own adventure books, adventure games and other fixed multi-linear narratives. The expressive form relies less on a sequence of events and behaves more like an architecture. The view of story construction as a type of architecture is shared by Jenkins [19]: 'in the case of emergent narratives, game spaces are designed to be rich with narrative potential, enabling the story-constructing activity of players. [...] it makes sense to think of game designers less as storytellers than as narrative architects.'

The act of creating narrative potential is an act of *story construction*, not story telling. That is, a story is constructed by game-play or interactions where the VGW or INS and its inhabitants are providing material for potential narratives as tellings of the story.

Players of games, users of systems and readers of INS pieces are in this text collectively labeled as *interactors* in Murray's sense [28] in order to designate their role as those traversing and experiencing a game or an INS. For denoting all those who act in a performative role, adding to the fiction or character of a game or INS world, the term *expressive agents* is used, to encompass human

---

[2] When Genette uses the word narrative he means 'the signifier, statement, discourse or narrative text itself' [15, p. 27]. The French word Genette uses for narrative is récit.

users and computational entities alike, such as non player characters (NPCs) or more abstract entities.[3] In summary, those traversing and experiencing a system are called interactors, those performing expressive actions are called expressive agents. Agents can be both expressive and experiencing, and driven by either human or computational intelligence, or be semi-autonomous.

3 Text Layers in Interactive Narrative Systems

When discussing story construction in the context of computer-based systems such as VGWs and INS I have previously found it is useful to divide story and narration into different layers [12] summarized in Fig. 1.[4] This way it is easier to communicate where in the structure something may be implemented, and what implications a new feature may have, e.g., for authoring rights and persistence. For instance, few designers would give creation rights to players on the architectural code layer because a change on that layer would change the rules of a whole INS or game world. Note that the layers in Fig. 1 refer to different layers of authored text, not to software architecture design.

Practically, these different text layers, and thus the narrative potential of the world are usually created by persons having different roles. The code layer is written by software engineers, the story layer by game designers and writers, while the discourse layer and the narrative layer are performed by players, game masters, and sometimes live teams or other persons having roles moderating the experiences within an INS or a VGW.

4 Code Layer

The code layer itself can generally be divided into three software layers. The bottom layer is the engine which consists of very general functions such as network and communication systems, the rendering of the system's interface, the sound system, the interface for animation, the handling of the terrain, the dialogue system, the media storage, and the physics system, which governs gravitation, forces, collisions and collision response.

Above this, there is the framework of the game, a layer of abstract representations of the game's structures such as classes of game agents, classes of behavioral control and systems for action control and communication. The engine is usually general and may be used in various game genres, but the framework tends to be more specific for its genre, implementing a generic system. Above the framework there is the scripting, that is the specific content programming, which mostly consists of data and the instantiated definitions specific to the given game or

---

[3] An example of an abstract entity that has an expressive and performative role could for example be weather, such as a storm god manifesting by changing the conditions in an environment.

[4] As noted earlier this lens for seeing narrative is adapted towards the creation of interactive narratives rather than analyzing them.

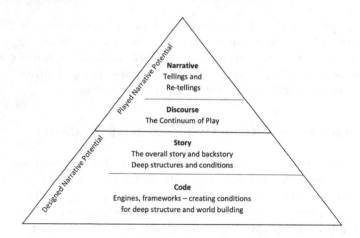

Fig. 1. Text layers in story construction

INS. These layers are co-ordinated to bring forth the media that become visible and audible to interactors, such as environments, characters, dialogues, music, sound effects and graphical user interfaces.

It is important to be aware of the implications that a certain engine or code base have for resulting play experiences and the conditions for creating narrative potential in a game world. The divisions of layers within the code layer are very general, the details vary from architecture to architecture. In order for the categorization to be useful in a production situation they can be derived from the production team structure: for example, if a game-engine group is assigned to create the engine layer, another group writes the framework and undertakes game programming. It is also vital to take coding that is done outside of the production team into account. In some cases it can be interactors coding. Cherny [9] shows an early example from LamdaMOO where players program personal and characteristic behaviors for their avatars that can be triggered by keywords typed by other players. In other, more recent cases, interactors may be computationally composed, such as Cook's Angelina system that produces level designs and content for them [10].

The Code layer is what creates the conditions for story constructors to create a deep structure for a game world or an INS. In Koenitz's model the code layer would correspond closest to the 'protostory', which in the SPP model denotes concrete content of an INS as a space for potential narratives. [22, p. 99] The protostory term is derived from prototype based programming that allows for dynamic changes of structures in run-time.

5   Story Layer

The deep structures of the potential stories are designed at the story layer – both dynamic and static elements. This aspect includes the forces motivating the actions of the characters, their goals and the specific abilities of each individual entity. At the discourse layer, these entities (mostly characters, but also more abstract forces like weather) manifest actual stories via performed actions by the interactor.

The story layer also includes the back-story, the explicit narrative framing by the game designers or INS authors. This back-story often has a branching structure where parts of it can be mandatory for the user to traverse in order to progress in the game world or INS. The story layer described here is what would be the equivalent of the narrative design in Koenitz' SPP model [22] as part of what he understands as the protostory.

We can take some aspects of a narrative to be essential, in particular ones that are necessary for an interactor to have a compelling experience, which makes them – in Koster's terms – a type of impositional narrative, in contrast to optional, but expressive narrative. The impositional stance can be found most often in single-player adventure games and hypertext narratives, where the overall story and its content are fixed, even though, when experienced, variations in chronology and sequencing can still create a varied experience.

In VGWs there is often a mix of different story construction techniques. Both Asheron's Call 2 [27] and Star Wars Galaxies [35] are good examples of game worlds that contain mixed strategies, from the linear to the fully emergent and from the impositional to the expressive. In Asheron's Call 2 a linear story arc is mandatory for players to go through in order to be able to get to new geographic areas in the game world. The VGW Star Wars Galaxies is an example of a world where players can perform quests that are connected to linear narratives, and are not mandatory for the development of PCs. In general, VGWs mix impositional and expressive story construction, the expressive stance being inherent, deriving from the code layer and implemented in the story layer to provide a framing to what agents and player characters are allowed to do depending on their states, in the form of dependencies, constraints and affordances.

5.1   The Deep Structure

Even if not all games contain a story in the same way as films, plays and novels do, they all contain a deep structure. Games like chess and solitaire contain deep structures; there are goals, driving forces and constraining rules for achieving the goals. In these examples though, the goals that drive the mechanics of game-play are part of the predefined conception of the game. This is not always the case in VGWs and INSes, where the interactors may define their own goals that are not always be foreseen by the designers.

The concepts of deep structure and surface structure are used by Greimas [16] and summarised by Rimmon-Kenan [30, p.10]: 'Whereas the surface structure of the story is syntagmatic, that is, governed by temporal and causal principles, the deep structure is paradigmatic, based on static logical relations among the elements.' Greimas' Actant Theory models static relations as relations among actants. Actants are entities that accomplish or submit to an act.

Budniakiewicz [3, p. 76] points out that the position of the object in the model has a double function: 'The positional value of the Object is doubly defined by the convergence of the actantial axes: both as an 'object of desire' and as an 'object of communication'.' Budniakiewicz reminds us that for Greimas the actant model and the actant grammar are foremost ways to extrapolate syntactic structure.

How can this be of use when discussing story construction? Actant theory is a conceptualization that breaks down the parts of a story into the force fields that make it possible for the narrative to come into existence. By applying this way of looking upon dynamic and static story elements it is possible to more clearly define the forces that, in Greimas' words, make up 'the semantic syntax' or the micro universe that a fictional world and its overall narrative consist of.

5.2   Action, Event, State and Antecedent Driving Forces

In the context of story construction it is necessary to make clear distinctions between action, event, and state, and in this way to be able to distinguish what implications an action has for one or several states. What states are affected depends upon an action's direction and sender. Greimas [17, p.176] defines the distinction between action and event in the following way: 'Whereas action is dependent only on the subject concerned with the organisation of his activity, event can be understood only as the description of this activity by an actant external to action.'

An *action* is, according to these terms, dependent on the subject that performs the action or activity. An *event*, on the other hand, is a description of the same event when the description is performed by an actant standing outside of the performed action. A *state* is held by an agent and is a result of all actions performed by the agent itself and by the actions performed by other agents aimed directly or indirectly at the first agent.

Budniakiewicz [3] asks what it means when someone says that 'we do' something. She means that verbs are 'unpacked' to make descriptions of antecedent states when someone contemplates an expression of 'something done'. Even though Budniakiewicz, just as Greimas, primarily studies syntactical structures, this terminology is useful in the current context. Budniakiewicz puts it in the following way:

> These antecedent states are the wants, the goals, and plans of the agent which are interconnected in a peculiar pattern of reasoning used by the agent both before and during the performance of action, when the agent is said to 'be doing' something. The reasoning has been named in traditional Aristotelian commentary a practical syllogism or inference.[...]
> Major premise: N wants to do O / bring about O.
> Minor premise: N considers that he cannot do O unless he does P.
> Conclusion: Therefore, N sets himself to do P / does P.

Put simply, an expressive agent performing a quest in may plan to, for example, find a dragon, kill it, take its treasure, give it to another character (that can be autonomous or another player character) and receive a reward for the trouble.

Ragnhild Tronstad [37] discusses what constitutes a quest and how only after its completion it becomes a story. For her, what constitutes the motivation for solving a quest is the search for its meaning (p. 81): 'To do a quest is to search for the meaning of it. Having reached this meaning, the quest is solved. The paradox of questing is that as soon as meaning is reached, the quest stops.'

In a VGW or an INS the experiencing agent who perform quests within the rules of the system are governed by the *antecedent driving-force* constituted by their long-term goals, plan or will. Tronstad argues that when the goal is reached, or the plan is carried out, or its will is satisfied, the driving-force of the agent is neutralized.

6 Discourse Layer and the States of the Agents

Discourse, in the context of games and IN Systems, is the sequence of experiences (expressed by signifiers in the game world) that an experiencing agent goes through.

It is in the discourse layer that the state of the expressive agent evolves. This would in many cases be the way a player character gains experience, skills, and personal history. A class (in terms of software) describing the type of the expressive agent also describes what types of action are possible for the expressive agent to perform and the possible basic obstructions against performing them. This constitutes the *action potential* of the expressive agent. When the expressive agent is instantiated for the first time (whether it is embodied or not), it contains its first conditioned state. The state of the expressive agent changes depending on its own actions, what actions are aimed at it by other agents and objects. The state can also change depending on influences by other elements specific to a game or an INS.

It is in the continuum of interaction with the system, in the discourse layer, that the interactors have, ideally, a sense of agency. Using the terminology of Mateas and Stern [25], the local agency may be a result of expressive agents having an impact on story element conditioned at the story layer. Global agency would be afforded by all parts of the story layer, eg also the conditions of the elements, goals and driving forces of actants, and perhaps even affecting the code layer.

7 The Fourth Layer of Narrative: The Re-Telling

The narrative layer of re-tellings consists of tales told about events and actions in an INS or a game world. An example would be a player telling someone about something that has happened during play.

Every play-through of a game, or a traversal of an interactive narrative, is unique, and therefore it is especially interesting to compare notes. The re-tellings occur in communicative everyday interactions, and through social media, in recordings displayed at Youtube or Twitch, or in the form of avatar diaries at

LiveJournal - there is a plethora of channels for re-tellings of experiences, sharing one's own experiences and getting to know others' unique and exceptional traversals.

Thus, re-tellings comes in many forms, and from authors with different degrees of closeness to the original creators of IN Systems. They also occur at automated system level, such as event logs parsed into a narrative, such as the player characters' diaries in Shenmue II [34]. This type of re-telling correspond with Koenitz's notion of product [22], eg, the recorded instantiated output.

Some VGWs' live teams write regular newsletters about what is happening in the world and have official web sites where this history is gathered and edited. An early example of this is when the developers of the social virtual world Second Life, Linden Labs, hired the journalist James Wagner, who, starting in 2003, reported on trends and happenings that were taking place in the virtual environment [39].

The official web sites of VGWs commonly have sections dedicated to narratives about what a player has experienced via her character, told from the character's point of view. It is also common for chronicles to be written by the most active players in a guild, highlighting marriages, wars that have been won and other important events.

A multitude of communication channels exist independently from the publishers of any game or INS which are used mainly for retelling of stories, one example being LiveJournal, a social networking service that is popular among players who create fictions about their game characters' experiences and thus can be understood as a specific form of fan fiction, [18].

7.1   The Tale of Alice and Kev

Let us consider 'Alice and Kev - The story of being homeless in The Sims 3'. It is a series of retellings of game experiences by Robin Burksinshaw. Burkinshaw created two characters (Alice and Kev), moved them into a place looking like an abandoned park, and removed all their remaining money. Then, he attempted to help them survive in the game without them taking career routes that would earn them money. About his narrative stance, Burkinshaw writes: 'I have attempted to tell my experiences with the minimum of embellishment. Everything I describe in here is something that happened in the game.' [4]

In the chapter 'Selflessness' the character Alice has after many hardships finally managed to get her first salary only to give it away to charity: [5]

Alice gets to work late, but not too late.
When her shift at the supermarket ends that evening, she has 100 hard-earned simoleons, but she is as exhausted as it is possible to be. She wobbles slightly after walking out the door, and only just manages to stop herself from losing consciousness there and then.
But she doesn't want to rest now. She's just come up with a new wish. It's a wish that would be easily fulfilled, but the idea scares and horrifies me. I don't want to grant it to her.
But it's her life, and her choice. I reluctantly let her do it.

She takes all of the money she has just earned, places it into an envelope, writes the name

of a charity on the front, and puts it into a mailbox.

Burkinshaw expresses in the text how his role as author/player becomes dramatic by the need to make a choice - he doesn't want Alice to give the money away, but lets her anyway, allowing her to act according to her character. Readers of Burkinshaw's text who have also played The Sims 3 [36] know what Burkinshaw is alluding to when Alice is 'as exhausted as it is possible to be', and what it means within the game rules that Alice has a wish. This adds to the degree of enjoyment when comparing and discussing the unique narrative experiences from the same game.

Burkinshaw's narrative has gained traction with other players. The chapter Selflessness has (as of 2018-08-01) 178 comments by readers. In the commentary, other players express that Alice feels real as a character, and that her gift to charity is beautiful. There is also more interpretative commentary, such as by the user Danuab: 'It doesn't mean anything. Alice has likely internalised her father's distaste and abuse and developed a negative self-concept. She isn't giving money away because she's altruistic, she's giving it away because she doesn't think she's worth it.'

The example of Alice and Kev shows that The Sims 3 as an INS not only affords the emergent story construction that is taken by players as meaningful enough to narrate to others, but also how the resulting second order narration merits its own critique and commentary by other players.

7.2 Re-Tellings as an Instrument for Critique

Based on the example above, I propose that The Sims 3 can be seen as a highly successful INS in terms of artistic quality and originality.

Conversely, I postulate that re-tellings of experiences from INS can be considered a fourth layer of narrative, and that these are indicators suggesting that the INS in question is 'well-made' or 'good' and had significant impact on the player. This means that a game or an INS - at its base level - has provided an experience that is significant or meaningful enough that it is worth telling someone else about. Re-tellings can be collected and analyzed in order to gain an increased understanding of what aspects of INSes are particularly well received. This method has been used for example by Lisbeth Klastrup for 'The Death Stories Project' [21]. Through a web form she gathered narratives from players describing death experiences. An important goal of the project was to find suggestions that may help designers to 'become better at designing worlds which give players experiences they want to tell stories about.'

I propose that re-tellings of experiences from traversals of INS could be used as an instrument for the critique of IN Systems. Using data-mining methods, the occurrence of re-tellings could be collected and used as an - admittedly somewhat blunt - indicator of a successful design. More in-depth analysis may provide pointers to what aspects of an INS are particularly interesting and why. Related work by Ringer and Nicolaou [31] use visual analysis of game streams (twitch) to detect game highlights based on player reactions.

Figure 2 summarizes the OC model, adding some tentative types of tellings and re-tellings in the column to the left. Future work includes a typology of fourth layer narratives.

Story Construction			
Designed Narrative Potential		**Played Narrative Potential**	
Code Layer	Story Layer	Discourse Layer	Narrative Layer
Engines, framework, and game programming. These together manifest the geographic structure as well as the conditions for the deep structure of the story and its construction.	The overall story or back story. The deep structure consisting of the individual expressive agents and the story elements. At the discourse layer, these manifest the overall story and possible side stories.	The continuum of play. The current dynamic states, experienced events, movements, and actions of the expressive agents that result in sequences of events: the actual story, or discourse.	Tellings and re-tellings. The narratives told about the actions and events in the game world or INS. The narratives are told both in-world and out-of-world.
Scripting Detailed programming of objects specific to the game or INS.		**Individual Story Discourse** The past of the expressive agent, a chronological sequence of the actions performed and the events experienced. This is the actual story of a specific expressive agent.	**Recorded system output** Product in the form of narrative discourse, recorded instantiated output from a system.
Framework - Abstract model of a world and system. - The glue between scripting and engine(s)	**Story Elements** The specific setup of expressive agents and story elements that are to be instantiated.		**Simultaneous retellings**. Ex: Streaming game play via Twitch or YouTube Gaming.
			Communicative re-tellings. Ex: "You won't believe what happened in the raid. We ..."
	Conditions Causal dependencies governing relations between specific agents and objects,	**State** The state of the expressive agent in the moment of interaction, defined by the construction of the class the agent is instantiated from, and from the agent's individual story discourse.	**Chronicles and Reporting.** Ex: guild scribes telling about marriages or funerals in VGWs, or reporters commissioned by game companies.
Engine, may include: - physics system; - graphics rendering system; - dialog system; - media storage; - communication layer - INS system. - etc.	**Goals, Driving Forces** Wills, motives, aspirations, and goals of the expressive agents.		**Narratives with artistic or authorial intent.** Avatar narratives, re-tellings of simulations (ex. Alice and Kev), fan-fiction.

Fig. 2. Story construction in games and INS

8 Conclusion

In this paper I postulated that the occurrence of player's re-tellings of diverse forms of interactive narratives (narrative video games, interactive documentaries and many others) are indicators of successful designs since they indicate that the underlying experiences were important enough to re-tell them. I described the re-tellings as a fourth layer of narrative, adding it to a three-fold structural model of interactive narrative systems as having (1) a base architectural layer giving conditions for a (2) second layer of narrative design, while a (3) third layer is the narrative discourse - eg. the unique, session-specific played or traversed sequences of events. I also suggested that analyses of corpuses of re-tellings can be used as instruments for critique of interactive narrative systems.

References

1. Aarseth, E.J.: Cybertext, Perspectives on Ergodic Literature. Johns Hopkins University Press, September 1997
2. Bolter, J.D.: Writing Space: The Computer, Hypertext, and the History of Writing. Lawrence Erlbaum Associates (1991)
3. Budniakiewicz, T.: Fundamentals of Story Logic: Introduction to Greimassian Semiotics. John Benjamins Pub. Co., Amsterdam (1992)
4. Burkinshaw, R.: Alice and Kev - The story of being homeless in The Sims 3. https://aliceandkev.wordpress.com/
5. Burkinshaw, R.: Selflessness—Alice and Kev. https://aliceandkev.wordpress.com/2009/06/16/selflessness/
6. Campbell, J.: The Hero with a Thousand Faces. Princeton University Press, Princeton (1949)
7. Cavazza, M., et al.: The IRIS network of excellence: integrating research in interactive storytelling. In: Spierling, U., Szilas, N. (eds.) ICIDS 2008. LNCS, vol. 5334, pp. 14–19. Springer, Heidelberg (2008). https://doi.org/10.1007/978-3-540-89454-4_3
8. Chatman, S.: Story and Discourse. Cornell University Press, London (1978)
9. Cherny, L.: "Objectifying" the body in the discourse of an object-oriented MUD. Stanford University, Technical report (1994)
10. Cook, M., Colton, S., Gow, J.: The ANGELINA videogame design system-part i. IEEE T. Comp. Intel. AI Games 9(2), 192–203 (2017). https://doi.org/10.1109/TCIAIG.2016.2520256, http://ieeexplore.ieee.org/document/7429751/
11. Danzyger, K., Rush, J.: Alternative Scriptwriting. Focal Press (1995)
12. Eladhari, M.P.: Characterising action potential in virtual game worlds applied with the mind module. Ph.D. thesis, Teesside University, September 2010
13. Fencott, C.: Agencies of Interactive Digital Storytelling (2003)
14. Fencott, C.: Virtual storytelling as narrative potential: towards an ecology of narrative. In: Balet, O., Subsol, G., Torguet, P. (eds.) ICVS 2001. LNCS, vol. 2197, pp. 90–99. Springer, Heidelberg (2001). https://doi.org/10.1007/3-540-45420-9_11
15. Genette, G.: Narrative Discourse - An Essay in Method. Cornell University Press, Ithaca (1983)
16. Greimas, A.J.: Sémantique structurale. Larousse (1966)
17. Greimas, A.J.: Narrative Semiotics and Cognitive Discourses. Pinter (1990)
18. Hellekson, K., Busse, K.: The Fan Fiction Studies Reader. University of Iowa Press, Iowa City (2014)
19. Jenkins, H.: Game Design as Narrative Architecture. The MIT Press, Cambridge (2003)
20. Juul, J.: A clash between game and narrative - a thesis on computer games and interactive fiction. Ph.D. thesis, University of Copenhagen (1999)
21. Klastrup, L.: The Death Stories Project. [Electronic Publication] (2006). http://www.death-stories.org/
22. Koenitz, H.: Towards a specific theory of interactive digital narrative. In: Interactive Digital Narrative: History, Theory and Practice (2015)
23. Landow, G.P.: Hypertext: The Converge of Contemporary Critical Theory and Technology. Johns Hopkins University Press, Baltimore (1992)
24. Laurel, B., Strickland, R., Tow, R.: Placeholder: landscape and narrative in virtual environments. SIGGRAPH Comput. Graph 28(2), 118–126 (1994)

25. Mateas, M., Stern, A.: Structuring content in the Façade interactive drama architecture. In: Proceedings of the First AAAI Conference on Artificial Intelligence and Interactive Digital Entertainment, AIIDE 2005, pp. 93–98. AAAI Press, Marina del Rey (2005)
26. Meadows, M.S.: Pause & Effect - The Art of Interactive Narrative. New Riders (2003)
27. Microsoft Corporation: Asheron's Call 2 - Fallen Kings [Computer Game - Virtual Game World]. Turbine Entertainment (2002)
28. Murray, J.H.: Hamlet on the Holodeck. The Free Press, New York (1997)
29. Propp, V.: Morphology of the Folktale. University of Texas Press, Austin (1968)
30. Rimmon-Kenan, S.: Narrative Fiction: Contemporary Poetics. Methuen & Co (1993)
31. Ringer, C., Nicolaou, M.A.: Deep unsupervised multi-view detection of video game stream highlights. In: Proceedings of the 13th International Conference on the Foundations of Digital Games - FDG 2018, pp. 1–6. ACM Press, New York (2018). https://doi.org/10.1145/3235765.3235781, http://dl.acm.org/citation.cfm?doid=3235765.3235781
32. Ryan, M.L.: Beyond Myth and Metaphor - The Case of Narrative in Digital Media. Game Studies, July 2001
33. Ryan, M.L.: Avatars of Story (Electronic Mediations), 1 edn. University of Minnesota Press (2006)
34. Sega AM2: Shenmue II [Consol Game]. Sega, Microsoft Game Studios (2001)
35. Sony Online Entertainment: Star Wars Galaxies: An Empire Divided. Lucas Arts [Computer Game - Virtual Game World], June 2003
36. The Sims Studio: The Sims 3. Elactronic Arts [Computer Game] (2009)
37. Tronstad, R.: Semiotic and Nonsemiotic MUD Performance. Holland (2001)
38. Vogler, C.: The Writers Journey. Michael Wiese Productions (1993)
39. Wagner, J.: Second Life: Notes from a New World. Electronic Publication (2003). http://secondlife.com/notes
40. Wardrip-Fruin, N.: Expressive Processing: Digital Fictions, Computer Games, and Software Studies. The MIT Press, Cambridge (2009)

Comparing Player Responses
to Choice-Based Interactive Narratives
Using Facial Expression Analysis

John T. Murray[1](✉)(iD), Raquel Robinson[2], Michael Mateas[3],
and Noah Wardrip-Fruin[3]

[1] University of Central Florida, Orlando, USA
jtm@ucf.edu
[2] University of Saskatchewan, Saskatoon, CA, USA
Raquel.robinson@usask.ca
[3] Expressive Intelligence Studio, University of California, Santa Cruz, USA
{michaelm,nwf}@soe.ucsc.edu

Abstract. Interactive storytelling balances the desire to create dynamic, engaging experiences around characters and situations with the practical considerations of the cost of producing content. We describe a method for assessing player experience by analyzing player facial expressions following key content events in *The Wolf Among Us* by Telltale Games. Two metrics, engagement and valence, are extracted for six participants who play the first episode of the game. An analysis of the variance and distribution of responses relative to emotionally charged content events and choices suggests that content is designed around events that serve to anchor player emotions while providing the freedom to respond through emotionally-motivated choice selections and content elicitors.

Keywords: Analyses and evaluation of systems · Media annotation
Facial expression analysis · Interactive storytelling · Emotion

1 Introduction

Emotionally compelling content is at the core of many contemporary choice-based storygames, such as those produced by Telltale Games. In contrast to open-world storygames or branching narratives, recent Telltale Games productions focus on a strong story with fewer branches and dramatically-motivated choices. This paper proposes a new method for assessing choice-based game content both for insights into interactive narrative design principles as well as evaluating game content effectiveness. Content in these games often elicits emotional responses and can be considered efficient when the same content elicits different player responses, representing variations in player experience.

The approach described in this paper could be applied both to existing commercially released storygames as well as experimental games, and further would

© Springer Nature Switzerland AG 2018
R. Rouse et al. (Eds.): ICIDS 2018, LNCS 11318, pp. 79–92, 2018.
https://doi.org/10.1007/978-3-030-04028-4_6

allow researchers to analyze existing corpora such as gameplay traversal videos published as performances on popular platforms such as Twitch. The method described in this paper can be used to compare content event volatility as an elicitor based on comparing player responses, and does not make claims about individual player experiences as there are only 6 participants in the present study. Instead, the method points to the value of comparing similar events in a player record in order to understand their context within a longer interactive experience when comparing responses by the same set of players.

We analyze encoded data using a set of player experiences which included video recordings of their facial expressions and assess the extracted expression values after key content locations in each traversal that were labeled by hand. For the study, we used the first three chapters of Telltale Game's *The Wolf Among Us* (*TWAU*) Episode 1 based on its critical success and popularity. We believe that annotating playthrough records with their important and related emotional and thematic content locations will enable greater insights into both the intended content design as well as compare methods for evaluating player responses. Annotating video playthroughs with content locations is particularly useful for storygames where the content length and timing varies and where other methods of assessment may not account for the immediate subjective reception of the presentation of content, such as speaker tone, pacing, and cinematic choices. These aspects are emphasized in this genre and are not as easily assessed through game telemetry or analyzing the topography of choice paths or more traditional content analysis.

Storygame content in choice-based cinematic adventure games (CCAGs) focuses on emotional decisions, events, and themes, and a successful game organizes content efficiently for maximum effect. This content consists primarily of performances (animations and voice-acting recordings) and writing (dialogue content) and is produced similarly to television content, incorporating work by writers, actors, and animators. Because of the cost of producing static content per minute of gameplay, studios that use this approach must maximize its use by reusing sound files of dialogue and animations as much as possible while creating the desired experience. *TWAU* demonstrates efficient and effective use of content that pulls players into the story, as evidenced by both the uniformity and variation in user responses to different content segments.

The content design accomplishes this feat by collocating positive and negative valenced emotional content events in such a way that players feel connected to the underlying story values while also given the freedom to express individual emotional responses. Emotionally charged events that consistently produce a similar response appear to anchor player emotions after sequences where the emotional responses vary. Dependent content tends to reward player emotional responses in subtle ways while supporting a diversity of possible expressions in choice options. Our analysis shows that the content strategy used in *TWAU* successfully elicits a combination of varied and consistent player responses from the same content segments by considering the *range* of variance in engagement and valence across the same content events. In effect, the difference in player response provides a means of evaluating how much the interpretation of the content can diverge or whether a single content event functions to anchor player emotional state despite player differences and previous choices.

Valence in affective science is one perceived dimension of emotion that varies from positively valenced emotions (such as joy) to negative (such as sadness or anger). While valence is a subjective perception of a feeling, it is often communicated to others through facial expressions. It is worthwhile to note that the visible expressions do not always line up with the as-felt experience and that different people express their feelings to different degrees. Through the process of annotating the content and reviewing player response data, we also observed the role that emotional events played in the game content. In particular, the same events could elicit a wide variety of emotionally intense experiences, which formed the core of the investigation into the causes of differing user responses to similar content events. These led to identifying events that functioned as emotional anchors that could provide the basis for choices and situations that provoked a range of responses and choices that expressed them.

These "anchors" appear designed to align player emotions regardless of the emotional variations in the previous content and served to point players feelings toward a particular target or mood. The encoding method presented here and its use in assessing player response data is a starting point for further refining label taxonomies and metrics for assessing player engagement and response.

2   Related Work

In the last two decades, there has been a renaissance in research into the human experience using computational methods, in part due to the rapid increase in the capabilities of computers, the development of efficient algorithms and the availability of sensors [18]. Approaches taken by researchers range from directly measuring and modeling players [29] to the creation of tools and instruments that measure games and record gameplay (also called play traces or traversals) [2,7, 13]. Concepts such as *fun, challenge,* and *flow* are often used to distinguish games from other types of narrative media and so do not naturally map onto moments that aim to evoke sadness or remorse in players. The interactive storytelling community recognizes this challenge and has developed a number of instruments to address it, such as Szilas' use of game telemetry in measure narrative content distributions and player behavior [26] and a standardized questionnaire that assesses player's experience during [25], or after playing a game [28]. Another use for such measures is to actively incorporate player responses into gameplay [6], though this paper focuses on the use of player response data to understand existing storygame content, particularly the role of emotion-eliciting events and choices. Some methods of measuring experiences have explored getting more precise and detailed data directly from EEG readings [1], but that approach presents barriers to adoption due to equipment requirements and experimental conditions. This paper describes a method that capitalizes on recent advances in machine learning and computer vision to examine both content and player responses using commodity webcams and existing traversal records.

Several systems were designed to aid in the analysis of player experience data once it was collected, including Microsoft's Tracking Real-time User Experience (TRUE) [8]. Data Cracker [12], a tool for online user experience evaluation, was built alongside the game *Deadspace 2* and with the input of the development team. Microsoft TRUE combined data analytics with specific measurement protocols built in, such as surveying users during gameplay. Microsoft TRUE's subjective analysis was accomplished by pausing the game every three minutes and prompting the players to answer a survey question. The system was deployed in a large-scale case study in a released game, providing evidence that the technique could provide valuable insights into aggregate datasets. Both Microsoft TRUE and Data Cracker focus on spatial and logical components that are key to the experience of many genres, whereas the present approach focuses on emotional story content often found in storygames. The method described in this paper aims to address both smaller sets of player records and already-released games without requiring instrumenting the system itself, making it useful in research contexts outside of a particular game development context and to researchers interested in broader trends in storygame production and content.

The thread that distinguishes games user research approaches from the more humanistic perspective on player experience is the former's use of the scientific method to verify results as well as its use of biometrics and telemetry. Ravaja et al., for instance, investigates the relationship between specific gameplay events and physiological measures [20, 21]. Nacke's dissertation [14] focuses on the relationship between subjective measures such as questionnaires and objective psychophysiological measures, whereas the present paper focuses on the relationships between narrative-specific content features and facial expression-derived metrics. Nacke calls the intersection of game studies and psychophysiological measures "affective ludology" [15].

The increasing availability of affordable biometric sensors has made applying computational methods to measure and classify emotional states more accessible [16], and motivate our investigation into how best to take advantage of them for assessing narrative-specific content features and responses.

2.1   Classifying Emotions

There are two primary classifications of emotion within the affective science research community. The first is a categorical measure, where a person's emotional state can be mapped to a discrete set of states such as fear, anger, happy or sad. The second is a set of continuous dimensions that represent arousal and valence. In addition to classifying the response emotion, affective science employs the term *elicitor* to label an event or condition that acts as a stimulus and gives rise to an emotional response. There are several competing models for how emotion arises, of which the most popular is the appraisal model.

Appraisal Model of Emotion. The emotional appraisal model has gained widespread support in the community [24]. The theory focuses attention on structural features of the situation and the agent experiencing emotion. It differs from other theories by emphasizing the dynamic interpretation of the situation of an agent over static associations between emotions and elicitors. It addresses many issues raised by previous theories such as stimulus-response. "A common pattern of appraisal is found in all the situations that evoke the same emotion" [24]. For example, losing a laptop may give rise to either joy or sadness based on the knowledge of whether it was insured, which can further classify whether the response was based on perceiving the event as a positive or negative valenced emotional response.

In *TWAU* and other games by Telltale Games, the primary game content consists of a sequence of emotionally charged situations, in which the player has severely constrained agency to shape the outcome of events. The player's moment to moment reactions are available for observation through facial expressions and biometric signals (Heart rate, Skin Conductivity) that correlate with physiological responses. The content itself, such as specific depicted actions, dialogue or visuals, is available for annotation through records of the gameplay video, providing the context and locations for these responses. The appraisal model suggests that an encoding method that incorporates features from the content, when compared with the various measurable signs of player affect, could be useful in understanding associations and variations between player responses.

Categorical Models of Emotion. These "basic emotions" are families of related states, each of which may include some temporal duration or even a mixture of different emotions. Paul Ekman conducted a seminal study documenting facial expressions from numerous cultures [3], during which several such emotional labels were found to be universal. The emotion categories are used as labels for particular expressions classified by the Affdex Software Developer Kit (SDK), a library produced by Affectiva [11], though in this paper we focus on the two dimensions of valence and engagement to analyze specific responses. Future work could expand to these emotional categories or incorporate other methods of self-report.

3   Method

The study design and the collection of the data were conducted collaboratively, as well as some of the initial annotations. We brought in seven graduate students to a user research lab to play the first episode of *TWAU* in a lab while being videotaped. None of the participants had played the game before, though we later learned that one had read the comics on which it was based. We discarded one participant's data due to technical issues. The remaining subjects had their heart rate and skin conductivity measured, and were encouraged to both use think-aloud as well as manipulate non-verbal self-report sculptures known as the Sensual Evaluation Instrument. We conducted interviews before and after each session and asked each participant to complete a survey. We focus in this paper on the facial expression-derived metrics of valence and engagement. A more detailed description of the various measures and their comparisons can be found in [23], however we constrain the present paper to the annotated events and the facial expression responses.

3.1   The Wolf Among Us

TWAU [27] received numerous positive critical reviews, becoming an exemplar of the CCAG subgenre and is often compared to other cinematic branching narratives in reviews and other critical commentary. In it, players take the role of the protagonist, Bigby Wolf. Bigby is the Sheriff of a town of immigrant fairy tale characters who are struggling with issues of class and race. Other characters include Toad, an owner of a tenement complex and Snow, Bigby's partner and assistant to the deputy mayor. In the words of Telltale Games founders, the story is "tailored" through the selection of options throughout gameplay. Other gameplay elements include timed sequences of prompted actions known as quicktime events and segments where the player controls a character to roam an area and discover content through selecting "hotspots". The primary mechanic is the timed selection of a conversational option which usually includes a silent option.

3.2   Measuring Affect

One of the primary ways by which computing systems can understand and classify facial expressions is through an existing taxonomy known as the facial action coding system (FACS). A Swedish anatomist, Hjortsjö [5], developed the original taxonomy, which Ekman and Friesen adapted and published in 1978 [4]. The system was updated in 2002 and has served as a gold standard for research on automated facial recognition and emotion classification [10]. The reasoning behind using visual images and movies to classify emotions is that humans are capable of recognizing emotions based on pictures alone and that these expressions are the result of combinations of common facial muscles. These combinations are called action units (AUs).

We used the Affdex SDK, an openly available toolkit that incorporates trained models that classify expressions into values assigned to both categorical emotions as well as engagement and valence metrics. Robinson et al. incorporated the Affdex SDK [11] into a software tool, All The Feels, which was used in the study to record player biometrics [22].

There are two metrics that can be extracted from the detected player response facial expressions based on sets of facial action units and which are provided by the SDK: *valence*, whose value can range from −100 (negative) to 100 (positive), and *engagement*, whose value ranges from 0 to 100[1]. Features from measures

---

[1] The specific AUs used in each metric can be found at Affectiva's website, https:// developer.affectiva.com/mapping-expressions-to-emotions/.

such as Galvanic Skin Response (GSR), which is the change in skin conductivity following a physiologically detectable event, can ideally be extracted using statistics. However, the dataset collected contained a number of artifacts that precluded it, including a large amount of participant movement, breathing, and talking and loss of sensor data during segments of the traversals. Future studies that seek to incorporate biometrics may want to employ more guidance for player movement or measure breathing to overcome these challenges.

3.3 Encoding

We recorded both players and the gameplay itself while playing the first three chapters of *TWAU* and used a prototype web-based video annotation tool to locate and label similar content events across different player-traversal records. Our approach is similar to Lorenzo et al.'s work with Cinematic, though the tool we used was designed for annotating and aligning gameplay videos with shared content in different locations [9].

The data consisting of labels and timecode ranges for each content event were exported, including any textual content. Event content was divided into options and events, which further was either independent or dependent on a particular selected option. This dataset was brought into R [19], where the player facial expression metrics were also imported. Both were aligned previously so that the index of each frame was relative to a shared reference time. Then, the data was filtered and processed based on the methods outlined in the following sections.

Content events are segments of storygame content where the characters perform. They can be either dialogue acts by a specific character or physical gestures. These segments were annotated and included in the dataset based on an evaluation of their subjective impact by one of the authors using the tool mentioned above. As a result, not every line of dialogue or action are present in the analysis, but only those which were assessed to be a potential elicitor. While this encoding method is fundamentally subjective, a future study is planned to compare assignment of labels to content segments from multiple annotators and their relation to the dataset and each other. Future studies should also compare baseline expressiveness using controlled elicitors that involve gameplay as opposed to static images or even videos.

Choice prompts are locations where players are given a set of options consisting of short text phrases that describe a type of performance that the player character could respond with to a given situation. They are often timed, and almost always include a default option where the player-character remains silent. These are directly linked to content events that play based on their selection and can also represent states that select future content events. This reference to prior decisions helps to reinforce the importance of such decisions, though these references may be subtle.

4   Results

Our analysis compares player responses to these two features: content events and choice prompts. The annotations include the frame index of the content itself and can be used to identify time windows for player response metrics during the time window. While each event may elicit emotional responses, the recorded response metrics may also be due to some other source than the annotated event. A simple set of criteria can classify content events according to the presence or absence of certain values in the player responses during the windows based on thresholds. A window starts at the beginning of an event and lasting until eight seconds after the completion. The window provides enough time to account for comprehension of the content and its implications, though it does mean there may be overlaps in the time windows with closely spaced events. The minimum and maximum of the set of values in each window is used to determine the label as listed in Table 1.

Table 1. Content labels based on player experience measurements

Label	Value	Calculation	Threshold
Engaged	Engagement	Max	80
Negative	Valence	Min	-50
Positive	Valence	Max > 50	50
Mixed	Valence	Max > 50 and Min < -50	$-50, 50$

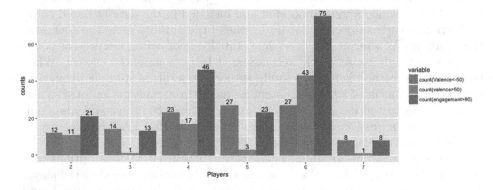

Fig. 1. Story event responses

Events. The counts for content events are charted in Fig. 1. For this analysis, ranges were set to the absolute values listed in the table and were based on our observations of the dataset, but a value based on an individual player's emotional tendencies across a given experience may yield more accuracy as each player may have a particular distribution.

In order to assess variation in player response, statistics for each player were collected for all content events that did not depend on an option or state. The variance was calculated based on the squared distribution of differences between each individual and the population mean for each time window's maximum and minimum valence and maximum engagement. The following tables are the result of sorting this dataset by each of the specified fields (in either ascending or descending order) and looking at the ten events that were located at either end.

Choices. For assessing choices, we also used an eight-second time window following each decision point and an engagement threshold of 70. The threshold is used to include an event if the value representing a player's engagement is greater than 70 for any frame in the time window. There were 51 unique choices in the three chapters included in the encoding, although not every player encountered every choice. For the purposes of this analysis, we looked only at choices which were presented to every player, shown in Table 2.

Table 2. Count of player response types to choices

Player	Positive valence	Negative valence	Mixed valence	Engagement
2	7	10	2	8
3	3	8	1	8
4	5	14	2	15
5	3	15	0	7
6	21	20	9	35
7	2	8	1	2

While the overall numbers reflect the expressivity of the other measures, this particular view shows balances and bias toward negative effects following choices, when we anticipated that there would be a higher percentage of choices that would have the with mixed or ambiguous labeled responses. There were also only a few choices that trigger both positive and negative effects. After totaling each choice using the method above, all choices that had resulted in at least one player response in each of the three categories (positive, negative, and mixed) were tallied.

While these results were promising for dividing player responses into groups, a method for comparing player responses was needed to assess whether content produced a variable set of responses.

The next analysis focused on ranking each content event according to the variance of player responses. In Table 3, each choice is listed along with the calculated variance across all players' maximum engagement, and choices were selected from 64 events that every player experienced.

Table 3. Highest **Engagement** variance content events FA: Faith Action, CS: Collin Speech, BuS: Beauty Speech, BA: Bigby Action, MS: Mirror Speech, WS: Woodsman Speech, FS: Faith Speech

EventID	Associated text	Variance
FA10	FAITH steps on an axe, looking determined	2992.21
FA18	FAITH removes her hand from Bigby's arm, turning away from him	2907.40
FA7	Faith crouches and begins to search the WOODSMAN	2804.27
CS120	People are scared of you	2751.96
BuS70	Please, Bigby... promise me you won't tell 2689.72 Beast you saw me	
BA16	Bigby turns, intending to pursue him	2648.50
MS119	Through powerful magic, her whereabouts are concealed. Unfortunately for you, "These lips are sealed."	2580.45
WS131	I'm the woodsman, you whore	2511.29
BS53	And I'm guessing it'd be bad for you to show up empty-handed	2510.43
FS52	A hundred...	2496.33

Table 4 lists events with the lowest variance of engagement, or where most players had a similar maximum engagement value following the event. The events seem to function as emotional anchors, providing either an independent anchor for the player experience or a more straightforward interpretation that provides clear emotional signals to guide players into a desired emotional state; for example, the mirror dialogue line is distinct in that it is clearly ambiguous about Faith's fate, and players respond to the different voice and intriguing information, which thus elicits interest.

Table 5 lists events where the variance in player's maximum detected valence in the time window varied the most in their responses. The response to these events depends heavily on other interactions and context, which may account for the variance. Another possibility is the particular characters involved, as some players either identified or responded very differently to the content depending on how they viewed the character involved. The most variance in player responses occurred following events Cr103 and Cr104, which followed a tense argument between Snow, Crane (the Deputy Mayor) and Bigby. The event is a significant clue for the next episode but timing their delivery after the emotionally tense argument was likely designed to cause a confused response.

These values suggest that categorizing and ranking content based on player responses can provide further insight into whether using the same content and strategically distributing it is successful in providing both personal and "tailored" experiences.

Table 4. Lowest **Engagement** variance content events. TS: Toad Speech, BfA: Bufkin Action. SS: Snow Speech, FA: Faith Physical Action, BS: Bigby Speech, Cr: Crane Speech

EventID	Associated text	Variance
TS2	Just cut me a break	910.66
BfA	Bufkin marks Faith as deceased in the Book of Fables	1338.95
GS89	Must be nice being the Sheriff. Do whatever the 1353.89 fuck you like	
SS105	Bigby do you have any idea what's going? on? How did this happen? Why her?	1389.58
FA19	Faith furrows her brows in anticipation	1413.93
BS123	You don't want me catching you out of glamour again	1461.81
Cr102	Any shred of evidence you two know what the hell you're doing?	1522.30
W30	Woodsman strangles Bigby	1612.23
FS54	I'll be fine	1619.13
FA20	Faith kisses Bigby on cheek	1682.78

Table 5. Highest **Valence** variance content events. TS: Toad Speech, BfA: Bufkin Action. SS: Snow Speech, FA: Faith Physical Action, BS: Bigby Speech, Cr: Crane Speech

	EventID	Associated text	Variance
59	Cr103	Call Vivian right this minute and let her know I'm coming in early for my... massage	2925.79
60	Cr104	And where is the bottle of wine you were to purchase?	2877.63
9	TS134	Furry pricked gobshite. Tell me how to spend my money. <Spit>	2610.97
10	TS136	You want the big bad wolf to take you away? Then get the fuck back inside	2610.97
6	TS122	Do you have any idea how much it costs to have an entire family in glamour?	2563.28
31	BA16	Bigby turns, intending to pursue him	2540.79
11	TJS135	The lights are shaking again	2537.51
45	Co81	Just gimme a drink, please!	2514.47
16	WS125	Aisle fuhged puhd yew in de ground	2424.48
18	WS131	I'm the woodsman, you whore	2393.37

5 Conclusions

We found that player responses could be analyzed based on the variance of engagement and valence as extracted using facial expression analysis. The results provided strong evidence that the content in *TWAU* successfully elicits a range of responses, with some content eliciting more variations in valence. As a result of the range in response variance, we propose emotional content anchors as an explanation for how content can reset the current scene intention and emotional state. For example, in *TWAU*, one of Toad's lines is "You going to just stand there?" This line conveys various facts and feelings simultaneously and has a strong emotional charge: it reminds the player of their scene intention (helping Toad with a disturbance, which may not have been clear from the introduction) while resetting their relationship back to an antagonistic one despite any previous positive expressions of sympathy. The accusatory subtext is unmistakable and is important for when Toad is cast in a suspicious light during a later scene in which Bigby is investigating Toad's lies.

Often story value charges at the end or beginning of a scene function either as anchors or are strongly related to player choices. Several dependent lines occur at the end of scenes to reinforce relationships, such as Beast's parting shot at Bigby when the player chooses the silent option and lets the elevator door close in his face. Beauty's warm thanks when Bigby promises to not tell Beast about her also reflects a strong reinforcement at the end of the beat for the player's (verbal) support. These emotional cues are strategically located either before or after a critical choice in a scene or at the beginning or end of a scene for maximum effect, reminding players of their decision to aid or hurt another character, and they often support closing scenes by providing dominant emotional notes.

Emotional content anchors, on the other hand, are present in all traversals and function as plot points that provide the backbone of the emotional trajectory of the scenes. They usually occur either at the beginning or the end of a beat. Examples include when Faith removes her arm from Bigby's after the concern for the Woodsman getting away, and the entire sequence of kissing Bigby at the end of Chap. 1 (serving to leave the player with the impression that Faith desires intimacy as well). The player character can also perform these actions. For example, Bigby's statement, "And I'm guessing it'd be bad for you to show up empty-handed," reminds players of the stakes of the situation and sets up the next decision. Interestingly, most players presented a negative valence expression during this speech act, in part responding to its implications. The expression itself is one of intimacy, whereby Bigby empathizes with Faith's situation, but the response is one where the player empathizes with Faith's situation as well. Bigby's action guides the player into the interpretation and the desired emotional take on the situation.

Future work should further investigate other factors such as expressiveness and classification of personality [17]. The distribution of responses indicates that the annotation method used may benefit from distinguishing between the intended feeling of a player and the enacted feeling of a character. For example, In humorous events, there is an opposite response (e.g., Toad's increasing frustration leads to laughter or amusement), though none of the characters are presenting a positive emotion. Further work in extracting character emotions using the techniques outlined in this paper could also be correlated with player responses.

References

1. Bruni, L.E., Baceviciute, S., Arief, M.: Narrative cognition in interactive systems: suspense-surprise and the P300 ERP component. In: Mitchell, A., Fernández-Vara, C., Thue, D. (eds.) ICIDS 2014. LNCS, vol. 8832, pp. 164–175. Springer, Cham (2014). https://doi.org/10.1007/978-3-319-12337-0_17
2. Drenikow, B., Mirza-Babaei, P.: Vixen: interactive visualization of gameplay experiences. In: Proceedings of the International Conference on the Foundations of Digital Games, p. 3. ACM (2017). https://doi.org/10.1145/3102071.3102089
3. Ekman, P.: An argument for basic emotions. Cogn. Emot. 6(3–4), 169–200 (1992)
4. Friesen, W.V., Ekman, P.: Facial Action Coding System: A Technique for the Measurement of Facial Movement. Consulting Pyschologists Press, Palo Alto (1978)
5. Hjortsjö, C.H.: Man's Face and Mimic Language. Studen litteratur (1969)
6. Jalbert, J., Rank, S.: Exit 53: physiological data for improving non-player character interaction. In: Nack, F., Gordon, A.S. (eds.) ICIDS 2016. LNCS, vol. 10045, pp. 25–36. Springer, Cham (2016). https://doi.org/10.1007/978-3-319-48279-8_3
7. Kaltman, E., Osborn, J., Wardrip-Fruin, N., Mateas, M.: Getting the GISST: a toolkit for the creation, analysis and reference of game studies resources. In: Proceedings of the International Conference on the Foundations of Digital Games, FDG 2017, pp. 16:1–16:10. ACM, New York (2017). https://doi.org/10.1145/3102071.3102092
8. Kim, J.H., Gunn, D.V., Schuh, E., Phillips, B., Pagulayan, R.J., Wixon, D.: Tracking real-time user experience (TRUE): a comprehensive instrumentation solution for complex systems. In: Proceedings of the SIGCHI Conference on Human Factors in Computing Systems, CHI 2008, pp. 443–452. ACM, New York (2008)
9. Lombardo, V., Damiano, R.: Narrative annotation and editing of video. In: Aylett, R., Lim, M.Y., Louchart, S., Petta, P., Riedl, M. (eds.) ICIDS 2010. LNCS, vol. 6432, pp. 62–73. Springer, Heidelberg (2010). https://doi.org/10.1007/978-3-642-16638-9_10
10. Martinez, B., Valstar, M.F., Jiang, B., Pantic, M.: Automatic analysis of facial actions: a survey. IEEE Trans. Affect. Comput. (2017)
11. McDuff, D., Mahmoud, A., Mavadati, M., Amr, M., Turcot, J., Kaliouby, R.E.: AFFDEX SDK: a cross-platform real-time multi-face expression recognition toolkit. In: Proceedings of the 2016 CHI Conference Extended Abstracts on Human Factors in Computing Systems, CHI EA 2016, pp. 3723–3726. ACM, New York (2016)
12. Medler, B., John, M., Lane, J.: Data cracker: developing a visual game analytic tool for analyzing online gameplay. In: Proceedings of the SIGCHI Conference on Human Factors in Computing Systems, pp. 2365–2374. dl.acm.org (2011)
13. Mirza-Babaei, P.: Biometric storyboards: a games user research approach for improving qualitative evaluations of player experience. Ph.D. thesis, University of Sussex (2014)
14. Nacke, L.: Affective ludology: scientific measurement of user experience in interactive entertainment. Ph.D. thesis, Blekinge Institute of Technology, Karlskrona (2009)

15. Nacke, L., Lindley, C.A.: Affective ludology, flow and immersion in a First-Person shooter: measurement of player experience. The Journal of the Canadian Game Studies Association (2009)
16. Nacke, L.E.: An introduction to physiological player metrics for evaluating games. In: Seif El-Nasr, M., Drachen, A., Canossa, A. (eds.) Game Analytics. Springer, London (2013). https://doi.org/10.1007/978-1-4471-4769-5_26
17. Paradeda, R., Ferreira, M.J., Martinho, C., Paiva, A.: Using interactive storytelling to identify personality traits. In: Nunes, N., Oakley, I., Nisi, V. (eds.) ICIDS 2017. LNCS, vol. 10690, pp. 181–192. Springer, Cham (2017). https://doi.org/10.1007/978-3-319-71027-3_15
18. Poria, S., Cambria, E., Bajpai, R., Hussain, A.: A review of affective computing: from unimodal analysis to multimodal fusion. Int. J. Inf. Fusion **37**, 98–125 (2017). https://doi.org/10.1016/j.inffus.2017.02.003
19. R Core Team: R: A Language and Environment for Statistical Computing. R Foundation for Statistical Computing, Vienna, Austria (2017). https://www.R-project.org/
20. Ravaja, N., et al.: The psychophysiology of video gaming: Phasic emotional responses to game events. In: Proceedings of DiGRA 2005 Conference: Changing Views - Worlds in Play, pp. 1–13 (2005)
21. Ravaja, N., Turpeinen, M., Saari, T., Puttonen, S., Keltikangas-Järvinen, L.: The psychophysiology of james bond: phasic emotional responses to violent video game events. Emotion **8**(1), 114–120 (2008). https://doi.org/10.1037/1528-3542.8.1.114
22. Robinson, R., Isbister, K., Rubin, Z.: All the feels: introducing biometric data to online gameplay streams. In: Proceedings of the 2016 Annual Symposium on Computer-Human Interaction in Play Companion Extended Abstracts, CHI PLAY Companion 2016, pp. 261–267. ACM, New York (2016). https://doi.org/10.1145/2968120.2987732
23. Robinson, R., Murray, J., Isbister, K.: You're giving me mixed signals! A comparative analysis of methods that capture players' emotional response to games. In: Extended Abstracts of the 2018 CHI Conference on Human Factors in Computing Systems, CHI EA 2018, pp. LBW567:1-LBW567:6. ACM, New York (2018). https://doi.org/10.1145/3170427.3188469
24. Scherer, K.R., Schorr, A., Johnstone, T.: Appraisal Processes in Emotion: Theory, Methods, Research. Oxford University Press, Oxford (2001)
25. Schoenau-Fog, H.: Hooked! Evaluating engagement as continuation desire in interactive narratives. In: Si, M., Thue, D., André, E., Lester, J.C., Tanenbaum, J., Zammitto, V. (eds.) ICIDS 2011. LNCS, vol. 7069, pp. 219–230. Springer, Heidelberg (2011). https://doi.org/10.1007/978-3-642-25289-1_24
26. Szilas, N., Ilea, I.: Objective metrics for interactive narrative. In: Mitchell, A., Fernández-Vara, C., Thue, D. (eds.) ICIDS 2014. LNCS, vol. 8832, pp. 91–102. Springer, Cham (2014). https://doi.org/10.1007/978-3-319-12337-0_9
27. Telltale Games: The Wolf Among Us (2013)
28. Vermeulen, I.E., Roth, C., Vorderer, P., Klimmt, C.: Measuring user responses to interactive stories: towards a standardized assessment tool. In: Aylett, R., Lim, M.Y., Louchart, S., Petta, P., Riedl, M. (eds.) ICIDS 2010. LNCS, vol. 6432, pp. 38–43. Springer, Heidelberg (2010). https://doi.org/10.1007/978-3-642-16638-9_7
29. Yannakakis, G.N., Spronck, P., Loiacono, D., André, E.: Player modeling. In: Dagstuhl Follow-Ups, vol. 6 (2013). https://doi.org/10.4230/DFU.Vol6.12191.45

Ludonarrative Hermeneutics: *A Way Out* and the Narrative Paradox

Christian Roth[1]([⊠]), Tom van Nuenen[2], and Hartmut Koenitz[1]

[1] HKU University of the Arts Utrecht, Nieuwekade 1, 3511 RV Utrecht,
The Netherlands
{christian.roth,hartmut.koenitz}@hku.nl
[2] King's College London, WC2R 2LS London, UK
tomvannuenen@gmail.com

Abstract. The practice of designing Interactive Digital Narratives [IDN] is often described as a challenge facing issues such as the "narrative paradox" and avoiding the unintentional creation of "ludonarrative dissonance". These terms are expressions of a perspective that takes narrative and interactivity as dichotomic ends of a design trajectory, mirroring an enduring discussion in game studies between positions often cast as ludologists and narratologists. The dichotomy of ludo versus narrative is, in itself, problematic and is often the source of the very conflict it describes. In this paper, we investigate this issue through the example of the cooperative game *A Way Out*, in which two players team up to break out of prison. The game is designed with a narrative twist, involving the escalation and final resolution of the game's competitive motif in the final scene. To understand the user experiences of this reveal, and the concomitant consequences, we engage in a discursive analysis of "Let's Play" videos as a largely untapped resource for research. By analyzing the interactions and performances in these videos, we can more clearly understand player responses to unsatisfying IDN design. As a result we introduce the notion of a 'hermeneutic strip', extending Koenitz' SPP model to locate and describe the involved processes of narrative cognition in IDN work.

Keywords: Interactive narrative design · Ludonarrative dissonance
Narrative paradox · Hermeneutics · Hermeneutic strip · SPP model
Role distancing

1 Introduction

The practice of designing Interactive Digital Narratives [IDN] is often described as a challenge that requires moderation between player freedom and the structured experience that interactive forms like video games internalize. Here, terms such as "ludonarrative dissonance" and "narrative paradox" are often used expressions of a perspective that takes narrative and interactivity as dichotomic ends of a design trajectory, reflecting the enduring trope of the narratology vs. ludology debate. However, as we will point out, the dichotomy of "ludo" versus "narrative" is in itself problematic, and is often the source of the very conflict it describes as a design challenge.

© Springer Nature Switzerland AG 2018
R. Rouse et al. (Eds.): ICIDS 2018, LNCS 11318, pp. 93–106, 2018.
https://doi.org/10.1007/978-3-030-04028-4_7

In practice, the terms "ludonarrative dissonance" [1] and "narrative paradox" [2] are used in relation to unsatisfactory user experiences in terms of agency and immersion [3]. Little is known, however, about the exact nature of the underlying issues, of the supposed tension between narrative and interaction. We investigate this issue through the example of Hazelight Studios' narrative action-adventure game *A Way Out* [4], in which two players team up to break out of prison and escape the authorities. We focus especially on player reactions to the showdown in the final scenes of the game where agency is suddenly revoked and the players are forced into a deadly confrontation from which there is no escape. In order to understand how this reveal and change of gameplay is experienced, we turn to the material of "Let's Play" videos on YouTube, which we consider a largely untapped resource for user-experience research. By analyzing the interactions and performances in these videos, we can more clearly understand player responses to IDN design.

This paper argues that the concept of ludonarrative dissonance is insufficient in describing situations where games let their players down due to tensions between gameplay and narrative constituents. We go on to suggest that the concept should, at least in this specific case, be extended and better defined by using the construct of *interpretation* of the ludonarrative to better accommodate the hybrid nature of the ludonarrative construct taking both player and game designer into account than the entrenched dichotomic ludology/narratology perspective.

2   Summarizing *A Way Out*

A Way Out is a game about the prison breakout of Leo and Vincent, two inmates who meet in jail and become partners in planning a daring escape. Convicted of robbery, assault and grand theft, Leo is introduced as a confident, pragmatic and headstrong character with a tendency towards violence. Vincent, on the other hand, has been sentenced for fraud, embezzlement and murder; he is portrayed as a smart, rational and reserved character. An unlikely pair, the two are united by their wish to take revenge on a common enemy – Leo's former boss, Harvey, who has framed Leo and killed Vincent's brother. Determined to make their escape, the two have to work together. Cooperation is required for most tasks, be it opening doors, subduing guards, hoisting each other up, or creating distractions so the other character can accomplish a task.

Teamwork is at the core of *A Way Out*'s game design, realized as cooperative activity for two players presented in a split screen. This configuration supports the narrative of the two characters being dependent on each other, while placing the respective players in the position of their avatars [5]. As Nitsche [6] argues, players understand the video game space and their movement therein by ways of narrative comprehension: a form of understanding of the events they trigger and encounter. To bolster the game's synergetic disposition, both characters' story unfolds simultaneously on the screen, allowing each player to see what the other one is experiencing. In certain situations, the screens merge, marking crucial points of interaction and shared experience. Once the two characters have escaped, action scenes are intercut with slower narrative segments, revealing the gradual development of friendship. Throughout the game players encounter dichotomic choices, usually juxtaposing Vincent's careful approach with Leo's brutish one. The narrative comes to a climax as both players finally confront and kill Harvey at his hideout in Mexico. Having fulfilled their mission, they return to the US, but in typical Hollywood fashion, the game has a twist up its sleeve. Vincent turns out to be an undercover cop whose sole reason for working with Leo is to get to Harvey. Feeling betrayed, Leo takes Vincent hostage, leading to a series of actions that culminate in a final showdown. Here, the game's dominant mode changes from one of cooperation (where players must help each other in order to proceed) to one of confrontation (where players can and, in the end, *must* harm each other in order to propel the narrative forward and achieve the game's objectives), mirroring the narrative of the betrayal and the resulting broken bond.

That is not to say that confrontation is absent beforehand: in fact, the game constantly plays off of the dialectic between competition and collaboration to increase the bond between players. From the start of the game, small, individual mini-games can be undertaken, such as doing pull-ups in prison, the results of which can be compared to the other player's tally. However, in the game's closing moments, narrative and gameplay shift dramatically from a mode that is mainly co-operative to one that is solely competitive. In the last interactive moment, players fight to reach a single weapon. Similar to earlier friendly competitions, the player who presses X faster gets to the weapon first. Once one of the characters reaches the gun, the game cuts to the perspective of that character within a slow-motion scene. The scene produces a radical shift in what, following Genette [7], we might call ludic mood: the way the designer allows events to unfold. We might say this is where the second betrayal occurs – this time, of the contract between the game and its players [8]. The narrative only advances when the trigger is pressed long enough so that the character in control raises his arm, aims for the other character's chest and then pulls the trigger. This is the only way to advance the narrative of this scene; any choice of non-participation just causes the game to pause.

3 Theoretical Background

3.1 Harmony, Dissonance and Narrative Paradox

<don't make me shoot him> ↑ I DON'T WANNA SHOOT HIM ↑

The above line is a Conversation Analysis excerpt from a Let's Play video of *A Way Out* [9]. The player, shouting at the game as he struggles to avoid killing his accomplice and co-player, is typical for the response of players in the final section of the game, having cooperated with the other player until this point. How can we understand these strong, disapproving responses? We might be tempted to call this a matter of 'ludonarrative dissonance', which is typically understood as the result of a disconnect between game mechanics and narrative. The concept was first offered in a rather terse blog post by Clint Hocking [1], who defines the concept loosely through the example of *Bioshock*. In the game, the "ludic contract" between player and game, – an objectivist morality that regards everything around them as a means to their own end – is in conflict with its "narrative contract", in which the player only progresses when they help an anonymous interlocutor over the radio. *Bioshock* thus contains a "disso-nance between what it is about as a game, and what it is about as a story" [1]. The concept has proven fruitful outside academic circles and is frequently applied in games journalism and public discourse.

In the case of *A Way Out*, if we take the game's dominant ludic mode to be that of collaboration, then, the narrative component seems incongruent, and – in the final scene – violates the "narrative contract" through the removal of agency, eliciting strong negative reactions.

We argue, however, that "ludonarrative dissonance" does not adequately describe this phenomenon, in part due to the unstable ontological premises of this term. While the term ludonarrative dissonance seems to evoke diachronicity – a tension or clash resulting from the combination of two disharmonious or unsuitable elements during a musical piece – the term very often describes its problem in holistic terms. A game either is ludonarratively dissonant, or it is not. The qualitative statement Hocking makes about his case study ("Bioshock seems to suffer from a powerful dissonance between what it is about as a game, and what it is about as a story") demonstrates this *pars-pro-toto* well. Of course, Hocking's example is not *entirely* ludonarratively dis-sonant: he notes that during the initial hours of his playthrough, what he experienced was more like what Pynenburg [10] calls "ludonarrative harmony", as he writes: "the game literally made me feel a cold detachment from the fate of the Little Sisters, who I assumed could not be saved." Harmony and dissonance seem, much like in music theory, co-dependent terms. Second, when understood in a particular way, ludonarra-tive dissonance may constitute what Gilbert Ryle [11] designated as a category-mistake, in which things belonging to a particular category are presented as belonging to a different one. We argue that the "ludic contract" Hocking describes is, upon closer inspection, another narrative contract: the world-making that players engage in through the game's mechanics is a cognitive achievement, and one in which their identification with "Randian objectivism" is a wholly narrative model, based on connected events. This is no attempt to drag up the problematic dichotomy of narratology versus ludology; instead, we mean this insofar as Jerome Bruner noted that "[w]e seem to have no other way of describing 'lived time' save in the form of a narrative." [12] of course, the player *does* engage with mechanics that are not (overtly) narrative in terms of their practical involvement. A reflection on what those mechanics mean, however, undoubtedly needs to consider the narrative aspect. This means we need to look more closely into the tension, between narrative aspects in a game, instead of stopping short at the definition of "mechanics". We will do so in the analytical section of this paper.

As mentioned, ludonarrative dissonance also implies ludonarrative harmony. Ludonarrative harmony refers to the successful syncing of both ludic and narrative aspects to build a consistent, immersive experience. When achieved, this harmony results in an internally consistent world that "feels right" [10]. As such, ludonarrative harmony seems to describe the status of the *well-functioning videogame*, and its par-ticularities are interesting to analyze. Interestingly, the lead designer of *A Way Out*, Josef Fares, has implemented cooperative gameplay before in *Brothers: A Tale of Two Sons* [13]. In *Brothers*, the game mechanics require players to use one gamepad stick for each of the two brothers they are controlling, reflecting the cognitively challenging task of cooperation. The older brother helps the younger one with different tasks –

notably, carrying him on his back while swimming. Later in the game the older brother dies, and the younger brother has to finish the journey alone. Players are left with one of the gamepad sticks to interact. Yet at the game's end, players are confronted with another stream to cross, and the younger brother refuses to go beyond the shore. The problem is overcome when players realize that the older brother is still there 'in spirit': both gamepad sticks can still be used. This narrative twist, told through the gameplay gambit of first taking away agency and then giving it back, has brought much praise to Fares and his design team. Similarly, in *A Way Out*, Fares' design fosters the bond between the characters (and the players) through cooperative gameplay right up to the climax of the game, where agency is taken away. In this case, however, it is never given back. Instead, the narrative design imposes either of two versions of an emotional ending, with one character dead. On an analytical level, the question is whether the observed problem is an instance of ludonarrative dissonance: the incongruence between what players assume based on what they have thus far experienced, and what the game designer has planned as the conclusion for the story.

Cliff Makedonski draws several conclusions from the notion of ludonarrative dissonance, considering designers responsible solely for the disruption. Overcoming the problem would either mean "focusing its efforts in a mostly linear direction", so that the player cannot make decisions that would put consistency at risk, or creating a proverbial map that spans the entire territory, and "molding a world where anything could happen" [3]. Of course, creating an IDN system that allows for such high levels of agency shifts the conversation to whether the resulting experience would still be meaningful for both player and the designer.

This brings us to the concept of narrative paradox [2, 14] which describes the inherent tension between authorship and participation, in which the player asserts agency, the freedom to take actions, while the game designer refuses to relinquish control of the narrative for the purpose of ensuring what they believe is a satisfying structure [15].

In IDN, interactors are encouraged to actively create belief by performing or, in effect, inhabiting a role [16]. This perspective assumes a fundamental distinction between agency and dramatic structure. A narrative is taken as a carefully woven product the storyteller crafts in order to create maximum impact. Herein lies the problem.

Costikyan [17] writes: "To the degree that you make a game more like a story – a controlled, pre-determined experience, with events occurring as the author wishes – you make it a less effective game. To the degree that you make a story more like a game – with alternative paths and outcomes – you make it a less effective story." However, this view has been challenged by a range of authors, including Jennings [18], Murray [16], Mateas [19] and Koenitz [20]. Thus, in order to be able to identify more precisely the tension caused by the ending of *A Way Out*, we need a better view of the ludonarrative relationship between players and designers. To do so, we need to return to the problem of what ludonarrative refers to in the first place.

3.2   Ludonarrative Hermeneutics

Adding to the confusion about ludonarrative dissonance is the fact that "ludonarrative" itself "is variously understood as a structural quality of the video game artifact, an experiential quality during the experience of a video game, or a high-level framework to understand video games." [21] In either case, as we mentioned in the last section, a number of scholars emphasize the difference to linear narrative manifestations and therefore work towards specific theories of video game narrative, seen as a variant of interactive digital narrative (IDN).

As Montfort [22] and Koenitz [23] clarify, an IDN artefact is not itself a narrative, it is an interactive computer program with the potential of instantiating narratives through user interaction. Koenitz reflects this aspect in his SPP model [20, 23], by understanding IDN as comprised of System, Process, and Product. Through the *process* of the player's engagement with the interactive narrative *system* by choices and other behavior - her performance (see also Knoller's perspective on "userly performance" [24]) - a concrete and personal narrative *product* is instantiated. Koenitz understands the IDN system as a prototype for all potentially instantiated narratives and thus as a *protostory*.

At any moment of reflecting on this narrative, it forms a story in the mind of the player. This is the ludonarrative expression of the hermeneutic circle, in which a text as a whole is established by reference to the individual parts and one's understanding of each individual part by reference to the whole. Yet, in the case of interactive digital narrative, the player also makes plans by evaluating the results of the interaction strategy so far, by speculating about paths not taken and by considering the current potential for interaction.

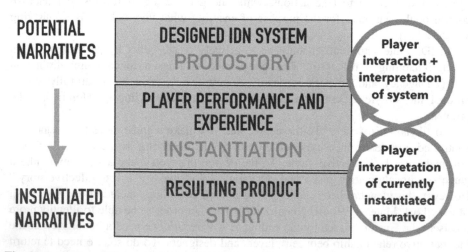

Fig. 1. Extension of Koenitz' SPP model [23] through implementation of a double-hermeneutic circle ('hermeneutic strip')

To illustrate how this system of ludonarrative hermeneutics works, we propose to extend Koenitz' SPP model [23] by adding a "hermeneutic strip", incorporating two interconnected loops of narrative interpretation processes (see Fig. 1).

The hermeneutic strip illustrates the player's narrative meaning-making process that happens (a) when players interact with the system and (b) when they interpret the instantiated narrative at any point of the experience. The latter can be understood as the classic hermeneutic circle, and together the two loops result in an interdependent double-hermeneutic circle of the IDN experience (cf. [25]).

In the 'upper hermeneutic circle' players are reflecting what the system allows them to do and what narrative they could extract, also in the sense of narrative game mechanics [26]. Within the 'bottom hermeneutic circle', then, players interpret the currently instantiated narrative. While players interact with an IDN system, they are continuously extracting information to understand past and present events and to plan their actions. As we mentioned above, this meaning-making process can be understood from a cognitive perspective on narrative. Following cognitive narratologists Herman [27] and Bordwell [28], Marie-Laure Ryan [29] narrative meaning is a cognitive construct, or mental image, built by the interpreter in response to the narrative construct (text in narratological terms). Intuitively, we might understand narrative as located with a narrative product like a printed book or a movie, however, the cognitive perspective stresses the point that narrative resides within the human mind as a mental construct. "… it does not take a representation proposed as narrative to trigger the cognitive construct that constitutes narrativity" [29]. Through interaction with a game such as *A Way Out*, players create mental narratives in an effort to make sense of the simulated environment and constantly check if their assumptions are consistent. New information leads to an updated projection, and conflicting information can lead to perceived dissonance. Thus, we understand IDN to have different narrative agents: on the one hand what is conveyed, implied, intended by the designer on a system level, and on the other hand what is performed, interpreted, assumed, expected, speculated and planned by the player. For the present discussion, we focus on player reactions to an IDN system. Through an analysis of these responses, we will now attempt to shed light on the potential dissonance players experience with the ending scenes of *A Way Out*.

4   Method: Analysis of Let's Play Videos

For our analysis of player responses to *A Way Out*'s narrative twist, and the way in which ludonarrative hermeneutics can be demonstrated, we turn to Let's Play (LPs) videos on the popular video platform Youtube. Let's Play is a style of videos documenting the playthrough of a video game, usually including commentary by the gamer. Glas et al. [30] identified LPs' potential for game archiving and exhibition purposes within cultural heritage institutions. Extending this perspective, we use LP as samples for the evaluation of user experiences. The first selective step consisted of watching a number of popular Let's Play videos (N = 40), showing up under the search query "A Way Out Let's Play". We narrowed the selection to 20 videos for the conversational analysis when the responses to the telling moment seemed not to yield any new insights.

For the purpose of this analysis we focus on two 'telling moments' at the end of the game, when the narrative twist takes place. In the first scene Vincent reveals that he is an undercover cop and Leo becomes aware of his betrayal. The second scene is the showdown in which Leo and Vincent fight each other, leaving one of them dead. We decided to exclude Let's Play heavily edited videos as we were interested in a recording situation that resembles an unedited think-aloud protocol. A smaller number of conversations (6) were then transcribed using the *Jefferson system*, one of the founders of conversation analysis (CA). [31, 32]. This method is interesting for several reasons. Reeves et al. [33] note that investigations into video game play developed from ethnomethodological and conversation analytic (EMCA) perspectives remain scarce. EMCA approaches the need to engage both with play as social action and the ways in which it is practically accomplished by players, "between players themselves, and between players and "the game" – as a moment-by-moment, sequentially organized activity" (ibid.) They do, however, offer the opportunity to focus in detail on the embodied act of play itself. Yet, EMCA typically attempts to work with what we could refer to as "naturalistic data": audio and video recording of activities that are, as much as possible, occurring in their original settings.

While the kinds of performative behavior that Let's Players demonstrate are likely not the same kinds of behavior found in everyday – and unrecorded – home scenarios, we contend that the performativity here allows us *more* insight, not less, into the ways in which players respond to the tensions arising out of the particular combination of gameplay and narrative. Youtubers "act out" their responses, often using what Ytreberg [34], following Goffman [35], refers to as a performative aspect of mass media, namely hyper-ritualizations and dramatic scriptings. The former involves a concentration and intensification of certain traits of unmediated behavior and interaction. The latter, Goffman notes, refer to "all strips of depicted personal experience made available for vicarious participation to an audience or readership" [35]. It is this dual nature of the Youtube performance that makes it indicative of the way players "ought" to respond to, in this case, a game. Goffman writes that "[the] deepest significance [of dramatic scriptings] is that they provide a mock-up of everyday life, a put-together script of unscripted social doings, and thus are a source of broad hints concerning the structure of this domain." We view the videos we analyze, then, as "over-performed" interactive narrative user experiences, telling of the ways in which games produce affective responses in their players.

To transcribe the findings of the LP sessions we turn to Conversation Analysis (CA): cf. [31, 32], which focuses on "the shape and form of the ways in which contributions to interaction form a connected series of actions", while attempting to "discover and describe the architecture of this structure: the properties of the ways in which interaction proceeds through activities produced through successive turns" [31]. In the process of annotation, we made use of the "Jefferson system" after its developer, the late Gail Jefferson. One of the additions we decided to make to this system is the inclusion of physical behavior, which due to the video format includes important interactional cues. We further made a distinction between physical player behavior (throwing the controller away) and in-game character behavior (pointing the gun towards something), as the latter is obviously controlled by the player but adds further contextual information.

5 Analysis

As the final confrontation between the characters commences, all of the players remained highly motivated to continue, as this event at first seems in line with the gradual escalation of the competitive elements that it has included from the beginning. Then, after a long fight scene between the characters Leo and Vincent (both badly wounded) stumble to a gun at the edge of the building. Still enthralled by the game's ludonarrative harmony, players shout and curse at each other as their movements bring them closer to the gun. Then, as one player reaches the gun, they are confronted with the results: the camera pans behind the winning character, and all they can do is to press the trigger.

In all of the analyzed LPs in which Vincent was the victor, players did not want to shoot the other, trying out a myriad of ways to avoid the outcome. Some temporarily put down the controller in refusal [9], others started playing meta-games with the mechanism of pointing the gun at the player [36]; yet others simply waited for a long time [37]. A closer look at a particular response of the players in The Let's Play channel *T&J Nexus* [38] demonstrates the disbelief of players as the game forces their hand and negates the ludonarrative harmony of comradery that has characterized the majority of the playthrough.

P Vincent: wha- aim, i don't wanna shoot. (.5)
P Leo: oh::: my god (.4)
P Vincent: i don't gonna i'm not gonna shoot (.) are you kidding me? {*switches be-*
         tween pointing and pointing away at Leo} (.3) do I have to? (.3) no,
         what if i don't. (.6) i don't wanna d(h)o this (.h) ↑ it's gonna f(h)orce
         me ↑
P Leo: (h) (.h) you don't have an option. (.3)
P Vincent: (h) i don't wanna do this (.3) I <u>really</u> don't wanna do this (.2)
P Vincent [holy shit]
P Leo: [ahh:: this is so] (.hh)
P Vincent: {*shoots*} ohh:: ↓ my god. ↓ why? (..) ohh:: come o::n
P Leo: (.hhh) (hhh)
P Vincent: fuck this ga::me. No:: i didn't w(h)ant it to e(h)nd like this

What we see here is a familiar "mapping" of players onto their characters, despite the fact they have played a round character for the entirety of the game – putting further tension on Troisi's distinction between "objective" and "subjective" narrative positions [39]. Players refer to their characters in first person yet simultaneously reflect on their own position as players. Additionally, they use the subject pronoun "it" to refer to the agency of the game itself, clearly no longer a "game" in the sense of "free movement within a more rigid structure" as Salen and Zimmerman [40] put it, but a system of predetermined choices. We also see players rationalizing the choices made by their characters and, instead of resisting, "playing along" and roleplaying as the idiosyncratic character they are playing. One player who gets to shoot while playing the cop, Vincent, rationalizes by saying "Well, it's my job" and "there's no honor among thieves" to his co-player. At the same time, players who control the character who shoots the other discursively distance themselves from the act they engage in. One player, while having used first and second person pronouns throughout the scene, slips into third person directly after his avatar shot the other.

P Vincent: ↑ why did he ↑ shoot im? (.) i mean i guess he-
P Leo: leo definitely was gonna kill him
P Vincent: ↑ yeah i mean ↑ he (.) had (..) all the right to

The player demonstrates what Goffman calls 'role distancing' [35] which pertains to the act of presenting one's 'self' as being removed or at a distance from the role one is being required to play. Role distancing is one strategy which allows the individual to play the role but to resist it – for example, by keeping your eyes open when asked to pray or say grace, you communicate to the group by role distancing, that you are making no commitment to the role. As such, people get to deny "the virtual self that is implied in the role for the allocating performers" [41]. While role distancing is a well-known trait from everyday life, it has as of yet not been connected to the complex performances of streamed video game play. Let's Players have to negotiate the space between themselves as performers vis-a-vis both the game (which fixes them into certain roles) and their potential audience (which may expect certain roles to be played). In this particular case, their linguistic behavior signals a dissonance not between their play and the narrative, but between their prior investment in the totality of their prior role and the new one they are forced to take. Taking stock of such conversations, where Glas [42] argues that "the aim with LP videos is not to create stories", we would strongly disagree. More than "annotating their game-play in real time" [43], Let's Players engage in all kinds of narrative life writing acts [44]. Moreover, it is the negotiation of that self that occurs in the moment that players are confronted with a forced action they do not subscribe to.

In sum, the use of role distancing in the broader narrative construction of "demonstrative play" that the Let's Play genre consists of, shows the subtle ways in which players are claiming authorship over the uncontrollable experience that the game offers. It also demonstrates that the dissonance, here, is not primarily one between mechanics and narrative, even if we would agree upon such a binary: there is not necessarily a tension between the narrative of the betrayed partner and the mechanical consequences that flow from that. Instead, the dissonance here arises between what we could describe as the hermeneutics of the designer and that of the player.

6 Discussion

The term 'ludonarrative' and related vocabulary ('video game narrative', 'narrative-focused game' 'interactive story') has been used to describe the phenomenon of narrative in interactive media. However, clear and generally accepted definitions of what this term actually entails are elusive. Accordingly, Koenitz states that no generally accepted definition of video game narrative exists as of yet [21]. He identifies a range of positions (e.g. the experience of a video game, its content and or an analytical perspective), which clearly demonstrate the vagueness of existing terminology. In this paper we have seen how current definitions of interactive narrative are not sufficient to describe the problems players have with the narrative of a particular game, and its narratively interpreted mechanics.

Again: the fact that we cannot conceptualize gameplay without a resort to narrative is not an attempt to police the borders of narratology and ludology. What it allows us to see is that there is a friction between the player's unfolding ideas about the characters they inhabit, and the designer's intended experience for that player. In this respect, ludonarrative dissonance describes the consequences of deeper-seated systemic tensions. In order to conceptualize this, we have proposed a different categorization by incorporating a hermeneutic approach to Koenitz' SPP model [23]. This conflict we identify lies beyond the moniker of ludonarrative dissonance: it is a disturbance in the interactive narrative experience caused by the unbridgeable distance between players' expectations (the assumptions they develop as they experience the narrative through gameplay, as shown in the *interaction and interpretation circle* in Fig. 1) and what is imposed by the designer, with the intention to create an engaging, immersive, and meaningful experience.

This view is supported by our analysis of Let's Play sessions as we observed players to be confused and in some cases even "rebelling" against the removal of agency, especially when the narrative that ensued subverted their conception of its integral unity. The hermeneutic strip we have introduced seemed to break, as the particular instantiation of the story turned out to differ (due to player agency) from the protostory players had imagined. This, we argue, demonstrates how players develop a sense for the level of granted agency, for instance when choosing to follow Leo's or Vincent's approach to the issues they encounter throughout the game.

As discussed above, IDN is a shared meaning-making activity between designer and audience. In the last interactive scene of *A Way Out*, shared meaning-making turns into an imposed narrative by the author. Here, the creator changes from the role of an interactive narrative designer, offering agency to the players, to the role of the traditional author who wants to convey a specific narrative meaning. Players revolt, when encountering the withdrawal of their agency as the co-creative process turns into an authored one, subverting their own co-created hermeneutical ideas about the 'protostory' (the set of all possible narratives) and the current concrete instantiation (the product created so far). This issue is related to the concept of design conventions as the conventional understanding of design methods by the audience [45]. *A Way Out*, in this context, applies the IDN design convention of "meaningful collaborative choice" throughout most of the game before finally frustrating audience's expectations when a novel, limiting interaction design is imposed.

This confusion leads to perceived dissonance, a rupture in the experience, leading to a break in the ludonarrative process. We argue that players, as a result of this interruption, instead of being invested in further narrative progression, started focusing on the change of their interaction experience – a move towards a meta-communicational level. As we know, in literature the "whole", as part of the hermeneutic movement, refers to the entirety of the story. When it comes to IDN, that whole is more than that: as the protostory it also refers to anything the player "could have done" as well. This is, in fact, what Murray [16] considers part of the transformative aspect of games: knowing that things could have been different is constitutive for the experience, as it makes one's decisions personally meaningful.

7 Conclusion

When creating interactive digital narrative systems, designers need to find a balance between player agency and a dramatic structure to offer a consistent, meaningful narrative. The resulting set of ludonarrative experiences is an essential part of narrative-rich games that cannot be ignored. Ludonarrative dissonance can be best understood as a temporal dissonance between the player's interpretation of the ludonarrative process and the interpretation of the overarching narrative (the instantiated narrative product created so far), and a function of the player's iterative hermeneutic oscillation.

"Ludonarrative dissonance" as an umbrella term does not explain the actual dissonances that occur and which can easily be misinterpreted as creating a false dichotomy between ludic and narrative elements. Our extended SPP model is a first step towards gaining a better understanding of such dissonant experiences. The challenge that lies ahead involves identifying and explaining the actual dissonances that can occur as the construction of narrative is tightly connected to our meaning-making. To understand the complex relationship between interaction and narrative it is crucial to include a cognitive perspective in the analysis. This destabilizes the dichotomy between "ludo" and "narrative", as narrative interpretation can be situated on several dimensions of the ludonarrative experience.

Future work might focus on expanding the IDN model to include the different narrative dimensions in between which dissonance can occur. Researchers might also investigate into temporal aspects and, for instance, the dissonance between different playthrough sessions (e.g. for systems that offer cross-session memory like *Save The Date*). In terms of methodology, a further exploration of Let's Play Videos as qualitative samples for the evaluation of the interactive narrative user experience is warranted – the fact that the captions of these videos can be computationally scraped is noteworthy.

A Way Out creates a collaborative experience, while highlighting the friction between collaboration and competition by which many friendships are characterized. Each player is capable of relating this "social model" to their own life. Interactive narratives, in other words, are significantly more flexible in achieving what Barthes called the writerly text, in which the reader is located as a site of the production of meaning, and for which the goal is to make the reader no longer a mere consumer, but a producer of the text [46]. Interactive Digital Narratives are not played for escapist motives alone but also for the transformative aspect: "The right stories can open our hearts and change who we are. [...] Enacted events have a transformative power that exceeds both narrated and conventionally dramatized events because we assimilate them as personal experiences." [47]

References

1. Hocking, C.: Ludonarrative Dissonance in Bioshock: The Problem of What Game is About. ETC Press, Pittsburgh (2007). http://clicknothing.typepad.com/click_nothing/2007/10/ludonarrative-d.html
2. Aylett, R.: Emergent narrative, social immersion and "storification". Presented at the 1st International Workshop on Narrative Interaction for Learning Environments, Edinburgh (2000)
3. Makedonski, B.: Ludonarrative Dissonance: The Roadblock to Realism (2012). https://www.destructoid.com/ludonarrative-dissonance-the-roadblock-to-realism-235197.phtml
4. Hazelight Studios: A Way Out (2013)
5. Klevjer, R.: What is the avatar? Fiction and embodiment in avatar-based singleplayer computer games (2006)
6. Nitsche, M.: Video Game Spaces. MIT Press, Cambridge (2008)
7. Genette, G.: Narrative Discourse, An Essay in Method. Cornell UP, Ithaca (1980)
8. Roth, C., Vermeulen, I.: Breaching interactive storytelling's implicit agreement: a content analysis of façade user behaviors. In: Koenitz, H., Sezen, T.I., Ferri, G., Haahr, M., Sezen, D., Çatak, G. (eds.) ICIDS 2013. LNCS, vol. 8230, pp. 168–173. Springer, Cham (2013). https://doi.org/10.1007/978-3-319-02756-2_20
9. Lets Play Pals: A Way Out - It Doesn't Have To Be Like This (End). https://www.youtube.com/watch?v=4Nvi3bguqoE
10. Pynenburg, T.: Games worth a thousand words: critical approaches and Ludonarrative Harmony in Interactive narratives. http://scholars.unh.edu/cgi/viewcontent.cgi?article=1069&context=honors
11. Ryle, G.: The Concept of Mind. University of Chicago Press, Chicago (2003)
12. Bruner, J.: Life as narrative. Soc. Res. **54**, 11–32 (1987)
13. Starbreeze Studios: Brothers: A Tale of Two Sons (2013)
14. Louchart, S., Aylett, R.: Solving the narrative paradox in VEs – lessons from RPGs. In: Rist, T., Aylett, R.S., Ballin, D., Rickel, J. (eds.) IVA 2003. LNCS (LNAI), vol. 2792, pp. 244–248. Springer, Heidelberg (2003). https://doi.org/10.1007/978-3-540-39396-2_41
15. Louchart, S., Aylett, R.: Narrative theory and emergent interactive narrative. Int. J. Contin. Eng. Educ. Life Learn. **14**, 506–518 (2004)
16. Murray, J.H.: Hamlet on the Holodeck: the Future of Narrative in Cyberspace. Free Press, New York (1997)
17. Costikyan, G.: Where stories end and games begin (2001). http://www.costik.com/gamnstry.html
18. Jennings, P.: Narrative structures for new media. Leonardo **29**, 345–350 (1996)
19. Mateas, M.: A preliminary poetics for interactive drama and games. Digit. Creat. **12**, 140–152 (2001)
20. Koenitz, H.: Towards a theoretical framework for interactive digital narrative. In: Aylett, R., Lim, M.Y., Louchart, S., Petta, P., Riedl, M. (eds.) ICIDS 2010. LNCS, vol. 6432, pp. 176–185. Springer, Heidelberg (2010). https://doi.org/10.1007/978-3-642-16638-9_22
21. Koenitz, H.: Narrative in video games. In: Lee, N. (ed.) Encyclopedia of Computer Graphics and Games, pp. 1–9. Springer International Publishing, Cham (2018). https://doi.org/10.1007/978-3-319-08234-9_154-12
22. Montfort, N.: Twisty Little Passages. MIT Press, Cambridge (2005)
23. Koenitz, H.: Towards a specific theory of interactive digital narrative. In: Koenitz, H., Ferri, G., Haahr, M., Sezen, D., Sezen, T.I. (eds.) Interactive Digital Narrative, pp. 91–105. Routledge, New York (2015)

24. Knoller, N.: The expressive space of IDS-as-art. In: Oyarzun, D., Peinado, F., Young, R.M., Elizalde, A., Méndez, G. (eds.) ICIDS 2012. LNCS, vol. 7648, pp. 30–41. Springer, Heidelberg (2012). https://doi.org/10.1007/978-3-642-34851-8_3

25. Karhulahti, V.-M.: Double fine adventure and the double hermeneutic videogame. Presented at the Foundations of Digital Games, New York, USA (2012)

26. Dubbelman, T.: Narrative game mechanics. In: Nack, F., Gordon, A.S. (eds.) ICIDS 2016. LNCS, vol. 10045, pp. 39–50. Springer, Cham (2016). https://doi.org/10.1007/978-3-319-48279-8_4

27. Herman, D.: Story Logic. U of Nebraska Press, Lincoln (2002)

28. Bordwell, D.: Poetics of Cinema. Routledge, New York (2007)

29. Ryan, M.-L.: Narrative Across Media: The Languages of Storytelling. University of Nebraska Press, Lincoln (2004)

30. Glas, R., de Vos, J., van Vught, J., Zijlstra, H.: Playing the Archive. In: Mol, A.A.A., Ariese-Vandemeulebroucke, C.E., Boom, K.H.J., Politopoulos, A. (eds.) The Interactive Past: Archaeology. Heritage & Video Games. Sidestone Press, Leiden (2017)

31. Wooffitt, R.: Conversation Analysis and Discourse Analysis. SAGE, London (2005)

32. Liddicoat, A.J.: An Introduction to Conversation Analysis. Bloomsbury Publishing, London (2011)

33. Reeves, S., Greiffenhagen, C., Laurier, E.: Video gaming as practical accomplishment: ethnomethodology, conversation analysis, and play. Top. Cogn. Sci. **9**, 308–342 (2016)

34. Ytreberg, E.: Erving Goffman as a theorist of the mass media. Crit. Stud. Media Commun. **19**, 481–497 (2010)

35. Goffman, E.: Frame Analysis: An Essay on the Organization of Experience. Northeastern University Press, Boston (1974)

36. GameGrumps: A Way Out: Finale - PART 20. https://www.youtube.com/watch?v=FWFMPkU0hKc

37. #TheEscapeBros: Ending - a Way Out [Co-Op] - Part 11. https://www.youtube.com/watch?v=WUfru2Gk92k

38. T&J Nexus: A Way Out, Vincent Ending (Spoilers Duh) Reaction ft Bes. https://www.youtube.com/watch?v=yXYLd0J2Lh0

39. Troisi, A.: Interactive Narrative Design in Mass Effect 2. Vancouver, Canada (2010)

40. Salen, K., Zimmerman, E.: Rules of Play. MIT Press, Cambridge (2004)

41. Goffman, E.: Encounters: Two Studies in the Sociology of Interaction. Allen Lane, London (1972)

42. Glas, R.: Vicarious play: engaging the viewer in Let's Play videos. Empedocles Eur. J. Philos. Commun. **5**, 81–86 (2015)

43. Newman, J.: Videogames. Routledge, New York (2013)

44. Eakin, P.J.: How Our Lives Become Stories: Making Selves. Cornell University Press, Ithaca (1999)

45. Roth, C., Koenitz, H.: Towards creating a body of evidence-based interactive digital narrative design knowledge: approaches and challenges. Presented at the AltMM 2017, Mountain View, CA 21 August (2017)

46. Barthes, R.: S/Z. Hill and Wang, New York (1975)

47. Murray, J.H.: Hamlet on the Holodeck. The Free Press, New York (2016)

The Myth of 'Universal' Narrative Models

Expanding the Design Space of Narrative Structures for Interactive Digital Narratives

Hartmut Koenitz[✉], Andrea Di Pastena, Dennis Jansen,
Brian de Lint, and Amanda Moss

Professorship Interactive Narrative Design, HKU University of the Arts Utrecht,
3500 BM Utrecht, The Netherlands
hartmut.koenitz@hku.nl, andrea.dipastena@gmail.com,
d.jansen5@students.uu.nl, briandelint@gmail.com,
a.moss.l@student.rug.nl

Abstract. In narrative game design and related practices, the role and function of narrative models is described as predominantly pragmatic. However, we see that many interactive digital narratives (IDN) including narrative video games derive their story structures from the same formulas connected to Joseph Campbell and Aristotle, adhering to the trajectory of the Hero's Journey and the dramatic arc. We engage with scholarly criticism exposing the supposed ubiquity of these structures and agree that the question of narrative models in interactive digital media requires both further exploration and intervention. We follow up on some proposed solutions by looking at non-Western narrative traditions to expand the corpus of narrative structures available to game designers and other narrative developers. With this paper we raise awareness of alternative structures and simultaneously introduce implementable narrative structures with the aim to expand the design space and range of analytical models for IDN.

Keywords: Interactive digital narrative · Narrative game design
Narrative structure · Analytical models · Narrative theory · Eurocentrism
IDN design

1 Introduction

In narrative game design and related practices, narrative is often used in a "pragmatic" way, as Marie-Laure Ryan [1] reminds us. Yet, the discourse surrounding narrative in both scholarship and the professional field does not address what this actually means in regards to narrative structures. In lieu of Ryan's claimed pragmatic conceptual flexibility, we see only a small number of dominant underlying models at play. In the so-called 'ludology vs. narratology' debate of early game studies [2–9], for instance, the idea of 'narrative' that the ludologists maintained (and fought against) was limited by a narrow perception of what the concept can entail – partially affected by the hegemony of certain narrative structures in the Western literary tradition [10]. Indeed, a large number of video games derive their narrative structures from formulas connected to the

© Springer Nature Switzerland AG 2018
R. Rouse et al. (Eds.): ICIDS 2018, LNCS 11318, pp. 107–120, 2018.
https://doi.org/10.1007/978-3-030-04028-4_8

concepts proposed by Joseph Campbell and Aristotle, adhering to the trajectory of the Hero's Journey [11] and the "classic dramatic arc" [12].

Following the criticism of the ubiquity of these structures by scholars such as Pamela Jennings [13], Marie-Laure Ryan herself [1], Barry Ip [14] and Hartmut Koenitz [10, 15, 16], we agree that narrative models in interactive digital media require both further exploration and intervention, and aim to follow up on some proposed solutions by looking beyond Aristotle and Campbell to non-Western narrative traditions to expand the corpus of narrative structures available to IDN designers and game developers. So far, this perspective has had only a limited impact on the design of interactive digital narratives and has not yet reached the status of 'credible alternative' to the dominant models. It seems peripheral awareness of structural alternatives is not enough; these structures also need to be supported by descriptions concerned with implementation. With this paper we address this dual challenge, by raising further awareness of alternative structures and by simultaneously introducing implementable narrative structures. For the purpose of this paper, our focus is primarily on examples from video games, however, we do take IDN as an expression that transcends several forms.

2   Defining Interactive Digital Narrative

First, we should elaborate on our understanding of the specific form of narrative for which we suggest alternative structures later in this paper. With the advent of the digital medium, the necessity for medium-specific perspectives of narrative has become increasingly clear. Katherine Hayles reminds us that in prior perspectives, the layer of mediated representation has been largely ignored and consequently challenges this practice by introducing "medium-specific analysis" [17]. Conversely, Liv Nausen raises awareness for the widespread "media blindness" in the humanities [18]. In this context, the limitations of established definitions of narrative by narratology scholars like Gerald Prince [19] and Gérard Genette [20] become clear, as they do not problematize the aspect of the medial representation. In that sense, Espen Aarseth's definition of cybertexts [21] is also media-blind due to his insistence on a media-agnostic perspective (including paper-based as well as digital forms). In contrast, the ludology vs. narratology debate, the former side takes narrative [22] to be properly at home only in non-interactive media: "Video games are not a narrative medium" [2] and thus effectively treats narrative as specific to non-interactive media (e.g. the comparison to novel and movies in [9]). This claim was repeated by Bogost as recently as 2017 [23].

A primary requirement for a definition of IDN is thus medium-specificity that prevents diverting to a different medium. Furthermore, this definition needs to account for the systemic nature of procedural artefacts, the interactive process and the linear, static recorded stories that result from this process (cf. [15]). Here, we extend Koenitz' previous definition [15] to more explicitly represent the role of the participant:

Interactive Digital Narrative is an expressive form in the digital medium, implemented as a computational *system* containing a *protostory* of potential narratives that is experienced through a *process* in which participants influence the continuation of the unfolding experience that results in *products* representing instantiated stories.

This definition has a number of consequences: (1) the author/screenwriter is transformed into the creator of a dynamic 'system'; (2) the audience now has at least some influence on the course of the narrative by engaging with that system; (3) IDN requires the presence of additional elements that allow for alternative paths to be realized.

This medium-specific perspective on narrative in interactive digital media also means that the narratives should be structured in such a way that they make use of the specific affordances of the digital medium [24, 25]. Jennings' proposal to look at African oral storytelling for more adequate structures is therefore well-founded [13], yet so far this suggestion has been underdeveloped, with Fox Harrell's work being a rare exception [26–28]. The reason, we believe, is in a dual challenge of (a) dominant models that marginalize knowledge of alternatives and (b) the lack of structural descriptions that lend themselves to concrete implementation in interactive media, which we discuss further in the next section.

3 Narrative Structure in IDN

3.1 Aristotelian Poetics and the Hero's Journey

The two most influential and pervasive narrative structures in the Western narrative tradition, regardless of medium, are the dramatic arc and the Monomyth/Hero's Journey. The former has its roots in Aristotle's *Poetics*, which prescribes a well-formed plot containing a beginning-middle-end structure wherein "the narrative increases in intensity to the climax and then gradually reaches an end parallel to the tone of its beginning" [13]. Yet, it is important to realize that Jennings' description (and similar interpretations by others) is the result of a Neo-Aristotelian re-interpretation that takes at least as much from Gustav Freytag's [29] five-act model of the dramatic pyramid, with exposition (beginning), rising action + climax + falling action (middle), dénouement (resolution) as from the *Poetics*. Furthermore, Aristotle's work is often misunderstood as a general description of narrative, when a closer reading actually reveals the opposite: it is a medium-specific understanding of narrative that distinguishes between epic (prose) and mimetic (dramatic) forms and focuses on the latter with a detailed analysis of the tragedy. Aristotle himself cautions his readers that narratives cannot simply be translated between epic and mimetic forms (and thus different media), arguing that episodic epic narratives are unsuitable for mimetic treatment.

The Hero's Journey, also known as the Monomyth, was first conceptualized by Joseph Campbell in his cross-cultural study *The Hero with a Thousand Faces* [30] and has subsequently been elaborated upon by others [14, 29, 30]. The Hero's Journey traces its protagonist's story roughly through the following stages:

1. Introduction of the hero's ordinary world;
2. A call to adventure, often initially rejected by the hero and then reluctantly answered;
3. The meeting with the mentor, who/which will guide the hero in their journey;

4. The crossing of the threshold, when the hero leaves their ordinary world and begins to face trials and challenges that test their resolve;
5. The preparation for and undergoing of an ultimate ordeal, when the hero faces their nemesis/shadow/foil;
6. The reward gained from this final task, and the hero's return home from their now-completed journey with that reward.

Though Campbell researched tales from around the world, the 'universal' structure he derived from those different stories aligns surprisingly well with Aristotle's and Freytag's "mono-orgasmic" [13] dramatic arc, in the sense that both structures follow similar patterns of exposition, rising tension/conflict followed by a climactic event that serves to de-escalate the central conflict, and a conclusion that often involves a return to the 'normal state of affairs' [11, 14]. In fact, many books on (screen)writing tend to unify the two structures without seriously problematising either [31, 32], and many of the most influential stories in Western culture seem to follow these structures very closely – e.g. *The Odyssey*, *Jane Eyre*, *Lord of the Rings*, and also the more contemporary example of *Star Wars*. Even though care is often taken to note that exceptions to this normative trend exist (both within and outside of Western narrative tradition), little attention is paid to such instances as anything other than exceptions that prove the rule.

3.2   The Inadequacy of the Hero's Journey for IDN

The idea that the dramatic arc/Hero's Journey is the paradigmatic, media-agnostic, universal form of narrative structure is problematic in several important ways. On a general level, it blinds us – scholars, writers, designers – to non-Western forms of narrative (as well as 20th century avant-garde forms), which come to be seen as 'more primitive' and/or 'less developed'. This perspective also prevents us to grasp the opportunity of IDN and conceive of radically different aesthetic experiences that might be brought about by interactive digital narratives which do not follow the dramatic arc/Hero's Journey structure. More specifically, the inadequacy of the Hero's Journey structure for IDN shows itself both in the narratives themselves and in our understanding of those narratives, with the common problem being that this model does not do justice to the affordances of interactive digital media (cf. Ruth Aylett's insight into the "narrative paradox" [25]). For instance, as with other media forms, many of the most popular and influential video games and game franchises seemingly trace the Hero's Journey in their narratives, which is exemplified most strongly by those games that provide their players with masculine power fantasies, such as first-person shooters (*Call of Duty* [33], *Half-Life* [34]) and role-playing games (*The Elder Scrolls* [35], *The Legend of Zelda* [36]), yet similar structures also seemingly exist in more 'docile' games like the puzzle adventure *Professor Layton* [37] and the point-and-click adventures like the *The Longest Journey* [38]. Yet, in a detailed analysis of narrative structures in games, Barry Ip consistently identifies a conflict between the model Hero's Journey/dramatic arc and actual implementations, as regularly more than 90 percent of a game is spent in the middle part of that structural model. Normally – read: in non-interactive media – that part would be expected to take up around half of that time [39]. This means one of two things: either, that this change violates the rules of the model and thus the resulting narrative is deficient; or, that this is actually an evolution that should be considered separately from the original. In his subsequent remarks, Ip tends to the former perspective, as he detects an "imbalance between the various acts has remained all but constant [throughout the past few decades], thus pointing toward the relative predictability, and obscure representation of game narrative" [39], which aligns well with observations and critiques on the conventions of IDN written by various others since the late 1990s [10, 11, 13, 16, 40–43].

Indeed, given the conflict between the forced application of the Hero's Journey structure on a conceptual level and actual implementations that set a different emphasis on game-appropriate aspects – as reported by Ip – it is no wonder that we find an all-too-frequently seen claim in academic and non-academic games criticism that "the narrative [...] and writing found in video games are often of poor quality" [44]. This sentiment is arguably further encouraged by the conventions of narrative delivery in games, which rely heavily on modalities that are not native or specific to interactive digital media, such as cutscenes and on-screen text [14, 39]. The dominant Western conception of 'narrative' as having a passive audience, as requiring a single protago-nist, a central conflict and a single climax – that is, as a Hero's Journey – is then clearly insufficient to unleash the potential that interactive forms like games have when it comes to novel expressive modes of narrative. This is especially obvious given that some of the most recent aesthetically interesting game narratives (such as *Dear Esther* [45] and *NieR:Automata* [56]) diverge from and defy the Hero's Journey.

What is needed instead, is a radical shift in the way designers and academics think of what interactive digital (game) narrative *could* and *should* be, which entails first and foremost doing away with "classical [Western] notions of narrative" [42] and dethroning the Hero's Journey as the standard narrative structure for IDN. In the following sections, our present contribution to this effort does this by presenting a variety of alternative structures for interactive narratives and tentatively suggesting some ways in which these structures might be applied.

4 Narrative Structures: Beyond the Hero's Journey

The methodology used to conduct this research combines textual analysis with literary review, using an approach akin to grounded theory. First, we conducted a literature review, searching for narrative structures already identified in previous research. In this stage, we noted several structures such as Kishōtenketsu [46], a conflict-free narrative structure originating in Chinese poetry and widely used in Korean and Japanese writing; the Robleto [47], a Nicaraguan narrative structure defined by a notable line of repetition; and frame narrative structures from the Indo-Arab literary and oral traditions which feature two to three distinct diegetic levels [48]. These particular narrative structures clearly demonstrate that viable alternatives exist and thus they already serve to expose the fallacy of assigning universal status to the Monomyth and the dramatic arc.

Yet, we do not want to stop here, as we aim to push the boundaries even more and thus have opted to focus on structures which have not yet been addressed at length by other (Western) scholars. In our primary research effort, we studied and analyzed a variety of narratives from Indian, Arab, indigenous North American, and Northern African literary traditions, as well as contemporary (postmodernist) works and Western interactive digital media. For the non-Western literary traditions we focused on pre-colonial works to preclude Western influence as much as possible. The selection of primary texts was based on accessibility and availability of English translations of local, oral stories found in anthropological research [49, 50] and recorded stories from indigenous, precolonial cultures. Using a neostructuralist approach, we scanned this selection, paying attention to how events and conflicts propelled the narrative forward, how different stages were announced and distinguished from each other, and whether or not tension factored into one particular stage, or the transition between stages.

We approached these narrative structures coming from a media landscape that is saturated by the Hero's Journey/dramatic arc. In contrast, we focus on alternatives and therefore the narrative structures we describe below represent a look at the fringes of Western literary tradition and beyond.

4.1 Etiological Oral Narratives

Stories that follow this structure do not end with a traditional conclusion, but rather with a lesson about how the story explains something about the state of the world today – usually some natural phenomenon.

This structure (see Fig. 1) is based on the etiological animal narratives recounted in Ruth Finnegan's *Oral Literature in Africa* [49]. They were used by the Kikuyu tribe from East Africa and the Limba tribe from Sierra Leone to explain the relationships between certain animals and the material world. Narratives that follow this structure begin with an introduction of the setting and the main characters. One of the characters is then indebted to another by accepting a service or goods from them, which serves as the inciting event. The next element is a failure to repay the debt, leading to a conflict with their creditor. After a period of pursuit, the debt is then finally repaid, willingly (often through alternative means than initially intended/planned) or by force (that is, as cunning revenge taken by the creditor). The narrative concludes with an etiological explanation, using events of the prior narrative as a justification of the current state of the natural world. While the earlier variants can be made manifest in an IDN design as the consequences of player choices, justification aspect could be realized by presenting players' earlier choices.

Etiological stories are commonplace in other cultures as well, and thus might serve as reference points for diverse audience groups. In Greek and Roman mythology we see stories that explain the origins of certain animals, many of which can be found in Ovid's Metamorphoses. There are also similarities to some Iroquois narratives which provide an etiological explanation of how the turkey buzzard got his suit or why the eagle defends native Americans [51].

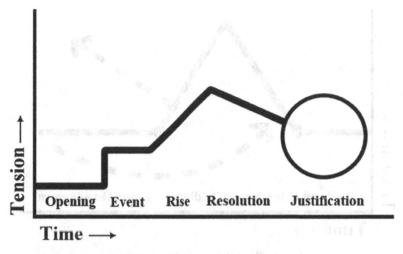

Fig. 1. Etiological structure

4.2   Bengali Widow's Narratives

The Bengali Widow's narrative structure either raises after the climax to a tragic outcome, when the protagonist is abandoned by her family, or folds back to see the protagonist becoming the antagonist to her son's bride.

We derived this narrative structure (Fig. 2) from the comparison of different narratives that circulate among the West Bengal population that focus on the powerlessness of the displaced widowed mother. In so doing, they provide a critical perspective on the status of the apparent stability women are assumed to have acquired upon marriage, which comes into question in West Bengal after the death of their spouse, especially if their children have already reached adulthood by that time [50]. Therefore, the Bengali widowed mother narrative wants to illustrate a less romanticized reality which many women face. At first sight, this narrative structure is reminiscent of the dramatic arc, however there is a crucial variation that is connected to the 'themes' of the narrative. The climax is not followed by a phase of dénouement; rather, the tension keeps growing, either with the narrative looping back on itself if the widowed mother becomes the antagonist (the mother-in-law) for the bride of her son – effectively repeating the cycle from marriage to close – or, by continuing forward to show the abandonment of the mother by her sons after the death of her husband, will end in a climax where her sons and daughters-in-law leave her beggared and alone. What is notable here is the underlying tension between the mother's expectations for how her sacrifices for her children will be repaid in the future and the reality of widowhood, as well as her gradually shifting role from protagonist to antagonist in the eyes of the younger generation of brides. Having two variants in a narrative is an aspect that can be made productive for IDN, as the different outcomes can be connected to players' choices. In addition, IDN could add additional varieties, e.g. an outcome in which the widow becomes a good friend and trusted advisor of the next generation of women.

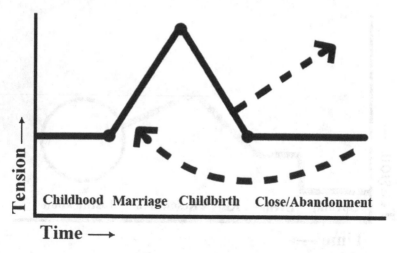

Fig. 2. West Bengali widow narratives

4.3 Ganga Comics

This structure is based on adaptations of Indian mythology in comics, in which the solution to one conflict also immediately causes the next conflict to arise.

The "Ganga" [52] comic provides another interesting narrative structure to study (Fig. 3). The "Ganga" comic is derived from the *Amar Chitra Katha* (ACK), an illustrated comic series depicting hundreds of tales from the *Rāmāyaṇa*, *Mahābhārata*, *Panchanatra*, and *Vasavadatta*, alongside a host of other plays, epics, and romances across the Indian subcontinent. This particular story stems from the *Mahābhārata*, a collection of mythological and instructive stories that revolve around a main narrative that recounts the power struggle between two groups of cousins, namely the Kauravas and the Pandavas. The *Mahābhārata* represents a seminal text for the growth of Hinduism, and it is understood as both Dharma (moral law) and Itihasa (history) [53]. The "Ganga" comic is a particular variety of this narrative that utilizes the affordances of its medium.

The narrative structure is arranged as a negotiation between the two poles of 'responsibility' and 'consequence'. The narrative begins with an initial instigating action (IA), which would have specific consequences (C1). The next step involves the search of a solution (S1), that eventually results in a sort of resolution (R1), which however would have other ongoing consequences (C2). These further consequences would begin the next part of the narrative, as the secondary instigation for further action, escalating and repeating until all major consequences are resolved. The "Ganga" comic narrative structure is characterized by a cumulative pattern, in which the consequences of the solution to each problem affect the overall narrative. This aspect also aligns well with the affordances of IDN; the idea of player choice affecting the problems/conflicts they will encounter later in the story is a powerful one with much potential for the creation of many individually different narratives from the same system.

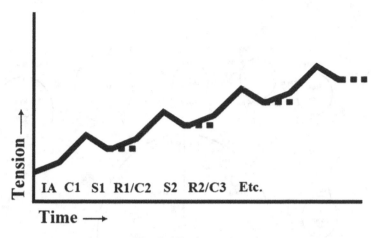

IA C1 S1 R1/C2 S2 R2/C3 Etc.

Fig. 3. Ganga comics

4.4 Sīra Narratives

The Sīra narrative structure has a central hub from which many smaller, episodic journey narratives depart and return, set within the larger frame of a community's survival and eventual demise.

Sīra narratives (Fig. 4) recount the circle of life and death of a Bedouin community known as the Banī Hilāl tribe. These narratives have the purpose of preserving the memory of brave warriors who vanished as the tribe achieved peace through struggle. More specifically, they narrate the adventures of the tribe as it traveled toward Tunisia in search of new pasturages. They feature an 'accurate' historical frame of the migration and conquest, while the actual narratives are "a series of intricate tales built on tension among a constellation of central characters" [54], involving several key male roles playing opposite a single female lead role.

The life of the Bedouin tribe is organized in a "pattern of repeating cycles" [54], which organize the progression of episodes as journeys, from the protagonists' birth to their death. Each episode narrates a journey, with varying characters and changing composition of events; the different and unique premises of every episode emphasize the significance of each individual journey. The dual nature of the 'journey theme', understood both as the search of new life and as war campaign, "sets up a vital tension of opposites", such as "famine-plenty, desert-pasture land, war-peace, life-death" [54]. Each episode starts with the Banī Hilāl council organizing the journey. However, during the expedition, an obstacle appears that obliges the travelers to go back and get ready anew. After that, they take on the journey again which will end successfully.

The variable episodic nature of these tales/journeys is suitable for the multiplicity that IDNs can offer. The overall journey topic fits well with the spatial affordances of interactive digital media [24]. Furthermore, the five-part structure of each tale/journey [55] (lack; departure; contract; violation; lack liquidated or new lack) provides ample opportunities to involve interactors/players in the unfolding narratives with a repeating succession of obstacles, tension build-up and continuing challenges.

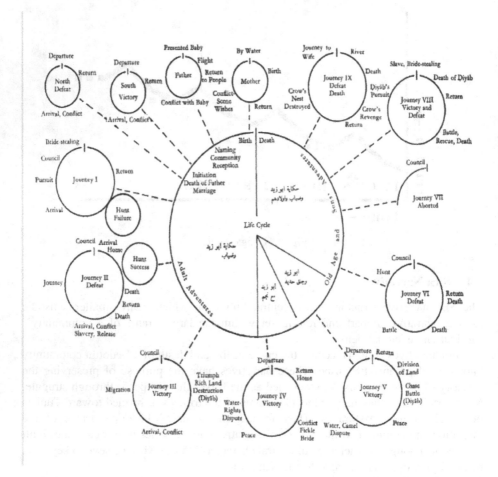

Fig. 4. Sīra structure [54]

4.5   Epiphanic Structure

This original structure features a cycle of conflict designed to create a moment of epiphany, which causes the player/interactor to suddenly understand the events of the narrative in a different light, and subsequently explores the narative again from the beginning to discover the consequences of this revelation.

While alternatives to established narrative structures have been discussed before, these discussions frequently lack a structural analysis. Moreover, established narrative structures like the Hero's Journey are gleaned from the analysis of linear, fixed media with no regard for the participatory aspect of interactive narrative. In contrast, the above structure (Fig. 5) is inspired by and partially based on the analysis of two playthrough sessions of PlatinumGames' 2017 action game *NieR:Automata* [56], in which players see the same events twice, but through the eyes of each of the two protagonists.

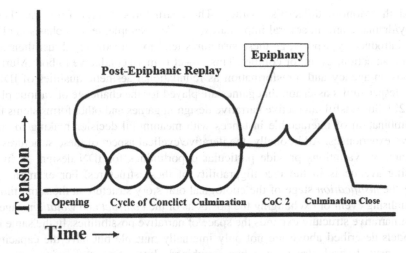

Fig. 5. Epiphanic structure

The first playthrough builds up to an epiphany, a realization or retrospective moment that radically re-contextualizes the events of that playthrough; the second playthrough then has players experience those same events with that epiphany in mind, which causes a (presumed) significant shift in the meaning that the player ascribes to their own actions and the actions of the protagonists. Another game that can be said to follow this structure is Paper Dino's *Save the Date* [57]. The structure can be described as follows:

1. Opening: the introduction of the storyworld;
2. Cycle(s) of Conflict (CoC): the protagonist(s) face(s) challenges – physical, battles and treasure hunts; emotional, relationships with other characters/actors; mental, piecing together clues about the storyworld's backstory – and overcome(s) them (or not);
3. Culmination: the fulfilment of the CoC's narrative purpose, its result;
4. Epiphany: a realization or retrospective moment, as a consequence of the culmination, that radically re-contextualizes the events of the CoC;
5. (optional) Post-epiphanic Replay(s): the *implicitly or explicitly acknowledged* repetition of the narrative after the epiphany that reconnects to the opening and may introduce/acknowledge the altered perspective;
6. Close: the conclusion of the narrative.

5 Concluding Remarks

In this paper, we describe a range of narrative structures from outside the dominant canon of western print literature and cinematic works. They represent an untapped opportunity for the design and analysis of IDNs. Conversely, our work exposes the idea of 'universal' narrative structures as a myth, as many alternatives exist to the dramatic arc and the Monomyth/Hero's Journey. These structures diverge from the 'Hero's Journey/dramatic arc' in several important ways. For example, less emphasis is placed on the introductory aspects, as these structures tend to immediately thrust their audience into an action, event, or conflict. This aspect is more conducive to both Murray's emphasis on agency and transformation as foundational aesthetic qualities of IDN as well as Jesper Juul's assertion that games are played for the challenge of various player skills [22]. Successful interactive narrative design in games and other forms stems from this combination of interactable instances with meaningful decision-making to create narrative experiences. Additionally, the iterative/cyclical aspect of these structures and their narrative variations provide particular opportunities for IDN design. A further promising avenue is in the reconfigurability of these structures. For example, presenting the *justification* stage of the etiological oral story structure at the same time as the initialising event or exchanging the positions of the *contract* and *violation* stages of the Sīra narrative structure expands the space of narrative possibilities. In the same line, the models described above are not only internally mutable but have the capacity to produce new, hybrid structures when combined. Interesting and unique ways of establishing narrative contingency and trajectory can come from deliberate, reasoned blending, for instance by overlaying the Sīra structure with the epiphanic stages of *epiphany* and *cycle of conflict*.

Our present paper is an initial effort, which can only start to explore the opportunities for IDN design beyond the supposed universal model of the Monomyth/dramatic arc. Further research is necessary and will most likely identify many more variants as well as entirely novel formulas. Furthermore, these new structures represent a challenge for analytical concepts and thus also call for the further development of theoretical perspectives. For instance, we need to improve our understanding of the process of translation from non-ergodic forms to IDN, e.g. by extending Ryan's [1] framework for categorizing narrative interactivity. Therefore, specific narrative structures should be subjected to critical enquiry and empirical evaluation to further investigate their particular qualities in respect to IDN design and theory. As they stand, these structures serve as a stepping stone for researchers and designers alike to successfully ascertain the expressive potential of IDN.

References

1. Ryan, M.-L.: Avatars Of Story. University of Minnesota Press, Minneapolis (2006)
2. Juul, J.: A clash between game and narrative. Danish literature (1999)
3. Juul, J.: Games telling stories. Game Stud. **1**, 45 (2001)
4. Aarseth, E.J.: Computer game studies, year one. Game Stud. **1**, 1–15 (2001)
5. Eskelinen, M.: The gaming situation. Game Stud. **1**, 68 (2001)
6. Frasca, G.: Ludologists love stories, too: notes from a debate that never took place. In: DIGRA Conference (2003)
7. Jenkins, H.: Game design as narrative architecture. In: Wardrip-Fruin, N., Harrigan, P. (eds.) First Person: New Media as Story, Performance, and Game. MIT Press, Cambridge (2004)
8. Murray, J.H.: From Game-Story to Cyberdrama. http://electronicbookreview.com/thread/firstperson/autodramatic

9. Aarseth, E.J.: Genre trouble. In: Wardrip-Fruin, N., Harrigan, P. (eds.) First Person: New Media as Story, Performance, and Game. MIT Press, Cambridge (2004)
10. Koenitz, H.: The "Story Arc"–a Ghost of Narrative Game Design. Presented at the DIGRA 2017 (2017)
11. Walk, W.: The Myth of the Monomyth. https://www.gamasutra.com/blogs/WolfgangWalk/20180514/318014/The_Myth_of_the_Monomyth.php
12. Fullerton, T., Swain, C., Hoffman, S.S.: Game Design Workshop. Morgan Kaufmann, Burlington (2008)
13. Jennings, P.: Narrative structures for new media. Leonardo 29, 345–350 (1996)
14. Ip, B.: Narrative structures in computer and video games: part 1: context, definitions, and initial findings. Games Cult. 6, 103–134 (2011)
15. Koenitz, H.: Towards a specific theory of interactive digital narrative. In: Koenitz, H., Ferri, G., Haahr, M., Sezen, D., Sezen, T.I. (eds.) Interactive Digital Narrative, pp. 91–105. Routledge, New York (2015)
16. Koenitz, H.: Narrative in Video Games. In: Lee, N. (ed.) Encyclopedia of Computer Graphics and Games, pp. 1–9. Springer International Publishing, Cham (2018). https://doi.org/10.1007/978-3-319-08234-9_154-1
17. Hayles, N.K.: Print is flat, code is deep: the importance of media-specific analysis. Poet. Today 25, 67–90 (2004)
18. Nausen, L.: Coda. In: Narrative Across Media, pp. 391–403. University of Nebraska Press (2004)
19. Prince, G.: A Dictionary of Narratology. University of Nebraska Press, Lincoln (1987)
20. Genette, G.: Narrative Discourse, an Essay in Method. Cornell University Press, Ithaca (1980)
21. Aarseth, E.J.: Cybertext. JHU Press, Baltimore (1997)
22. Juul, J.: Half-Real. MIT Press, Cambridge (2005)
23. Bogost, I.: Video Games Are Better Without Stories. https://www.theatlantic.com/technology/archive/2017/04/video-games-stories/524148/?utm_source=atlfb
24. Murray, J.H.: Hamlet on the Holodeck: the Future of Narrative in Cyberspace. Free Press, New York (1997)
25. Aylett, R.: Emergent narrative, social immersion and "storification." Presented at the 1st International Workshop on Narrative Interaction for Learning Environments, Edinburgh (2000)
26. Harrell, D.F.: Walking Blues Changes Undersea: Imaginative Narrative in Interactive Poetry Generation with the GRIOT System. (2006)
27. Harrell, D.F.: Cultural roots for computing: the case of african diasporic orature and computational narrative in the GRIOT system. Presented at the Proceedings of the Digital Arts and Culture Conference, Perth, Australia (2007)
28. Harrell, D.F.: Phantasmal Media. MIT Press, Cambridge (2013)
29. Freytag, G.: Die Technik des Dramas (1863)
30. Campbell, J.: The Hero with a Thousand Faces. Harper & Row, New York (1949)
31. Field, S.: Screenplay: The Basics of Film Writing. Random House Publishing Group, New York (1979)
32. Yorke, J.: Into the Woods: A Five-Act Journey Into Story. The Overlook Press, New York City (2014)
33. Infinity Ward: Call of Duty (2003)
34. Valve: Half-Life (1998)
35. Bethesda Softworks: The Elder Scrolls I: Arena (1994)
36. Nintendo: The Legend of Zelda (1986)
37. Level-5: Professor Layton and the Curious Village (2007)

38. Funcom: The Longest Journey (1999)
39. Ip, B.: Narrative structures in computer and video games: part 2: emotions, structures, and archetypes. Games Cult. **6**, 203–244 (2011)
40. Koenitz, H.: Five theses for interactive digital narrative. In: Fernández-Vara, C., Mitchell, A., Thue, D. (eds.) Interactive Storytelling: 7th International Conference on Interactive Digital Storytelling, ICIDS 2014, Singapore, Singapore, November 3-6, 2014, Proceedings, pp. 134–139. Springer International Publishing, Cham (2014). https://doi.org/10.1007/978-3-319-12337-0_13
41. Ferri, G.: Narrative structures in IDN authoring and analysis. In: Koenitz, H., Ferri, G., Haahr, M., Sezen, D., Sezen, T.I. (eds.) Interactive Digital Narrative. Routledge, New York (2015)
42. Calleja, G.: Narrative involvement in digital games. Presented at the Foundations of Digital Games (2013)
43. Calleja, G.: Game narrative: an alternate genealogy. In: Digital Interfaces in Situation of Mobility (2015)
44. Tavinor, G.: Art and Aesthetics. In: Wolf, M.J.P., Perron, B. (eds.) The Routledge Companion to Video Game Studies. Routledge (2014)
45. The Chinese Room: Dear Esther (2008)
46. Fernandes, S.: Curated Stories. Oxford University Press, Oxford (2017)
47. Reinhart, D.: Narrative Structure. http://narrativestructures.wisc.edu/home
48. Irwin, B.D.: What's in a frame? The medieval textualization of traditional storytelling. Oral Tradit. **10**, 27–53 (1995)
49. Finnegan, R.: Oral Literature in Africa. Open Book Publishers, Cambridge (2012)
50. Lamb, S.: The beggared mother: older women's narratives in West Bengal. Oral Tradit. **12**, 54–75 (1997)
51. Powers, M.: Stories the Iroquois Tell Their Children. American Book Company, New York Cincinnati Chicago (1917)
52. Seshadri, L., Havaldar, S.S.: Ganga. Amar Chitra Katha, 515 (1975)
53. Hiltebeitel, A.: Rethinking the Mahabharata. University of Chicago Press, Chicago (2001)
54. Connelly, B.: The structure of four bani Hilāl tales: prolegomena to the study of Sira literature. J. Arab. Lit. **4**, 18–47 (1973)
55. Connelly, B., Massie, H.: Epic splitting: an Arab folk gloss on the meaning of the hero pattern. Oral Tradit. **4**, 101–124 (1989)
56. PlatinumGames: NieR:Automata (2017)
57. Cornell, C.: Save the Date (2013)

Predictability and Plausibility
in Interactive Narrative Constructs:
A Case for an ERP Study

Bjørn Anker Gjøl[1(✉)], Niels Valentin Jørgensen[1], Mathias Ramsø Thomsen[1],
and Luis Emilio Bruni[2(✉)]

[1] Aalborg University Copenhagen,
A. C. Meyers Vænge 15, 2450 Copenhagen, Denmark
bjornankergjol@gmail.com, nieller0304@gmail.com, mathundert@gmail.com
[2] Augmented Cognition Lab, Aalborg University Copenhagen,
A. C. Meyers Vænge 15, 2450 Copenhagen, Denmark
leb@create.aau.dk

Abstract. It is a common assumption that subjects unconsciously construct storyworlds in their minds when experiencing a narrative. In this article we suggest that this construction includes imagined rules and constraints that if violated may affect the subjects' suspension of disbelief. In this direction, we examine whether the cognitive processing of people experiencing interactive narratives varies based on whether the outcomes of their actions are perceived to be predictable and plausible, according to the narrative context. In order to explore this hypothesis, we devised an event-related-potential experiment and created a video game featuring a number of player-instigated narrative events within three different categories: (a) predictable-plausible, (b) unpredictable-plausible, and (c) unpredictable-implausible. Based on the analysis of the N400 and P600 ERP components, our results show that there is a significant detectable difference between the three categories. Additionally, the results strongly indicate that experiencers of interactive narratives do indeed create storyworlds' rules and constraints in their minds, and that the imagined rules of these worlds can be felt to be broken by implausible events.

Keywords: Predictability · Plausibility · Narrative cognition
Interactive narratives · Psychophysiology · EEG · ERP · N400 · P600

1 Introduction

The cognitive turn in narratology [1,2] has been almost concomitant with the advent of the transmedial world of storytelling. In this context, Ryan suggested that a story is not simply a "thing" that can be read or told, but should rather be considered as "a mental image, a cognitive construct that concerns certain types of entities and relations between these entities" [1]. The interest on cognitive narratology [1,2] and "narrative cognition" [3,4] have opened a whole new set

© Springer Nature Switzerland AG 2018
R. Rouse et al. (Eds.): ICIDS 2018, LNCS 11318, pp. 121–133, 2018.
https://doi.org/10.1007/978-3-030-04028-4_9

of questions regarding how we cognitively interpret and experience narratives [5]. Most of the work in this direction have concerned linear fictional narratives in different media [1]. There is however an increasing interest in investigating the cognitive and psychophysiological aspects of interacting with different kinds of applications that qualify as interactive narratives, including several genres of video games [6]. The cognitive turn in narratology claims that the narrative function is an essential part of how the human mind functions, suggesting that narratives can act as a "cognitive tool for meaning-making" [7] and is "part of the fundamental nature of the self" [8].

Therefore, under this perspective, a narrative exists not on the paper, the game, or the film, but as a *storyworld* in the mind of the experiencer, a "form of possibility and potentiality in our imagination" [7]. Consumers of narratives build "mental models of the narrative world" [5], a contextual framework that is constantly updated as the narrative unfolds. As such, interactive narratives convey two stories: The author/designer's story and the cognizer's story [9], the latter allegedly being the more important of the two, as it relies on the subject's involvement with - and impact on - the application itself. In this paper we suggest that experiencers of interactive narratives unconsciously construct these storyworlds with relatively stringent sets of rules and constraints, that outcomes of events can be described in terms of how *predictable* and *plausible* they are when compared with the constructed rules of the storyworld, and finally, that these narrative "features" are psychophysiologically measurable.

2   Predictability and Plausibility

Predictability can be defined as the degree to which something can be regarded as being likely to happen in the future, often as a consequence of something else that is currently happening or has previously happened [10]. Predictability can be said to be an important aspect of most narratives - the more predictable a plot is, the less likely the narrative is to captivate an audience. On the other hand, in narrative terms, *plausibility* can be defined as how reasonable or probable an event or happening is in relation to the experiencer's internal storyworld [11]. For example, in a typical fantasy-themed novel it would be plausible that a wizard conjures up a fireball and throws it at a troll, an event which would be considered highly implausible in a classic crime novel. As such, predictability and plausibility are closely related when put in a narrative context. Both terms have to do with the *probability* of specific events and outcomes - but where predictability is closely related to *plot* and suspense, plausibility has more to do with *themes*, *rules* of the storyworld, and suspension-of-disbelief.

2.1   Related Terms

Narrative predictability is intrinsically related to *suspense* and *surprise* [3]. While the present study will not explicitly explore the relation to suspense, the relation to surprise can hardly be avoided. If something unexpected happens, the mind is bound to experience some degree of surprise, be that an outcome that brings a "resolution of suspense" [3] or as a result of the event being totally unexpected and therefore unpredictable.

Plausibility on the other hand may be related to "realism". In a study, based on interviews with 47 participants with focus on various TV shows [12], "media realism" is conceptualised by deriving a number of contributors to realism. One of these contributors resulted to be the "plausibility of the portrayed events or behaviors". What was meant by this was to which extent events and behaviours in the shows corresponded with what could happen in real-life situations. The biggest offenders were supernatural events as well as "impossibly harmonious family relationships". Plausibility was "the most readily articulated" conceptualisation of media realism, and can thus be considered of high importance to how stories are perceived. A related term mentioned by several participants was *narrative consistency*. In order to appear realistic, a narrative should be "internally coherent" and not contradict itself. In order for events to appear plausible to the rules and constraints of an internal storyworld, then, events should be comparable to real-world situations, and/or be consistent with what is expected within the fictional world.

Finally, the concept of storyworlds and plausibility can be related to *Suspension of disbelief* (SOD). The term SOD dates as far back as 1817, and in today's usage can be described as a participant's willingness to accept a simulation as being real [13]. For example, while "realness" is not necessarily what is desired in new media such as video games, players are usually required to accept the game world as being internally consistent. Therefore, the possibility to form in their minds a consistent storyworld, with its own specific rules and constraints, may require players to suspend their disbelief. In turn, the inability to suspend their disbelief may be directly correlated with the inability to create and/or maintain a consistent, mental storyworld - at least in cases where the game world is not identical to the real, immediate world of the player.

2.2   Storyworld Consistency

What will be examined here is, in a sense, the consistency of the internal storyworld, via the *degree* of predictability of the narrative outcomes prompted by players' actions. While one might consider predictability to be binary (either an outcome is predicted or not), we suggest, cognitively speaking, that there are levels to *how* predictable an event may be. Specifically, whether the outcome of the player's action, while unpredictable, *makes sense* in the storyworld set up by the narrative (i.e., a *plausible* outcome), or whether it is outside the presumed or accepted range of possibilities for the storyworld (i.e., an *implausible* outcome). These situations are exemplified in Fig. 1. It can also be hypothesized that the storyworld will fall apart, and the players left unable to suspend their disbelief, if the consistency of the storyworld is heavily violated, or broken repeatedly.

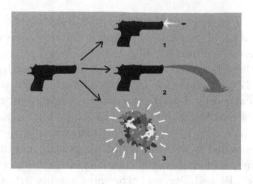

Fig. 1. An example of different outcomes to pulling the trigger on a gun in a "real-world" context. Three possible outcomes after pulling the trigger may be: (1) the guns fires, a predictable outcome. (2) the gun squirts water, an unpredictable, but plausible, outcome, as water guns do exist. (3) the gun turns into a bouquet of flowers, an unpredictable and implausible outcome.

3   Narrative Cognition

The purpose of this study is to examine whether the cognitive processing of people experiencing interactive narratives somehow varies based on whether the outcome of their actions are perceived to be contextually predictable and plausible, or not. In this direction we advance the following experimental hypothesis: the degree of predictability and plausibility of the stimuli presented in a video game significantly affect the cognitive processing of persons experiencing such stimuli.

The emerging field of narrative cognition [3] attempts to characterize the narrative function in humans as a fundamental cognitive mode. Focusing on the use of psychophysiological measures, combined with phenomenological instruments and behavioral observations, it intends to build bridges between classical and cognitive narratology on the one hand, and cognitive neurosciences on the other. Psychophysiological methods are thus considered as a very useful tool for examining the cognitive processes of experiencing narratives.

One such psychophysiological measure is electroencephalography (EEG), a non-invasive method for measuring the weak, electrical signals produced in the cerebral cortex, via metal electrodes placed on the subject's scalp [14]. Many studies featuring EEG use Event-Related Potentials (ERPs), which are signal patterns measured at very precise time points when specific events occur in the stimuli. An ERP component is characterized by three parameters: the amplitude of the signal, the precise time of its occurrence after the given event, and whether the voltage difference is negative (N) or positive (P) [15]. Usually, in order to "clean" the signal from unwanted noise, several ERPs are recorded for the same type of event and consequently averaged [16] in order to get the template for each type of event. These averaged "sequences" are then considered an expression of the immediate cognitive processing of the stimulus [15], revealing information about, among other things, the subject's emotions, behaviour, and awareness [14]. In other words, ERPs are used as a tool for describing somewhat localized neural activity in response to specific events [15]. Several studies have combined psychophysiological measures with video games, but few have utilized EEG measures [6], and even fewer have done so with game narratives in mind [3].

There are some well-studied ERP components that may be relevant for investigating predictability and plausibility. One of these is the N400, a negativity typically measured as peak values or mean voltages within a time window of 300–500 ms [17]. It was first reported by Kutas and Hillyard in 1980 [18], as a reaction to reading "semantically inappropriate words", e.g. "he took a sip from the transmitter". Since the early 1980s, what the N400 actually measures has been highly debated. There was almost consensus that the N400 component was a response to semantic violations (not only verbally but also visually and multisensorially). However, the consensus has shifted to interpret N400 as a reaction to both semantic congruency and incongruency in the stimuli, with differences marked by the amplitude of the signal [17]. Therefore the most accepted explanation nowadays is that the amplitude of the N400 "reflects'contextual integration' and mental effort required to integrate an item into context" [16]. The N400 has been proven to be related to expectancy of words in a sentence (also known as cloze probability in ERP studies), eliciting more negative peaks for less expected (lower cloze probability) than for more expected (higher cloze probability) semantic associations [17,19]. The bulk of research that has gone into the N400 component has revolved around written texts; however, N400 effects have been investigated for many other types of stimuli as well, e.g. spoken words, environmental sounds, facial expressions, drawings, and films [17]. Thus, it can be assumed that this component can also be triggered by unpredictable outcomes of player actions in a game. Whether the N400 component is also affected by plausibility has been tested for written sentences, but results have so far been inconclusive [20]. However, the P600, a late positivity associated with "syntactically anomalous sentences" [21], has been speculated to be related to plausibility: "when a critical noun is mildly implausible in the given sentence (...) integration difficulties arise due to the unexpectedness but they are resolved successfully, thereby eliciting an N400 effect. When the noun is deeply implausible however, (...) a strong conflict arises; integration fails and reanalysis is triggered, eliciting a P600 effect." [22]. Further research [23,24] has indicated that the component is triggered when information conflicting with a subject's preconception regarding the rules governing the context is broken, and when reanalysis of these rules has thus to be performed. If this is valid, then P600 effects should also be detected when the rules of a person's mental storyworld are broken, indicating in fact that these rules do exist in the minds of those experiencing a narrative.

4   Experimental Design and Implementation

In order to explore our hypotheses, we created a video game featuring a number of player-instigated narrative events within three different categories: (a) predictable (and by default considered also plausible) events, (b) unpredictable-plausible events, and (c) unpredictable-implausible events.

In order to confirm whether the in-game events are actually perceived as consistent or inconsistent with the storyworld as intended, all participants were also required to fill in a questionnaire following their experience, posing questions about the perceived plausibility of in-game events.

The game, *Quality Control*, is an audio-visual experience in which the player takes the role of a soviet-era conveyor belt worker, doing routinary control work in an industrial facility. The game scene can be seen in Fig. 2. Our assumption was that having a real-world theme (in this case a well-known historical context) would prompt players to build real-world expectations towards the game-world as well, i.e.: if the outcome of an interaction would have been implausible in the historical context of the eastern block in the 1980s, it would be considered implausible in the game world as well.

Fig. 2. The game scene in *Quality Control*, featuring a work desk, a conveyor belt, a product to be inspected on the conveyor belt (in this case, a safe), and the lever used to approve/discard products.

After pulling a lever on the work desk, the conveyor belt transports a random product into the view field placing it in front of the player. The player inspects the product by interacting with different parts of it - e.g.: buttons, pull strings, dials and valves - in order to check whether the product behaves as it should, based on the outcome of the interaction (i.e.: auditory and/or visual feedback). Nine different types of products were implemented, each featuring either one or two interactive elements. When interacted with, these elements can produce one of three different outcomes: (1) an outcome that is predictable and plausible according to the narrative context (i.e.:, the product works as intended), (2) an outcome that is unpredictable but plausible (i.e.: the product is broken), and (3) an outcome that is unpredictable and implausible (i.e.:, the product somehow behaves unrealistically in relation to the narrative situation). An example of each type of outcome can be seen in Fig. 3.

After completing the inspection of a product, the player pulls the lever either up or down, deciding whether the product should be, respectively, discarded or

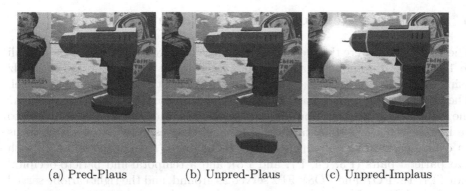

(a) Pred-Plaus   (b) Unpred-Plaus   (c) Unpred-Implaus

Fig. 3. An example of the different outcomes of interacting with a drill (pulling the drill trigger). The predictable-plausible outcome (a) is simply the drill bit rotating. The unpredictable-plausible outcome (b) is the battery being ejected, falling out of view. Finally, the unpredictable implausible outcome (c) is the drill ring a round of bullets as if it was a machine gun.

approved. This procedure is repeated a set number of times for nine "working-days", each day featuring a new product. The first spawned product of its kind always produces predictable and plausible outcomes, giving the player an idea of how the product should work. Following this, each interactive part of the product can be in one of the 3 states, decided semi-randomly when the product is spawned. In total, each player experiences 28 unpredictable-plausible inter-actions, 28 unpredictable-implausible interactions, and 94 predictable-plausible interactions. These interactions were spread out on the 9 different product types of which the actual numbers varied, based on the number of interactions per product.

5   Procedure

The sample population consisted of 20 male participants, of which 95% were in the age group 22–29. Most participants considered themselves to be "gamers", with 85% of them rating 4 or 5 on a 5-point Likert scale with the question "To which degree would you consider yourself a gamer?". The time they spend playing video games was evenly spread out between 2 to 30 h a week.

   The experiment took place in the Augmented Cognition Lab at Aalborg University, Copenhagen. Participants were brought in the lab one at a time, and asked to fill out the first part of a questionnaire, containing a consent form and basic demographic questions. Participants were then informed about the controls and goal of the game (but not about the rules of the game world). Following this, the electrode cap was placed on their heads, the electrodes filled with conductive gel, a pair of Bose SoundTrue Ultra in-ear headphones fit in their ears, and the EEG recording software and game started. After finishing the game, the electrodes cap was removed, and the second part of the questionnaire, with questions regarding the plausibility of the in-game interactions, was administered.

6   EEG Data Recording and Treatment

The EEG signals were time-locked to intervals going from the onset of the stimuli to 1000 ms post-stimulus in a continuous recording at a sampling rate of 256 Hz using an elastic cap with an array of 13 Ag/AgCl electrodes with conductive gel. The electrodes were placed according to the international 10–20 system [25]. As the N400 has a broad distribution in the cerebral cortex, but has been proven to be largest over centro-parietal sites [15,20], electrodes were placed with a focus on centro-parietal measurement - along the midline (Fz, Cz, Pz, and Oz), with two parietal pairs (P3, P4, P7, and P8), and a temporal-and parieto-occipital pair (T7, T8, PO7, and PO8). FPz served as ground, and the right earlobe served as reference. The electrodes were connected to a g.tec g.GAMMAbox and taken through a g.tec g.USBamp amplifier and DAC converter, and from there the signal was recorded by a desktop computer using the Simulink MATLAB plugin and g.tec's g.BSanalyze.

The raw ERP data was cleaned up and analysed using g.tec's g.BSanalyse software. In order to clean it up, the data was bandpass filtered using a Butterworth filter between 0.05 and 100 Hz, a notch filter removing electrical noise between 50 and 60 Hz was applied, and artefacts (eyeblinks and noise) were removed.

All of the predictable-plausible ERPs were averaged per participant, as was the unpredictable-plausible and unpredictable-implausible ERPs, and the three outcome categories were compared to each other pair-wise through visual analysis of the generated graphs (see below). Also displayed on the graphs were areas that were significantly different from one another according to a Mann-Whitney U test. A p-value of $p < 0.05$ for the Mann-Whitney U test was considered enough to be a significant difference. Following this, the grand averages for the 3 conditions across all participants were analysed in the same way.

7   Results

7.1   Questionnaires

As expected, players found that some of the outcomes were implausible. Furthermore, it was determined that participants more or less "grew accustomed to" these narrative-breaking elements, resulting in a lesser cognitive impact as more of them were encountered. All in all, the answers to the questionnaires fit with the observations and notes taken from the interviews.

7.2   Individual Subjects' ERP Analysis

Predictable-Plausible vs. Unpredictable-Plausible. Comparing the "normal", predictable-plausible, interaction outcomes to the unpredictable-plausible outcomes revealed very similar responses from participant to participant. No significant differences were present for any subject, for any electrode, at any time in the averaged ERPs. An example of this can be seen in Fig. 4. While no significant differences were traceable for this pairwise comparison, there was a constant pattern in the graphs: all participants showed some degree of a late positivity on the Fz, Cz, Pz, P3 and P4 electrodes. Most of the other electrodes also showed this positivity for some participants, but not as consistently as the above mentioned 5 electrodes.

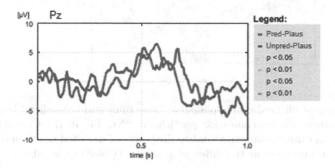

Fig. 4. Averages of ERPs for all predictable-plausible (green line) and unpredictable-plausible (blue line) interaction outcomes for participant "Nr. 2" in the Pz electrode. The absence of yellow, orange and light green points evidences lack of significance differences between the curves (see Fig. 5 for a different situation). (Color figure online)

Predictable-Plausible vs. Unpredictable-Implausible. Comparing these two pairs revealed a different story: all electrodes showed significantly higher amplitude responses to the unpredictable-implausible interaction outcomes (according to a Mann-Whitney U test) for parts of the 500–700 ms time window. The effect was more consistent for some electrodes than others - again, Fz, Cz, Pz, P3 and P4 were most consistent, with unpredictable-implausible interaction outcomes being significantly higher than the "normal" predictable-plausible outcomes for more than 50% of the participants. A very good example can be seen in Fig. 5.

Also worthy of note is the N400 spikes observed for most electrodes, most consistently for the parietal electrodes (Pz, P3, and P4). However, in most cases, there were no significant differences between the conditions. Finally, all electrodes showed cases of a late negativity following the P600, in a time window of approximately 700–900 ms. In many cases, the negativity was significantly larger for the unpredictable-implausible outcomes, but there was no real visible pattern for which electrodes, and for which participants, this negativity occurred.

The final pair (Unpredictable-Plausible vs. Unpredictable-Implausible) showed the same tendencies as the previously mentioned pair, with the unpredictable-implausible outcomes having significantly higher amplitude responses for some cases, albeit less consistently than when weighed against the "normal" predictable-plausible outcomes.

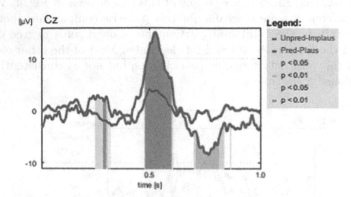

Fig. 5. Averages of all predictable-plausible (blue line) and unpredictable-implausible (green line) interaction outcomes for participant "Nr. 14" in the Cz electrode. The green, yellow and orange columns visualize the points of detected significance difference between the two outcomes at the different p-values. (Color figure online)

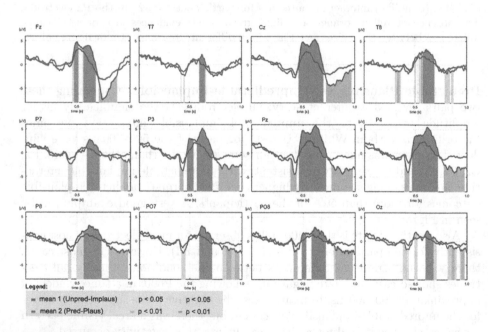

Fig. 6. Grand averages (for each electrode) of the unpredictable-implausible outcomes (green lines) compared to grand averages of predictable-plausible outcomes (blue lines), showing higher significant positivity in the 500–700 ms time window, and higher significant negativity following this, for the unpredictable-implausible interaction outcomes at most electrode sites. (Color figure online)

7.3   Grand Averages

Averaging the data from each participant, and constructing grand averages for each outcome pair, reveals much the same tendencies as the individual data sets - only more prominent. The predictable-plausible vs. unpredictable-implausible outcomes again yields the strongest results (as seen in Fig. 6).

In the 300–500 ms time window, where N400s are usually found, there are significant amplitude differences in (albeit very brief) periods of negativity around 400 ms after stimulus onset. This effect is seen for all parietal electrodes (Pz, P3, P4, P7, P8), the parieto-occipital pair (PO7, PO8), the temporal pair (T7, T8), and Oz. The only electrodes that have not picked up on a significant N400 difference are the Fz and Cz electrodes.

In the 500–800 ms time window, all twelve electrodes recorded very significantly ($p < 0.01$) higher amplitudes for the unpredictable-implausible outcomes, for durations between 50–300 ms, and most notably on the Cz, Pz, P3, and P4 electrodes. This was the most prevalent effect observed in the data.

Finally, from approximately 800–1000 ms, most electrodes elicited a late negativity for the unpredictable-implausible outcomes (the only electrode showing no sign of this was the T7 electrode).

The unpredictable-plausible vs. unpredictable-implausible comparison follows much the same pattern as the one shown in Fig. 6, i.e.: significant higher positivity for the unpredictable-implausible outcomes beginning approximately 500 ms after stimulus onset, followed by a late negativity. The effects were most prominent for the Cz, Pz, P3, P4, P8, and PO8 electrodes. The only big difference between this comparison and the previous one was that no significant differences in N400 effects were observed, except for a period of only a few milliseconds on the Pz electrode. The predictable-plausible vs. unpredictable-plausible pair comparison showed the same tendencies seen for individual participants, that is, no significant differences appeared at any time, for any electrode.

8   Discussion

Looking at the individual trials as well as the grand averages paints a very clear picture: as expected from the literature on the N400 and P600 ERP components, across several electrodes both the unpredictable but plausible and the unpredictable-implausible outcomes produced significantly higher N400 spikes when compared to the "normal" predictable results. Additionally, the implausible outcomes resulted in significant P600 activity when compared to the other outcomes. These results clearly support that predictability and plausibility of stimuli affects cognitive processing. Furthermore, as nothing was explained to the participants about the "rules" of the game-world, these results strongly indicate that experiencers of interactive narratives do indeed create "storyworlds" in their minds [1,2], constantly updated mental models of the narrative and the fictional world in which it takes place, and that the imagined rules of these worlds can be broken, even if they are not explicitly stated. Finally, this experiment also supports the view that N400 and P600 components can be observed in non-verbal audio-visual events, and not just as responses to written words, and that an increase in N400 amplitude reflects "minor" unresolved issues with "contextual integration" [16], and by extension can be related to predictability; while increases in P600 amplitudes reflect a failed attempt at integration [22], and therefore can be related to plausibility [12].

9 Conclusions

From our results we can conclude that for audio-visual experiences the amplitude of N400 components is inversely correlated to the predictability of narrative events, whereas the amplitude of P600 components is inversely correlated with the plausibility of such events, and that predictability and plausibility may be important elements for experiencers of interactive narratives and their cognitive construction and mental imagining of storyworlds.

The rather consistent spikes of P600 activity observed across subjects indicate that virtual representations of objects can, when behaving anomalously, elicit the same ERP response as for language processing of semantic anomalies [26]. Perhaps, this hints to the importance of the non-verbal and contextual aspects of narrative cognition. Further research is needed to understand whether the P600 is consistently related to the narrative context of the storyworld (considering also fantasy worlds), or whether it is simply occurring in breaks with reality. In order to assert with more property whether these results actually relate to the violation of the individual's narrative constructs, and the consequent suspension of disbelief that they entail [13], future work could consider a systematic comparison between the workings of predictability and plausibility in different levels and kinds of narrativity. In this direction, the levels of predictability and plausibility could be conceptualized as a function of the imagined storyworld afforded to the experiencer by the narrative material, and his or her subjective propensity for suspension of disbelief.

Acknowledgment. We would like to thank Morten Porsing and Philip Andreas Kingo for their help in the early stages of this project, and in particular their help in creating the game Quality Control, and Andreas Wulff-Jensen for his help in setting up the experiment at the Augmented Cognition Lab at Aalborg University.

References

1. Ryan, M.L.: Avatars of Story, New edn. University of Minnesota Press, Minneapolis (2006)
2. Herman, D.: Storytelling and the sciences of mind: cognitive narratology, discursive psychology, and narratives in face-to-face interaction. Narrative **15**, 306–334 (2007)
3. Bruni, L.E., Baceviciute, S., Arief, M.: Narrative cognition in interactive systems: suspense-surprise and the P300 ERP component. In: Mitchell, A., Fernández-Vara, C., Thue, D. (eds.) ICIDS 2014. LNCS, vol. 8832, pp. 164–175. Springer, Cham (2014). https://doi.org/10.1007/978-3-319-12337-0_17

4. Sanford, A.J., Emmott, C.: Mind, Brain and Narrative. Cambridge University Press, Cambridge (2012)
5. Ryan, M.L.: Narratology and cognitive science: a problematic relation. Style **44**(4), 469–495 (2010)
6. Kivikangas, J.M., et al.: Review on psychophysiological methods in game research. In: Nordic DiGRA Conference, Stockholm, Sweden, 16–17 August 2010, Nordic Digra (2010)
7. Lee, Y.: Narrative cognition and modeling in new media communication from peirce's semiotic perspective. Semiotica **2012**, 181–195 (2012)
8. Bruni, L.E., Baceviciute, S.: On the embedded cognition of non-verbal narratives. Sign Syst. Stud. **42**, 359–375 (2014)
9. Rouse III, R.: Game Design: Theory and Practice, 2nd edn. Wordware Publishing, Plano (2005)
10. Oxford English dictionary. https://en.oxforddictionaries.com/definition/predict. Accessed 15 Dec 2017
11. Oxford English dictionary. https://en.oxforddictionaries.com/definition/plausibility. Accessed 15 Dec 2017
12. Hall, A.: Reading realism: audiences' evaluations of the reality of media texts. J. Commun. **53**(4), 624–641 (2006)
13. Muckler, V.C.: Exploring suspension of disbelief during simulation-based learning. Clin. Simul. Nurs. **13**(1), 3–9 (2017)
14. Teplan, M.: Fundamental of EEG measurement. Meas. Sci. Rev. **2**, 1–11 (2002)
15. Duncan, C.C., et al.: Event-related potentials in clinical research: guidelines for eliciting, recording, and quantifying mismatch negativity, p300, and n400. Clin. Neuropsychol. **120**, 1883–1908 (2009)
16. Kuitunen, A.: Integrated semantic processing of complex pictures and spoken sentences - evidence from event-related potentials (2007)
17. Kutas, M., Federmeier, K.D.: N400. Scholarpedia **4**(10), 7790 (2009)
18. Kutas, M., Hillyard, S.A.: Reading senseless sentences: brain potentials reflect semantic incongruity. Science **207**(4427), 203–205 (1980)
19. Frishkoff, G., Tucker, D.: Anatomy of the N400: brain electrical activity in propositional semantics. University of Oregon, Brain Electrophysiology Lab (2000)
20. Kutas, M., Federmeier, K.D.: Thirty years and counting: Finding meaning in the N400 component of the event-related brain potential (ERP). Annu. Rev. Psychol. **62**(1), 621–647 (2011)
21. Regel, S., Meyer, L., Gunter, T.C.: Distinguishing neurocognitive processes reflected by P600 effects: Evidence from ERPs and neural oscillations. PLoS One **9**(5), e96840 (2014)
22. Meerendonk, N.V.D., Kolk, H.H.J., Chwilla, D.J., Vissers, C.T.W.M.: Monitoring in language perception. Lang. Linguist. Compass **3**(5), 1211–1224 (2008)
23. Maganioti, A.E., Hountala, C.D., Papageorgiou, C.C., Kyprianou, M.A., Rabavilas, A.D., Capsalis, C.N.: Principal component analysis of the P600 waveform: RF and gender effects. Neurosci. Lett. **478**, 19–23 (2010)
24. Brouwer, H., Fitz, H., Hoeks, J.: Getting real about semantic illusions: rethinking the functional role of the P600 in language comprehension. Brain Res. **1446**, 127–43 (2012)
25. Jasper, H.H.: The ten-twenty electrode system of the international federation. Electroencephalogr. Clin. Neurophysiol. **10**, 371–375 (1958)
26. Chow, W.Y., Phillips, C.: No semantic illusions in the "semantic P600" phenomenon: ERP evidence from mandarin chinese. Brain Res. **1506**, 76–93 (2013)

Meta-communication Between Designers and Players of Interactive Digital Narratives

Colette Daiute[(✉)] [ID], Robert O. Duncan [ID], and Fedor Marchenko [ID]

The City University of New York, New York, NY, USA
cdaiute@gc.cuny.edu

Abstract. This study addresses a typically silent dimension of Interactive Digital Narrative (IDN) theory and practice – meta-communication between designer and player. Meta-communication involves directly sharing thoughts and feelings the designer and player have during the development process. We refer to this interaction as "meta-communication" to distinguish it from comments about behavior, such as mentioning options chosen and evaluations of the IDN product. To address foundational questions about meta-communication in the IDN process, we conducted a research workshop with undergraduate novice IDN designers. Participants worked through a series of *Twine* IDN design-play sessions and made their meta-communication explicit using a think-aloud protocol. Transcriptions of the think-aloud sessions and notes made by designers and players during the IDN design process were analyzed for expressive functions, such as stating confusion or emotion. Analyses of the IDN designs identified structural features such as nodes and connections. Results of quantitative and qualitative analyses revealed that the frequency and type of meta-communications relate to the complexity of the final product (connection density). This study contributes a practice-based research approach accounting for inter-subjective dimensions of the IDN experience, thereby adding measurable psychological constructs to IDN theory.

Keywords: Interactive digital narrative theory · IDN pedagogy
Interactive digital narrative research methods · Designer & player interaction

1 Designer-Player Meta-communication

IDN scholars have argued that IDN designers can benefit from learning about the mind of the player in real time [1, 2]. This meta-communication, where designers and players express their thoughts and feelings during IDN development, is typically silent. Interacting in this way involves players' and designers' sharing their subjective states, rather than making comments primarily about their behaviors or game features [3, 4]. Prior theory has explained the unique co-authoring quality of IDN, the importance of game mechanics, and the potential of such a contingent creative process for moral, social, and affective development [2, 5, 6]. Current behavioral measures may be sufficient for assessing player engagement and entertainment in IDN games. IDN design and players' authorship of the IDN may, however, develop via unanticipated reflections expressed in comments such as, "Ha, ha, I'm into this!"; "I'm confused"; "Wow, you

© Springer Nature Switzerland AG 2018
R. Rouse et al. (Eds.): ICIDS 2018, LNCS 11318, pp. 134–142, 2018.
https://doi.org/10.1007/978-3-030-04028-4_10

really tricked me there"; or "That sure was a creepy outcome". Making such subjective thoughts and feelings explicit could be especially useful among novice IDN designers as they learn to consider the player and to develop strategies, vocabulary, and aesthetics of IDN design for the player's uptake. Understanding the engagement process in psychological terms may, thus, offer insights for expanding IDN pedagogy and assessing cognitive or emotional outcomes of serious games [7]. Implementing research with novice undergraduate IDN designers could also reveal approaches and concerns before students are overly trained with basic IDN design techniques or assumptions about the effectiveness of play testing one's own designs. Experience with player-designer interaction could, moreover, increase students' motivation to learn complex game strategy, as well as to increase their appreciation of other players' diverse perspectives and needs.

Consistent with IDN scholars who advocate increased understanding of players' cognitive processes, a recent study applying theory and methods of cognitive science and human development to IDN provided a foundation for further inquiry into the player reflections and the complexity of their IDN designs [3]. This paper presents an extended analysis of a workshop with student IDN designers and players to address several research questions: (1) What meta-communications do novice IDN players and designers express during a two-hour introductory design-play processes? (2) How do those interactions (number and type) relate to measures of IDN design complexity? (3) How does this process of meta-communication inform IDN research, theory and practice?

2   Methods

Sixteen undergraduates from the York College undergraduate research pool volunteered to participate in the study.

2.1   The *Twine* IDN Workshop

After an orientation to the workshop process and informed consent, participants used *Twine* to create a basic IDN. *Twine* has been used successfully with beginning IDN designers, because of its accessible text-based tools and basic game mechanics [8–10]. Over four iterative phases, participants alternated between designing their IDN and playing a peer's in-process design. Instructions to the participants appeared in folders on computers in two adjacent rooms, where they were encouraged to think aloud and summarize comments in writing. Think-aloud audio and video were captured using a GoPro Hero 4 Session. Materials included a file with basic components of the *Twine* authoring tool, several *Twine* IDNs to play, step-by-step instructions for becoming familiar with *Twine* and the workshop activities, a template for designing one's own IDN, a prompt to think aloud to one's partner, and an interview template. During the two-hour session, participants were cued by the experimenter to switch rooms/roles (i.e., from designer to player and *vice versa*) every 15 min.

2.2   Data and Data Analyses

Designer-Player Meta-communication. The research team compiled participants' oral and written reflections into an ATLAS.ti 8 database using "expression categories" from the 2017 pilot study [3] and expanded to account for additional data for this study. A qualitative data analysis process of identifying the expressive function of each thought unit (sentence, clause) for all the think-aloud sessions was applied to generate categories, documented with category definitions and examples in a code book, and applied again to ensure stability [11]. Categories applied to all sentences and clauses include Affect:Me (1st person), Cognition:Me (1st person), Cognition:Other (2nd or 3rd person), IDN features, CoDesign, Evaluation, Process, Recap, and Surface focus. Figure 1 presents an analyzed excerpt.

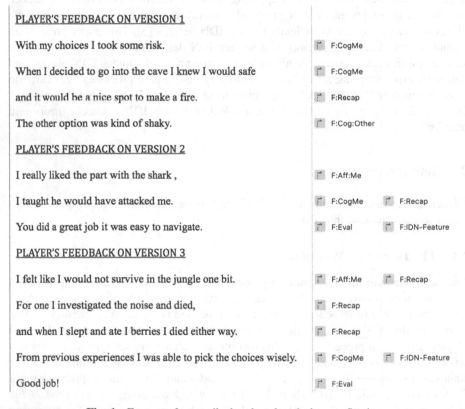

Fig. 1. Excerpt of transcribed and analyzed player reflection

Analyses of the *Twine* IDN Designs. Objective measures of IDN design complexity included a measure of *connection density* and an analysis of IDN elements. The *connection density index* was derived from analysis techniques in graph theory that measure the complexity of networks in terms of their density [12]. The complexity of a network in IDN design refers to the number of connections with a given number of nodes. The *connection density index* sums the total number of connections and divides by the total number of nodes. In *Twine* terminology, nodes are represented as "cards" (or "passages"); connections are represented by arrows extending to and from cards. This measure classifies networks as more densely connected (index greater than 1) or less densely connected (index less than 1). For a hyper-text genre like *Twine*, relatively more connections among passages characterizes designs of higher complexity because they more fully engage their player's authorship, that is the player's implementation of choices available in the IDN design.

Twine **IDN Elements.** IDN scholars have proposed categories that account for narrating as an interactive rather than a linear process [2, 5, 6, 13]. Consistent with such IDN theory, we applied IDN scholar Aarseth's ontic categories. These were augmented with an element emphasized in narrative theory to account for character depth [11, 14], which meta-communication might also spark. Without pre-determination of the differential use or value of these IDN qualities, we analyzed transcriptions of screen shots of the final IDNs (as shown in Fig. 2 with *Twine* syntax) by each participant for IDN elements, including world, character (agent), psychological state, object, event, and connection type.

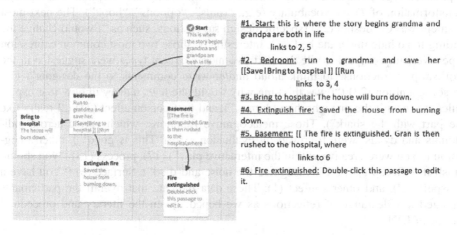

Fig. 2. A *Twine* IDN and transcription of passages and connections

The hypothesis of this study was that greater frequency and use of diverse categories of designer-player meta-communication would correlate positively with greater *Twine* design connection density.

Relating Designer-Player Meta-communication to *Twine* IDNs. Correlations between the number and type of individuals' expressive reflections (to and from the partner) and IDN connection density measures were computed. Correlation coefficient matrices were created comparing reflections to designers and from designers. Both the number of reflections and the types were compared to the number of nodes, the number of connections, and the connection density. The most telling correlations were between the number and variety of reflections and the connection density. To acknowledge that giving and receiving reflections to a partner's design are within a zone of proximal development (mutual understanding and activity) during interactive learning [14], we also computed combined meta-communication reflections, IDN connection density indices, and analyses of IDN elements for all dyads.

Participant Interviews. Interview questions requested participants' post-participation assessments from their perspectives as designers and as players about what they learned, what surprised them, and what they would change in the workshop process. Participant responses were examined for what they said in particular about sharing their thoughts and feelings and their suggestions for future research and practice.

3 Findings: What Meta-communications Do Novice IDN Players and Designers Express During a Two-Hour Design/Play Processes with *Twine*?

The analysis of expressive reflection categories indicates that player-design meta-communication is a unique dimension of IDN interactivity. The most frequent expression type focused on IDN features (49), indicating the adoption, sharing, and transformation of *Twine* vocabulary (e.g., "cards", "options", "hook"). The next most frequent was Co-design (28) (specific design suggestions, such as "I would change the ending to go hide under the bed…"). Interestingly, those two most common expression types were unprompted, while the next two most frequent types were suggested in the workshop instructions "to think aloud and/or write comments to the designer": first person cognition (23) ("I was thinking why would she have a diary of how to escape a killer if she isn't the one who hired him…"); and first person affect (23) ("I really like the part with the shark"). Those metacognitive functions, which varied across individuals and dyads, were followed by evaluation (19) ("This is good!"), other's cognition ("You were creative within the interactive play") (17), process (13) ("you should finish it"), Recap (12) ("I investigated the noise and died"), Surface (6) ("You have a misspelling"), and other's affect (1). These data indicate that overall the participants engaged a wide range of reflections as we hoped, given the literary and procedural nature of IDN.

4 Findings: What Are the Features of Beginning *Twine* IDN Designs?

Individual connection density indices, computed as the number of connections divided by the number of nodes, ranged from 0.5 to 1.64. The number of story nodes (passages/cards) ranged from 5 to 24, while the number of connections spanned from 4 to 38. The connection density indices for dyads (designer-player cohorts) ranged from 0.96 to 1.59.

The IDN design elements (on cards) patterned as rich in events (average of 14.5 across the sixteen designs) and characters (average of 9.6) with some psychological character depth (average of 2.7). World elements (5.4) and object elements (3.1) occurred less frequently on average. Interestingly, when examined in terms of player options, events predominated (average of 7.4) followed by spatial options such as moving to a certain room (average of 3.1). Character options and character psychological state options (alternative choices) were few (one participant offered character options, while character motives appeared in 4). Four connections did not lead to any option and were categorized as "broken".

5 Findings: How Do Player-Designer Meta-communications Relate to IDN Design Complexity?

To explore the relationship between measures of IDN complexity and reflections, several correlations were conducted. Participants who gave more varied reflections created more dense stories, ($r(14) = 0.53$, $p = 0.03$). Participants who gave more reflections created more dense stories ($r(14) = 0.41$, $p = 0.11$). Participants who received more varied reflections created less dense stories ($r(14) = -0.47$, $p = 0.07$). Participants who received more reflections created less dense stories ($r(14) = -0.38$, $p = 0.15$). While many of these correlations are not statistically significant, there is a trend suggesting that participants who deliver more and varied reflections are better engaged and create more complex stories. Conversely, participants who receive more reflections may be distracted or overwhelmed by the feedback and produce less complicated stories. These results are consistent with research on peer collaboration indicating those who offer more suggestions to partners improve their outcomes more than partners who offer fewer suggestions [15, 16].

Shifting the connection density analysis to dyad effects showed, moreover, that the relationship between number and variety of comments offered to one's partner is not a zero sum game. Combined dyad connection density scores (which include relatively higher and lower individual scores across all the individuals) showed that some dyads created designs assessed at greater than 1.0 connection-to-passage designs and thus relatively rich in options for players, while other pairs offered relatively fewer options for their players as indicated by index scores under 1.0. This computation was done for all dyads, revealing a continuum of the most to least expressive dyads.

For example, dyad 7 shared the most reflections (33) of all the dyads, while dyad 6 shared the fewest (14). Correspondingly, the connection density index of dyad 7 was above 1.0 while that of dyad 6 was below. To explore these relationships in qualitative detail as appropriate for this novel IDN research method, we present detailed analyses for the most and least expressive dyads as contrasting cases of meta-communication, as shown in Table 1.

Reflections emphasized by the most successful dyad in terms of their final designs include cognitive expressions about one's own and others' cognitions, IDN features, Co-design expressions, and a Recap (although this was relatively rare across individuals). In contrast, the least successful dyad emphasized their own affect, evaluations of partners' designs, and general comments about process. As shown in Table 2, the contrasting IDN features across the most and least successful dyads are also informative.

Table 1. Percent reflection phrases of different types by the most successful dyad (7) and least successful dyad (6)

Dyad	Affect mine	Cog. mine	Cog. other	IDN feature	Co-design	Eval	Process	Recap/surface
7	9	21	12	12	12	9	3	21/0
6	29	4	0	7	7	29	14	0/0

Table 2. Twine IDN elements used by the most and least successful dyads

Dyad	World	Characters	Psych states	Objects	Events	Connections
7	7	29	12	2	33	16 event
6	7	22	3	9	21	11 event

Dyad 7 partners emphasized characters, character psychological states, events and event connections. In contrast, dyad 6 participants emphasized objects. As with the case study comparisons for expressive reflections, these descriptions suggest the value of using these analytic tools in a study with more participants and design drafts over time. Overall, these findings are remarkable for a two-hour intervention, which we qualify for not having a control group.

6   Conclusion and Implications for Future Research and Practice

This study offers the concept - meta-communication between designer and player – and a research approach with tested objective measures. Correlation analyses of the individuals' connection density indices revealed that designers who *gave* more varied types of reflections and more reflections overall created more complex IDN stories. This result that feedback to another leads to richness of one's own design suggests the value of partnership and of encouragement to think beyond procedural behaviors and the artifact to the humanistic aspects of IDN, which are after all, a major dimension of IDN appeal. Comments about specific design elements and procedures were also expressed in this study, but results indicate that meta-communications about participant psychosocial states had a concrete positive impact on final designs. Analyses of the participant interviews indicated student excitement about the workshop and willingness to do it again.

The method of this study is worth implementing in IDN classes, with additional discussion about how understanding the higher order psychological state of the player might be leveraged to create increasingly complex IDN worlds and processes. The IDN design instructor could, for example, learn about students' mastery of IDN vocabulary, as occurred by participants in this study with relatively high frequency, and that could guide subsequent work with the students. Another kind of insight to consider with students could be based on observations of think-aloud or written comments about player thoughts and feelings, as these are connected to IDN elements (world, character, etc.) and thus the psychological versus behavioral value of the emerging design. An examination of the connection density of in-process designs could be computed by students themselves and thus might provide another way to consider the complexity of game mechanics.

Although a rich descriptive foundation for future research and practice, this study requires replication, ideally in pedagogical contexts. Specific changes indicated for the future include increasing the number of participants, increasing the amount of time and number of sessions learning *Twine* (or other IDN authoring system), collecting records of play and draft designs during player reflection sessions, and adding a comparison group not engaged in the think-aloud process.

In conclusion, this novel approach to designer-player meta-communication illustrates how IDN is about more than behaviors, as in digital games of skill. Focus on the psychosocial realm of IDN, which we hear as players-designers ponder, project, and emote provides provocative material for IDN theory.

References

1. Dubbelman, T.: Narrative game mechanics. In: Nack, F., Gordon, A.S. (eds.) ICIDS 2016. LNCS, vol. 10045, pp. 39–50. Springer, Cham (2016). https://doi.org/10.1007/978-3-319-48279-8_4

2. Koenitz, H., Dubbelman, T., Knoller, N., Roth, C.: An integrated and iterative research direction for interactive digital narrative. In: Nack, F., Gordon, A.S. (eds.) ICIDS 2016. LNCS, vol. 10045, pp. 51–60. Springer, Cham (2016). https://doi.org/10.1007/978-3-319-48279-8_5

3. Daiute, C., Duncan, Robert O.: Interactive imagining in interactive digital narrative. In: Nunes, N., Oakley, I., Nisi, V. (eds.) ICIDS 2017. LNCS, vol. 10690, pp. 282–285. Springer, Cham (2017). https://doi.org/10.1007/978-3-319-71027-3_26

4. Knoll, T.: The think-aloud protocol. In: Drachen, A., Mirza-Babaei, P., Nacke, L. (eds.) Games User Research. Oxford University Press, Oxford (2018)

5. Murray, J.H.: The tale of two boyfriends: a literary abstraction strategy for creating meaningful character variation. In: Koenitz, H., Ferri, G., Haahr, M., Sezen, D., Sezen, T.I. (eds.) Interactive Digital Narrative, pp. 121–135. Routledge, New York(2015)

6. Koenitz, H.: Towards a specific theory of interactive digital narrative. In: Koenitz, H., Ferri, G., Haahr, M., Sezen, D., Sezen, T.I. (eds.) Interactive digital narrative, pp. 91–105. Routledge, New York (2015)

7. Granic, I., Lobel, A., Engels, R.C.M.E.: The benefits of playing video games. Am. Psychol. **69**(1), 66–78 (2014)

8. Friedhoff, J.: Twine: a platform study. In: Proceedings of DiGRA (2013)

9. Tran, K.M.: Her story was complex: a twine workshop for ten- to twelve-year-old girls. E-Learn. Digit. Media **13**(5–6), 212–226 (2016)

10. Klimas, C.: Twinery: Twine Homepage (2009). https://twinery.org/

11. Daiute, C.: Narrative Inquiry: A Dynamic Approach. Sage Publications, Thousand Oaks (2014)

12. Rubinov, M., Sporns, O.: Complex network measures of brain connectivity: uses and interpretations. NeuroImage **52**, 1059–1069 (2010)

13. Aarseth, E.: A narrative theory of games. In: Proceedings of the International Conference on the Foundations of Digital Games, FDG 2012, pp. 129–133. ACM, New York (2012)

14. Daiute, C.: A relational theory of human development in the 21st century crisis of violence and displacement. Hum. Dev. **59**(2–3), 128–151 (2016)
15. Lundstrom, K., Baker, W.: To give is better than to receive: The benefits of peer review to the reviewer's own writing. J. Second Lang. Writ. **18**, 30–43 (2009)
16. Diab, N.M.A.: A comparison of peer, teacher and self-feedback on the reduction of language errors in student essays. System **57**, 55–65 (2009)

A Framework for Creative Teams of Non-fiction Interactive Digital Narratives

Nicole Basaraba(✉)

Trinity College Dublin, Dublin, Ireland
nicole.basaraba@adaptcentre.ie

Abstract. Interactive digital narratives (IDNs) have been widely studied in the format of video games and in the fiction genre, but less attention has been focused on the creative process and non-fiction. There are many IDN formats such as interactive cinema and transmedia stories and with these increasingly complex narrative forms, there are more people involved in the creation beyond the author of the text, such as graphic designers, programmers, curators, photographers and other specialists. Considering the affordances and limitations of new media is also increasingly important for IDN creation. This article takes a media-centred approach and adapts the principles of rhetoric to create a framework that aims to support the process of collaborative authorship of non-fiction IDNs in different formats.

Keywords: Interactive digital narrative · Non-fiction · Rhetorical theory

1 Introduction and Background

Interactive digital narrative (IDN) theory was first proposed by Koenitz [1] whose analysis of different formats (e.g., interactive fiction, interactive cinema, video games, etc.) showed that IDNs are comprised of the three main components: the system, process, and product. Regardless of format, IDNs are expressive digital narratives realised in a system containing potential narratives that are experienced through a process that results in products [1] or emergent narratives. Since IDN theory was established, Koenitz et al. [2] identified different possible approaches and key requirements for its future development. This article takes a medium-centred approach to show how digital media impact non-fiction IDN creation. This paper outlines a proposed framework for non-fiction IDN system creation based in rhetorical theory and best practices in human-computer interaction (HCI), which is currently being tested in ongoing research.

This PhD research is supported by the ADAPT Centre and is supervised by Drs. Owen Conlan, Jennifer Edmond, and Peter Arnds of Trinity College Dublin, Ireland.

© Springer Nature Switzerland AG 2018
R. Rouse et al. (Eds.): ICIDS 2018, LNCS 11318, pp. 143–148, 2018.
https://doi.org/10.1007/978-3-030-04028-4_11

In current practices, many creators release a digital work into the world hoping it will be successful without consulting potential users in advance [3] and there is a sense of urgency to adopt new media technologies as they emerge to remain relevant and engage with the public in novel ways. However, digital communication production involves complex choices regarding audience, content, technology, and media [4]. Existing frameworks for creating IDNs have focused on developing different authoring tools and element-driven approaches [5–7] which categorise narratives into components such as pattern, path, goal, action, outcome and event. Different authoring tools have answered certain questions and problems, but they commonly focus on video games and system developers are also the content creators so less attention has been paid to the creative process [8]. Element-driven approaches rely on specific terminology and become a challenge for IDN creators who may come from different disciplines or industries (e.g., novelists, journalists, educators, or museologists) and require easy-to-follow composition guidelines. Thus, there still is a gap between the descriptions of IDN and the current, natural practices of creators [9].

IDN authoring studies have also focused on fictional narratives. Aristotle's *Poetics* is often referred to when examining and creating fictional IDNs [10], but scholars [11,12] have noted that *Poetics* is an inadequate narrative model for the complexity of IDNs, and especially for non-fiction IDNs which have communication goals and call for different composition considerations. The IDN creation process has been compared to African storytelling - a circular rather than linear process - [11] and oral storytelling [13] which adapts to specific audiences and their responses. Considering these techniques, Aristotle's *Rhetoric*, with origins in oral traditions and emphasis on persuasion/purposeful communication, is more applicable for non-fiction IDN composition. Rhetorical theory is an applied art; it generates principles, not rules that are always interpreted and adjusted for different situations [14]. The art of storytelling is subjective or "fuzzy" and it is difficult to define a one-size-fits-all method for creating different IDNs but many scholars agree that the medium affects the message [15–18] and rhetoric, with its long history of use, can formalise the process of non-fiction IDN creation. The following media-centred rhetorical framework for IDN creation leaves creators with the artistic licence to use the narrative techniques (e.g., poetics) and specific tools best suited to the genres of their narratives while guiding decision-making that considers how media will affect the rhetoric. The following outline of a proposed non-fiction IDN creation framework is being tested in ongoing research in a case study and aims to be useful for collaborative creative teams.

2   A Framework for Creating Non-fiction IDN Systems

Phase 1: Know Your Audience. It is important to consider the audience by conducting demographic research or user modelling. Key questions to answer may include: Who is the IDN for? Where are they from? Which age group(s) do they fall into? What is their level of digital literacy? What information might they know about the IDN topic already and what information do they need to know? [19].

Phase 2: Define the Communication Goals. To measure IDN success, the rhetorical goals to be evaluated in later product testing need to be defined. For example, is the IDN aiming to communicate a feeling, theme, clear message, specific learning outcomes, or a call to action? Are there multiple messages being communicated? What type of experience is being created or what emotional response is desired from the audience?

Phase 3: Delivery. Digital delivery influences the production, design, and reception of narratives and ability to achieve rhetoric [20]. IDN systems include the hardware on which the artefact is delivered and the software containing the "protostories" [1]. The medium (hardware) and authoring tools (software) can impact creative expression and require considerations of which affordances are necessary to achieve the rhetorical goals. IDNs can use a single medium or use multimedia (i.e., transmedia) and the software depends on the IDN media format(s), complexity of narrative, and project budget. Software selection will require individual project-based research and future platform/software studies [21] would be useful for IDN creators to cross-compare of affordances and constraints for narratives with different purposes, formats, and genres. As the medium and authoring tool selection affects the ability to communicate the message and also depend on the content gathered during "invention", there may be a back-and-forth process between the "delivery" and the following "invention" phases.

Phase 4: Invention. IDN invention involves searching for and gathering materials to create persuasive works [22]. This includes considering multimodal resources, existing remixed content and which tools/software can accommodate the content [22]. There is now a specialisation that allows each mode to carry part of a message for which it is best equipped as different modes have different affordances [18] and IDN creators need to consider which semiotic mode of communication is best suited for each type of narrative content/topic [23]. Reality-based technologies (e.g., VR, AR, MR) offer new opportunities, especially for non-fiction narrative communication. IDNs could also include remixed content, which is often user-generated, includes commentary, opinions and creative ideas. Digital media support and encourage a participatory culture [24] and once an IDN is created, it may later be remixed by users which could also be reviewed in phase 7: "revision".

Phase 5: Arrangement. Arrangement involves considering the procedural rules for interactivity and the narrative structure. IDN arrangement is determined in part by the creators and users to create emergent narratives. IDN systems involve the arrangement of multiple protostories that emerge from user interaction and as opportunities for interaction increase, it raises the possibility of ludonarrative dissonance—the conflict between narrative interactivity and structure [50] of becoming an issue. The narrative structure helps maintain immersion and avoid ludonarrative dissonance [25]. One tool to help determine interactivity level is Ryan's [26] five levels of interactivity that range from low to high. IDN systems offering high levels of interactivity (i.e., agency) through artificial intelligence (AI) have a major impact on the narrative arrangement/structure because AI (e.g., via an AI drama manager) provides new choices and paths. The rules for linking protostory content is determined through a narrative structure. Examples of protoype IDN structures include those identified by Ryan [26] (e.g., the Vector, Braided Plot, and Action Space) and Schoenau-Fog [27, 28] (e.g., IDEM, STDM).

Phase 6: Design. For many IDN formats, the style or aesthetics pertain to the interface design, including options like colour, font choice, layout, appropriate use of media, and usability [22]. The interface design choices need to be intuitive for the user and could be used to create more meaning depending on how the multimodal content is delivered. The aesthetics need to clearly identify how to navigate through the content and present options for user interaction. The interface design impacts how long a user will interact with an IDN and it contributes to their level of immersion. Historically, artists made a work within a single medium so the interface and the work were one in the same but in new media they are separate, which presents opportunities to create multiple interfaces for the same material to be accessed from a "database" of multimodal material [29]. Thus, IDNs can have a single digital interface or multiple. As many issues with IDN consumption are technical, the "design" and "delivery" are important phases for rhetorical success.

Phase 7: Revision. In more recent scholarship, the rhetorical principle of "memory" has generally been overlooked because print and digital media technologies diminished the need for memorisation. Eyman [22] argues that the memory in the digital medium refers to the creators' knowing how to store, retrieve, and manipulate information. However, these skills may be covered by different creators involved in the process and they need to be considered during "delivery". It is proposed that the principle of "memory" be reframed to "revision". Instead of developing a narrative and delivering it into the world in a one-to-many linear manner, IDNs have the potential to be a work in progress. As per HCI best practices, testing the technical aspects of interaction and understanding the audience's response will determine if the IDN achieves rhetorical goals, if it needs to be updated, re-released or if a subsequent or spin-off narrative is possible. There is an opportunity to create stronger rhetoric through revision, remixing, and/or further response to the audience's reaction and interaction with the text. IDNs could also continually be expanded through user-generated content or, if permitted, a level five interactivity [26] which would allow consumers to directly modify the original IDN.

3   Conclusion

While this framework, only outlined above, does not cover every creative decision that is required for non-fiction IDN creation, it aims to act as a guideline or roadmap to facilitate media-centred choices for creative teams in digital humanities and creative industries. This framework is presented in seven phases, but the process should be cyclical, involve a negotiation between phases, and evolve as the IDN production progresses. It aims to aid collaborate authorship in considering how the properties of digital media and interactivity affect the IDN and ability to achieve rhetorical purposes. This framework could be supplemented with more artistic-driven approaches and format-specific creation tools.

References

1. Koenitz, H.: Towards a theoretical framework for interactive digital narrative. In: Aylett, R., Lim, M.Y., Louchart, S., Petta, P., Riedl, M. (eds.) ICIDS 2010. LNCS, vol. 6432, pp. 176–185. Springer, Heidelberg (2010). https://doi.org/10.1007/978-3-642-16638-9_22

2. Koenitz, H., Haahr, M., Ferri, G., Sezen, T.I.: First steps towards a unified theory for interactive digital narrative. In: Pan, Z., Cheok, A.D., Müller, W., Iurgel, I., Petta, P., Urban, B. (eds.) Transactions on Edutainment X. LNCS, vol. 7775, pp. 20–35. Springer, Heidelberg (2013). https://doi.org/10.1007/978-3-642-37919-2_2

3. Warwick, C.: Studying users in digital humanities. In: Warwick, C., Terras, M., Nythan, J. (eds.) Digital Humanities in Practice, pp. 1–21. Facet Publishing, London (2012)

4. Sheppard, J.: The rhetorical work of multimedia production practices: it's more than just technical skill. Comput. Compos. 26(2), 122–131 (2009)

5. Swartjes, I., Theune, M.: A Fabula model for emergent narrative. In: Göbel, S., Malkewitz, R., Iurgel, I. (eds.) TIDSE 2006. LNCS, vol. 4326, pp. 49–60. Springer, Heidelberg (2006). https://doi.org/10.1007/11944577_5

6. Carpentier, K., Lourdeaux, D.: Diegetization: an approach for narrative scaffolding in open-world simulations for training. In: Mitchell, A., Fernández-Vara, C., Thue, D. (eds.) ICIDS 2014. LNCS, vol. 8832, pp. 25–36. Springer, Cham (2014). https://doi.org/10.1007/978-3-319-12337-0_3

7. Damiano, R., Lombardo, V., Pizzo, A.: Formal encoding of drama ontology. In: Subsol, G. (ed.) ICVS 2005. LNCS, vol. 3805, pp. 95–104. Springer, Heidelberg (2005). https://doi.org/10.1007/11590361_11

8. Koenitz, H.: Five theses for interactive digital narrative. In: Mitchell, A., Fernández-Vara, C., Thue, D. (eds.) ICIDS 2014. LNCS, vol. 8832, pp. 134–139. Springer, Cham (2014). https://doi.org/10.1007/978-3-319-12337-0_13

9. Szilas, N., Marty, O., Réty, J.-H.: Authoring highly generative interactive drama. In: Balet, O., Subsol, G., Torguet, P. (eds.) ICVS 2003. LNCS, vol. 2897, pp. 37–46. Springer, Heidelberg (2003). https://doi.org/10.1007/978-3-540-40014-1_5

10. Laurel, B.: Computers as Theatre. Addison Wesley, Boston (1991)

11. Jennings, P.: Narrative structures for new media: towards a new definition. Leonardo 29(5), 345–350 (1996)

12. Rieser, M.: The poetics of interactivity. In: Rieser, M., Zapp, A. (eds.) New Screen Media: Cinema/Art/Narrative (2002)

13. Murray, J.: Hamlet on the Holodeck: The Future of Narrative in Cyberspace. The Free Press, New York (1997)

14. Sullivan, P., Porter, J.E.: Opening Spaces: Writing Technologies and Critical Research Practices. Greenwood Publishing Group, Greenwich (1997)

15. McLuhan, M.: Understanding Media: The Extensions of Man. McGraw-Hill, New York (1964)

16. Bolter, J.D., Grusin, R.: Remediation: Understanding New Media. MIT Press, Cambridge (2000)
17. Ryan, M.L.: On the theoretical foundations of transmedial narratology. In: Kindt, T. (ed.) Narratology Beyond Literary Criticism: Mediality, disciplinarity, p. 6. Walter de Gruyter (2005)
18. Kress, G.: Literacy in the New Media Age. Routledge, New York (2003)
19. Rosinski, P., Squire, M.: Strange bedfellows: human-computer interaction, interface design, and composition pedagogy. Comput. Compos. **26**, 149–163 (2009)
20. Ridolfo, J., Hart-Davidson, W. (eds.): Rhetoric and the Digital Humanities. University of Chicago Press, Chicago (2014)
21. Monfort, N., Bogost, I.: Racing the Beam. Library of Congress, USA (2009)
22. Eyman, D.: Digital Rhetoric: Theory, Method, Practice. University of Michigan Press, Ann Arbor (2015). https://doi.org/10.3998/dh.13030181.0001.001
23. Sanchez-Mesa, D., Aarseth, E., Pratten, R., Scolari, C.: Transmedia (storytelling?): a polyphonic critical review. Artnodes E-J. Art, Sci. Technol. **18**, 8–19 (2016)
24. Jenkins, H.: The cultural logic of media convergence. Int. J. Cult. Stud. **7**(1), 33–43 (2006)
25. Hocking, C.: Ludonarrative Dissonance in Bioshock. Click Nothing, 7 October 2007. http://clicknothing.typepad.com/click_nothing/2007/10/ludonarrative-d.html
26. Ryan, M.-L.: Narrative as Virtual Reality 2: Revisiting Immersion and Interactivity in Literature and Electronic Media. Johns Hopkins University Press, Baltimore (2015)
27. Schoenau-Fog, H., Bruni, L.E., Khalil, F.F., Faizi, J.: Authoring for engagement in plot-based interactive dramatic experiences for learning. In: Pan, Z., Cheok, A.D., Müller, W., Iurgel, I., Petta, P., Urban, B. (eds.) Transactions on Edutainment X. LNCS, vol. 7775, pp. 1–19. Springer, Heidelberg (2013). https://doi.org/10.1007/978-3-642-37919-2_1
28. Schoenau-Fog, H.: Adaptive storyworlds. In: Schoenau-Fog, H., Bruni, L.E., Louchart, S., Baceviciute, S. (eds.) ICIDS 2015. LNCS, vol. 9445, pp. 58–65. Springer, Cham (2015). https://doi.org/10.1007/978-3-319-27036-4_6
29. Manovich, L.: The Language of New Media. MIT Press, Cambridge (2001)

A Multidimensional Classification of Choice Presentation in Interactive Narrative

Sergio Estupiñán[⊠], Brice Maret, Kasper Andkjaer,
and Nicolas Szilas

TECFA, FPSE, University of Geneva, 1211 Geneva 4, Switzerland
{sergio.estupinan,kasper.andkjaer,
nicolas.szilas}@unige.ch

Abstract. This article approaches the question of choice in interactive narratives and presents a multidimensional classification model based on a selection and characterization of 31 existing works. The methodology for establishing such a classification is detailed, which considers composing elements, functions, aesthetic considerations, and mechanics for choice presentation. This article uses an observational approach for analyzing interactive narratives based in theoretical considerations.

Keywords: Choice · Interactive narratives · Taxonomy

1 Introduction

Interactive Digital Narrative (IDN) aims at letting the audience play an active role in the unfolding of a story, put in theatrical terms, breaking the fourth wall [1]. With few exceptions, this implies offering choice to the user. While many articles—mostly in academia but also in game design—have discussed the consequences of these choices on the narrative experience (e.g. [2]), and how the story should reconfigure according to the user's intervention (e.g. [4]), surprisingly little has been said of the choice itself; that is the situation in which a user is faced with various alternatives and must choose one of them.

What is the impact of the choice design on the interactive narrative experience? A notable study by Mawhorter and colleagues [3], tackles this subject by seeking to understand how choices affect users and how choice structure is related to the user experience. In particular, they identified a certain number of patterns in the choice structure that could provide a well-defined effect to the user, such as the dead-end option, false choice, blind choice, etc. In this article, we aim to extend this work by focusing only on one aspect of choice: the way choice is represented to the user.

Research on IDN design has largely focused on story structures, that is, the semantic level (in the four-level model proposed by Spierling for IDN [5]). However, the concrete presentation of the choice situation—its careful multimodal design (what would correspond to the syntactic level in [5])—has great impact on the interactive narrative experience. This impact could be studied following an experimental methodology, but prior to such an enterprise we considered it necessary to first delimit

© Springer Nature Switzerland AG 2018
R. Rouse et al. (Eds.): ICIDS 2018, LNCS 11318, pp. 149–153, 2018.
https://doi.org/10.1007/978-3-030-04028-4_12

the design space: given a choice situation provided by a crafted story or an IDN engine, what are the different possibilities to present choices to a user? This has resulted in the current multidimensional classification of choice, a taxonomy that could serve as inspiration to creators of interactive narratives.

2   Method

Since not every user intervention in an interactive narrative is a choice, a first distinction becomes to define choice as a *situation in which the user has to decide between a certain number of explicit options*. This definition discards works based on free interfaces [6], such as interactive fictions using a natural language input interface. According to [3], choice is composed by framing, options, and results: framing refers to the content that might lead the user to interpret a choice in a certain way, options refer to the alternatives, and results to what is delivered when an option is selected. This work focuses exclusively on the mediatic representation of these three components.

To build the taxonomy, we selected interactive narratives complying with the above definition that we could have direct access to, or videos of users interacting with them. It resulted in a body of 31 works (Table 1) from the following genres: Visual novels employing dialogs between different characters, Adventure games whose focus is primarily narrative along with a mix exploration and problem solving, and Cinematic adventure games where the character can move around and interact.

Table 1. List of interactive narratives examined for establishing the taxonomy

A story as you like it	Tales from the Borderlands - Episode 1: Zero Sum
Amnesia: Memories	The Doom Beneath
Batman: The Telltale Series - Episode 1: Realm of Shadows	The Eye of Emerald
Beach Bounce	The Lion's Song - Episode 1: Silence
Beyond: Two Souls	The Royal Trap
Do not Take This Risk	The Stanley Parable
Emily is Away	The Walking Dead - Episode 1: A New Day
Fahrenheit: Indigo Prophecy	The Wolf Among Us - Episode 1: Faith
Hakuoki: Stories of the Shinengumi	Three Fourths Home
Hatoful Boyfriend	To Be or Not To Be
Heavy Rain	Tokyo Twilight Ghost Hunters
King's Quest - Episode 1: A Knight to Remember	Toradora Portable
Mass Effect: Andromeda	Until Dawn
Minecraft: Story Mode - Episode 1: The Order of the Stone	Warhammer 40'000 Legacy of Dorn - Herald of Oblivion
Norn9: Var Commons	Zero Escape: Zero Time Dilemma
Steins: Gate 0	

3 Classification

The resulting classification is presented below, see Fig. 1.

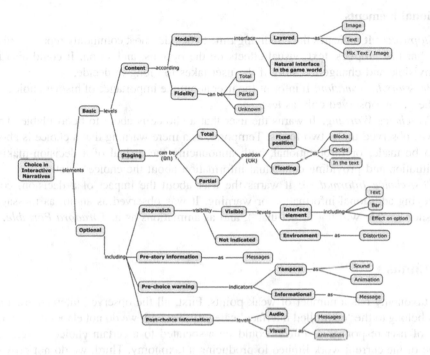

Fig. 1. Multidimensional classification of choice in interactive narratives

3.1 Categories

Basic Elements

- *Content:* Represents the information given about the options. It includes two sub-categories: modality and fidelity; according to [3], modality is the form that takes the option leading to a result, whereas fidelity expresses the difference between the content of the option and its result.
  - Modality: It includes images (symbolizing actions, objects), text (words or sentences), or a blend representing both the main message and conveying additional information (such as the tone with which a message will be transmitted, as in *Mass Effect*). We call them 'Layered' interfaces since they're situated in dedicated screen areas. In contrast, other options are rendered as part of the environment in which the story takes place ('Natural interface in the game world').
  - Fidelity: We observed different cases: when what is uttered by the character matches exactly the content in the option ('Total'), when a difference is introduced ('Partial'), and when the execution is hidden to the user ('Unknown').

- *Staging:* It refers to the actual representation of the options. In most of the observed works all the options were visible at the same time ('Total'), in some other works the user has to interact with the interface to make the options visible ('Partial'). We also observed a subsequent separation concerning positioning ('Fixed', 'Floating').

Optional Elements

- *Stopwatch:* It indicates the remaining time to decide; most commonly represented as a bar that empties, text, visual effects on the options, and so on. It could also be invisible and change the story if the user takes too long to decide.
- *Pre-story Information:* It informs the user about the importance of his/her choices in the game, observed only as text.
- *Pre-choice Warning:* It warns the user that a choice is about to be available. This was observed under two forms: Temporal, as a mere warning that a choice is about to be made, or Informational, both announcing the arrival of a decision-making situation and providing contextual information about the choice situation.
- *Post-choice Information:* It warns the user about the impact of a decision, conveying additional information or warning. It was observed as audio, as messages (such as "He will not forget that"), and as animations as in *Toradora Portable*.

4 Limits

The taxonomy has a number of weak points. First, all the observed interactive narratives belong to the 'controlled interface' category. Second, we do not elaborate on what kind of user responses or effects could be associated to a certain choice design, the scope of the current work limited to producing a taxonomy. Third, we do not provide annotations for each work of the corpus concerning the choice dimensions it features.

5 Conclusion

Following an observational approach based on a body of 31 interactive narratives, this article proposes a multidimensional classification of choice, characterizing different elements, functions, mechanics and aesthetic considerations found to be part of the presentation of choice. This taxonomy may inspire designers of interactive narratives to come up with combinations of elements for presenting choice to users in their works.

In general, this taxonomy borrows from and extends previous research in the field [3]; it wants to be seen as a guide for advancing the discussion on how interface design and choice mechanics influence the perception of narrative or could be used to evoke or alleviate certain responses on the users, such as frustration, enjoyment, and engagement.

Acknowledgements. This research would not have been possible without the financial support from the Swiss National Science Foundation under grant No. 159605 (N. Szilas, principal investigator).

References

1. Koenitz, H., Ferri, G., Haahr, M., Sezen, D., Sezen, I.T. (eds.): Interactive Digital Narrative – History, Theory and Practice. Routledge, New York (2015)
2. Mateas, M., Stern, A.: Procedural authorship: a case-study of the interactive drama facade. In: Digital Arts and Culture (DAC) (2005)
3. Mawhorter, P., Mateas, M., Wardrip-Fruin, N., Jhala, A.: Towards a theory of choice poetics. In: Proceedings of 9th International Conference Foundation Digital Games (2014)
4. Riedl, M., Saretto, C.J., Young, R.M.: Managing interaction between users and agents in a multi-agent storytelling environment. In: Proceedings of the Second International Joint Conference on Autonomous Agents and Multiagent Systems, pp. 741–748 ACM, New York (2003)
5. Spierling, U.: Interaction design principles as narrative techniques for interactive digital storytelling. In: Koenitz, H., Ferri, G., Haahr, M., Sezen, D., Ibrahim Sezen, T. (eds.) Interactive Digital Narrative - History, Theory and Practice, pp. 159–173. Routledge, New York (2015)
6. Szilas, N.: Stepping into the interactive drama. In: Göbel, S., et al. (eds.) TIDSE 2004. LNCS, vol. 3105, pp. 14–25. Springer, Heidelberg (2004). https://doi.org/10.1007/978-3-540-27797-2_3

Narrative Consistency across Replays of Pro-social Interactive Digital Narratives

Jonathan Barbara[1,2][✉] [iD]

[1] Leuphana University of Lüneburg, Lüneburg, Germany
jbarbara@stmartins.edu
[2] Saint Martin's Institute of Higher Education, Schembri Street, Hamrun, Malta

Abstract. Studies showing the influence of pro-social interactive digital narratives on their participants' appreciation of the modelled situations are subject to having the participants perceiving their interaction as meaningful and being able to clearly understand the consequences of their actions. This paper suggests the supplementary use of the Narrative Consistency criterion to assess the participants' understanding of the modelled social context by measuring how the interactive narrative's outcomes meet their expectations across replays.

Keywords: Interactive narratives · Criticism · Narrative consistency

1 Introduction

Traditional linear narratives are limited in modelling the complex narratives of today's society because they present a single outcome that has already been chosen by the author. On the other hand, interactive narratives present a narrative form that allows for situated empathy in relation to personal choices and consequential outcomes. If modelled well and consistently across replays, interactive narratives can inform the audience of the intricate machinations underlying today's political and social fabric.

Studies using Interactive Digital Narratives (IDNs) have explored the plight of homeless single parents [21], persons living in a refugee camp [20], and illegal immigrants from Mexico into the United States of America [11]. Their findings show that exposure [11], meaningful interaction, clear consequences of actions [20], and appreciation [21] were necessary, while enjoyment, reaching a successful ending, and duration of exposure were not necessary for encouraging prosocial behaviour [20, 21] and causing positive affective dispositions towards the marginalised social group [11]. Meaningful interaction requires a good choice of game mechanics as highlighted by Mulier and Crawford who suggest that a bad choice of interaction may belittle *"complex social situations into simple rational choices"* [9]. Such an outcome would reduce, rather than attract, empathy towards the target communities.

The above studies measured the effect of IDNs on participants beyond hedonistic entertainment by combining existing audience response measuring tools or modified forms thereof. These include measuring for responsibility, empathic concern, appreciation and enjoyment, narrative engagement, and text comprehension [21], and affect in the form of familiarity, admiration, acceptance, affection, approval, sympathy, warmth, and similarity [11]. Other studies have tried to bridge practice with theory by mapping 12 user experience dimensions to the 3 experiential aesthetic qualities of digital media as proposed by Murray [10], being usability, effectance and autonomy in the agency category; flow, presence, role-identification, curiosity, suspense, and believability in the immersion category, and eudaimonic appreciation, affect, and enjoyment in the transformation category [17].

Measurement of meaningful interaction and clear consequences of action was carried out in a study using event-indexing models and perceived difference in outcome [4]. Another study suggests that the narrative provides a context that raises desirable actions for the player, whose satisfaction lies in those actions being afforded by the underlying computational model [22].

However meaningful interaction and clear consequences of action were measured along a single session by having participants revisit their choices and, with the benefit of hindsight, assess the consequentiality of each choice [4]. By measuring such criteria across multiple replay sessions of the same IDN will allow the participant to compare outcomes not only with hypothetical expectations [22], but also with actualised outcomes as supported by the IDN.

I thus propose to measure meaningfulness of interaction and clear consequence of action through the narrative consistency of the player's interactions across replays within an IDN.

2   Dimensions of Narrative Consistency in IDNs

The role of narrative consistency in the evaluation of IDNs has been highlighted at various points throughout the past two decades of their scholarly consideration [1, 7, 8, 13, 15, 18]. The challenge increases when attempting to generate multiple possible narratives with similar levels of quality and length [6] while maintaining a high replay value [16].

I suggest that IDNs' unique nature of presenting not one, but a multitude of possible narrative manifestations, provides two dimensions along which narrative consistency may be evaluated: along a single narrative (intra-narrative configuration [12] and coherence [14]) and across the multiple narratives through inter-narrative fidelity as presented in Fisher's Narrative Paradigm [5].

The methodology used by most studies is to only analyse a single run per player, asking them to judge the outcome of their actions based on expectations raised by the story up to that point. This is where intra-narrative coherence is used to gauge the consequentiality of actions by comparing the actual with the expected outcome within the actual narrative generated.

Inter-narrative fidelity measures the difference in narrative outcome based on the different (or same) actions taken between sessions. This requires analysis of consequentiality of action across multiple sessions by the same player. This repeated exposure would help the player generate a mental mapping between choice and outcome through experience across the multiple generated narratives. This mapping would raise outcome expectations to each choice made, which is tested once the realised outcome is presented.

When a system is objectively analysed to be free from internal contradictions by being perceived to be coherent across replays, the level of narrative consistency reported by the user could reflect their understanding of the societal model that the interactive narrative is attempting to portray.

3   Evaluating Narrative Consistency in IDNs

In the abovementioned studies, the criteria that come closest to narrative consistency are narrative understanding [3], believability [17], eudaimonic appreciation [20] and effectance [17].

Narrative understanding was a criterion developed for narrative engagement with narrative media in general, not particularly interactive ones. Thus it makes no distinction between understanding the narrative as a result of the author's intent and the narrative resulting from the user's actions or decision making. While both are of importance, we wish to focus on the evaluation of the user's understanding of the consequences of their own interactions, and suggest its own specific measurement [3].

Skov and Andersen define a believable character as one that causes the player to suspend disbelief that they are interacting with an AI controlled character [19]. Roth and Koenitz relate suspension of disbelief to narrative plot evolving *"in a plausible way, and characters reacting in a credible manner"* [17]. In the case of plot, they ensure to have a "consistent dramatic arc" when testing between different candidate conventions in another study [18]. As for which characters are being assessed for consistency, it is clarified later on when believability is used as a criterion on non-player characters and their behaviour, and not for the player's character (whose actions and consequences we are interested in here) [17].

With respect to eudaimonic appreciation, this is a criterion that covers aesthetic pleasantness and personal gratification derived from comparing one's real life experience (and not previous experiences exposed to through other narratives) with the narrative's character(s) as they deal with hardship [20].

Effectance, as a dimension in the agency category, may be the closest to narrative consistency. A user will perceive effectance when responses are meaningful and coherent to their actions. It measures the user's perceived effect of their interactions on the narrative: in both the short and the long term, referred to as local and global effectance respectively [17]. A study that measures effectance in IDNs tested the effect of replay on effectance by having participants have a second go at playing *Façade* [16]. While the findings report that replay had a positive effect on effectance, this was only measured through two items that measured impact and direct effect on the narrative outcome, such that the study could only suggest that a more coherent and meaningful narrative would result in higher perceived effectance.

4 The Narrative Consistency Scale

With the relevance of IDNs to the complex societal models of contemporary culture, persuasion of the user is highly dependent on their understanding of the represented phenomenon. Thus, assessing the narrative consistency of an IDN under development, and thereafter assessing the perceived narrative consistency from the user is crucial to ensuring an effective experience with the desired outcome in signification that is not misinterpreted or misunderstood. While effectance measures the perceived level of impact a user's interaction has on the narrative, it does not indicate whether the outcome has met expectations implied by the action and to what level.

I hereby suggest the adoption of the Narrative Consistency Scale [2], as a complementary tool to Roth's and Koenitz's evaluation toolbox [17], in order to assess the meaningfulness of the outcome relative to the actions taken, especially in the long term consequences of global effectance [17]. Such a scale would have experiences deemed to be Consistent when the same actions taken across different sessions have led to same results. They would be Cohesive when different actions have led to an understandably different result while they would be deemed Irrelevant when different actions have led to a totally irrelevant result. On the negative consistency side of the scale, experiences would be deemed to be inconsistent when taking different actions have led to an unexpected result while taking the same actions but leading to an unjustifiable different result would be deemed to be Conflicting.

This paper therefore suggests the measurement of meaningful interaction with clear consequence of actions through the use of the Narrative Consistency Scale and encourages empirical research to support or reject this claim.

5 Conclusion

IDNs can contribute to cultural studies by providing a model of societal behaviour within which readers can partake in the action and through whose effectance they can better understand the hidden machinations of the portrayed phenomenon. A high-quality criticism of IDNs should focus on their ability to explain such models to the user by providing narratively consistent outcomes relative to their in-game actions. As empirical research is the method of choice in the new wave of IDNs based on intelligent systems that act as surrogates for the author's intent, supplementing existing questionnaires with scales specific to narrative consistency can help enhance the quality and effectiveness of IDNs in explaining target societal models to IDN consumers. Such a scale can be used at prototype stage to assist in the development of effective IDNs as well as a means to validate an IDN's user experience by allowing the user to express the resulting narrative outcome relative to their own expectations based on the interaction they effected throughout the experience. This can help contribute to a high-quality criticism that not only assesses the structural make-up of the narrative engine but also the resultant narrative experiences of the interacting audience.

References

1. Aylett, R.: Emergent narrative, social immersion and "storification". In: Proceedings of the 1st International Workshop on Narrative and Interactive Learning Environments, pp. 35–44 (2000)
2. Barbara, J.: Towards measuring consistency across transmedial narratives. In: Schoenau-Fog, H., Bruni, L.E., Louchart, S., Baceviciute, S. (eds.) ICIDS 2015. LNCS, vol. 9445, pp. 243–250. Springer, Cham (2015). https://doi.org/10.1007/978-3-319-27036-4_23
3. Busselle, R., Bilandzic, H.: Measuring Narrative Engagement. Media Psychol. **12**(4), 321–347 (2009)
4. Cardona-Rivera, R.E., et al.: Foreseeing Meaningful Choices. In: Proceedings of the Tenth Annual AAAI Conference on Artificial Intelligence and Interactive Digital Entertainment (AIIDE 2014)
5. Fisher, W.R.: Human Communication as Narration: Toward a Philosophy of Reason, Value, and Action. University of South Carolina Press, Columbia (1989)
6. Green, M.C., Jenkins, K.M.: Interactive narratives: processes and outcomes in user-directed stories. J. Commun. **64**(3), 479–500 (2014)
7. Koenitz, H., Dubbelman, T., Knoller, N., Roth, C.: An integrated and iterative research direction for interactive digital narrative. In: Nack, F., Gordon, Andrew S. (eds.) ICIDS 2016. LNCS, vol. 10045, pp. 51–60. Springer, Cham (2016). https://doi.org/10.1007/978-3-319-48279-8_5
8. Luo, L., et al.: A review of interactive narrative systems and technologies: a training perspective. Simulation **91**(2), 126–147 (2015)
9. Muriel, D., Crawford, G.: Video Games as Culture. Routledge, New York (2018)
10. Murray, J.H.: Hamlet on the Holodeck: The Future of Narrative in Cyberspace. Simon and Schuster, New York City (1997)
11. Parrott, S., et al.: A test of interactive narrative as a tool against prejudice. Howard J. Commun. **28**(4), 374–389 (2017)
12. Rabinowitz, P.J.: Before Reading: Narrative Conventions and the Politics of Interpretation. Cornell University Press, Columbus (1987)
13. Riedl, M.O., Bulitko, V.: Interactive narrative: an intelligent systems approach. Ai Mag. **34**(1), 67 (2012)
14. Riedl, M.O., Young, R.M.: Narrative planning: balancing plot and character. J. Artif. Intelligence Res. **39**, 217–268 (2010)
15. Rieser, M.: Interactive narratives: a form of fiction? convergence. Int. J. Res. New Media Technol. **3**(1), 10–19 (1997)
16. Roth, C., et al.: Exploring replay value: shifts and continuities in user experiences between first and second exposure to an interactive story. Cyberpsychology Behav. Soc. Netw. **15**(7), 378–381 (2012)
17. Roth, C., Koenitz, H.: Evaluating the user experience of interactive digital narrative. In: Proceedings of the 1st International Workshop on Multimedia Alternate Realities, pp. 31–36. ACM (2016)
18. Roth, C., Koenitz, H.: Towards creating a body of evidence-based interactive digital narrative design knowledge: approaches and challenges. In: Proceedings of the 2nd International Workshop on Multimedia Alternate Realities, pp. 19–24. ACM (2017)
19. Skov, M.B., Andersen, P.B.: Designing interactive narratives. In: Proceedings of the 1st International Conference on Computational Semiotics in Games and New Media, pp. 59–66 (2001)

20. Steinemann, S.T., et al.: Increasing donating behavior through a game for change: the role of interactivity and appreciation. In: Proceedings of the 2015 Annual Symposium on Computer-Human Interaction in Play, pp. 319–329. ACM (2015)
21. Steinemann, S.T., et al.: Interactive narratives affecting social change. J. Media Psychol. (2017)
22. Wardrip-Fruin, N., et al.: Agency reconsidered. breaking new ground: innovation in games, play, practice and theory. In: Proceedings of DiGRA 2009 (2009)

Sketching a Map of the Storylets Design Space

Max Kreminski[(⊠)] and Noah Wardrip-Fruin

UC Santa Cruz, Santa Cruz, CA 95064, USA
{mkremins,nwardrip}@ucsc.edu

Abstract. Linear and branching narrative structures are widespread in games, but limited in their dynamism and expressiveness. We consider the alternative *storylets model* of interactive narrative content, in which a game's narrative is assembled from a database of discrete, reorderable narrative "chunks" or "modules" known as *storylets*. This paper represents a first attempt to map out the design space of storylet-based narrative systems in games. We define the common elements of storylet-based systems; categorize such systems along several distinct dimensions; and survey implementations of such systems in existing games.

Keywords: Interactive narrative design · Procedural narrative

1   Introduction

Linear and branching narrative structures are widespread in games, and for good reason: they give the designer precise control over the story's direction, are easy to implement, and have been thoroughly explored by existing games. However, these narrative structures also place natural limitations on a game's narrative dynamism, replayability, and expressiveness [13].

The *storylets model* represents one potential alternative way to structure narrative content in games. Under this model, a game's narrative is assembled over the course of a playthrough from a database of discrete narrative "chunks" or "modules" known as *storylets*. Both the player and the game have a degree of control over which storylets will be chosen and in what order: the availability of storylets is dependent on the current game state, which player actions may alter, and players might even be permitted to choose which of the available storylets they want to play next. In this sense, under the storylets model, the player does not pass through a story dictated up front by the game's designer. Rather, the player and the game work together to assemble a story from the modules at their disposal, with both having some ability to influence the direction of the story as it is built.

This paper represents a preliminary attempt to map out the design space of storylet-based interactive narrative systems. By surveying existing storylet-based systems, we aim to identify similarities and differences between them and categorize the differences into several independent dimensions of variation.

© Springer Nature Switzerland AG 2018
R. Rouse et al. (Eds.): ICIDS 2018, LNCS 11318, pp. 160–164, 2018.
https://doi.org/10.1007/978-3-030-04028-4_14

2   Defining Storylets

2.1   Common Elements and Precondition Types

The term "storylet" first appeared in the game *Fallen London* [2] (originally titled *Echo Bazaar*), and referred to the player-selectable mini-stories from which the bulk of the game's narrative was composed [4]. These storylets were gated by *qualities*: numerical stats pertaining to the player character, with values varying based on the player's choices. We use the term more broadly; for our purposes, storylets are discrete, self-contained, and reorderable modules of narrative content, gated by preconditions that determine whether they can be presented to the player at any given moment in time. Some types of preconditions are especially common; in particular, many games use preconditions to restrict access to storylets based on the player character's current location in the game world, effectively binding storylets to certain locations. For instance, in StoryNexus [3] games such as *Fallen London*, nearly all storylets are location-bound.

An interesting extension of preconditions can be seen in *Starfreighter* [7], where *parametrized storylets* augment preconditions with *dynamic queries* that treat the game state as a database. These queries search for characters, inventory items, and so on that meet certain criteria and "bind" them to named parameters. A parametrized storylet may only be presented to the player if all of its parameters are successfully bound; a single parametrized storylet may also be satisfiable by several different sets of parameters, and which parameter bindings are chosen can impact both how the surface text of the storylet is instantiated and what effects the storylet will have on the game state (Table 1).

2.2   Repeatability

Can a single storylet be shown to the player more than once? Different systems answer this question in different ways. In some games, such as *The King of Chicago* [16,17], storylets are never repeatable: each storylet may be encountered once and only once in the course of a single playthrough. In some systems, the opposite is true: all storylets are repeatable unless designers take special care to prevent the repetition of particular storylets by means of hand-authored preconditions. Still other systems provide a means by which designers may select, on a per-storylet basis, whether or not this storylet is intended to be repeatable.

2.3   Internal Structure

Narrative content within storylets may be structured in a variety of ways. The simplest possible storylets contain fixed, static text. Other systems extend this mechanism by allowing for the substitution of variables from the game state into otherwise static text templates.

Still other games and systems allow for greater dynamism in storylet-internal content. Dynamic assembly of content pairs well with reusable storylets; if a single base storylet may be expanded or instantiated in multiple distinct ways

Table 1. Selected existing games and systems that make use of storylets to structure narrative content, classified according to the dimensions discussed.

Game or system	Precondition types	Repeatability of storylets	Internal structure of storylets	Content selection architecture
Epitaph	Quality check	Never repeatable	Replacement grammar; templated text	Player choice (from simple list); random selection
Façade	Quality check	Author chooses per-storylet	Recursive (storylets are drama managers with their own content pools)	Drama manager
Ice-Bound [14]	Quality check	Never repeatable	Replacement grammar; templated text	Player choice (via complex interface, requiring exploration)
Reigns	Quality check; location	Usually repeatable	Branching	Weighted random selection
Starfreighter	Dynamic query	Usually repeatable	Branching; replacement grammar; templated text	Weighted random selection
StoryAssembler	Quality check	Author chooses per-storylet	Branching; replacement grammar; templated text	Pathfinding/search
StoryNexus	Quality check; location	Usually repeatable	Branching	Player choice (from simple list)
The King of Chicago	Quality check	Never repeatable	Branching	Salience-based

depending on the game state or on random selection of alternatives, this may help to mask the fact that content is being repeated or mitigate the potentially boredom-inducing effect of verbatim repetition on the player.

Some systems structure storylets internally as replacement grammars, with the grammar being used to instantiate a fresh variant of the text content each time the storylet is reused. The procedural narrative idlegame *Epitaph* [5] uses this approach [6]. Other systems may permit storylets to feature internal branching, effectively enabling the author to approach each storylet as a miniature Choose Your Own Adventure story. Many existing games use this approach, including both StoryNexus games and *Reigns* [12].

In addition, these approaches may be freely mixed with one another. *Starfreighter* in particular uses a hybrid of all of the approaches mentioned here.

2.4   Content Selection Architectures

There are many ways for a system to choose which storylet it will present to the player next. Each of these mechanisms is an example of what Michael Mateas terms a *content selection architecture* [10,11] – a means by which an interactive narrative system decides what content to present – for storylet-based systems. These content selection architectures may be combined in arbitrary ways.

One of the simplest possible approaches is to present players with an interface that allows them to select for themselves, from all the currently available storylets, which one they would like to play next. This is the approach used in StoryNexus games. Alternatively, an equally straightforward but opposite approach is to make a simple random selection from the pool of available storylets.

Weighted random selection extends simple random selection with an additional layer of complexity: a "weight" for each available storylet is calculated based on the current game state, making some storylets more likely to be selected than others. *Reigns* uses a weighted random approach, framing it in terms of a "deck of cards" metaphor: a storylet (or "card") that is highly relevant to the current game state may be dealt into the "deck" multiple times [1].

A related approach, *salience-based selection*, compares the actual current game state to an "ideal" game state with which each storylet is tagged and selects the storylet that represents the closest match. Some storylets, tagged with highly specific state conditions, match the game state only rarely but are especially relevant when selected; others, tagged with highly generic state conditions, are used as fallbacks when none of the more specific storylets represent a good match for the current state. *The King of Chicago* takes this approach.

One uncommon approach to selecting storylets involves the use of pathfinding or search algorithms on a graph of possible future directions for the story to take. One example is StoryAssembler [15], which maintains an internal "story spec" detailing the storytelling goals it wishes to accomplish and searches for paths through the database of storylets that can effectively fulfill these goals. Similarly, in Emily Short's *Glass* [19], player and non-player characters take turns "steering" a conversation through a graph of interconnected discussion topics, with the goal of successfully steering the conversation onto specific topics. Short refers to this approach as *waypoint narrative* [18].

Perhaps the most potentially complex approach involves the use of a full-fledged *drama manager* to determine which storylet should be presented next. This is the approach taken by *Façade* [8], an "interactive drama" in which narrative content is structured as a pool of "beats" and a drama manager makes selections from this pool in response to the player's actions [9].

3   Conclusions

This paper represents a first attempt to map out the design space of storylet-based narrative systems in games. We provide a definition of storylet-based systems grounded in their common elements; identify four independent dimensions (precondition type, repeatability of storylets, internal structure of storylets, and content selection architecture) along which such systems can vary; and classify several existing systems according to this taxonomy. Future work may extend this analysis by characterizing the relative advantages and disadvantages of storylet-based narrative systems, as well as some of the common challenges and design patterns involved in authoring content for storylet-based narrative games.

References

1. Alliot, F.: The casual (but regal) swipe: creating game mechanics in Reigns. https://www.gdcvault.com/play/1024278/The-Casual-(but-Regal)-Swipe. Accessed 25 Jul 2018
2. Failbetter Games: Fallen London. http://fallenlondon.storynexus.com. Accessed 25 Jul 2018
3. Failbetter Games: StoryNexus. http://www.storynexus.com. Accessed 25 Jul 2018
4. Kennedy, A.: Echo Bazaar narrative structures, Part two. http://www.failbettergames.com/echo-bazaar-narrative-structures-part-two. Accessed 25 Jul 2018
5. Kreminski, M.: Epitaph. https://mkremins.itch.io/epitaph. Accessed 25 Jul 2018
6. Kreminski, M.: History generation in Epitaph. https://mkremins.github.io/blog/history-generation-epitaph. Accessed 25 Jul 2018
7. Kreminski, M.: Starfreighter. https://mkremins.itch.io/starfreighter. Accessed 25 Jul 2018
8. Mateas, M., Stern, A.: Façade. https://games.softpedia.com/get/Freeware-Games/Facade.shtml. Accessed 25 Jul 2018
9. Mateas, M., Stern, A.: Structuring content in the Façade interactive drama architecture. In: Artificial Intelligence and Interactive Digital Entertainment (2005)
10. Mateas, M.: Introduction to content selection architectures (unpublished lecture slides)
11. Mateas, M.: More content selection architectures (unpublished lecture slides)
12. Nerial: Reigns. http://nerial.co.uk/reigns-original. Accessed 25 Jul 2018
13. Reed, A.A.: Changeful tales: design-driven approaches toward more expressive storygames. Diss, UC Santa Cruz (2017)
14. Reed, A.A., Garbe, J.: The Ice-Bound Concordance. http://www.ice-bound.com. Accessed 25 Jul 2018
15. Samuel, B., et al.: Leveraging procedural narrative and gameplay to address controversial topics. In: International Conference on Computational Creativity (2017)
16. Sharp, D.: Story vs. game: the battle of interactive fiction. http://web.archive.org/web/20040404061317/www.channelzilch.com/doug/battle.htm. Accessed 25 Jul 2018
17. Sharp, D.: The King of Chicago. https://classicreload.com/the-king-of-chicago.html. Accessed 25 Jul 2018
18. Short, E.: Beyond branching: quality-based, salience-based, and waypoint narrative structures. https://emshort.blog/2016/04/12/beyond-branching-quality-based-and-salience-based-narrative-structures. Accessed 25 Jul 2018
19. Short, E.: Glass. http://inform7.com/learn/eg/glass/index.html. Accessed 25 Jul 2018

Creating and Sharing Interactive Narrative Design Knowledge – A Multipronged Approach

Hartmut Koenitz[✉], Christian Roth, and Teun Dubbelman

HKU University of the Arts Utrecht,
Nieuwekade 1, 3511 RV Utrecht, The Netherlands
{hartmut.koenitz, christian.roth,
teun.dubbelman}@hku.nl

Abstract. When it comes to interactive digital narrative design, there is both a lack of formal training and formal knowledge. Yet, at the same time, the job title of "narrative designer" exists in many places, and many critically and commercially successful interactive digital narratives (IDN) have been realized during the past three decades. This means that interactive narrative design knowledge is mostly private, earned "the hard way" through trial, error, and intuition. The problem with this state of affairs is that design knowledge can be shared only with great difficulty, due to its use of private – and therefore inaccessible – vocabulary. In this paper, we describe a multipronged approach to the creation and sharing of formal design knowledge. We reference our empirically based method to identify and verify design conventions, outline a formal vocabulary (an ontology), describe an online platform for the collection of convention candidates and associated events to foster collaboration between scholars and practitioners.

Keywords: Interactive narrative design · Design conventions
Design concepts · Ontology · Open online platform
Empirical design knowledge

1 Introduction

When it comes to interactive digital narrative design, there is both a lack of formal training and formal knowledge. Yet, at the same time, the job title of "narrative designer" exists in many places, and many critically and commercially successful interactive digital narratives (IDN) have been realized during the past three decades, as narrative games (e.g. Adventure [1], King's Quest [2], Monkey Island [3], The Last Express [4], Dear Esther [5], Heavy Rain [6], The Walking Dead [7], Firewatch [8] and Oxenfree [9]) and other manifestations, including interactive documentaries (e.g. Fort McMoney [10], Last Highjack Interactive [11]), installation pieces (e.g. Text Rain [12] and others [13]), journalistic 'interactives' (e.g. [14, 15]), VR and AR works [16–18], and Electronic Literature pieces [19].

This discrepancy – between a considerable body of work and the lack of formal resources stems from the fact that interactive narrative design knowledge is mostly

R. Rouse et al. (Eds.): ICIDS 2018, LNCS 11318, pp. 165–170, 2018.
https://doi.org/10.1007/978-3-030-04028-4_15

private, earned "the hard way" through trial, error, and intuition. The problem with this state of affairs is that design knowledge can be shared only with great difficulty, due to its use of private – and therefore usually inaccessible – vocabulary.

In this paper, we detail the implementation of our multipronged approach [20] to address these issues. Individual measures are:

- an empirically-based method to identify and verify design conventions [21–23]
- the development of a formal vocabulary (an ontology), which we hope to establish as widely-used 'lingua franca' for designers and researchers [33]
- an online platform for the collection of convention candidates, which opens our effort to a wider community of practitioners and researchers
- the organization of local events to raise awareness of interactive narrative design amongst practitioners and industry.

2   Verifying Interactive Narrative Design Conventions

2.1   Defining Design Conventions

We have previously described Design Conventions [23]. Essentially, we differentiate two levels: abstract 'design concepts' and concrete design methods – the latter we understand as 'design conventions' which we have defined as "concrete design methods to create conventional comprehension and effects in interactors." [21–23] Design concepts are higher-level categories that describe and overarching function, e.g. "scripting the interactor" (StI) [24] or "delayed consequences" [25].

We also position Design Conventions and Concepts vs. "Design patterns" [26], a concept originating in architecture, that has been applied to describe games design [27, 28]. The issue with patterns is the varying levels of abstraction, which makes comparisons difficult and also means that one collection cannot be used to extend another one [27].

2.2   Verification

To verify a design convention candidate, we use a combined qualitative and quantitative approach, specifically an extended version of Roth's measurement toolbox [28]. Concretely, this means the creation of two nearly identical IDNs that differ only in the use of the convention candidate. The effect of these two different variants on the user experience (A/B testing) are then compared in a post-test-only randomized experimental setup. In the case of a significant positive impact in line with the intention of the convention candidate and a sufficient effect size, the convention is verified for the given context [21–23]. The database also collects replication studies with different artefacts, using the same design conventions, and similar or different samples to further prove validity.

3   A Specific Ontology for IDN Conventions

Previous work was undertaken on ontologies for videogames [29–31] and similar typologies [32]. These efforts were focused on creating general formal descriptions. In contrast, our effort is more focused and dedicated solely on a vocabulary to describe interactive narrative design. In the following section we briefly present a first public version (1.0) (c.f. [33]).

	Top-level category	*Second-level category*/description
1	Proposers	Names of submitters
2	Convention name	Design convention (DC, verified) or candidate (DCC, unverified)
3	Design concept	Conjunction with an overarching category
4	Primary function	Purpose of a convention
5	General description	Further explanation
6	Examples	Artefacts implementing the proposed DC(C)
7	Design intention	high-level design perspective regarding *guidance*, *goal setting*, *challenge*, *reward*, *distraction*
8	Intended effects	Concrete effects on user interaction and user experience in the categories of *agency*, *immersion* and *transformation* [21, 24]
9	Production impact	*Costs* (work hours) and *professional requirements* (e.g. writing skills, modelling/animation skills, programming skills)
10	Manifestation	*Sense level* (visual, auditory, olfactory, gustatory, tactile …); *implementations* (text, graphics, tangible user interface elements), *relationships* (mechanics, rules)
11	Application	*Form* (narrative games, interactive novels, interactive documentaries, interactive installation, …), *genre* (action, thriller, comedy, …), *visual representation* (2D, 3D, 2.5D, independent), *physical representation* (screen-based, installation, mobile, VR, AR, MR, …), *platform* (console, PC, smartphone, tablet, platform independent, …), *user input type* (keyboard, mouse, touch screen, standard gamepad, motion controller, …)
12	Interdependence	Conjunction with other design approaches
13	Cultural dependence	DC(C) requires a specific societal or historical context
14	Research status	References to existing studies that empirically tested/verified DCs

Examples entries can be found here: http://interactivenarrativedesign.org/DC/.

4 Online Platform

In order to enable participation from the community we have created an online platform at http://interactivenarrativedesign.org/DC/ including an online form to submit design convention candidates. As stated earlier [33], we connect a number of goals with this endeavor, in particular, the growth of design knowledge through collaboration between diverse researchers and also practitioners. Therefore, we position the Design Convention database as:

(a) a tool that allows researchers and practitioners to enter design conventions candidates (names of contributors will be clearly visible and we will moderate the entries to assure quality)

(b) an open basis for research that enables researchers to test and verify design convention candidates (and take credit for their work)

(c) a means to improve the ontology through scholarly and practitioner's feedback

(d) a growing resource for interactive narrative designers to look up verified design conventions.

In our view this approach creates all-around benefits for the community: contributions are clearly listed, topics that need more research are easily identified and can be picked up by researchers worldwide, including replication studies.

5 Local Events

Research is in danger to be disconnected from the practice. In order to engage with the practitioners and other interested parties, we plan a series of events. A local conference will serve as a kick-off meeting to discuss early results, industry perspectives and question of collaboration. Then, ongoing meetups will build a community to foster mutual understanding and collaboration, for example on design conventions, but also on the development of programs for formal education.

6 Concluding Remarks

This work documents our ongoing, multipronged research and community-focused effort in creating and sharing interactive narrative design knowledge. This includes the collection of empirically verified design knowledge, a related ontology with the goal of providing a 'lingua franca' for the dialogue between research, education and application, a public online platform in order to enable collaboration and a series of ongoing events to engage a wider community of scholars and practitioners in an effort to move the community forward.

References

1. Crowther, W.: Adventure [Video Game] (1976)
2. Sierra On-Line: King's Quest (1980)

 3. Lucasfilm Games: Monkey Island (1990)
 4. Smoking Car Productions: The Last Express (1997)
 5. The Chinese Room: Dear Esther (2008)
 6. Quantic Dream: Heavy Rain [Video game] (2010)
 7. Telltale Games: The Walking Dead [Video game] (2012)
 8. Campo Santo: Firewatch [Video Game] (2016)
 9. Night School Studio: Oxenfree (2016)
10. Dufresne, D.: Fort McMoney. http://www.fortmcmoney.com (2013)
11. Submarine Channel: Last Hijack Interactive. Submarine Channel (2014)
12. Utterback, C., Achituv, R.: Text Rain (1999)
13. Sorensen, V.: Emergent Storytelling: Interactive Transmedia Installation for Digital Cultural Heritage. Presented at the Museums and the Web 2014, Silver Spring, MD (2014)
14. The Financial Times: The Uber Game (2017)
15. Thomson Reuters: Getting Inside Taser (2017)
16. la Peña, de, N.: Project Syria (2014)
17. The Guardian: 6 × 9 (2016). https://www.theguardian.com/world/ng-interactive/2016/apr/27/6x9-a-virtual-experience-of-solitary-confinement
18. Viana, B.S., Nakamura, R.: Immersive Interactive Narratives in Augmented Reality Games. Presented at the Cham (2014)
19. Hayles, N.K., Montfort, N., Rettberg, S., Strickland, S.: Electronic literature collection 1. Electronic Literature Organization (2006)
20. Koenitz, H., Dubbelman, T., Knoller, N., Roth, C.: An integrated and iterative research direction for interactive digital narrative. In: Nack, F., Gordon, Andrew S. (eds.) ICIDS 2016. LNCS, vol. 10045, pp. 51–60. Springer, Cham (2016). https://doi.org/10.1007/978-3-319-48279-8_5
21. Roth, C., Koenitz, H.: Evaluating the user experience of interactive digital narrative. Presented at the 1st International Workshop, New York (2016)
22. Roth, C., Koenitz, H.: Towards creating a body of evidence-based interactive digital narrative design knowledge: approaches and challenges. Presented at the AltMM 2017, Mountain View, 21 August 2017
23. Koenitz, H., Roth, C., Dubbelman, T., Knoller, N.: What is a convention in interactive narrative design? In: Nunes, N., Oakley, I., Nisi, V. (eds.) ICIDS 2017. LNCS, vol. 10690, pp. 295–298. Springer, Cham (2017). https://doi.org/10.1007/978-3-319-71027-3_29
24. Murray, J.H.: Hamlet on the Holodeck: The Future of Narrative in Cyberspace. Free Press, New York (1997)
25. Koenitz, H.: Design approaches for interactive digital narrative. In: Schoenau-Fog, H., Bruni, L.E., Louchart, S., Baceviciute, S. (eds.) ICIDS 2015. LNCS, vol. 9445, pp. 50–57. Springer, Cham (2015). https://doi.org/10.1007/978-3-319-27036-4_5
26. Alexander, C., Ishikawa, S., Silverstein, M.: A Pattern Language. Oxford University Press, Oxford (1977)
27. Koenitz, H., Roth, C., Knoller, N., Dubbelman, T.: Clementine Will Remember That – Methods to establish design conventions for video game narrative. Presented at the Proceedings of the 2018 DiGRA International Conference The Game is the Message, Torino, Italy, July 2018
28. Roth, C., Vorderer, P., Klimmt, C., Vermeulen, I.: Measuring the user experience in narrative-rich games: towards a concept-based assessment for interactive stories. Entertainment Interfaces (2010)
29. Zagal, J.P., Mateas, M., Fernández-Vara, C., Hochhalter, B., Lichti, N.: Towards an ontological language for game analysis. Presented at the DIGRA Conference 2005 (2005)

30. Zagal, J.P., Bruckman, A.: The game ontology project: supporting learning while contributing authentically to game studies. Presented at the Proceedings of the 8th international conference on International conference for the learning sciences (2008)
31. Karhulahti, V.-M.: Fiction puzzle: storiable challenge in pragmatist videogame aesthetics. Philos. Technol. **27**, 201–220 (2014)
32. Elverdam, C., Aarseth, E.J.: Game classification and game design: construction through critical analysis. Games Cult. **2**, 3–22 (2007)
33. Koenitz, H., Roth, C., Dubbelman, T.: Engaging the community in collecting interactive narrative design conventions. Presented at ChiPlay 2018, Melbourne (2018). https://doi.org/10.1145/3270316.3271533

Exploring Bloom's Taxonomy as a Basis for Interactive Storytelling

Sarah Harmon[✉] and Seth Chatterton

Bowdoin College, Brunswick, ME 04011, USA
{sharmon,schatter}@bowdoin.edu

Abstract. Prior work has called for Bloom's taxonomy of learning objectives to be incorporated in educational games, but little research has explored how to achieve this within a generative context. We formalize aspects of Bloom's taxonomy as logical assertions, thereby enabling metaphorical bridges to be generated between learning objectives and narrative elements. Through this lens, we present an example of a dynamic narrative framework driven by Bloom's cognitive model.

Keywords: Bloom's taxonomy
Computer-supported cooperative work
Educational interactive narrative

1 Introduction

Storytelling is a believable, memorable, and entertaining method of fostering learning that resonates with students from diverse backgrounds [1]. However, ensuring that interactive narratives successfully meet defined learning objectives is a crucial, yet complex task [20]. While cognitive models for learning objectives such as Bloom's taxonomy [12] exist, they have yet to be formalized as part of a dynamic, generative interactive narrative system from the start of the design process [6]. We seek to structurally analyze the logic behind common learning objectives as suggested by Bloom's taxonomy.

2 Related Work

Bloom's taxonomy of educational objectives defines six levels of cognitive objectives: *Remember, Understand, Apply, Analyze, Evaluate,* and *Create.* Recent work has sought to use this taxonomy to drive static playable experiences. For instance, games for teaching cybersecurity were developed that connected puzzle games with the *Remember* level, shooter games with *Understand*, problem-solving games with *Apply*, and what they termed capstone games with *Analyze, Evaluate,* and *Create* [3]. Conversely, Ibrahim et al. developed crossword puzzle and shooter games that applied the *Remember, Understand* and *Analyze* levels [10]. To date, Bloom's taxonomy continues to be used as a consistent basis for educational game design and learning outcome assessment [15,19].

© Springer Nature Switzerland AG 2018
R. Rouse et al. (Eds.): ICIDS 2018, LNCS 11318, pp. 171–175, 2018.
https://doi.org/10.1007/978-3-030-04028-4_16

Beyond considering Bloom's taxonomy for the design of instructional games, researchers have also explored how Bloom's taxonomy might inform computer-aided question generation, organization, and assessment. Teo and Joy, for instance, suggested that concept relations and Bloom's cognitive levels could give rise to a reusable set of question templates [17]. We postulate that this kind of ontology-based question generation could be useful as part of an interactive narrative framework in several ways. First, it can be useful when developing questions for students to answer, as in the original work. Second, logical queries founded on the same kinds of concept relations can be generated in a similar way and used to expand details in a given narrative scene. We use both of these methods in our example implementation.

3   Bloom's Taxonomy and Interactive Narrative

3.1   Learning Objectives as Logical Formalisms

We encoded eighteen primary tasks related to the levels specified in Bloom's taxonomy as logical constructions. These tasks are as follows: define, list, locate, match, order (*Remember*), explain, defend, draw (*Understand*), compute, classify (*Apply*), assess, differentiate (*Analyze*), critique, recommend (*Evaluate*), and compose as a set of four categories, namely compose_algorithm, compose_poem, compose_skit, and compose_song (*Create*). These tasks were selected due to their popularity in educational assessment [5], as well as their prior integration in games [21]. Each task also describes observable and measurable behavior, which is a key aspect of an effective learning objective [2,13]. By representing these kinds of tasks in first-order logic, we are able to use the event calculus [11] to reason over constraints about both the learning objectives and world knowledge within the full context and knowledge base of a narrative scenario.

3.2   System Architecture

Content Library. To initialize its knowledge base, the system first must understand basic facts (*assertions*) about the world, including encoded tasks relating to Bloom's taxonomy. In separate sections of the library, we have also encoded facts and rules to represent general world knowledge (e.g. *type_of(apple, fruit)*) as well as knowledge specific to a fantastical universe (e.g. *type_of(ghost, monster)*, *capable_of(ghost, fly)*, and so on). The content library also stores metadata related to any multimedia (images, videos, etc.) beyond the narrative text that is shown in the final realization.

Premise Generation. When a story is instantiated, an overall motivation for the player to engage with the game is generated. The underlying foundation of this motivation is selected at random from a list of basic human values [14]. Incorporating a goal founded on a universal value provides players with a potentially relatable long-term goal from the start of play, and has been shown to be a potentially useful technique in interactive narrative generation [7].

Building Scene Foundations. When the system needs to make a decision about how to represent a specified learning goal in the narrative world and generally construct a scene, procedural content generation and case-based reasoning techniques are combined with logical queries to satisfy preconditions and link selected events with consequences. This approach is broadly inspired by the imaginative recall process used by Minstrel [18], a story generator that has been recently reviewed and updated for research use [8, 16]. Because both world knowledge and the underlying concepts and rules of learning objectives are expressed as logical formalisms that may freely interact within our implementation, it is possible to create links between them.

Memory. A *core memory unit* keeps track of the system's past generations. This is useful input for a set of inner exhaustion mechanics, which helps guarantee any new generations are novel [16]. In addition to providing valuable information to ensure the system generates novel scenes and does not emphasize one learning objective in particular, the core memory unit is used as a record of the player's history. As such, it may be queried to gather information about the player's past successes and choices during the development of new scenes.

Realization. Once the assertions and rules behind a scene have been fleshed out, we use the Rensa narrative representation framework to transform and realize the generated assertions related to the scene's telling as simple English sentences [9]. The teacher can write or modify their own logical assertions in natural language to personalize the knowledge base for their classroom context.

4   Discussion

Despite the fact that Bloom's taxonomy does not necessarily use formal language, we have shown here that tasks corresponding to learning objectives can be represented in a logical form and thereby serve as a basis for computational systems. Going forward, it is important to consider several limitations of the current work. For instance, the example tasks do not require extensive planning on the student's part and are not necessarily productive for every possible subject area. Future work should seek to develop further examples of interactive narrative driven by cognitive models of learning objectives, and evaluate the effectiveness of these implementations in practice. Given the tendency for these types of models to be misconstrued [4], we suggest that it will be important for researchers from theoretical and practical perspectives to work in tandem.

References

1. Barzaq, M.: Integrating sequential thinking thought teaching stories in the curriculum. Action Research, AlQattan Center for Educational Research and Development QCERD (2009)
2. Bers, T., Swing, R.L.: Championing the assessment of learning: The role of top leaders. Higher education assessment: Leadership matters, pp. 3–26 (2010)
3. Buchanan, L., Wolanczyk, F., Zinghini, F.: Blending Bloom's taxonomy and serious game design. In: Proceedings of the International Conference on Security and Management (SAM), p. 1. The Steering Committee of The World Congress in Computer Science, Computer Engineering and Applied Computing (WorldComp) (2011)
4. Case, R.: The unfortuate consequences of Bloom's taxonomy. Soc. Educ. **77**(4), 196–200 (2013)
5. Gregory, G.H., Chapman, C.: Differentiated Instructional Strategies: One Size Doesn't Fit All. Corwin press, Boca Raton (2012)
6. Gunter, G., Kenny, R.F., Vick, E.H.: A case for a formal design paradigm for serious games. J. Int. Digit. Media Arts Assoc. **3**(1), 93–105 (2006)
7. Harmon, S.: An expressive dilemma generation model for players and artificial agents. In: Twelfth Artificial Intelligence and Interactive Digital Entertainment Conference (2016)
8. Harmon, S., Jhala, A.: Revisiting computational models of creative storytelling based on imaginative recall. In: Schoenau-Fog, H., Bruni, L.E., Louchart, S., Baceviciute, S. (eds.) ICIDS 2015. LNCS, vol. 9445, pp. 170–178. Springer, Cham (2015). https://doi.org/10.1007/978-3-319-27036-4_16
9. Harmon, S.M.: Narrative encoding for computational reasoning and adaptation. Ph.D. thesis, University of California, Santa Cruz (2017)
10. Ibrahim, R., Yusoff, R.C.M., Omar, H.M., Jaafar, A.: Students perceptions of using educational games to learn introductory programming. Comput. Inf. Sci. **4**(1), 205 (2010)
11. Kowalski, R., Sergot, M.: A logic-based calculus of events. In: Schmidt, J.W., Thanos, C. (eds.) Foundations of knowledge base management. Topics in Information Systems, pp. 23–55. Springer, Heidelberg (1989). https://doi.org/10.1007/978-3-642-83397-7_2
12. Krathwohl, D.R.: A revision of Bloom's taxonomy: an overview. Theory Pract. **41**(4), 212–218 (2002)
13. QM: Quality matters: Higher education rubric. Annapolis, MD (2014)
14. Schwartz, S.H.: The refined theory of basic values. In: Roccas, S., Sagiv, L. (eds.) Values and Behavior, pp. 51–72. Springer, Cham (2017). https://doi.org/10.1007/978-3-319-56352-7_3
15. Söbke, H., Londong, J.: Educational opportunities of a social network game. In: Göbel, S., Ma, M., Baalsrud Hauge, J., Oliveira, M.F., Wiemeyer, J., Wendel, V. (eds.) JCSG 2015. LNCS, vol. 9090, pp. 63–76. Springer, Cham (2015). https://doi.org/10.1007/978-3-319-19126-3_6
16. Tearse, B., Mawhorter, P., Mateas, M., Wardrip-Fruin, N.: SKALD: minstrel reconstructed. IEEE Trans. Comput. Intell. AI Games **6**(2), 156–165 (2014)
17. Teo, N.H.I., Joy, M.: Evaluation of an automatic question generation approach using ontologies. In: European Conference on e-Learning, p. 735. Academic Conferences International Limited (2016)
18. Turner, S.R.: Minstrel: a computer model of creativity and storytelling (1993)

19. Vahldick, A., Mendes, A.J., Marcelino, M.J., Roberto, P.: Computational thinking practiced with a casual serious game in higher education. Gamification-Based E-Learning Strategies for Computer Programming Education, p. 26 (2017)
20. Whitton, N.: Learning with Digital Games: A Practical Guide to Engaging Students in Higher Education. Routledge, New York (2009)
21. William, W.A.I., Tait, R.J.: Game having multiple game activities, US Patent 6,279,909 (2001)

A Tool for Interactive Visualization
of Narrative Acts

Nicolas Szilas, Monika Marano, and Sergio Estupiñán[(✉)]

TECFA, FPSE, University of Geneva, CH 1211 Geneva, Switzerland
{nicolas.szilas, sergio.estupinan}@unige.ch

Abstract. Authoring for Interactive Digital Storytelling (IDS) requires reasoning in formal paradigms which has proven to be a difficult task. One of such paradigms is the narrative act, understood as "actions on actions". We compiled a catalog of narrative acts and made it publicly available as an online interactive visualization tool. A preliminary evaluation deemed this 'living' tool as useful for inspiring authors of IDS systems.

Keywords: Narrative act · Visualization · Authoring

1 From New Writing Practices to New Authoring Tools

Research and innovation in the field of IDS tend to show that this emerging media calls for more abstract ways of writing [4]. Writing plain text is replaced by creating structures, parametrizing algorithms, creating logical conditions, handling variables. More particularly, some IDS systems involve writing abstract actions that are "actions on actions". For example, Chris Crawford's Storytron [1] uses verbs such as Promise, Advice in the core mechanics of the narrative engine. Authors need to create such verbs and then implement them into the system. Similarly, the narrative engine IDtension is based on a number of action types, such as Dissuade, Congratulate, Ask for assistance [3]. We call these complex actions types "narrative acts".

Beyond technical difficulties for creating proper data structures, IDS authors may not come easily with an idea of which narrative act to use, let alone which parameters. This situation encouraged us to create a catalog of narrative acts so that authors could either borrow from for story writing or to create novel narrative acts taking inspiration from the indexed ones. The catalog was built from multiple sources including IDS systems, narrative theories, agent languages, speech act theory. At the time of writing it contains 223 narrative acts, enriched with various descriptors.

This catalog is rather large and valuable as such, but narrative acts are not easily retrievable if data is only structured as a table or a spreadsheet. In addition, the catalog wants to be inspirational for authors, not only enabling them access but also engaging them in browsing and discovering narrative acts. Therefore, we propose to design and implement a visualization tool based on appropriate visualization techniques.

R. Rouse et al. (Eds.): ICIDS 2018, LNCS 11318, pp. 176–180, 2018.
https://doi.org/10.1007/978-3-030-04028-4_17

2   The Visualization Interface

Information visualization is an active domain in Human-Computer Interaction, studying how to visually represent information so that it is best understood by a user of a computer system. Methods of representation depend on the type of data represented, in our case the main structuring element of the catalog is a hierarchical organization of narrative acts. They are grouped into six main domains, each decomposed into classes containing narrative acts. For example, the narrative act *Promising* belongs to the *Decision* domain, contained in the *Commitment* class.

A number of methods to represent hierarchical information exist, including trees, tree maps, sunburst, circle packing. We chose the sunburst visualization for its readability [2]. Figure 1 represents the home view of the visualization tool: domains are represented by six sectors of different colors, classes and narrative acts represented in the same color range with a lower degree of saturation. The visualization is interactive at several levels. First, when a portion of the disk is rolled-over (a domain, class or narrative act), the corresponding description is detailed on the right panel.

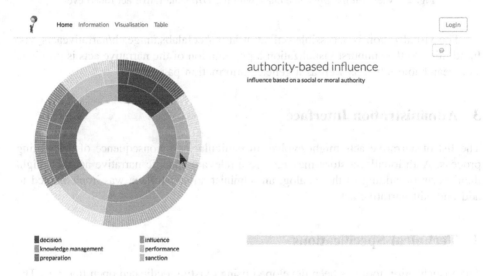

Fig. 1. Main page of the visualization with one class rolled-over.

In Fig. 1, the mouse is positioned at the specific class, "Authority-based influence" (see Fig. 2)

Second, when an element is clicked, an animation reconfigures the sunburst placing the selected element in the center and the sub-elements around it. In Fig. 2 the *Influence* domain was clicked, the visualization now focuses on the narrative acts under this domain. Similarly, all the elements can be rolled-over: the narrative act *Order* is rolled-over in Fig. 2 providing all corresponding information. It is then possible to zoom in on a class and then on a specific narrative act.

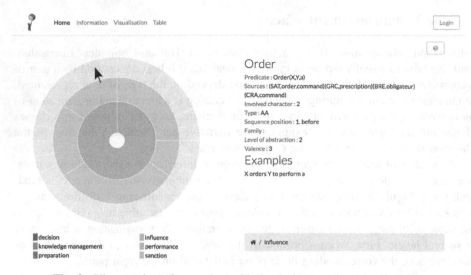

Fig. 2. View on the *Influence* class with the *Order* narrative act rolled-ever.

The visualization is accessible online at http://tecfalabs.unige.ch/narrativeacts_vis/ In addition to the sunburst visualization a presentation of the narrative acts is provided as a searchable table, as well as a general information page.

3   Administration Interface

The list of narrative acts might evolve, in particular as a consequence of the writing process. Additionally, a story may require a relevant specific narrative act that might then worth be adding to the catalog, an administration interface was implemented to add and edit narrative acts.

4   Technical Specifications

The visualization tool has been developed using existing dedicated open libraries. The general web functionalities were programmed using the *Bootstrap* framework. Narrative acts data and their hierarchical organization is stored using a *MySQL* database. Transactions between the website and the database rely on three additional frameworks, namely *Slim*, *Twig*, and *Eloquent*. Data is formatted in *JSON*. Finally, the sunburst visualization was implemented in *D3.js*, a JavaScript library for advanced data visualization.

5 Preliminary Evaluation

A qualitative usability study was carried out with four participants with knowledge in linguistics or IDS authoring. The goal of the evaluation was to assess if (1) the tool is usable; (2) users could find a certain narrative act they search for (and how); and (3) if the visualization was useful for free exploration of narrative acts.

Participants were given a series of five tasks, such as "could you retrieve the definition of the *Knowledge* domain?" in order to assess the tool usability. Two tasks targeted the utility of the visualization: first, authors were asked to tag an existing story with proper narrative acts, then they were asked to continue the story with the help of the visualization tool. Next, they were invited to add a narrative act in the database via the administration interface. At the end, participants filled out a questionnaire covering their perception of the visualization, difficulties in comprehension, perceived usefulness of the visualization tool, and suggestions for improvement.

The four participants managed to use the tool, despite some reported usability issues when navigating the catalog. They all managed to finish the tasks battery, were enthusiastic regarding the tool, and found it appropriate to complete the tasks they were asked to perform. The table view was perceived as more appropriate than the visualization when it comes to searching for a specific narrative act. Conversely, the visualization appeared more relevant when searching a narrative act according to its domain and class. The usability issues were considered to design the current version of the visualization tool.

6 Conclusion

Based on a catalog of 223 narrative acts, an interactive visualization tool was implemented and made available online to any IDS author involved in handling narrative acts. An interesting extension of this work could consist in connecting the catalog to an IDS engine so that actions related to a given narrative act could be executed (as text, animated images, 3D behaviors, etc.) in order for the author to get a better grasp of a certain narrative act.

Acknowledgements. This research would not have been possible without the financial support from the Swiss National Science Foundation under grant No. 159605 (Fine-grained Evaluation of the Interactive Narrative Experience, N. Szilas, principal investigator).

References

1. Crawford, C.: Chris Crawford on Interactive Storytelling, 2nd edn. New Riders, San Francisco (2012)
2. Stasko, J., Zhang, E.: Focus + context display and navigation techniques for enhancing radial, space-filling hierarchy visualizations. In: Mackinlay, J.D., Roth, S.F., Keim, D.A. (eds.) Proceedings of IEEE Symposium on Information Visualization 2000 – INFOVIS 2000, pp. 57–65. IEEE Computer Society (2000)

3. Szilas, N.: A computational model of an intelligent narrator for interactive narratives. Appl. Artif. Intell. **21**(8), 753–801 (2007)
4. Szilas, N., Richle, U., Dumas, J.E.: Structural writing, a design principle for interactive drama. In: Oyarzun, D., Peinado, F., Young, R.M., Elizalde, A., Méndez, G. (eds.) ICIDS 2012. LNCS, vol. 7648, pp. 72–83. Springer, Heidelberg (2012). https://doi.org/10.1007/978-3-642-34851-8_7

A Research on Storytelling of Interactive Documentary: Towards a New Storytelling Theory Model

Chanjun Mu$^{(\boxtimes)}$

City University of Hong Kong, Hong Kong, China
Chanjunmu2-c@my.cityu.edu.hk

Abstract. Interactive documentary is a new genre that narrates the real and enables audience interact with reality through interactive digital technologies. This genre has grown with the development of interactive digital technology and documentary practice. It indicates a need to understand the various new perceptions of interactive documentary storytelling not only for theoretical value but also for practical guide use. However, relatively, existed studies are not comprehensive in this field, even the definition and boundary of this category are still blurry. Interactive documentary, as a wide and independent genre, demands its own storytelling system and philosophy to break through the fog and remedy the gap. My doctoral research divides this wide genre into two streams: interactive documentary film (I-Doc Film) and interactive documentation, offering some important insights into storytelling of these two compositions and aiming to build new systematic theory. Currently, my research seeks to address questions in two preliminary directions: (1) The current storytelling features and system of western and eastern I-Doc film practice; (2) The storytelling of interactive documentation as curating method and digital heritage. Based on literature review in relevant field and case studies of representative artworks and projects, a series of interviews from related artists, scholars, research group and practitioners in the industry, as well as empirical study will be conducted to enrich this research.

Keywords: Interactive documentary · Interactive digital storytelling

1 A New Storytelling Theory Model of Interactive Documentary: Start from Two Streams

Compared with traditional documentary which has already built a generally accepted definition, interactive documentary, because the genre, characteristics, technology are still under rapid change, is facing difficulty to form a unified and effective definition. Through research, I find this problem could be solved by means of taxonomy. First, we need admit that interactive documentary contains two streams, interactive documentary film (I-Doc Film) and interactive documentation. They are two independent branches under the genre, having their own features but also some overlaps.

As I-Doc film stream, interactive documentary is "a new category based on interaction and film" [1], arising from the initial experimentation with interactive films,

© Springer Nature Switzerland AG 2018
R. Rouse et al. (Eds.): ICIDS 2018, LNCS 11318, pp. 181–184, 2018.
https://doi.org/10.1007/978-3-030-04028-4_18

where physical, rather than cognitive activity is used to navigate live within the existing material (video or film) [2]. As a new branch and variation of tradition documentary film, it shows the influence from interactive technologies and audience physical participation. In terms of the content, it shares many common features with traditional documentary film. The most important character is that this genre has a complete storytelling structure: start-rising-turning-(climax)-ending and contains a purpose to argue something or convey some opinion. This is also the biggest difference between I-Doc film and interactive documentation.

However, many scholars treat interactive documentary as a more expanded genre, which includes web-docs, transmedia documentaries, serious games, locative docs, interactive community media, docu-games, virtual reality non- fiction, ambient literature and live performance documentary. Some scholars think that any project that "starts with the intention to engage with the real, and that uses interactive digital technology to realize this intention could be treated as interactive documentation" [3]. And any documentary that "uses interactivity as a core part of its communication mechanism" is an interactive documentary [4]. Therefore, the genres that belong to interactive documentary but have no relationship with traditional documentary film background or features could be interpreted as interactive documentation. Interactive documentation stream has a much more broader definition and boundary. It also asks for Interactive technologies and audience physical participation. It has storytelling content but often without a complete storytelling structure, showing purpose of presenting instead of argue something. Based on such a broader definition, interactive documentation could contain much more specific categories, such as interactive installation artwork, serious game, navigating artwork or product, and VR artwork.

Currently, there are plenty of studies focusing on the storytelling of interactive documentary. Scholars discuss and argue concentrating on the following aspects: time and space of digital media storytelling (broken time and space, disappeared boundary), structure types (tree structure, net structure, layer structure, etc.), storytelling features (nonlinear, interactive, emergent, programmable, immersive and flexible), new identities of authors and readers and their relationship (The author acts as the architect while the reader as the editor or agent). However, the discuss is scattered like jigsaw, and the technologies and methods such as VR for interactive documentary creating are always under fast change and update. So, the storytelling research ought to follow the steps of the practice, basing on the clarification of taxonomy, to build an "always under upgrading" storytelling theory model which has clear boundary and structure for interactive documentary.

2   Research Work

At present, through a series of literature review and case studies, I have carried on a systematic research and have concluded the storytelling theory system of I-Doc film stream. At the same time, taking Chinese interactive documentary as the representative of eastern I-Doc film, I have studied the historical procedure in which Chinese documentary started to employ and be reshaped by emerging digital technologies, as well as the current practice situation and features of Chinese I-Doc film. I also did some field study and empirical study by participating in the 2016 Shanghai Youth Documentary Festival, helping conduct the VR special screening unit. This film festival invited the most famous Chinese documentary directors and scholars like Zhou Hao and du Haibin to be involved in the experience and discussion. During the forums, everyone expressed their views and shared their own experience or feelings. Through a series of discuss and interviews, I collected many valuable opinions and materials. Especially in VR interactive documentary field, this category is full of great potential to explore.

3 Results

So far, the main theory outcomes of my research work are summarized as following:

- As essential compositions, the media, author, audience and content constitute the interactive documentary storytelling system. Under the influence of digital era, each of them presents fresh narrative characteristics. The media is constantly innovating and providing upgrading creative means and platforms for interactive documentary. The identity of author and audience becomes more and more complex, even begins to overlap and shift with each other. Audiences own more rights and higher status in storytelling, while authors give up their domination in some extend. In this case, in fact, authors are required to show much stronger and more comprehensive ability while design the storytelling. Therefore, the interactive documentary authors start to play some new roles such as programmer, curator, new media artists, etc.
- The storytelling structure of interactive documentary deviates from the traditional linear storytelling structure and change to nonlinear structures such as tree structure, mesh structure, parallel structure and instant generated structure. It presents increasingly possibilities in interactive documentary storytelling.
- Interval of storytelling is a promising solution for the contradiction between immersive and interactive. As is known to all, experiencing a complete storytelling requires the audience to immerse in the story plot, but the interactive behavior will undoubtedly make the experience pause, thus breaking the immersive feeling. There are various immersive that people probably experience in many situation: sensor-muscle movement immersive; cognitive immersive; emotional immersive, spatial immersive and psychological immersive [5]. How to protect the immersive and fluency of storytelling from interactivity is still a big challenge [6]. After previous research, I notice that making use of the interval in storytelling to enhance immersive and interactivity at the same time is possible. We should try to grasp the key intervals as breakthrough to design proper interactivity and make further investigation.
- VR documentary is forming a new industry, and mobile VR cinema is a highlight. Even though the storytelling of VR documentary is still very simple and in an early stage, more and more practice is involved in this field. Many mainstream and independent documentary filmmakers admit this genre is full of potential. Besides, the emergence of mobile VR cinemas such as IQUT [7] indicates a significant trend in the future, which means a new era for VR content. It may help VR content become the industry of next generation instead of traditional cinema.

4　Status and Next Steps

Through the first phase of research, I have prepared basic theory and information of the practice situation and storytelling features of interactive documentary. I realize the interval in storytelling maybe a solution for contradiction between immersive and interactivity.

Next, I will do further work on summarizing and comparing the similarities and differences between western and eastern I-Doc film storytelling. And an empirical study about the interval of storytelling in interactive documentary is going to be conducted, by making a short I-Doc film which applied my research theory about interval. I will focus on designing the intervals in interactive storytelling, then combine with some user studies to test the effects. A systematic study of the interactive documentation stream will be launched as well. The National Palace Museum of Taipei is selected to be the first case study, which is one of the most typical "digital interactive" museum in the world. The digital interactive technologies are widely used as curating methods and digital heritage in the exhibitions. I will start a field study and conduct some interviews in National Palace Museum of Taipei as my first step of investigation about interactive documentation stream.

References

1. Almeida, A., Alvelos, H.: An interactive documentary manifesto. In: Aylett, R., Lim, M.Y., Louchart, S., Petta, P., Riedl, M. (eds.) ICIDS 2010. LNCS, vol. 6432, pp. 123–128. Springer, Heidelberg (2010). https://doi.org/10.1007/978-3-642-16638-9_16
2. Castells, AG.: The Interactive Documentary. Definition Proposal and Basic Features of the New Emerging Genre. In: Mcluhan Galaxy Conference, Conference Proceedings, pp. 367–378 (2011)
3. Gaudenzi, S.: What is an i-doc? I-Docs Homepage. http://i-docs.org/about-interactive-documentary-idocs/. Accessed 25 July 2018
4. Galloway, D., McAlpine, K.B., Harris, P.: From Michael Moore to JFK reloaded: towards a working model of interactive documentary. J. Media Pract. **8**, 325–329 (2007)
5. Bjork, S., Holopainen, J.: Patterns in Game Design, p. 423. Charles River Media, Boston (2004)
6. Castells, AG.: Mapping Trends in interactive non-fiction through the lenses of interactive documentary. In: Interactive Storytelling: 7th International Conference on Interactive Digital Storytelling, ICIDS 2014, pp. 160–161(2014)
7. Liang L.: No Longer Has to Go to the Cinema, Iqiyi IQUT, To Start a New Era of Film Watching, Sohu News, http://www.sohu.com/a/232657426_116776. Accessed 25 July 2018

Agency and Authorship in Ludic Narrative Environments

Samantha Schäfer(✉)

Winchester School of Art, University of Southampton, Southampton, England
s.schafer@soton.ac.uk

Abstract. The evolution of new media forms in the context of contemporary 'convergence culture' [7] renders the entertainment industry increasingly interactive and participatory, encouraging 'gamelike' narrative forms that rely on the audience's participation and agency [11, p. 3]. This doctoral research investigates choice-making in ludic environments – here, video games and transmedia storytelling – as spatial practice, in which the virtual and physical structures of the text allow the player/participant's navigation, orientation, and (physical and mental) self-positioning within a choice-based system. Choice-making practices will be addressed through textual analysis and ethnographic research.

Keywords: Game space · Agency · Game narratives · Navigation Transmedia storytelling

1 Introduction

Approaching convergence culture from a ludological perspective, my doctoral research focuses on the player/participant's narrative choice-making practices in video games and transmedia storytelling as theorised by Jenkins [7]. With transmedia storytelling being frequently likened to core concepts in video games [5,11], this research aims at gaining insights into the ways in which we experience and make choices in interactive narratives that are both contained within and traverse the boundaries of a single medium.

My research conceptualises video games and transmedia storytelling as playful, i.e. *ludic environments*, and investigates the player/participant's narrative engagement in the context of agency and interactivity as spatial practices. Agency itself is a commonly researched phenomenon in game studies and the computer is often regarded to have spatial properties [10]. However, the relationship between choice-making in terms of narrative development and spatial practices is not investigated as clearly, which defines the gap in which this research is situated. Focusing first on choice-making on the level of the video game through textual analysis and ethnographic research, this engagement will then be applied to a wider interactive context, wherein interactivity does not emerge from technical aspects only, but from the wider organisation of a convergent, participatory project in transmedia storytelling.

© Springer Nature Switzerland AG 2018
R. Rouse et al. (Eds.): ICIDS 2018, LNCS 11318, pp. 185–189, 2018.
https://doi.org/10.1007/978-3-030-04028-4_19

2   Research Design

2.1   Rationale and Research Question

This doctoral research is concerned with the spatial practices that drive agency, i.e. the player's ability and desire to make choices from a number of pre-designed choices that are embedded in the technical structures of the text [13]. I argue that spatial navigation is closely related to agency and decision-making in video games, and indeed video games often focus on the exploration of a storyworld [6,7,9,12]. In the context of ludic environments, I distinguish between two modes of engagement, the *topographical* and *choice space*. The former defines the phys- ical elements of the game world, whereas the latter defines the navigational properties of the game world as informed by the player's narrative decisions, encompassing technical and perceived agency as the players situate themselves within the choice structures available to them in the computer game. On the level of the video game, I propose to investigate choice-making on the basis of the overall game design, i.e. narrative structures and techniques, and the player's choices both in design and actual engagement. These questions will then be extrapolated to transmedia storytelling as a more open ludic environment by investigating how the different media platforms contribute to the construction of the narrative within a transmedia project and what kinds of navigational choices users make in their consumption of the project, including the ways in which they can exert agency and authorship within the project.

Based on this rationale, this research is defined by one main research question: *How are navigational practices used to drive the player's/participant's agency and authorship in the construction of narratives in ludic environments?* Firstly, and in its essence, this question addresses the concept of agency and its often controversial relationship to narrative. Secondly, and more specifically, it is con- cerned with the virtual and physical structures that allow the navigation, orien- tation and (physical and mental) self-positioning of the player/participant within a choice-based system.

2.2   Methodology

The methodological approach consists of the combination of textual analysis and ethnographic research, and is driven by two sub-questions:

- What is the role of player agency within the construction of video game narrative?
- How do participants navigate complex narratives across different media platforms?

The first question addresses the narrative structures and techniques of the respective texts, the degree of agency that is given to the user, and the ways in which players can and do navigate the narrative on a game level. The second question extrapolates the results from the game analysis to the relationships between the different media platforms in a transmedia setting, addressing the ways in which they contribute to the construction of the narrative and the ways in which audiences exert agency within the project.

The qualitative method of *textual analysis* will be used to investigate the narrative design of video game and transmedia storytelling project, and will therefore provide the starting foundation in answering both sub-questions. On the level of the video game, textual analysis revolves primarily around the narrative and interactive elements, including interface studies and interaction maps as suggested by Consalvo and Dutton [2]. On the level of the transmedia franchise, textual analysis focuses on the way the narrative is developed across the different media platforms, particularly focusing on migratory cues and negative capability as described by Long [8].

Building on the results of the textual analysis, ethnographic research can give more definitive insights into the choice-making practices of the player-participant through participant observation in the context of 'observer as participant' [1, p. 164] (sub-question 1) and focus groups (sub-question 2). During the participant observation, participants will play a section of a video game selected on the basis of textual analysis, which would ideally be narrative-heavy and offer players different levels of engagement. The play session will then be followed by a semi-structured interview in which certain player choices can be investigated more closely. In the play session, the screen and voices (of myself and the participant) will be recorded, whereas the interview will only record audio; this approach is taken to address the elusiveness of gameplay and the difficulty of theorising one's often intuitive choices after gameplay has ended, as noted by Giddings and Kennedy [4]. In the focus groups, participants will be able to investigate and discuss their everyday engagement with a transmedia franchise and the consumption choices that they make, possibly through methods such as visually mapping out the engagement. This approach would also give insights into whether different types of audiences have different approaches to a transmedia project, which can be connected to the notion of 'tiering' [3].

2.3   Participants

The participants for the study will be recruited locally. Selection aspects may include the level of engagement with the franchise, previous knowledge of the video game, gaming experience (such as how much time participants typically spend playing video games), and media preferences. Participants who qualify for the study will be divided into two groups: those who typically play the video games of their preferred franchises, and those who prefer to focus on the other media in the franchise. The participants will take part in the gaming and interview session individually, and will be brought together for the focus group, either in their separate groups or as one bigger group depending on the initial sample size.

2.4   Case Studies

At the time of writing, the selection of video game case studies has not yet been finalised. As the game analysis revolves around the player's choice-making practices, potential case studies may include *The Walking Dead* and *The Wolf Among Us* by Telltale Games, *Life is Strange* by Square Enix, or *Heavy Rain* and *Detroit: Become Human* by Quantic Dream. A pilot study will provide the opportunity to test a number of video games in the context of choice-making, as well as to test and refine the ethnographic aspect of the methodology. On the level of the transmedia franchise, two case studies have currently been chosen: *Assassin's Creed* (2007-present) and *The Walking Dead* (2003-present). In both franchises, the individual media platforms, such as video game, television series, or novels, occupy distinct spaces within the overall narrative and expand the storyworld with information that is not necessarily given in all platforms. In accessing or rejecting different texts in those franchises, then, audiences would be able to curate their own narrative experience.

3   Status of the Research Work

3.1   Framework and Methodology

My doctoral research has so far focused on establishing a theoretical framework and a preliminary methodology; as of yet no analysis has been undertaken. The focal point during this time was to situate the project within the field of game studies and transmedia storytelling, recognising the navigational properties of choice-making as fundamental link between these two areas. Specifically, I developed the idea of 'choice space' and situated this within a theoretical framework of agency and spatiality. In the future, the idea of choice space needs to be further incorporated within ludology and spatial theories.

3.2   Future Work

The next step in my doctoral research is to further refine the notion of choice space and to extend the current theoretical framework. Ethical approval has been obtained in order to conduct a pilot study, in which I will test different aspects of the methodology to further develop the research design. The pilot study will involve participant observation of gameplay for some of the proposed case studies to refine the proposed methodological approach and to collect preliminary data on choice-making processes in narrative agency across different types of games. Following the results of the pilot study, the research design will be finalised and ethical approval will be sought for the commencement of the full ethnographic study.

References

1. Brennen, B.S.: Qualitative Research Methods for Media Studies. Routledge, New York (2013)
2. Consalvo, M., Dutton, N.: Game analysis: developing a methodological toolkit for the qualitative study of games. Game Stud. **6**(1) (2006). http://www.gamestudies. org/0601/articles/consalvo_dutton
3. Dena, C.: Transmedia practice: theorising the practice of expressing a fictional world across distinct media and environments. Ph.D. thesis, University of Sydney (2009). http://www.christydena.com/phd/
4. Giddings, S., Kennedy, H.W.: Little Jesuses and *@#? -off robots: on cybernetics, aesthetics and not being very good at Lego star wars. In: Swalwell, M., Wilson, J. (eds.) The Pleasures of Computer Gaming: Essays on Cultural History, Theory and Aesthetic, pp. 13–32. McFarland (2008)
5. Harvey, C.B.: Fantastic Transmedia: Narrative. Play and Memory across Science Fiction and Fantasy Storyworlds. Palgrave Macmillan, London (2015)
6. Jenkins, H.: Game design as narrative architecture. In: Wardrip-Fruin, N., Harrington, P. (eds.) First Person: New Media as Story, Performance, and Game. MIT Press, Cambridge (2004)
7. Jenkins, H.: Convergence Culture, When Old and New Media Collide. New York University Press, New York (2006)
8. Long, G.: Transmedia storytelling: business, aesthetics and production at the Jim Henson company. Master's thesis, Massachusetts Institute of Technology (2007)
9. Murray, J.: Hamlet on the Holodeck: The Future of Narrative in Cyberspace. The MIT Press, Cambridge (1997)
10. Murray, J.: From game story to cyberdrama. In: Wardrip-Fruin, N., Harrigan, P. (eds.) First Person: New Media as Story, Performance, and Game, pp. 2–11. MIT Press, Cambridge (2004)
11. Rose, F.: The Art of Immersion. Norton & Co., New York (2011)
12. Stockburger, A.: Playing the third place: spatial modalities in contemporary game environments. Int. J. Perf. Arts Digit. Media **3**(2–3), 223–236 (2007)
13. Wardrip-Fruin, N., Mateas, M., Dow, S., Sali, S.: Agency Reconsidered. In: DiGRA 2009 - Proceedings of the 2009 DiGRA International Conference: Breaking New Ground: Innovation in Games, Play, Practice and Theory. Brunel University (2009). http://www.digra.org/wp-content/uploads/digital-library/09287.41281.pdf

Practices in Games

Playing with Vision: Sight and Seeing as Narrative and Game Mechanics in Survival Horror

Mads Haahr[✉][iD]

Trinity College, University of Dublin, Dublin, Ireland
mads.haahr@tcd.ie
https://www.scss.tcd.ie/Mads.Haahr/

Abstract. A considerable number of survival horror titles use the modification of sight and seeing, in particular the disruption and enhancement of the same, as important elements in relation to story and game mechanics. Examples range from simple obscuration of the gameworld by mist and darkness to highly sophisticated approaches that direct break the fourth wall with visual effects that belong not to the game world but to the player's reality. Grouping the approaches under five headings—obscuration, distortion, mediation, perspectivity and disruption—this paper presents a comparative analysis of ten survival horror titles with a view to understanding how sight and seeing are used as story elements and narrative mechanics across the genre.

Keywords: Survival horror · Narrative mechanics
Comparative readings

1 Introduction

The survival horror video game genre is broad, consisting of games that use violence and shock as the primary means to scare players (e.g., recent games in the *Resident Evil* series) to games that use a more psychological approach to horror (e.g., games in the *Silent Hill* series). While all survival horror games tend to incorporate elements from both ends of this spectrum, titles generally situate themselves quite clearly at one end or the other in terms of their main focus. Story always plays an important part in survival horror titles. For example, Kirkland observes that "[s]urvival horror has an intrinsic relationship with story and storytelling media" [5, p. 62], a relationship that has been explored also by researchers like Perron [10,13] and Krzywinska [6].

Perhaps the most important genre convention for psychological horror is the underpowered (often defenseless) protagonist, who is ill equipped to deal with the horrors with which they are confronted. In addition to obvious gameplay elements, such as the presence/absence of weapons, ammunition and health packs,

© Springer Nature Switzerland AG 2018
R. Rouse et al. (Eds.): ICIDS 2018, LNCS 11318, pp. 193–205, 2018.
https://doi.org/10.1007/978-3-030-04028-4_20

many titles also use the modification of sight and seeing, for example the disruption and enhancement of the same, as crucial elements in relation to story and mechanics.

This paper presents a comparative analysis of a range of ten survival horror titles with a view to understanding how sight and seeing are used as story elements and game mechanics across the genre, in particular in relation to the emotional effect that the games are intended to have on their players. Particular attention is given to the way the games use sight and seeing to create feelings of dread and suspense, but other elements of horror are treated as well. There is a considerable body of work on the use of emotion in horror, and in particular in the context of games, Perron's work [12,13] on the *Silent Hill* series is highly significant.

I have found five distinct ways in which the games engage with sight and seeing and will discuss them in sequence, drawing examples from the ten titles. Finally, I will discuss broader narrative themes before concluding the paper.

2   Obscuration

In this paper, I use the term "obscuration" to mean "to cover something so that it cannot be seen" [1].

As a game design feature, obscuration (and consequently, revelation) is used in many survival horror games, and examples of its use range from very simple to highly complex. At the former end of the spectrum is a straightforward obscuration of the gameworld, such as the mist shrouding the town in *Silent Hill 2* (2001) or the darkness obscuring the village in *Siren* (2003), both shown in Fig. 1.

Light and darkness have of course been subject to considerable related work. In the context of *Resident Evil 4* (2005), Niedenthal writes that "the distribution of light and dark illumination ... displays a logic that enhances player vulnerability through obscurity." [8, p. 176]. On the specific topic of fog, Perron has analysed its use in the *Silent Hill* series [13], including its "unending" appearance. However, for the purposes of this paper, we are mainly interested in the fog's obscuratative power.

Fig. 1. Obscuration: the fog in *Silent Hill 2* and the darkness in *Siren*.

Taking away the visual abilities of the player as well as the player character is in good accord with the genre convention of the underpowered protagonist. The absence of proper vision emphasises the vulnerability of the player character to unseen threats, puts the player on edge and taps into primordial fears: We are not sure what lurks in the dark (or in the fog), but it is sure not to be pleasant.

In games that use obscuration, the way in which light is created is often highly significant. In *Silent Hill 2*, the protagonist James finds the only light source in the game (see Fig. 7) attached to a dress that belonged to his deceased wife Mary. Appropriating the light, James wears it on his heart for the rest of the game (see Fig. 7). The narrative function of the light is clear: James' personal mystery and his descent into the dark underworld of Silent Hill is associated with his wife; she (or, uncovering the truth about her) is at the same time the object of his quest, the force that propels him and the power that allows him to progress. The light source of course also serves a gameplay function, allowing James to shed light on an, albeit small, section of Silent Hill universe.

A newer survival horror title, *Among the Sleep* (2014) features perhaps the most underpowered protagonist of all: a two-year old child who goes in search of mommy who has disappeared. The house is dark and scary, but the toddler carries a teddy bear that not only serves as a companion and guide, but who can also be hugged tight to generate a modicum of light. Although Teddy as a character serves an important narrative purpose in *Among the Sleep*, his function as a light source is primarily in relation to gameplay, rather than story. Nevertheless, the game mechanical coupling of the creation of light to the hugging of the companion has the wonderful effect of getting the player to steer the toddler around the house, crawling on all fours and clutching the treasured bear throughout the game. The game mechanic in this fashion supports the role-play aspect of the game by encouraging the player to behave in character.

A third title, *Amnesia: The Dark Descent* (2010), bases a more complex gameplay around the absence, presence and creation of light. The game uses a sanity mechanic where the protagonist Daniel, whose aim it is to escape from Catle Brennenburg, loses sanity from (amongst other things) being in the dark. Daniel can use tinderboxes found throughout the castle to light candles, which are also found throughout the castle. The light created in this fashion helps Daniel explore the game world, and staying in the light for periods of time also helps him recover sanity, but in addition it makes Daniel more visible to the deadly monsters that roam the castle. Furthermore, and unlike the light sources found in *Silent Hill 2* and *Among the Sleep*, the number of tinderboxes is limited, requiring Daniel to use them economically.

Perception (2017) bases almost its entire gameplay around obscuration and revelation. In this title, the player takes on the role of Cassie, a blind woman who explores Echo Bluff, a haunted mansion in Gloucester, Massachusetts. During the game, Cassie encounters ghosts of past inhabitants of the mansion as well as a deadly opponent called The Presence. Being blind, Cassie navigates Echo Bluff by echolocation, which the game simulates through monochromatic visuals, outlining rooms and their features instantly but briefly in response to sounds coming either from the environment (e.g., hissing radiators, as well as radios and television sets that Cassie can turn on or off) or directly from Cassie herself (i.e., her footsteps or the tapping of her cane). Similarly to the light sources in *Amnesia: The Dark Descent*, Cassie's cane causes noise that attracts The Presence and therefore has to be used carefully. The gameplay encourages the player to tap economically and to memorize the layout of the gameworld to the greatest extent possible—essentially to construct a mental map of the house, very much like a blind person might develop highly accurate spatial memory of a physical environment.

Game designers like Adams talk about a game's "internal economy" [3], and it is of course common that a game action that has benefit to the player comes at a cost, e.g., purchasing upgrades for weapons. In survival horror, the double-edged nature of the light as a useful—even necessary—game object with dangerous side effects is a variation of this, and it constitutes a particular convention for the survival horror genre. In addition to *Amnesia: The Dark Descent* and *Perception*, the convention is found also in *Silent Hill 2* as well as *Among the Sleep* where the light enables sight but it also attracts monsters. In survival horror, "double-edging" (if that is a word) is common for other types of game objects too; for example, slightly more powerful weapons, such as guns, tend to be noisy and hence attract further monsters. I will give more examples related to sight and seeing later on, too.

3   Distortion

In this analysis, I use the term "distortion" to describe "a change in the way that something looks, sounds or behaves so that it becomes strange or difficult to recognize" [1].

I have found two games that use visual distortion to great effect. In *Haunting Ground* (2005), the protagonist is a young woman Fiona whose aim it is to escape from a castle. Fiona's struggle is not against Lovecraftian monsters or demons from her past, but against a patriarchal control over her body—as an object for food, sexual gratification and impregnation. In this way, *Haunting Ground* boasts a very different enemy from most survival horror titles.

Haunting Ground has a game mechanic in which Fiona's distress level can increase, either as the result of shock or of physical injury. If her distress level gets too high, Fiona flicks into full-blown panic, and this is a serious affair. It causes serious visual distortion (see Fig. 2), as well as a heavy layer of audio drones, panting and screaming, which is distracting for the player. The player also loses partial control of Fiona; when panicking she can only run at full speed, but she does not obey all the player's directional commands and sometimes runs in the opposite direction.

Overall, full-blown panic is a pretty detrimental affair, leaving the player struggling for control, and losing the game a lot of the time. While the loss of control over Fiona's body that the player experiences resonates well with the game's overall theme of Fiona's own struggle against patriarchal control of her

Fig. 2. Distortion: visual distortion in *Haunting Ground* and *Amnesia: The Dark Descent.*

body, the visual distortion serves no real narrative function—it is mainly an aesthetic effect to disorient the player.

Another game that uses visual distortion is *Call of Cthulhu: Dark Corners of the Earth* (2005), a game based on H.P. Lovecraft's writings, particularly his 1936 story "The Shadow over Innsmouth." The protagonist in *Dark Corners of the Earth* is Jack Walters, a private detective who during an investigation into a mysterious cult is confronted with horrific sights as well cosmic horrors that make him lose sanity if he looks at them. This creates an incentive for the player to direct Jack's gaze away from the horrors, but since it is necessary to look at the horrors to progress in the game, the result is a well thought out tension between the need to look at the horrors and the penalty for doing so. This is another example of double-edging; it is useful (even required) to look at the horrors, but it increases the risks.

Dark Corners of the Earth is faithful to genre conventions for games based on Lovecraft's universe in that it features a "sanity" game mechanic, not unlike the one in *Amnesia: The Dark Descent* or the "panic mechanic" found in *Haunting Ground.* When Jack loses too much sanity, the game distorts his vision as well as his hearing and also adds sounds of Jack muttering to himself. Like *Haunting Ground*, it changes the sensitivity of the controls, making it difficult for the player to steer the protagonist.

In terms of sensory fidelity, the distortion used in *Dark Corners of the Earth* is considerably more representational than *Haunting Ground.* It feels almost too realistic, creating an experience that is immersive to the degree of being really uncomfortable. Where the distortion used in *Haunting Ground* creates anxiety and perhaps a modicum of panic in the player, the effect easily leads to frustration and resignation. *Dark Corners of the Earth* uses a first-person perspective, so the realistic distortion of Jack's vision directly affects the player's vision, and the consequent immersion is deeply unpleasant. Instead of the frustration and resignation that arises from *Haunting Ground*, the effects in *Dark Corners of the Earth* tend to result in dizziness and nausea. Choose your poison.

Amnesia: The Dark Descent, as we discussed before, also uses visual effects to denote Daniel's loss of sanity, causing visual and auditory hallucinations. The visual hallucinations are distortions in Daniel's perception of the game world that cause his vision to blur and bulge in a fashion that is dizzying and unpleasant to the player. (See Fig. 2.) The effect is similar to that used in *Dark Corners of the Earth*, so I will not go into further detail here.

It should be noted that other games use distortion in a more secondary capacity, such as the sightjacking feature of *Siren* that we will discuss shortly, but they are primarily aesthetic devices rather than highly integral to the story or gameplay, so I will not discuss them further here.

4 Mediation

In this paper, I use the word "mediation" to mean "intervention in a process or relationship; intercession" [2]. We consider this separate from obscuration/revelation in that mediation involves a direct intervention in the process of seeing, typically a distinct layer between the seer and the observed. We could consider "distortion" a type of mediation, but to classify something as "mediation" we expect a more sophisticated type of intervention, something that can also reveal rather than merely obscure.

There are some titles in which a vision-enhancing mediative object is used either to overcome darkness and reveal what is hidden. Examples include the camera obscura in *Fatal Frame 2* (2003) and the nightvision video camera in *Outlast* (2013). Whether magical or technological, these mediative objects connect the "ordinary" game world with a hidden supernatural (and invariably frightening) game world that would otherwise not be visible to the characters. Other researchers have written on the topic of mediation and remediation, in particular Kirkland [4] and Nitsche [9], the latter who has explored the role of the camera obscura from the *Fatal Frame* games very deeply.

The camera obscura in *Fatal Frame 2* is a wonderfully complex object, and its importance in the story is matched by its role in the gameplay. First, the camera works as a scanner, allowing the main protagonist Mio, accompanied by her sister Mayu, to examine her surroundings for paranormal phenomena to see and photograph things that she would not normally be able to see. Importantly, the camera also functions as a weapon. By photographing a hostile ghost, Mio inflicts damage on it, eventually causing it to recede into the nothingness from whence it came. The idea of photographing ghosts to exorcise them is of course evocative of the old myth that having your photo taken will capture your soul. (See Fig. 3.)

A powerful gameplay tension exists in the use of the camera, since looking through the viewfinder decreases Mio's field of view significantly and makes moving around a much slower affair. Hence, when Mio uses her only mode of attack, she becomes very vulnerable. A further complication is that looking through the lens of the camera obscura sometimes attracts the ghosts' attention and draws them towards Mio. In this way, the camera allows Mio to look deeper

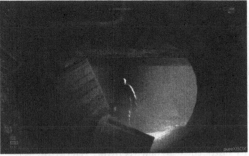

Fig. 3. Mediation: *Fatal Frame 2* and *Outlast.*

into the fabric of the world, but it narrows her field of view and it seems the things that lurk in the depths indeed look back. True to genre convention, the double-edged nature of the camera is clear: its power comes with a risk.

The camera obscura's mediative powers are also used at the gameplay level, for example in the context of the gatekeeper ghosts, or door spirits, that block certain doors. To exorcise a gatekeeper ghost, Mio must first photograph it. The photo will show a different location to that photographed, which Mio must then find and photograph separately. After this, she can return to the gatekeeper for another photo, which will now finally exorcise the ghost and open the door. In one particular puzzle, the secondary location is a room with a small hole in the wall through which Mio must photograph a ghost in an adjacent room. The many layers highlight how much fun the game has with sight and seeing and with mediation. At the semiotic level, what is the signifier and the signified? *Fatal Frame 2* mixes them up deliberately. Everything points to something else.

As mentioned, the 2013 title *Outlast* also features a camera, although a less complex one than that found in *Fatal Frame 2*. The camera in *Outlast* is a video camera with night vision, which allows the main character Miles Upshur to navigate the dark Mount Massive Asylum psychiatric hospital. (See Fig. 3.) The night vision camera is a purely technological object with no supernatural powers, and the batteries required to drive it become an important game resource which must the scavenged throughout the hospital. Unlike *Fatal Frame 2*, the video camera's role as a mediative object is also purely defensive—filming the enemies does not affect them—but recording the enemies serves a narrative function in that it may unlock additional story content about them.

5   Perspectivity

The term "perspectivity" can mean "The quality or condition of being limited by or confined to a particular mental perspective or point of view" [2]. In this paper, I use it to denote this type of perspective restriction, but I also use it a little more broadly, to denote a game's engagement with (predominantly visual) perspective as a narrative and game mechanical technique. In a broader context,

Perron has written a thorough analysis of the use of perspective in horror games, in particular its artful use in the *Silent Hill* series [13].

Strange camera angles are a genre convention in survival horror. The camera through which the player gazes on the scene is sometimes (but not all the time) placed in strange locations, and the focal length of the virtual lens is sometimes (but not all the time) either too wide or too narrow in comparison to human eyes. The effect on the player is they feel as if someone is watching the player character and perhaps this someone's eyes are not quite human. The result is a slight unsettlement, the subtle awareness that there are monsters in the world, and that they are watching. (See Fig. 4.)

Fig. 4. Perspectivity: strange points of view in *Silent Hill 2*.

At the same time, but secondarily, the player may also feel like a voyeur, taking on a certain aspect of this imagined monster by virtue of adopting its vision. *Silent Hill 2* is exemplary in that it uses many perspectives that seem inhuman, either because they are too high too low, too wide or even directly (and not unlike James' wife in the story) from beyond the grave (see Fig. 4).

A few titles take highly sophisticated approaches to the use of perspective. *Siren* (2003) features "sightjacking," a psychic power possessed by each of the thirteen characters in the game, even the non-playable ones and monsters, like the undead shibito. It works like a radio scanner, allowing the sightjacker to "tune in" to other characters in the area, to pick up their sensory input, to see what they see, hear what they hear. The sightjacking ability is purely passive (meaning the sightjacker cannot control the sightjacked) and is in fact undetectable to the sightjacked. In the sightjacking view, the protagonists (some of which are player-controlled) are marked with crosshairs, as shown in Fig. 5.

Siren is also a highly repetitive game, and it forces the player to engage with the same material again and again. The player must revisit earlier stages, go through the same areas, encounter the same monsters repeatedly. The revisiting happens with the same characters (essentially replaying a level to find things that were missed on the first playthrough) as well as with different characters (seeing slightly different things, perhaps left behind by an earlier character). Repetition and circular structures are not uncommon in survival horror, as has been documented by Perron [11], but *Siren* creates an entire game experience around it.

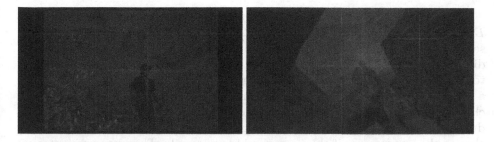

Fig. 5. Perspectivity: sightjacking in *Siren*. The screenshots show opponent views of the protagonists.

The repetition and use of changing perspectives in *Siren* result in a gameplay that is primarily about getting to know the gameworld, by looking at all its areas from different perspectives again and again, seeing them as one player-controlled character, then as another, then as the first again, then seeing them as an undead shibito. What does the monster see? Does it see me? Does it see my companion? How does seeing work?

Call of Cthulhu: Dark Corners of the Earth also uses changing perspective but in a different way and to a different effect. Krzywinska has observed that this game changes the player's point of view to see the world from the monsters' perspective and this reminds the player that they are being hunted, and it is by something that is "not in any way human" [7, p. 273]. Krzywinska also observes that in that game, the perspective changing technique is "thematically and narratively motivated ... rather than directly ludic" [7, p. 273]. This clearly differentiates *Call of Cthulhu: Dark Corners of the Earth* from *Siren* in which perspectivity was used primarily for gameplay purposes. While the changing perspective in *Siren* also supports the narrative, its primary function is ludic.

6 Disruption

In this paper, I use the term "disruption" to mean "a problem or action that interrupts something and prevents it from continuing" [2]. I consider disruption distinct from obscuration in that it has an interruptive character, i.e., it creates a temporary break in a process of seeing, a break that when it ends results in the resumption of the interrupted process. Furthermore, for an effect to qualify as a disruption, it must be not be directly activated by the player. For this reason, the sightjacking feature in *Siren* does not qualify as a disruption.

I have not found many games that use disruption, and from a game design perspective, it is a risky effect to use, because it will either remove control or perception from the player or change one or both of them dramatically. From a game design point of view, this is fraught with problems, because the disruption may easily become too disorienting, and therefore annoying and frustrating, to the player.

The genre's main example of disruption in relation to sight and seeing is *Eternal Darkness: Sanity's Requiem* (2002). This title is famous for its pioneering sanity effects, which are both visual and auditory, and which come in many different varieties. In *Eternal Darkness: Sanity's Requiem*, the player steers a total of twelve different characters through a Lovecraftian conspiracy that spans a total of two millenia. The game features plenty of monsters, and if a player character is seen by a monster, he or she loses sanity. If the character's sanity drops too low, the game may disrupt the play experience with hallucinations that change the appearance of the game world temporarily. The player may steer a character into a room and suddenly see the head of the character chopped off and the character stagger around like a headless chicken. The walls may start to bleed, or the room may be upside down and the character walking on the ceiling. Regardless of the effect, after a few moments, a white flash restores the view of the gameworld to its normal appearance, accompanied by the sound of the character in agony lamenting, "This can't be happening." (See Fig. 6.)

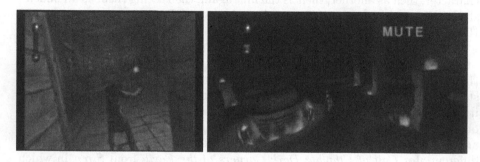

Fig. 6. Disruption: sanity effects in *Eternal Darkness: Sanity's Requiem*. (Color figure online)

The disruptions are surprising and amusing, and despite the fact that they temporarily prevent the gameplay from continuing, they remain surprising and amusing throughout the game. The wide range of possible effects, and the humorous relief that results when the player recognizes them for what they are, mean that the visual disruptions do not become repetitive or annoying, even after a while.

While some of the sanity effects change the appearance of the game world, *Eternal Darkness: Sanity's Requiem* is particularly famous for the sanity effects that attempt to affect the real world, i.e., effects that try to break through the fourth wall. Examples include the effect of making a fly appear to crawl across the player's television screen or of simulating the effect of the television set being set to mute or game console being unplugged, resulting in a blank blue screen and a confused player. (See Fig. 6.) In this fashion, *Eternal Darkness: Sanity's Requiem* attempts not only to disrupt the playable characters' sense of sight, but also the player's.

7   Narrative Aspects

In this section, we will delve deeper into the ways in which the games use sight and seeing not merely relevant for the interaction but also as narrative elements in a broader context. We have already discussed how the creation of light in *Silent Hill 2* resonates with the game's main theme, but it is worth nothing also that the game's main villain, Pyramid Head, is blind. (See Fig. 7.) The protagonist and antagonist are placed in opposition by their design. James sees, albeit with difficulty, but Pyramid Head represents the refusal to see, his eyes hidden behind a thick layer of metal. This is James' central struggle in the story: the tension between confronting the truth about the past or refusing to.

Fig. 7. Sight, seeing and blindness in *Silent Hill 2*.

In *Perception*, the apparitions of the house's former inhabitants are also of interest. These phantoms are not dangerous but are simple replays of past events, i.e., their function is narrative, rather than ludic. They appear as luminescent figures through which Cassie can see the interior of the house clearly. In this way, they offer a different type of revelation than the game's echolocation mechanic, one that is tied to the ghosts themselves, rather than to sound or player actions. Their visual representation links the ghosts to seeing in terms of narrative, underlining that the game (like so many other survival horror titles) is about revealing the past. Pay attention to the ghosts, and you will see clearly.

In *Eternal Darkness: Sanity's Requiem*, the game's story consistently draws attention to vision and casts it as being unreliable. An 814 AD bishop in France bleeds from the eyes, while a wrongfully imprisoned 1760 AD doctor locked up in an asylum curses his captors, "may the rats eat your eyes!" (See Fig. 8.) The game even deliberately contradicts itself to mark sight as unreliable, for example in the opening scene where the police detective who welcomes the main protagonist Alexandra Roivas to the mansion where her grandfather has been murdered says "there is not much to see" but immediately then proceeds to describe the scene as "not a pretty sight." The unreliability of vision pervades the game's story in this regard, preparing the player for disruption, constantly saying "don't believe your eyes" and "don't trust what you see."

Fig. 8. Emphasis on sight and seeing in *Eternal Darkness: Sanity's Requiem* and *Fatal Frame 2*.

Fatal Frame 2 also references sight and seeing and contrasts blindness with vision. In one ending (see Fig. 8), the final cut scene shows the protagonist Mio having lost her sight. This ending results if the player chooses to run away rather than complete the game to its final stage, essentially if she refuses to see the game to its end. Similarly to *Silent Hill 2* and *Perception*, the story in *Fatal Frame 2* emphasises the importance of *seeing* what it was that happened in the past and contrasts vision with blindness to this effect.

8   Summary

In this paper, we have explored how a total of ten titles engage with sight and seeing and how they link vision to narrative and game mechanics in different ways. Perhaps, and in spite of its age, *Eternal Darkness: Sanity's Requiem* seems to be the game that does both of these things, most consistently and ambitiously.

While all games that engage with sight and seeing ultimately aim to affect the player's vision, nearly all of them do it by affecting the player character's vision. This of course makes sense because the player primarily experiences the game world through the player character. *Eternal Darkness: Sanity's Requiem* is also particularly ambitious (in fact, uniquely so) in its attempt to affect the player's vision directly, i.e., by breaking through the fourth wall.

Generally speaking, the best game designs tend to use what I think of as "resonating design" in which a single element (like sight and seeing) appears as a common theme taking different forms across the game's story, mechanics and aesthetics. To my game design students, I mention *Asteroids* (1979) as the first game I know of that had a highly resonating design, basing its game mechanics as well as aesthetics firmly in real physics and in visual styles associated with deep space, such as star maps. As this paper has shown, sight and seeing constitute a theme that is sufficiently broad to allow it to be used to create such resonating designs, not in just a single title but across many.

References

1. Macmillan dictionary (2018)
2. Oxford dictionaries (2018)
3. Adams, E.: Fundamentals of Game Design. New Riders (2010)
4. Kirkland, E.: Resident evil's typewriter: survival horror and its remediations. Games Cult. 4(2), 115–126 (2009)
5. Kirkland, E.: Storytelling in survival horror video games. In: Perron, B. (ed.) Horror Video Games: Essays on the Fusion of Fear and Play, pp. 62–78. McFarland, Jefferson (2009)
6. Krzywinska, T.: Hands-on horror. Spectator **22**(2), 12–23 (2002)
7. Krzywinska, T.: Reanimating lovecraft: the ludic paradox of Call of Cthulhu: dark corners of the earth. In: Perron, B. (ed.) Horror Video Games: Essays on the Fusion of Fear and Play, pp. 267–287. McFarland, Jefferson (2009)
8. Niedenthal, S.: Patterns of obscurity: gothic setting and light in Resident Evil 4 and Silent Hill 2. In: Perron, B. (ed.) Horror Video Games: Essays on the Fusion of Fear and Play, pp. 168–180. McFarland, Jefferson (2009)
9. Nitsche, M.: Complete horror in fatal frame. In: Perron, B. (ed.) Horror Video Games: Essays on the Fusion of Fear and Play, pp. 200 219. McFarland, Jefferson (2009)
10. Perron, B.: Coming to play at frightening yourself: welcome to the world of horror video games. In: Aesthetics of Play, pp. 14–15 (2005)
11. Perron, B.: The heuristic circle of gameplay: the case of survival horror. In: Gaming Realities: A Challenge for Digital Culture, pp. 62–71 (2006)
12. Perron, B.: Horror Video Games: Essays on the Fusion of Fear and Play. McFarland, Jefferson (2009)
13. Perron, B.: Silent Hill: The Terror Engine. University of Michigan Press, Ann Arbor (2012)

"The Link Out"

Towards a Theory of Epiphany in Digital Games

Andrea Di Pastena, Dennis Jansen(✉), Brian de Lint,
and Amanda Moss

Professorship Interactive Narrative Design, HKU University of the Arts Utrecht,
Nieuwekade 1, 3511 RV Utrecht, The Netherlands
andrea.dipastena@gmail.com, briandelint@gmail.com,
d.jansen5@students.uu.nl, a.moss.1@student.rug.nl

Abstract. In this paper, we take up the subject of epiphany in digital games, inspired by Espen Aarseth's claim in *Cybertext* that epiphany serves as one half of a "pair of master tropes [that] constitutes the dynamic of hypertext discourse: the dialectic between searching and finding typical of games in general". This article investigates the continuities and discontinuities between the literary epiphany and the hypertext epiphany, and subsequently theorizes the different types of epiphanies that occur in various digital games. We argue that epiphany in digital games is experienced by the player instead of the fictional protagonist, and that this experience can be brought about by ludic or narrative elements (making either a 'ludic' or a 'narrative epiphany'), or by the collaboration of those elements (a 'ludonarrative epiphany'). In addition, we distinguish between epiphany on a 'local', meaning small-scale and context-specific, and a 'global' scale, pertaining to the entirety of the game system. We conclude that an improved understanding of epiphany in digital games contributes to the maturation of digital games as a medium, since it allows both designers and scholars to better understand the medium-specific ways in which games can evoke certain feelings and emotions within their players.

Keywords: Epiphany · Aporia · Digital games · Ludonarrative
Ludic system · Narrative system

1 Introduction

"The epiphany [...] is the sudden revelation that replaces the aporia, a seeming detail with an unexpected, salvaging effect: the link out. The hypertext epiphany, unlike James Joyce's 'sudden spiritual manifestation' [...] is immanent: a planned construct rather than an unplanned contingency." - Espen Aarseth, *Cybertext* [1].

Several questions arise from the second sentence in Aarseth's statement. Who is the 'receiver' of the epiphany, the protagonist/avatar or the reader/player? How can a 'planned construct' simultaneously have an 'unexpected, salvaging effect'? How different is the 'immanent' hypertext epiphany from its Joycean literary counterpart, which is not only spiritual but also refers to a "secular experience" [3]? None of these matters are further specified in *Cybertext*, and Aarseth's subsequent claim that aporia

© Springer Nature Switzerland AG 2018
R. Rouse et al. (Eds.): ICIDS 2018, LNCS 11318, pp. 206–216, 2018.
https://doi.org/10.1007/978-3-030-04028-4_21

and epiphany serve as a "pair of master tropes [that] constitutes the dynamic of hypertext discourse: the dialectic between searching and finding typical of games in general" [1] has since gone undiscussed in game scholarship, with one exception. In an online article, Katherine Hayles notes that "searching for keys to a central mystery" is a common trope in electronic literature such as hypertexts, inherited from digital games [10]. This argument is dismissed by Aarseth himself, who proceeds to disconnect hypertext and games entirely: "The real father of electronic literature is not computer games, but the computer interface itself. And the result, in the form of hypernovels [...] is no hybrid, it is literature" [2]. This provocative stance is at odds with his equally provocative, though far less inflammatory argument in *Cybertext*, and the reasoning behind this change of heart is never fully explained. We seek to pick up the thread of epiphany in cybertexts by studying and clarifying its occurrence in one type of cybertext: digital games. We investigate the continuities and discontinuities between the literary epiphany and the hypertext epiphany, and subsequently theorize different types of epiphanies that occur across three digital games.

2 Epiphany in Historical Context

In this paper we employ the notion of epiphany as it is defined by the Oxford Dictionary: "A moment of sudden and great revelation or realization". This definition is the product of the distance created between the original divine connotations of the word and its purely etymological origin through its modern utilization. The word originates from the Greek ἐπιφάνεια, *epipháneia*, which is a combination of ἐπι and φαίνειν, that roughly translates to 'manifestation' or 'appearance'. It was primarily used to describe the appearance of a deity to a worshipper [15]. The word came into use in Christian circles, among which it delineated specifically the manifestation of "God's presence within the created world" [3]. Later, the epiphany became an important aspect of nineteenth and twentieth century literature, wherein this specific form took a more secular approach to the experience of epiphany as a hidden divine aspect becoming manifest. William Wordsworth described sublime revelations when observing natural phenomena, which some scholars have now come to understand as epiphanies [7]. James Joyce's description of this form of epiphany within the semi-autobiographical *Stephen Hero* lays the foundation for a now fundamental understanding of the concept within literary studies (cf. [5, 14, 27]). The titular character describes how an ordinary object had revealed its true self to him through a sudden flash of revelation: "Its soul, its *whatness*, leaps to us from the vestments of its appearance. The soul of the commonest object, the structure of which is so adjusted, seems to us radiant. The object achieves its epiphany" ([13]; emphasis ours).

What makes this definition particular is that Joyce disconnects the epiphany from its originally divine sense and focuses it rather on the mundane aspects of life, and how gaining a new understanding of these aspects is close in relation to this divine inspiration. Irene Hendry explains the three aesthetic principles bound to the epiphany as Joyce and other modernist writers use it: *integritas*, *consonantia*, and *claritas* [11]. *Integritas* refers to the observation of a single thing as *one* thing; *consonantia* is the subsequent perception of the thing as "complex, multiple, divisible, separable, made up of its parts and their sum". Lastly, *claritas*, or 'radiance', is connected to the notion of *quidditas*, realizing the 'whatness' of a thing:

> This is the moment which I call epiphany. First we recognise that the object is one integral *thing*, then we recognise that it is an organized composite structure, a thing in fact: finally, when the relation of the parts is exquisite, when the parts are adjusted to the special point, we recognise that it is that thing which it is. ([13]; original emphasis).

Finally, Scott Berkun takes a decidedly more pragmatic approach and describes the epiphany as the final piece of a puzzle, which completes the picture and allows for a clear understanding of what is (re)presented. He describes the action of fitting the final piece as feeling different than those before, "in comparison to the simple action of fitting [them] into place, we feel the larger collective payoff of hundreds of pieces' worth of work" [6]. Berkun also feels that the work that came before is just as important to the moment of epiphany as the moment itself: "the last piece isn't any more magical than the others, and it has no magic without its connection to the other pieces" [6].

3   Epiphany in Digital Games

Unlike the modern literary epiphany, which is experienced by a character within the fiction of the text, the hypertext epiphany as Aarseth theorizes it appears to be experienced by the player through interaction with complex, responsive digital systems. Berkun's discussion of epiphany as the 'collective payoff' of multiple elements working in conjunction with each other, then, appears to stand closer to Aarseth's conception of the 'immanent' hypertext epiphany than the literary epiphany. Similarly to hypertexts, digital games as interactive systems are geared towards incorporating feedback from the player into meaningful outputs. Subsequently, the medium-specific interactive modalities of digital games are constructed to, when combined with each other, afford an epiphanic experience for the player. In other words, the payoff experienced by the player is manifested by a sudden understanding of the relationship between the player's visible and invisible interactions with these complex systems and these systems' interactions with each other, all of which are necessarily planned, designed and constructed. Accordingly, epiphany in hypertexts and digital games is *immanent* – non-transcendent, bounded – precisely because it is contained within these interactive systems. Jonathan Blow's *The Witness* [26], for example, explores this notion through environmental storytelling and puzzles. In this game, epiphanies are not derived from arbitrary actions and symbols, but from instantaneous awareness of the 'whatness' of the game's simulated behavior and environments [4].

The sense of *aporia* in such a puzzle game, where the player is 'stuck', is replaced by an epiphany when "suddenly something happens in your mind where you understand exactly what [the problem] was about, what was going on" [4]. Aarseth places the hypertext epiphany in dialectical opposition to aporia, defined by Nicholas Rescher as "any cognitive situation in which the threat of inconsistency confronts us" which is resolved only by "a plausibility analysis that enables the chain of inconsistency to be broken" [23]. For digital games and hypertexts, the 'threat of inconsistency' that is aporia is built through the player's interaction with, and understanding of, ludic and narrative elements and is resolved by means of a sudden realization of the internal logic of these elements, the moment that breaks the perceived inconsistency: the digital game epiphany. The player's own pre-existing literacies of digital, hypertext, or game systems and interfaces (also known as "ludoliteracy" [28]) may aid in avoiding a state of aporia, but developers and designers can also exploit this knowledge to subvert player expectations and encourage aporetic moments, which in turn primes the player to search for an epiphanic moment that will reinstate consistency to their understanding of their interactions with the system. This is not to say that the aporia-epiphany dialectic is connected to notions of player skill and mastery: an aporetic state is not necessarily an indication of low player skill, and epiphany is not the same as attaining 'full mastery' of a game system – though understanding a system's 'whatness' may be an important step towards it.

In placing the player as the subject of epiphany, the object of epiphany must be found somewhere within the game, that is, in the holistic interrelation of the components of these phenomena. From this perspective, Aarseth's determination that the hypertext epiphany leads to an 'unexpected, salvaging effect' for the player can be qualified by looking at the aspects of a hypertext/game that factor into the epiphany that is eventually experienced by the player, namely the ludic and narrative elements.

Ludic and Narrative Systems

Our apparent separation of ludic and narrative elements requires some further elaboration. The surface-level systems that the player consciously interacts with are the ludic and narrative systems. Narrative systems in digital games share some similarities with other media, such as film, the book/novel, and theatre, particularly when the narrative system does not meaningfully interact with or map onto other systems in the game [12, 20, 24]. We see narrative systems in digital games as being in line with Hartmut Koenitz' theoretical framework for interactive narrative design, containing elements such as the environment, assets, settings, and narrative vectors [16]. Mechanics that are typically framed as part of the narrative system include dialogue navigation, diegetic user interfaces, audiovisual representations; in other words, any mechanic which explicitly serves to establish narrative elements such as characters, events, etc. Bearing this in mind, we identify the ludic system as those mechanics which the game does not frame as having 'narrative implication': this frequently (but not always) includes spatial navigation and movement, non-diegetic user interfaces, and combat systems, among others. When mechanics are not given immediate or overt narrative meaning, they qualify as part of the game's ludic system.

Ideally, both the ludic and narrative systems are intertwined to form a single coherent game system; this is the case in all three case studies we address in Sects. 3.1 and 3.2 of this paper. Unfortunately, many games tend to frame the ludic and the narrative as separate systems that coexist (or sometimes even compete) in the digital game space – and indeed, for many digital games the story still serves as nothing more than a "narrative shell" [18] to contextualize their ludic system. This distinction we have made is highly arbitrary, as the ludic and narrative systems can and do overlap often enough. However, (academic) games criticism continues to draw similarly troubled dichotomies, mostly as a result of the yet-unresolved 'ludology versus narratology' debate – a fault Aarseth is not innocent of, either (cf. [2, 9, 17]). Given that this discourse is so pervasive that it becomes nearly impossible to evade, we choose to adopt it with a critical lens, as it is still useful to pinpoint which aspects of a game system contribute to the epiphanic moment as it is experienced by the player. This typology enables us to analyze which specific elements of the game bring about epiphany for the player, be they framed narratively or ludically, or both. Let us be clear, however, that the primary purpose of our own ludic/narrative distinction is to be comprehensible within the current state of game scholarship, and that it does not stem from a belief that game and narrative are somehow two irreconcilably different concepts.

Local vs. Global Epiphany

As a second typological tool, this time to qualify the different 'scales' on which epiphany can take place, we propose the notion of 'local' and 'global' epiphany, inspired by Mateas and Stern's distinction between "local" and "global agency" [19]. This idea is useful especially in the context of digital games as systems that players must engage with in order to eventually achieve a certain understanding of them. Thus, players can experience a sudden revelation that is "immediate, context-specific" and would shed light on a nearby, single element of the game's system; a *local epiphany*. On the other hand, they may have an epiphany that would reveal the meaning, the true nature, the "global shape" of the system in its entirety; a *global epiphany*. Local epiphanies can be seen as suddenly realizing the solution to a single puzzle or problem, whereas global epiphanies provoke a more radical, grand-scale understanding of the system in which those individual problems are situated.

3.1   Ludic Epiphany in *the Witness*

The first type of epiphany that we discern within digital games is *ludic epiphany*. This form is specifically focused around the ludic system and the player's understanding of it. A game that models this type of epiphany, both locally and globally, with particular clarity is *The Witness* by Jonathan Blow. In an interview with Leigh Alexander, Blow explains that one of the primary goals of *The Witness* was modeling the feeling of epiphany [4]. The environments in *The Witness* were crafted with purpose, every single aspect of the island that the players get to explore has an element of intentionality and simplicity. The goal of this is to have the player engage with a complicated system that does not obfuscate its particularities in the hopes of fostering epiphany, both locally and globally. First the player is taught the general idea that will govern the puzzles within the game, which are like small mazes that the player must solve by drawing the solution. The solution seems simple at first, when the mazes are just about finding the way to the exit while evading their many dead ends, but as the game continues, more and more different mechanics are added to the mazes that complicate this simple notion. *The Witness* directly addresses the player's lack of knowledge by having them face a seemingly insurmountable challenge prior to providing the tools for a solution. It confronts the player with their own aporetic state before leading them to the puzzle sequences which are constructed in such a way that they lead the player towards a moment of understanding, resolving their aporia. Quite like the puzzle piece that Berkun describes, the sequence allows for the moment of clarity, the moment of epiphany, to take place at any of these panels, but the subsequent puzzles are just as important to the player's growing understanding because they test the hypotheses formed by the player; "it's not [...] the magic moment that matters much, it's the work before and after" [6]. This creation of understanding comes from a local ludic epiphany, which happens on a smaller scale and it is particular to a single element of the ludic system (see Fig. 1).

Fig. 1. The pathway to epiphany [26]

However, *The Witness* also features a global ludic epiphany, a moment that shifts the player's understanding of the system to such a degree that they will regard the gameworld as if with an entirely new set of eyes. The puzzles in *The Witness* have a very particular shape, the starting point is bulbous and the end point tapers off, various aspects of the environment on the island that house these puzzles reflect this iconic shape. This at first might seem to be a purely aesthetic choice, but a few curious individuals might actually attempt to 'solve' these environmental puzzles and find out that indeed there is a whole secondary layer of puzzles hidden in plain sight. This realization completely recontextualizes the game's environments and changes the overall view that the player has on the game and its gameplay systems; this is a global ludic epiphany.

3.2   Ludonarrative Epiphany

We discern two additional types of epiphany in digital games: narrative epiphany and ludonarrative epiphany. *Narrative epiphany* within digital games can be equated with the hypertext epiphany which Aarseth discusses in *Cybertext*. He points out that within hypertext fiction the concept of epiphany indicates the revelation, or the understanding, of the narrative system itself [1]. That is, while the Joycean literary epiphany is understood as an aesthetic experience [11], within hypertexts, and especially digital games, narrative epiphany is not only an aesthetic experience which 'reveals the true nature of an object', but is also part of the structure of hypertexts themselves.

Progressing through a hypertext fiction is a matter of accepting aporia and pursuing epiphany, in the sense that the selection of one path would preclude following another one, so that one part of the story is 'revealed', while another remains 'unknown'. However, the main difference between narrative epiphany and the other two is that the former does not require spatial navigation to engage with the narrative – after all, navigating a hypertext is merely the clicking/following of hyperlinks. Given that we consider digital games to be those cybertexts that involve not only such narrative navigation but also spatial navigation and interaction within that space, we do not discuss narrative epiphany in further detail here. Instead, we turn to *ludonarrative epiphany*, for which the narrative system and the ludic system are inextricably intertwined and together produce a great revelation/realization about the digital game as a whole. We discuss two games that model ludonarrative epiphanies in similar, yet different ways: *Oxenfree* and *NieR:Automata*.

Corollaries of Epiphany in *Oxenfree*

Oxenfree [21] is a graphic adventure game that models both local narrative epiphanies and global ludonarrative epiphanies. The story follows the events of a group of teenagers who go to an ostensibly inhabited island for a weekend party. Alex, the protagonist, accidentally opens a portal to another dimension that traps the teenagers in a time-loop. The goal of the game is to rescue Alex and her friends and bring them home. The game does not have many mechanics: it allows the player to walk across the different areas, to select dialogue lines – in this way, it is possible to affect the story, shaping it according to the player's decisions – and to tune the radio with the singularities around the island. These singularities provide additional background information on the story, and it is precisely through them that players can experience a local narrative epiphany. Indeed, by collecting all these 'bits of story', they may realize what past events have led to the current situation. Thus, they find out that a woman called Maggie Adler was the cause of everything, when she inadvertently gave the order to attack a submarine loaded with nuclear weaponry that was sailing close to the shores of the island. This epiphany is related only to the narrative system of the game, and it does not affect its ludic elements. Rather, it permits the player to understand parts of the story, thus gaining a better comprehension of some aspects of the ongoing narration.

On the other hand, to understand *Oxenfree* in its entirety, the player has to experience a final, global ludonarrative epiphany. After Alex has rescued her friends and they are all on the ferry back to the mainland, she discusses the events that have happened and that would happen afterwards. However, at one point her voice starts glitching and suddenly she is talking about going to an island with her friends for a weekend party. It is in this moment that the game gives the player the "continue timeline" option (see Fig. 2). Thus, *Oxenfree* narratively motivates an aspect of the gameplay, that is the possibility of re-playing it. In this way, players can try different options to experience different endings. In order to keep track of the choices players have made in previous playthroughs, the player can leave hints and messages in specific places. *Oxenfree*'s global ludonarrative epiphany is given precisely by the understanding of the relationship between those two mechanics and the time-looped structure of the narrative. Alex cannot break out of the loop, she is trapped there for good. Even though players try different things, eventually the protagonist always find herself at the 'beginning' of the time-loop. The hints left by the users over the course of the game contribute to create the global ludonarrative epiphany: *Oxenfree*'s story is endless, and it does not have a univocal finale, no ultimate conclusion. The game's story ends only in the moment the player stops playing. Through different playthroughs, which are narratively motivated by the 'continue timeline' option and the hint mechanic, the game constructs its ludonarrative epiphany. Therefore, the understanding of the dynamics in play between these two mechanics and the looping narrative manifests *Oxenfree*'s nature.

Fig. 2. Continue timeline? [21]

Recontextualizing Conflict in *NieR:Automata*

Ludonarrative epiphany in action role-playing game *NieR:Automata* [22] comes in the first two 'playthroughs' of the game, which both chronicle the same events but switch perspectives between the two protagonists across those playthroughs. During the first playthrough, when the player controls the female combat android '2B', the game sets up an oppositional relationship between the human-made androids and the alien machines who invaded Earth. Multiple characters in the game tell us that the machines are dangerous, warmongering creatures out to destroy all androids and whatever still remains of humanity. Correspondingly, the vast majority of machines that the player encounters will be hostile and attack on sight, leaving the player no other choice but to fight back. Even those machines that are not immediately hostile, such as those that have occupied an abandoned amusement park, can be easily taken to be a threat – especially considering that there is often one machine in the group that *will* attack the player, which quickly leads to escalation. As the player progresses through the story, going through the motions of what one might expect of a typical-yet-engaging action RPG, they increasingly get the sense that something is quite off. This opposition is contrasted with displays of 'human-ness' by the machines, for example when 2B and her partner, '9S', encounter a group of machines trying to emulate human sexuality and child care (see Fig. 3).

Fig. 3. Trying to be human, in their own way [22]

By the end of the first playthrough, it has become clear that the machines are not mindless robots and that, in fact, many machines have no desire to fight and are even afraid of the androids. The second playthrough, as mentioned, follows the same events as the first but switches the player's perspective to 9S, who also happens to be one of the most vocal proponents of the oppositional frame, with lines like "they're just imitating human speech, they don't have any feelings". The player visits the same places, encounters the same characters, and mostly engages in the same combat scenarios. This time, however, the content of the dialogue and the fighting mechanics are radically recontextualized, with the player's understanding of what is happening completely different now than during the first playthrough. In the first playthrough, the machines' actions and speech were the elements that challenged the established frame of reference; in the second, it is the dialogue with other androids that causes the tension, which serves to expand upon and drive home the 'point' of the incited epiphanic moment. The game uses its "ludonarratively dissonant game design" [25] to set up the conditions for aporia and global ludonarrative epiphany, contrasting the rigid actantial model of 'androids = helpers; machines = enemies' enforced by the ludic system with the rhetoric of blurred lines conveyed by the narrative system (insofar as the two can even be considered separate in this case) to great effect. In other words, the competitive friction between ludic and narrative systems, "ludonarrative dissonance" [25], is actually a strength in this case, rather than a weakness. The moment of epiphany is ludonarrative because the player's altered understanding of narrative relationship between androids and machines also affects their understanding of their ludic interactions with the machines. During the second playthrough, the player once again has to kill many machine lifeforms who, as it turned out in the first playthrough, might not have any urge to fight at all. The game thereby heavily leans into the player's presumed ludoliteracy of action RPGs, which leads them to expect that the primary mode of interaction with their opponents is through combat. The combat does not feel like righteous battle anymore, instead coming across as senseless slaughter, as 'going through the motions', as "cutting through hundreds of robots like butter because [...] that's what you have to do to complete the game, right?" [8].

4 Concluding Remarks

Making any generalizable statements regarding digital games and player experience is a fundamentally problematic exercise, and we are indeed critical of adopting Aarseth's normative claim that the aporia-epiphany dialectic constitutes any medium's "master tropes" [1]. There are many types of games, players and experiences, which inhibits any assertion that the game system necessarily constructs aporia for the purpose of leading the player to epiphany, or that the player actually experiences epiphany even when the game system is constructed with this dynamic in mind. For instance, a game's ludic and narrative systems may present aporia in a manner that, when resolved, does not grant a sudden revelation of the 'whatness' of an object or system, but rather emphasizes the need to master certain skills in order to solve the puzzles or conflicts presented within the game. Likewise, both global and local epiphanies might be experienced outside of the game through, for example, extensive paratextual engagement on the part of the player in the form of theorycrafting or lore analysis. The cognitive experience of epiphany during gameplay, as well as outside of the game through engagement with game objects and paratexts in online discussions, or simply "while you're reaching for the cat food at the store" [4] is worthy of further research. Similarly, further study that engages in comparisons between reader, audience and player will deepen our phenomenological understanding of the embodied experience of epiphany.

Our three analytical case studies appear to use some of the affordances most commonly connected to digital games as a medium to set up the aporia-epiphany dialectic; for instance, *NieR:Automata* does this by sending conflicting messages through various ludic and narrative elements before allowing the player to understand and reconcile those inconsistencies, thereby resolving the aporetic state into epiphany. Such consideration of epiphanic experiences by means of game systems – that is, making explicit the aporia-epiphany dialectic in a variety of digital games – has the potential to provide game designers with the conceptual tools necessary to devise new design practices oriented around intentionally constructing epiphanies. Ultimately, an improved understanding of epiphany in digital games contributes to the maturation of digital games as a medium, since it allows both designers and scholars to better understand the medium-specific ways in which games can evoke certain feelings and emotions within their players.

References

1. Aarseth, E.: Cybertext: Perspectives on Ergodic Literature. The John Hopkins University Press, Baltimore (1997)
2. Aarseth, E.: Genre trouble. In: Wardrip-Fruin, N., Harrigan, P. (eds.) First Person: New Media as Story, Performance, and Game. The MIT Press, Cambridge (2004)

3. Abrams, M.H.: A Glossary of Literary Terms, 7th edn. Heinle and Heinle, Boston (2011)
4. Alexander, L.: The Witness : Modeling epiphany (2014). https://www.gamasutra.com/view/news/218953/The_Witness_Modeling_epiphany.php. Accessed 12 Jul 2018
5. Beja, M.: Epiphany in the Modern Novel. University of Washington Press, Seattle (1971)
6. Berkun, S.: The Myths of Innovation. O'Reilly, Sebastopol (2010)
7. Bidney, M.: Patterns of Epiphany: From Wordsworth to Tolstoy, Pater, and Barrett Browning. Soutern Illinois University Press, Edwardsville (1997)
8. Black, H.: Why NieR:Automata could only work as a game (spoiler analysis) (2017). https://www.youtube.com/watch?v=_yfA94EpeqM&
9. Frasca, G.: Ludologists love stories too: Notes from a debate that never took place. In: Copier, M., Raessens, J. (eds.) Level-up: Digital games research conference proceedings. Utrecht University, Utrecht (2003)
10. Hayles, K.: Cyber|literature and Multicourses: Rescuing Electronic Literature from Infanticide (2001). http://www.electronicbookreview.com/thread/electropoetics/interspecial. Accessed 16 Jul 2018
11. Hendry, I.: Joyce's epiphanies. Sewanee Rev. **54**, 449–467 (1946)
12. Jennings, P.: Narrative structures for new media: Towards a new definition. Leonardo **29**, 345–350 (1996)
13. Joyce, J.: Stephen Hero. New Directions Publishing, New York (1963)
14. Kelly, D.: Joycean epiphany in seamus deane's reading in the dark. In: Tigges, W. (ed.) Moments of Moment: Aspects of the Literary Epiphany. Rodopi, Amsterdam (1999)
15. Kim, S.: Literary Epiphany in the Novel, 1850-1950: Constellations of the Soul. Palgrave Macmillan, New York, NY (2012)
16. Koenitz, H.: Towards a specific theory of interactive digital narrative. In: Koenitz, H., Ferri, G., Haahr, M., Sezen, D., Sezen, Tİ. (eds.) Interactive Digital Narrative: History, Theory and Practice. Routledge, London (2015)
17. Koenitz, H.: Narrative in video games. In: Lee, N. (ed.) Encyclopedia of Computer Graphics and Games. Springer International Publishing AG, Cham (2018). https://doi.org/10.1007/978-3-319-08234-9_154-1
18. Manovich, L.: The Language of New Media. The MIT Press, Cambridge, MA (2001)
19. Mateas, M., Stern, A.: Structuring content in the Façade interactive drama architecture. In: Young, R.M., Laird, J.E. (eds.) Artificial Intelligence and Interactive Digital Entertainment. AAAI Press, Menlo Park (2005)
20. Murray, J.H.: Hamlet on the Holodeck: The Future of Narrative in Cyberspace, 2016th edn. The Free Press, London (2016)
21. Night School Studio: Oxenfree [PC]. Night School Studio (2016)
22. PlatinumGames: NieR:Automata [PC]. Square Enix (2017)
23. Rescher, N.: Aporetics: Rational Deliberation in the Face of Inconsistency. University of Pittsburgh Press, Pittsburgh (2009)
24. Ryan, M.-L.: Avatars of Story. University of Minnesota Press, Minneapolis (2006)
25. Seraphine, F.: Ludonarrative dissonance: Is storytelling about reaching harmony? Academia (2016)
26. Thekla, Inc.: The Witness [PC]. Thekla, Inc. (2016)
27. Tigges, W.: The significance of trivial things: towards a typology of literary epiphanies. In: Tigges, W. (ed.) Moments of Moment: Aspects of the Literary Epiphany. Rodopi, Amsterdam (1999)
28. Zagal, J.P.: Ludoliteracy: Defining, Understanding, and Supporting Games Education. ETC Press, Pittsburgh, PA (2010)

Narrative-Led Interaction Techniques

Felipe Breyer[1]([⊠]), Judith Kelner[2], Daniel Ferreira[1],
José Paulo Teixeira[1], Paulo de Lima Filho[1],
Pedro Henrique Mendonça[1], and Givanio Melo[2]

[1] Federal Institute of Pernambuco, Recife, PE, Brazil
felipebreyer@recife.ifpe.edu.br
[2] Federal University of Pernambuco, Recife, PE, Brazil

Abstract. Despite the efforts of game companies to cut production costs, they spent more resources on developing items, animations, and special effects each year. One way to reuse game characters' animations is to change the interaction techniques that trigger such game actions. An interaction technique is a specific way to use an interaction device to perform an interaction task. Our research focused on eight interaction techniques for the digital button: *Press, Rhythmic Press, Hold, Hold and Release, Opportunity Press, Quick Press, Time-Limited Hold*, and *Pump*. To make these changes significant for the player, the game narrative must support them. We defined a model to guide game designers in making these modifications based on the interaction techniques' characteristics. This model offers two possibilities, increasing or decreasing the interaction techniques' complexity. As we did not find existing cases on the market nor in the literature, we developed a game and used the decreasing complexity approach as a proof of concept. In this way, we demonstrate how it is possible to change interaction techniques without adding new animations or items to the game. We hope that game designers can use our model to change interaction techniques while keeping the game narrative coherent and refreshing the player's experience.

Keywords: Interaction technique · Narrative · Game design
Character evolution · Player experience

1 Introduction

In game environments, players' experience is easily influenced by their characters' abilities and how these relate to game mechanics and narrative. Lessard and Arsenault [10] emphasize that characters can serve as subjective interfaces within the game environment. In this way, the player experiences the game world through the lens of the character and assumes their abilities and limitations. In turn, Larsen and Schoenau-Fog's model [9] emphasizes the relation between game mechanics and its narrative context, which creates meaning for the user. Game designers have explored these two ideas in different ways to create interesting experiences.

Considering characters' abilities, game designers usually adopt incremental approaches to stimulate the feeling of progress and achievement as players experience the game. That is, as the player advances in the game, he or she unlocks new action,

R. Rouse et al. (Eds.): ICIDS 2018, LNCS 11318, pp. 217–229, 2018.
https://doi.org/10.1007/978-3-030-04028-4_22

moves, and items. In *Bayonetta* [11], for example, the player earns about fifty different attacks throughout the game. However, to produce such a content, the development team needs to create new items, animations, and code altogether. This work adds extra costs to the project, regardless of whether the player uses them or not. This problem is also common in games that use branching narratives: when following a path, the player will give up another, and once the game is over, most players will not always play it again. As such, some narrative possibilities may never be explored, and the extra work put into the development of alternative paths may never be fully appreciated by the players. For example, *Heavy Rain* [12] has seventeen different endings, requiring at least seven playthroughs to see them all.

A common approach to deal with the heavy load of content related work is to re-use such content throughout the game. For example, in *Brothers: A Tale of Two Sons* [16], the player controls two brothers simultaneously. At some point in the game, the older brother dies, which then disables some controls representing the older brother's absence. Later on however, the game reestablishes these controls, and from that point on, the younger brother acquires his older brother abilities. Games can also let the player customize some rules. For instance, in *Remember Me* [5], the game allows the player to change the effects of the character's attack sequences with healing and/or extra damage capabilities.

To bind interaction devices and game rules, game designers need to choose interaction techniques. Usually, game designers assign interaction techniques to the player's character actions and they remain unchanged throughout the game, which is thought to avoid adding too much cognitive load to the players, thus affecting their learnability. But learning the game should be part of the fun [18]. Conversely, we believe that designers can refresh the user's experience by changing interaction techniques. This approach reuses items and animations within a game, requiring only new code to be produced. However, to grant meaning for such changes, the game's narrative must support them. In this manner, our research's objective is to demonstrate how interaction techniques can be applied as narrative tools.

2   Related Works on Narrative Interaction Design

Interaction design is structured by three elements working together: interaction tasks, interaction techniques, and interaction devices [7]. The interaction *tasks* comprise the basic action units performed by a user, and they are performed using an interaction *technique* through an input *device*. Over the years, researches have created new interaction devices to enhance storytelling.

Shen and Mazalek [14] developed *PuzzleTale*, a tangible puzzle game for interactive storytelling. *PuzzleTale* makes use of tangible puzzle pieces on the surface of an interactive table. Assembling the pieces can affect the characters and create a flexible story context, allowing the users to explore and compose the story. In turn, Wang et al. [20] developed *StoryCube*, a cubic tangible interaction device composed of seven buttons, one joystick, with an elastic band so a toy can be tied in the front of the box. *StoryCube* is also equipped with a NFC reader to identify the attached toy and an accelerometer to collect motion data. More recently, Krishnaswamy et al. [8] developed

Iyagi, an immersive storytelling tool for healthy bedtime routine, built with a smart projector, motion-sensing object tags and a smartphone application. Sullivan's et al. [17] created *Loominary*, a game platform that plays Twine games using a rigid heddle tabletop loom as a controller. All these are custom devices, but the default controller for the current game console generation is the gamepad.

About interaction tasks, researchers such as Dubbelman [6], and Larsen and Schoenau-Fog [9] explored different narrative functions of game mechanics. Game actions are a part of game mechanics and are the equivalent for interaction tasks in the game design jargon. Dubbelman's [6] explains that is possible to re-characterize a game action for narrative purposes through the action's visual representation and its goal in the game. However, the new visual representation still needs new items or animations.

Still, Sim and Mitchell [15] claim that manipulating the player's ability to control his/her character allows them to experience different characteristics in the game and can add emotional impact to the narrative. But the authors only identify the possibility to do so by enabling and disabling interactions during the game.

Interaction tasks and devices have been used to create interactive storytelling, but we were unable to find researches applying interaction techniques for this purpose. Therefore, our research aims to expand the idea of characterization of the player's actions for narrative purposes described by Dubbelman [6] to the characterization of the interaction technique that triggers the action. Instead of creating a unique interaction device we will focus on the digital button which is the simplest and common interaction device.

3 Interaction Techniques Classification Model

Our work is based on the interaction techniques classification model proposed by Breyer et al. [2], their model is based on three characteristics. The first is the Effort required from the player's character to perform such an action; it could take any form of effort, such as physical or mental effort. The second characteristic is the Duration that the character takes performing the action, and finally, the Context in which the character finds itself. Each characteristic is valued from positive to negative in a semantic difference scale. Positive value of Effort is called High, while negative value is called Low. Positive value of Duration is called Continuous and negative corresponds to Instantaneous. Positive value of Context is defined as Specific and negative is General. Considering that each of the three characteristics has two variations, the authors combined them and created eight different categories of interaction techniques. Based on the eight categories, the authors defined a set of interaction techniques for five different devices, including the digital button. Since the digital button is the most common interaction device found in the gamepads of the current console generation, our research will focus on it. So, the interaction techniques for the digital button are: *Press, Rhythmic Press, Hold, Hold and Release, Opportunity Press, Quick Press, Time-Limited Hold*, and *Pump*.

3.1   Press (Low, Instantaneous, General – LIG)

The player must press the button for a short period at any time during the game. This interaction technique represents immediate actions with low effort for the player character in a general game context.

3.2   Rhythmic Press (High, Instantaneous, General – HIG)

The player must press the button multiple times at predetermined intervals. The avatar's animation should show its high effort, and this high effort is represented by the player by the difficulty associated with the need of pressing the button following a specific rhythm to perform the action successfully. Keeping up with the rhythm for multiple interactions escalate the difficulty for the player. If the player misses the timing for one press, he/she must start the interaction again or cause an unintended effect. The game must allow access to the actions represented by this interaction technique in a general game context, also ensuring a clear feedback to the users while they take action. For example, this would mean a sequence of even more powerful attacks while the player keeps a specific pace for consecutive button presses.

3.3   Hold (Low, Continuous, General – LCG)

As long as the player holds down the button, the action is performed. Thus, this kind of interaction technique should be used to represent low-stress load, prolonged and accessible actions regardless of the context. The game designer should consider for how long this action will be performed to avoid user fatigue or discomfort. This interaction technique is commonly applied to a button to make the player's character defends itself.

3.4   Hold and Release (High, Continuous, General – HCG)

The player must hold down the button for a few seconds and then release it in order to complete the action. This interaction technique attempts to represent the avatar's effort to the player through the inability to access the action directly, requiring some time until the action becomes available. Hence, the period that the player kept the button pressed should be associated with the action outcome, so this interaction technique must be associated with a high effort continuous action, available in a general game context. Game rules must limit both the time and the resulting intensity of the action. For example, the player must hold down a button and release it to finish the action causing the player's character to unleash a more powerful attack proportional with the time the button was held down.

3.5   Opportunity Press (Low, Instantaneous, Specific – LIS)

The player must press the button quickly in a specific situation temporarily created by the game to successfully trigger the action. This kind of interaction technique must be used for actions with low effort and instantaneous duration, however, available for a brief period determined by the specific game context. The difference between *Press* and *Opportunity Press* interaction techniques is that the *Opportunity Press* requires the game to create the opportunity in which the player will choose whether or not to activate the interaction device. *Opportunity Press* is considered an interaction technique indicated to represent actions of low effort because the condition in which it can be used is taught to the player so that he can practice and learn to identify and even anticipate the situation in which he can activate it, often occurring throughout the game. The game should previously explain to the player the situations in which he/she can access this feature, so that it may be possible for the player to choose whether or not to perform the action, as well as to prepare in advance for such. In case of failure to perform the interaction technique accurately, the player should be penalized, so that the user is aware of the risk/benefit relationship when trying to trigger the action. This interaction technique could be found in games representing counter-attacks made against the player character.

3.6   Quick Press (High, Instantaneous, Specific – HIS)

The player must press the button when requested by the game within a short period to trigger the action. The surprise and the consequent sense of urgency represent for the user the high effort made by the player's character. In turn, the short time interval in which the action is available represents the instantaneous duration and the specific context. While the feedback to this type of action should represent the effort required by the player's character, it is important not to distract the user. When creating, for example, an animation as feedback to the correct activation of the action, the game designer should consider that the user's attention would be split between the animation displayed on the screen and the wait for the indication to interact. Thus, it should still be possible for the user to activate the command when required and understand what's going on in the game. Distinct from *Opportunity Press*, the player is obliged to perform the *Quick Press* correctly to progress in the game. This interaction technique is commercially known as Quick Time Events.

3.7   Time-Limited Hold (Low, Continuous, Specific – LCS)

To complete the action successfully, the player must hold down the button for a predetermined period, in a specific context established by the game and without external interruptions to his/her character. In case of interruptions and consequently change of the player's character state, the action must be stopped and restarted. The game interface should inform the player about the progression of the action so that it can examine whether it is or is not a favorable moment for trying to complete the action. In this way, the user can decide whether to stop the action or continue it. For example, this interaction technique could be used to search defeated enemies for loot in their pockets.

3.8   Pump (High, Continuous, Specific – HCS)

The player must press the button multiple times as fast as possible for a few seconds to trigger the action correctly. The access to this type of action must be controlled by the game through specific contexts because it requires high effort from both the avatar and the player. Since this factor is exacerbated due to the continuous and repetitive stress through which the player is put, he/she may have difficulty in performing other tasks simultaneously. This interaction technique could represent in the game the action of pushing a large boulder.

4   Interaction Techniques for Narrative Purposes

Interaction techniques are assigned to evoke a certain experience to the game action [2], so changing the interaction technique of a game action could bring another meaning to the game. Considering the three interaction techniques' characteristics and their values, it is possible to establish transitions between them. Once established the interaction technique's transitions, we considered two approaches, to increase or to decrease the complexity of the interaction technique assigned to a game action. By decreasing the interaction technique's complexity, the game designer would be "increasing" the players' skills at an appropriate pace as they progress through the game [4, 18]. For example, in an action game, at first, the *Pump* interaction technique is assigned to a special attack; afterwards, the interaction technique changes to *Hold and Release* (Fig. 1). This change removes the specific context from the game action, allowing the player to perform the special attack whenever he or she wants during the game. It is important to point out that the change in the interaction technique should not impacts the game balance [1]. Thus, the game designer should make the proper adjustments in other game elements to account for this easier action trigger, for example, increasing the number of enemies in the scenario or including more resistant ones.

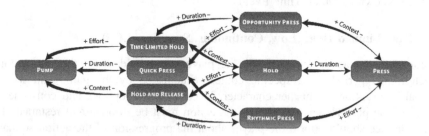

Fig. 1. Interaction techniques' transitions.

Conversely, we can increase the interaction technique's complexity to rise the player's challenge [13]. For example, in a game from the action genre, a game action can be initially performed by the *Press* interaction technique and at a later game stage the technique changes to the *Rhythmic Press*, therefore increasing the effort required to perform it (Fig. 1). Considering the interaction techniques' relations, from *Pump*, the most complex interaction technique, to *Press*, the simplest of them, we got six possible transformations:

1. Pump ↔ Time-Limited Hold ↔ Hold ↔ Press
2. Pump ↔ Time-Limited Hold ↔ Opportunity Press ↔ Press
3. Pump ↔ Quick Press ↔ Opportunity Press ↔ Press
4. Pump ↔ Quick Press ↔ Rhythmic Press ↔ Press
5. Pump ↔ Hold and Release ↔ Rhythmic Press ↔ Press
6. Pump ↔ Hold and Release ↔ Hold ↔ Press

It is important to note that in all cases the narrative must contextualize the change in interaction techniques to prevent the user from becoming frustrated, also allowing the game designer's intention to be acknowledged by the players [19].

5 Applying Interaction Techniques for Narrative Purposes

We were unable to find an example that uses interaction techniques for narrative purposes on both the game market and the literature; instead, a project team composed by the authors developed a game as proof of concept for the proposed model of designing interaction techniques based on narrative demands. The conceptual design of the game was divided into three stages: knowledge leveling, ideation, and implementation. During the knowledge leveling stage, the project coordinator explained and practiced the concept of interaction techniques for narrative purposes to the other team members composed by four undergraduate students in graphic design at Federal Institute of Pernambuco. During ideation, the team participated in two brainstorming sessions. The first session defined the game theme and its general narrative, and used the platforms action genre as constraint. The selected idea, chosen by a simple voting process, was the prehistoric era theme with a caveman as the player's character. The second brainstorm session had the purpose of deepening the idea from the first one. Before the second brainstorm session, the team defined that the approach used in the proof of concept game would be to decrease the complexity of interaction techniques. Besides walk and jump, the team created a set of six actions for the player's character and the interaction techniques assigned to them (Fig. 2). The six actions were:

Fig. 2. Player's character actions.

- attack with club to kill enemies in close combat;
- throw rocks to kill enemies from afar;
- eat meat to heal hit points;
- ignite the torch with rocks to light the way;
- call reinforcements with the blow horn as a special attack;
- escape from trap.

To challenge the player's character abilities, the team created four obstacles: enemy cavemen from a rival tribe, monkeys who throw fruits from the top of trees, traps to the player's character, and dark caves that restricts the player's character vision. Finally, the team implemented the game prototype using Unity engine in pixel art style (Fig. 3).

Fig. 3. Game prototype's screenshots.

6   Decreasing the Complexity of Interaction Techniques for Narrative Purposes

The game follows the journey of a young caveman aiming to become an adult member of his tribe, and for this, he must become stronger and stand out among others tribe members. In this way, the game uses the approach of decreasing the interaction techniques' complexity. For example, the action "attack with club" will begin the game with the *Pump* interaction technique (i.e. the player must press a button many times to complete the action) to show the character effort in lifting its weight, also needing some time to accomplish such a feat and being unable to carry the club with himself. By the fourth and last stage, the player's character is stronger and can attack with his club easily at any time using the *Press* interaction technique (i.e. the player must press a button only once to complete de action). Table 1 shows the actions and interaction techniques applied to each stage.

The game narrative was based on a simplified version of the Hero's Journey [3], showing cutscenes between game stages (Fig. 4). Each cutscene, in addition to telling part of the story, also shows the new interaction techniques for the following stage, which works as a tutorial as well.

The opening cutscene shows the player's character on his 16th birthday as he must attend a trial to become an adult tribe member – this passage represented the call to adventure from the Hero's Journey. Stage 1 shows the player's character with his initial abilities, still weak, without knowledge of survival, and without permission to carry the

Table 1. Interaction techniques assigned for the game actions in each stage.

Game actions	Interaction techniques			
	Stage 1	Stage 2	Stage 3	Stage 4
Attack with club	Pump	Hold and release	Rhythmic press	Press
Throw rock	Pump	Hold and release	Hold	Press
Eat meat	Pump	Time-Limited Hold	Hold	Press
Ignite torch with rocks	Pump	Time-Limited Hold	Opportunity Press	Press
Call reinforcements with the blow horn	Pump	Quick Press	Opportunity Press	Press
Escape from trap	Pump	Quick Press	Rhythmic Press	Press

Fig. 4. Old tribe shaman teaching the player's character

blow horn that summons the other tribe members. In this stage, all six actions use the Pump interaction technique. After completing Stage 1, the displayed cutscene shows the player's character equipped with his club and rocks, and leaving his tribe's camp to start Campbell's road of trials.

At the beginning of Stage 2, the player's character is stronger, being able to carry his club and rocks. So the *Pump* interaction technique is replaced by *Hold and Release* (i.e. the player must hold the button down for a few seconds and release it to finish the action), altering the Context characteristic from Specific to General. The character is also more agile, being able to escape from traps and to call for reinforcements with the blow horn faster. To represent this change, the *Pump* interaction technique is altered to *Quick Press* (i.e. the player must press the button when prompted by the game), reducing the action's Duration from Continuous to Instantaneous. Additionally, at this moment the player's character is more skilled at igniting the torch with rocks and eating meat, so the Pump interaction technique is replaced by *Time-Limited Hold* (i.e. the player must hold the button down for a predetermined time period), reducing the Effort from High to Low. Upon completing Stage 2, the cutscene shows the old tribe shaman teaching the player's character how to prepare the meat to take it with him on his journey (Fig. 4), as the Meeting with the Goddess from the Hero's Journey.

To continue with the player's character evolution, the interaction techniques are changed again at Stage 3. The actions "ignite torch with stones" and "attack with club" then have their Duration reduced from Continuous to Instantaneous. Thus, their interaction techniques changed from *Time-Limited Hold* to *Opportunity Press* (i.e. the player must press the button in a specific situation created by the game to complete the action), and *Hold and release* to *Rhythmic Press* (i.e. the player must press the button a couple of times at predetermined intervals), respectively. Similarly, the interaction techniques for the actions "eat meat" and "escape from trap" change from *Time-Limited Hold* and *Quick Press* to *Hold* (i.e. the player must hold the button down to perform the action) and Rhythmic Press, reducing the Context from Specific to General. Finally, the "throw rock" and "call reinforcements with the blow horn" actions have their Effort characteristic reduced from High to Low, resulting in the change of interaction techniques *Hold and Release* to *Hold*, and *Quick Press* to *Opportunity Press*. Upon the Stage 3 completion, the cutscene shows the player's character receiving the right to carry the blow horn and being accepted as an adult member of the tribe, reaching Apotheosis from the Hero's Journey.

At Stage 4, all three characteristics, Effort, Duration, and Context, are set to their lowest values, i.e. the interaction techniques of all actions were replaced by the *Press* interaction technique. As a result, the player's character then reaches the peak of his abilities. After Stage 4, the final cutscene shows the player's character celebrating with other tribe members the victory over the rival tribe, as Master of Two Worlds from the Hero's Journey.

7 Discussion

The team adopted some strategies to maintain balance throughout the game. Regarding the level design, the team progressively increased the number of enemies placed along the stages. Also, the team brought obstacles closer, placing traps and monkeys together as to allow the player's character to be within the monkey's attack range while trying to break free from the trap.

About game mechanics, it was necessary to include two game mechanics to limit the player's character abilities. The first mechanic was introduced at Stage 3, when the meat became a collectible item along the stage. This change in game design was necessary due to the change in the interaction techniques, from *Time-Limited Hold* to *Hold*, allowing the player's character to recover hit points at any time. However, the player's character would be limited to the amount of meat he previously picked up, subtracting his meat stock every time he ate meat. The second mechanic was introduced at Stage 4, in which the project team added a cooldown effect for the action "call reinforcements with the blow horn". This mechanic was necessary due to the change from *Opportunity Press* interaction technique to *Press*, thus, the player's character could call reinforcements at any time during Stage 4. However, the player could only use this ability again after sixty seconds, to avoid falling into the problem of having one winning strategy. It is important to point out that these game design changes required new code only, without the need for new animations.

It is also possible to change only some interaction techniques from stage to stage instead of all of them (as in our game) to ease the game's learning curve. That could lead to needing more passages from the Hero's journey. The current game used five passages of the Hero's journey to support the game narrative, however, Campbell [3] lists seventeen stages. Thus, we believe that other quantities and combinations of stages can be used to tell stories through games.

8 Conclusion and Future Work

For commercial games, the development team should create as many animations as possible to give a good-looking visual effect. But, some of these animations could be reused by changing their interaction technique instead of creating new ones. We believe that this approach could at least increase the usage of one animation, hence, bringing some benefits to the development process.

This work demonstrated how to apply interaction techniques as a game narrative supporting tool. To do so, we developed a game prototype as proof of concept, in which interaction techniques were intentionally changed along the game in view of the narrative demands. As such, the controls over the player's character were different in every game stage based on the characteristics of that stage, which enabled a coherent chain of changes. We proposed six paths that the interaction techniques can be altered, by increasing or decreasing the interaction technique's complexity. So, the game designer should be aware of his intentions when choosing which approach to apply in the game design to convey the proper meaning to the game actions. The game prototype used the decreasing complexity approach, in which interaction techniques progressed from more to less complex over time, while also increasing the ease with which the players could perform the corresponding actions. We also discussed the impacts that this approach brought to game balancing. If well applied, we believe that the interaction techniques for narrative purposes can create an innovative player experience without too much work for the development team and with little load to players' cognition, as the interaction techniques would be changing to become ever easier.

As future work, we will explore three possible paths. First, we will investigate further the increase complexity approach. We will do so by developing a new game prototype in which we can analyze the impacts of this increased complexity on the game balance (i.e. a story about a character losing his strength due to some illness as the game progresses and he searches for the cure). Then, we intend to investigate how to combine the increase and decrease complexity approaches in a mixed way. This would require some careful game design to keep the game mechanics balanced. Also, we will explore changing two interaction technique's characteristics at once, which may create a harder learning curve for the player. All these approaches will require new game prototypes to be developed. Finally, we will run user evaluations to analyze their experience, to understand how timely changes in interaction techniques can impact players' learnability and enjoyability during the game. We believe that game narratives have the potential to shape the choices of interaction techniques throughout the game and to be a key to unlock new players' experiences.

Acknowledgments. This research has been supported by the Federal Institute of Pernambuco.

References

1. Adams, E., Dormans, J.: Game Mechanics: Advanced Game Design. New Riders, Berkeley (2012)
2. Breyer, F., Kelner, J., Clua, E.: Multi-device classification model for game interaction techniques. Int. J. Hum.-Comput. Interact. **34**(8), 716–731 (2018)
3. Campbell, J.: The Hero With a Thousand Faces, 3rd edn. New World Library, Novato (2008)
4. Desurvire, H., Caplan, M., Toth, J.A.: Using heuristics to evaluate the playability of games. In: CHI 2004 Extended Abstracts on Human Factors in Computing Systems, pp. 1509–1512. ACM, Vienna, Austria (2004)
5. Dontnod Entertainment. Remember Me. PlayStation 3, 3 June 2013
6. Dubbelman, T.: Narrative game mechanics. In: Nack, F., Gordon, Andrew S. (eds.) ICIDS 2016. LNCS, vol. 10045, pp. 39–50. Springer, Cham (2016). https://doi.org/10.1007/978-3-319-48279-8_4
7. Foley, J.D., Wallace, V.L., Chan, P.: The human factors of computer graphics interaction techniques. IEEE Comput. Graph. Appl. **4**(11), 13–48 (1984)
8. Krishnaswamy, M., Lee, B., Murthy, C., Rosenfeld, H., Lee, A.S.: Iyagi: an immersive storytelling tool for healthy bedtime routine. In: Proceedings of the Eleventh International Conference on Tangible, Embedded, and Embodied Interaction, pp. 603–608. ACM, Yokohama, Japan (2017)
9. Larsen, B.A., Schoenau-Fog, H.: The narrative quality of game mechanics. In: Nack, F., Gordon, Andrew S. (eds.) ICIDS 2016. LNCS, vol. 10045, pp. 61–72. Springer, Cham (2016). https://doi.org/10.1007/978-3-319-48279-8_6
10. Lessard, J., Arsenault, D.: The character as subjective interface. In: Nack, F., Gordon, Andrew S. (eds.) ICIDS 2016. LNCS, vol. 10045, pp. 317–324. Springer, Cham (2016). https://doi.org/10.1007/978-3-319-48279-8_28
11. PlatinumGames. Bayonetta. PlayStation 3, 29 October 2009
12. Quantic Dream. Heavy Rain. PlayStation 3, 23 February 2010
13. Schell, J.: The Art of Game Design: A Book of Lenses, 2nd edn. CRC Press, Boca Raton (2015)
14. Shen, Y.T., Mazalek, A.: PuzzleTale: a tangible puzzle game for interactive storytelling. Comput. Entertain. (CIE) **8**(2), 11 (2010)
15. Sim, Y.T., Mitchell, A.: Wordless games: gameplay as narrative technique. In: Nunes, N., Oakley, I., Nisi, V. (eds.) ICIDS 2017. LNCS, vol. 10690, pp. 137–149. Springer, Cham (2017). https://doi.org/10.1007/978-3-319-71027-3_12
16. Starbreeze Studios. Brothers: A Tale of Two Sons. PlayStation 3, 3 September 2013
17. Sullivan, A., McCoy, J.A., Hendricks, S., Williams, B.: Loominary: crafting tangible artifacts from player narrative. In: Proceedings of the Twelfth International Conference on Tangible, Embedded, and Embodied Interaction (TEI 2018), pp. 443–450. ACM, New York, NY, USA (2018)

18. Sweetser, P., Wyeth, P.: GameFlow: a model for evaluating player enjoyment in games. Comput. Entertain. (CIE) **3**(3), 1–24 (2005)
19. Rusch, D.C.: Making Deep Games: Designing Games with Meaning and Purpose. CRC Press, Boca Raton (2017)
20. Wang, D., He, L., Dou, K.: StoryCube: supporting children's storytelling with a tangible tool. J. Supercomput. **70**(1), 269–283 (2014)

Perceived Agency as Meaningful Expression of Playable Character Personality Traits in Storygames

Liting Kway[(✉)] and Alex Mitchell

Department of Communications and New Media,
National University of Singapore, Singapore, Singapore
litingk@u.nus.edu, alexm@nus.edu.sg

Abstract. Academic discussion about agency has shifted towards agency as something the player perceives, rather than necessarily involving visible and lasting effects within a storygame. Existing work suggests players experience perceived agency even when no consequences result from their choices, due to various features and techniques used in storygames. This paper aims to understand the experience players have when engaging with choices and playable characters when playing storygames that produce a sense of perceived agency. We conducted retrospective protocol analysis and interviews with 15 players who played one of three games, *The Wolf Among Us*, *Oxenfree* and *Kentucky Route Zero*. Our findings suggest that perceived agency arises both from the player's ability and willingness to engage in meaningful expression of the playable character's personality within constraints, resulting in the creation of a unique playable character, and from the system's recognition of this expression of the playable character's personality through appropriate feedback.

Keywords: Perceived agency · Choice · Characters · Meaningful expression

1 Introduction

Early views of agency emerged from Murray's notion of agency as "the satisfying power to take meaningful action and see the results of our decisions and choices" [1]. Wardrip-Fruin et al. argue that agency should be seen as an improvisational act between player and system, where the player's motivations are backed by the system's ability to dynamically support player expectations [2]. Videogames adopting this form of agency are what Reed calls *storygames*: "a playable system, with units of narrative, where the understanding of both system and narrative, and the relationship between them, enables a traversal through the work" [3]. Recently, scholars have argued that attempts to design for theoretical agency are misguided; focus should instead be placed on perceived agency [4, 5]. To explore how players describe their experience of perceived agency, we conducted an observational study of players' responses to three storygames: *The Wolf Among Us* (TWAU) [6], *Oxenfree* [7] and *Kentucky Route Zero* (KRZ) [8]. Our findings suggest that a player's sense of perceived agency arises both from their ability and willingness to partake in meaningful expression of the playable

© Springer Nature Switzerland AG 2018
R. Rouse et al. (Eds.): ICIDS 2018, LNCS 11318, pp. 230–239, 2018.
https://doi.org/10.1007/978-3-030-04028-4_23

character's personality traits which results in the creation of unique playable characters that are theirs alone, and from the system's recognition of this through appropriate feedback.

2 Related Work

Agency has traditionally been studied from a systemic perspective that focuses on balancing the affordances and constraints of a system [9]. More recently, this has shifted to a focus on perceived agency. Tanenbaum and Tanenbaum have described *commitment to meaning* as agency that arises when a player is only able to perform a single action, but is fully committed to carrying out that action [10]. Referring to choice-based videogames, they argue that designers should reframe agency in terms of understanding player motivations, so as to fulfill the expectations of the player [10]. Cheng notes how a player's inability to take action can also be viewed as *representational agency* where players fully empathize with their characters at a particular moment [11]. Furthermore, Day and Zhu propose that videogames contain Agency Informing Techniques, such as user interface cues, that lead players to believe that they have had an impact in a videogame because they are provided with feedback from the choices they make [4]. This suggests that agency no longer has to be seen from an "action and impact paradigm".

In his analysis of *Balloon Diaspora* [12], Weir proposes a similar outlook in what he calls *emotional agency*, where choices do not have a major impact on the overall events of the game [13]. Weir argues that even without consequence, emotional agency is present due to the "meaning and significance" of the player's choice. Expanding on this, Kway and Mitchell propose that emotional agency is closely related to a player's attachment to the videogame's characters and to the choices they make [14]. In their close readings of TWAU, *Oxenfree* and KRZ they note that emotional agency does not arise from players seeing large-scale consequences in the long term, but instead manifests from the build-up of small, seemingly inconsequential but sentimental decisions made when interacting with other characters.

3 Research Problem

While perceived agency has been studied by many scholars, only a few have conducted empirical studies on how it can arise [5, 15, 16]. In one such paper, Fendt et al. found that players experienced a sense of agency as long as there was contextual feedback provided, regardless of whether there was a change in the ending of the interactive narrative [15]. Apart from this, most papers that explore perceived agency have involved close reading analysis of narrative videogames [4, 11, 14, 17]. As mentioned above, Kway and Mitchell argue that a player's experience of emotional agency, seen as a form of perceived agency, is closely tied to the sentiments that the player holds towards the characters in the storygame [14]. Since existing literature suggests that perceived agency is highly subjective and related to a player's choices during gameplay, we ask the following question: How do players actually describe their experience of perceived agency when making choices in a storygame?

4 Method

To explore this question, we conducted an empirical study of 15 participants each playing one of three videogames: TWAU, *Oxenfree*, and KRZ. Participants were recruited from an undergraduate research class. The researchers were not involved in teaching the class. A total of 12 female and 3 male participants, aged 18 to 24, took part in the study. The three games were selected following Kway and Mitchell [14], who argue that these videogames have the potential to produce a sense of perceived agency. These games all have a strong focus on the player's relationship with the playable character, and also showcase a range of player impacts on outcome.

4.1 Study Procedure

Each participant's previous exposure to the three videogames was assessed to ensure that they were not allocated to a videogame that they had prior knowledge of. As all three of the videogames require several hours of gameplay to complete, participants were only asked to play until a designated scene, resulting in an average of twenty-five minutes of play per participant. This ensured some consistency across the three videogames, and that the participants could reach an appropriate level of understanding of the playable and non-playable characters (NPCs) and the general narrative arc.

Screen and audio recordings of the participants' playthroughs were taken. A retrospective protocol analysis was employed to gather insights into the participants' experience [18, 19]. Following the playthrough, the screen recordings were replayed and paused whenever the player had to make a decision. Participants were prompted to explain how they made decisions for each choice. This was followed by a semi-structured interview to probe for further insights. Transcriptions were prepared by a single researcher, and thematic analysis was performed to identify recurring issues.

5 Findings

Across the three games, the player's connection to the playable character seemed to be central to their experiences of choice-making. The findings also suggest that perceived agency can arise when players are afforded the opportunity to affect how characters perform in the game. However, there were also participants who felt indifferent towards the playable character and approached the content more analytically. We now discuss these findings in more detail.

5.1 Managing the Playable Character's Personality and Relationships

Choice-making was strongly tied to the participants' identification with the playable character and the playable character's relationships with the NPCs. These participants took many steps to identify the playable character's personality traits as suggested by the narrative and dialogue that they were given.

Tension Between Shaping the Character and Ensuring Character Consistency. Participants felt the need to ensure that their actions led to a consistent characterization of their playable character, which guided them in their decision-making process. However, some of the participants mentioned they alternated between the characterization that was 'given' to them and their own need for self-expression. As participant 1 said when playing Bigby in TWAU: "I thought I was staying true to what the game wants this character to be, but then again, ... I [also] want to personalize this game for me?"

In terms of self-expression, the participants' ability to make choices was the main way they could affect the personality of the playable character. As participant 6 explains: "It [one of the choices] feels too emotional. ... [Shannon] doesn't sound like a very emotional person, based on the character I made of her based on the choices I made previously." The choices participants made were crucial in contributing to their sense of agency, because it reflected how they wanted the playable character to behave.

In contrast, participant 7 felt choices in KRZ were not as expressive as they hoped:

"I don't know what his character is about to be honest. I wouldn't say Conway is me, nor is he him. Sometimes I feel like he's all over the place. ... The choices are more of an informative style. I'm not sure if there's more of a personality in these choices."

This suggests that the types of choices present guided how the participants made their decisions. Choices that encouraged expression of personality seem easier for participants to resonate with, as opposed to choices that were about gathering information.

Managing Relationships Between Characters. In addition to paying attention to how their choices impacted the playable character's personality, participants were also constantly managing the feelings of the playable characters and NPCs within the fiction of the game. For example, when playing *Oxenfree* several participants showed a sense of protectiveness towards Jonas, Alex's step-brother in the game, and were almost always prioritizing his feelings over other characters' feelings, as noted by participant 12:

"The conversation we had was private ... It feels like it was not something that was easy for [Jonas] to open up to. And Ren seems quite loud-mouthed, and maybe if I kept it a secret, Jonas would appreciate it, and it'll be good for the game later on."

This was also seen in TWAU, when some participants found themselves having to engage in conversations diplomatically to maintain the balance of Fabletown while also staying true to Bigby's role as a sheriff. This was highlighted by participant 10:

"As I play the game, my intention is that, if he's the good guy, then he should have good relationships with everyone else. So then uh, my options would then be more geared towards trying to find out, which, what are the different characters personality are like in the game, and how I can steer my options to be more aligned with their character, saying things that they want to hear, so as to improve their relationships."

Most participants were concerned with how the NPCs viewed the playable character, which became a key motivation in their decision-making. However, this intention was often at odds with the perception that their actions were constrained by game objectives. We discuss this tension between game objectives and character roles in the next section.

5.2   Game Objectives and the Playable Character's Role

The presence or absence of game objectives was an important factor when making choices. Having a game objective meant that participants could attribute decisions to the development of the playable character, whereas an absence of game objectives allowed participants to make choices to better understand the characters in the storygame.

Understanding Game Objectives Through Character Roles and Vice Versa. Participants who engaged with TWAU were able to determine game objectives through the role of their playable character, Bigby. Some expressed their urge to carry out the role of a sheriff, with participant 1 noting that this was a key factor when making decisions:

> "I relate to him cause I feel the sense of needing to do something... I mean I'm not like the protagonist or anything, but I know that I need to do something to move forward or something or to actually be of use to somebody, so I feel that he shares that sense of, the need for action, to do something, to be relevant."

For participant 1, the need for action was emphasized in their observation about staying true to Bigby's character through the decisions they were helping Bigby make when interacting with the other characters.

The idea that there would always be a game objective to fulfill was also important to players who felt that there were more objectives later in the game. With reference to *Oxenfree*, participant 12 noted that their choices tallied with how they usually approach narrative videogames where the game objectives are initially hidden from players:

> "At the start, cause I don't know everyone's motives and I don't know what the game objective is, so I feel the best approach is to be neutral first. ... It felt like it was more logical for me to not burn all my bridges right at the start."

Participant 12 was constantly juggling their desire to protect Jonas and Ren and their goal to be as 'nice' to everyone as possible at the start, as they were still lacking information about the game objectives at the beginning of the game.

Tension Between Game Objective and Playable Character's Role. Participants who played KRZ were confused as to what the main story thread was, latching onto the one clear goal of completing the delivery when making decisions. They attributed this to their characterization of Conway. According to participant 6, "Conway's just trying to get his job done... He keeps wanting to deliver stuff, but he keeps getting interrupted". Participant 7 also noted that the choices they were given were for different purposes:

> "I figured that the first [choice] would put me on the straight path to what I am doing and the second one would give me some more interesting dialogue or something like that. ... If I had just asked him so where's Dogwood Drive, I would just go straightaway, and that's at that point just clicking through a game. So I want to figure out what the characters do in the game."

Participant 7's observations suggest that even when players are given options to help them pursue a game objective, they still want to first understand how the game objective is related to the character's motivations. For participant 8, it was only when they realized that the game was not what it seemed that they shifted from making choices to accomplish a game objective to making choices for character development:

"I think it was the moment that like I realized that like Dogwood Drive wasn't real. And I was like... okay... It's not real, yet, I need to make a delivery. So at that point I was like okay there's something more, than just this guy going to somewhere to drop some antique off. So I was like at this point in time I was just trying to find out everything that was going on, as much as I can, basically. Yeah."

These observations reflect Reed's definition of a storygame as "a playable system, with units of narrative, where the understanding of both, and the relationship between them, is required for a successful traversal" [3]. While some participants were able to derive game objectives from the role of the playable character, others had the opposite perspective, seeing objective as a means to develop the playable character's characterization. This highlights the need to understand both game objectives (the playable system) and characterization (units of narrative) in order to proceed in the storygame. This understanding develops over time and as part of the iterative process of choice-making. We discuss the need to develop this understanding over time in the next section.

5.3   Time Needed to Develop a Connection with the Playable Character

The act of choice-making contributed to the participants' perceived agency, provided that it was also supported by contextual responses from the system. This sense of perceived agency parallels what previous studies have called *emotional agency* – where time and a commitment to making sense of the characters and the narrative is essential before players feel a sense of attachment to the characters [13, 14]. Consistent engagement with choices was required before participants could experience emotional agency.

For example, participant 14 pointed out that they felt that Jonas would have avoided revealing more about himself regarding his past history in jail at the beginning of the game, even if the player had chosen to try to probe more into his backstory:

"I feel like even if I chose the 'jail' option, he wouldn't have said anything much. Cause at that point they're not super close and they haven't had talks to each other. So the jail, he would evade the question and maybe later he would bring it up again."

For participant 14, this observation supported their faith in the coherence of *Oxenfree*'s design, which they felt would eventually satisfy their curiosity about Jonas' backstory, as long as they took time to allow Alex and Jonas to open up to each other.

Development of a connection to characters over time was also present in KRZ. Although some were initially ambivalent towards the dog who accompanies Conway, most players wanted to ensure that the dog did not enter the mines. As participant 8 notes:

"I kept going back to Homer [the dog] cause like I thought that I needed to tell him to stay there. ... Cause like poor Homer, I don't want you to die, if you die poor Conway would be all alone. I mean like, there's a reason why he's still following him right? So, yeah. But then he just sat there, so I'm like okay you just stay there."

In contrast, participants who had little exposure to choices that were closely related to the playable character's role in the game were somewhat indifferent towards the playable character. For participant 5, the result of the quick-time event at the beginning of TWAU came from their motivation of not wanting to lose the game:

"For me, it was just like, shit. I can't lose. Not really like a, shit, he can't die or lose. More of how this sets me in the progress of the game. ... Uhm, I'm playing the character, but it's more of a I cannot lose."

For participant 5, there was a clear distinction between them losing and Bigby dying, the latter being something that they were less concerned about. Participant 8 also notes that the interactions in KRZ were too fast-paced for them to have any meaning: "The time you encounter with the character, I feel like it's not enough to have a relationship, that kind of thing, with the other characters." Overall, the participants expressed the need for sufficient time and interactions with the characters before they were able to establish any form of attachment to them. This influenced the way they made decisions, and was reflected in their explanations about the motivation behind their actions.

6 Discussion

In this section, we attempt to understand how the players' act of choice-making can help crystallize our conception of perceived agency, building on existing literature and the findings above. The findings suggest that the player's connection with their playable character was central to their choice-making, provided that they had sufficient interactions with the characters. This supports existing research that has shown how storygames can lead to players experiencing a form of perceived agency [13, 14]. We suggest that this sense of perceived agency is aided by the participants' belief in the playable system that the storygame provides [3], and by participants' attempts to try to create a unique playable character as supported by the synthesis of the narrative intended by the game designer and the participants' agency when making choices.

The relationship between game objectives and character attachment reflects how storygames operate, as "the ludic mechanisms and narrative content, and the way they interrelate, are both required for a successful traversal" [3]. By advancing both goals – that of fulfilling the 'main' objective that they derived from the game, and managing the personality of their playable character – players can enjoy a form of emotional agency, when the decisions they have made hold sentimental value due to their attachment to the characters [14]. Parallel to this is the player's commitment to meaning [10], whereby the player's intent to fulfil the game objective is supported by the conversations they engage in between the playable character and the NPCs.

Every choice made by the player contributes to a clearer understanding of how the playable character should perform. When players receive feedback from their choices, they believe that they have had some meaningful impact on the storygame. As such, we argue that the specific consequences of a choice begin to factor very little in the player's decision-making processes. As Participant 7 notes, "If I had just asked him so where's Dogwood Drive, I would just go straightaway, and that's at that point just clicking through a game". This suggests that even in the presence of a clear objective, players would prefer to find out more about the characters first. Agency therefore moves from focusing on the large-scale consequences of choices towards the affective significance of the choice instead. Players believe they have exercised agency because they have changed the way the characters behave as a result of choices they have made. Therefore, having many choices with global impact does not necessarily mean a greater sense of agency, since players are likely to base agency on their own subjective feelings [4].

Finally, players must consistently engage with choices that allow for the expression of the playable character's personality traits for perceived agency to arise [13, 14]. In storygames where the game objective is absent or too ambiguous, we suggest that opportunities for the player to deepen their attachment to the characters through meaningful expression of the playable character's personality traits should be provided. Meaningful expression is not a matter of *what* the character does and *what* happens to the story when players make choices, but rather, *how* the character does it and *how* this reflects on the playable character. Klimmt et al. argue that character identification in videogames is a dynamic process as players are constrained by the fixed traits of the playable character, although they are afforded flexibility in identifying with the character beyond those traits [20]. As such, identification occurs when players look at what the playable character should achieve through the game objectives, before they partake in any performative actions aligned with the playable character's traits.

A player's sense of perceived agency can then be viewed as their ability and willingness to partake in meaningful expression of the playable character's personality traits within constraints, which results in the creation of a unique playable character that is theirs alone. Perceived agency is further supported by the system's recognition of this meaningful expression through appropriate feedback. When players engage with game mechanics that allow them to identify with playable characters and form deep bonds with them, they are able to experience a stronger sense of perceived agency.

7 Conclusion

This study explored how agency is described by players when playing storygames. We suggest that perceived agency is related to a player's ability to engage in meaningful expression of playable character personality traits within constraints. This allows for the creation of a unique playable character as determined by both the playable system and the player's own desires. The system's recognition of this through appropriate feedback allows the player to feel a sense of perceived agency within the storygame.

It is important to acknowledge the limitations of our study. We have not attempted to establish generalizability in terms of our interview findings, but rather, we are highlighting the rich, personal experiences of our participants with regards to their play experience in these particular storygames. Rather than establishing strongly validated claims, we highlight the subjective nuances of perceived agency through qualitative interviews with these participants, something that has not been done in previous research. Future work to expand on this research will include conducting quantitative experiments with the aim to confirm the validity of these findings.

References

1. Murray, J.H.: Hamlet on the Holodeck: The Future of Narrative in Cyberspace. MIT Press, Cambridge (2017)
2. Wardrip-Fruin, N., Mateas, M., Dow, S., Sali, S.: Agency reconsidered. In: Proceedings of the 2009 DiGRA International Conference: Breaking New Ground: Innovation in Games, Play, Practice and Theory, West London, UK (2009)
3. Reed, A.: Changeful tales: design-driven approaches toward more expressive storygames (2017)
4. Day, T., Zhu, J.: Agency informing techniques: communicating player agency in interactive narratives. In: Proceedings of the 12th International Conference on the Foundations of Digital Games, pp. 1–4. ACM Press (2017)
5. Thue, D., Bulitko, V., Spetch, M., Romanuik, T.: A computational model of perceived agency in video games. In: Proceedings of the Seventh AAAI Conference on Artificial Intelligence and Interactive Digital Entertainment, pp. 91–96. AAAI Press, Stanford (2011)
6. Telltale Games: The Wolf Among Us. Telltale Games, San Rafael (2013)
7. Night School Studio: Oxenfree. Night School Studio, Glendale (2016)
8. Elliott, J., Kemenczy, T.: Kentucky Route Zero. Cardboard Computer, Chicago (2013)
9. Mateas, M.: A preliminary poetics for interactive drama and games. In: Wardrip-Fruin, N., Harrigan, P. (eds.) First person: New Media as Story, Performance, and Game, pp. 19–33. MIT Press, Cambridge (2004)
10. Tanenbaum, K., Tanenbaum, J.: Commitment to meaning: a reframing of agency in games. In: Proceedings of the Digital Arts and Culture Conference 2009 (2009)
11. Cheng, P.: Waiting for something to happen: narratives, interactivity and agency and the video game cut-scene. In: Proceedings of DiGRA 2007 Conference: Situated Play, pp. 15–24 (2007)
12. Elliot, J., Kemenczy, T.: Balloon Diaspora. Cardboard Computer, Chicago (2011)
13. Weir, G.: Analysis: incidental character choices in Balloon Diaspora (2011). http://www.gamasutra.com/view/news/124604/Analysis_Incidental_Character_Choices_in_Balloon_Diaspora.php
14. Kway, L., Mitchell, A.: Emotional agency in storygames. In: Proceedings of the 13th International Conference on the Foundations of Digital Games. ACM Press, Malmö (2018)
15. Fendt, M.W., Harrison, B., Ware, S.G., Cardona-Rivera, R.E., Roberts, D.L.: Achieving the illusion of agency. In: Oyarzun, D., Peinado, F., Young, R., Elizalde, A., Méndez, G. (eds.) ICIDS 2012. LNCS, vol. 7648, pp. 114–125. Springer, Heidelberg (2012). https://doi.org/10.1007/978-3-642-34851-8_11
16. Cardona-Rivera, R.E., Robertson, J., Ware, S.G., Harrison, B., Roberts, D.L., Young, R.M.: Foreseeing meaningful choices. In: Proceedings of the Tenth AAAI Conference on Artificial Intelligence and Interactive Digital Entertainment, pp. 9–15. AAAI Press, Raleigh (2014)
17. MacCallum-Stewart, E., Parsler, J.: Illusory agency in Vampire: The Masquerade – Bloodlines. Dicht. Digit. **37** (2007)
18. Ericsson, K.A., Simon, H.A.: Protocol Analysis: Verbal Reports as Data. MIT Press, Cambridge (1993)

19. Knickmeyer, R.L., Mateas, M.: Preliminary evaluation of the interactive drama facade. In: Proceedings of the Conference on Human Factors in Computing Systems (CHI 2005), p. 1549. ACM Press, Portland (2005)
20. Klimmt, C., Hefner, D., Vorderer, P.: The video game experience as "true" identification: a theory of enjoyable alterations of players' self-perception. Commun. Theory **19**, 351–373 (2009)

Filling in the Gaps: "Shell" Playable Characters

Trena Lee[✉] and Alex Mitchell

Department of Communications and New Media,
National University of Singapore, Singapore, Singapore
trena.lee@u.nus.edu, alexm@nus.edu.sg

Abstract. In this paper we propose a new character type, the "shell" playable character, which differs from the standard playable character types of avatars or "rich" characters. These "shell" characters are neither complete "blank slates" for the players to project themselves onto, nor do they provide enough information to be considered "well-rounded" characters with complete personalities and backstories. Drawing on the concepts of *leerstellen* and ambiguity, we explore this new playable character type through comparative close readings of three games: *INSIDE*, *Emporium*, and *The Stanley Parable*. Our findings suggest that "shell" playable characters are characters that encourage players to develop their own understanding of the character, enabled through gaps and ambiguities that allow players the space to "fill" up the character with an interpretation of who the character could be, and to view the character as a separate entity rather than simply an extension of the player.

Keywords: Playable character types · Player interpretation · Ambiguity Gaps

1 Introduction

In games, the playable character is often viewed as an important figure, forming a bridge between the player and the game world through choices the player makes in the game [1–4]. Current literature on playable character in games has mainly focused on two character types: avatars (directly representing the player) and "rich" characters (characters with their own personalities and backstories) [5–7].

However, an interesting character type has surfaced in recent games that does not fit into these two categories. While these characters appear to be avatars due to their apparent lack of backstory or personality, simultaneously they are potentially "rich", as the game hints at a story behind them, albeit one left open to the player's interpretation. Through an analysis of three games – *INSIDE* [8], *Emporium* [9], and *The Stanley Parable* [10] – we explore how these characters do not fit either the avatar or "rich" character categories, and propose a new category: "shell" playable characters.

The paper begins by exploring current literature on the player-character relationship between the existing two character types. Next, we describe the research problem and explain the methodology and findings. We bring these findings together to propose a

© Springer Nature Switzerland AG 2018
R. Rouse et al. (Eds.): ICIDS 2018, LNCS 11318, pp. 240–249, 2018.
https://doi.org/10.1007/978-3-030-04028-4_24

preliminary definition of the "shell" playable character. Finally, we conclude with a brief summary, the limitations of this paper, and suggestions for future work.

2 Related Work

One of the concepts describing the attachment between the player and playable character is Character Attachment (CA), defined as "an individual's feelings of (a) friendship and (b) identification with a video game character when an individual is (c) willing to suspend disbelief, (d) feels responsible for the game character, and (e) feels in control of the game's character's actions" [11: p. 516] In short, CA describes the psychological merging of player's and playable character's minds, leading to the player identifying themselves as the character during gameplay [12–16].

Building upon the ideas of attachment and shifting self-perceptions, studies have been conducted into how this applies to avatars [4–6]. Avatars are commonly defined as the player represented physically within the game-world [6]. Beyond physically, avatars are also a form of social representation, being tied to the player's reputation in the game community [17]. Studies also show that the more similar the avatar to the player's characteristics, the more connected players feel to the avatar, suggesting that players prefer for avatars to represent themselves (the player) [18–20].

Studies have also been done on "rich" characters with their own clearly established personalities and backstories [3, 7]. Unlike avatars, players playing "rich" characters play as if they are navigating the game-world as, for example, Lara Croft [21]. For this type of character, Lankoski argues, "the personality traits of a character are an amalgam of traits inferred from features fixed by the game (predefined functions and goals structure) and features the player has imposed upon the character (e.g. by selecting skills and augmentations)" [21: p. 302]. Researchers have found that players tend to forget they are playing a game during gameplay. For example, players felt guilty making antisocial choices against NPCs, thus showing that they identified with the characters and interacted as though engaging with the characters in real-life, with real-life societal norms in place [22]. Mallon and Lynch conclude that characterisation of playable characters is important because players desire meaningful relationships with the game and its characters [7]. Doing so helps players connect with the playable character and thus care about their character's feelings and what happens to them [7].

3 Research Problem

In recent years, unlike the usual avatar and "rich" character, games that seem to be utilising a different playable character type and associated player-character relationship have emerged. Unlike Mallon and Lynch's strongly characterized playable character, in these games the player is often "guiding" the character while interpreting hints so as to form their own unique interpretation of who the character is, instead of being restricted by a set of character-defining choices provided within the game [7]. The player is thus given space to freely interpret the character instead of "filling" the character with "me but in the game world" (an avatar), or through preset storylines and choices provided by the game designers (a rich character). In this paper, we investigate this new player-character relationship and how this character type arises from the game mechanics, defining what we refer to as a "shell" playable character.

4 Methodology

For this paper, we conducted close readings [23] of three recent games that include the third playable character type described above: *INSIDE*, *Emporium* and *The Stanley Parable*. Close readings are often used to "reveal insights into the design of games, and also into the variety of pleasures afforded by the game experience, such as imagination, emotion, kinesthetic engagement, narrative immersion, and ludic flow" [23: p. 289], thus allowing in-depth preliminary exploration of whether such a character type indeed exists, and if it does exist, how this character type should be defined. This method involves multiple playthroughs of the games, during which the play experience is analyzed through a carefully chosen set of "analytical lenses" [23: p. 304].

To develop an understanding of the emerging category of "shell" characters, we draw on existing theories from related fields that can help to explain how players fill the gaps that exist in characters, and the techniques used by game designers to provide information while still leaving some gaps. Specifically, the analytical lenses used in the close readings are based on Iser's theory of *leerstellen*, and (narrative) ambiguity.

In the field of literature, *leerstellen* (meaning 'blanks' or 'gaps') is used to describe aspects of a text which leave gaps for readers to fill with their own imagination, reconstructing the work by using their background assumptions to fill in missing pieces [24]. Iser posits that readers should be given freedom to fill in gaps however they imagine, and that there is no 'best' interpretation [25–27]. The text, then, is a collaboration between writer and reader, in which the text guides how it should be read but does not determine the end-product of the reader's interpretation [25].

Ambiguity in text has been defined as "a poetic device [where] multiple meanings of a word or phrase are at work in poetry" [28: p. 210]. Building from the idea of multiple potential meanings, Buck, Sobiechowska and Winter argue that the author-reader role is one where "[w]riters are not told by readers what their story 'really' means [...] neither do writers tell readers what the 'real point' of the story is, i.e. what the writer had 'intended': rather, the story is a neutral ground, where different worlds of experience can intersect and interact" [29: p. 23]. Rather than leaving gaps, the use of ambiguity allows for multiple readings of the text, all of which could potentially be "true". Thus, in contrast to *leerstellen*, ambiguity does not result from a lack of information, but rather from the usage of information in such a way as to cause readers to question more deeply and ponder the truth about the story or characters in a work, creating their own interpretations based on their experience of the text.

5   Findings

Partial or inconsistent characterisation seemed to be a strong factor in suggesting that playable characters have undiscovered stories to be explored, stories that can be filled in with the player's own interpretations based on surface hints provided by the game. Choices were found at times to provide too much information about the playable character, but also interestingly to possibly preserve the "shell" nature of the character if this information led to ambiguity about the character's personality or backstory. We also found that "shell" characters, unlike other playable character types, create a clear sense of separation between the player and playable character, leading to a somewhat different player-character relationship. We now discuss these findings in more detail.

5.1   Partial or Inconsistent Characterisation

The use of partial or inconsistent characterisation to create gaps or ambiguity is one way that all three games developed the sense of a "shell" playable character.

In *INSIDE*, the focus is on a generic young boy with pale skin and dark hair. The only thing that stands out about him is his bright red shirt. In one scene, the player has to make the boy imitate the movements of mind-controlled humans; any mistakes lead to the guards noticing that the boy is not mind-controlled, and then killing him. In the background, other non-controlled humans can be seen spectating, all dressed in black with dark hair. The boy, whom I initially saw as generic, was now seen as special: his red shirt clearly differentiates him from the others. This small, differentiating detail in the boy's design motivated the main question that plagued me for the rest of the game: what makes him special, and why does he have to avoid detection instead of being with the other non-controlled humans? Though the game did not impose a specific personality or backstory on the boy, his characterisation as "special" compared to the other characters implied a deeper story to be discovered behind the boy, suggesting he was more than simply an avatar representing me in the game world.

Similarly, in *Emporium*, the playable character is a generic boy. However, in contrast to *INSIDE*, here the perception of a "shell" character is formed through the boy's interactions with another character – the old man. Despite the player controlling the boy, the narration in the game mostly takes place from the old man's point-of-view. For example, on a pier, the old man describes the boy's actions, saying: "He said nothing. Just clung to my hand tightly." The constant second or third-person reference to the boy (instead of say, "*You* said nothing...") led me to feel that the boy is not an avatar representing me, but rather is a character of his own separate from my control, especially as the old man often describes the boy performing actions that I had no part in selecting, such as holding the old man's hand. The old man, therefore, seems to be the player's guide to learning more about the boy's yet-to-be-discovered story.

Unlike *INSIDE* and *Emporium*, where gaps in characterisation lead to a sense of a "shell" character, in *TSP* every thought and action of Stanley is described by the narrator, who portrays Stanley as a generic office worker. However, this detailed sharing of information about Stanley and his thoughts eventually led me to question whether the narrator is truly reliable. For example, in repeat playthroughs, upon stepping into the boss's office I encountered different versions of the dialogue. In one version, Stanley is fearful and breaks down in the office, but in another, he is still hopeful for a solution to his predicament. Unlike in the previous two games, here the gaps the player deals with are not blanks but rather are filled with ambiguity, due to the different descriptions of Stanley offered by the narrator. Although Stanley first appears to be a "rich" character, the conflicting versions of Stanley described by an increasingly unreliable narrator suggest that the narrator could never have been describing the "real" Stanley, instead leaving it to the player to decipher which is the "real" Stanley.

5.2   Choices

The use of choices and the information conveyed by those choices was another way that the three games made use of gaps or ambiguity to create a feeling that the playable character was something other than either an avatar or a rich character.

INSIDE features linear gameplay with no branching choices, as all puzzles only have one solution. For example, to solve one puzzle, the boy has to suck chicks into a giant machine, using them as projectiles to knock down a box to reach the next platform. My feeling of dissonance during this scene, resulting from not wanting to harm the chicks but having to do so to proceed, helped me to distance myself from "being" the boy. I thought of the use of the chicks as an autonomous action on his part, rather than a reflection of what I myself would do in that situation. Through many of these events, I began to form the impression that either the boy was willing to do anything to proceed even if it was cruel, or that this type of behavior was commonplace in the game-world. While it could be argued that the player does have control over the boy's behaviour, as they control his movements and actions, the player ultimately is only complying with the game's demands because of its linear, one-solution structure.

In contrast, most of the choices in *Emporium* are what Mawhorter et al. call flavour choices – choices that do not impact the overall course of game events even though they impact the player's game experience [30]. These choices tend to reveal information about the character, potentially allowing the player to learn more about the character and his background. However, most of the choices and responses in *Emporium* are somewhat abstract and poetic, leading to more questions than answers about who the boy is. As I experienced further dialogue choices, I came to understand that the key to knowing who the boy was lay not only in details revealed through the choices, but also in figuring out his relationship to the old man. For example, the train station dialogue painted a moody image of both characters in my mind, through the description of the boy showing the old man a wilted dandelion, while not explicitly telling me what the "silence" that they both wanted was, nor the significance of the wilted dandelion. While the choices provided some information, they were akin to a puzzle with missing pieces, gaps left for me to fill with my own interpretations.

In TSP, choices are very important, as the different paths the player takes do actually lead to different endings. However, the narrator is always one step ahead of the player, saying things such as "When Stanley came to a set of two open doors, he entered the door on his left." As 'Stanley', if the player then goes through the right door, the narrator will try to stay in control of the story, saying, "This was not the correct way to the meeting room, and Stanley knew it perfectly well. Perhaps he wanted to stop by the employee lounge first, just to admire it". Here, while the narrator *tells* the player to 'be Stanley' and go through the left door, this idea of what Stanley is supposed to do is also shown to be flexible, as the narrator 'shapes' another version of Stanley when the player goes through the right door instead. My choices thus, while seemingly having a meaningful impact on the narrator's story flow, ultimately were subjected to the narrator's whims. As a result of the narrator's need to fully control Stanley's story, Stanley became an ever-changing enigma of a character. In TSP, having choices eventually led to many inconsistencies and ambiguities, ultimately leaving me with more questions than answers as to who 'Stanley' might be.

5.3 Role of the Player

As seen in previous studies, the focus when viewing the role of the player has usually been on the idea of the player feeling as if they *were* the playable character, implying that the role of the player during gameplay is to be the character [16]. However, in the case of the "shell" character, there is potential for the player's role to straddle the space between being behind the computer and being within the game-world.

In *INSIDE*, during one of the puzzles, the numbers "04" can be seen on a glass panel, suggesting that the player is viewing the boy from a room behind the glass panel. Furthermore, there are scientists with a clear view into the room where the boy is located. However, despite him swimming past them to solve the puzzle, they do not seem to notice him, a stark contrast from earlier, where one mistake could cause an adult to notice the boy and try to kill him. The revelation of the player's apparent "location" within the game world as being in a lab watching the boy suggests that the player's character might actually be a scientist in the game monitoring the boy, rather than the boy himself. The intriguing implication of this is that with the "shell" character the player does not assume the usual position of "being" the main playable character, but instead possibly plays another, somewhat ambiguous, role in the game.

Similarly, in *Emporium*, the tension between the player controlling the boy and yet only being told information about the boy from old man's perspective implies that the role of the player is not one of "being" the boy. For example, in the train station, the old man mentions: "It was in this waiting room that I first met the boy." However, my first encounter with the old man had been in the emporium, not the train station. This simple statement by the old man raised questions within me as to what history they shared and what their relationship was, beyond what I had directly experienced when playing the game. It suggested that they had a history prior to the game, creating a knowledge gap that I, the player, had to fill with my own interpretations. This highlighted the distance between the boy and I, because he had a history with the old man that I could never truly know. The boy was the boy, and my role was perhaps that of a disembodied being who guides the boy while listening to the old man's musings.

TSP also suggests this idea of a player role separate from the playable character. Throughout the game the narrator switches between addressing the player ("you") and addressing "Stanley", implying that the two are separate entities. This is most evident in the "Broom Closet" ending, where after the player has Stanley stay in the broom closet for some time, the narrator sarcastically assumes the player is dead, and requests for a second player to replace the player at the computer. Through this sequence, the game suggests that the player is replaceable and separate from Stanley, as any other player can take over and the game will proceed as usual, with no impact on Stanley's story. Unlike most games where I would expect to feel like I am "Stanley", TSP breaks this connection and highlights the player's role as what it really is: a player behind a computer screen, a player with seemingly complete power over the player character and yet bound within the pre-programmed outcomes of the game world.

6 Discussion

From the close readings, it appears that "shell" playable characters are characters the player can only describe in interpretative terms, and that the "player" and "playable character" roles are distinctly separate. We now discuss these findings in more detail.

6.1 Interpreting What Is not There and What May Be There: Gaps and Ambiguity

Through the close readings of *INSIDE* and *Emporium*, we have explored how the character's appearance and behaviour can draw players' attention to the lack of explanation about who the playable characters are exactly. As games do not solely rely on dialogue, what the player sees happen on-screen contributes to their idea of who the playable character is [20]. When characters are given information only through the game environment without any dialogue, such as in *INSIDE*, players have to rely on their imagination or past experiences to derive meaning from what is shown (and what is not shown). In other words, players have to fill in "gaps" when information is not given and decide the "truth" when information provided has more than one possible interpretation. *Emporium* shows that making choices in games can provide more information about the playable character, but rather than clearing up the player's questions, abstract choices and responses can instead make things more ambiguous. In TSP, the narrator gives "too much" information, and yet not enough consistent information to determine what is true and what is not. The narrator provides conflicting, ambiguous information with insufficient evidence behind each viewpoint to determine which is the truth. Stanley's true identity is left open to interpretation by the player.

From these games, we see that what defines a "shell" character is not the amount of information revealed about the character per se. Rather, it is whether the information given is incomplete or conflicting, providing no clear answer as to who the character is exactly. Who the character is has to be interpreted based on these gaps and ambiguities. As with the idea of *leerstellen*, in which the text is a collaboration between writer and reader [25], here the designer hints at the character's story and yet also gives the player some control over the story by allowing them to interpret both story and playable character. Designer and player thus create the game's meaning hand-in-hand.

6.2 We Are Connected, yet I Am not You and You Are not Me

Initially, due to the generic features of the characters in the games we have analyzed, the player starts off feeling that the character is an "avatar". Players tend to perceive avatars as virtual representations of themselves within the game [17]. Therefore, if "shell" characters were seen as avatars, it is possible that players would not bother to uncover who the characters really are, viewing them simply as representations of themselves. However, in *INSIDE* my initial impression of the boy as generic and thus "blank" soon changed when I realised that he seemed to have a backstory as suggested by hints in the game. Due to these hints, the player-character relationship I formed with the boy became not one of seeing him as "me" within the game-world (as an avatar), but rather, as one in which I was guiding this boy with an unknown backstory through the game.

At the same time, "shell" characters seem to imply a (hidden) rich backstory for the player to discover, suggesting they could also potentially be experienced as "rich" characters. For "rich" characters, the playable character's identity is a combination of features predetermined by the game and choices made by the player as the playable character [20]. Similarly, for "shell" characters, the playable character's identity is a combination of hints and gaps left within the game and the player's interpretation of this information. The difference here is that choices are not meant to define the character, but instead serve as a source of ambiguity and gaps for the player to interpret.

However, this is not the most important difference. A "shell" character truly moves away from being a "rich" character when the player realizes the true nature of the player's role within the game. In *INSIDE*, for example, the positioning of the "player" behind the laboratory screen implies that the player has a separate role within the game, perhaps as a scientist monitoring the boy. In *Emporium*, the strangeness of how the player chooses the boy's responses to the old man and yet the old man talks about the boy in third-person, as if having a conversation directly with the player, seems to suggest a disembodied role for the player instead of playing as the boy. This is most strongly seen in TSP, as the game goes against the usual idea that when playing the player should suspend her disbelief and forget that she is playing a game [22], and instead foregrounds the fact that the player is sitting in front of the computer screen, with no true presence in or power over the pre-programmed game world.

Therefore, with a "shell" playable character, players are encouraged to view the character as more than a "puppet" or avatar they control in the game, but instead as a character in its own right that the player cares about. However, at the same time, the "shell" character is not a "rich" character, as details are left for the player to fill in with their own unique interpretations. This difference from the two usual player character types is further emphasized when the role of the player is suggested to be one that is entirely separate from the playable character, subverting the usual expectations of "being" the playable character during gameplay and instead making it clear that the player and the playable character are two different entities, joined by the game.

7 Conclusion

Through close readings of three games, *INSIDE*, *Emporium*, and *The Stanley Parable*, we have explored how "shell" characters are not simply a middle ground between avatars and "rich" characters, but instead form a unique, new playable character type. "Shell" playable characters are characters that allow players to derive their own interpretations of the character, attempting to untangle who the character is from ambiguities and gaps within the game. The playable character is thus not just an extension of the player herself. Instead, the player feels herself to be a separate entity within the game, one with no real influence over the game world due to her position of being outside the game-world and in front of a computer. By identifying this new playable character type and its characteristics, this paper provides a foundation for future empirical studies that can more clearly define how this playable character type may be identified and categorized, and how it may be used in future game designs.

References

1. Taylor, L.: When seams fall apart: video game space and the player. Game Stud. **3**(2) (2003). http://www.gamestudies.org/0302/taylor
2. Yee, N.: The demographics, motivations, and derived experiences of users of massively multi-user online graphical environments. Presence Teleoperators Virtual Environ. **15**(3), 309–329 (2006)
3. Taylor, N., Kampe, C., Bell, K.: Me and Lee: identification and the play of attraction in the walking dead. Int. J. Comput. Game Res. **15**(1) (2015). http://www.gamestudies.org/1501/articles/taylor
4. Papale, L.: Beyond identification: defining the relationships between player and avatar. J. Games Crit. **1**(2), 1–12 (2014)
5. Kastenmüller, A., Greitemeyer, T., Fairclough, S., Waite, D., Fischer, P.: Playing exergames and sporting activity. Soc. Psychol. **44**(4), 264–270 (2013)
6. Mccreery, M.P., Krach, S.K., Schrader, P., Boone, R.: Defining the virtual self: personality, behaviour and the psychology of embodiment. Comput. Hum. Behav. **28**(3), 976–983 (2012)
7. Mallon, B., Lynch, R.: Stimulating psychological attachments in narrative games: engaging players with game characters. Stimul. Gaming **45**(4–5), 508–527 (2014)
8. INSIDE: Playdead (2016)
9. Emporium: Tom Kitchen (2017)
10. The Stanley Parable: Galactic Café (2013)
11. Lewis, M.L., Weber, R., Bowman, N.D.: "They May Be Pixels, But They're MY Pixels:" developing a metric of character attachment in role-playing video games. CyberPsychol. Behav. **11**(4), 515–518 (2008)
12. Bowman, N.D., Schultheiss, D., Schumann, C.: "I'm Attached, and I'm a Good Guy/Gal!": how character attachment influences pro- and anti-social motivations to play massively multiplayer online role-playing games. Cyberpsychol. Behav. Soc. Netw. **15**(3), 169–174 (2012)
13. Klimmt, C., Hefner, D., Vorderer, P., Roth, C., Blake, C.: Identification with video game characters as automatic shift of self-perceptions. Media Psychol. **13**(4), 323–338 (2010)
14. Klimmt, C., Hefner, D., Vorderer, P.: The video game experience as "True" identification: a theory of enjoyable alterations of players self-perception. Commun. Theory **19**(4), 351–373 (2009)
15. Cohen, J.: Defining identification: a theoretical look at the identification of audiences with media characters. Mass Commun. Soc. **4**(3), 245–264 (2001)
16. Hart, C.: Getting into the game: an examination of player personality projection in videogame avatars. Int. J. Comput. Game Res. **17**(2) (2017). http://www.gamestudies.org/1702/articles/hart

17. Carter, M., Gibbs, M., Arnold, M: Avatars, characters, players and users: multiple identities at/in play. In: Proceedings of the 24th Australian Computer-Human Interaction Conference, pp. 68–71 (2012)
18. Hooi, R., Cho, H.: Avatar-driven self-disclosure: the virtual me is the actual me. Comput. Hum. Behav. **39**, 20–28 (2014)
19. Jin, S.A.: Self-discrepancy and regulatory fit in avatar-based exergames. Psychol. Rep. **111** (3), 697–710 (2012)
20. Trepte, S., Reinecke, L.: Avatar creation and video game enjoyment. J. Media Psychol. **22** (4), 171–184 (2010)
21. Lankoski, P.: Player character engagement in computer games. Games Cult. **6**(4), 291–311 (2011)
22. Weaver, A.J., Lewis, N.: Mirrored morality: an exploration of moral choice in video games. Cyberpsychol. Behav. Soc. Netw. **15**(11), 610–614 (2012)
23. Bizzocchi, J., Tanenbaum, J.: Well read: applying close reading techniques to gameplay experiences. In: Davidson, D. (ed.) Well Played 3.0: Video Games, Value and Meaning, pp. 289–315. ETC Press, Pittsburgh (2011)
24. Iser, W.: The reading process: a phenomenological approach. New Lit. Hist. **3**(2), 279–299 (1972)
25. Iser, W.: The Act of Reading: A Theory of Aesthetic Response, 1st edn. Johns Hopkins University Press, Baltimore (1997)
26. Brinker, M.: Two phenomenologies of reading: ingarden and iser on textual indeterminacy. Poet. Today **1**(4), 203–212 (1980)
27. Karhulahti, V.: An ontological theory of narrative works: storygame as postclassical literature. Storyworlds J. Narrat. Stud. **7**(1), 39–73 (2015)
28. Bahti, T.: Ambiguity and indeterminacy: the juncture. Comp. Lit. **38**(3), 209–223 (1986)
29. Buck, A., Sobiechowska, P., Winter, R.: Professional Experience and the Investigative Imagination: The Art of Reflective Writing, 6th edn. Routledge, London (1999)
30. Mawhorter, P., Mateas, M., Wardrip-Fruin, N., Jhala, A.: Towards a theory of choice poetics. In: Proceedings of the 9th International Conference on the Foundations of Digital Games (2014)

A Model for Describing Alternate Reality Games

Ryan Javanshir[✉], Beth Carroll, and David E. Millard

University of Southampton, Southampton, UK
{rjlg15, E.Carroll, dem}@soton.ac.uk

Abstract. Alternate Reality Games (ARGs) are a form of transmedia story-telling that are difficult to describe and analyse due to their inherent ephemerality and use of multiple media channels. But critical analyses of ARGs and a deeper understanding of how they work are needed for both improvements in ARG design theory, and to aid in the preservation of ARG content and structure. This paper presents a way to describe and analyse ARGs, the ARG Descriptive Model (ADM), that combines together features from several existing approaches to create a more holistic description of an ARG. The ADM is then applied to two case studies to demonstrate how it can be used to model the media channels, potential navigation routes between these channels, and how these channels evolve over time. The paper shows that this approach can be applied to create a basis for a common methodology for ARG analyses.

Keywords: Alternate Reality Games · Narrative · Transmedia storytelling

1 Introduction

Alternate Reality Games (ARGs) are a form of transmedia story [10, 13] that seek to layer a fictional world on top of reality and provide a story in the process [3, 8, 11, 12]. Though the Web is one of the major channels for delivery, ARGs deliver their content to players using a number of media channels, and sometimes include multiple game mechanics that require varying levels of interaction from players [7, 8, 11].

Several considerations must be made when analyzing ARGs: their contents span multiple media channels, their content is often hidden, and they are commonly ephemeral [8]. However, in order to analyse an ARG, it must first be described and its media channel components need to be identified.

There have been several attempts made to create models and frameworks that can be used to describe different aspects of ARGs [4, 5, 9, 15, 16]. However, these attempts are limited in that they do not give a 'scene by scene' breakdown of an ARG, showing which media channels were used, how they linked to each other, when they became 'live', and how they changed over time.

This paper presents the ARG Descriptive Model (ADM), which attempts to build upon this existing work and address these limitations. We first explore the prior work on defining and modelling ARGs, we then describe our methodology for iteratively developing the model, present the model itself, and finally demonstrate the model by applying it to two case study ARGs: *Overwatch: Sombra ARG* and *Cloverfield ARG*.

© Springer Nature Switzerland AG 2018
R. Rouse et al. (Eds.): ICIDS 2018, LNCS 11318, pp. 250–258, 2018.
https://doi.org/10.1007/978-3-030-04028-4_25

2   Background Literature

Initial design documents are sometimes used to describe ARGs [6]. Such design documents are created by the producers and are used as the blueprint or script of their respective ARGs. What these documents focus on is varied, reflecting the genre of the ARG being created. In a similar way, attempts in academia have sought to create retrospective design documents, by modelling different aspects of ARGs. The 'ARG Analysis Form', developed by Ciancia [4], documents which channels were used, the overall story as a written account, and an action flow showing how events are conveyed to participants. It can be used as a general summary, but does not provide any information on how channels update over time. An alternative approach is taken by Ruppel, who models ARGs as network graphs that allow the identification of traits, such as the amount of incoming and outgoing connections into any given channel [15]. This technique concerns itself with the relationship between the elements of the network, but not the content of those elements. Despite this, Ruppel argues that by portraying ARGs as a graph, it provides insight into the design of the ARG, such as the potential user journey through the network. Looking more at the content of channels, de Beer's model [5] seeks to show how narrative, game action and player participation evolves over time. A 'component' is an action that occurs in the ARG. Disregarding the specificity of a channel, de Beer provides a timeline of components, showing which one's players will encounter. For example, the ARG may start with a narrative component, to a game component and then back to narrative. Being channel agnostic, the model does not provide any details as to which channels these components were embedded, or how channels evolved over time. Finally, Stanescu et al.'s work [16] seeks to model the player's journey through their choices. Players start in one place, and are then presented with choices, with each choice presenting new choices. This however only works effectively for single player, linear ARGs, where there are choices to be made.

The wider field of narratology can provide some insight into how ARGs could be modelled [2]. ARGs layer a fictitious world (the *fabula*) onto to the real world (creating the *story*) that is manifested in the form of multiple media channels (creating the narrative *text*). This allows us to distinguish between different types of time within the experience. For example, Tomashevskij separates *fabula time* from *story time*, with the former being 'hypothetical time' in which the events occur inside the fictional world, and the latter being 'narrating time', being the chronology of the text or the order in which content is given to the audience [17]. The telling of a story can then be broken up into constituent 'events', which are defined as 'a change of state manifested in discourse by a process statement in the mode of Do or Happen' [14].

3   Methodology

In our work we wanted to develop a model that captured the key elements identified in previous work: media channels, potential navigation routes, channel evolution over time, and the events of the ARG. We undertook an iterative development process, analysing a series of ARGs and exploring how they might be deconstructed in such a way that these features are captured. In each iteration the model was applied to the ARGs, modelling problems were identified, and the model evolved to accommodate them.

The ARGs were selected based on the following criteria:

Practicality. The ephemeral nature of many ARGs mean that they cannot be replayed, so any data used to model the ARG must have existed in the form of third party post mortems, blogs, videos, wikis, summaries or any archived content that has been left over. Only ARGs that had such data were selected.

Diversity. ARGs use a variety of techniques such as levels of audience interaction, different media channels and different puzzles. When expanding our set of ARGs we attempted to choose those with characteristics not already in the set.

Motivation. ARGs are made for a wide variety of reasons, e.g. for the promotion of products such as films and games, to reveal a story associated with a product, or as a standalone experience. When expanding our set of ARGs if alternatives were present that had the same characteristics, we chose those that had a different motivation.

We began our analysis with *19 Reinos* (HBO, 2015). This is a relatively recent, popular ARG, with a high practicality value – due to the presence of a case study around the experience on the producer's webpage. We then began to expand this set, evaluating potential ARGs using the ARG Wikipedia page.[1] The Wikipedia list provided useful information such as the title, developer, story summary, gameplay summary and scale. This information was then used to see whether an ARG fulfilled the criteria. The scale provided insight into practicality (the more popular it was, the more third party content there would be), the story and gameplay summary provided diversity considerations, and the developer, story summary and further reading of the ARG identified the reason for production. In total we included twenty ARGs in this process (shown in Table 1).

4 The Model

ADM is based around the concept of a *channel*, a subset of a media channel that is defined by its boundary. For example, two text-based websites communicate their content in the same way, but will have their own channel (denoted as W1 and W2), because their content is different and in two separate domains. Channels can also be differentiated by space, for example two live performances in different locations will each receive their own channel. Table 2 shows the superset of channels in our analysis.

The periodicity of the channels is also recorded, with any change to the channel spawning a new *instance*. An instance will remain until another instance takes its place. For example, blog W1 contains two posts on Monday, but on Tuesday there are three posts. W1 will spawn a new instance because of this and will be known as W1(1).

Instances have values that describe their *interactivity* and *state*. For interactivity an instance is *passive* if the audience do not have to engage with the instance to consume the content, e.g. watching a film or reading a book, and *active* if the audience have to interact

---

[1] https://en.wikipedia.org/wiki/List_of_alternate_reality_games. accessed: 19/09/2018.

Table 1. ARGs used to create the ADM.

ARG title	Practicality	Diversity	Motivation
GoT: 19 Reinos	Case study	Linear & episodic content	Promotion
Batman: Why So Serious?	3rd party	Role play	Promotion
Conspiracy for Good	3rd party	Role play	Social benefit
The Beast	3rd party	Network of clues	Promotion
Dexter ARG	3rd party	Live events & streaming	Promotion
Afterbirth ARG	3rd party	Linear	Promotion
The Black Watchman	Perm' game	Single player	Standalone
Waking Titan	3rd/archive	Network of clues	Add' Story
Oxenfree	3rd/archive	Linear	Add' Story
Cloverfield ARG	3rd/archive	Network of clues	Promotion
Majestic	3rd party	Episodes, NPC roles	Standalone
Year Zero	3rd party	Network of clues	Political
Frog Fractions 2	3rd/archive	Clues in Steam games	Promotion
I Love Bees	3rd party	Events, role play & clues	Promotion
Super 8 ARG	3rd/archive	Network of clues	Promotion
10 Cloverfield Lane ARG	3rd/archive	Network of clues	Promotion
Westworld	3rd party	Network of content	Promotion
Xi	3rd party	Games console based	Standalone
Cathy's Book	3rd/archive	Physical book based	Standalone
Overwatch: Sombra ARG	3rd party	Linear	Add' Story

Table 2. Examples of unique channels.

Media channel	Examples of unique channels
Website (non-social)	Domains
Website (social)	Profiles, product pages, forum threads, messenger conversations
Email	Addresses
TV, film and video	Films, episodes, single uploaded video and video playlists
Telephone	Payphones and telephone numbers
Live performance	Location and time
Physical artefacts	Newspapers, documents, posters, stickers etc.

with the instance such as emailing a character or talking to them over the phone. We refer to interaction in a functional sense, meaning media is passive when non-ergodic in the way described by Aarseth [1]: *"where the effort to traverse the text is trivial, with no extranoematic responsibilities placed on the reader except (for example) eye movement and the periodic or arbitrary turning of pages"*. Hence posting on Twitter is interactive but watching a video is not. Concerning state, an instance is *live* if it cannot be accessed in its original form after it has occurred, e.g. a live performance, and *static* if the content is still available in its original form after an update. Table 3 shows examples of instances with different state and interactivity values.

Table 3. Instance state and interactivity.

	Passive	Active
Live	e.g. live theatre	e.g. live action role play
Static	e.g. YouTube video	e.g. video game

Links are connections between channels or instances that represent potential navigational paths, for example hyperlinks between websites, automatic loading of channels e.g. website links to a YouTube video after twenty seconds of inactivity, or direct referral to another channel e.g. 'go to www.google.com'.

A *scene* is associated with channels and instances that are playable at any given time, used similarly to books, plays, films and some games. This will illustrate which updates occurred before or after others, as well as which ones occurred around the same time. A scene signifies the narrating time.

A *description* is the description associated with an instance, and captures free form notes about the story, nature of the puzzles or audience engagement.

ADM therefore models an ARG as a set of channels, with each channel comprised of a sequence of instances that are part of a scene. Each instance contains links, interactivity/state values, and a description. This model can be used in both written (shown in Table 4), and visual form, with the visual form being used to illustrate the model in this paper. Figure 1 is an example ARG that starts off (top left) with a static website, that leads to a live stream, then later to a computer game, and finally to a live event.

Table 4. Model of a single channel.

Name of Channel					
Instance	Scene	Links	Interactivity	State	Description

5   Case Studies

This section will apply ADM to two case studies, to demonstrate how the model can be applied, and to show how it reveals the underlying structure of ARG experiences. Table 5 includes the abbreviations used in the visual model.

5.1   Overwatch: Sombra ARG

Overwatch: Sombra ARG (Blizzard, 2017) was made to create interest around a new character, called Sombra, to feature in the multiplayer-only game *Overwatch*. *Overwatch; Sombra ARG* was an add-on for *Overwatch* players and provided diegetic content not in the game.

Figure 2 shows the model applied to *Overwatch: Sombra ARG*. The model shows that the ARG was a linear experience, with new channels becoming involved and new instances spawning steadily over time. Much of the content at the beginning was static and passive (scenes 1–7), allowing latecomers to view much of the backstory. The largely active and live content (scenes 8–16) involved Sombra communicating with the community via websites, emails and forum posts. The ARG concluded at Blizzcon, a live conference hosted by Blizzard, that saw Sombra hack into one of the shows and reveal her identity. This provided both a conclusion to the ARG for those who knew about it, and an introduction to the new character to those who had no idea the ARG existed. This reveal was then uploaded as a video for posterity.

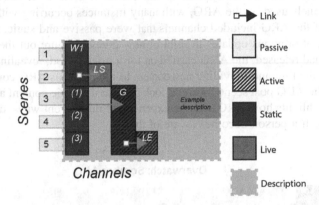

Fig. 1. An example ARG

Table 5. Abbreviations

Abbr.	Word	Abbr.	Word	Abbr.	Word
W	Website	P	Paper	LE	Live event
F/W	Forum	E	Email	C	Comic
MS	MySpace	G	Game	F	Film
B	Blog	PH	Phone	DVD	DVD
Y	YouTube	TW	Twitter	TR	Trailer
A	Audio recording	VID	Video	BR	BluRay

5.2   Cloverfield

The *Cloverfield ARG* (Bad Robot, 2007) was created in 2007 to promote the upcoming *Cloverfield* (Bad Robot, 2007) movie, set to release in 2008. The ARG started with a hub website and trailer. The hub website was used to connect players to some of the other channels of the ARG, like Myspace pages of different characters that feature in the film. Over time, fictitious companies and organisations were identified, with their website updates providing their backstory and current operations. One of these was Tagruato, a deep sea drilling company that had recently been the victim of a catastrophic event that saw one of their drilling stations collapse. This event was reported by fictitious news reports from around the world, that were uploaded to YouTube.

Figure 3 shows the model applied to the *Cloverfield ARG*. It shows the large amount of channels used by the ARG, with many instances occurring within the same scene. Much of the ARG included channels that were passive and static, allowing the players to look at previous updates in light of new clues to figure out the connection. Once the film had released, the ARG carried on for a brief period, revealing events that happened after the film and providing newcomers to the previous ARG content. People introduced to the ARG post scene 24 could look back at the static content as a historical record. This highlights how ARGs can be experienced in different ways, depending on the time in which a person becomes aware of them.

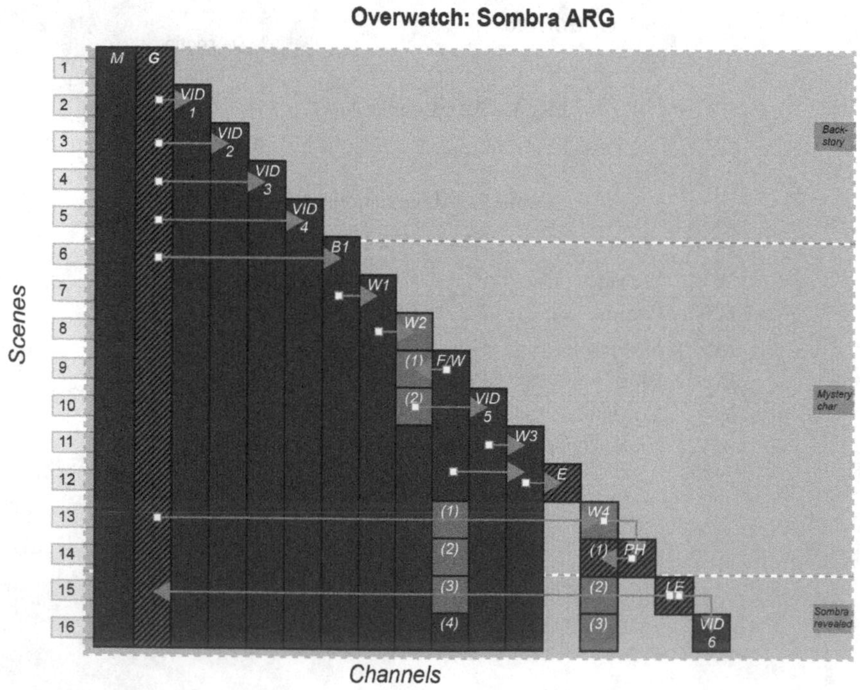

Fig. 2. Overwatch: Sombra ARG

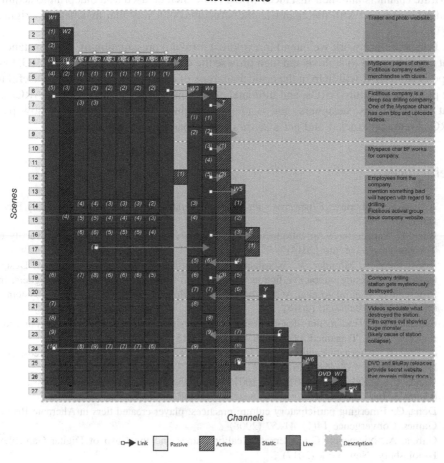

Fig. 3. Cloverfield ARG

6 Conclusion

This paper has presented ADM, a model that describes ARGs that can be used as a basis for analysis. The model was created and refined using a diverse set of twenty ARGs that were selected based on the availability of data, technical diversity, and difference in the motivation for their production. The model differs from previous work in that it captures media channels, potential navigational routes, and time. Two case studies were then presented to demonstrate ADM, showing that the model successfully models ephemeral ARGs with scenes that show what content is available at any given time.

Potential applications of ADM are as a planning tool, aiding in the creation of a design document, or as a retrospective tool to model ARGs. This may aid ARG researchers in understanding the structure of ARGs and how they evolve over time. It is hoped that ADM could also aid in the preservation of ARG content, identifying separate channels and their instances which could then be used as a blueprint to acquire content associated with the channels and structured in a way that matches the original ARG.

For our future work we intend to explore a formal representation of ADM instances that could be used to archive and then browse the content and structure of an ARG. Our hope is that ADM will help in the critical analysis of existing ARGs, would be useful in the planning of future ARGs, and ultimately might help in the preservation of ARGs so that future writers, designers, and academics might be able to understand how past ARGs were constructed and get a sense of what participants experienced.

References

1. Aaseth, E.: Cybertext: Perspectives on Ergodic Literature. Johns Hopkins University Press, Baltimore (1997)
2. Bal, M.: Narratology: An Introduction to the Theory of Narrative, 3rd edn. University of Toronto Press, Toronto (2014)
3. Bonsignore, E., Moulder, V., Neustaedter, C., Hansen, D., Kraus, K., Druin, A.: Design tactics for authentic interactive fiction: insights from Alternate Reality Game designers. In: Proceedings of 32nd Annual ACM Conference on Human Factors in Computing Systems - CHI 2014, pp. 947–950 (2014)
4. Ciancia, M.: Transmedia design framework. Design-oriented approach to transmedia research. Int. J. Transmedia Lit. 1(1), 131–145 (2015)
5. de Beer, K.: Alternate Reality Games (ARG) as innovative digital information sources. Libr. Hi Tech 34(3), 433–453 (2016)
6. Dena, C.: ARG Design Charts (2007). http://www.christydena.com/online-essays/arg-design-charts/
7. Dena, C.: Emerging participatory culture practices: player-created tiers in Alternate Reality Games. Convergence 14(1), 41–57 (2008)
8. Garcia, A., Niemeyer, G.: Alternate Reality Games and the Cusp of Digital Gameplay. Bloomsbury, New York (2017)
9. Hansen, D., Bonsignore, E., Ruppel, M., Visconti, A., Kraus, K.: Designing reusable alternate reality games. In: Proceedings of the SIGCHI Conference on Human Factors in Computing Systems - CHI 2013, p. 1529 (2013)
10. Jenkins, H.: Convergence Culture. New York University Press, New York (2006)
11. Kim, J., Allen, J., Lee, E.: Alternate Reality Games. Educ. Week Digit. Dir. 51(2), 36–42 (2008)
12. Phillips, A., Thompson, B., Alexander, B., Dena, C., Barlow N.: 2006 Alternate Reality Games White Paper. IGDA ARG SIG (2006)
13. Pratten, R.: Getting started with transmedia storytelling. CreateSpace Independent Publishing Platform (2015)
14. Prince, G.: A Grammar of Stories: An Introduction. Mouton, The Hague (1973)
15. Ruppel, M.: Visualizing transmedia networks: links, paths and peripheries. Ph.D. thesis, University of Maryland (2012)
16. Stanescu, R., Olsson, C., M.: Designing a conceptual framework for reusable Alternate Reality Games. Master's thesis, University of Malmo (2014)
17. Tomashevskij, B.: Russian Formalist Criticism: Four Essays. University of Nebraska Press, Lincoln (1965)

Frammenti: The ARG About Erasing Memories, That Was Forgotten

Serena Zampolli(✉)

H-Farm, Roncade, Italy
serena.zampolli@h-farm.com

Abstract. "Frammenti" was released in 2009 and it was Italy's first Alternate Reality Game. It consisted of a television series and an online game of solving enigmas collaboratively. The development of the project is here retraced basing on interviews lead with its director, screenwriter, game designer. Since the budget was limited, production had to get creative and resourceful in the way they strengthened the emergent narrative by getting involved in first person with the players, both in the virtual and real world.

Keywords: Alternate Reality Game · Interactive digital storytelling
Frammenti · H-Farm

1 Introduction

In 2009, more than one thousand people took part in a secret online operation to save the world from a terrible chemical attack: they were all players in Italy's first Alternate Reality Game: "Frammenti".

"Frammenti" was a pioneering experience, but there are few written records about it, and so far only in Italian[1]. This is why it seems important to write about it, so that it can be included as case study in the map of interactive digital storytelling.

This work is a short recollection of what happened during the designing and deployment of "Frammenti", and it bases on interviews carried with director Valerio Di Paola, screenwriter Gianluca Marino, and game designer Fabio Salvadori[2] (Sect. 2), followed by a comparison of "Frammenti" with other ARGs of the time (Sect. 3). It closes with some takeaways from this experience (Sect. 4).

---

[1] One academic paper about "Frammenti" was published in 2014 and then again in 2016 [1, 2]. In addition, in 2017 a MA thesis analysing the role of video games in learning included "Frammenti" as a case study [3].

[2] At the time of "Frammenti"'s production, Di Paola and Marino were working for Shado, and Salvadori was working for Log607.

© Springer Nature Switzerland AG 2018
R. Rouse et al. (Eds.): ICIDS 2018, LNCS 11318, pp. 259–264, 2018.
https://doi.org/10.1007/978-3-030-04028-4_26

2   Frammenti: Italy's First ARG

"Frammenti" was Italy's first Alternate Reality Game (ARG). Its story revolved around journalist Lorenzo Soare: he had lost his memory, and could rebuild it only by solving a series of puzzles he himself had left behind (therefore the title "Frammenti", "fragments"). He did so with the help of the online players (referred to as "The Activists"), and discovered that the pharmaceutical industry Marlow & Kurtz had created a pill that could erase memories and wanted to dissolve it in the sewages of some major city to manipulate the population and take over the world; he had found out about it and so they had kidnapped him and erased his memory.

"Frammenti" consisted of two parts: an Italian television series broadcasted on Current Italia in 2009, and an online platform designed to have players cooperate in solving the puzzles and unlock the episodes[3].

Here we revisit the main steps of the project. It started in the first half of 2008, the game mechanics were defined during the Fall of 2008, and filming of the series took place in the Spring of 2009 (Sect. 2.1). The show was aired from October to December 2009, with the game unfolding in parallel (Sect. 2.2).

2.1   How It All Started: Concept, Pre-production, and Production

In 2008 a startup named Log607, specialised in gamification[4], partnered with a startup named Shado[5], specialised in video production, to develop an interactive narrative that would unfold partly online and partly in a television series.

They asked writer Simone Sarasso to write a story that could accommodate a series of enigmas. Then, Log607 started working on developing the game mechanics. They imagined a narrative structure with multiple and intersecting paths, but soon realized filming all the possible scenes would exceed their budget. So they decided to create a linear story for the television series, and trigger emergent narrative in the online part.

They divided the story into episodes, designed an enigma for each episode, and scattered clues along all the series. This work was meticulous and started long before the series' release. For example, a clue was an advertisement published on a local newspaper in January 2009: the episode referring to it was aired in November 2009.

Meanwhile Shado took care of writing a screenplay that would fit the game mechanics and filmed it (Fig. 1).

2.2   Release of "Frammenti": The ARG Experience

"Frammenti" was aired every Thursday from October 29, 2009 to January 21, 2010, for a total of twelve episodes. The website went online as soon as the first episode ended.

---

[3] The series is still available and can be watched on the website frammenti.tv.

[4] The previous year Log607 had created the Whai Whai city guides, unconventional city guides which had users walk around the city to solve a series of puzzle and unlock the episodes of a story. They were the first step of the path leading to "Frammenti". For more information: http://www.whaiwhai.com/en/.

[5] Both startups were "growing" in H-Farm, an innovative hub located in Roncade, Italy.

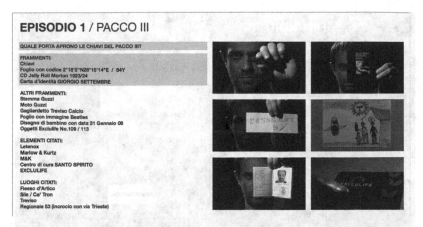

EPISODIO 1 / PACCO III

QUALE PORTA APRONO LE CHIAVI DEL PACCO III?

FRAMMENTI:
Chiavi
Foglio con codice 2°18'5"N26°15'14"E / 54Y
CD Jelly Roll Morton 1923/24
Carta d'identità GIORGIO SETTEMBRE

ALTRI FRAMMENTI:
Stemma Guzzi
Moto Guzzi
Gagliardetto Treviso Calcio
Foglio con immagine Beatles
Disegno di bambino con data 31 Gennaio 08
Oggetti Exclulife No.109 / 113

ELEMENTI CITATI:
Letenox
Marlow & Kurtz
M&K
Centro di cura SANTO SPIRITO
EXCLULIFE

LUOGHI CITATI:
Fiesso d'Artico
Sile / Ca' Tron
Treviso
Regionale 53 (incrocio con via Trieste)

Fig. 1. First page of the internal dossier of the team at Log607. It specifies: enigma, "fragments" or clues (main and secondary ones), story's elements cited in the episode, places cited in the episode.

During its run, a total of 1199 people connected to take part in the solving of the puzzles (Fig. 2).

Log607 had designed the online part to trigger cooperation among the users, so that they could leverage on a wide range of abilities and knowledges to solve the puzzles[6]. This not only worked, but the players were faster than they expected. Log607 had to find a way to adapt: they inserted fake accounts in the online community to provide help or distraction, and somehow control the timing of the solving.

Adaptation was a constant for Log607 in this project. For the whole duration of the series, they closely monitored the community and reacted according to the players' moves.

- They modified the first 30 s of each television episode so that it would give account of what had happened that week online. That was the only moment Log607 could use to align the television series with the online story.
- Even though the episodes were set and it was not possible to change the main story, in the online part Log607 expanded some of the characters' backstories to create additional storylines.
  Most of all, they gave more relevance to a mysterious character named J, who acts as Lorenzo's guide. He appears few times in the series, but is often narrating the episodes as voiceover. Log607 used this character heavily to interact with the players online, and steer the story where they wanted it to go.
- Log607's members engaged in first person with the players. For example, after Episode 4, a group of players got convinced that the Treviso's stadium (featured in

---

[6] The community forum is no longer available, but "the Activists" created a Wiki dedicated to "Frammenti" where, in addition to detailed information on each episode, they also provide useful insights on how they collectively solved the enigmas. The wiki can be reached following this link http://it.noletenox.wikia.com/wiki/.

Fig. 2. "Frammenti" website's page dedicated to the first episode of the series

some scenes) hid important clues and organized to go investigate there. When the people at Log607 realized it, they had two of them disguise as motorcyclists, go to the stadium and meet the players to hand them an envelope with additional clues.

The latter reveals a high level of engagement on the part of some of the players. A smaller group of approximately 40 people were so active online and so passionate that Log607 organised a final puzzle for them: it lead them to the H-Farm headquarters, where they met the cast and crew, and they watched the last episode together.

3 "Frammenti" Compared to Some Contemporary ARGs

"Frammenti" was released in 2009. The references Log607 had were: 42 Entertainment's "I love bees" (2004), produced for the launch of video game "Halo 2"; "Year Zero" (2006), an ARG based on the homonymous Nine Inch Nails concept album; Swedish "The truth about Marika" [4], which had been aired the previous year.

In 2009 much was still to be invented in terms of ARG, especially in Italy which did not offer previous examples. However, we know there were also other cases that resemble what "Frammenti" wanted to achieve; for example 2001 "The Beast" to market Steven Spielberg's movie "AI", which involved three million active participants.

"Frammenti" triggered a way smaller reaction than that: the community that was active for the whole run consisted of a group of around 120–150 people, with a hard core of around 40 people, who showed a very high level of engagement with the media content under all five measures used for transmedia storytelling[7]: Attention;

---

[7] Despite being presented as an ARG, "Frammenti" can also be considered an example of Transmedia Storytelling. It includes all four elements of the Transmedia Radar (Pratten, 2001: 52): Story, Experience in the real-world, Participation of the audience, Gaming.

Evaluation; Affection; Advocacy; Contribution [5]. Like for "The Beast" several of them remained active after the end of the game.

Something that sets "Frammenti" apart from other ARGs is its resourcefulness. The budget was low for such an ambitious project, so the producer teams filmed in locations close to H-Farm headquarters and involved coworkers as actors. This lead to unexpected consequences: since many of the players lived close to the area of filming, when the community started researching every single element of the series[8], some of them decided to scout the places of the story in person. That is how, one day, a group of Activists presented themselves in front of screenwriter Marino's house. He contacted the Log607 team and (as they had done for the stadium) they decided to sustain the fantasy: instead of sending the intruders away, they had Marino scribble a note (whose content was consistent with the story) and send his wife to deliver it to the Activists.

"Frammenti" saw the boundaries between reality and game get more and more blurry, and it is very interesting to observe how the constraints of a small budget transformed into an opportunity to explore the boundaries of ARG.

4   Conclusion

The strengths of "Frammenti" were two: attentive community management and improvisation. They guaranteed a superlative game experience despite the low budget. Log607 achieved this result by creating a solid structure, and defining meticulously the narrative world they were moving in, so that they could improvise with ease. The interactions between ARG designers and players allowed for emergent narrative and was sustained by improvised encounters in real life, that are a peculiarity of this project.

Acknowledgments. The author would like to thank Gianluca Marino, Fabio Salvadori, and Valerio Di Paola for sharing their experience with "Frammenti". She would also like to thank Giulia Pozzobon for helping put all the pieces together.

References

1. Leonzi, S., Ciofalo, G., Di Paola, V.: Frammenti di un discorso transmediale. In: Morreale, D. (ed.) Transmedia e Co-Creazione - Intermediari grassroots e pubblici online nella produzione transmediale italiana, pp. 77–86. Aracne, Roma (2014)
2. Leonzi, S., Ciofalo, G., Di Paola, V.: Frammenti di un discorso transmediale. In: Morreale, D. (ed.) Teorie e pratiche dell'esperienza transmediale (2016). Emerg. Ser. J. **5**
3. Moroni, G.: Videogiochi e apprendimento: la posizione di James Paul Gee. Tesi di Laurea in Scienze della Formazione e dell'Educazione, Università Guglielmo Marconi. Relatore Prof. Domenico Morreale (2017)

---

[8] When the players researched the owners of some fake websites created specifically for the ARG, they discovered the name of Log607 and started monitoring all the output Log607 would produce (some of it not at all related to the series).

4. Nani, A.: Sanningen om Marika - the truth about Marika. A transmedia case study. Tallinn University (2011). Link: https://truthaboutmarika.files.wordpress.com/2011/12/the-truth-about-marika-a-transmedia-case-study.pdf. Accessed 15 July 2018
5. Pratten, R.: Getting started in transmedia storytelling a practical guide for beginners. CreateSpace (2011)

Structuring Digital Game Stories

Elizabeth Goins[✉]

Rochester Institute of Technology, Rochester, NY, USA
esggsh@rit.edu

Abstract. This paper describes ongoing research towards a new model of video game storytelling involving structural manipulation of space and interactivity.

Keywords: Spatial storytelling · Environmental storytelling · Narrative Space-time · Video games

1 Introduction

No matter where you place them along the narrative-ludic poles [1], video games are experiences that take place in a computer generated space. Indeed, it is the spatial elements of virtual environments that help define the underlying structures unique to video game experiences [2]. Game-based storytelling can immerse players in a world of art, sound and story with an immediacy unique to the medium. However, video games, by and large, do not fully reach their storytelling potential: "They can, very literally, fashion any sort of space they care to dream. But for all this power, and all the narrative potential of space and place, most videogames follow a fairly traditional route to storytelling, using the space only to supplement a linearly (as opposed to spatially) told narrative" [3]. The question then arises of how structural and formal game elements should be manipulated to tell stories in a way unique to virtual interactive game media.

Space has been acknowledged as an essential parameter of video games and interactive media, [3–5] with storytelling defined as privileging "spatial exploration over plot development" [7]. Notions of game narrative evolved to define environmental storytelling as being either embedded, evoked, emergent and enacted [8]. These definitions point to the idea that space itself can convey meaning albeit in a supportive, rather than primary, role [8, 9]. Building on concepts of environmental storytelling, researchers and designers began to consider more complex and dynamic structures [10] that could support immersion within gameplay and narrative [11], or, in a refinement called indexical storytelling, allow players to create their own meaning from icons, indices and symbols [12]. These works indicate that it is not only space that is unique to game-based storytelling but also interactivity [10, 13].

In older media like film, drama and print, formal and structural elements are used to analyze individual art works. Film makers and writers know well how to exploit elements like camera angles, editing methods to link shots, sentence, and paragraph structures to construct meaning. However, the definition and relationship between the formal elements of game-based storytelling are not fully established or understood. Instead there are a number of different models that have been proposed. Fullerton [14]

© Springer Nature Switzerland AG 2018
R. Rouse et al. (Eds.): ICIDS 2018, LNCS 11318, pp. 265–269, 2018.
https://doi.org/10.1007/978-3-030-04028-4_27

envisions game design as divided between formal, dramatic and dynamic elements where formal elements are considered to be things like modes of interaction, rules, objectives, resources, boundaries and outcomes. Primitive elements have been forwarded as game anatomy: components, actions (both player and component) and goals [15]. Also, pattern frameworks for "describing games based upon the activities you as a player perform within them" [16]. In relating the form of computer games to other media forms Myers [17] declares that, "the experience of computer game play is more properly compared to the experience of reading poetic language."

These studies clearly indicate a need to understand how games might structure stories and convey meaning to players. However, the proposed models do not take into consideration both the structural elements of video games and the ludo-narrative processes associated with video game making. The literature stops short of clearly defining the underlying structural and formal components essential for designers to leverage the storytelling potential of interactive virtual environments and games. The purpose of this research is to propose a new model describing how meaning can be created through structural manipulation of space and interactivity – not in support of traditional filmic and textual narratives – but as a primary media specific method of storytelling in interactive game spaces.

2 Structuring Space and Time

Film manipulates notions of time to form experience from sequence and connection; shaping them into creative configurations that structure meaning [18, 19]. How then does the medium of the video game construct meaning? Huber [20], in an analysis of the *Final Fantasy* series, mapped activities that took place on different screens, or game spaces. He found that as the series evolved, so did the nature of the game structure into both spatial and temporal zones, "it is impossible to disentangle space from time. We must therefore focus on the relationality of space-time rather than of space in isolation." Zagal and Mateus [21] developed a conceptual tool for analyzing temporality in video games via the relationships between temporal frames such as "sequential frames (e.g., different frames for different levels), and co-existing frames (e.g., fictive and game-world temporal frames often co-exist in a game)." These works suggest that video games create meaning from the juxtaposition and relationships between structural units of both time and space.

LeFebvre [22, 23] argues that space is a social construct formed from the interplay of a triad (perceived space, conceived space and lived space) as individuals negotiate constructed (real, urban) space. As we travel through the real world, we change it and it in turn shapes us, thus we create our own narratives and identity [22, 24]. Is it possible that the negotiation of a virtual environment by a player will lead to narrative construction in a way that reflects that of the real world?

In film we understand how editing practices like cuts on action or fades can impact the narrative. The structural units of the video game environments are also combined in ways that impact player experience and they may be used to create meaning. In a virtual environment, players encounter a series of spaces often called maps or scenes that represent distinct spatial elements. Scenes are organized in different ways depending on the requirements of the game that typically fall into several main categories: User Interfaces (Save/load/options screens, maps of the game world, resources and character information, journals, quests/tasks/stats), loading screens, discreet geographical areas, streamed geographical/topographical areas for large open worlds, and levels. From this organizational perspective, designers create both the temporal and spatial structures of the game. The experiences may be structured in a linear way to move players forward through a sequence. The scenes may be non-linear and accessed in an open world format, loading scenes may be used to indicate temporal or spatial changes, user-interfaces may be used to pull players out of the environment thus breaking flow or they may be diegetic.

Player movement through the space is also structured, typically via objectives and quests. Quests combine a textual command or guide that requires the player to move through the environment to complete a series of tasks thus structuring, to varying degrees, access to space and temporal sequences. Designers may choose to make quests purely pragmatic as a tutorial, for example. Or designers can create quests that are narrative units where the player interacts with a world full of metaphor [25].

At this somewhat abstracted perspective, the game structure can be understood in terms of LeFebvre's triad [22, 23] as "conceived space." That is, space formed through knowledge, signs, and codes in which "representations of space" are used by planners, architects, and other specialists who divide space into separate elements that can be recombined as needed. Game designers, like architects, structure the relationships between these different elements to convey meaning by organizing space and structuring movement through the space.

3 Playing Space and Time

In the previous section, scenes were considered in the abstract, from the design perspective, to show how units could be organized. However, the player also encounters these units from a closer perspective, one in which they are placed in a virtual space. Each scene, be it UI or the representation of a place, is made up of a large number of elements: artwork, sound, hidden triggers, NPCs, interactable objects, and code linked specifically to the scene. It is at this level that the player fully encounters the game world.

The environment in which the player exists can be thought of as analogous to LeFebvre's lived (representational) space where the world is experienced through the mediation of images and symbols: the interior of a castle, a tavern, a region of an open world. It is also at this level that elements of environmental storytelling are encountered. Spaces will evoke pre-existing cultural connections and contain embedded narratives that inform the player of the history of the space.

As every game designer knows, interactivity is a powerful means to shape player experience and convey meaning. Player agency allows active participation and negotiation of meaning within the game, however meaningless the choices might be. Mechanics allow players to explore, run, shoot, collect and construct things. Mechanics also define the ways in which the player will interact with the environment and these affordances contribute to meaning making. Interaction and game mechanics correspond to ideas of LeFebvre's perceived space where (urban) reality is produced by the collective, and the rhythms of work, residential, and leisure activities bring space into contact with society and establish spatial practice. Often, game designers focus on inventing bespoke mechanics that customize unique interactions around which gameplay and narrative are designed. However, LeFebvre's ideas of rhythms and their interaction with the symbolic elements of lived space suggest that standard mechanics might be manipulated in conjunction with the art and structure of the environment to convey different meanings. Additionally, relationships between scenes can construct rhythms of movement at a more abstract level.

Environmental storytelling does not directly address the aspect of time, nor does the work of LeFebvre, but instead they hint at, or assume, temporality. In environmental storytelling [8] for example, enacted modes assume a timeline as actions must occur over time within space. On the other hand, embedded narratives exist in the player's present time frame but convey stories that have already happened. Likewise, LeFebvre's [23] notion of perceived space, or spatial practice, comprises activities and work rhythms that produce (urban) reality. In game environments, as in those of the real world, individuals negotiate objects and spaces full of meaning through interacting with the world around them over time.

4   Conclusion

Games create stories through the interactions of three components: (1) the organization of high level scene structures and interactions, (2) environments (spaces) filled with symbolic objects and metaphors and, (3) interactions with the game world that occur over time. Games can do more than support filmic or textual narratives, they can create their own types of stories derived from the affordances of the medium itself. This model proposes that meaning can be made in virtual worlds in much the same way as it is constructed in the real world. Games are constructed and played in a manner that parallels that of socially constructed space as described by LeFebvre (see Table 1). As in LeFebvre's model, it is important to note that it is the dialectical tension between game space, time and interactivity that are important for constructing meaning.

Table 1. A table illustrating the relationship between LeFebvre's triad and two essential components of video games (space-time, and interactivity)

LeFebvre	Game space	Game interactivity
Conceived space	Scenes, UI, maps	Objectives, quests, tasks
Perceived space	Rhythms, movement	Mechanics
Lived space	Objects, art, symbols, metaphors, NPCs	

References

1. Aarseth, E.: A narrative theory of games. In: Proceedings of the International Conference on the Foundations of Digital Games, pp. 129–133. ACM, Raleigh (2012)

2. Nitsche, M.: Video Game Spaces: Image, Play, and Structure in 3D Worlds. The MIT Press (2008)
3. Biswas, S.: Videogames and the art of spatial storytelling (2016). https://killscreen.com/articles/videogames-and-the-art-of-spatial-storytelling
4. Aarseth, E.: Allegories of Space. The Question of Spatiality in Computer Game. In: Eskelinen, M. and Raine, K. (eds.) Cybertext Yearbook 2000, (Jyväskylä: University of Jyväskylä (2001)
5. Murray, J.H.: MIT Press: Hamlet on the Holodeck: the future of narrative in cyberspace. The MIT Press, Cambridge (2001)
6. Aarseth, E.: Allegories of space. In: Borries, F. von, Walz, S.P., and Böttger, M. (eds.) Space Time Play. Birkhäuser Architecture, Basel (2007)
7. Jenkins, H.: Narrative spaces. In: Borries, F. von, Walz, S.P., and Böttger, M. (eds.) Space Time Play. Birkhäuser Architecture, Basel (2007)
8. Jenkins, H.: Game design as narrative architecture. In: Wardrip-Fruin, N., Harrigan, P. (eds.) FirstPerson: New Media as Story, Performance, and Game, pp. 118–130. MIT Press (2004)
9. Carson, D.: Environmental Storytelling: Creating Immersive 3D Worlds Using Lessons Learned from the Theme Park Industry (2000). https://www.gamasutra.com/view/feature/131594/environmental_storytelling_.php
10. Schoenau-Fog, Henrik: Adaptive storyworlds. In: Schoenau-Fog, Henrik, Bruni, Luis Emilio, Louchart, Sandy, Baceviciute, Sarune (eds.) ICIDS 2015. LNCS, vol. 9445, pp. 58–65. Springer, Cham (2015). https://doi.org/10.1007/978-3-319-27036-4_6
11. Watfen64: Nitty Gritty: Creating A Fetching Environmental Narrative In Games. https://tay.kinja.com/nitty-gritty-creating-a-fetching-environmental-narrati-1796259731
12. Fernández-Vara, C.: Game Spaces Speak Volumes: Indexical Storytelling. In: Proceedings of DiGRA 2011. p. 13 (2011)
13. Mhamdi, C.: Interpreting games: meaning creation in the context of temporality and interactivity. Mediterr. J. Soc. Sci. 8, 39–46 (2017)
14. Fullerton, T.: Game Design Workshop: A Playcentric Approach to Creating Innovative Games, 3rd edn. A K Peters/CRC Press, Boca Raton (2014)
15. Lankoski, P., Björk, S.: Formal analysis of gameplay. In: Lankoski, P., Björk, S. (eds.) Game Research Methods, pp. 23–35. ETC Press, Pittsburgh (2015)
16. Bjork, S., Holopainen, J.: Patterns in Game Design. Charles River Media, Hingham (2004)
17. Myers, D.: Play Redux: The Form of Computer Games. University of Michigan Press, Ann Arbor (2010)
18. McLuhan, M., Lapham, L.H.: Understanding Media: The Extensions of Man. The MIT Press, Cambridge (1994)
19. Bordwell, D.: Narration in the Fiction Film. University of Wisconsin Press, Madison (1985)
20. Huber, W.H.: Epic Spatialities: the production of space in Final Fantasy games. Third Pers. Authoring Explor. Vast Narrat., pp. 373–384 (2009)
21. Zagal, J.P., Mateas, M.: Analyzing time in video games. In: Lankoski, P., Björk, S. (eds.) Game Research Methods, pp. 37–55. ETC Press, Pittsburgh (2015)
22. Ronneburger, K.: Henri LeFebvre and Urban everyday life : in search of the possible. In: Goonewardena, K., Kipfer, S., Milgrom, R., and Schmid, C. (eds.) Space, Difference, Everyday Life: Reading Henri Lefebvre. Routledge (2008)
23. Lefebvre, H.: The Production of Space. Wiley-Blackwell, Malden (1992)
24. Proshansky, H.M., Fabian, A.K., Kaminoff, R.: Place-identity: physical world socialization of the self. J. Environ. Psychol. 3, 57–83 (1983)
25. Howard, J.: Quests: Design, Theory, and History in Games and Narratives. A K Peters/CRC Press, Wellesley (2008)

Player Identity and Avatars in Meta-narrative Video Games: A Reading of *Hotline Miami*

Luca Papale[1(✉)] and Lorenzo Fazio[2]

[1] IUDAV–VHEI, Solofra, Italy
lucapapale88@gmail.com
[2] Badgames.it, Milan, Italy
lorenzokobefazio@gmail.com

Abstract. Video games are a suitable territory to experiment and play with identity, thanks to the use of avatars, which let players put themselves in someone else's shoes, project values on blank slates or bond with virtual characters upon which they have a partial agency. Through the case study of *Hotline Miami*, this paper aims to examine how games can push players to actively question their identity, agency and role in the game's systems and narrative. The end point of the paper is defining a new category of avatar, the meta-avatar, which elicits a sense of identity instability in the players, leading them to have a more conscious approach to the gameplay experience.

Keywords: Video games · Avatar · Identity · Identification · Hotline Miami

1 Identity, Simulation and Avatars

Developing a sense of identity has historically been linked to, among other things, territory, ancestry and profession [2–4]. In comparison, current generations are turning into digital nomads, always ready to shift careers, and proficient in more than one language, which is itself something that impacts identity, personality and behavior [5–8]. In this context of liquid modernity [9], it's presumable that the same sense of identity stability felt by previous generations is harder to achieve. Noting how the notion of "self" has become extremely unstable, academics from various fields have been talking about the so-called "culture of simulation" that seems to have become the norm in the search and definition of identity [10–13].

Video games are the perfect breeding ground for identity games, which find their keystone in the avatar, a graphical representation that, in the context of virtual spaces, allows representing oneself and interacting with others and the environment [14]. Fraschini [15] pinpoints four macro-categories of avatars or "digital prostheses", to use his definition. The *transparent digital prosthesis* is not "actorialized", has no characterization, and has a mere agentive function in the game world, as it lets the player

---

Parts of this paper are an abridged, updated and translated reworking of excerpts from a previous publication by the authors [1].

© Springer Nature Switzerland AG 2018
R. Rouse et al. (Eds.): ICIDS 2018, LNCS 11318, pp. 270–274, 2018.
https://doi.org/10.1007/978-3-030-04028-4_28

operate in it; the player's identity is untouched by the interaction with and through this kind of prosthesis; examples of it are *Bejeweled* [16] and digital versions of games like chess and solitaire. The *vehicle digital prosthesis* implies a minimal alteration of the player's identity, and it is present in all those instances in which the player is tasked to drive or control any kind of vehicle as main game mechanics; this is the case for most racing games or vehicle simulation games, like *Gran Turismo* [17]. The *mask digital prosthesis* is recurrent in most first-person games and implies an identity overlapping between the avatar and the player; for the duration of the game, the player assumes the avatar's identity, implicitly accepting its values and characteristics; an example could be the Doom Guy of *DOOM* [18]. Finally, the *character digital prosthesis*, typical of action-adventures or graphic adventures, implies the maximum degree of characterization of the avatar, and for this reason players tend to have a dialectic relationship with it, resulting in an ambiguous pattern of identity alteration; an example could be Lara Croft from *Tomb Raider* [19].

Starting from this classification, Papale [20, 21] proposes a comprehensive scheme of the various degrees of characterization of avatars, and of the ways players interact with them. Choosing the concept of *identification* as the starting point, intended as a process that involves the player assuming and assimilating the behaviors and traits of the controlled avatar, Papale then outlines the psychological mechanisms defined as *empathy*, *sympathy*, *projection* and *detachment*.

It should be noted that the psychological mechanisms triggered in players while interacting with their avatars, and the emotions felt, are rarely stable and unambiguous. They are, instead, influenced by the game flow, the player's current state of mind and the gaming environment. This impossibility of clearly framing the player in a specific role is consciously exploited by some games, to push players to question their agency and identity. One way of achieving this is to place emphasis on the gap between the avatar, which has specific motives but is controlled by someone else, and the player, who has a moral code but is forced to act inside the system of rules, bottlenecks and constraints dictated by the software and its developers.

2 Interactive Ambiguity in *Hotline Miami*

In *Hotline Miami* [22], set in the 80's USA of an alternate timeline, the player controls a killer, Jacket,[1] who, after receiving instructions via code messages left on his voicemail, raids several locations with the goal of exterminating everyone on the premises, always wearing an animal mask to conceal his identity.[2] After a brief tutorial, the game starts with a dreamlike sequence that sees Jacket standing in a dim-lit, messy room, facing three people sitting in armchairs and wearing, respectively, a mask of a horse (Don Juan), a rooster (Richard) and an owl (Rasmus).

---

[1] The majority of characters in the game have no name, and this also applies to the protagonist, who is referred to as Jacket in online discussions and academic papers [23].

[2] Every mask has a name, in strong opposition to actual characters who, as said above, are usually anonymous. The masks could be interpreted as a visual representation of a multiple personality disorder suffered by the protagonist [23].

Don Juan: And who do we have here? Oh, you don't know who you are..? Maybe
we should leave it that way?

Richard: But I know you. Look at my face. We've met before... Haven't we?

Rasmus: I don't know you! Why are you here? You're no guest of mine!

Don Juan: Do you really want me to reveal who you are? Knowing oneself means
acknowledging ones [sic] actions. As of lately you've done some terrible
things...

Richard: You don't remember me? I'll give you a clue... Does April the 3rd mean
anything to you? I believe that was the day of our first encounter. You
look like you might be remembering something [22] ...

After the end of the cutscene, the first level starts, with Jacket wearing the
mask/personality of Richard – this is their "first encounter"; thus we can infer that the
several playable missions are actually memories being re-enacted by Jacket.

From this very first dialogue, some peculiarities catch the eye. First of all, the game
starts right away to break the fourth wall by addressing at the same time both the player
and the avatar. In fact, the line "Oh, you don't know who you are..?" is a subtle meta-
narrative innuendo, considering that at this point of the game the player still doesn't
know who he or she "is" – that is, the player is unaware of the avatar's identity.
Moreover, the three masked figures have their own distinct personalities and registers,
and while they are speaking, the lights in the scene change color, recalling the ones of a
traffic light. Don Juan (green light) is reassuring and seems to want to shield the
protagonist from a terrible truth, with a phrasing rich with accommodating questions;
Rasmus (red light) is hostile, speaks with a lot of exclamations and is clearly distancing
himself from Jacket; Richard (yellow light), finally, is calm, neutral and balanced, his
way of speaking being abundant with ellipses and rhetorical questions. We can assume
that the three masked figures are fragments of Jacket's psyche: Don Juan is the part of
him that is trying keep him safe, Rasmus represents denial and self-loathing, and
Richard is the awareness creeping beneath the surface.

After an escalation of violent missions, Jacket meets the three masked figures once
again. A dialogue takes place, and the following bit is especially relevant.

Richard: [...] Before you go, here's [sic] four questions to ponder. Question number
one: Do you like hurting other people? Question number two: Who is
leaving messages on your answering machine? Question number three:
Where are you right now? And the final question: Why are we having this
conversation [22]?

Richard's questions are ambivalent. If, in a way, they are diegetically motivated
and directed to the avatar, on the other hand it's clear that they are also meant to reach
out to the empirical players. Does the player enjoy violence? Does he or she ever stop
to think about the actions carried out in the game? Is the player inside the game, outside
of it, or somewhere in between two worlds?

From this point on, the plot puts on stage ambiguous characters and apparently
inexplicable situations. During Chapter 7, Jacket faces another assassin, dressed like a

biker, and kills him; however, towards the end of the game, the plot "rewinds" and the roles get reversed. The player now controls the biker and, this time around, he kills Jacket. The two storylines can't possibly coexist in the same narrative frame as they stage two conflicting versions of what happened during the fight. One possible explanation could be that the player is in presence of unreliable narrators and that neither of the two versions of the story is fully true. Possibly, not everything we see as players is really happening: Visions of talking corpses and fuzzy continuity are often accompanied by white noise, a visual commentary about the unreliability of the avatars' perception [23].

Put in the uncomfortable position of having to play as two opposing avatars and to kill both of them at the hands of the other, players find themselves facing an identity crisis, aggravated by the top-down view that creates an evident gap between their point of view and the avatars' one. Users are thus forced to constantly re-negotiate their role in the story and to doubt what they are experiencing.

3   Conclusions

This analysis paves the way for the identification of a new type of digital prosthesis, the meta-avatar, gifted with the ability to instill deep identity instability in players (Table 1).

Table 1. An updated classification of digital prostheses.

Type of prosthesis	Characterization	Alteration of player's identity	Example
Transparent	None	None	Mouse cursor
Vehicle	Minimal	Minimal	Car pilot
Mask	Minimal	Maximum	Doom guy
Character	Maximum	Ambiguous	Lara Croft
Meta-avatar	Ambiguous	Unstable	Jacket

In this scenario of fragmented, nomad identity, video games could prove themselves to be a useful tool. By playing around with the concept of identity and actively questioning themselves when playing games like *Hotline Miami* and other titles that employ a meta-avatar or other meta-narrative techniques, players can maybe learn something about themselves, provided that they maintain a conscious and vigilant approach to the gameplay experience.

References

1. Papale, L., Fazio, L.: Teatro e videogiochi: Dall'avatāra agli avatar. Edizioni Paguro, Mercato San Severino (2018)
2. Knight, D.B.: Identity and territory: Geographical perspectives on nationalism and regionalism. Ann. Assoc. Am. Geogr. **72**(4), 514–531 (1982). https://doi.org/10.1111/j.1467-8306.1982.tb01842.x

3. Tutton, R.: "They want to know where they came from": Population genetics, identity, and family genealogy. New Genet. Soc. **23**(1), 105–120 (2004). https://doi.org/10.1080/14636770420001896606

4. Gibson, P.: Identity and career (Doctoral dissertation). Retrieved from Swinburne Research Bank (2001). http://hdl.handle.net/1959.3/26020

5. Nash, C., Jarrahi, M.H., Sutherland, W., Phillips, G.: Digital nomads beyond the buzzword: Defining digital nomadic work and use of digital technologies. In: Chowdhury, G., McLeod, J., Gillet, V., Willett, P. (eds.) iConference 2018. LNCS, vol. 10766, pp. 207–217. Springer, Cham (2018). https://doi.org/10.1007/978-3-319-78105-1_25

6. Ervin, S.: Language and TAT content in bilinguals. J. Abnorm. Soc. Psychol. **68**(5), 500–507 (1964). https://doi.org/10.1037/h0044803

7. Ervin-Tripp, S.: An analysis of the interaction of language, topic, and listener. Am. Anthropol. **66**(6), 86–102 (1964). https://doi.org/10.1525/aa.1964.66.suppl_3.02a00050

8. Koven, M.E.J.: Two languages in the self/the self in two languages: French-Portuguese bilinguals' verbal enactments and experiences of self in narrative discourse. Ethos **26**(4), 410–455 (1998). https://doi.org/10.1525/eth.1998.26.4.410

9. Bauman, Z.: Liquid Modernity. Polity Press, Cambridge (2000)

10. Turkle, S.: Growing up in the culture of simulation. In: Denning, P.J., Metcalfe, R.M. (eds.) Beyond Calculation: The Next Fifty Years of Computing, pp. 93–104. Springer, New York (1997). https://doi.org/10.1007/978-1-4612-0685-9_7

11. Miller, C.R.: Writing in a culture of simulation: Ethos online. In: Coppock, P. (ed.) The Semiotics of Writing: Transdisciplinary Perspectives on the Technology of Writing, pp. 253–279. Brepols, Turnhout (2001)

12. Pecchinenda, G.: Videogiochi e cultura della simulazione: La nascita dell''homo game', 3rd edn. Editori Laterza, Milano/Bari (2010)

13. Essig, T.: Psychoanalysis lost – and found – in our culture of simulation and enhancement. Psychoanal. Inq. **32**(5), 438–453 (2012). https://doi.org/10.1080/07351690.2012.703571

14. Merriam-Webster Online. https://www.merriam-webster.com/dictionary/avatar. Accessed 24 Jul 2018

15. Fraschini, B.: Videogiochi & new media. In: Bittanti, M. (ed.) Per una cultura dei videogames: Teoria e prassi del videogiocare, 2nd edn, pp. 99–135. Edizioni Unicopli, Milano (2004)

16. PopCap Games: Bejeweled. PopCap Games (2001)

17. Polyphony Digital: Gran Turismo. Sony Computer Entertainment (1998)

18. id Software: DOOM. GT Interactive (1993)

19. Core Design: Tomb Raider. Eidos Interactive (1996)

20. Papale, L.: Beyond identification. Defining the relationships between player and avatar. J. Games Crit. **1**(2), 1–12 (2014)

21. Papale, L.: Per una tassonomia delle relazioni corporee e mentali tra giocatori e personaggi dei videogiochi. Imago **12**, 221–230 (2016)

22. Dennaton Games: Hotline Miami. Devolver Digital (2012)

23. Caracciolo, M.: Unknowable protagonists and narrative delirium in American Psycho and Hotline Miami: A case study in character engagement across the media. Acta Univ. Sapientiae Film and Media Stud. **9**, 189–207 (2014)

Throwing Bottles at God: Predictive Text as a Game Mechanic in an AI-Based Narrative Game

Max Kreminski(✉) and Noah Wardrip-Fruin

UC Santa Cruz, Santa Cruz, CA 95064, USA
{mkremins,nwardrip}@ucsc.edu

Abstract. We present *Throwing Bottles at God*, an experimental interactive narrative game that makes use of a predictive text writing interface as both a game mechanic and a means by which to deliver narrative content. The player steps into the role of @dril, a well-known pseudonymous social media personality with a distinctive writing style, and authors short snippets of text while receiving suggestions from the game as to which word @dril might use next – suggestions supported by word pair frequency data extracted from the corpus of all existing tweets by the actual @dril. The game represents a first attempt to use AI-based game design to heighten the player's awareness of AI algorithms, specifically predictive text algorithms, as they play a role in the player's day-to-day life. It also blurs the line between player-authored and developer-authored narrative content by inviting players to freely mix snippets of developer-authored text into their own in-game social media posts as they compose them, resulting in player-assembled messages that embed sequences of words drawn both from an external corpus (the @dril corpus) and from developer-authored narrative content.

Keywords: Interactive narrative design · AI-based game design

1 Introduction

Predictive text writing interfaces, which monitor text as a user types it and offer a small set of suggested next words that can be inserted immediately after the cursor, have become a nearly ubiquitous part of the text composition interface on modern smartphones. They represent a small algorithmic intervention into the process of text composition, with which smartphone users interact on a daily basis. However, the question of what effects (if any) the involvement of these assistive algorithms might have on the creative process of text composition seems to have gone largely undiscussed.

AI-based game design [6], a game design methodology that places AI agents or algorithms in the foreground of gameplay rather than relegating them exclusively to a background or supporting role, may present one potential strategy for

© Springer Nature Switzerland AG 2018
R. Rouse et al. (Eds.): ICIDS 2018, LNCS 11318, pp. 275–279, 2018.
https://doi.org/10.1007/978-3-030-04028-4_29

heightening player awareness of the roles and affordances of AI algorithms. Digital games are uniquely well-equipped to critique or comment on AI algorithms: because they are made of code, they can directly embed "playable" versions of the algorithms they are intended to comment on, thus giving players a chance to experience what it is like to interact with these algorithms firsthand or from the "inside". Moreover, systems such as *Say Anything* [5] have successfully leveraged AI algorithms to create playful collaborative writing experiences. Perhaps, then, AI-based game design techniques could be applied to AI algorithms that play a regular role in players' daily lives. A game that uses predictive text as a game mechanic, for instance, could raise interesting questions of algorithmic co-authorship (among other issues) in the player's mind. In this paper, we present one such game.

2   Predictive Text as a Game Mechanic

Throwing Bottles at God is an experimental AI-based interactive narrative game that casts the player in the role of `@dril` [3], a well-known pseudonymous social media personality with a distinctive (and frequently profanity-laden) writing style that functions as a parody of self-important social media personalities. In the game, `@dril` is presented as a recipient of prophetic visions who must post on Twitter in order to communicate what he has seen to the world and thereby avert the catastrophic future the visions portend.

Central to gameplay is the use of predictive text as a game mechanic. The player character's only way of interacting with the game world is by writing and posting messages to the in-game mock Twitter interface; thus, in order to make progress in the game and explore the narrative, the player is required to compose social media posts of their own in the style of the `@dril` character. The player is assisted in this task by a predictive text interface that looks at what they have written so far and provides real-time feedback on what words the actual `@dril` might be most likely to use next. At any time while composing a message, the player may click on one of these suggested next words to insert it at the end. These suggestions are based on word pair frequency data extracted from the corpus of all existing tweets by the actual `@dril`; the game essentially uses a Markov model "trained on" the corpus of all existing `@dril` tweets to help the player author text in the `@dril` style.

The game's narrative content is structured as a partially ordered sequence of largely self-contained vignettes. Each of these vignettes is written in the style of a hallucinatory "dream vision" that predicts some future scene or event, usually foreboding and darkly humorous in tone. When the player attempts to compose a new in-game social media post using the predictive text writing interface, there is a chance that one of the suggested prediction slots will be randomly allocated to a vignette appropriate to this point in the player's progress through the game, such that repeatedly clicking on this prediction slot will cause the player to "write out" the complete text of the vignette, one word at a time, into the text input box.

Because any given suggested word may thus be drawn either from a vignette or from the corpus of words present in actual @dril tweets, and because the player only has indirect control over which words will appear as suggestions, this design creates a sense of ambiguity as to whether the @dril corpus, the vignettes, or players themselves are most responsible for the final content of a message they have composed.

The intended effect of this design is to heighten the player's perception that they are receiving or channeling some sort of divine inspiration when they rely on the predictive text interface to write. This is inspired by the way in which predictive text writing interfaces are sometimes used to perform a kind of AI-based "divination" – for instance in the kinds of predictive text "games" that are sometimes played on social media, wherein participants manually type in the beginning of a sentence as a prompt, use predictive text to fill in the rest of the sentence, and share the result [4,7]. It is also inspired by the perceived lack of agency that participants in Ouija board sessions who believe in the supernatural power of their chosen divination method tend to report [1]; ideally, players in *Throwing Bottles at God* will experience a similar sense of diminished personal responsibility while still in fact exerting a significant influence on the structure, content and overall coherency of the messages they compose.

By encouraging players to interact with predictive text in an explicitly playful way, as well as by estranging them from the more familiar aspects of writing with predictive text (both by basing the bulk of the suggestions on the unfamiliar, frequently alarming @dril corpus and by inserting preauthored narrative content into the suggestions at random), *Throwing Bottles at God* aims to call attention to the ways in which algorithmic suggestions influence the way players write. The game can be judged as a success if players then take this heightened awareness with them when they walk away from the game and return to interacting with predictive text writing interfaces in their daily lives.

3   Other Design Elements

3.1   Evaluation of Player-Composed Messages

Once the player posts a message to the in-game social media feed, the message is evaluated to assign it a numeric score. This semi-random score is used to determine how many in-game likes and reposts the message will receive, and by how much the player's in-game follower count will change as a result of posting it. In order to nudge the player toward making use of the predictive text algorithm's suggestions while also encouraging them to deviate from the suggested choices at times, messages are scored according to what proportion of their text is drawn from suggestions rather than hand-typed by the player. A message in which approximately half the words are drawn from suggestions and half are hand-typed would score the highest, while messages that are entirely hand-typed or entirely composed of suggested words would score the lowest. However, the player is not explicitly made aware of how the scoring mechanism works; it is our hope that this will encourage players to actively experiment with how they compose text in an attempt to discover the precise nature of the relationship between their approach to authoring and how their messages are received by their in-game "audience".

3.2   Generative NPC "Dialogue"

Throwing Bottles at God features an in-game mock Twitter feed, populated with social media posts from a variety of non-player characters (NPCs). Each of these NPCs is built around a Tracery [2] grammar that generates posts in a particular style. Periodically, the game selects an NPC at random and uses that NPC's associated grammar to generate a snippet of text that it can add to the feed.

Many of these grammars were created by volunteer contributors. Because Tracery is relatively easy to use and provides a consistent framework for authoring text generators, it was fairly straightforward to integrate NPCs created by over a dozen different volunteers into a single project. The juxtaposition of these different NPCs in the in-game Twitter feed creates an impression of chaotic polyvocality, mirroring the subjective experience of using Twitter in real life.

4   Conclusion

We presented *Throwing Bottles at God*, an experimental AI-based interactive narrative game that makes use of predictive text as a game mechanic and a means of conveying a (partially player-authored) narrative. It is our hope that the game, as a first step toward using AI-based game design practices to comment on or critique everyday AI algorithms, will leave players with a heightened awareness of the ways in which algorithmic assistance influences their writing process.

References

1. Andersen, M., Nielbo, K.L., Schjoedt, U., Pfeiffer, T., Roepstorff, A., Sørensen, J.: Predictive minds in Ouija board sessions. Phenomenol. Cogn. Sci. **17**(3), 1–12 (2018)
2. Compton, K., Kybartas, B., Mateas, M.: Tracery: an author-focused generative text tool. In: Schoenau-Fog, H., Bruni, L.E., Louchart, S., Baceviciute, S. (eds.) ICIDS 2015. LNCS, vol. 9445, pp. 154–161. Springer, Cham (2015). https://doi.org/10. 1007/978-3-319-27036-4_14
3. @dril. https://twitter.com/dril. Accessed 21 Aug 2018
4. People are writing their own epitaphs using predictive text and they are pretty profound. https://www.independent.ie/world-news/and-finally/people-are-writing-their-own-epitaphs-using-predictive-text-and-they-are-pretty-profound-36452010. html. Accessed 24 Sept 2018
5. Swanson, R., Gordon, A.S.: Say anything: a massively collaborative open domain story writing companion. In: Spierling, U., Szilas, N. (eds.) ICIDS 2008. LNCS, vol. 5334, pp. 32–40. Springer, Heidelberg (2008). https://doi.org/10.1007/978-3-540-89454-4_5

6. Treanor, M., et al.: AI-based game design patterns. In: Proceedings of the 10th International Conference on Foundations of Digital Games, FDG (2015)
7. What Does Predictive Text Do? People On Twitter Are Using Predictive Text To Write The Story Of Their Lives, & The Results Are Equal Parts Poetic & Bizarre. https://www.bustle.com/p/what-does-predictive-text-do-people-on-twitter-are-using-predictive-text-to-write-the-story-of-their-lives-the-results-are-equal-parts-poetic-bizarre-3226156. Accessed 24 Sept 2018

The Story Pile - Representing Story in the Board Game Mind Shadows

Mirjam Palosaari Eladhari[(✉)] [iD]

Södertörn University, Alfred Nobels allé 7, 141 89 Huddinge, Sweden
mirjam.palosaari.eladhari@sh.se

Abstract. Mind Shadows illustrates how story can be represented in board games. Here, the game is described, along with design considerations regarding event documentation and co-authoring. In analog games these activities, needs to be designed in a manner that integrate them into game-play, in a manner that is not too cumbersome for the players.

Keywords: Board games · Story construction · Story games
Co-creation

1 Introduction

Mind Shadows is a board game for two or three players where players cooperatively aim to overcome Shadows - in-game representation of players' own real world problems. The main aim of the design was to create play situations where players in cooperation can better understand situations in their everyday lives that are difficult or emotionally complex, and by this understanding find ways to cope with these situations.

2 Playing Mind Shadows

Mind Shadows is played in three phases, Set-up, Enactment and Reflection. In the *Set-up*, players start with describing something that is difficult to cope with on a card in writing, which then becomes the opponent in the game, the Shadow, see Fig. 1. By doing so, they create an understanding of the challenges they will meet and thus, create a mental model of what they and their co-players interact with in the next phase - by observing what the Shadow does, how their co-players act, and by reflecting upon how they act themselves. Figure 2 shows the set-up of a two-player session.

In the *Enactment* phase each player has a board that represents their emotional state, and a hand of support cards (see Fig. 3). The Shadow acts as a special NPC that is controlled in turn by the players who roll the dice to determine which destructive card or player-authored action it will put in play. In this way all players experience the actions of their friends' Shadows. To counter the actions of a shadow, players monitor each others' wellbeing, finding ways

R. Rouse et al. (Eds.): ICIDS 2018, LNCS 11318, pp. 280–284, 2018.
https://doi.org/10.1007/978-3-030-04028-4_30

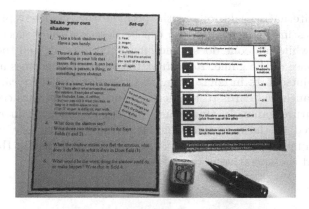

Fig. 1. Making a Shadow MindShadows.

make to each other happy, and lending each other support when in a state of vulnerability. Concretely, this means that players choose support actions from their hand (see Fig. 3), or author new support-cards to help each other. Players win together by diminishing the strength of the respective shadow, represented as bars on the Shadow's board.

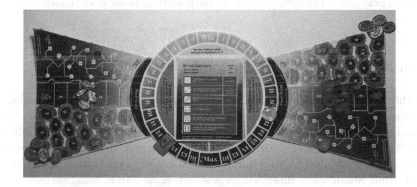

Fig. 2. Mind Shadows v1 board game set up for two players.

During play a "story pile" is created, consisting of the used cards and authored events, helping players to keep track of who did what. During the enactment phase, players talk; inventing supportive actions, describing them, and enacting them by for example hugging, applauding or giving context-relevant compliments. Thus, players partake in continuous co-authoring of the scenario they are playing. As observed during testing, players spend a lot of time in conversation about how to respond to a Shadow's action, and how they can best help each other. About three fourths of the player-authored support cards were specially aimed at helping their friend(s) in their particular contexts, offering support and alternative solutions to the problem the Shadow represented. The player activities in this second phase can be described as Reflection-**in**-action [5], occurring while someone does something, reflects on it, and then continues. In the final phase of the game, *Reflection*, the story pile becomes a summary of the players' joint efforts in confronting their Shadows. Players can now choose to add newly authored cards to the deck for future games, thus cohelp another friend, in a future game. In this phase, players are engaged in reflecting-**on**-action, triggered by the narrative which is a result of their play-session. They consider which methods might be useful in real-life, and whether they should be kept to expand the narrative potential of the deck.

Fig. 3. An example of the hand of cards at the players disposal in the enactment phase.

3   Development and Design Considerations

Over the course of three years, ten iterations of the game have been considered in 18 documented play tests. The play tests were of the participatory design flavor, and the majority included domain experts, who advised about the following areas: therapy, counseling, story construction, graphic design, user experience design, board game design, and game mechanic design and balancing. This version of Mind Shadows is intended as a stand-alone game, but future work will explore uses for therapeutic situations.

Representing story in analog games poses interesting practical challenges.[1] In digital systems, event logs can be rendered as narratives (eg. stories that are told). In a board game however, event-logging needs to be made part of the game play in a way that is not too cumbersome for the players. Many solutions were tested and discarded until the designer settled onto the concept of a "story pile" of cards as the resulting story, inspired by the practice of storing game states in Microscope [4]. Figure 4 shows the cards that represent narrative elements. Another interesting aspect is co-creation: in what manner, and to what extent, is it possible to entice players to add their own content?

---

[1] The word story here means a temporal sequence of events, the content that a narrative is about, in Genette's sense. [2, p. 27].

Fig. 4. Story Cards. The top row are those of the Shadow, the bottom row are support- and event cards.

During play testing and redesigning it emerged that a balance between game mechanics and play situations are necessary to achieve the main aim of the game: facilitate conversations in which real world situations can be approached, deconstructed, and reconstructed to gain deeper understandings through cooperative play. A crucial aspect in this regards was the construction of a Safe Space (see [1] for further detail), inspired by the tradition of psychodrama [3] as well as "cozy" game design [6]. Another important decision was to eliminate the possibility of egocentric behavior - players can only help others, not themselves, and cannot perform hostile actions [7].

Availability. Mind Shadows is produced under the independent label Otter Play. Version 1 of Mind Shadows is available for download as a printable at http://www.otter-play.com. In order to play the game the following materials are necessary: A printer, paper, scissors (for cutting out the boards, cards and game pieces), a six sided die, and a pen.

References

1. Eladhari, M.P.: Bleed in, Bleed Out - a design case in board game therapy. In: DiGRA 2018 - Proceedings of the 2018 DiGRA International Conference: The Game is the Message, Turin, Italy (2018)
2. Genette, G.: Narrative Discourse - An Essay in Method. Cornell University Press (1983)
3. Moreno, J.L., Moreno, Z.T.: Psychodrama, vol. I. Beacon House, New York (1959)
4. Robbins, B.: Microscope - a fractal role-playing game of epic histories. Lame Mage Productions [Boardgame] (2011)
5. Schön, D.A.: The Reflective Practitioner: How Professionals Think in Action. Basic Books (1983)

6. Short, T., et al.: Group report: coziness in games: an exploration of safety, softness, and satisfied needs. In: The Twelfth Annual Game Design Think Tank Project Horseshoe, Comfort, Texas (2017)
7. Taylor, S.E., Klein, L.C., Lewis, B.P., Gruenewald, T.L., Gurung, R.A.R., Updegraff, J.A.: Biobehavioral responses to stress in females: tend-and-befriend, not fight-or-flight. Psychol. Rev. 3(107), 411–429 (2000)

Margaret's

Esther Doorly[1]([⊠]) [iD] and Kelly McErlean[2]([⊠]) [iD]

[1] Trinity College Dublin, Dublin, Ireland
doorlye@tcd.ie
[2] Dundalk Institute of Technology, Dundalk, Ireland
kelly.mcerlean@dkit.ie
https://www.dkit.ie/creative-arts-media-music

Abstract. Margaret opened her hair salon in Ballymoney, Co. Antrim, Northern Ireland in 1959. It's still there.

In recent years, despite dwindling customers and limited opening hours, *Margaret's* remains a bustling community hub for an aging clientele.

Yet during the Troubles (Northern Ireland Conflict) of the late 20th century *Margaret's* was an important, non-sectarian feminist centre for Catholic and Protestant women to meet, talk and most crucially, hold their town together.

Keywords: Women · Northern Ireland conflict
Transmedia documentary

1 The Story

In a small town in Northern Ireland during the troubles, from early Tuesday morning to late Saturday evening, hairdresser Margaret and her 'regulars' openly debated media reports of regional and national affairs and collectively agreed upon a mutually acceptable narrative, their version of events. The result was a functioning local society which held it together in the midst of a violent ethno-nationalist conflict. These business women, housewives, factory workers and shop employees kept a strife-torn world together for their families today and tomorrow.

As a young female entrepreneur in this rural market town, Margaret wanted her salon bookings to be sought after. Her intended customers were the town 'sophisticates' rather than the 'hoi polloi' whom she felt she could never win over. In 1961, just 3 weeks after the birth of her first child, she travelled alone to London to take a colouring course and to research customer service in such an upmarket, cosmopolitan setting. On her return she introduced a number of hospitality features that created a warm, convivial atmosphere that set her apart from the competition. She gradually introduced the latest colouring services that were previously unavailable in the area. For many years, business boomed.

© Springer Nature Switzerland AG 2018
R. Rouse et al. (Eds.): ICIDS 2018, LNCS 11318, pp. 285–288, 2018.
https://doi.org/10.1007/978-3-030-04028-4_31

With this story we have collected and digitised a range of cultural artefacts [1]. We interviewed a number of women who now in their later years feel they are ready to speak about some of their experiences. Certain issues and events were clearly still too raw and had to be avoided.

Together and individually they relayed their stories to us. They made it clear that in the midst of the political and nationalistic conflict of the 70s and 80s, a weekly visit to their hairdresser was an absolute must. Kathleen, a long-standing customer and close personal friend said, "No matter what you did in the week, whatever you had on or had to do, you always made sure you went to *Margaret's*. Because that was where you learned what was really going on in the community."

Some 25 years ago, when Margaret's husband passed away, Kathleen and many other customers rallied to her aid. For many months they quietly took on various roles within the business to keep everything going.

During the series of interviews Kathleen was a most forthcoming documentary participant. She spoke openly of the challenges women faced during the Troubles. In a working class community stretched to its limit, they ran businesses and raised children under incredibly difficult circumstances and sometimes failing marriages. Kathleen was considerably vocal and seemed to want to get her story on record. She was frank, blunt and relatively unrestrained, talking about her various businesses and land deals. She died suddenly some 10 days after our interview. It was as if she had been holding on for us to come and speak to her.

On camera, Margaret demonstrates the courtier-like skills she often used to assess the religious inclination (Protestant or Catholic) of new, unknown customers. During the Troubles, this was an important ability. It was always necessary to gather background information when meeting new people. Synthesised correctly, this knowledge would frame a conversation from that point onwards. A series of seemingly innocuous questions concerning the weather, traffic and local awareness functioned as an exercise in highly selective data gathering, followed by a statistical analysis of pertinent information. An informed guess took place and the conversation moved forward, in one direction or another. An interactive text version of this exchange is envisaged as a Twine-based non-linear narrative.

2   Methodology

Margaret's is a transmedia narrative which uses digital storytelling techniques [3] to create a work of social anthropology. It includes voice recordings, video interviews, documentary footage, a photo essay [2] of the town and text-based content. This collection of story elements will be published as an interactive website, hosted at http://www.StoryFort.ie. The story will be promoted via the social media reach of the authors and their respective websites Storyfort.ie and Elocutionroom.com.

The audiences' interactive engagement and resulting narrative immersion will be perspectival. This transmedia story deliberately lacks technological complexity in order to ease the audience into a non-linear story space. An interactive user-experience will include scene-setting video that plays automatically. The story elements will be formatted on the page to avoid clutter.

The audience will have the opportunity to listen to both sides of this religious divide, with locals talking about the same events/time but with rather different frames of reference. In considering the minutiae of their lives [4], this transmedia story will highlight the cultural differences that exist within traditional Northern Ireland communities, Differences which are often subtle, yet poignant.

More people are ready to share their experiences of this time and the authors intend to continue to gather content, parsing the language for keywords and phrases that indicate certain life experiences within a specific time and place. They are also considering the creation of a series of geo-located audio narratives, told by the people who lived the experience, which will exist virtually across Northern Ireland.

References

1. Barker, G.: Interview with Christian Patterson, Bottom of the Lake. Hotshoe, Contemporary Photography, Issue 186, pp. 34–45 (2013)
2. Lingwood, J.: FT Magazine. Rediscovered Italy: Luigi Ghirri's 1970s photographic landscapes.   https://www.ft.com/content/10d2887c-4ccd-11e8-97e4-13afc22d86d4. Accessed 3 Sept 2018
3. McErlean, K.: Interactive Narratives and Transmedia Storytelling: Creating Immersive Stories Across New Media Platforms. Routledge, New York (2018)
4. Perec, G.: Species of Spaces and Other Pieces. Penguin Classics, England (2008)

Narrative Game Mechanics
and Interactive Fiction

Kirsty Michelle McGill[(⊠)] [iD]

University of Bedfordshire, Bedfordshire LU1 3JU, UK
kirsty.mcgill@study.beds.ac.uk

Abstract. This doctoral research aims to develop the ongoing understanding of narrative game mechanics and establish its presence within interactive fiction. Research to define and understand the narrative effects of game mechanics is a current topic of academic debate [4–7] and relates to the question of 'how do games tell stories' [8]. Building on this work from key researchers [4–8], this study aims to carry out several textual analyses to identify potential narrative producing game mechanics. In addition, an interactive fiction game using the platform Twine has been created. Feedback will be collected from the Twine game and used to enhance further iterations of it. As part of the study an analytical structure has been developed which has drawn upon several theoretical approaches [14–21]. This framework, in its preliminary stages, has four levels: Actions, Aesthetics, Mechanics and Narration to identify and analyze potential narrative game mechanics present within interactive fiction. Currently, two textual analyses have been carried out and these have been supplemented with Youtube 'Let's Play' videos. The first and second versions of the interactive fiction game have been launched and feedback gathered. Preliminary conclusions indicate that narrative game mechanics require further defining. The information mechanic identified as part of this study, and its relationship to how it progresses a narrative, requires further examination. The framework designed has also shown the potential to be applied to both interactive fiction and video games.

Keywords: Narrative game mechanics · Interactive fiction · Video games
Let's play · Game mechanics · Textual analysis

1 Research Work

Interactive fiction remains an area of interest for academic study. Although it has retained an established audience, it is currently less prevalent in popular culture [1–3]. However, interactive fiction offers a unique medium through which the developing concept of narrative game mechanics [4–7] can be explored. The concept of narrative game mechanics ties into the emerging academic question of 'how do games tell stories' [8].

The goal of this study is to investigate, analyze and understand the potential narrative game mechanics within, primarily, interactive fiction but also video games. The theory of "machinic texts" [9] and N. Katherine Hayles' understanding of "print is flat

© Springer Nature Switzerland AG 2018
R. Rouse et al. (Eds.): ICIDS 2018, LNCS 11318, pp. 289–292, 2018.
https://doi.org/10.1007/978-3-030-04028-4_32

and code is deep" [10] gives merit to the potential for these two media forms to overlap due to their shared nature of reading and play existing together.

This research-led practice [11] study involves several textual analyses and, in addition, the design of an interactive fiction game using the platform Twine [12]. To gather feedback from the interactive fiction an online forum has been created. This feedback will be used to enhance further iterations of the game but it is not critical to the ongoing study. The primary purpose of the game, used in conjunction with the textual analyses, is as a reflective and exploratory tool to see if and how narrative game mechanics are presented within interactive fiction. There is also the potential that there may be medium specific narrative game mechanics present in interactive fiction but not in video games. For the purposes of this study it is the process of creating an artefact that is more important than the artefact itself [13].

2 Analytical Framework

In order to attempt to understand narrative game mechanics a media-specific analysis [9] is required. For the purposes of this study an analytical framework has been designed drawing upon several theoretical approaches [14–21] relating to narrative, game studies and interactive fiction. This analytical structure is still in its preliminary stages and will develop as the study progresses; additional theories will be factored in to further develop the framework.

The analytical structure currently has four levels: Actions, Aesthetics, Mechanics and Narration. Influenced by Roland Barthes' model for the structural analysis of narratives [16] and the MDA framework [19] the four outlined levels are intended to work in progression and have integrational links. Barthes gives the example of the integrational link between a phoneme, word and sentence that is required to produce meaning. This same link can be applied to narrative game mechanics- the mechanic alone is not enough to contribute to the narrative but viewing it within the expanded context of the game allows meaning to be derived.

The Actions level of the preliminary analytical structure is the lowest level and consists of the basic actions a player can take such as picking up objects (within a video game) or clicking on links (within an interactive fiction). This leads to the Aesthetics level, based on Hunicke et al's partial list of aesthetic classifications [19], which looks at how the actions are presented within the game's context. The genre of the game contributes to this level as certain actions will encourage the narrative of the genre e.g. the action of using magic exists more naturally within (but is not exclusive to) the fantasy genre. The third level, which is the Mechanics level, focuses on how the identified actions are used with the game's aesthetic setting. An example of this would be the action to *crouch*. Depending on the context and aesthetic of the game this could become the mechanic of *sneak* or *hide*. The action carried out by the avatar is to move from a standing position to a crouching one but the player, influenced by the game's aesthetic, views this action as the mechanic to *sneak* or *hide*. The last level is Narration and, as with Barthes' understanding of this level [16], this level is unclear. What this level is trying to establish is what, if any, meaning can be established from the executed mechanic. It can be assumed that a narrative game mechanic has been successful if meaning/narrative has been interpreted by the player once they reach this final level. However, this level is indistinct as it is dependent on player interpretation and each player may find different interpretations.

To combat the ambiguity of the Narration level Youtube [22] 'Let's Play' videos have been used as a method of observing other player interpretations. These videos have been used to supplement my own interpretations as part of the textual analyses carried out. Although the use of Let's Play videos for analytical purposes is still in a nascent stage it has been noted that they can be viewed as a paratext of the video games [9]. Let's Play videos also allow for players reactions and understandings to be observed [23] and players create their own narrative through their play experiences [24].

3 Status and Next Steps

At present two textual analyses, one interactive fiction and one video game, have been carried out using the analytical structure outlined. A key idea that has emerged from the work completed so far is the notion of an 'information mechanic'. Within interactive fiction this is observed as purposely not providing the player with a piece of information; which leads to the player having to interpret the games events. It is believed that this purposeful ambiguity allows the content of the text to function as a type of mechanic. This idea is still to be explored further but may prove to be present in video games as well. This mechanic is, more likely, to be observed in wordless games (games with little or no dialogue/text) with the ambiguous visuals taking the place of the text present in interactive fiction.

It is proposed to carry out a further two textual analyses and apply the developed structural framework. At the time of writing the first and second versions of the Twine interactive fiction has been launched and feedback has been collected. The feedback gathered from the first version has been analyzed and has contributed to the second iteration of the interactive fiction. The feedback from the second version is currently being analyzed. A third version of the interactive fiction will be created following the analysis of the feedback collected from the second version.

References

1. Pope, J.: 'Where do we go from here?' Responses to interactive fiction: narrative structures. Reading pleasure and the impact of interface design. Convergence Int. J. Res. New Media Technol. **16**(1), 75–94 (2010)
2. Mangen, A., Van der Weel, A.: Why don't we read hypertext novels? Convergence Int. J. Res. New Media Technol. **23**(2), 161–181 (2017)
3. Miall, D., Dobson, T.: Reading hypertext and the experience of literature. J. Dig. Inf. **2**(1) (2001). https://journals.tdl.org/jodi/index.php/jodi/article/view/35/37. Accessed 5 Mar 2017
4. Dubbelman, T.: Narrative game mechanics. In: Nack, F., Gordon, A.S. (eds.) ICIDS 2016. LNCS, vol. 10045, pp. 39–50. Springer, Cham (2016). https://doi.org/10.1007/978-3-319-48279-8_4

5. Dubbelman, T.: Repetition, reward and mastery: the value of game design patterns for the analysis of narrative game mechanics. In: Nunes, N., Oakley, I., Nisi, V. (eds.) ICIDS 2017. LNCS, vol. 10690, pp. 286–289. Springer, Cham (2017). https://doi.org/10.1007/978-3-319-71027-3_27

6. Larsen, B.A., Schoenau-Fog, H.: The narrative quality of game mechanics. In: Nack, F., Gordon, Andrew S. (eds.) ICIDS 2016. LNCS, vol. 10045, pp. 61–72. Springer, Cham (2016). https://doi.org/10.1007/978-3-319-48279-8_6

7. Hjaltson, K., Christophersen, S., Togelius, J., Nelson, M.: Game mechanics telling stories? An experiment (2015). http://julian.togelius.com/Hjaltason2015Game.pdf. Accessed 28 Mar 2017

8. Sim, Y.T., Mitchell, A.: Wordless games: gameplay as narrative technique. In: Nunes, N., Oakley, I., Nisi, V. (eds.) ICIDS 2017. LNCS, vol. 10690, pp. 137–149. Springer, Cham (2017). https://doi.org/10.1007/978-3-319-71027-3_12

9. Mukherjee, S.: Video Games and Storytelling: Reading Games and Playing Books. Palgrave Macmillan, UK (2015)

10. Hayles, N.: Print is flat, code is deep: the importance of media-specific analysis. Poetics Today 25(1), 67–90 (2004)

11. Smith, H., Dean, R. (eds.): Practice-Led Research. Research-Led Practice in the Creative Arts. Edinburgh University Press, Edinburgh (2009)

12. Twine. http://twinery.org/. Accessed 12 July 2018

13. Rust, C., Mottram, J., Till, J.: AHRC research review: practice-led research in art, design and architecture (2007). http://arts.brighton.ac.uk/__data/assets/pdf_file/0018/43065/Practice-Led_Review_Nov07.pdf. Accessed 05 June 2017

14. Aarseth, E.: Cybertext: Perspectives on Ergodic Literature. Johns Hopkins University Press, Baltimore (1997)

15. Barthes, R.: The Pleasure of the Text. Farrar, Straus and Giroux, France (1975)

16. Barthes, R.: Image, Music. Text. Fontana Press, London (1977)

17. Barthes, R.: S/Z: An Essay. Hill and Wang, New York (1998)

18. Ensslin, A.: Literary Gaming. MIT Press, Cambridge (2014)

19. Hunicke, R., LeBlanc, M., Zubek, R.: MDA: a formal approach to game design and game research (2004). http://www.cs.northwestern.edu/~hunicke/MDA.pdf. Accessed 20 Sept 2017

20. Ryan, M.: Narratives as Visual Reality: Immersion and Interactivity in Literature and Electronic Media. The Johns Hopkins University Press, Baltimore and London (2001)

21. Ryan, M.: Narrative as Virtual Reality 2: Revisiting Immersion and Interactivity in Literature and Electronic Media. Johns Hopkins University Press, Baltimore (2015)

22. Youtube. https://www.youtube.com. Accessed 14 July 2018

23. Burwell, C.: Game changers: making new meanings and new media with video games. English J. 106(6), 41–47 (2017)

24. Kerttula, T.: "What an Eccentric Performance": Storytelling in Online Let's Plays. Games and Culture. First published online 21 November 2016

Practices in Virtual Reality

Measuring User Experience on Interactive Fiction in Cinematic Virtual Reality

Maria Cecilia Reyes$^{(\boxtimes)}$ (iD)

Università degli Studi di Genova, Genoa, Italy
maria.cecilia.reyes@edu.unige.it

Abstract. This paper proposes a methodology to measure User Experience (UX) dimensions on Interactive Fiction in Cinematic Virtual Reality (IFcVR), in order to evaluate the effectiveness of IFcVR as a narrative form and as a vehicle for different types of messages. The presented methodology merges Human Computer Interface (HCI) evaluation techniques with Interactive Digital Narrative (IDN) user dimensions, and gathers both qualitative and quantitative data by mixing different types of instruments. An experimental evaluation of an interactive VR fiction film functional prototype demonstrates the viability of the proposed methodology while gathered data shows a positive acceptance by the participants to IFcVR as an entertaining and immersive experience.

Keywords: Cinematic virtual reality · Interactive digital narrative
Interactive fiction in cinematic virtual reality · Hyperfiction
Medium-conscious narratology · User experience measurement

1 Interactive Fiction in Cinematic Virtual Reality

While Virtual Reality (VR) develops as a narrative medium, more filmmakers are attracted by the possibility of producing VR artefacts through the capture of reality with 360° video cameras. In recent years, the term Cinematic VR (cVR) has been used to name this kind of immersive experiences in which the story unfolds in a traditional linear way with the novelty of the 360° environment that, if delivered through a Head Mounted Display (HMD), creates an immersive VR experience and, to some extent, an interactive experience since the user decides what to look at within the visual sphere. From a cinematic point of view, research on audiovisual language is studying how to tell engaging linear stories in Virtual Environments (VEs), with the aim to develop an autonomous audiovisual and narrative language for VR [1], and in particular for cVR [2]. In the same way, VR as a medium and its various user interfaces are continuously under research and development [3], as users send feedbacks and new experiences are developed.

Even though VR is intended as an interactive medium, because it requires from the user a "lean in" [4] behaviour, VR experiences based on 360° video find themselves in opposition to the interactive nature of VR, since users can not modify the VE neither change the course of the story. However, the nature of VR allows the creation of interactive narrative structures that can be navigated through several kinds of Human Computer Interfaces (HCI), offering the user different levels of agency [5] and

© Springer Nature Switzerland AG 2018
R. Rouse et al. (Eds.): ICIDS 2018, LNCS 11318, pp. 295–307, 2018.
https://doi.org/10.1007/978-3-030-04028-4_33

decisional power upon the course of the story, hence enhancing the cVR user experience (UX). The term Interactive Fiction in Cinematic Virtual Reality (IFcVR) is proposed to stand for an Interactive Digital Narrative (IDN) VR experience based on 360° video narrative units (NU) [6] with an interactive structure based on IF or hyperfiction [7]. At the time, the aesthetics, narratological and interactive theoretical foundations have been studied in order to identify the main aspects to be considered on the creation of interactive immersive fiction films [8]. These aspects have guided the creation process of the interactive immersive film prototype "ZENA", from the screenwriting framework [9] to the functional prototype to be tested.

The current scarcity of IFcVR experiences has a direct consequence in the lack of research on: production workflow (from development to post-production), potential applications, and assessment tools for measuring UX in terms of enjoyment and engagement. This lack of user feedback hinders the creation of a medium-conscious narratology [10] for IFcVR as a hybrid genre. The measurement of UX is the basis of the design and improvement of successful system and interfaces, as UX measures user's satisfaction achieving pragmatic and hedonic goals [11]. HCI evaluation techniques and measurements [12, 13] can partially help to evaluate the usability aspects (effectiveness, efficiency, satisfaction, learnability, accessibility and safety) [11] of the IFcVR system, but it lacks in measuring the perceptive and narrative immersion, and the enjoyment of the interactive narrative experience, as they do not take into consideration the narrative aspects which are peculiar to cVR and IDN. Contributing to fill these gaps is the aim of this study.

This exploratory research is driven by the following questions: (1) Does IFcVR provide engaging narrative experiences able to deliver coherent messages and stories? (2) Which aspects of IFcVR should be measured in order to evaluate the quality of the experience? (3) Is IFcVR perceived as a filmic experience rather than a gaming one?

In order to answer these questions, the IFcVR functional prototype "ZENA" was submitted to user testing. This paper proposes a full evaluation protocol for IFcVR that gathers qualitative and quantitative data based on standard HCI evaluation techniques that, besides usability, comprises IDN User Dimensions [14]. In addition, the proposed evaluation protocol works out three *ad hoc* instruments: an observation grid, a questionnaire and a semi-structured interview. The paper illustrates the proposed protocol through its pilot application to the IFcVR prototype "ZENA". Findings show users' impressions on IFcVR and discusses its suitability and effectiveness as an interactive narrative and entertaining artefact.

2   A Framework Proposal for IFcVR User Experience Evaluation

The IDN User Experience Dimensions offer an interdisciplinary approach that can be applied to a wide range of technologies and narratives. Starting from this analytical framework, Table 1 presents a breakdown of the categories proposed by Roth and Koenitz [14], and adds some specific categories specifically related to cVR and IFcVR. These categories respond on one side to the cinematic experience in VR (e.g.: realness of the cVE, cinematic continuity [15], audiovisual flow, type of hotspot if visual or auditory, intuitive use of the hotspots, visual exploration of the space Vs interest on the scene events, use of spatial audio, use of diegetic or extradiegetic audio) and on the other to the IF features (e.g.: use of text as a guide for the decision-making, length of the decision-making moments, use of diegetic and extradiegetic hotspots, understanding and remembrance of the story, filmic experience Vs gaming experience, desire of repeat the experience).

Table 1. IFcVR user experience measurement categories of analysis

Agency	System's Usability
	Autonomy (Intuitive use of HCI to activate the Hotspots; Use of Text as a Guide for the Decision-making; Length of the decision-making moments; Type of hotspot if visual or auditory; Use of Diegetic and Extradiegetic Hotspots)
	Effectance
Perceptual immersion	Realism of the cVE
	Presence
	Flow (Audiovisual: awareness of the Camera Position, awareness of Editing Cuts between shots. Interactive: type of interaction feedback)
	Use of Spatial Audio
Narrative immersion	Cinematic Continuity
	Understanding of the story/remembrance
	Believability
	Role Identification
	Curiosity
	Visual exploration of the Space Vs Interest on the Scene Events
	Use of Diegetic and Extradiegetic Sound (Voice Over, Music)
Transformation	Sense of "Living" the Film Vs Video Game Feeling
	Aesthetic Pleasantness/Eudaimonic Appreciation
	Positive or Negative Affect
	Desire of repeat the experience
	Enjoyment

Even though linear cVR is considered itself as a form of IDN, IFcVR adds a level of interactive creation and reading. In this sense it is possible to identify both levels as follows: (1) Local (cVR assessment): aspects related to what happens inside each NU and (2) Global (IDN assessment): aspects related to how users navigate between nodes that conduct to the final IDN outcome.

Local Assessment - Aspects related to Cinematic Virtual Reality. As a place-based experience, the effects on emotion, enjoyment and narrative flow regarding IFcVR rely on what happens within each NU. On a first level, UX is based on what occurs within the *scene-space* and the interaction consists in what user chooses to see. Data collection instruments such as head tracking [16, 17], body movements and biometrics [18–20] software have been used to measure the behaviour and emotional involvement of the user during the immersive experience in correlation to what is seeing-living within the *scene-space.*

Since IFcVR is mostly based on 360° video, aspects related to the level of realism offered by the video, image and cinematic techniques, such as the position of the camera or the internal and external cuts, as well as by the use of the spatial audio [21] and the diegetic or extradiegetic sound (voice over, music, effects) can be used to prove the quality of the cinematic VR experience and its audiovisual language.

Global Assessment - Aspects related to Interactive Digital Narrative. In IFcVR, during each *scene-space,* users face decision-making moments that represent the agency level offered by IFcVR. Users make their choices based on the information given by the NU and the level of engagement they are experiencing. Agency in IFcVR, where the VE can not be modified by the users, can be measured by the intuitive use that the users can do of the proposed HCI to make choices that will change the course of the story, or to activate the hotspots that offer extra-information. Hence, HCI measurements that regard usability parameters (such as time on task, time to learn, number of errors, etc.), help to reflect the level of effectance and autonomy that influence the enjoyment of the overall interactive experience.

3   The IFcVR Evaluation Protocol

The evaluation protocol was tested on "ZENA", a 20 min long IFcVR functionally prototype based on an Interactive Fiction structure whose NUs were developed using 360° video for a Cinematic VR experience. The screenplay of the prototype follows an interactivized version of the Hero's Journey [22], in which user decisions affect the protagonist's actions during the course of the story. "ZENA" has a longer length than traditional VR short films, in an attempt to create an experience that can be perceived as a traditional film. The prototype was shot in Genoa's Old Town labyrinth of narrow streets called "vicoli". Each scene was recorded in 4 K 360° video, with stereo audio (questions regarding spatial audio were not included in the questionnaire) and hotspots are activated by head-tracking gaze. During the evaluation, the experience was played through a Samsung Gear device.

3.1   Design

The procedure was divided into two moments in order to undertake separately the Local and the Global Assessment, as shown in Table 2. The *During-the-Experience* phase corresponds to the local assessment and analyzes aspects related to the cVR quality of each NU, and consequently to the *decision-making* moments. While the *After-the-Experience* phase corresponds to the global assessment, evaluating user's final journey, that is the output resulting from the instantiation process. User's characteristics and tendencies questions were included into the *After-the-Experience* questionnaire.

Table 2. Procedure design

	Analysis	Methods
User characteristics	Participant Tendencies	Consensus Demographic Data Expertise level in Film, Videogames and VR
During the experience	Local Assessment (cVR): Scene-Space	User's Journey System Recording Observation of Body Movements Think-aloud Protocol
After the experience	Global Assessment (IDN): Final Journey	Questionnaire Semi-structured Short Interview

3.2 Participants

The prototype was tested by a total of 60 participants, one user at a time, in the age range 12–64 years old ($M = 30.46$, $SD = 15.02$), in three different sessions organized by groups: G1 = Genoa's middle and high school students (24), G2 = adults non residents in Genoa (19), G3 = videomakers and/or researchers (17). 66.7% were female. Participants were asked if they are residents of Genoa or if they have visited the city in the past in order to differentiate the sensation of *being* in the city of residents and non-residents. 56% of the participants were residents, and 95% of them had been in Genoa at least once. G3 group was differentiated in order to highlight expert view on cinematic language, VR development and new media applications.

Among the participants, 33.3% were enrolled in high school, 10% in middle school, 6.7% already had a Bachelor's degree, 25% had a Master's degree and a 15% were enrolled or already finished their PhD programme and 10% had a technical diploma. As concerns the physical discomfort of participants, such as nausea or use of glasses, 51.7% of the participants wear glasses while a 36.7% often suffers from motion sickness.

Participants were asked about their knowledge, expertise and use frequency of videogames, cinema and VR. 3.3% play videogames every day, 5% play weekly, 36.7% play occasionally and 55% never play. This 55% corresponds to the participants older than 40 years. Regarding film consumption: 51.7% watch more than one film a week, 26.7% at least one film a week, 18.3% few times a month and only 3.3% few times a year. As concerns knowledge about film production, 41.7% reported inter-mediate, 38.3% basic, 11.7% none and 8.3% expert. 63.3% have never used before a VR HMD. 43.3% did not have any knowledge about VR production, a 46.7% had a basic knowledge, a 8.3% a intermediate knowledge, while a 1.7% were VR experts.

Therefore, the test included a group of people used to watch films very often but not to play videogames, and neither knowing or using VR HMDs. Hence, for them the cinematographic language is natural, allowing us to evaluate if the cinematic narrative in the 360° environment is perceived as fluid in spite of the alternative navigation paths. On the other hand, their little use of video games and VR systems allowed us to have a clearer idea of how intuitive and easy to use is the interactive system for the non-expert user.

In 68.3% of the cases, the experience ran in a fluid way and without technical errors. 25.8% experimented an error due to the expiration of the decision-making time, while 5.9% experimented some kind of system errors or freezing that were corrected immediately.

3.3 During the Experience

The first phase of the evaluation process starts from the moment in which the opportunity to live the experience is offered to the user. This is the first decision that the user must make, if s/he accepts or not to be isolated in a neo-reality that will disconnect them, for some minutes, from their own reality. In absence of technological tools as motion sensors, biometric sensors or VR analytics software, for the evaluation of the prototype three types of qualitative data were collected simultaneously and correlated through an observation grid (see Table 3) while the users were experiencing the film: User's Journey System Recording, Observation of Body Movements and the Think-aloud Protocol [23].

Table 3. During-the-experience observation grid

N.U	Time	System recording	User observation	Think-aloud
		• Scene • Space	• Move in place • Walk around • Touch attempts • Head movement • Others	• Attitude • About the Story • About the Space • About the Prototype • Discomfort • System Usability

Participants were not asked to express their thoughts, but left free to speak up their feelings and impressions when they wanted, so as the think-aloud process would not interfere with the enjoyment of the experience. The aim of this data choice is to correlate body movements, feelings and thoughts, together with what the user was observing at a specific time inside the *scene-space* or NU. This correlation allows us to analyse the construction of the scene from the cVR point of view, analyze how much a user follows a scene or prefers to observe the space, and to understand the mental and emotional process of each user when choosing one way or the other.

During-the-Experience, users and system can be recorded in video. The video recording was carry out with G3 participants: User's navigation path was recorded by mirroring the HDM vision on a computer, while user's body movements and think-aloud were recorded with a video camera. The video recording allows to complete the observation grid at a later time.

3.4 After the Experience

Once the experience was over, a questionnaire and a short semi-structured interview were submitted to all participants, to gather user's retrospective quantitative and qualitative data regarding the overall journey in relation to agency, perceptive and narrative immersion, and transformation aspects (enjoyment, aesthetic pleasantness, affect) and the level of physical discomfort. The mixed method allowed a better comprehension of UX aspects related to their cognitive remembrance and understanding of the story, their feeling of presence within the cVE, their level of enjoyment, and their feelings in determining if the IFcVR experience was enjoyed as a film or as a videogame.

Questionnaire. The questionnaire takes into account aspects related to the immersive experience, as well as those related to the interactive narrative. It is organized in three blocks: User Characteristics, During and After the experience. Table 4 presents the structure of our questionnaire, that merges the ITC-SOPI questionnaire [24] measure the Sense of Presence in Cross-media Experiences, together with specific questions based on the toolbox for the evaluation of User Experience of Interactive Digital Narrative [11]. Finally, some questions were added from the Simulator Sickness Questionnaire (SSQ) [25] in order to spot the physical discomfort caused by the IFcVR artefact.

Table 4. Structure of the IFcVR questionnaire

User dimensions	Categories	N°Q
User information	Demographic data	4
	Knowledge (Expertise) and Use of: Films, Videogames and VR	6
	Nausea tendency and use of glasses	2
Agency	System Usability	3
	Autonomy	4
	Effectance	3
Perceptive immersion	Realism of the cVE	6
	Presence	5
	Flow	2
Narrative immersion	Curiosity and Suspense	4
	Believability	5
	Role Identification	5
	Sound (Voice Over, Music)	2
	Scene Vs Space	4
Transformation	Enjoyment	4
	Film Vs Videogame Feeling	3
	Affect	4
Physical discomfort	General Discomfort	2
	Visual Discomfort	2
	Nausea	3

The final questionnaire for IFcVR contains a set of 73 questions: 6 questions on demographic data, 6 questions on User's knowledge and consume of films, videogames and VR. 57 questions have a response option of five-point Likert scale (1 = strongly disagree; 5 = strongly agree), 1 is a multiple choice question with constructed answer: *which one was your favorite character and why?* and 3 were open questions: *what was your favorite scene and why?, what was your favorite place and why?* and a open comment about the experience.

Semi-structured Short Interview. The interview consisted in a short dialogue in which users were invited to share their thoughts and feelings about the experience in a retrospective way. The questions covered several topics that allowed us to understand the Transformation aspect from different points of view: Cognition about the story and the journey, Enjoyment and Affective aspects of the IFcVR experience. Table 5 presents the main questions that were asked to the participants.

Table 5. Structure of the IFcVR semi-structured short interview

	Questions
IQ1	Can you tell us what the story was about?
IQ2	Can you relate your journey? (Remembrance of the navigation path and the choices lead them to the specific ending)
IQ3	What aspects of the story catch your attention? (characters, places, sounds, etc.)
IQ4	What was your feeling about the Virtual Experience? (Impressions about the VR experience)
IQ5	Do you have any suggestion for future improvements or projects?

4   Findings

The results presented in this paper are intended to be representative of the kind of information that can be gathered by implementing the proposed evaluation protocol. At the same time, the presented data aims to recognize matters about IFcVR narrative and interactive validity, its level of engagement and the balance between filmic and gaming user fruition feeling offered by the artefact. Data regarding specific subjects of the prototype were left out of the following results, even though some meaningful insights and correlations were taking into account.

4.1   During the Experience

The observation grid provided data that allowed us to note an overall appreciation of the story. The confrontation between the system mirroring along with user movements, allowed us to see that the majority of the participants looked for the figure of protagonist everytime they found themselves in a new NU, and once the character was spotted then they felt free to visually explore the space. This corresponds to a high level of narrative immersion, in particular to role identification, curiosity and suspense. Their body movements were noticed to follow the movements and actions of characters in the scene, especially in some scenes that were designed to make the user turn around while following the characters, or to look for the hotspots in space. Regarding body movements, it was also possible to identify that some users moved around in the room, while others simulated walking during moving camera scenes or tryed to touch characters and objects during the experience, in an attempt to interact with the cVE. This active body attitude mostly characterized people without previous experience with HMD, that were more than half of participants. Two participants took off the HMD, one of them was afraid and refused to continue the experience, while the other one needed a time to accept to be isolated and then restarted watching the film.

The Think-aloud recording provided some insights about the feeling of presence. In general, participants used of the verb *To Be* in present tense or used the first person to describe situations (e.g. "I am at the tower", "I don't trust the master"). Most participants from G1 shared feelings regarding the story (e.g.: they talked to characters to give them instructions, or they spoke to themselves about the choices to make). As adults non residents, G2 participants shared comments about the novelty of the VR experience and the places that they remembered from Genoa. G3, formed by video makers and researchers, shared thoughts about the quality of the audiovisual experience (e.g.: "I can feel the different heights of the camera", "the cuts between scenes are practically imperceptible") and about the system usability by asking questions about the technical development of the experience.

4.2 After the Experience

Questionnaire. Participants took 10 min in average to complete the questionnaire. The results presented in Table 6 show the average by subcategories and the corresponding standard deviation. In terms of *Agency*, Usability and Effectance had the highest score, while Autonomy shows a slight lower score. Regarding *Perceptual Immersion*, the data show a high level of Presence, Flow and also Realism of the cVE. *Narrative Immersion* shows a lower score if compared with perceptual immersion, being Believability the lower result with a $M = 3.5$, while Curiosity and Role Identification show a higher level. In this category, items as Visual Exploration of the Spaces, Voice Over Narrator and Music Role in Engagement were included to measure how these aspects increase Narrative Immersion. The results show that these three items have helped users to get immersed in the story. In *Transformation* terms, the overall Enjoyment of the experience shows a $M = 4.54$, while Affect a $M = 3.95$.

Into the Transformation category two questions were included regarding if using the artefact raised a feeling similar to watch a film or to play a videogame. The results show a very close balance between both feelings: 54% for film, while the feeling of being playing a videogame resulted 46%. The last part of the questionnaire, dedicated to the *Physical Discomfort*, reported low scores, being the Visual Discomfort the most problematic aspect $M = 2.65$.

Even though the data set offered by the questionnaire presents low scores related to Narrative Immersion, the open questions complemented the information related to the narrative immersion showing very positive results that also allowed interesting correlations. For example: the favorite place corresponds also to the favorite scene; during

Table 6. Results of the questionnaire

User dimensions		M =	SD =
Agency	Usability	4.22	0.24
	Autonomy	3.94	0.15
	Effectance	4.08	0.32
Perceptual immersion	Realism of the cinematic VE	4.08	0.99
	Presence	4.13	0.38
	Flow	4.24	0.03
Narrative immersion	Curiosity	3.75	0.64
	Believability	3.5	0.611
	Role Identification	3.7	0.20
	Visual Exploration of the Spaces	4.64	0.15
	Voice Over Narrator	4.35	0.68
	Music role in engagement	3.98	0.87
Transformation	Enjoyment	4.54	0.12
	Affect	3.95	0.07
Physical discomfort	General Discomfort	1.78	0.40
	Visual Discomfort	2.65	0.23
	Nausea	1.80	0.43

the scenes shot in the labyrinth of narrow streets of the historical center, participants felt high levels of suspense and curiosity, and some of them felt them so real to remember the characteristic smells of the historical center. The favorite character was Lorenzo, protagonist and character that followed user choices, with a 35% of the appreciation.

Semi-structured Short Interview. The short interview, 5 min average, helped to measure the level of understanding of the story and how participants remember it. All participants could elaborate a recap of the main plot of the story (IQ1), and also relate the stages and the decisions they made during the experience, reconstructing clearly their navigation path (IQ2). Some of the participants reported their feeling when choosing the path of the experience: "I started again after completing the route. I wanted to continue, as if it was not enough Probably in large part I was guided by my intuition. I had little way of "consciously choosing". I felt guided, more than capable of deciding my destiny".

They could also elaborate on the aspects that catch their attention (IQ3). Some repeated answers included: be able to see the city in a different way, a respondent commented "I think I saw more of the city in this experience rather than in my 15 years of life". The story and the characters were considered interesting, with comments on the personality of the characters, the acting quality, and how the turn of the events surprised them. Another aspect highlighted was the sound: "I liked sound effects (the ambient, the sea, when I went back to the past the music was from the middle ages, the sound of people talking). A representative comment regards the coherence of the film: "Being able to choose the paths of the character is good fun as it has a logical consequence. (e.g.: the choice *I'm lost* leads Lorenzo to the church which in my eyes makes a lot of sense)".

About the feeling of the Virtual Experience (IQ4), impressions are quite positive if we take in consideration that 63.3% of the participants had never worn a HMD before. Comments about the feeling in the majority of the cases were adjectives to describe the experience, while others extended the answer: "Good experience to escape from the stress of daily life", "Nice but tiring", "At first I was a bit fearful, then I had fun". Some answers correspond to some technical aspects of the cVR experience: "It is very strange not to see my own body", "The graphic quality is still low and can be improved", "It is possible to optimize the times in which we have to make choices". Finally, giving suggestions for future improvements or projects (IQ5), some highlighted the value of the experience regardless of the genre of film they experienced, and imagined applications for tourism or education.

5 Conclusions and Further Work

The evaluation protocol proposed in this paper showed to provide the necessary information to measure the effectiveness of the IFcVR as an interactive digital narrative, as well as it offered detailed information regarding specific aspects related to the prototype. The outputs of the pilot application of the protocol to be highlighted include: (i) The division of the procedure design into "During and After the Experience" and its correspondence with the Local and Global evaluation was useful to distinguish aspects related to the cVR and later to the IFcVR. (ii) The analog and low cost instruments used to gather both quantitative and qualitative data (observation grid, questionnaire, semistructured interview), complemented each other and offered a deep overview of the user experience, not only in terms of system usability but also in terms of narrative and perceptive inmersion.

The final outcome of the methodology confirms the effectiveness of IFcVR for the transmission of various types of messages in an entertaining experience. Users appreciated the veracity of the cVE, they felt immersed in the story and enjoyed the possibility of choosing the path to follow. A significant result is presented by the balance of the IFcVR as an experience that is situated in the middle between the film and the video game. The cinematographic sensation was high, and the fact of having an active role enriched the development of the experience. The most critical aspect was the error caused by the expiration of the decision-making time, which 25.8% of the participants experienced. Further research and projects intend to propose strategies to overcome the technical limit that the inherent duration of the video presents to the moments of interaction.

Upcoming assessment of the methodology includes more accurate quantitative research by using biometric and motion sensors into the *During-the-Experience* phase, an improvement of the questionnaire in order to provide information about some specific elements that were left out the test, as the aesthetic pleasantness (some aesthetic aspects were included as helpers for Narrative Immersion), or Suspense (even though some participants related the feeling of suspense, specific questions were not included).

The tested prototype contained subtitles, a novelty in VR experiences, further testing will include the measure of this aspect.

References

1. Aylett, R., Louchart, S.: Towards a narrative theory of virtual reality. Virtual Reality **7**, 2–9 (2003). https://doi.org/10.1007/s10055-003-0114-9
2. Lasse, T., et al.: Missing the point: an exploration of how to guide users' attention during cinematic virtual reality. In: Proceedings of the 22nd ACM Conference on Virtual Reality Software and Technology (VRST 2016), pp. 229–232. ACM, New York (2016). https://doi.org/10.1145/2993369.2993405
3. Sutcliffe, G. et al.: Reflecting on the design process for virtual reality applications. Int. J. Hum.–Comput. Interact., 1–12 (2018). https://doi.org/10.1080/10447318.2018.1443898
4. Vosmeer, M., Schouten, B.: Interactive cinema: engagement and interaction. In: Mitchell, A., Fernández-Vara, C., Thue, D. (eds.) ICIDS 2014. LNCS, vol. 8832, pp. 140–147. Springer, Cham (2014). https://doi.org/10.1007/978-3-319-12337-0_14
5. Murray, J.H.: Hamlet on the Holodeck: The Future of Narrative in Cyberspace. MIT Press, Cambridge (1997)
6. Koenitz, H.: An iterative approach towards interactive digital narrative – early results with the advanced stories authoring and presentation system. In: Chiu, D.K.W., Wang, M., Popescu, E., Li, Q., Lau, R. (eds.) ICWL 2012. LNCS, vol. 7697, pp. 59–68. Springer, Heidelberg (2014). https://doi.org/10.1007/978-3-662-43454-3_7
7. Montfort, N.: Twisty Little Passages: An Approach to Interactive Fiction. MIT Press, Cambridge (2005)
8. Reyes, M.C.: An epistemological approach to the creation of interactive VR fiction films. In: Nunes, N., Oakley, I., Nisi, V. (eds.) ICIDS 2017. LNCS, vol. 10690, pp. 380–383. Springer, Cham (2017). https://doi.org/10.1007/978-3-319-71027-3_48
9. Reyes, M.C.: Screenwriting framework for an interactive virtual reality film. In: Proceedings 3rd Immersive Research Network Conference iLRN 2017, pp. 92–102 (2017). https://doi.org/10.3217/978-3-851-25-530-0-15
10. Wolf, W.: Narratology and Media(lity): The transmedial expansion of a literary discipline and possible consequences. In Olson, G. (ed.) Current Trends in Narratology, pp 145–180. De Gruyter, Berlin (2011)
11. Bevan, N.: Classifying and selecting UX and usability measures. In: International Workshop on Meaningful Measures: Valid Useful User Experience Measurement (2008)
12. Bevan, N., Carter, J., Earthy, J., Geis, T., Harker, S.: New ISO standards for usability, usability reports and usability measures. In: Kurosu, M. (ed.) HCI 2016. LNCS, vol. 9731, pp. 268–278. Springer, Cham (2016). https://doi.org/10.1007/978-3-319-39510-4_25
13. Issa, T., Isaias, P.: Sustainable Design: HCI, Usability and Environmental Concerns. Springer, London (2015)
14. Roth, C., Koenitz, H.: Evaluating the user experience of interactive digital narrative. In: Proceedings of the 1st International Workshop on Multimedia Alternate Realities (AltMM 2016), pp. 31–36. ACM, New York (2016). https://doi.org/10.1145/2983298.2983302
15. Magliano, J.P., Zacks, J.M.: The impact of continuity editing in narrative film on event segmentation. Cogn. Sci. **35**, 1489–1517 (2011)
16. Bala, P., Dionisio, M., Nisi, V., Nunes, N.: IVRUX: a tool for analyzing immersive narratives in virtual reality. In: Nack, F., Gordon, Andrew S. (eds.) ICIDS 2016. LNCS, vol. 10045, pp. 3–11. Springer, Cham (2016). https://doi.org/10.1007/978-3-319-48279-8_1

17. Rothe, S., Hußmann, H.: Guiding the viewer in cinematic virtual reality by diegetic cues. In: De Paolis, L.T., Bourdot, P. (eds.) AVR 2018. LNCS, vol. 10850, pp. 101–117. Springer, Cham (2018). https://doi.org/10.1007/978-3-319-95270-3_7
18. Bian, Y., et al.: A framework for physiological indicators of flow in VR games: construction and preliminary evaluation. Pers. Ubiquit. Comput. **20**(5), 821–832 (2016). https://doi.org/10.1007/s00779-016-0953-5
19. Hou, G., Dong, H., Yang, Y.: Developing a virtual reality game user experience test method based on EEG signals. In: 2017 5th International Conference on Enterprise Systems (ES) (2017). https://doi.org/10.1109/es.2017.45
20. Cipresso, P., et al.: Low-cost motion-tracking for computational psychometrics based on virtual reality. In: De Paolis, L.T., Mongelli, A. (eds.) AVR 2014. LNCS, vol. 8853, pp. 137–148. Springer, Cham (2014). https://doi.org/10.1007/978-3-319-13969-2_11
21. Aspöck, L., Kohnen, M., Vorlaender, M.: Evaluating immersion of spatial audio systems for virtual reality. J. Acoust. Soc. Am. **143**(3), 1829 (2018). https://doi.org/10.1121/1.5036003
22. Campbell, J.: The Hero with a Thousand Faces. New World Library (2008)
23. Janni, N., Torkil, C., Carsten, Y.: Getting access to what goes on in people's heads?: reflections on the think-aloud technique. In: Proceedings of the Second Nordic Conference on Human-Computer Interaction (NordiCHI 2002), pp. 101–110. ACM, New York (2002). https://doi.org/10.1145/572020.572033
24. Lessiter, J., Freeman, J., Keogh, E., Davidoff, J.: A cross-media presence questionnaire: the ITC-sense of presence inventory. Presence Teleoperators Virtual Environ. **10**(3), 282–297 (2001). https://doi.org/10.1162/105474601300343612
25. Kennedy, R., Lane, N., Berbaum, K., Lilienthal, M.: Simulator sickness questionnaire: an enhanced method for quantifying simulator sickness. Int. J. Aviat. Psychol. **3**(3), 203–220 (1993). https://doi.org/10.1207/s15327108ijap0303_3

Director's Cut - Analysis of Aspects of Interactive Storytelling for VR Films

Colm O. Fearghail[1(✉)], Cagri Ozcinar[1], Sebastian Knorr[1,2], and Aljosa Smolic[1]

[1] V-SENSE, School of Computer Science and Statistics, Trinity College Dublin,
The University of Dublin, Dublin, Ireland
{ofearghc,ozcinarc,smolica}@scss.tcd.ie
[2] Communication Systems Group, Technical University of Berlin, Berlin, Germany
knorr@nue.tu-berlin.de

Abstract. To explore methods that are currently used by professional virtual reality (VR) filmmakers to tell their stories and guide users, we analyze how end-users view 360° video in the presence of directional cues and evaluate if they are able to follow the actual story of narrative 360° films. In this context, we first collected data from five professional VR filmmakers. The data contains eight 360° videos, the directors cut, which is the intended viewing direction of the director, plot points and directional cues used for user guidance. Then, we performed a subjective experiment with 20 test subjects viewing the videos while their head orientation was recorded. Finally, we present and discuss the experimental results and show, among others, that visual discomfort and disorientation on part of the viewer not only lessen the immersive quality of the films but also cause difficulties in the viewer gaining a full understanding of the narrative that the director wished them to view.

Keywords: 360° film · Storytelling · Director's cut · Virtual reality

1 Introduction

The ability to create a visual narrative in a film has seen over a century of professional experimentation and developments. In cinema, the development of a visual narrative can be seen with the start of continuity editing, where the film is cut from one scene to another to tell the story [22,23] effectively. This allows for the viewer to create a mental model of the scene and the position of the characters and objects in it, which allows the viewer to orientate themselves within the scene as the camera moves to different locations after cuts happen.

There are a number of methods used by directors in order to direct viewers attention [10]. The effectiveness of these can be seen in traditional cinema in the 'tyranny of film' effect that a Hollywood style of film-making has [15]. In 360° film-making, however, these conventions must be adapted as this new format has intrinsic features that differ from traditional cinema, such as the viewer being free to explore the entire scene. This also causes difficulties in cutting from scene

© Springer Nature Switzerland AG 2018
R. Rouse et al. (Eds.): ICIDS 2018, LNCS 11318, pp. 308–322, 2018.
https://doi.org/10.1007/978-3-030-04028-4_34

to scene as the director cannot be sure of where a person may be looking in the 360° film, *i.e.*, it puts an increased importance on the ability of the director to guide attention.

Some of the factors being used to guide the viewers' attention can be categorized into the directional cues: sound, environment and motion/action. Motion or action can either be present in the scene or due to the motion of the camera itself. Actors can be used to direct attention by the viewer matching their eyeline or by directly addressing the camera.

Given the rapid pace of development, it is crucial that filmmakers in the medium understand how the use of the techniques that they are using in a 360° format affects the viewers ability to follow and enjoy a narrative. Hence, the motivation of this paper is to study visual attention of users in the presence of directional cues within professionally produced 360° films. In this context, we first collected data from five professional virtual reality (VR) filmmakers. The data contains eight 360° videos, the director's cut, which is the intended viewing direction of the director, plot points and directional cues used for user guidance (see Sect. 3.1 for details). Then, we performed an extensive experiment with 20 test subjects viewing the videos while their head orientation (*i.e.*, the viewing direction) was recorded. During and after the experiment, the participants were asked to answer general and video related questions (see Sect. 3.2 for details).

Finally, we present and discuss the experimental results in Sect. 4 by comparing the director's cut with the users' viewing direction and by evaluating the users' answers to the questionnaires. Our findings show, among others, that adapting directional cues from traditional filmmaking seems to work well to attract users' attention but the potential for visual discomfort must be considered alongside managing the orientation of the viewer to ensure an immersive experience. The entire dataset is publicly available with [12][1], where a new scan-path similarity metric and its visualization is presented.

2   Related Work

Four techniques that have traditionally formed the 'tools' that filmmakers rely on to tell their stories are cinematography, mise-en-scene, sound, and editing [24]. The expansion of these tools into VR, however, requires each to be re-evaluated as the viewer is free to look in any direction of the 360° film without the direct control of the filmmaker.

One of the most central ideas to the notion that continuity-led film grammars [3] are also applicable to cinematic VR is the ability of the director to predict and indirectly control the user's viewport [16]. Serrano *et al.* [21] investigated continuity editing in VR video in the context of segmentation theory [13]. Their findings include that continuity of action across cuts by aligning the regions of interest between them is best suited to fast-paced action while misaligning these regions of interest or action discontinuity between cuts leads to more exploratory

---

[1] https://v-sense.scss.tcd.ie/?p=2477.

behavior from the viewer. In addition, a survey was carried out in [11] which aimed to measure the effect of cut frequency on viewers disorientation and their ability to follow a story. Their findings suggested that if the point of interest remains consistent across cuts, a high frequency does not increase disorientation or affect the ability to follow the story.

Table 1. Description of the dataset. The *Help* video is the training video.

Video	Content description	Resolution	FPS	Duration
Help [9]	Science fiction film: alien destroys buildings and objects; slow moving camera	3840 × 2160	30	1 m
360Partnership	Documentary: urban Indian quarters and schools; camera mostly static with long shots	3840 × 1080	30	6m17s
Cineworld	Commercial: dark interior with forced viewer attention by use of graphic arrows on screen; moving camera	2560 × 1280	30	1 m
DB	Commercial: bright lit interior and exterior scenes; slow paced moving camera	4096 × 1024	30	3m58s
Jaunt	Commercial: scene of a parties interior. Actor addresses camera. Slow moving camera	2304 × 1152	60	2m52s
Smart	Commercial: camera point of view inside moving car; fast movement outside of car	2880 × 1440	60	2m7s
Luther	Tourism: various German interior and exterior sites; high amount of cuts; camera mostly static	4096 × 2048	30	4m25s
Vaude	Commercial: scenic mountain exteriors and factory floor interior; slow moving camera	4096 × 2048	30	2m25s
War	Education: exterior trenches in World War 1; mostly static camera	4096 × 1152	25	3m25s

To direct the viewer in a 360° narrative short, Nielsen *et al.* [17] investigated two methods; one where the orientation of the virtual body was faced in the region of interest, the other where the viewers' attention was guided by the use of implicit diegetic guidance, in this case, a firefly. They found that the viewers preferred the firefly method of guiding attention and that forcing the viewer's attention by orientating the virtual body increased visual discomfort. A similar approach to non-narrative 360° videos can be found in [14]. Blur was also evaluated as a method to direct the viewer within a virtual environment in [7] and a 360° video in [4].

Padmaneban *et al.* [19] introduced a motion sickness predictor for stereoscopic 360° video based on a machine learning approach. Their findings show that conflict in motion and not the presence of motion itself cause sickness, if users were allowed to freely move their heads with the virtual scene. Finally, Pavel *et al.* [20] developed a 360° video player with two features; a viewport-orientated technique and active reorientation. Viewport-orientated techniques reorient the shot at each cut so that an essential content lies in the viewer's field of view. Active reorientation is performed by the viewer pressing a button to reorient the shot to the important content immediately. Finally, an analytics tool was developed for 360° video in [2] that allows to select areas in the scenes that were key to the story.

3   Methodology

For our studies, we used a dataset of eight monocular 360° videos for testing. The dataset has a wide range of content types including documentary, advertisement, tourism, and education. Each 360° video is in the equirectangular format with various resolutions and frame rates. Table 1 describes the characteristics of the 360° videos used in this work.

3.1   Collection of Data from Professional Filmmakers

To collect relevant and useful information about the intended viewing direction of the filmmakers, the used directional cues and essential plot points for the given set of 360° videos, we first let five filmmakers manually create a scan-path, the so-called *director's cut*, which represents the intended viewing direction, by setting position markers in the equirectangular format of their own videos. The setting of the position markers was done with The Foundry's professional compositing software *Nuke*[2] using the *Tracker* node. More details about the process can be found in [12].

Together with the director's cut, the filmmakers were asked to provide additional information about plot points and directional cues used to attract attention of the viewers. In particular, the filmmakers were asked to provide the level of importance for the story ("plot point", "essential plot point", "not relevant") and the intended viewing behavior ("maintain attention", "free exploration", "not relevant") within certain frame ranges. Besides this, the following directional cues were requested:

1. Sound ("character/object", "other sound cues")
2. Environment ("brightness/contrast/color", "visual effects elements", "other environment cues")
3. Motion/action ("camera motion", "character/object motion", "other motion cues")

---

[2] https://www.foundry.com/products/nuke.

3.2 Collection of User Data

Apparatus and Test Subjects. To collect users' scan-paths and answers from the prepared questionnaires for a given set of 360° videos, the publicly available test-bed in [5,18] is modified to allow video playback, continuously recorded participants' head orientation with the current time-stamp and video name.

In parallel with the video, the audio data was sent to the integrated headphone of an head mounted display (HMD), which was the Oculus Rift consumer version in this work.

Subjective experiments were conducted with 20 participants (16 males and four females). Participants were aged between 22 to 46 with an average of 30.8 years. 50% of the participants had a medium familiarity with visual attention studies; 35% and 15% of the participants had no and high familiarity with visual attention studies respectively. Furthermore, eight participants wore glasses during the experiment, and all of the participants were screened and reported normal or corrected-to-normal visual acuity.

Questionnaires. In addition, we prepared a general questionnaire for the entire experiment to evaluate the subjective experience of the test subjects and a questionnaire for each test video to collect additional information for each test subject in order to trace back potential anomalies for the statistical evaluation of the scan-paths vs. directors' cuts. The general questionnaires $\{Q_1^g \ldots Q_7^g\}$ and the video related questionnaire $\{Q_1^v \ldots Q_{15}^v\}$ are listed in Tables 2 and 3, respectively.

Test Procedure. Subjective tests were performed as *task-free* viewing sessions, *i.e.*, each participant was asked to look naturally at each presented 360° video while seated in a freely rotatable chair. Each session, which lasted approximately 30 min, was split into a training and a test session. During the training session, one minute of the *Help* [9] 360° video was played to ensure a sense of familiarity with the viewing setup. Then, during the test session, the test videos were randomly displayed while the individual viewport trajectories (*i.e.*, the center location of the viewport) were recorded for each participant.

After each presented video, we inserted a short questionnaire period where the test subjects were asked to answer the questions in Table 3, while a mid-gray screen was displayed. Before playing the next 360° video, we reset the HMD sensor to return to the initial position. Finally, after all videos had been presented, the test subjects had to answer the general questions Q_1^g to Q_7^g as outlined in Table 2.

4 Analysis and Discussion

4.1 Comparison of Scan-Paths

In order to measure the similarity between the scan-paths, i.e., the director's cut and the head orientations of the users, we calculated the angles between both for each frame of the video sequences.

Figure 1 shows both, the scan-paths together with the viewport area and the plot points. With respect to the latter, only five of the eight videos included plot points which are highlighted in red. The user's scan-path is here the average across all test subjects and thus only gives an indication of the average viewing direction.

4.2 Evaluation of General Questionnaire

The general questions and the number of participants' answers to the point-scale questions, Q_1^g and Q_2^g, are listed in Table 2. With respect to Q_1^g, only two test subjects felt sick during the experiment. The rest either did not feel sick (thirteen participants) or were not sure if they felt sick (five participants). The majority of the participants felt medium (twelve participants) or highly (seven participants) engaged/immersed with the 360° content.

Table 2. General questionnaire.

Question	Answer	Answer (# of participants)
Q_1^g: Did you feel sick?	A_1^g: "no"/"maybe"/"yes"	(**13**, 5, 2)
Q_2^g: How engaged/immersed do you feel with the 360 content in general?	A_2^g: "low"/"medium"/"high"	(1, **12**, 7)
Q_3^g: Did any issues occur when wearing the HMDs?	A_3^g: free answer	
Q_4^g: Was there anything you disliked?	A_4^g: free answer	
Q_5^g: Which video did you like most?	A_5^g: free answer	
Q_6^g: What was most effective in attracting your attention for the entire dataset?	A_6^g: free answer	
Q_7^g: Any further comments you would like to share?	A_7^g: free answer	

Furthermore, for question Q_3^g, "*Did any issues occur when wearing the HMD?*", ten of the participants commented on the problem of low-resolution playback of 360° video as an essential issue. We observed that the content resolution has a significant impact on the quality of the immersive experience for VR. A similar result was also previously reported in the MPEG survey for VR [6]. The effect of motion also has a significant impact on the viewing experience. As observed in Q_4^g, five participants complained about the motion in the *Smart* video. Four participants (the highest number) liked the *Vaude* and *DB* videos the most, as observed by the answer to question Q_5^g. With respect to question Q_6^g, most of the participants mentioned that the appearance of actors (six participants), audio (four participants), and overlays (four participants) were the most effective in attracting participant attention for the entire dataset. Finally, none of the participants commented on question Q_7^g.

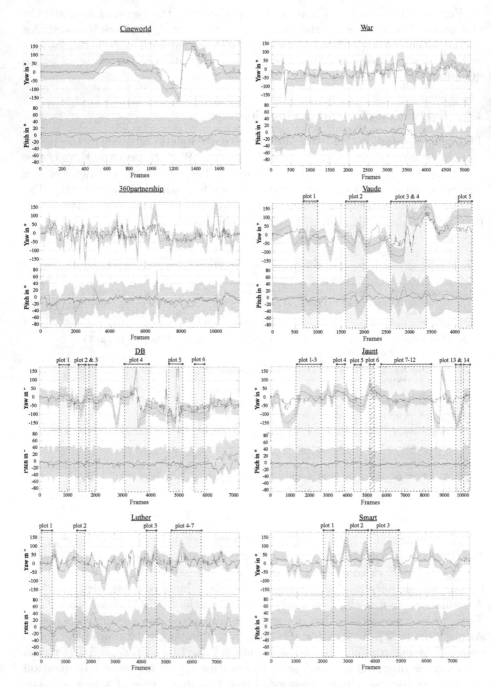

Fig. 1. Similarity measures: Director's cut (dark green) with viewport area (light green), average user's scan-path (black) and plot point areas (red). (Color figure online)

Table 3. Video related questions and number of participant answers ("no", "maybe", "yes") to the point-scale answered questions.

Question	Answer	Video	Answer (# of participants)
Q_1^v: Did you feel any discomfort?	A_1^v: "no"/"maybe"/"yes"	all videos	see Table 4
Q_2^v: Did you feel immersed in the environment/engaged with the video?	A_2^v: "no"/"maybe"/"yes"	all videos	see Table 4
Q_3^v: Did you feel any disorientation?	A_3^v: "no"/"maybe"/"yes"	all videos	see Table 4
Q_4^v: What was most effective in attracting your attention?	A_4^v: free answer	all videos	see text
Q_5^v: Any further comments you would like to share?	A_5^v: free answer	all videos	see text
Q_6^v: Which of the people passing by do you remember?	A_6^v: free answer	*Smart*	see text
Q_7^v: Did anything in particular stand out?	A_7^v: free answer	*Vaude*	see text
Q_8^v: Did you find the arrows helpful?	A_8^v: "no"/"maybe"/"yes"	*cineworld*	(**10**, 1, 9)
Q_9^v: Did you pay attention to the overlays?	A_9^v: "no"/"maybe"/"yes"	*Jaunt*	(0, 3, **17**)
Q_{10}^v: Did you feel like you picked up the main information of the story?	A_{10}^v: "no"/"maybe"/"yes"	*DB*	(2, 6, **12**)
Q_{11}^v: Did it give you a good sense of life in the trenches?	A_{11}^v: "no"/"maybe"/"yes"	*War*	(**9**, 2, **9**)
Q_{12}^v: Did you see someone dying?	A_{12}^v: "no"/"maybe"/"yes"	*War*	(3, 3, **14**)
Q_{13}^v: Did you feel a good sense of children's life in India?	A_{13}^v: "no"/"maybe"/"yes"	*360partnership*	(1, 2, **17**)
Q_{14}^v: Did you notice the overlays in the factory?	A_{14}^v: "no"/"maybe"/"yes"	*Vaude*	(5, 5, **10**)
Q_{15}^v: Did you find the Luther character helpful?	A_{15}^v: "no"/"maybe"/"yes"	*Luther*	(5, 5, **10**)

4.3   Individual Evaluation of Videos and Video Related Questionnaires

The video related questionnaire with its 15 questions is presented in Table 3, where questions Q_1^v to Q_5^v are questions which were asked for all videos, while Q_6^v to Q_{15}^v are video specific questions. Questions Q_1^v to Q_3^v and Q_8^v to Q_{15}^v are questions using a 3-point-scale with possible answers "no", "maybe", "yes", respectively. The number of answers of the 20 test subjects and eight test videos for the questions Q_8^v to Q_{15}^v and Q_1^v to Q_3^v are reported in Tables 3 and 4, respectively. In the following, we evaluate the findings first for each video separately.

360partnership. This video, shot in a documentary style, hoped to give the viewer a good sense of the environment and conditions of the children that the program helps with live in India. The director provided a scan-path as to how they would prefer the viewer to watch the video but did not consider any part particular to be essential enough to the videos understanding to be considered a plot point. This is reflected in the strong variation of the yaw in Fig. 1, which is an indication for exploratory behavior of the users. However, information was relayed through the use of audio commentary, so there were no plot points displayed visually within the scene. This video was also found to be the least disorientating of the videos, with only one participant answering 'maybe' (Q_3^v); the shots were long enough that the viewer could take their time in exploring

Table 4. Answers ("no", "maybe", "yes") to the point-scale answered questions (in terms of no. of participants) for all test subjects.

Video	Q_1^v	Q_2^v	Q_3^v
360Partnership	(**16**, 2, 2)	(2, 4, **14**)	(**19**, 1, 0)
Cineworld	(**12**, 2, 6)	(**13**, 2, 5)	(9, 1, **10**)
DB	(**18**, 1, 1)	(6, 1, **13**)	(**15**, 3, 2)
Jaunt	(**17**, 0, 3)	(4, 2, **14**)	(**16**, 2, 2)
Smart	(**9**, 5, 6)	(5, 1, **14**)	(**15**, 1, 4)
Luther	(**16**, 1, 3)	(2, 5, **13**)	(**17**, 1, 2)
Vaude	(**15**, 1, 4)	(2, **7,11**)	(**14**, 2, 4)
War	(**13**, 4, 3)	(3, 5, **12**)	(**12**, 4, 4)

the environment at a relaxed pace. From the received answers of the video questionnaires, when asked: *"what was most effective in attracting your attention?"* (Q_4^v), five participants found that text overlays were the most effective, the movement and direction of people was the second most common response with four participants. All participants except one felt that it gave them a good idea as to the challenges that the children shown in the video are required to face in daily life (Q_{13}^v), and four participants answered 'maybe' when asked if they found the video to be engaging (Q_2^v) while two participants answered 'no'.

Cineworld. This video took the style of a first-person shooter that would be more commonly seen in a video game such as Doom [1] and applied it to a cinema interior. The area of interest was ringed by a circle which was very clearly illustrated the area where the director intended the viewer to look. This was further emphasized by the use of two large arrows to either side that pointed directly towards it. At certain times in the video, this circle turned at a sharp 90°. Here, the filmmaker intends that the viewer would turn likewise in the same direction. For instance, the first time that this occurs in the video is at frame 515. As it can be seen in Fig. 1, degrees of the yaw angle increase with this sharp turn.

The use of this as a mechanism caused discomfort, with twelve participants answering 'yes' to (Q_1^v), and disorientation, with ten participants answering 'yes' to (Q_3^v). The effect of the confusion experienced by the viewer made *Cineworld* also score lowest for engagement with only five participants feeling engaged by the video and two participants answering 'maybe' (Q_2^v).

Nine of the participants said that they found the arrows helpful (Q_8^v) in knowing where to look. From the Fig. 1 it is clear that there was a delay in the viewers orientating themselves in the direction the arrows indicated. Two responses made to (Q_5^v) help to explain this behavior, one being that the movement of the arrows was uncomfortable and the other that the arrows were too forceful in commanding attention.

DB. This video had six plot points and was a commercial in which the viewer could see the use of technology in transforming modern banking. The presence of the viewer was used in different ways in various scenes. At the start the viewer is directly addressed by the family's matriarch. For the rest of the video the viewer has more of an observatory role. In later scenes the viewer is addressed directly again.

At plot number four, for example, the director used a number of graphics, in this case, furniture appearing in a room, behind two characters as they walked around a room at frame number 3,300. The response of the viewers can be seen in Fig. 1. The mean shows that viewers followed it but most did not make a full bodily turn in the chair but rather followed it until the point that they could rotate their neck across to the other side in order to pick up the action.

DB had the lowest score on discomfort (Q_1^v), with 18 participants answering 'no'. In attracting attention (Q_4^v), the movement and placement of actors were the most effective for with six participants followed by graphics and overlays that were imposed into the scene with five participants mentioning them as the most successful in leading their attention (Q_5^v). Finally, the voice-over dialogue was present in only the left ear and was mentioned by four participants (Q_5^v).

Smart. The *Smart* video made use of three plot points. The level of importance did not differ too much between the plots points highlighted in the video. This video was more about the viewer experiencing a sense of fun and excitement as they were driven through the city.

Smart also had the highest score for discomfort (Q_1^v). The reason for this score might be a sharp turn at the end of the video and the fast motion of the car. The turn starts just after frame number 6,450 and in Fig. 1 it can be denoted by the viewers leaving the directors scan-path before rejoining it again once the turn was completed just after frame number 7,000. The car itself operated as an agency for the movement and gave the viewer a familiar setting in where they could anticipate how and where to look, and the path that the car would be following, along the road. The sharp turn at the end made a full 180° and was unexpected for viewers and, as mentioned by seven participants (Q_5^v), was a reason for discomfort. Because of these reasons, viewers experienced vection or perceived self-motion which lead to the discomfort reported in the experiment. *Smart* also has, together with *360Partnership* and *Jaunt*, the highest score for immersion (Q_2^v) with fourteen participants answering 'yes', which would lead to suspect that a familiar setting or agency can increase the immersion as long as this setting or agency operates in the manner that the viewer would expect it to. The video has just one single shot and no cuts, *i.e.*, it is more natural and thus may increase the feeling of being present. The direction perceived from the principal actor and the movement of the car and the direction that it was moving in, both mentioned by six participants, were the most frequent answers as to what attracted attention (Q_4^v). The band playing music, which was in the direction of the camera motion, was the most memorable of the people that the car passed (Q_6^v) with nine participants mentioning it.

Jaunt. There were 14 plot points in the video that had a high level of importance for the viewer to follow as can be seen in Fig. 1. The director used the principal actor along with graphical overlays to attract and direct attention within the video. The video consisted on just one scene without any cuts and this could be a reason for it scoring highly for engagement (Q_2^v), with fourteen participants answering that they did feel immersed in the environment; two answered maybe and four answered that they did not.

When asked about the overlays that were used in the video (Q_9^v) 17 participants answered 'yes', the rest answered 'maybe'. The audio was the highest answer when it came to attracting attention (Q_4^v) mentioned by seven participants followed by the direction of the principal actor, mentioned by six participants. *Jaunt* had the second lowest score on discomfort (Q_1^v), with only three participants answering that they felt discomfort.

Vaude. Among the directorial cues received, five were cues that had a high level of importance for the viewer to follow and considered to be essential occurring to the director. The most of these plot points consisted of a dialogue delivered by the principal actor as she addressed the camera directly. Given the commercial nature of the video, the narrative, in this case, was the relating of information about the product, as per plot points 1 and 2, where the principle actor talked directly to the camera. During plot point 2, the use of overlays were again used, and when asked (Q_{14}^v) five participants did not notice them, and five participants answered 'maybe'.

The direction of the principal actor was the most frequent answer when asked what device was the most effective in attracting the attention of the viewer (Q_4^v) with eight participants mentioning it. The line up of cuts in between shots noticeable for a number of viewers, with four participants mentioning it as an additional comment (Q_5^v), they found that the area of interest was not matched correctly across a cut, it caused them to have to find it again after a cut happened.

The main causes of discomfort (Q_1^v) were the vibrations when the camera was mounted on a bicycle with four participants mentioning in response to (Q_5^v), which might have had a bearing on people not noticing the Panda figure around frame 2,600 in Fig. 1, which was in the director's cut.

Luther. The video had an animated character, a Playmobil character that took the appearance of *Luther*, imposed on a number of shots and across a few cuts. There was a mixed reaction to the use of this character which can be seen in response to (Q_{15}^v). For this question, five of the participants found that the use of this character distracted from their ability to freely explore the environment while others found it helped to orient themselves around the area of interest, *i.e.*, the character of *Luther*. One viewer's response was that if he had lost track of the character, he would spend time looking for him while the scene changed which disorientated him even further.

Luther also had the highest number of shots and the shortest scene length. Four participants mentioned for (Q_5^v) that there was too much information as the scenes were perceived to be changed too quickly. Only two participants found the video to disorientate them (Q_3^v), and three participants found the video to cause discomfort (Q_1^v).

War. The *War* video, which was educational, was the second highest scoring video for disorientation (Q_3^v). In this video, two allied soldiers were shown in a trench and then a firefight was displayed at night.

Taking place in a nighttime environment, the most common response to (Q_4^v) was the bright lights that were used in the film with four participants mentioning so that start at frame number 2,970. A flare used to attract the attention of the viewer upwards while the scene cut below at frame number 3,440 was mentioned by three participants to the same question and can be seen in Fig. 1 as a large increase in the pitch of the directors cut.

The dark environment alongside the hand-held movement of the camera in the later part of the video caused discomfort for three participants (Q_4^v).

4.4   Overall Findings and Discussion

From the data collected and the responses to the questionnaire, it would appear that viewers prefer to have their attention led rather than forced. This finding was also reported in [17]. The shot lengths for the videos that scored highest for engagement were longer than those that scored more lowly, which allowed the viewer time to freely explore the environment without having to worry about the shot changing before they had time to do so. Audio and the direction of the principle actor were the two most significant factors for the attracting of attention across all the videos. Another factor that had a significant influence on the engagement of the video was the orientation of the viewer. If the viewer becomes disorientated within the scene, they also become disorientated in the narrative the director is displaying. This also causes problems for viewer immersion as they are more worried about missing the area of interest than enjoying the video. One way that can happen is a bad match of action across the cuts. The disorientation can be emphasized even further if a cut happens when the viewer is already disorientated from a previous cut. Not only should action match across scenes but other factors such as scale should also be taken into account.

Motion/Action. The motion was used in various ways by the videos. *Smart* was most evident in the use of it as a device in order to transport the viewer through the narrative. However, this was also a conflicting cue with respect to action cues to the left and right of the camera path. There was camera movement in a number of the videos, and it was received with mixed reviews in terms of effectiveness based on the manner used and the personal preference of the viewer. One answer to (Q_4^v) made on the *Smart* was that it was faster than walking speed and this was the cause of the discomfort that the participant felt. One factor that did have a very noticeable impact when camera motion was used was how stable the camera was when the motion was taking place. In general, camera motion was accepted when it was clear to the viewer along what track that the motion would be taking place.

The use of actors in other to direct the viewer within the scene was used successfully in a number of the videos. *Vaude, BD, Jaunt* and *Smart* all used the principle character in order to direct the viewer. However, the interaction between the viewer and the animated character in *Luther* differs from one in which people are used. There are many advantages in the use of a person to direct attention across the scene, which is learned behavior from childhood to focus on what other people are looking at or what they have their attention directed towards. It also gave the viewers a clear idea as to where to look, and in general, the principle actor was easy to find within the scene.

Environment. Environmental cues including visual effects were used by a number videos also, most noticeably by *360partnership, DB, Vaude* and *Jaunt. Luther* and *Vaude* had a large number of scenic locations often dominated by a landmark building such as Wartburg castle, which had the effect of attracting the viewers' attention and often let the viewers explore freely the scenery. However, in *Vaude*, the environmental cues were also conflicting cues with respect to drawing attention to the actual product. Many of the videos used graphics in various ways to better illustrate information at various points. They also served as a method to guide attention, perhaps most effectively in *DB*. In general across the videos, the use of graphics clearly showed the viewer the area of interest in the scene that they were watching.

Sound. Even though sound is known to aid visual processing in VR [8], they did not solely form plot points provided by the directors of the films. Sound cues that were provided were often used in conjunction with visual ones. *Luther* at various times gave commands to the viewer such as at frame number 570 when the voice-over said "look around you" in order to encourage exploratory behavior from the viewer and later at frame number 4,430, more directly by telling the viewer to "take a look to the right". *Vaude* used audio in the form of dialogue from the principle actor to direct attention, such as at frame number 1,582 where she directly addresses the camera from the factory floor.

5   Conclusion

While traditional directing techniques can serve to lead viewer attention in 360° film, there are a number of differences required in the conceptual approach of their use. 360° film means moving from a window onto a world to being present within one. Rather than directing the viewer to conceptualize their environment through a series of images, the task is to orientate the viewer within one. This orientation is even more crucial when a cut is present, as the viewer is required to re-orientate themselves in the space of the new scene and disorientation will lessen the quality of the immersive experience. The nature of adapting these traditional directorial cues to 360° will require a directorial approach that moves away from using a time based sequence of images into one that makes use of the spatial nature of virtual reality. Further studies on this dataset including the introduction of a new metric for scan-path comparison were carried out in our paper [12] which offers an intuitive visualization for use in a post-production environment.

Acknowledgment. This publication has emanated from research conducted with the financial support of Science Foundation Ireland (SFI) under the Grant Number 15/RP/2776.

References

1. Doom [PC CD-ROM], 10 December 1993
2. Bala, P., Dionisio, M., Nisi, V., Nunes, N.: IVRUX: a tool for analyzing immersive narratives in virtual reality. In: Nack, F., Gordon, A.S. (eds.) ICIDS 2016. LNCS, vol. 10045, pp. 3–11. Springer, Cham (2016). https://doi.org/10.1007/978-3-319-48279-8_1
3. Bolle, R., Aloimonos, Y., Fermüller, C.: Toward motion picture grammars. In: Chin, R., Pong, T.-C. (eds.) ACCV 1998. LNCS, vol. 1352, pp. 283–290. Springer, Heidelberg (1997). https://doi.org/10.1007/3-540-63931-4_228
4. Danieau, F., Guillo, A., Dore, R.: Attention guidance for immersive video content in head-mounted displays. In: 2017 IEEE Virtual Reality (VR), pp. 205–206. IEEE, Los Angeles, March 2017. https://doi.org/10.1109/VR.2017.7892248
5. De Abreu, A., Ozcinar, C., Smolic, A.: Look around you: saliency maps for omnidirectional images in VR applications. In: Proceedings of the 9th International Conference on Quality of Multimedia Experience (QoMEX), pp. 1–6. IEEE, Erfurt, May 2017. https://doi.org/10.1109/QoMEX.2017.7965634
6. The MPEG Virtual Reality Ad-hoc Group: Summary of survey on virtual reality. Technical report N16542, JTC1/SC29/WG11, ISO/IEC, Chengdu, CN, October 2016
7. Hillaire, S., Lecuyer, A., Cozot, R., Casiez, G.: Depth-of-field blur effects for first-person navigation in virtual environments. IEEE Comput. Graph. Appl. **28**(6), 47–55 (2008). https://doi.org/10.1109/MCG.2008.113
8. Hoeg, E.R., Gerry, L.J., Thomsen, L., Nilsson, N.C., Serafin, S.: Binaural sound reduces reaction time in a virtual reality search task. In: 2017 IEEE 3rd VR Workshop on Sonic Interactions for Virtual Environments (SIVE), pp. 1–4, March 2017. https://doi.org/10.1109/SIVE.2017.7901610
9. Justin (Director), L.: Help (2015). http://www.imdb.com/title/tt4794550/
10. Katz, S.D.: Film Directing Shot by Shot: Visualizing from Concept to Screen. Gulf Professional Publishing, Boston (1991)
11. Kjær, T., Lillelund, C.B., Moth-Poulsen, M., Nilsson, N.C., Nordahl, R., Serafin, S.: Can you cut it?: an exploration of the effects of editing in cinematic virtual reality. In: Proceedings of the 23rd ACM Symposium on Virtual Reality Software and Technology, p. 4. ACM, Gothenburg, November 2017
12. Knorr, S., Ozcinar, C., O Fearghail, C., Smolic, A.: Director's cut - a combined dataset for visual attention analysis in cinematic VR content. In: The 15th ACM SIGGRAPH European Conference on Visual Media Production, London, UK, December 2018
13. Kurby, C.A., Zacks, J.M.: Segmentation in the perception and memory of events. Trends Cogn. Sci. **12**(2), 72–79 (2008)

14. Lin, Y.C., Chang, Y.J., Hu, H.N., Cheng, H.T., Huang, C.W., Sun, M.: Tell me where to look: investigating ways for assisting focus in 360 video. In: Proceedings of the 2017 CHI Conference on Human Factors in Computing Systems, pp. 2535–2545. ACM, Denver, May 2017

15. Loschky, L.C., Larson, A.M., Magliano, J.P., Smith, T.J.: What would jaws do? the tyranny of film and the relationship between gaze and higher-level narrative film comprehension. PloS one **10**(11), e0142474 (2015)

16. Mateer, J.: Directing for cinematic virtual reality: how traditional film director's craft applies to immersive environments and notions of presence. J. Media Pract. (author-produced version) **18**(1), 14–25 (2017). https://doi.org/10.1080/14682753.2017.1305838

17. Nielsen, L.T., et al.: Missing the point: an exploration of how to guide users' attention during cinematic virtual reality. In: VRST 2016 Proceedings of the 22nd ACM Conference on Virtual Reality Software and Technology, pp. 229–232. Munich, Germany, November 2016. https://doi.org/10.1145/2993369.2993405

18. Ozcinar, C., Smolic, A.: Visual attention in omnidirectional video for virtual reality applications. In: 10th International Conference on Quality of Multimedia Experience (QoMEX), Sardinia, Italy, May 2018

19. Padmanaban, N., Ruban, T., Sitzmann, V., Norcia, A.M., Wetzstein, G.: Towards a machine-learning approach for sickness prediction in 360 stereoscopic videos. IEEE Trans. Visual. Comput. Graphics **24**(4), 1594–1603 (2018)

20. Pavel, A., Hartmann, B., Agrawala, M.: Shot orientation controls for interactive cinematography with 360 video. In: Proceedings of the 30th Annual ACM Symposium on User Interface Software and Technology, pp. 289–297. ACM (2017)

21. Serrano, A., Sitzmann, V., Ruiz-Borau, J., Wetzstein, G., Gutierrez, D., Masia, B.: Movie editing and cognitive event segmentation in virtual reality video. ACM Trans. Graphics **36**(4), 47:1–47:12 (2017). https://doi.org/10.1145/3072959.3073668

22. Smith, T.J.: An Attentional Theory of Continuity Editing (2006)

23. Smith, T.J., Levin, D., Cutting, J.E.: A window on reality: perceiving edited moving images. Curr. Dir. Psychol. Sci. **21**(2), 107–113 (2012)

24. Vosmeer, M., Schouten, B.: Project orpheus a research study into 360° cinematic VR. In: Proceedings of the 2017 ACM International Conference on Interactive Experiences for TV and Online Video, TVX 2017, pp. 85–90. ACM, New York (2017). https://doi.org/10.1145/3077548.3077559

Spatial Storytelling: Finding Interdisciplinary Immersion

Asim Hameed[✉] and Andrew Perkis

National University of Science & Technology (NTNU),
7491 Trondheim, Norway
asim.hameed@ntnu.no

Abstract. This paper is part of an ongoing transdisciplinary research into immersion. In specific, it focuses on Spatial Storytelling to examine the narrative technique in conjunction with Spatial Presence, a commonly accepted subtype of Presence. How our real-life occupation is a constant narrative making exercise and how storytelling is ingrained in our movement in space. It is argued here that immersion and presence models stand to benefit from spatial theory, particularly, the body of work surrounding spatial practices and narratives. Further, that the incorporation of spatial theory adds to the necessary versatility required in approaching immersion, which has been thus far dominated by positivist empiricism. Contributions of a theorized space are also found missing from interactive storytelling and videogames where subject/object interactivity is seen as mere actions performed inside a given space whereas the paper argues that space is learnt through such involvement.

Keywords: Immersion · Presence · Spatial Storytelling · Spatial practice

1 Overview

When BBC unveiled its coverage of the FIFA World Cup 2018 in Russia, it did so by announcing a dedicated high-tech broadcast trial in VR. A first-time-ever VR experience that was designed to give audiences: "…taste of the future", said BBC [1]. The "fully immersive" experience of the matches transported viewers into a simulated hospitality box at the stadium. One did not only watch a live game but also had access to highlights packages and on-demand content. Additionally, it was possible to scan information on each game, lineups and overall stats of the tournament.

Such experiences are congruent with the state of contemporary society where pervasive media systems have rendered physical space into a data-space. Terms like "fully immersive" and "as-if-real" have become synonymous with the coming of age of audiovisual, multimodal and interactive media capable of occupying our perceptual system and simulating environments that evoke a feeling of 'being there' [2–4], or thereabouts [5]. Referring to the BBC Sports VR app, the user encounters a spatial experience inside an interior space, a hospitality box, which serves a virtual double of a generic hospitality box in some Russian stadium. The richness of experience here is extracted from providing a virtual experience where users could feel *as-if* they truly were in Russia. The experience does not limit itself to a mere delivery of a live

R. Rouse et al. (Eds.): ICIDS 2018, LNCS 11318, pp. 323–332, 2018.
https://doi.org/10.1007/978-3-030-04028-4_35

broadcast. In fact, to enrich this VR experience, the virtual hospitality box lets users interact with other media within, doubling on the illusion. The potential of content selection makes users feel more involved. This positively plays to secure user attention while providing interaction, both considered vital for rich experiences [6].

In this paper we discuss such efforts for richness, realness and/or believability. Is interactivity with virtual objects inside simulated environments enough to instill a sense of immersiveness or presence in the user? Or is it a multi-user shared experience of sociability in these virtual environments that makes them real? Perhaps it's the authorship and agency that comes with content generation and manipulation, which can summon that all evasive feeling of as-if-real? These questions are of interest when creating spectacular synthetic/narrative/virtual environments that would imbue a willful suspension of disbelief or presence. This paper is part of an ongoing body of work aimed at understanding and being able to use digital storytelling to create compelling new immersive media. In doing so, we must depart from the monodisciplinary, and/or multidisciplinary, approaches with an intent to support transdisciplinary endeavors in as far as concepts of immersion and presence are concerned.

The paper considers Spatial Storytelling, as a subgenre of Interactive Digital Storytelling, building on traditions of immersive theatre and invites input from mediapsychology and spatial studies, particularly spatial thinking and spatial narratives. It adopts a media philosophical approach to examine, through case studies, the role of participatory spatial narratives to offer a reformulation of the theoretical modelling of topics related to electronic simulations and extended realities.

2   Immersive New Media

2.1   Immersion and the Spatial Presence Models

The consequential challenges posed by such immersive and interactive new media have resulted in an abundance of theory surrounding Immersion and Presence [7–10], while producing notable frameworks [11–13] over the years. However, these frameworks are many, and incoherent, which is effectively due to the interdisciplinarity and multidimensionality of Presence research. Apropos to media technologies, Spatial Presence has emerged as the most relevant subtype of Presence in line with the theories of machine-mediated telepresence and teleoperation [14]. This interest has yielded a more concentrated evaluation of Spatial Presence as a "psychological" [13] "state of consciousness" [12] defined as "the subjective experience of a user or onlooker to be physically located in a mediated space" [6] even though one is not. From a mediapsychological standpoint, there are two aspects involved:

1. a simulated spatial environment where one feels located;
2. for that mediated environment to offer perceivable options for activity [15].

In effect, most Spatial Presence models view Immersion as a "sensation of being enveloped" [13] by such media-based environments. Wirth et al. [15], refine this to the "features that give rise to Presence" by stating that, "presence is conceptualized as the experiential counterpart of immersion". Mel Slater's framework for Immersive Virtual

Environments (FIVE) [12], divides the achievement of Spatial Presence into three phases of *place illusion* (I am here), *plausibility* (this is happening), and *body ownership* (it is my body). Each is a separate stage and arguably each requires a varied palette to be effective. However, this interdisciplinary potential is not fully utilized when immersion is limited to a system characteristic alone, i.e., the input properties of the mediated technology to provide stimuli (vividness) and afford action (interactivity) [11, 16, 17]. Immersion as technology or immersion as the experience of being enveloped by technology for place illusion empirically enables researchers to quantify otherwise subjective mediated experiences. As sensorimotor contingencies, i.e. to map and match the user's proprioception; and information it affords the senses (visual, haptic, aural, etc.), it's possible to study immersion as a technically measurable property of the system.

Such frameworks reinforce positivist models that favor data-oriented approaches to perception and representation in these media forms, i.e. to design a simulated spatial environment where one would feel present, and that any such design would be possible through thorough mapping. In this way, as a system property, immersion is thus reducible to a degree of correspondence—higher fidelity of display and tracking yields greater level of immersion—enabling a "productionist metaphysics" [18]. This has led to a vastly Euclidean interpretation of three-dimensional simulated space, which signifies a preoccupation with low-mimetic realism [19] or skeuomorphs; often confused with believability [20].

In contrast, we can also find works that bring interdisciplinarity vis-à-vis immersive and interactive media [21–24], and concentrate on the other two aspects of *plausibility* and *ownership* in the same way. These works are usually at the intersections of hard science and digital humanities, which discuss immersive and interactive new media drawing from fields as diverse as art, narratology, ludology, social anthropology, phenomenology, and psychology to name a few. That for believability, a place illusion is not enough and that the plausibility of reality is enriched through factors like sociability, delight, play, etc. Our interest remains in cultivating immersion on such interdisciplinary lines (See Fig. 1) finding encouragement in projects from within virtual reality and gaming sectors that are turning to low-tech features, such as involved narrative and social participation, to enhance the immersive qualities of their applications and products [25–28].

2.2 Immersion in Interactive Digital Narratives

We find Interactive Digital Storytelling, or Interactive Narrative Design, suitable because it propositions a position at the crossroads of narratology (the study of narratives and socio-cultural narrative structures), ludology (the study of gameplay and design) and HCI (human-computer interaction). Murray's [29] identification of the four essential properties found in computer-based narrative media can be viewed in parallel with Mel Slater's framework. Murray talks of *procedural* (computational), *participatory* (interactive), *spatial* (experiential) and *encyclopedic* (database) properties. Elements are utilized for believability, which must be achieved in congruity to real-life in order for immersive experiences to evoke presence. In other words, it is not only enough to immerse a user into a simulated space but to provide potential for

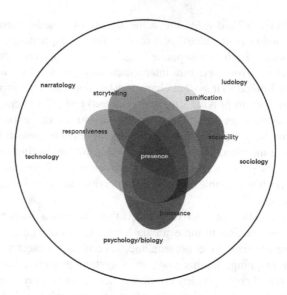

Fig. 1. Immersion radar illustrates the various overlapping influence factors on presence.

believability through additional properties, which too are immersions. Consequently, it can be reasoned that to attain better congruence immersion shall include system immersion [12], but also refer to *absorption & engagement* [30], *strategic and tactical immersion* [30], *imaginative immersion* [31], *challenge-based immersion* [31], *ludic immersion* [32], and *narrative immersion* [32]. Together, they make immersion an interdisciplinary concern.

With Interactive Digital Storytelling, we find a media experience, which utilizes a storytelling engine (system) offering action possibilities (interactivity) to intentionally influence the narrative (immersive) experience. Unlike most Spatial Presence models where an immersive experience is predominantly interpreted inside a simulated spatiality, narrative here, pursues that pivotal role. Narrative, however, is not to a binary categorization of stories non-stories. Instead, it is the potential for 'storiness' that is valuable [32]. Ryan's theorization of narrative as a "semiotic object" is important in this regard since she conceptually develops narrative for use across varied media, i.e. as a cognitive template.

Spatial Storytelling. In continuation, we explicate the aforementioned cognitive template in its application inside Spatial Storytelling. Cognitive templates can be understood as mentally designed codes or stored templates used for the comprehension of our environment. This bottom-up information processing goes by piecing together disparate data to arrive at a bigger and bigger picture. Like this, they aid in the interpretation of experience and shaping an individual's perception of reality [33]. The term 'storiness' can then be the potential for furnished possibilities of a given environment (natural or artificial) for a narrative unfolding.

A good example for 'storiness' is Spatial Storytelling, not just because it foregoes linguistic traditions and textual form, but for putting storiness to great effect. Spatial

Storytelling works by spatially engaging a user inside a mediated environment whose discovery through exploration advances a non-linear narrative, and where space is the essential communication medium. Inspired by 'immersive theater' [34], it closely follows environmental storytelling in creating preconditions for immersive narrative experiences in four possible ways [35]:

1. ability of spatial stories to evoke pre-existing narrative associations;
2. provide a backdrop where narrative events unfold;
3. embed narrative information within their mise-en-scene,
4. provide resources for emergent narratives.

Immersive theater has been learning from environmental storytelling. A good example is the theater company Punchdrunk [34] who allow their audience the liberty to watch and move as they choose. Further, they involve visual, aural, olfactory and tactile elements to evoke phenomenological multi-sensory experiences. More recently game designers have adopted similar approaches [36, 37]. Through Spatial Storytelling, they attempt to restructure narratives from temporal to spatial bodies of information—narratives distributed across the game space. This appropriation is easier for games since they do not rely on temporal markers common to narratives like "once upon a time…" or "the next day…", etc. Games are usually characterized by spatiotemporal markers, that is, we point at a certain 'thereness' (dungeon, lake, downtown library, etc.) to communicate how far we are in a game; space relays information on time. Hence the readiness witnessed in game design towards Spatial Storytelling. This research considers it to be a compelling model useful for stimulating presence in immersive environments, largely due to its induction of a variety of immersions.

3 Immersive Spatial Narratives

3.1 We Are Immersed in Space

By shifting focus towards space, Spatial Storytelling turns to the narrative potential of locations and places in our everyday life. It is space, marked with disparate anchors of locations and places, each carrying meaning, temporal significance and past memories, which serves as the backdrop against which our individual life stories unfold. Space also works as a force field simultaneously accumulating formal, psychological and ideological histories, discourses, and economies over time—irreducible to and from any one aspect [38].

Everything 'takes place' in this space. Therefore, our actions are a "*spatial practice*" [39] "that shapes, and is shaped by, the social, economic, political and cultural" [40] forces within this space. In time, this enriches our *spatial literacy*. Our movement, participation, action, and recreation *inscribe* meaning within this space through the repetitive patterns of a daily routine. These spatial inscriptions emerge over denominated temporal cycles of days, weeks, months and years during our interaction with space, resulting in "*spatial narratives*". "Through practice, we transform it into a place of meaning and value": De Certeau [41].

3.2   Time and Space

In spatial theory, space is defined as the "physical setting in which everything occurs". Whereas, place is, "the outcome of the social process of valuing space; a product of the imaginary, of desire, and the primary means by which we articulate with space and transform it into a humanized landscape." [42]. While time and space have been long recognized as the criteria for studying everyday life. Western social theories have been favorably modeled around time, dispassionately assuming compliance from space. This position of dominance is most obvious when one considers the separation of history from geography. To this effect, spatial theory studies offer reflectivity and point at the "[…]implicit subordination of space to time […]" [43]. From a media-philosophical perspective previously absent cross-disciplinary discussions from politics, geography, archaeology, and narratology among other, are fundamental in framing discourses on the co-evolution of space and time with media systems, and for their re-conceptualization in the current age of extended realities.

Returning to our discussion on immersion and presence, one can observe similar binary tendencies in immersive media, particularly in the construction of immersive virtual environments (IVE) and a close "reenactment of Cartesian ontology" [22, 24]. This is evidenced in most Spatial Presence models that treat space as an a priori given; a Cartesian box; a Euclidean XYZ model. These are not self-acquired positions rather cultural values inculcated through traditions of Western technoscience. The conceptualization of space as a container is an attractive proposition for its ease of offering a completeness to its elusive nature [44]. Such an *ontic* position assumes the world (space) to be present-to-hand. In Heideggerian phenomenology we find a challenge to this model contending that space is learned—one learns it—through involvement [45]. Space, it postulates, is an "artifact" [46], which we constantly innovate and mold through our active participation. By being in space we create space, our agency is consumed by the continuous production of space [47]. Space is not a mere container nor an a priori. In fact, it is "an experiential environment whose qualia and character are produced through behavior, ritual, and human activity" [47].

3.3   Body and Space

Activity, our immediate involvement, finds a bodily interpretation in theories of embodied cognition. Space allows for action and movement, which is performed *through the body as a tool*, over a temporal cycle of time—making a narrative. Space is experienced through the body. We can observe this in terms of spatial literacy; if you compare spatial descriptions like north, south, vertical, horizontal, etc. to more experience-based descriptions such as lying down, in front of, straight up, etc. we'd find a better understanding of the latter set. This is because humans, from their childhood, develop through a bodily experience of space, which helps them in learning and understanding space (spatial literacy).

This spatial literacy is made possible by affordances, which are furnished action possibilities in an environment (space). A core concept for embodied psychology models and now widely adopted in interface and interaction (UX) design. It is vital not to confuse or restrict affordances to mere things one does inside an environment (natural or artificial). In fact, they are a relational complementarity between subject/environment, subject/object, object/environment, all at the same time [48]. Affordance are both projectable and non-projectable, for example, a door presents a projectable property of opening but can also have a non-projectable property of one being excited to open the door for your friends; the latter we learn from our experience in space. In his Spatial Presence model, Schubert et al., refer to these as "anticipated" actions that help in presence, they call them a "cognitive feeling". Such research developments in theorizing Spatial Presence are refreshing for they bring a psychological model closer to its phenomenological counterpart.

3.4 A Way Forward with Spatial Storytelling

The insistence upon a Cartesian way of seeing-the-world (mind over body, the subject over the object) has more in common with renaissance perspectivism than with space. Our example of the BBC VR hospitality box is the most recent illustration of such representationalism. Such inclinations prevail over immersive media industries and, as previously discussed in relation to data-oriented system immersion, remain a popular conceptualization for research models and frameworks.

Alternatively, there are encouraging niche research projects like Holojam [27, 49], developed by the NYU Future Reality Lab, which creates interactive, participatory and shared immersive experiences. It is a nonpartisan approach with low-tech solutions integrating sociability through a collective activity. Holojam employs multiple immersions for effectivity, proving a useful precedent for study. Users are represented as stick figures as opposed to photorealist avatars, walking around a shared space where other users, local and remote, are there to interact with and contribute in making spatial art. Holojam makes use of a *participatory spatial narrative* experience inside an immersive environment where users can talk, observe, and physically interact with one another and the space.

Holojam can be viewed as a Spatial Storytelling model that favors believability to realism. It achieves this through: one, transporting physical objects into the ambient virtual space (place illusions) to create familiarity; two, requiring participation (plausibility); three, a participation not only with the virtual environment but social too, meaning, interaction with other users; four, these multi-user interactions are used for collaborative activity (increase sense of ownership); and five, the activity takes place in a shared virtual space allowing remote users to congregate. Through a shared (social) activity performed in space (spatial practice), participants create unique narratives that they can reflect on.

4 Conclusions

In conclusion, this paper notes that Spatial Storytelling presents promising theoretical interstices, which can help in the development of more cohesive models for immersion and presence. It creates an opportunity for technicians, designers, narrators, and theorists to contribute inside a diverse team. It identifies some immediate research directions for pushing forward interdisciplinary research on immersion, such as: evaluation of immersive experiences using system-based immersion against immersive media that involve multiple immersions; assessing narrative content-generation and manipulation as an influence factor on the quality of immersive experiences; using spatial literacy exercises to improve body ownership of subjects; and assessing ease-of-use in mixed-reality and virtual-reality applications through the benchmark of spatial practice.

There is a burgeoning growth of immersive media products dominated by gaming apps that provide entertainment material for a content-craving consumer market. To make the most of this anticipation, new media applications have to be seen as exciting new paradigms that require to be explored in their own right. Passive content inside simulated spaces shows little consideration for the potential of the medium. Spatial Storytelling offers a chance at agency to the user inside immersive media to focus on believability not realism that is congruent with the narrative of our daily lives.

References

1. BBC Sports page. https://www.bbc.com/sport/football/44305845. Accessed 1 July 2018
2. Pausch, R., Proffitt, D., Williams, G.: Quantifying immersion in virtual reality. In: Proceedings of the 24th Annual Conference on Computer Graphics and Interactive Techniques, pp. 13–18. ACM Press/Addison-Wesley Publishing Co., LA (1997)
3. Burdea Grigore, C., Coiffet, P.: Virtual Reality Technology. Wiley-Interscience, London (1994)
4. Spagnolli, A., Gamberini, L.: Immersion/emersion: presence in hybrid environments. In: Proceedings of Presence 2002: 5th Annual International Workshop, Porto, Portugal (2002)
5. Bowman, D.A., McMahan, R.P.: Virtual reality: how much immersion is enough? Computer 40(7), 36–43 (2007)
6. Hartmann, T., Wirth, W., Vorderer, P., Klimmt, C., Schramm, H., Böcking, S.: Spatial presence theory: state of the art and challenges ahead. In: Lombard, M., Biocca, F., Freeman, J., IJsselsteijn, W., Schaevitz, R. (eds.) Immersed in Media, pp. 115–135. Springer, Cham (2015). https://doi.org/10.1007/978-3-319-10190-3_7
7. Biocca, F.: Lighting a path while immersed in presence: a wayward introduction. In: Lombard, M., Biocca, F., Freeman, J., IJsselsteijn, W., Schaevitz, R. (eds.) Immersed in Media, pp. 1–9. Springer, Cham (2015). https://doi.org/10.1007/978-3-319-10190-3_1
8. Lombard, M., Jones, M.T.: Defining Presence. In: Lombard, M., Biocca, F., Freeman, J., IJsselsteijn, W., Schaevitz, R. (eds.) Immersed in Media, pp. 13–34. Springer, Cham (2015). https://doi.org/10.1007/978-3-319-10190-3_2
9. Slater, M.: A note on presence terminology. Presence Connect 3(3), 1–5 (2003)
10. Mestre, D., Fuchs, P., Berthoz, A., Vercher, J.L.: Immersion et présence. In: Le traité de la réalité virtuelle, 1st volume, p. 309-38. Ecole des Mines de Paris, Paris (2006)
11. Morie, J.F.: Ontological implications of Being in immersive virtual environments. In: The Engineering Reality of Virtual Reality 2008. SPIE, USA, vol. 6804, article id. 680408 (2008)
12. Slater, M., Wilbur, S.: A framework for immersive virtual environments (FIVE): speculations on the role of presence in virtual environments. Presence Teleoperators Virtual Environ. 6(6), 603–616 (1997)

13. Witmer, B.G., Singer, M.J.: Measuring presence in virtual environments: a presence questionnaire. Presence **7**(3), 225–240 (1998)
14. Steuer, J.: Defining virtual reality: dimensions determining telepresence. J. Commun. **42**(4), 73–93 (1992)
15. Wirth, W., et al.: A process model of the formation of spatial presence experiences. Media Psychol. **9**(3), 493–525 (2007)
16. Biocca, F.: The cyborg's dilemma: progressive embodiment in virtual environments. J. Comput.-Mediat. Commun. **3**(2) (1997)
17. Zeltzer, D.: Autonomy, interaction, and presence. Presence Teleoperators Virtual Environ. **1**(1), 127–132 (1992)
18. Coyne, R.: Heidegger and virtual reality: the implications of Heidegger's thinking for computer representations. Leonardo **27**(1), 65–73 (1994)
19. Davies, C., Harrison, J.: Osmose: towards broadening the aesthetics of virtual reality. ACM SIGGRAPH Comput. Graph. **30**(4), 25–28 (1996)
20. Vanderbilt, T.: These tricks make virtual reality feel real. Nautilus **32** (2016). http://nautil.us/issue/32/space/these-tricks-make-virtual-reality-feel-real. Accessed 28 July 2018
21. McMahan, A.: Immersion, engagement and presence. In: The Video Game Theory Reader, 1st edn., pp. 67–85. Routledge, NY (2003)
22. Davies, C.: Osmose: notes on being in immersive virtual space. Digit. Creat. **9**(2), 65–74 (1998)
23. McLellan, H.: Virtual realities. In: Handbook of Research for Educational Communications and Technology, 4th edn., pp. 457–487. Springer, London (1996)
24. Morie, J.F.: Performing in (virtual) spaces: embodiment and being in virtual environments. Int. J. Perform. Arts Digit. Media **3**(2–3), 123–138 (2007)
25. Qvortrup, L.: Introduction — welcome into the interface. In: Qvortrup, L. (ed.) Virtual Interaction. Interaction in Virtual Inhabited 3D Worlds, pp. 1–18. Springer, London (2001). https://doi.org/10.1007/978-1-4471-3698-9_1
26. Nilsson, N.C., Nordahl, R., Serafin, S.: Immersion revisited: a review of existing definitions of immersion and their relation to different theories of presence. Hum. Technol. **12**(2), 108–134 (2016)
27. Perlin, K.: Future Reality: how emerging technologies will change language itself. IEEE Comput. Graph. Appl. **36**(3), 84–89 (2016)
28. De la Peña, N., et al.: Immersive journalism: immersive virtual reality for the first-person experience of news. Presence Teleoperators Virtual Environ. **19**(4), 291–301 (2010)
29. Murray, J.H., Murray, J.H.: Hamlet on the Holodeck: The Future of Narrative in Cyberspace. The Free Press, New York (1997)
30. Adams, E.: Fundamentals of Game Design, 3rd edn. New Riders, Indianapolis (2014)
31. Ermi, L., Mäyrä, F.: Fundamental components of the gameplay experience: analysing immersion. In: Worlds in Play: International Perspectives on Digital Games Research, vol. 37(2), pp. 37–53 (2005)
32. Ryan, M.-L.: Narrative as virtual reality. In: Narrative as Virtual Reality: Immersion and Interactivity in Literature and Electronic Media, 1st edn. John Hopkins University Press, Baltimore (2001)
33. Solso, R.L., McCarthy, J.E.: Prototype formation of faces: a case of pseudo-memory. Br. J. Psychol. **72**(4), 499–503 (1981)
34. Eglinton, A.: Reflections on a Decade of Punchdrunk Theatre. TheatreForum **37**, 46 (2010). Questia Online
35. Jenkins, H.: Game design as narrative architecture. In: First Person: New Media as Story, Performance and Game, 1st edn., pp. 118–130. MIT Press, Cambridge (2004)

36. Upload VR Gaming page. https://uploadvr.com/exclusive-preview-loading-human. Accessed 30 June 2018
37. IDNA page. https://www.metalocus.es/en/news/idna-%E2%80%93-spatial-storytelling. Accessed 3 July 2018
38. Rakatansky, M.: Spatial narratives. In: Strategies in Architectural Thinking, 1st edn., pp. 198–221. MIT Press, Cambridge (1992)
39. Gilded age plains city page. http://gildedage.unl.edu/narrative/topics.php?q=theory#refn01. Accessed 6 July 2018
40. Lefebvre, H., Nicholson-Smith, D.: The Production of Space. Basil Blackwell, Oxford (1991)
41. de Certeau, M.: The Practice of Everyday Life, 2nd edn. University of California Press, Berkeley (1984)
42. University of Texas Spatial Theory Homepage. https://sites.utexas.edu/religion-theory/bibliographical-resources/spatial-theory/overview. Accessed 7 July 2018
43. Soja, E.W.: Postmodern Geographies: The Reassertion of Space in Critical Social Theory. Verso, London (1989)
44. Neuhaus, F.: Body space and spatial narrative. In: Emergent Spatio-temporal Dimensions of the City: Habitus and Urban Rhythms, pp. 37–54. Springer, Cham (2015). https://doi.org/10.1007/978-3-319-09849-4_3
45. Coyne, R.: Thinking through virtual reality: place, non-place and situated cognition. Techné Res. Philos. Technol. **10**(3), 26–38 (2007)
46. Dunn, S.: Space as an Artefact: a perspective on 'Neogeography' from the digital humanities. In: Digital Research in the Study of Classical Antiquity, 1st edn., pp. 53–72. Ashgate, Burlington VT (2010)
47. Drucker, J.: Humanities approaches to graphical display. Digit. Hum. Q. **5**(1), 1–21 (2011)
48. Gibson, J.: The theory of affordances. In: Perceiving, Acting, and Knowing: Toward an Ecological Psychology, 1st edn., pp. 67–82. University of Michigan, Michigan (1977)
49. Velho, L., Lucio, D., Carvalho, L.: Situated participatory virtual reality. In: Proceedings of XVI Simposio Brasileiro de Jogos e Entretenimento Digital, Curitiba, Brazil (2017)

Cue Control: Interactive Sound Spatialization for 360° Videos

Paulo Bala[1,2]($\boxtimes$), Raul Masu[1,2], Valentina Nisi[1,3], and Nuno Nunes[1,4]

[1] Madeira-ITI, Funchal, Portugal
{paulo.bala,raul.masu,valentina.nisi,nnunes}@m-iti.org
[2] FCT/U. Nova de Lisboa, Lisbon, Portugal
[3] UMA, Funchal, Portugal
[4] IST/U. of Lisbon, Lisbon, Portugal

Abstract. In the 360° videos, the role of sound became crucial as it not only contributes to the participant's level of Presence (the feeling of being in the virtual environment) but can also provide viewers with a periodical awareness of their surroundings; therefore, audio can guide user attention toward desired points. In this sense, the sonic elements of a 360° video assume an interactive role, as sounds become notifying elements or icons. In the paper, we describe Cue Control, an audio editor that facilitates the creation of soundtracks for 360° videos. The user can control the location of the sonic elements by positioning the sounds in the virtual 3D space following the desired timeline; Cue Control automatically creates a cue list of the spatial soundtrack events for playback. The software also allows for different interactive modalities of playback, adapting the cue list to the viewpoint of the user. We conducted a small pilot study where Cue Control was used to assemble the soundtrack of two 360° videos. According to the data gathered, we present some preliminary reflections about the use of sound to guide users' attention in 360° videos towards points of interest.

Keywords: Spatial sound · 360° video · Sonic interaction design

1 Introduction

The usage and design of sound in 360° video should combine soundtrack and sonic interaction design principles, with audio playing both the role of the soundtrack and sonic feedback. For example, concerning storytelling in 360° VR, sound plays a vital role in peripheral awareness [1]. This ability is supported by a considerable amount of work on the spatial and binaural rendering of sound for VR, to provide a realistic listening experience; however, there is a disconnect on how creators can use these techniques for narrative purposes.

Given the importance of narrative development in the video context, we argue that manipulation of sound in 360° videos should take into account on the need of the plot and the interactive context of the user's experience. Current

© Springer Nature Switzerland AG 2018
R. Rouse et al. (Eds.): ICIDS 2018, LNCS 11318, pp. 333–337, 2018.
https://doi.org/10.1007/978-3-030-04028-4_36

solutions for 360° video, pre-render audio, not allowing interactivity during the viewing. Based on this, we designed and developed Cue Control, an audio editor that allows the creation of dynamic and interactive soundtracks for 360° videos. During runtime, these cues lists create spatially rendered sounds, capable of dynamically adapting to the viewer's point of view. We also discuss a pilot study on the viewer's perception of audio in 360° videos where we used Cue Control.

2   Audio Perception in Interaction

Audio as objects and events: The relation between human and sounds is a complex phenomenon that involves perceptive, psychological and cultural elements [2]. Pasnau proposes the idea that we should treat sounds as an "object of the hearing", identifying the sound with the vibrating motion of the object that produces the sound [4]. O' Callaghan [5] expanded the idea, arguing that sounds are events in which a moving object produce sound. Nudds [6] combined these previous ideas, arguing that hearing informs us about both objects and events of the surrounding environment.

Listening Modalities: Gaver defined two modalities of listening: musical listening and everyday listening, arguing that in everyday listening, people tend to listen to the source rather than to the properties of the sound itself [7]. In this case, humans tend to classify the object or the event. This listening modality is directly connected with the concept of sound as an object. This proposal has been applied in the development of sound icons for notification purposes.

Shifting the Function from Acousmatic Sounds to Auditory Icons: Sound that in a traditional film context are produced by something that is outside the view (e.g., birds chirping in a field) are defined as acousmatic sounds by Chion [8]. In the context of 360° videos, these become sonic representations of events and convey information about events that are happening outside the viewpoint. In this sense, those sounds assume an active role in the relation between the viewer and the video, echoing the idea of icon proposed by Gaver [9].

3   Cue Control

For 360° video, the standard workflow of a sound designer encompasses using digital audio workstations for the treatment of captured audio and the inclusion of new audio cues, relying on ambisonics to render 3D sound fields in a spherical format around a point in space (the viewer). On runtime, decoding to a binaural stereo output allows users with standard headphones to distinguish spatial distributions of sound [3]. Using pre-rendered audio results in a linear experience, that while responsive to position and orientation of the user is not adaptive to the cue list structure. In striving for interactivity, audio samples should be played in discrete sound sources and have them mixed in real time according to the position of the camera [10]. Cue Control is a software application for designing non spatial and spatial audio for 360° Video, using sound object rendering

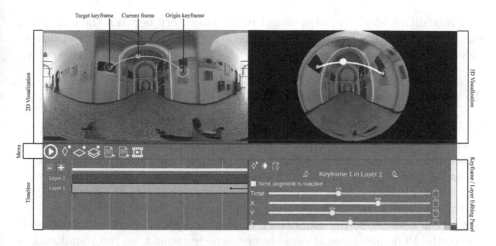

Fig. 1. Cue control spatializer

(virtual sound sources in 3D space using as input mono audio data). By spatializing these virtual objects, an audio designer can create a dynamic and interactive spatial audio scenario. Cue Control was built using the Unity engine and is composed of two components: Cue Spatializer (used to create a cue list representative of the audio behavior) and Cue Playback plugin (used in the deployed Unity applications to have audio playback consistent with the cue list). Cue Spatializer and consequently the cue list borrows an interface metaphor common in editing or animation software: layers containing keyframes, arranged in a timeline. Layers correspond to an audio source, while keyframes correspond to a change in the internal state of the audio source. The internal state of a keyframe is represented by the longitude (x coordinate in the equirectangular texture), latitude (y coordinate in the equirectangular texture), and distance (distance between the audio source and the origin of the Cartesian system, matching the location of the camera). The Cue Spatializer interface is composed of a 2D and 3D visualization of the equirectangular video, a menu, a timeline (displaying the cue list and an interactable slider for video playback), and editing panels for layers/keyframes properties (see Fig. 1).

After loading a video, the user can create layers from the menu or shortcuts and keyframes by directly clicking on 2D visualization; the new keyframe assumes the x and y coordinate of the pixel where the user clicked. In the 2D and 3D visualizations, the user can observe and hear the changes in audio during the video playback. At any moment in time, the position of a source in 3D space is calculated based on the internal state of the start and end keyframe of a segment (origin and target), with the x and y pixel coordinates being transformed into longitude and latitude coordinates. From this point, orthodromic distance can be used to get the shortest path between the origin and target and based on the current frame and distance, place the audio source on that path in world space. The user can select how the audio cues are interpreted (during runtime) in 3 modalities: static (placing sound in the trajectory between the origin and target), guiding (placing sound halfway between the desired location and current viewpoint) and exploration (placing sound only if it is in the current viewpoint).

4   Pilot Study and Future Work

In order to test the use of spatial soundtrack for interactive notification, we conducted a small pilot study with 5 participants, where they were asked to watch two equirectangular videos (a city tour and a safari tour). For this study, we used Cue Spatializer in the static modality and designed the soundtracks with the aim of guiding viewers' attention toward specific points of interest (POIs). In the city video, the POIs (buildings, monuments, and Christmas lights) do not produce sound, so the soundtrack is solely composed of music. In the safari video, the POIs are animals capable of producing sound, so the soundtrack is composed of sound effects and music.

While data are currently under analysis, we report here preliminary observations based on exit interviews. In both videos, sound appears to effectively notify the viewers about the position of POIs. In the city video, despite that not all the participants oriented themselves using the soundtrack, a considerable number of participants ($N = 4$) generally understood that the music was pointing at POIs. In one case, a participant had strong positive feedback, declaring that the spatial manipulation of the music was fundamental for him to orient himself. This case reflects the musical listening modality as described by Gaver [7], in which the perception process focuses on the properties of the sound itself and its elements (in this case, position of the sound). Even in the absence of discrete icons that idiomatically represented the POIs, sound spatialization allowed the music to convey enough information about the environment of the video.

In the safari video, sounds were generally used to locate the different animals; in this case, the spatial manipulation of music appears to be less important as more people stressed the role of sound effects for navigation. For example, one participant declared that the presence of sound (in a scene when birds appeared) was fundamental for him to start to gaze at the sky. Indeed, the participant stated that, before the first bird sound, he was unsure about where to look. The dominance of sound effects over music may be because sound effects (animal grunts, steps, and so forth) are direct representations of the POIs, providing the users peripheral awareness of the location and identity of the POI. In this case, the everyday listening modality is representative of how our participants use sound, focusing directly on the object or event that produces the sound.

While current results are promising, future work will strive to examine different soundtracks (e.g. spatial sound effects or multi-track music) and other interactivity modalities of Cue Control: guiding modality and exploration modality.

Acknowledgments. The project has been developed as part of MITIExcell (M1420-01-0145-FEDER-000002). The author Paulo Bala wishes to acknowledge FCT for supporting his research through the Ph.D. Grant PD/BD/128330/2017.

References

1. Pope, V.C., Dawes, R., Schweiger, F., Sheikh, A.: The geometry of storytelling: theatrical use of space for 360-degree videos and virtual reality. In: CHI Conference on Human Factors in Computing Systems 2017, pp. 4468–4478. ACM, Denver (2017)
2. Garner, T.A.: Sound and the virtual. In: Echoes of Other Worlds: Sound in Virtual Reality. PSS, pp. 47–82. Springer, Cham (2018). https://doi.org/10.1007/978-3-319-65708-0_3
3. Serafin, S., Geronazzo, M., Nilsson, N., Erkut, C., Nordahl, R.: Sonic interactions in virtual reality: state of the art, current challenges and future directions. IEEE Compu. Graph. Appl. **38**, 31–43 (2018)
4. Pasnau, R.: What is sound? Philos. Q. **49**, 309–324 (1999)
5. OCallaghan, C.: Sounds and events. In: Sounds and Perception, pp. 26–49. Oxford University Press, Oxford (2009)
6. Nudds, M.: Sounds and Space. In: Sounds and Perception, pp. 69–96. Oxford University Press, Oxford (2009)
7. Gaver, W.W.: What in the world do we hear? An ecological approach to auditory event perception. Ecol. Psychol. **5**, 1–29 (1993)
8. Chion, M., Murch, W.: Audio-Vision: Sound on Screen. Columbia University Press, New York (1994)
9. Gaver, W.W.: Synthesizing auditory icons. In: Proceedings of the INTERACT93 and CIII93 Conference on Human Factors in Computing Systems, pp. 228–235. ACM (1993)
10. Marks, A.: The Complete Guide to Game Audio: For Composers, Musicians, Sound Designers, Game Developers. CRC Press, Berkeley (2012)

Social Viewing in Cinematic Virtual Reality: Challenges and Opportunities

Sylvia Rothe[1($\boxtimes$)], Mario Montagud[2], Christian Mai[1],
Daniel Buschek[1], and Heinrich Hußmann[1]

[1] Ludwig Maximilian University of Munich, Munich, Germany
sylvia.rothe@ifi.lmu.de
[2] University of Valencia & i2CAT Foundation, Valencia, Spain

Abstract. Cinematic Virtual Reality (CVR) has been increasing in popularity in the last years. However, viewers can feel isolated when watching 360° movies with a Head-Mounted Display. Since watching movies is a social experience for most people, we investigate if the use of Head Mounted Displays is appropriate for enabling shared CVR experiences. In this context, even if viewers are watching the movie simultaneously, they do not automatically see the same field of view, since they can freely choose the viewing direction. Based on the literature and experiences from past user studies, we identify seven challenges. To address these challenges, we present and discuss design ideas for a CVR social movie player and highlight directions for future work.

Keywords: Cinematic Virtual Reality · 360° video · Social viewing

1 Introduction

360° movies are attracting widespread interest in a number of applications, like education, entertainment and news. Users highly benefit from the possibilities to freely look around and explore the presented scenes, either to entertain themselves or to gain a better understanding of the movie content.

In Cinematic Virtual Reality (**CVR**) viewers watch 360° movies via Virtual Reality (VR) devices. By using an HMD, the viewer can feel immersed within the scenes and freely choose the viewing direction. In contrast to traditional cinema or TV, each CVR viewer has an own display and gets isolated of the surrounding environment when watching a movie via HMD. The drawback of these systems is the associated visual and mental separation from other people, i.e. social isolation. Natural discussion, like pointing at interesting objects in the video or keeping the awareness about what the others focus is on, is impeded by the HMD.

In this work, we identify key challenges and related design aspects that are crucial for efficiently supporting social awareness and interaction when watching movies together remotely. We provide an overview of the current research state and identify seven open challenges. While further challenges may exist, these seven challenges are important for a first design approach. For each of these challenges, we propose potential approaches and future work directions.

© Springer Nature Switzerland AG 2018
R. Rouse et al. (Eds.): ICIDS 2018, LNCS 11318, pp. 338–342, 2018.
https://doi.org/10.1007/978-3-030-04028-4_37

2 Challenges and Approaches for Social Viewing in CVR

2.1 Challenge 1: Viewport Sharing

One of the main problems for social viewing via HMDs is the difference of the users' FoV and the missing awareness of the other's viewport. Being unaware of where co-watchers are looking at within the 360° scenes can lead to difficulties of understanding. A first approach is to **frame** the viewport of the co-watcher [1]. So, the viewport is visible, if the viewports are overlapping (Fig. 1 left). For finding the viewport of the co-watcher, which is off-screen, an arrow can be used [1].

Fig. 1. Approaches to show the viewport of a co-watcher. Left: Viewport shown by a frame; Right: Viewport shown by a display

Another approach is the **picture-in-picture (PIP)** method [2], where a little screen shows the co-watcher's FoV (Fig. 1 right). This has the advantage of visually showing the other's viewport, independent on the own viewing direction, but the disadvantage of covering a larger area of the display. So, the possibility of switching it off should be explored. The PiP-screen can be placed on that display side which is closer to the target.

2.2 Communication

A key issue in social viewing is the communication. In CVR the viewer does not know where the others are looking at. Why is he or she laughing? How can a viewer indicate details in the movie which are not necessarily in the FoV of the other viewers?

Voice chat is one possibility to communicate in social viewing. Although voice chat increases the social awareness [3], it can reduce the viewing experience because of distraction. Chatting could be replaced or extended by a simple **sign language** realized by gestures or controllers, to show emoticons to the co-watcher.

To inform the co-watcher about **PoIs** out of the screen, we plan to transfer methods used by gliders for collision avoidance. An example is shown in Fig. 2 left. The slide bar at the bottom shows if the PoI is on the right or on the left side. The slider on the right shows if the PoI is higher or deeper than the own viewing direction. Another example can be seen in Fig. 2 right, where the direction is shown by a circle and the height by a slider. In this way, participants will be able to distinguish between viewport awareness and signalling a PoI.

Fig. 2. Collision avoidance methods of gliders transferred to indicate the PoIs of the co-watcher. Left: The PoI is on the left side behind the viewer, below the viewing direction; Right: The PoI is on the left side behind the viewer, below the viewing direction.

2.3   Social Awareness

Another challenge for social viewing via HMDs is to provoke the feeling of "being together". Watching a movie together in the cinema or TV, the fellow is perceived in the periphery of the view. Even though "silent" feelings cannot be heard, they can be recognized by postures or gestures.

Voice chat and visualization of the co-watcher's viewport enable awareness of the other persons. Another way for increasing the social awareness is to include video chat windows via PiP. Figure 3 shows two examples. In the left one, the front-view of the co-watcher is displayed in the middle of the screen, even if the viewer turns the head. The right one is very similar to the situation of viewing a movie together in cinema or TV. The PiP is placed on the side of the viewer and shows the co-watcher from the side.

Fig. 3. Left: PiP of the co-watcher in front of the viewer. The co-watcher is always in the FoV; Right: PiP of the co-watcher on the side. The co-watcher can be seen, turning the head right.

2.4   Synchronization/Navigation

Synchronization of the media playout across the involved devices is a key requirement in social viewing [4, 5]. By providing this, all distributed users will perceive the same events at the same time. This involves designing and adopting the appropriate communication and control protocols, monitoring algorithms, reference selection strategies and adjustment techniques. Likewise, media synchronization must be preserved after issuing navigation control commands (e.g. play, pause, seek) in a shared session.

2.5   Input Device

For navigation as well as for communication, non-disturbing input methods need to be adopted. We think **graphical elements** on the display or controlling via **speech** disturb the viewing experience. One approach is to use **gestures**, because gestures are a natural method for interaction [6]. Other approaches are head/view-based, and controller-based methods. In [7] some of these methods were compared, head and controller-based methods achieving the best results, since there were some problems in gesture recognition. For our first test we used **controllers** to be sure the actions were triggered on purpose.

2.6   Role Concept

To define the relation between the viewers, two role concepts are conceivable: non-guided and guided. The **non-guided** approach is based on assigning the same roles and permission to all viewers. This can originate conflicts in case of highly active communications. Likewise, the display can become overloaded when information about all users is shown. The **guided** approach consists of differentiating two roles: the guide and the follower. The guide will be taken as the reference for communication and synchronization and will be the only participant with the navigation functionalities enabled. To allow more interactive and flexible sessions, the roles of guide and followers can be dynamic exchanged. A **slave** mode, where the follower is synchronized in time and viewing direction to the guide, causes simulator sickness [1]. However, it can be a helpful in asymmetric environments with non-VR collaborators.

2.7   Asymmetric Environments

Social viewing should also be possible for participants using different devices. Gugenheimer et al. [8] implemented ShareVR, which enables users of the real world to interact with users in a virtual world. They studied asymmetry in visualization and interaction. A novel social viewing concept is considered in [9], consisting of a multi-screen scenario in which different users play a different role: observer (TV), assistant (tablet) and inspector (HMD). The inspector's viewport is streamed to the TV to allow the remaining users being aware of the 360° scenes, thus overcoming isolation and stimulating interaction. This and the guidelines in [8] will be taken into account in our work.

3   Conclusion and Future Work

In this work, we have identified and addressed key challenges to enable social viewing in CVR. For a shared experience, viewers need new methods of communication and viewport awareness. The field of social viewing in CVR is relatively new and it needs more research and knowledge about the viewers' behaviour. The described approaches are one step to explore this field. Based on this work, we will compare the approaches among other relevant aspects. The aim is to define a design space for social CVR.

References

1. Nguyen, C., DiVerdi, S., Hertzmann, A., Liu, F.: CollaVR: Collaborative In-Headset Review for VR Video. In: Proceedings of the 30th Annual ACM Symposium on User Interface Software and Technology - UIST 2017, pp. 267–277. ACM Press, New York (2017)
2. Lin, Y.-T., Liao, Y.-C., Teng, S.-Y., et al.: Outside-in. In: Proceedings of the 30th Annual ACM Symposium on User Interface Software and Technology - UIST 2017, pp. 255–265. ACM Press, New York (2017)
3. Geerts, D., Vaishnavi, I., Mekuria, R., et al.: Are we in sync?: synchronization requirements for watching online video together. In: Proceedings of the SIGCHI Conference on Human Factors in Computing Systems, pp. 311–314 (2011)
4. Montagud, M., Boronat, F., Stokking, H., van Brandenburg, R.: Inter-destination multimedia synchronization: schemes, use cases and standardization. Multimed. Syst. **18**, 459–482 (2012). https://doi.org/10.1007/s00530-012-0278-9
5. Boronat, F., Montagud, M., Marfil, D., Luzon, C.: Hybrid broadcast/broadband TV services and media synchronization: demands, preferences and expectations of Spanish consumers. IEEE Trans. Broadcast. **64**, 52–69 (2018). https://doi.org/10.1109/TBC.2017.2737819
6. O'Hagan, R.G., Zelinsky, A., Rougeaux, S.: Visual gesture interfaces for virtual environments. Interact. Comput. **14**, 231–250 (2002). https://doi.org/10.1016/S0953-5438(01)00050-9
7. Pakkanen, T., Hakulinen, J., Jokela, T., et al.: Interaction with WebVR 360° video player: comparing three interaction paradigms. In: 2017 IEEE Virtual Reality (VR), pp. 279–280. IEEE (2017)
8. Gugenheimer, J., Stemasov, E., Frommel, J., Rukzio, E.: ShareVR: enabling co-located experiences for virtual reality between HMD and non-HMD users. In: Proceedings of the 2017 CHI Conference on Human Factors in Computing Systems - CHI 2017, pp. 4021–4033. ACM Press, New York (2017)
9. Núñez, A., Montagud, M., Fraile, I., Gómez, D., Fernández, S.: ImmersiaTV: an end-to-end toolset to enable customizable and immersive multi-screen TV experiences. In: Workshop on Virtual Reality, co-located with ACM TVX, Seoul, South Korea (2018)

Making New Narrative Structures with Actor's Eye-Contact in Cinematic Virtual Reality (CVR)

Dong-uk Ko, Hokyoung Ryu[✉], and Jieun Kim[✉]

Hanyang University, 222, Wangsimni-ro, Seongdong-gu, Seoul, South Korea
east@easthug.com, {hryu, jkim2}@hanyang.ac.kr

Abstract. With an advent of the VR market, using 360-degree cameras to create Cinematic VR (CVR) experiences opened up a prominent question that can challenge the traditional film narratology. Additional fields of view are allowed so the viewers in CVR can move their heads to choose more attentive and informative scenes, but frequent scene changes are not welcomed due to VR nausea. These technical drawbacks (and/or advantages) demand a new narratology for CVR, in particular, how the director of CVR can convey certain narratives to the viewers in conjunction with how he/she can attract the viewers to look at the acting persons in the 360-degree scenes. In this study, we employed well-established underpinnings of both eye contact and gaze, by which the acting persons in CVR can effectively convey the narrative structure, and, at the same time, more attentiveness from the viewer in CVR can be ensured. We completed two versions of CVR, one with the traditional film narratology and the other for the new CVR narratology (i.e., eye contact and gaze) proposed in this article, and are now in the stage of evaluation. Our preliminary results showed that the viewers in the CVR film with more eye contact and gazes effectively presented the narratives of the film and also were more satisfied with the CVR environment.

Keywords: Cinematic Virtual Reality · Narrative · Eye contact

1 Introduction

The filming industry recently applied VR technologies to create new media content; for instance, the Cinematic Virtual Reality (CVR) using 360-degree cameras is now widely applicable in some genres [1]. Major studios in Hollywood have often developed previews or trailers with CVRs and some film festivals (e.g., Sundance, SXSW, etc.) have newly introduced CVR-related categories [2, 3]. However, the means of effectively conveying the narratives to the viewer in CVR is still difficult and elusive because viewers can choose what to see in CVR [4].

The current shooting protocols in CVR have mainly borrowed from the traditional film grammar (e.g., cut-editing grammar, short-take conventions, etc.). However, CVR allows the viewer's intentional choices (i.e., by one's head movement) of the scenes in

© Springer Nature Switzerland AG 2018
R. Rouse et al. (Eds.): ICIDS 2018, LNCS 11318, pp. 343–347, 2018.
https://doi.org/10.1007/978-3-030-04028-4_38

the 360-degree environment, so that the director's tools to convey the narratives (e.g., zoom-in-and-out, close-up and etc.) do not work well anymore.

The aim of this article is to investigate a CVR directing style that can make the viewer effectively attend the CVR narrative being conveyed by the director, while being able to choose around the viewing perspectives in the 360 CVR environment. It is hypothesized that the viewer's attentive mechanism will be interactively triggered by acting persons; otherwise, the viewers will look away from the director's narrative to pay attention to more personally interesting scenes in the 360 CVR environment (see Fig. 1).

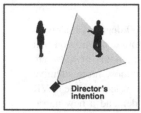  

| Traditional Film Environment | Cinematic VR Camera Environment | Cinematic VR Viewer Environment |

Fig. 1. Film & Cinematic VR environment

2   Cinematic VR and Acting Person-Audience Interaction

CVR cannot effectively follow traditional film grammar (i.e. shot, scene, sequence), in particular, short-take and frame-editing (see Fig. 2(a)) is not highly applicable to CVR. The CVR film, in nature, tends to have a number of long-takes that have not been much employed in the traditional film production [5]. As shown in Fig. 2(b), the 360-degree camera is located in the center of the mise-en-scene set, so the scene can be fully viewed in all directions (therefore, even the director should not be found in all the shooting scenes). This makes the long-takes more desirable in CVR, and this further gives the viewer a virtual realistic impression that s/he is co-present with the acting persons.

It is interesting that this "long-take" convention is often used in theatrical performances [5]. The audience in the theatre watches the acting persons in the stage through the "fourth wall" like a one-way mirror [6]. This invisible fourth wall, which France's Denis Diderot [6] coined, would separate the audience from the acting persons, but allow the acting persons to freely present different plots in the different play settings. Indeed, the theatrical performance is far more realistic than the film, and this fourth wall makes a weaker visual realism and co-presence.

Immersive theatre overcomes this limitation [7]. In immersive theatre, the audience is not merely a passive bystander, but it serves as a part of the narrative or the plot, so that often are the changes of the acting person's utterances, gestures and/or movements in response to the audience's feedback. In effect, the break-down of the traditional conception of the "fourth wall" helps the audience to feel more co-present with the acting persons and the narrative structure seems to be perceived as more personal, immersive and realistic [8].

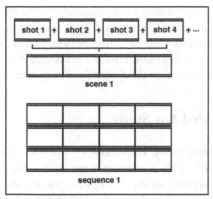
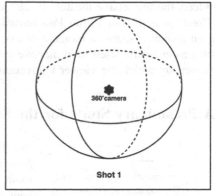

Fig. 2. a. Grammar of the shot in traditional film/**b.** Grammar of the shot in Cinematic VR

CVR has many commonalities with immersive theatre [9]. It can present the entire 360-degree space around the viewer in CVR (Fig. 2(b)), so the viewer can feel as if he or she is in the film, like the audience in immersive theatre. Our study, in this regard, proposes the eye-contact interaction technique that the acting persons can apply in the CVR, which helps the viewer have more immersive and co-present feeling with the acting persons and to discern the narrative to be more realistic.

3   Actor's Interaction in Cinematic VR with Eye Contact

3.1   Eye Contact: From Taboo to New Grammar

Eye contact is a single strong non-verbal tool in many communication skills. A literature review of gaze and eye contact [10] shows that one's gazes to a person or an object can provide emotional information of the beholder, regulate the interaction of the counterpart, express the intimacy between people, and facilitate particular service and task goals.

Interestingly, this direct eye contact between the acting person and the audience has been tabooed [11] in the traditional film grammar. Instead, the traditional film techniques manipulate a sense of space by changing how the actor's gaze can be best framed to convey the director's narrative (i.e., art of frame). While CVR has thus far struggled to reconcile such narrative control by the standards of the traditional film, thanks to the viewer's interactivity with HMD (Head Mounted Display), we believe that CVR should have a new practice of combining all of the performing elements through a careful orchestration of the physical spaces captured by the 360-degree camera. In particular, the expertise of CVR acting persons lies not only in their presentation of the narrative through attentive cues for the viewer, but also in their subtle delivery management of the narrative for the CVR viewer, why they did that, and what they do the next.

Indeed, the immersive theater has already established such practices. For instance, in *"The Drowned Man"* from Punchdrunk theatre [12], explicit interactivity occurs when an audience shares a moment of eye contact with an acting person. Hence, the attentive mechanisms used in immersive theatre might hint how the CVR can manage the viewer, by which the viewer inadvertently captures the flow of the narrative.

4 A Preliminary Study for the Scaled-Up Study

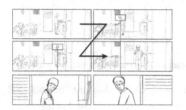

Fig. 3. Storyboard of the CVR *"Confessions" - Scene 1 [A man is humming and making food. The man turns his head and makes eye contact with someone and talks. "Will my father like it? I haven't seen him in a few years. Would he like it? In fact, it is the first time that I show my father who I love. I'm so nervous." His awkward smile is full of eyes for his loved one.]*

Fig. 4. Storyboard of the CVR *"Confessions" - Scene 2 [The house is all messed up. A man sitting on the front of the refrigerator. Trace of tears remained and the cheeks are reddish. The man looks at someone with a bitter smile. "Are you okay? ... Sorry. Because of me... Why does he do that? just... I don't want a big one. It's not like that ..." He looks at the photo frame on the floor. There is a picture of him and a man.]*

We filmed two CVR versions - titled as *"Confessions"*, with a running time of 5 min. The main narrative of this CVR was that an adolescent actor was to invite his father for a family dinner at his house, in order to introduce his fiancé. While cooking, he gave many worrying utterances about this dinner and his father (these utterances are the main medium to deliver the narrative. Note that more eye contact and gaze were employed in one of the CVR versions, and the other was not the case). The party turned into a disastrous event, and the viewer might understand why this happened in the final ending scene, however, the cue for this understanding was hidden in the CVR setting. This intervention was deliberate to see if the viewer with more eye contact or gazes from the acting person would better rate the CVR film and narratives.

In detail, the narrative conveyed by the adolescent actor consists only of his monologues, and no other acting persons appeared in the CVR. To complete this narrative, we applied two functional purposes of eye contact and gaze - "Providing Information", and "Task Goals". In this CVR, the viewer tends to be his fiancé, because the adolescent actor keeps talking whilst maintaining eye-contact with the viewer (see Fig. 3). This is an example of the function purpose - "Providing Information". In a similar vein, in the last scene, the actor gazed at the photo frame, without any utterances (see Fig. 4). This was intentional to guide the viewer's eye movement to the photo frame, to understand why his father was upset and the dinner was ruined. This is an example of function purpose - "Task Goals".

Again, the first version was to facilitate less eye contact or gazes, and the second for the other way around. In our preliminary pilot study, we found that gazing at the photo frame was helpful to attend to the narrative of the film in this CVR. We now plan to carry out a scaled-up usability study. In particular, we are interested in applying the Eye Tracker [13] to quantitatively measure the fixation time and the prime visual areas of the viewer. In conjunction with the interview data with viewers, we can interpret how the narrative structure is being built up by the acting person's eye contact and gazes.

References

1. MacQuarrie, A., Steed, A.: Cinematic virtual reality: evaluating the effect of display type on the viewing experience for panoramic video. In: 2017 IEEE Virtual Reality (VR), pp. 45–54. IEEE (2017)
2. Sundance institute. https://www.sundance.org/festivals/sundance-film-festival#/
3. SXSW. https://www.sxsw.com/
4. Mateer, J.: Directing for cinematic virtual reality: how the traditional film director's craft applies to immersive environments and notions of presence. J. Media Pract. **18**(1), 14–25 (2017)
5. Chang, W.: Virtual reality filmmaking methodology (animation producing). TECHART: J. Arts Imaging Sci. **3**(3), 23–26 (2016)
6. Stevenson, J.: The fourth wall and the third space. Center for Playback Theater, New York (1995)
7. LaFrance, M.: The disappearing fourth wall: law, ethics, and experimental theatre. Vanderbilt J. Entertain. Technol. Law **15**, 507 (2012)
8. White, G.: On immersive theatre. Theatre Res. Int. **37**(3), 221–235 (2012)
9. Pope, V.C., Dawes, R., Schweiger, F., Sheikh, A.: The geometry of storytelling: theatrical use of space for 360-degree videos and virtual reality. In: Proceedings of the 2017 CHI Conference on Human Factors in Computing Systems, pp. 4468–4478. ACM (2017)
10. Kleinke, C.L.: Gaze and eye contact: a research review. Psychol. Bull. **100**(1), 78 (1986)
11. Britten, B.: From Stage to Screen: A Theatre Actor's Guide to Working on Camera, pp. 103–107. Bloomsbury Publishing, London (2014)
12. Biggin, R.: Immersive Theatre and Audience Experience. Palgrave Macmillan, Basingstoke (2017). (Chapter 3)
13. Tobiipro. https://www.tobiipro.com/

Jonathan Swift: Augmented Reality Application for Trinity Library's Long Room

Néill O'Dwyer[1](✉) (iD), Jan Ondřej[2], Rafael Pagés[2],
Konstantinos Amplianitis[2], and Aljoša Smolić[2]

[1] Department of Drama, Trinity College Dublin, Dublin, Ireland
odwyernc@tcd.ie
[2] V-SENSE, School of Computer Science and Statistics, Trinity College Dublin,
Dublin, Ireland

Abstract. This demo paper describes a project that engages cutting-edge free viewpoint video (FVV) techniques for developing content for an augmented reality prototype. The article traces the evolutionary process from concept, through narrative development, to completed AR prototypes for the HoloLens and handheld mobile devices. It concludes with some reflections on the affordances of the various hardware formats and posits future directions for the research.

1 Introduction

This project is an interdepartmental collaboration between *V-SENSE* – a computer science research group in Trinity College, led by Professor of Creative Technologies, Aljoša Smolić, exploring virtual reality (VR) and augmented reality (AR) technologies – and the Library of Trinity College, which, under the leadership of librarian, Helen Shenton, is seeking to enhance its future accessibility programme by harnessing new interactive digital media. The goal was to conceive and build an innovative digital application that employs cutting-edge hard and software to enrich the visitor experience in the Long Room [1]. As an experimental and synergetic collaboration, the project benefits both parties. On one hand, *V-SENSE* gets an opportunity to build digital content on the basis of rich, engaging and famous cultural subject matter, e.g. rare, historical books, artefacts and sculptures, not to mention the breath-taking building itself. On the other hand, the library gets a cutting-edge interactive application that affirms its commitment to innovatively harnessing digital technologies towards constantly improving its accessibility to visitors, while also solidifying its immovable presence as guardian and proponent of Trinity's, and Ireland's, rich academic legacy.

2 Concept Development

From the outset it was agreed that there is no substitute for the real experience of being present in the Long Room. Therefore, the goal was to devise a narrative/concept that augments the visitor experience, and does not try to compete with the library's crucial

R. Rouse et al. (Eds.): ICIDS 2018, LNCS 11318, pp. 348–351, 2018.
https://doi.org/10.1007/978-3-030-04028-4_39

business model, based on real tourist footfall, i.e. a narrative that draws people in, as opposed to acting as a virtual substitute. An AR app suits this demand because, as per Azuma's three-tiered definition, AR merges real and virtual worlds, permits real-time interaction, and perceptually aligns digital information with real objects in geometric space [2]. It emerged that what was needed was a narrative that helps escort visitors through the library by pointing out rare artefacts, books and manuscripts [3]. There are numerous marble busts of famous historical figures – such as Socrates, Bacon, Swift, Hamilton, etc. – that line the central aisle of the Long Room. For the purposes of the prototype, these busts provide an interesting basis for subject matter. The concept that emerged was that an AR avatar would feature beside each bust imparting a whimsical, idiosyncratic anecdote linked to the Long Room and its context. The interactive tour would consist in visitors discovering peripheral stories that help draw their attention to the multitude of historical, architectural and archival details, procuring a deeper, more enriching experience of the world heritage site. The project is a practice-as-research experiment supported by the findings of Sommerauer and Müller, who quantitatively demonstrate that 'museum visitors learned significantly more from augmented exhibits than from nonaugmented exhibits, perceived AR as a valuable add-on of the exhibition, and wish to see more AR experiences in museums in the future' [4].

2017 marked the 350th anniversary of (famous Trinity scholar) Jonathan Swift's birth, so we decided to focus on his character for the prototype. Thus, the objective was to conceive a short, whimsical anecdote about Swift, and to produce the content for interactive AR viewing. Jane Maxwell, Principal Curator of TCD Library, assisted with drafting up a light-hearted yet informative script that engages visitors along the lines of humour interwoven with historical fact. The innovation that this project brings to the discourse on AR apps for museums is that it displays 3D volumetric content using real actors, costumes and video, not animated avatars developed natively in software. Free viewpoint video (FVV) is the technique we used for creating the avatar [5]. FVV is a volumetric video technique that 'offers the same functionality that is known from 3D computer graphics. The user can choose an own viewpoint and viewing direction within a visual scene, meaning interactive free navigation. In contrast to pure computer graphics applications, FVV targets real world scenes as captured by real cameras' [6].

3 Technical Process

The FVV process entails recording live action using multiple cameras that surround the actor, who performs in an enclosed green screen environment. The footage is stitched together, at the post production stage, using optimised computer vision algorithms. Accurate 3D reconstruction demands maximum scene coverage and image over-lap. Thus, twelve video cameras were strategically placed in a 360 degree arc. After the footage is captured it is prepared for the complex postproduction stage. Video and audio recordings, from all cameras, are synchronised to ensure all data frames concur, temporally and spatially. The actor is chroma-keyed and then exported as a series of raw images and thresholded silhouette masks. The camera positions are calculated in a 3D virtual geometry, and then all elements are used to reconstruct the 3D geometry based on the following techniques: shape-from-silhouette (SfS) [7], obtained from the silhouette mask; and multi-view stereo (MVS) [8], via a 3D point cloud. 'All data are then combined using 3D fusion techniques, resulting in volumetrically complete and accurate 3D models' [9]. A separate 3D model is generated for each frame of video. Input images are used to colour the corresponding models using a multi-view texturing technique [10], producing a series of fully textured, photorealistic models [11]. Iterating through these at 30 frames per second constitutes the basis of volumetric video. When the sequence is complete, it is compiled in a game engine. A custom script dynamically loads a textured mesh for each frame. Finally, the app is exported as an executable file, for the Microsoft HoloLens, or a handheld device, such as a tablet or smart phone.

4   Augmented Reality App

The app functions on the condition that the user wanders through the tangible space and uses pattern recognition technology to activate individual stories linked to the artefacts they are viewing. In the case of this prototype, it is the bust of Jonathan Swift that is recognised by the app, which triggers the volumetric video to load and begin playing back, hence the character of Swift appears as an AR hologram beside the original statue. The sequence executes in its entirety, from start to finish [12]. Considered singularly, the prototype video is linear, but the way it is triggered is interactive. It is easy to see how, using a repertoire of such video sequences, this model can be scaled-up as an interactive meta-narrative, involving each of the other busts in the Long Room, not to mention the plethora of books and manuscripts of historical significance.

5   Conclusion

The project was presented to the library's steering committee in May 2018, and we are currently awaiting feedback as to whether the proposal will be adopted to the future digital access programme. The prototype was well received, but we have yet to record qualitative user feedback [13]. The AR solution fulfils the brief by enhancing the visitor experience and does not attempt to offer an alternative to visitors being physically present at the historical site. It would be feasible to deploy iOS and Android versions in the near future, however handheld devices have shortcomings – 'they force the visitor to hold the guide and to look at its screen', thereby tiring the hands and drawing attention from real exhibits [14]. By providing a wearable screen and aligning information with reals object, the version for HoloLens is a richer user experience. However, although impressive for technical demos, its high cost is currently prohibitive of ambitions to furnish the numerous Long Room visitors each with a headset.

The deployment of AR technologies in archival and museological contexts is exciting, but also comes packaged with challenges and shortcomings. Harnessed in the right way they maintain the potential to enhance and enrich human experience; but, if used incorrectly, they can curtail it. The quality of FVV technology that is so beneficial is that it demands human performativity, thus affording collaboration between the performing arts and the computer sciences. By capturing real actors telling human stories, FVV content conserves a strong presence of humanity in a technology that is so often criticised for creating solipsistic worlds, devoid of human intersubjectivity.

Acknowledgments. Principle Investigator: Aljosa Smolic; Director/Producer: Néill O'Dwyer; Technical Team: Jan Ondřej, Rafael Pagés, Konstantinos Amplianitis; Script: Jane Maxell and Néill O'Dwyer; Actor: Jonathan White; Make-up artist: Roisín Condon; Costume designer: Sara Ben-Abdallah; Costume supplied by the Abbey Theatre Costume Department. This publication has emanated from research conducted with the financial support of Science Foundation Ireland (SFI) under the Grant Number 15/RP/2776.

References and Notes

1. The Trinity College Long Room is a Unesco World Heritage Site, which accommodates in excess of one million visitors per annum
2. Azuma, R.T.: A survey of augmented reality. Presence Teleop. Virt. Environ. **6**(4), 355–385 (1997). https://doi.org/10.1162/pres.1997.6.4.355
3. Library staff remark on the tendency of visitors to stroll through the Long Room taking in general, sweeping vistas, ultimately overlooking fine details and archival treasures
4. Sommerauer, P., Müller, O.: Augmented reality in informal learning environments: a field experiment in a mathematics exhibition. Comput. Educ. **79**, 59–68 (2014). https://doi.org/10.1016/j.compedu.2014.07.013
5. The core research team of behind this production have since spun out into an innovative start-up company, entitled Volograms <https://volograms.com>
6. Smolic, A., et al.: 3D video and free viewpoint video-technologies, applications and MPEG standards. In: IEEE International Conference on Multimedia and Expo 2006, pp. 2161–2164 (2006)
7. Kutulakos, K.N., Seitz, S.M.: A theory of shape by space carving. In: The Proceedings of the Seventh IEEE International Conference on Computer Vision 1999, vol. 1, pp. 307–314 (1999)
8. Schönberger, J.L., et al.: Pixelwise view selection for unstructured multi-view stereo. In: Leibe, B., Matas, J., Sebe, N., Welling, M. (eds.) ECCV 2016. LNCS, vol. 9907, pp. 501–518. Springer, Cham (2016). https://doi.org/10.1007/978-3-319-46487-9_31
9. O'Dwyer, N., et al.: Samuel Beckett in Virtual Reality: Exploring narrative using free viewpoint video. Leonardo JA System. MIT Press, Cambridge (2018)
10. Pagés, R., et al.: Seamless, static multi-texturing of 3D meshes. Comput. Graph. Forum **34**(1), 228–238 (2015). https://doi.org/10.1111/cgf.12508
11. Pagés, R., et al.: Affordable content creation for free-viewpoint video and VR/AR applications. J. Vis. Commun. Image Represent. (2018). For a complete description of the technical pipeline see https://doi.org/10.1016/j.jvcir.2018.03.012
12. See prototype test video here: https://youtu.be/TcVz0iTAa8g
13. It is intended that the demo at ICIDS will afford an opportunity for garnering such data
14. Vainstein, N., et al.: Towards using mobile, head-worn displays in cultural heritage: user requirements and a research agenda. In: Proceedings of the 21st International Conference on Intelligent User Interfaces-IUI 2016, pp. 327–331. ACM Press, Sonoma (2016). https://doi.org/10.1145/2856767.2856802

Leaving the Small Screen: Telling News Stories in a VR Simulation of an AR News Service

Torbjörn Svensson[1(✉)], Lissa Holloway-Attaway[1],
and Etienne Beroldy[2]

[1] University of Skövde, Skövde, Sweden
{torbjorn.svensson, lissa.holloway-attaway}@his.se
[2] École d'Ingénieurs de l'université de Nantes, Nantes, France
etienne.beroldy@etu.univ-nantes.fr

Abstract. This paper describes a demo of a Virtual Reality simulation of an interactable news service for Augmented Reality. The aim of the prototype is to implement it for user testing of new forms of news-interaction, leaving the small screen of mobile applications and entering into a 'virtual' world instead. This system can potentially be used for subjects other than news interactions and would be suitable as a test-platform for other kinds of AR-based digital storytelling. An advantage for a VR simulation is that current AR technology in the form of AR headsets/glasses are still in technical infancy, and therefore they are quite limited, both when it comes to field of view and for handling dynamic outdoor environments.

Keywords: VR simulation · Augmented Reality · Interactive news

1 Introduction

Local news journalism is often described as important for the local community and a crucial tool for local democracy [1, 2]. The focus of local newspapers is not only 'objectively' reporting what has happened, but also offering analysis of current affairs and presenting a platform for reader discussions. To engage readers, news stories should offer interaction, and one might then conclude that the digital format for local newsreaders has thus evolved to reach their readers. However, the digitalization of news has not been as revolutionary as other forms and genres, for example the transfer to the digital format for music, film or games. The way one interacts with music or game distribution platforms has changed more significantly over the last 15 years than news, from boxed artifacts to on-line distribution with many additional side-services. Digital news is generally fairly conventional and follows print formats, often with a long list of headlines and small images, along with additional links to related news articles. In comparison, music has undergone a much deeper transition, from the first digital product, the Compact Disc, via MP3 files and sharing on Napster, to digital distribution in iTunes, to streamed content on platforms like Spotify. With Spotify, some of the possibilities from the pre-digital age have even returned, most significantly with playlists that are a "digital echo" of the old mix-tape.

© Springer Nature Switzerland AG 2018
R. Rouse et al. (Eds.): ICIDS 2018, LNCS 11318, pp. 352–355, 2018.
https://doi.org/10.1007/978-3-030-04028-4_40

Currently, news, at least among younger generations, is primarily consumed on mobile devices [3, 4] with comparably small screen sizes that hinder readers from having an overview and which often limits their ability to customize news flow. An opportunity for digital formats that is seldom addressed is the possibility to geo-locate both the user and the actual news item. The combination of a world-simulation around the user with relevant localized digital information and almost infinite screen space are just some of the promises of future AR (Augmented Reality) systems. To that end, on this research demo, we explore the possibilities for intensifying news interaction in a geo-located simulated AR news environment to discover the key features such a virtual world might afford for readers.

The purpose of this demo/prototype is to escape the limitations of small screen mobile platform news interactions, and instead create a simulation of a news experience that removes news from the limitations of mobile device and moves it into 'the world' to focus attention on location-based interactions with other news readers/users. In this way, news becomes a more inclusive and immersive interactive storytelling environment, where a primary focus is to provide an environment for multiple news readers/users to discuss local, location-based, news items. Much research suggests that the creation of location-based environments to support storytelling provides an effective backdrop for creating personalized, embodied user-experiences [5]. Other studies consider the critical design of architectural and exhibition spaces suggest that storytelling may be enhanced by creating 'worlds' that move between physical and digital environments and/or that re-center a user's sense of their own body by developing their 'isovist,' or perceptual fields, [6–9]. Given the proposed Mixed Reality design elements for future news encounters (via AR), these studies support our research. One of the benefits of the system is the use of text and the possibility to use voice to comment on news items. Text has the advantage of being inherently non-linear, since one can skip over sections to have a very quick overview of an entire message to find points of interest without waiting for a video or sound file to load. The demo platform could also be used for content other than news, for example for testing any kind of location-based interactive AR narrative, a guide system, a heritage site, or any other built environment or landscape suitable as a storytelling backdrop.

2 Building Blocks of a Location-Based AR News Service

This prototype is not intended to mimic a conventional game system, as it has no scoring system or a finite goal. However it does share some features with games, as with some design features that are derived from how games function in terms of engaging players. According to Rigby and Ryan [10] Self Determination Theory, a psychological needs satisfaction theory, is one way to explain the motivation to play digital games. Players are motivated to play and engage in games, by their need for achieving satisfaction in the areas of Autonomy, Competence and Relatedness: Autonomy focuses on their freedom of choice and a feeling of not being controlled by others when taking action; Competence focuses on users finding the right level of challenge and having feedback to judge their progress; Relatedness focuses on how one needs to have a connection to other players, to feel meaningful to others. In the design of this AR/VR news platform, autonomy satisfaction is catered to by allowing the user to move freely and to choose which news items to engage with, as opposed to confronting a fixed, scrolling list of news items, as commonly found on mobile news platforms. Relatedness satisfaction gives the user both the possibility to comment and to read others comments based on the article and to react/see others' reactions to the news through simple emojis. Using a voice to text/text to voice interface is targeting competence satisfaction for users.

3   Description of the System

The application is made with Unity 2018.1.1. The application is made for Open VR systems and uses a SQLite Database to keep track of data. It needs Windows 10 because it uses the Unity engine Windows speech API for voice to text/text to voice conversion. The user has freedom of movement and can move around a simulated city by walking in the Vives "play area" and further via a standard teleportation system. Users can then enter into, and interact, with news objects, represented by spheres, by putting the spheres on their heads. Literally immersing them in news stories. After reading and interacting with the news item, users exit out of the news items in the same way, just by lifting the sphere to their heads a second time.

Fig. 1. Outside and Inside a News Item, with comment and reaction box.

Once the user is "inside" a news item, there are different possibilities for interaction. The user can read and scroll through the news, the news text can be moved around freely inside the news item bubble. The user can take the microphone and speak to create a comment which can then be validated or deleted. When validated, it is added to the news item on a separate panel and can be moved around, as with digital news articles. The user can also post a reaction to the article. Currently only four reactions are possible, surprised, happy, angry or sad, and they are symbolised by emojis. To choose a reaction the user puts the white ball in the corresponding box. For placing the news items at the user's location and for managing users and comments, there is also a developer mode. A map overview makes it easy to add and delete news on the city map, as well as a system of player login/identification to connect comments to separate users and to retrieve data concerning the player behaviour. This mode also helps facilitate a user and usage analysis.

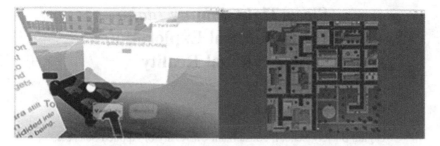

Fig. 2. A comment is validated and interface for placing news item.

4 Status and Next Steps

The VR simulation has been further developed during Autumn 2018 and will be used for testing on a target group of young (16–25) potential future users of AR local news services. Methods used for study of user behavior will be a mix of recorded data from the test sessions (for example: paths taken, time of engagement and interactions made), a UES (User Experience Scale) survey and talk-aloud sessions while watching replays of the test session.

References

1. Strömbäck, J., Djerf-Pierre, M., Shehata, A.: The dynamics of political interest and news media consumption: a longitudinal perspective. Int. J. Public Opinion Res. **25**(4), 414–435 (2012)
2. Shehata, A., Strömbäck, J.: Mediation of political realities: media as crucial sources of information. In: Esser, F., Strömbäck, J. (eds.) Mediatization of Politics: Understanding the Transformation of Western Democracies, pp. 93–113. Palgrave Macmillan, London (2014)
3. Jervelycke Belfrage, M.: Både slumpmässig och planerad. Ungas nyhetskonsumtion i sociala medier. Arbetsrapport (2016)
4. Westlund, O.: Nyhetsjournalistik i en mobil tidsålder: En genomgång av tio viktiga forskningsområden. Norsk medietidsskrift **24**(02), 1–12 (2017)
5. Tuan, Y.: Space and Place: The Perspective of Experience. University of Minnesota Press, Minneapolis and London (1977)
6. Benedikt, M.L.: To take hold of space: isovists and isovist fields. Environ. Plan. B Plann. Des. **6**(1), 47–65 (1979)
7. Wineman, J.D., Peponis, J.: Constructing spatial meaning: spatial affordances in museum design. Environ. Behav. **42**(1), 86–109 (2010)
8. Bardzell, J., Bardzell, S.: What is critical about critical design? In: Proceedings of the SIGCHI Conference on Human Factors in Computing Systems. ACM (2013)
9. Rouse, R., et al.: MRx design and criticism: the confluence of media studies, performance and social interaction. Digital Creativity **26**(3–4), 221–227 (2015)
10. Rigby, S., Ryan, R.M.: Glued to Games: How Video Games Draw us in and Hold us Spellbound. ABC-CLIO, Santa Barbara (2011)

Sleep Tight Johnny Idaho
A Multicultural Exploration into Virtual Reality

Nick Verouden[1], Mirjam Vosmeer[2(✉)], and Alyea Sandovar[2]

[1] Digital Society School, Amsterdam University of Applied Sciences,
Postbus 1025, 1000 BA Amsterdam, The Netherlands
n.w.verouden@hva.nl
[2] Lectoraat Play & Civic Media, Amsterdam University of Applied Sciences,
Postbus 1025, 1000 BA Amsterdam, The Netherlands
m.s.vosmeer@hva.nl, alyea@tinthue.com

Abstract. For this summer school project, four student teams in different cities across the world worked simultaneously on the same VR assignment, about visualizing the role of digital technology in society in the year 2030.

Keywords: Virtual reality · Digital society · Intercultural design

1 Introduction

In the summer of 2018 the Design Across Cultures programme of the Digital Society School in Amsterdam launched the first 'VR Summer school across cultures'. Together with the Play and Civic Media department, the VR Base and a consortium of international partners (Hanyang University, New York Medialab and Kyoto Sangyo University), we wanted to explore how to use VR to think about the future of our digital society from a cross-cultural perspective.

Over a period of three weeks, four multidisciplinary teams across the world worked together to translate a fragment of the dystopian Dutch novel *Sleep Tight Johnny Idaho* by the Dutch author Auke Hulst into a VR experience [1]. The novel is set in the year 2030, in a future where digital technology is used by the government to constantly monitor each individual.

With this innovative project, we aimed to challenge participants to think about the impact of digital technology on our personal lives and in society through a VR experience. We believe that VR provides new, experiential and immersive ways of storytelling that enable producers to visualise and reflect on issues like this [2].

A reason for setting up this project was to develop a collaborative and co-creative approach, in which we contributed to Digital Society School's mission to fight 'design waste', which refers to the throwing away of valuable work form the design process.

Our main interest was to get the four teams to collaborate, and share their insights and ideas. Teams were instructed to help each other in the design and coding process, and communicate, mainly electronically, for the duration of the project. Because remoteness and dispersion of work were key characteristics of the project, the teams

R. Rouse et al. (Eds.): ICIDS 2018, LNCS 11318, pp. 356–358, 2018.
https://doi.org/10.1007/978-3-030-04028-4_41

had to rely on digital technology for their communication. They shared weekly video vlogs between the teams, in which they recorded their progress, organised online hangouts and held virtual milestone check-in meetings, with the goal of sharing learnings and discussing progress. Slack, a cloud-based team collaboration tool, was used for everyday communication between teams and coaches and as a "virtual coffee machine" where information could be exchanged informally.

2 Cultural Diversity

At the closing of the summer school, each of the four teams presented a working VR prototype. Interestingly, all teams interpreted the book through their own lens. In Amsterdam, participants emphasised the neutral dimension of their virtual reality experience, leaving it up to the user to judge for themselves, while the NYC Medialab team for instance focussed on privacy and surveillance issues that played a role in the book. Each of the experiences allowed us to see how different cultural contexts think about the impact of technology on society in 2030 in their own way.

The VR summer school showed that there is cultural diversity in how designers understand, evaluate and shape the integration of digital technology in society. If we recognise that sustainable ways of dealing with digital technology involve diverse approaches and perspectives, intercultural dialogue becomes vital. Dialogue amongst cultures prevents design waste and provides a deeper base of knowledge toward solutions of today's societal problems. A dialogue is about collective thinking and inquiry, nicely summarised by Isaacs [3] as 'the art of thinking together'. This implies that participants recognise and respect differences, and are able to talk about them in constructive ways, both in face-to-face and online environments.

3 Demos

In this demo session, we will present the VR prototypes that were developed by our teams in Seoul, New York and Amsterdam.

Seoul

As the user enters she is presented with a beautiful calm scene. Flowers are blooming, calm music plays in the background, and the user can explore a nature filled world. Suddenly the scene changes and the user finds herself in the middle of a Blade Runner-like world with sky scrapers as high as the eye can see. The user can see citizens walking around the world. As she walks around, she notices that every citizen in the world has information about them above their heads, revealing intimate details about the person and their life.

Amsterdam

As the user enters the scene, she finds herself facing a dashboard. Through a video, the Artificial Intelligence system explains to the user her role to monitor the citizens and report any issues that she sees. Videos are shown to explain to the user what she is expected to do when other citizens that are not behaving appropriately. Next the user is thrust into an Amsterdam scene, where she can see citizens interacting within the world. As she moves around she can see an Amsterdam world of the early 1900's, a colorful world, with beautiful buildings, fresh air and with animated features and fountains. She can look around and see the world. The scene changes again and the citizen is now in the current world, a dark gray-like world, with tall buildings and faceless citizens.

New York City

This is composed of one scene only. As the user enters the scene, she finds herself facing a dashboard. Through a video, the Artificial Intelligence system explains to the user her role to monitor the citizens and report and issues that she sees. Detail videos explaining what the user must do in order to report the citizens are presented.

Acknowledgements. This project is partially funded by SiA RAAK – Nationaal Regieorgaan Praktijkgericht Onderzoek. Very special thanks to the amazing student teams and their coaches at the four summer school locations for developing the prototypes.

References

1. Hulst, A.: Slaap zacht, Johnny Idaho. Ambo/Anthos Uitgevers, Amsterdam (2015)
2. Vosmeer, M., Schouten, B.: Interactive cinema: engagement and interaction. In: Mitchell, A., Fernández-Vara, C., Thue, D. (eds.) ICIDS 2014. LNCS, vol. 8832, pp. 140–147. Springer, Cham (2014). https://doi.org/10.1007/978-3-319-12337-0_14
3. Isaacs, W.: Dialogue and the Art of Thinking Together: A Pioneering Approach to Communicating in Business and in Life. Random House, New York (1999)

Faoladh: A Case Study in Cinematic VR Storytelling and Production

Declan Dowling[1](✉), Colm O. Fearghail[2](✉), Aljosa Smolic[2](✉),
and Sebastian Knorr[2,3](✉)

[1] Tile Films Ltd, Dublin, Ireland
declan.t.dowling@gmail.com
[2] V-SENSE, School of Computer Science and Statistics,
Trinity College Dublin, The University of Dublin, Dublin, Ireland
{ofearghc,smolica}@scss.tcd.ie
[3] Communication Systems Group, Technical University of Berlin, Berlin, Germany
knorr@nue.tu-berlin.de

Abstract. Portraying traditional cinematic narratives in virtual reality (VR) is an emerging practice where often the methods normally associated with cinematic storytelling need to be adapted to the 360° format. In this paper we investigate some proposed cinematic practices for narrative storytelling in a cinematic VR film set in late 9th century Ireland that follows the perilous journey young Celt as he evades being captured by Viking raiders. From this we will analyze the fidelity of those practices with results collected from YouTube Analytics.

Keywords: 360-video · Virtual reality · Storytelling
Cinematography · YouTube Analytics

1 Introduction

In contrast to traditional cinema, where the viewer perceives the world through a window i.e. the cinema screen, cinematic VR allows a person to be present within the world by wearing a head-mounted display (HMD) [2]. This poses a new challenge for filmmakers as it necessitates the expansion of cinematic language to an immersive, border-less format. In this paper, we introduce a case study in cinematic VR storytelling and production for the VR film *Faoladh* [1]. We investigate some proposed cinematic practices for narrative storytelling in a cinematic VR film set in late 9th century Ireland that follows the perilous journey young Celt as he evades being captured by Viking raiders.

2 Adapting Cinematic Storytelling to VR

Four techniques that have traditionally formed the 'tools' that filmmakers rely on to tell their stories are: cinematography, sound, editing and mise-en-scene [3]. The expansion of these tools into VR, however, requires each to be re-evaluated.

© Springer Nature Switzerland AG 2018
R. Rouse et al. (Eds.): ICIDS 2018, LNCS 11318, pp. 359–362, 2018.
https://doi.org/10.1007/978-3-030-04028-4_42

Modern cinematography often uses as combination of light, movement, angles and focus to tell a story. With VR the viewer takes control of the camera and can look in any direction so angles become less effective narrative devices while camera position and movement become more critical to the viewers perception and level of comfort. A popular method for focusing viewer attention in traditional cinema is depth of field (DOF) which can draw attention to aspects of the scene in relation to its distance from the camera. VR cameras like the Google Odyssey used in this production, often rely on small sensor arrays with little to no DOF. Although it is possible to simulate DOF in post production via stereoscopic disparity, without the frame of the cinema screen it is a much less effective tool for focusing viewer attention in VR.

Spatial audio can be an effective tool to guide the viewer to another area of the scene as are directional cues by the actors present within, but VR also poses technical challenges in terms of staging and performance due to restrictions in editing. Quick cuts can disorient the viewer necessitating longer takes which results in staging and performances more closely aligned to traditional theater and deep focus cinematography which became quite popular in the 1940s with films such as Orson Welles Citizen Kane.

3   Deep Focus Staging

In Figs. 1 and 2 we see a staging plan and the resulting shot from a pivotal scene where the hero stares directly towards the dramatic death of the monk stage right, while a line is drawn from the villains arrow towards the hero leaving only a single prop the user can interact with to block its path. The objective is to draw the viewers attention from the hero > drama > threat > resolution.

Fig. 1. Staging plan

In Fig. 2 a heatmap collected from over 200 viewers is additionally overlaid to the shot, which shows a focus on the threat and solution with little attention is given to the hero or drama. From this we can conclude that the position of

Fig. 2. A YouTube Analytics heatmap collected from over 200 viewers

the camera, its proximity to the hero and the fact we can't see his face creates a narrative cue similar to a traditional over shoulder or 3rd person perspective where the viewer will look in the direction the hero is facing as opposed to at the hero.

4 Narrative Pacing

Filmed at the Irish National Heritage Park, a three-act story was built around each of the parks main locations. To reduce cuts and mitigate audience fatigue, a continuous path was plotted with intermediate rest stops throughout (see shoot plan in Fig. 3).

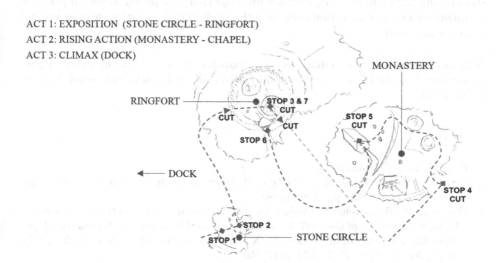

Fig. 3. Shoot plan at the Irish National Heritage Park

A YouTube Analytics chart of relative audience retention (see Fig. 4) shows audience interest peaks at 3:27 which corresponds with the scene from section 3 but is shortly followed by a dip in retention which coincides with a lull in the rising action portion of the film at 3:55 (see Stop 5 in Fig. 3).

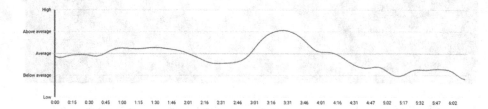

Fig. 4. YouTube Analytics chart of relative audience retention

Relative audience retention shows a YouTube video's ability to retain viewers during playback by comparing it to all YouTube videos of similar length. When the graph is higher, it indicates how many more viewers kept watching the video for that timeframe compared to the same timeframe in other YouTube videos[1].

5   Conclusion

Giving the audience the ability to look in any direction and accompanying this with a perceived sense of presence can cause underlying narrative cues such as the 3rd person effect or a lull in pacing to disrupt narrative flow and interrupt storytelling in cinematic VR. Further investigation is required to list all possible adaptations of cinematic practices and the underlying narrative devices virtual reality can reveal.

Acknowledgment. This publication has emanated from research supported in part by a research grant from Science Foundation Ireland (SFI) under the Grant Number 15/RP/2776.

References

1. Faoladh. http://faoladh.net/
2. Smith, S., Marsh, T., Duke, D., Wright, P.: Drowning in immersion. In: Proceedings of UK-VRSIG, vol. 98, pp. 1–9 (1998)
3. Vosmeer, M., Schouten, B.: Project Orpheus a research study into 360° cinematic VR. In: Proceedings of the 2017 ACM International Conference on Interactive Experiences for TV and Online Video, TVX 2017. pp. 85–90. ACM, New York (2017). https://doi.org/10.1145/3077548.3077559

---

[1] https://support.google.com/youtube/answer/1715160.

Cinematic VR as a Reflexive Tool for Critical Empathy

Sojung Bahng[✉]

Sensilab, Faculty of Information Technology,
Monash University, Melbourne, Australia
sojung.bahng@monash.edu

Abstract. This practice-based research aims to develop cinematic VR as a reflexive device for exploring critical empathy. Critical empathy is a concept that emphasizes the limitations and complications of empathy from reflexive perspectives. Many artists and filmmakers have become increasingly interested in using VR as a creative medium for evoking empathy. However, the complexity of the empathic process in reflexive contexts has not been considered sufficiently. Current cinematic VR is focused on creating an immersive illusion to induce a sense of presence or embodied experience rather than eliciting reflection. Although VR technologies have been developing rapidly, there are obvious gaps between physical reality and virtual reality in terms of embodiment and bodily presence. Those gaps do not necessarily need to be erased to create immersive illusions; rather, they can be used effectively as a new method of storytelling and as aesthetic techniques for promoting self and social reflection. The practical exploration of the creation of a new method of immersive storytelling could add substantive insight to understanding cinematic VR, which can be seen as a reflexive device as well as a sociocultural tool for critical empathy.

Keywords: Virtual reality · Cinematic VR · Critical empathy
Immersive storytelling · Reflexivity

1 Introduction

Virtual reality (VR) offers a distinctive, fully immersive and personalized experience. Its characteristic first-person view enables the audience to embody themselves with virtual characters or situations, making them feel as if they are present within an environment [1]. Many artists and filmmakers have tried to create artworks or films that provoke empathic experiences through VR technologies. American entrepreneur and artist Chris Milk proclaimed at a TED conference in 2015 that the ultimate future of VR is to make an empathy machine [2]. However, thinking of VR as empathy machine makes simple assumptions regarding degrees of embodiment and presence leading directly to the quality of the empathetic experience [3].

Empathy is generally understood as the capacity to feel or share another person's emotions [4]. If one literally tries to see the world of another thorough one's own eyes, then one needs to keep both self- and other-centered perspectives simultaneously.

© Springer Nature Switzerland AG 2018
R. Rouse et al. (Eds.): ICIDS 2018, LNCS 11318, pp. 363–366, 2018.
https://doi.org/10.1007/978-3-030-04028-4_43

The process of empathy requires knowledge of oneself and the ongoing critical awareness and reflection of that knowledge [5]. *Critical empathy* is a concept that emphasizes the complexity of the empathic process in reflexive contexts. Critical empathy is not only the process of imaging another person's point of view or emotional state but also being aware of the limitations and complications of empathy [6].

Current cinematic VR is focused on creating an immersive illusion rather than provoking awareness and reflection, but cinematic VR can also be seen as a way to create reflexive contexts. Although VR technologies have been developing rapidly, there are obvious limitations that make complete immersion difficult in a virtual world. The challenge comes from the technical limitations of current VR technologies, but it also comes from the fundamental gap between physical reality and virtual reality. This gap does not need to be erased to create immersive illusions; rather, it can be used effectively as a new method of storytelling and as motivation for exploring aesthetic techniques that encourage self and social reflection. The practical exploration of new storytelling methods and unconventional aesthetic techniques can provide substantive insight into the development of cinematic VR. The aim of my practice-based research is to explore the use of cinematic VR as an artistic medium and reflexive device for critical empathy.

2   Conceptual Framework

Marie-Laure Ryan argued that the fundamental natures of immersion and interactivity are contradictory. She said that reconciliation of immersion and interactivity requires the presence of a participant's body in VR, so the language of interaction should become a gesture, and any-reflexive dimensions should be erased so as not to destroy the illusion or sense of presence [7]. I agree that effective coexistence with immersion and interactivity in VR is related to the sense of the body. However, I argue that the reflexive dimension should not be removed and that certain factors of alienation from the virtual world can be used as storytelling methods for promoting critical awareness or reflection. This closely relates to the Brechtian concept of alienation effects, which break the illusion of drama and increase audience self-awareness and reflexivity [8].

In my practice-based research, I aim to manipulate the different levels of immersion and interactivity that create empathic engagement to affect the reflexive dimensions of storytelling. I want to employ bodily presence and embodiment as tools to induce empathic identification or projection, and exploit the gaps between physical reality and virtual reality as tools for prompting critical awareness and reflection.

This use of immersion is based on the interpretations of Slater and Wilbur. They defined immersion in VR as a quantifiable factor of a technology and described immersion as being inclusive, extensive, surrounding, and vivid. Matching is also a significant element of immersion, which is the correspondence between the participant's body movement and the information generated by the system [9]. The interactivity of VR is generally understood as user's power to modify the environment [10]. In a 360° movie, interactivity is defined as looking around and exploring an interactive sequence within the 360° environment [2]. Further to this we can consider interactivity as the degree to which an audience can navigate in and affect an environment.

Applying different levels of immersion and interactivity relates to inducing the different senses of embodiment and presence. However, exploring different methods of manipulating immersion and interactivity also creates "gaps" between virtual and physical reality, which can be used as storytelling methods or aesthetic techniques for inducing reflexive dimensions.

3 My Cinematic VR Projects

Based on the conceptual framework, I propose the creation of three cinematic VR projects using different levels of interaction and immersion in each project to develop a better understanding of storytelling for critical empathy. All the works will address issues of alienation, disconnection, and loneliness, which can ultimately lead to deeper understandings of critical empathy. The first work is *Floating Walk – Gangnam Kangaroo,* a 360° video that uses low-level immersive and interactive technology. This work is already completed.

Floating Walk – Gangnam Kangaroo is a cinematic essay about myself as a young Korean woman living in Australia. I go on a journey of self-confrontation to the root of my unclear but painful emotion and discover that historical traumas have affected my identity. To create effective immersive storytelling for this work, the factors of immersion, interactivity and narrative are used as follows:

- Immersion: The mobile-based monoscopic HD 360° video was used for this work, so its vividness is considered quite low. Matching is very limited since the audience is not permitted to move around.
- Interactivity: The audience can only look around in the panoramic world.

I used readily available and limited immersive and interactive technologies to deliver my personal story. Since I only used a portable small camera (Ricoh-Theta S), I could bring it anywhere and film anytime. Due to this, I could capture very intimate and private scenes since people rarely noticed the existence of my camera.

The medium of 360° video and the level of immersion and interactivity were well aligned with my artistic intentions. I invited the audience to participate in exploring virtual and floating identities. In VR, audience members can embody the spaces of two different countries, but they are positioned as floating selves in the physical and the virtual spaces. Although they are in a virtual space with me, they cannot modify the situation or environment. These limitations aim to support the process of questioning identity and for participants to critically reflect on their own identity while in the virtual world.

To support the sense of alienation and defamiliarization, I often composited together a half-Melbourne and half-Seoul environment, prompting the audience to question where they are located. The camera was not deliberately removed from view in order to remind the audience that they are not physically part of the virtual world; I even intentionally revealed the camera while I asked questions about self-perception and identity.

The second project is *Anonymous.* This is currently a work in progress. For this project, I am using real-time 3D graphics combined with gaze interaction. The story introduces an old man who lives alone in a small room. Participants wearing an HMD can observe his solitary daily activities, such as eating and watching TV. The environment and character are created with cardboard texture; the audience senses they are in a cardboard box. The audience's role is that of the character's dead wife, whose soul lingers in physical objects in the room. Their visual perspective is that of a portrait of his dead wife hanging on the wall. Additionally, participants can 'inhabit' other objects by gazing at them, and thus observe the man's life from different perspectives.

When the audience takes the role of the physical embodiment of the dead wife's soul, they can phenomenologically experience a position and situation of alienation and disembodiment from their lives. The unfamiliar and poetic experiences of loneliness and death might lead to empathizing with the old man in this work but also critically reflecting on their lives and deaths from the perspective of an alienated person.

4   Future Steps

I will complete *Anonymous* first, then I will start to create the third project that applies a higher level of immersion and interactivity. I will create a navigable, immersive environment with gesture-based interaction. The project will be related to the issues of narcolepsy and depression. Making creative works and building the theoretical framework will be a dialectical and iterative process.

References

1. Vosmeer, M., Schouten, B.: Interactive cinema: engagement and interaction. In: Mitchell, A., Fernández-Vara, C., Thue, D. (eds.) ICIDS 2014. LNCS, vol. 8832, pp. 140–147. Springer, Cham (2014). https://doi.org/10.1007/978-3-319-12337-0_14
2. How Virtual Reality Can Create the Ultimate Empathy Machine (2015). https://www.ted.com/talks/chris_milk_how_virtual_reality_can_create_the_ultimate_empathy_machine
3. Sutherland, E.A.: No, VR Doesn't Create Empathy. Here's Why (2017). https://www.buzzfeednews.com/article/ainsleysutherland/how-big-tech-helped-create-the-myth-of-the-virtual-reality#.kpVplqqq4
4. Kunyk, D., Olson, J.K.: Clarification of conceptualizations of empathy. J. Adv. Nurs. 35(3), 317–325 (2001)
5. Leake, E.: The (Un) knowable Self and Others: Critical Empathy and Expressivism. Critical Expressivism: Theory and Practice in the Composition Classroom, pp. 149–160 (2015)
6. DeStigter, T.: Public displays of affection: political community through critical empathy. Res. Teach. Engl. 33(3), 235–244 (1999)
7. Ryan, M.L.: Narrative as Virtual Reality 2: Revisiting Immersion and Interactivity in Literature and Electronic Media, vol. 2. JHU Press, Baltimore (2015)
8. Brecht, B.: Brecht on Theatre. Bloomsbury Publishing, London (2014)
9. Slater, M., Wilbur, S.: A framework for immersive virtual environments (FIVE): speculations on the role of presence in virtual environments. Presence Teleop. Virtual Environ. 6(6), 603–616 (1997)
10. Ryan, M.L.: Immersion vs interactivity virtual reality and literary theory. SubStance 28(2), 110–137 (1999)

Practices in Theater and Performance

Partners: Human and Nonhuman Performers and Interactive Narrative in Postdigital Theater

Rebecca Rouse[⊠]

Rensselaer Polytechnic Institute, Troy, NY 12180, USA
`rouser@rpi.edu`

Abstract. Media performance scholarship has largely not engaged with innovative work in the incorporation of technology in mainstream theater, pursuing instead a nearly exclusive focus on non-narrative works of media performance such as electronic music, dance, and installation art. This article provides a corrective to this absence, and highlights creative work from the 19th century onward with technologies in service of interactive storytelling in theater. Cornerstone concepts in the media performance field are examined, as well as possible anxieties behind the relative exclusion of narrative theater from the field. The concept of partnership is put forth as a way of understanding human and non-human performer relationships in postdigital culture, and a call for collaboration across disciplines including interactive narrative, games, electronic literature, artificial intelligence, and architecture is discussed. The practice-theory divide is bridged with a closing discussion of the author's work in creative practice in the field.

Keywords: Theater · Postdigital · Interactive narrative · Non-Human

1 Performance in Postdigital Culture

1.1 Entering Real-Time

We have entered the era of "real-time" media. What will this mean for storytelling in media that have always been real-time, such as theater, for example? Canned media, which must progress in one predefined direction only and contain only one expression or outcome are children of the early 20th century, while real-time, responsive, or playable media have emerged as the dominant offspring of the early 21st century. At a recent professional development seminar held Epic Games to promote its Unreal 4 game engine, it was emphasized proudly, over and over, that rendering was no longer required in the game engine, everything was real-time. This rhetoric of speed and transparency neatly compliments the current cultural obsessions with reality media, such as virtual and augmented reality, and even reality tv.

In the culture of real-time media, we have often been described as postdigital [1–4]. This term has had shifting meanings over time and across disciplines since at least the early 2000's including computer music, art and aesthetics, museum studies, games and cultural heritage. Performance studies scholar Matthew Causey has argued for a definition

© Springer Nature Switzerland AG 2018
R. Rouse et al. (Eds.): ICIDS 2018, LNCS 11318, pp. 369–382, 2018.
https://doi.org/10.1007/978-3-030-04028-4_44

of postdigital performance focused on resistance to the digital, claiming that postdigital performance works "can be understood as *thinking digitally*, embodying an activist strategy of critique within and against postdigital culture's various ideological and economic strategies of control, alienation, and self-commodification" [5; p. 432]. This perspective feels too narrow to me (and perhaps too optimistic in terms of 'resistance,' a point I will return to later) given one hallmark of the postdigital as a time of breaking down traditional or modernist boundaries between human/other, official/amateur, producer/consumer, high culture/kitsch, etc.

The postdigital is not only destructive, but is also generative of new ways of seeing, speaking, listening, and acting—all of which we are still in the process of theorizing and understanding. What is clear is that our world has fundamentally changed; even Walter Benjamin's auratic, unmediated mountaintop from 1935 no longer exists: "If, while resting on a summer afternoon, you follow with your eyes a mountain range on the horizon or a branch which casts its shadow over you, you experience the aura of those mountains, of that branch" [6]. That vista is long gone, not only because of environmental threats and overdevelopment, but also because of the collective cultural consciousness focused on capturing vistas for display on Instagram. Like the perceptual shifts described in Erwin Panofsky's *Perspective as Symbolic Form* [7] and John Berger's *Ways of Seeing* [8], we are becoming postdigital in how we see and interpret reality and images as well.

Theater scholar and artist Mark Sussman's examination of the history of techno-magic on stage and how human-machine relations have been understood through time is helpful in grounding this discussion [9]. Sussman refers to the 1748 La Mettrie's influential phrase *l'homme machine* as a core concept for the 18th century lens of understanding the human body as a machine, or body as automaton [10]. Sussman then describes the shift in understanding in the 19th century, towards anthropomorphized machines (as opposed to mechanized humans). A recent contribution from Ashley Ferro-Murray and Timothy Murray traces technological integration in performance across a series of phases, outlined as "the mechanical age, the televisual age, and the age of the Internet" [11]. This analysis is helpful in delineating large-scale shift related to technology in performance. Building on Ferro-Murray and Murray's work, and Sussman's analysis, we might describe the 20th century human-machine relationship as "extensions of man," to cite Marshal McLuhan's work [12], and then later in the 20th century, we might focus on a tighter coupling represented by the cyborg figure, written about so influentially by Donna Haraway [13]. Haraway again, presciently, provides a concept for understanding the human-machine relationship in our own early 21st century as a de-centered, hybrid, reciprocal partnership, in which she suggests our blended bio-mechanical-digital offspring might be regarded as "oddkin" [14]. It is this characterization of the subjectivities inhabiting the postdigital (human and non-human oddkin) that I find productive for rethinking human and non-human performer relationships on stage.

1.2   Liveness in Real-Time

One of the most influential 20th century scholarly conversations about the relationship between technology and performance is often referred to as 'the liveness debate.' Now that we have a much wider array of technologies in play in performance, beyond canned or linear media, how should we understand this line of thought, which has had major influence on the trajectory of the field? The liveness debate refers primarily to two works: Peggy Phelan's 1993 publication *Unmarked: The Politics of Performance* [15] and Philip Auslander's 1999 book *Liveness: Performance in a Mediatized Culture* [16], which was in part written as a response to Phelan's publication. While many scholars have weighed in during the intervening years, continually putting these two works in conversation with one another as a way of demarcating boundaries of the field, it is helpful to revisit the two works to note a commonality in their work that often goes unremarked upon: both sides of this debate conceptualize digital technology as an anti-theatrical force, and performance as a whole is conceptualized in both cases as somehow essentially mismatched with technology. Neither Phelan's nor Auslander's viewpoint serves to support innovative practice with digital technology in traditional theater, because of the oppositional way in which technology and theater are positioned. This is significant, because these two works have served as a cornerstone for digital performance technology in the intervening decades, and their influence continues to resonate powerfully. It is also worth noting that while other theorists have placed these two works in direct conversation with one another, Phelan and Auslander each write from very different perspectives and with different aims. This difference should be highlighted, in order to make clear the ways in which the two works talk past one another.

Auslander's writing centers on an economic model, which emphasizes the pervasive, unavoidable nature of late capitalism. His argument hinges on the belief that it is no longer possible to avoid entanglement with dominant culture, which he defines as mediatized, because capitalism controls all aspects of production and reception. He emphasizes this as a corrective to Phelan's work, which seeks to define the ontology of performance as one of resistance against dominant ideologies. It must be pointed out, that as astute as Auslander's critique may be of Phelan's work, he offers no alternative solutions. Again, this is because on a fundamental level, he is engaged in a different project.

Phelan writes from a cultural studies perspective, developing interpretations of many types of performances with the aim of carving out the possibility of an oppositional stance within dominant culture. Phelan is explicitly not interested in theater, however, which she characterizes as an oppressive part of dominant consumer culture which reifies the scopophilic, male gaze discussed so famously in Laura Mulvey's essay on Hollywood film [17]. None of Phelan's performance examples come from mainstream theater. Instead, Phelan analyzes performative works from Adrian Piper, Robert Mapplethorpe, Cindy Sherman, the Guerrilla Girls, a reproductive rights group, and others. While Auslander does discuss some examples of mainstream or commercial theater, only lackluster and disappointing examples are brought forward, to reinforce his thesis that media has "dominated" theater and degraded the stage as a space of creativity. Following up on Auslander's argument that media is poised to kill theater, roughly twenty years later today, we might expect to find all traces of theater stamped out in the wake of the highly advanced automated show control technologies available. And yet, the monster lives! Theater's Frankenstein-like capability to combine and absorb components, conventions, and techniques from other cultural arenas allows it to rise from the (oft proclaimed) ashes, again and again.

Indeed, these highly advanced automated show control technologies are in use across many genres of performance today—not only the Broadway touring shows that Auslander so disparages, but also in what are referred to as avant-garde or experimental performances, such as Andrew Schneider's *After* [18]. These performances carry on a long tradition of precise actor-machine synchronicity, dating back at least to Josef Svoboda's *Laterna Magika* performance experiments at the Brussels'58 Expo [19]. These works are spectacles of system automation, incorporating human as cyborg or cog-in-the-machine, and can be beautiful and interesting in their own right. While the remainder of this paper will focus on performances incorporating real-time or responsive technologies, and not canned or linear media systems, this focus is not meant as a denigration of other types of work and approaches; there is room on the stage for everyone. In fact, as noted in Jay David Bolter's keynote address at ISEA'11, *The Digital Plenitude and the End of Art* [20], this type of non-hierarchical cultural plethora is one of the hallmarks of the postdigital.

It must be acknowledged, there is a long history of debating what theater is for, or what it should do. In broad terms, the most ancient roots of theater might be found in ritual, religious ceremony, and liturgical drama—all meant to solidify social power structures, guide cultural norms, and soothe anxieties about the hereafter [21, 22]. Court theater might be understood as functioning to reify the greatness of the monarch and justify claims to power, while enlightenment theater educated a new middle class how to think, behave, and maintain power structures in the new economic order. The contemporary genre of performance referred to by many names including media performance, digital theater, virtual theater, and digital dramaturgy is at least in part a reaction against the new postdigital cultural order (or disorder) and functions to maintain a power structure focused around mostly white, male academics and artists working to preserve a so-called avant-garde, which is privileged by the Art (capital A as in High Art) market. One of the ways in which this boundary maintenance takes place is the relative invisibility of folk or popular forms in the study of digital performance. This leads to the question: what are the real anxieties in postdigital performance? Semiotic slippages between the human, animal and machine? Or a sense of erosion between High Art, scholarship, and the (already) encroaching postdigital plethora?

In Defense of Story. An excellent recent contribution to the field, Bay-Cheng, Parker-Starbuck, and Saltz's coauthored "Performance and Media: Taxonomies for a Changing Field" [23] provides a brilliant overview of the scholarship in media and performance over the past several decades. The summary, besides being a valuable tool as a guide to the field, makes clear a glaring omission: the field has avoided text-based, mainstream theater. That is, the field has neither focused on examples of traditional, script-based narrative theater as objects of study, and has likewise (or perhaps due to this neglect) not identified narrative, story, or playwright as significant components in the multitude of frameworks, lenses, and taxonomies that have been developed. An early work in the field first published in German in 1999 and only later translated to English in 2006, Hans-Thies Lehmann's *Postdramatic Theater* [24] concluded that computational media had unseated the primacy of text—meaning story and script—in theatre for the 20th century. It seems this assertion was met with near unanimous agreement in the scholarship that followed. David Barnett's work stands as a notable exception [25]. In addition to this neglect of mainstream theater by the bulk of media performance scholarship, work on puppetry and mask has been for the most part treated separately as well. As John Bell has noted "[...] puppets, masks, and objects have always had a strong connection to folk theatre, popular theatre, and religion, but (or perhaps consequently) they have rarely been subjects of sustained systematic academic attention in this century" [26, p. 15]. What a missed opportunity, not having the scholarship on digital technologies (and mostly screen technologies) in conversation with this significant legacy of technology in performance; the history of performing objects.

The lack of scholarship on technology in mainstream plays impoverishes the larger field, and cuts off theater as an acknowledged site of potential and ongoing innovation. Instead, media performance scholarship has focused on a particular avant-garde, which we must acknowledge is not really new, stemming directly from early 20th century modernism such as Oskar Schlemmer's *Kunstfiguren*, and now must be considered a solidified tradition and not experimental work. While the contemporary work has taken an aggressively anti-narrative tone, it's interesting to note that predecessor Schlemmer had always intended to later re-incorporate narrative into his work. He had identified narrative as a particularly complex, difficult element, and due to his constructivist, medium-centrist approach, began his performance experiments working with the most basic elements: "We confess that up to now we have cautiously avoided experimenting with this element of language, not in order to de-emphasize it, but conscious of its significance, to master it slowly" [27, p. 91]. Unfortunately, Schlemmer was never able to carry his work forward to the point of reintroducing narrative, as the second world war cut his career short.

The contemporary anti-narrative approach in this tradition comes at a high cost particularly in terms of accessibility, meaning the works produced often require highly specialized literacies to access, and are most often created by and for privileged white male audiences. Yet, this genre of work often claims for itself an attitude of resistance —against *what* is not always clear, yet is often assumed to be capitalism. This avant-garde and it's accompanying scholarship positions more accessible, popular work as 'commercial'—a distinction which is somewhat disingenuous given these avant-garde performances and venues also charge admission, and some are quite expensive to access such as international biennales, high tech venues such as ZKM, BAM, EMPAC, Banff, and international festivals such as the fringe festivals.

In addition, the media upon which the media performance field is built has complicity always already designed into the system - from the deplorable late capitalist material conditions of production of the technology, to the media archeology of these technologies as military training and simulation systems. The farther back one looks, the more dubious the claim of 'resistance' becomes. Langdon Winner has famously critiqued the view of technology as apolitical in his landmark essay *Do Artifacts Have Politics?* [28], debunking the myth that technologies can be separated from use, emphasizing their entanglement in non-neutral forces from the moment of conception. So while this avant-garde tradition of media performance work certainly should be studied, it should not be the *only* genre studied within the purview of media and performance scholarship, to the exclusion of others. As early as the 1920s, a group of scholars were calling for attention to be paid to popular forms. Semiotician and linguist Pyotr Bogatyev's 1923 study of the Czech puppetry tradition makes a powerful argument for "the study of folk theatre [...] as it is not a fragment of the past or an artistic relic [...] folk drama lives and evolves together with the people, reflecting their own most pressing needs and everyday poetics" [29, p. 101]. This argument can be extended to make a case for why we must include commercial, mainstream, or community theater today as objects worthy of study in postdigital performance.

These popular forms of theater are still highly narrative, resisting Lehmann's and others' claims that we are postdramatic as a culture. While some scholars may refer to these works as throwbacks, outmoded, or passé, the fact remains these works enjoy a sizable audience, and this is the type of theater most people in America encounter today, from elementary school plays to touring Broadway productions, to much of college-level theater education. The theater that starts with a play script and tells a story to an audience is far from dead, and our cultural interest in story at large continues unabated. There is great political power in story today, meaning today is not the moment to ignore story or take an anti-narrative stance. We live in what might be a golden age of story, when a good story, repeated again and again, is taken for fact. That, of course, is propaganda, which may be best refuted by offering alternative storylines. Luckily there are brilliant playwrights today, and from decades and centuries before us, who have penned plays (yes, stories) that continue to resist dominant power structures and oppression, and remain relevant today. For just one example among many, Max Wellman's *Sincerity Forever* [30] comes to mind. Published in 1990, at a contentious moment in the culture wars we once again find raging at a fever pitch, the play opens with this scene, which remains chillingly relevant:

Scene One
A beautiful summer's night in the outskirts of Hillsbottom. Two girls sit in a parked car talking about things. Both are dressed in Ku Klux Klan garb.
JUDY: Molly, do you know why God created the world they way he did? So complicated, I mean?
(Pause.)
MOLLY: Nope.
JUDY: Because I've been thinking about it, and I just get more and more puzzled.
MOLLY: So do I.
JUDY: Because if there is a divine plan it sure doesn't look it, very divine, that is. Or planlike. It looks kinda like a mess.

Wellman goes on to bring us into a (not so) strange world in which KKK members openly share their views, an African-American woman is Jesus, and mystic alien furballs have overrun the earth. Beyond the clear need for stories like these in our current fractured, frictional political state, it is a missed opportunity to find the discussion of storytelling and narrative mostly absent from the scholarship on digital performance, as other fields continue to engage deeply with narrative (such as interactive fiction, games, and artificial intelligence). These fields could use shared expertise on what makes storytelling effective across different aims, and could in turn share new ideas about storytelling with postdigital playwrights.

2 The Postdigital Playwright

What does the postdigital offer the playwright? The playwright creates a script to facilitate action and response, hence the need for stage directions. Reflecting the plasticity of the stage, stage directions can range from pedestrian to fantastical, to the practically lyric [31]. The playwright writes for multiple readers, all of whom are active readers: the director, designers, crew, cast, and audience. Theater (yes, scripted plays) are *by nature* interactive. The play comes into being through enactment by the actors or players. The play script is, and has always been, an interactive text. And, for much of theater history, the audience was overtly interactive as well. The convention of a silent, apparently passive, internally interpretive audience as a necessary part of scripted theater is a more recent development. As Richard Butsch reminds us in his excellent study on the development of American audiences, spectators were active until "the Jacksonian era in the 1830s and 1840s, the upper classes grew to fear such working class sovereignty [...] Elites labeled exercises in audience sovereignty as rowdyism, [...] redefining it as poor manners rather than an exercise of audience rights" [32, p. 5].

Pushing back against this relatively new form of passivity, the early 20th century avant-garde began a focus on reclaiming the inclusion of the audience member in the performance. This inclusion of the audience member as performer continued, reaching a high point with late midcentury environmental theatre, and creative works such as Allan Kaprow's happenings and Lee Breuer's *The Gospel at Colonus*. Given the current craze for interactivity, however, we must remember that just because something is participatory or interactive, it is not necessarily good. Today, sometimes this move to include the audience is done in an authoritarian manner, such as Ant Hampton's *The Extra People*, in which audience members are ordered around the performance space for an hour with no explanation, via individual instructions delivered through iPod headphones [33]. Sometimes audience participation is a shallow move that includes no dramaturgical impact, as in the audiences' navigation of the complex multiscreen but ultimately meaningless performance space in Peter Stamer, Jörg Laue, and Alain Franco's *26 Letters to Deleuze* [34]. Sometimes, however, audience participation is exciting, and lends meaningful intimacy to a story experience, as in the second act of Maria Irene Fornes' *Fefu and Her Friends*, when the audience enters the set of the main character's home, to take part in a set of three scenes in close quarters with the performers [35].

While focused on exploring the interaction between performer and audience member, the avant-garde may have overlooked another form of interactivity that is equally fascinating and generative—the interaction between performers, human and non-human. Interactivity can be participated in, but it can also be a spectator sport. Sport, in fact, is partly defined by people watching others interact. Brecht himself wrote on the connections between sport and theater [36], concluding theater could gain from incorporating some of the real-time uncertainty of sport (perhaps now more possible given our real-time technologies). And of course today we have eSports, where spectators watch others play videogames, and theater is still with us in the traditional spectatorial form, with an audience seated watching others, who like gamers are also referred to as players.

2.1 Postdigital Performers: Human and Non-human Partners

What does it mean for dramatic narrative text to introduce technological interactivity in partnership with human performers? Do narrative play structures need to change? Or, is it the case that plays are always interactive already, and the stage is an extremely plastic environment - even more plastic than the page, making traditional theater an ideal laboratory for experimentation in postdigital performance. Building on his earlier work on a taxonomy for digital theater, David Z. Saltz identifies in a more recent iteration of his work "five functions that media can play in relation to the live performer's actions: scene, prop, actor, costume, and mirror" [37, p. 97]. Media as actor is of particular interest given real-time technologies' capabilities for responsivity. The response is a defining characteristic of the modern actor, with most modern theories of actor training, from Stanislavsky to Grotowski and beyond focusing on developing responsiveness as a valued skill. Saltz defines media-as-actor as "[related to] by the performer as an autonomous agent, a subject in its own right, with sentience and volition. [...] The relationship between the live performer and the virtual actor here is not instrumental, as it is with a virtual prop, but *responsive*" [37, p. 100]. Thus the media-as-actor is characterized by responsiveness, or at least, the illusion of responsiveness.

For the postdigital era it may be more interesting to focus on this interaction between human and non-human performers, instead of a modernist focus on the interaction between performers and audience. The media-as-actor might be conceived of today as a *partner,* as opposed to more limited conceptions of media as *alien* (a threatening force to be kept out of theater - such as Auslander and Phelan both describe), as *servant* (who does what the human master commands and remains invisible), or as *tool* (which is visible but inert, and understood as malleable or neutral). In many scenarios, we often ask, How did the technology perform? Given this new perspective on media-as-actor as postdigtial partner, we might begin to ask instead, How did the technology play? How playful was it? How expressive? Was it a generous partner? Performance scholar Matthew O'Hare has cited generosity as an important component in performance partnerships with technology, based on his research in actor training methods [38]. The possibility emerges that real-time media can afford us increasingly generous partnerships.

In understanding this responsive, potentially generous partnership between human and non-human performers on the postdigital stage, looking to research on puppetry and performing objects may be helpful. Steve Tillis' category of the 'media figure' is defined as a "figure whose performance is made possible through technological mediation [39 p. 182]. Tillis includes CGI, stop motion animation, motion capture animation, animatronic figures, and figures in cel animation in this group. Tillis notes that similar to puppets, the media figure most often excels in a non-naturalistic role, meaning the media figure (at least at this point in time) poses no threat in terms of a replacement for human performers. Instead, we might think of these media figures as our partners, as messy human-machine collaborations, or as Haraway's oddkin.

Stephen Kaplin's "Puppet Tree" taxonomy for organizing thinking around performing objects based on the physical distance from the human body is very useful [40], and by reframing this perspective slightly, shifting the focus away from the human body and to the space between the human and non-human bodies or entities, and to the qualitative nature of these collaborative relationships, this taxonomy becomes useful for understanding the postdigital stage. While focusing on the material distance between human body and performing object is important for understanding some of the core material constraints and affordances of particular object, this literal distance is just one important quality among many that describe the human-non-human performer relationship. By shifting the frame of reference away from the human, and de-centering the human, we might instead focus on the qualitative and reciprocal nature of the relationship between non-human and human performers, focusing on qualities such as responsivity, generosity, playfulness, and creativity in terms of how we discuss and value these collaborations.

In addition, we could expand the range of Kaplin's taxonomy to also include things at much larger scale in which bodies and objects interact, such as the performance environment. In terms of environment, I refer not only to the set or backdrop for the performance, but also the larger structure such as a theatre building or performance venue. It is a common saying in theatre that 'the set directs the play;' a comment that recognizes the power of space in storytelling, but of course the theatre building also to some degree determines what is possible for the set. With the advent of robotic architecture, or the incorporation of responsive, live technologies into building practices as described by Weller and Do [41] we may have an opportunity in our postdigital era to revisit some of the tantalizing but unbuilt collaborations between architects and theatre directors, such as Walter Gropius and Erwin Piscator's *Total Theatre* from 1927 [42], and Cecil Price and Joan Littlewood's *Fun Palace* from 1968 [43]. Space should not be overlooked as a potential generative, creative non-human performing partner.

3   Postdigital Theater Histories and Contemporary Practices

The postdigital does not define a break from the past so much as continuations along multiple trajectories in a simultaneous, de-centered fashion. Focusing on narrative script-based theater and histories of human and non-human performance partnerships, including responsive spaces, we find many inspiring examples to draw from. Early works, of course, incorporate linear media, meaning the responsiveness of the media partner is a tightly rehearsed illusion. However, as mentioned above, this type of work continues today, and so cannot be conveniently ascribed to a set of technologies or time period. While this particular trajectory at large has not been highlighted by media performance scholars, and much work remains to be done in the excavation of this history, I share here an initial, incomplete set of examples, listed in chronological order. In each case I share references to more detailed information about the production:

- 1840s - 1850s: John Banvard performs proto-documentary style narratives live in front of scrolling panoramic paintings of the Mississippi River. With paintings scrolling in real-time to represent the actual speed of a journey down the river, the performances lasted several hours [44]. These performances tour around the world, and influence advanced moving panorama attractions around the turn of the century [45].

- 1898: Lincoln J. Carter's play *Chattanooga* includes simulated interaction between on-stage performers and filmed train action, projected at the back of the stage [46].
- 1907: Horace Goldin's magic act opens with a film showing him riding up to the theatre in a taxi, then physically entering the stage, followed by a simulated interaction between himself on stage and the cab driver projected on film [47].
- 1914: Winsor McCay's vaudeville act *Gertie the Dinosaur* builds on his experience as a 'chalk talk' vaudeville performer and early animator. The performance includes tightly rehearsed simulated interaction between McCay on stage and the projected dinosaur, including the illusion of McCay becoming transferred to the animated world at the end of the act [48].
- 1927-1931: Erwin Piscator directs multiple productions with innovative uses of film on stage, including most notably *Hoopla, Wir Leben!* and *Rasputin* (1927). The production of *Hoopla!* includes a multi-story set on a turntable, mounted with multiple projection surfaces, and incorporates film imagery not only as scenery but with expressionist effects, and to display animated text translations of morse code communications between performers [49]. Rasputin is performed on a set that also has multiple projection surfaces, constructed in a globe or shell-like shape, all mounted on a rotating turntable, and covered with reflective projection material [50]. Piscator also develops accompanying theoretical work, parsing the multiple dramaturgical functions of film on stage as didactic, dramatic, and as commentary [51].
- 1948-2002: Scenographer Josef Svoboda's long and storied career includes a multitude of examples of inspired experiments with technology in theater, opera, and dance. Of particular relevance for the concept of performing in partnership with media are his works stemming from *Laterna Magika*, originally exhibited at Expo'58 in Brussels. Svoboda continues to innovate on the techniques for creating the illusion of responsivity between live performer and film, even in his final production, *Graffiti*, in 2001 [19, 52].
- 1967 - 1990: Filmmaker and theater director Radúz Činčera develops projects billed as interactive films, but which incorporate complex interweavings of filmic and theatrical storytelling with interactive technologies, audience participation, and theatrical performance. Key performances include *Kineautomat*, developed in partnership with Josef Svoboda and shown at the Czechoslovak Pavilion at Expo67 in Montreal in 1967, and *Cinelabyrinth*, developed for the Osaka World Expo in 1990 [53].
- 1970 - today: Scenographer William Dudley continues to explore a variety of technologies, mechanical and digital, in traditional theater today, including mechanized seating platforms, a fog screen projection display, and 360-degree projection surfaces. While his uses of technology are more limited to traditional scenic functions, they are interesting examples of environmental or immersive approaches in narrative theater. Notable productions include *The Big Picnic* (1994), *Hitchcock Blonde* (2003), *The Woman in White* (2004), and *Peter Pan in Kensington Gardens 360* (2009) [54].

- 1990s - today: Director and performance scholar David Z. Saltz's work is explicitly focused on integrating responsive technologies including pressure sensors, motion capture, and robotics in performance with strong dramaturgical justification. Notable productions include *Kaspar* (1999), *The Tempest* (2000), an ongoing *commedia dell'arte* project involving both robotic and human performers [55, 56].
- 2006: Playwright Elizabeth Meriwether's *Heddatron*, a scifi comedy in which a pregnant housewife is abducted by robots and forced to perform Hedda Gabler. The script calls for "functioning robots or at least something on wheels with recorded dialogue" [57].

I have also contributed productions to this trajectory, emphasizing the potentials of responsive media as partners. My production of Sophie Treadwell's *Machinal* (2004) cast a robot in the role of the priest, emphasizing the callous, mechanical nature of the society portrayed in the piece. My 2007 musical adaptation of Georg Büchner's *Woyzeck*, co-created with composer Brendan Padgett, choreographer Kyle Shepard, and media designer Michelle Moon Lee, used augmented reality to bring interactivity to a script in which the author had never prescribed an order for the scenes, to allow audiences to construct their own pathways through the narrative. A 2013 production of Haruki Marukami's *after the quake*, created in collaboration with director Melissa Foulger, used a gesture controlled projected waveform to bring the play's giant, earthquake-causing worm to life. More recently, I collaborated with media designer Marc Destefano on a production of Thornton Wilder's *Our Town* (2017), utilizing a 360-degreee projection screen and gesture-based system that displayed procedurally generated artworks, derived from hand-painted and hand-drawn works commissioned for the production from artist Clare Johnson. The screen responded to the Stage Manager character's movements, extending his dramaturgical power as a puppet master to pull the audience into the world of the play. Also in 2017, my adaptation of Henrik Ibsen's *Peer Gynt*, created together with orchestra and choir director Nicholas DeMaison and sculptor Jefferson Kielwagen, combined physical and digital media to experiment with scale and playful shifts between modes of representation. Giant sculptural puppets, a full orchestra and chorus, live narrator, and miniature toy theatre augmented by live projection at massive scale, came together to emphasize the comic and surreal qualities of the narrative.

The aim of the timeline sketched above, along with the addition of my own work, is to begin to bring together a restorative history of mainstream theater's innovations with responsive technologies, both in the postdigital era today and the analogue prehistory. I hope others will add citations to this initial collection, including their own works.

4 Conclusion

In conclusion, the category of media theater work that engages creatively with technologies as postdigital partners and continues to incorporate the rich tradition of dramatic storytelling stands as a relatively untapped area in media performance scholarship, also ripe for collaboration with adjacent fields including games, interactive narrative, artificial intelligence, electronic literature, architecture, puppetry, and performing object work that are likewise concerned with responsive technologies and narrative. Unlike the critique of interdisciplinary in Grotowski's description of the 'Rich Theatre,' which "depends on artistic kleptomania," the disciplinary crossings open to postdigital theatre have the potential to develop creative, generous human and non-human partnerships, surpassing the decorative dystopia envisioned by Grotowski [58]. The goals of this paper have been to highlight the work both historical and contemporary in this under-examined area, as well as seek to unravel some of the reasons behind its relative lack of inclusion in the scholarly literature. In addition, I have put forth the concept of partnership as particularly relevant for the postdigital theater maker, building on work from Haraway, Saltz, O'Hare and others to claim the responsive technological actor as a viable cast member for the postdigital narrative stage. I hope these theoretical moves will help to expand and extend the conversation, and further bridge intersecting disciplines.

In tandem with the scholarly conversation, I hope this paper will help inspire further work in practice in responsive technologies in narrative theater. My own work will also continue in this direction. Again in collaboration with media designer Marc Destefano, I will direct Sondheim and Wheeler's *Sweeney Todd* in early 2019, using facial projection mapping to create responsive masks for Sweeney's victims, who will transform under his murderous clutches, appearing to share the same face with the actor portraying the judge character, who is Sweeney's ultimate aim. Also planned for performance in 2019, I am co-authoring with Lissa Holloway-Attaway an original play that will feature multiple characters connected to the ecological threats facing the Baltic Sea, including invasive species, refuse, and a robot who will tell a procedurally generated speculative future folktale, using an AI story generator to navigate a corpus of Baltic story materials.

References

1. Cascone, K.: The aesthetics of failure: "Post-digital" tendencies in contemporary computer music. Comput. Music J. **24**(4), 12–18 (2000)
2. Parry, R.: The end of the beginning: normatively in the postdigital museum. Mus. World **1** (1), 24–30 (2013)
3. Cramer, F.: What is 'Post-Digital'? In: Postdigital Aesthetics, pp. 12–16. Palgrave Macmillan, London (2015)
4. Holloway-Attaway, L., Rouse, R.: Designing postdigital curators: establishing an interdisciplinary games and mixed reality cultural heritage network. In: Ioannides, M., Martins, J., Žarnić, R., Lim, V. (eds.) Advances in Digital Cultural Heritage. LNCS, vol. 10754, pp. 162–173. Springer, Cham (2018). https://doi.org/10.1007/978-3-319-75789-6_12
5. Causey, M.: Postdigital performance. Theatr. J. **68**(3), 427–441 (2016)
6. Benjamin, W.: The Work of Art in the Age of its Technological Reproducibility, and Other Writings on Media. Harvard University Press, Cambridge (2008)
7. Panofsky, E., Wood, C.S., Wood, C.: Perspective as Symbolic Form. Zone Books, New York (1991)
8. Berger, J.: Ways of Seeing. Penguin, UK (1972)
9. Sussman, M.: Performing the intelligent machine: Deception and enchantment in the life of the automaton chess player. TDR/Drama Rev. **43**(3), 1–96 (1999). 8 pp.

10. de La Mettrie, J.O.: L'Homme machine ...(par La Mettrie). De l'imp. de'Elie Luzac, fils (1748)
11. Ferro-Murray, A., Murray, T.: Technologies of performance: machinic staging and corporeal choreographies. In: A Cultural History of Theatre in the Modern Age, vol. 6. Bloomsbury, New York (2017)
12. McLuhan, M., Lapham, L.H.: Understanding Media: The Extensions of Man. MIT Press, Cambridge (1994)
13. Haraway, D.: Manifesto for cyborgs: science, technology and socialist feminism in the 1980s. Social. Rev. **80**, 65–108 (1985)
14. Haraway, D.: Staying with the Trouble: Making kin in the Chthulucene. Duke University Press, Durham (2016)
15. Phelan, P.: Unmarked: the Politics of Performance. Routledge, New York (1993)
16. Auslander, P.: Liveness: Performance in a Mediated Culture. Psychology Press, New York (1999)
17. Mulvey, L.: Visual pleasure and narrative cinema. Screen **16**(3), 6–18 (1975)
18. Schneider, A.: After. Live performance in EMPAC, Troy, NY, 10 April 2017
19. Burian, J.: Josef Svoboda: theatre artist in an age of science. Educ. Theatr. J. **22**(2), 123–145 (1970)
20. Bolter, J.D.: The Digital Plenitude and the End of Art. Address presented at ISEA: international symposium on electronic art, Istanbul Turkey, 18 September 2011
21. Nagler, A.M.: A Source Book in Theatrical History: Twenty-five Centuries of Stage History in More Than 300 Basic Documents and other Primary Material. Dover Publications, New York (1959)
22. Brockett, O.G., Hilda, F.J. (eds.): History of the Theatre, 10th edn. Pearson, New York (2007)
23. Bay-Cheng, S., Parker-Starbuck, J., Saltz, D.Z.: Performance and Media: Taxonomies for a Changing Field. University of Michigan Press, Ann Arbor MI (2015)
24. Lehmann, H.T.: Postdramatic Theatre. Routledge, London (2006)
25. Barnett, D.: When is a play not a drama? two examples of post dramatic theatre texts. New Theatr. Q. **24**(1), 14–23 (2008)
26. Bell, J.: Puppets, masks, and performing objects at the end of the century. TDR/Drama Rev. **43**(3), 15–27 (1999)
27. Schlemmer, O., Moholy-Nagy, L., Molnar, F.: The Theater of the Bauhaus. Wesleyan UP, Middletown (1961)
28. Winner, L. Do Artifacts have politics? Daedalus, pp. 121–136 (1980)
29. Bogatyrev, P.: Czech puppet theatre and Russian folk theatre. TDR/ Drama Rev. **43**(3), 97–114 (1999)
30. Wellman, M.: Sincerity Forever. Broadway Play Publishing Inc., New York (1990)
31. Williams, T.: The Glass Menagerie. New Directions, New York (1944)
32. Butsch, R.: The Making of American Audiences: from Stage to Television 1750-1990. Cambridge UP, Cambridge (2000)
33. Hampton, A.: The Extra People. Live performance in EMPAC, Troy, NY, September 10 (2015)
34. Stamer, P., Laue, J., Franco, A.: 26 Letters to Deleuze. Live performance in EMPAC, Troy NY, 22 March 2014
35. Fornes, M.I.: Fefu and Her Friends. PAJ Publications, New York (1977)
36. Brecht, B.: Emphasis on sport. In: Brecht on Theatre: The Development of an Aesthetic, pp. 6–9 (1964)

37. Saltz, D.Z.: Sharing the stage with media: a taxonomy of performer-media interaction. In: Performance and Media: Taxonomies for a Changing Field, pp. 93–125. University of Michigan Press, Ann Arbor MI (2015)
38. O'Hare, M.: Points of Contact: An Actor-Centered Approach for the Design of Interactive Environments for Theatre Performance. Doctoral Dissertation, Department of Electronic Arts, Rensselaer Polytechnic Institute (2018)
39. Tillis, S.: The art of puppetry in the age of media production. TDR/ Drama Rev. **43**(3), 182–195 (1999)
40. Kaplin, S.: A puppet tree: a model for the field of puppet theatre. TDR/ Drama Rev. **43**(3), 28–35 (1999)
41. McDermott, J.F.: Banvard's Mississippi panorama pamphlets. Pap. Bibliogr. Soc. Am. **43**(1), 48–62 (1949)
42. Weller, M.P., Do, E.Y.: Architectural robotics: a new paradigm for the built environment. In: EuropIA, vol. 11, pp. 19–21 (2007)
43. Gropius, W., Wensinger, A.S., Schlemmer, O., Moholy-Nagy, L.: The Theater of the Bauhaus. Wesleyan University Press, Middletown (1961)
44. Price, C., Littlewood, J.: The fun palace. In: The Drama Review: TDR, pp. 127–134 (1968)
45. Huhtamo, E.: Illusions in Motion: Media Archaeology of the Moving Panorama and Related Spectacles. MIT Press, Cambridge (2013)
46. Waltz, G.: Filmed scenery on the live stage. Theatr. J. **58**, 547–573 (2006)
47. Solomon, M.: Up-to-date magic: theatrical conjuring and the trick film. Theatr. J. **58**, 595–615 (2006)
48. Canemaker, J.: Winsor McCay: His Life and Art. Harry Abrams, New York (2005)
49. Giesekam, G.: Staging the screen: the use of film and video in theatre. Macmillan International Higher Education (2007)
50. Piscator, E.: The political theatre: a history 1914-1929. Avon Books, New York (1978)
51. Innes, C.: Piscator's 'Rasputin'. Drama Rev. TDR **22**(4), 83–98 (1978)
52. Burian, J.M.: The Secret of Theatrical Space: The Memoirs of Josef Svoboda. Applause, New York (1993)
53. Hales, C.: Cinelabyrinth: the pavilion of forking paths. In: Nunes, N., Oakley, I., Nisi, V. (eds.) ICIDS 2017. LNCS, vol. 10690, pp. 117–125. Springer, Cham (2017). https://doi.org/10.1007/978-3-319-71027-3_10
54. Rouse, R.: A new dramaturgy for digital technology in narrative theater. Doctoral dissertation in Digital Media, School of Literature, Media and Communication, the Georgia Institute of Technology (2013)
55. Saltz, D.Z.: Live media: interactive technology and theatre. Theatr. Top. **11**(2), 107–130 (2001)
56. Wright, A.: What a mechanical performance! Bravo! In: The New York Times, Theater Section, 5 July 2012
57. Meriwether, E.: Heddatron. Playscripts, New York (2006)
58. Grotowski, J. Towards a Poor Theatre. In: Towards a Poor Theatre, pp. 15–26, Routledge, New York (2012)

'What Country, Friends, Is This?' Using Immersive Theatre Practice to Inform the Design of Audience Experience in *Estate 360°*

Scott Palmer[(✉)]

University of Leeds, Leeds LS2 9JT, UK
s.d.palmer@leeds.ac.uk

Abstract. This paper focuses on issues arising from the making of an experimental interactive 360-degree video that emerged from a relational 'immersive' site-specific theatre project for a public audience that was staged in historic grounds in South Florida, USA in April 2017. This work was undertaken with academics from University of Miami, Kim Grinfeder and Stephen Di Benedetto. The specific nature of the performance event, the filming of aspects of this experience and the post-production processes each raise significant questions relating to the development of methods of 'interactive' digital storytelling for 'immersive' audience experience. The role of theatre practice and performance design in developing these mediated experiences seems to be an important element that has largely been ignored in thinking about how digital immersive experiences might be created.

The video *Estate 360°* was first published on-line in January 2018 and is freely available to download: https://interactive.miami.edu/estate/.

Keywords: 360-degree video · Immersive theatre · Performance Design for audience experience · Interactive film · Scenography

1 Context

1.1 Background

This paper outlines the process, key issues and initial findings relating to the audience experience of an interactive 360-degree video based on a site-specific, relational, theatrical performance. Research questions have emerged from the practice: What are the principles and working methods that have arisen from this relatively new practice and how might performance knowledge be valuable in the future development of this medium? How might our experience link to the findings of the only other currently published academic writing that deals explicitly with immersive theatre, storytelling and 360-degree video? This paper therefore represents the first attempt to analyse some of the multiple aspects at play in what was originally framed as an opportunity for experimentation in translating a relational theatrical performance to the 360-degree interactive video medium.

R. Rouse et al. (Eds.): ICIDS 2018, LNCS 11318, pp. 383–391, 2018.
https://doi.org/10.1007/978-3-030-04028-4_45

1.2   Overview

Estate 360° (2018) is an experimental interactive video made in collaboration with students and researchers at University of Miami, Fl. USA. It emerged from a relational site-specific performance '*ESTATE*' staged in a heritage site on Florida's East coast in April 2017. Delivered via the smartphone screen and head-mounted display (HMD), this 'immersive' experience offers a digital simulacrum of the live performance in which the viewer, like the original audience, is asked to navigate the environment as witness to a multitude of characters and their stories. *Estate 360°* seems to raise key questions and new possibilities for exploring performance documentation but more importantly in the context of this paper, for the creation, development and design of audience experience using both theatre practice and 360° filming and VR technologies and techniques.

The original site-specific performance *ESTATE* (2017) was created through an extensive, collaborative, devising process that began with professional writers taking part in the Miami-Dade Playwright Development Programme and then developed in rehearsal with students and staff from the University of Miami's Department of Theatre Arts. The premise of the performance is outlined briefly below but it is important to note that an open creative process, beginning on-line six months earlier, allowed for multiple ideas to be tested and refined, re-written and then experimented with further within the rehearsal room before finally being translated to the external site. The importance of play within a devised process has been articulated elsewhere in relation to iterative design processes focused on audience experience in relation to digital content (e.g. Palmer 2006, Palmer and Popat 2007, Bayliss et al. 2009). A similar approach in this rehearsal and devising process was instrumental to the development of performed content and playful interactions continued through elements of improvisation in the final performance. Unfortunately because of time constraints, there was little opportunity for similar playful experimentation between the performers and the technology and technologists in the making of the 360-degree video.

2   ESTATE - Audience Experience as a Felt Scenography

The performance title and premise emerged directly from the 444-acre Deering Estate on the shores of Biscayne Bay and played on the multiple definitions of the term 'Estate' that were incorporated both implicitly and explicitly within the performance. The real and imagined histories of this place suggested rich territory for the development of dramatic material situated in a landscape that from pre-history to the present has been inscribed by stories of migration, invasion and occupation but where many of the traces of the past have been deliberately erased.

In considering contemporary notions of expanded scenography, Arnold Aronson draws on de Certeau's notion of space as a practised place and suggests that "we may say that human activity, and the sites of human activity, become performance through the application of scenography – the process of transforming a landscape into a meaningful environment that guides performers and spectators alike through a visual and spatial field imbued with meaning" (Aronson et al. 2017: xv). Although written

about contemporary scenography as a whole, these words take on a particular resonance when applied directly to the site-specific performance of *ESTATE* and they
neatly articulate both the underlying premise of the performance and the importance of
the designed audience experience.

The performance of *ESTATE* was created for an audience in small groups after
sunset when the Estate was usually closed to the public. This was a promenade performance with no division between actor space and audience space and centred on an
open, multi-layered dramaturgy that offered audiences individual choice about where to
go and what to experience. This structure with over-lapping narratives is typical of
many theatre works by companies who create 'immersive' performances and allowed
the audience considerable autonomy to negotiate the various one-to-one encounters
with performers, often in close proximity. This deliberate use of proxemics to establish
relationships between participants, actors and the spaces of the two houses was a key
scenographic strategy that defined the nature of the performance and became central in
the decision to explore how 360-degree video might work with this same subject
matter.

The role of the environment and design of the audience experience is at the heart of
post-dramatic performance work such as *ESTATE* where the combination of site and
written text combined to create new meanings. Aronson argues that:

"Scenography makes the underlying structures of representation visible, presenting
the spectator with multiple (and sometimes contradictory) understandings that expand a
literal text. Meaning is replaced by relationship. This is most apparent in site-specific
works in which scenography is not a newly created aesthetic product but a transformation of existing space and structures. Site-specific scenography foregrounds the
spectators' interaction with the surrounding environment and their increased awareness
of the emblematic signs inherent within the space." (Aronson et al. 2017, xvi) Rather
than viewed at a distance, *ESTATE* was centred on a scenography that was designed to
be felt and experienced. It both responded to and incorporated the qualities of the site.
The audience were situated within the work; some of them experiencing a well-known
space anew – transformed by the darkness and the aesthetic experience on offer; others
were overwhelmed by the novelty of the theatrical experience that began with a series
of vignettes in which the audience were first guided around the outside lawns, coastline
and pathways and then left to their own devices to explore the internal rooms and
spaces of the two houses. Crucially the design of this experience allowed for a gradual
immersion within a theatrical world of multiple narratives in which the audience
members were framed as co-creators. This framing is markedly different to the experience of sudden immersion experienced when using the HMD.

Adam Alston has suggested that models of immersive theatre experience such as
those of Shunt or Punchdrunk might be thought of as 'experience machines' (2016). In
using this term there is a clear analogy to the experience of computer gaming where the
participant is invited to enter a designed environment usually with a specific goal in
mind. In recent theatre practice, this 'goal' is usually framed around encounters in
which the audience are asked to make sense of fragmentary aesthetic experiences. The
particular qualities of *ESTATE* therefore, in part a guided tour and part a series of
intimate encounters, seemed to provide an ideal opportunity to experiment in order to
discover how a performance that was predicated on felt scenography and intimate one-

to-one encounters might translate to a new experience using the technology of the HMD and interactive 360-degree video.

3   Adapting Immersive Performance to 360-Degree Video

Although filmed in daylight, the *Estate 360°* video captures some of the qualities of the original night-time performance and offers a distinctly different audience experience that is now delivered via the smartphone screen and HMD. Unlike 360-degree films available on platforms such as YouTube, *Estate 360°* combines elements of game navigation via the Wonda VR app that allows some limited interaction. It provides a degree of control and autonomy within the world through the use of arrows that appear on screen as virtual buttons superimposed on the filmed environment. This interactivity allows the experiencer to choose to leave scenes that may not sustain interest and to explore choices of different pathways within the film – which is directly analogous to the live theatrical experience that was offered in *ESTATE*. This type of navigational experience has been compared to that of first-person computer games such as *Myst* (1993) where the player is left to explore the world to piece together a series of clues and has the freedom to move between linked areas. Other writing has drawn parallels between computer gaming and 'immersive' theatre practice (e.g. Klich 2015, Biggin 2017) but this paper specifically focuses on the nature of the experience offered through the format of the interactive 360-degree video.

3.1   Spatial Relationships in 360-Degree Video

Research relating theatre and performance practices to the development of 360-video techniques appears to date to be very limited. In a key recent study by Pope et al. (2017) there is both a recognition of the absence of studies in this field (p. 4476) and also a clear acknowledgement of both the value of 'immersive' performance practices and the central role of space in making meaning: "Theatre practitioners' expertise in manipulating spatial interactions has much to contribute to immersive recorded content." (p. 4468). This scientific study analyses the use of proximity/affect in 360 films using theatre directors and actors within a studio setting and specially commissioned script. The research team made the analogy between the VR/HMD experience and live performance: "Like VR, theatre is a fixed point 360° experience in which the audience is free to look anywhere, so expertise in theatre can inform VR cinematography." (p. 4468)

While this study might have generated important empirical data relating to the impact of proxemic relationships, there is little in their conclusions that might surprise a theatre practitioner familiar with the complexity of rehearsal and devising processes in making relational work for live audiences: "The complex ways in which theatre directors approach space, as a technical challenge and semantically loaded space, have much to contribute to the emerging art form of immersive recorded media." (sic) (p. 4477). While the value of performance practitioners in the development of interactive and immersive digital content may not yet be widely acknowledged or their potential fully recognised, in placing this expertise firmly in the hands of the theatre director, the research team appear to have taken a rather over-simplistic view of immersive theatre practices which are rarely predicated on the hierarchical models and single auteur of traditional or commercial theatre.

The focus in their study on old-fashioned notions of 'blocking' in terms of fixing the actor's positions in space "one of the most important parts of conveying the identity and relationships of characters *on stage.*" (p. 4470 my italics) while assisting in explaining the importance of proxemic relationships to the ways in which theatrical scenes make meaning, also suggests a theatrical model where the human body is decoded from afar. Discussions of stage left and right are unhelpful in the immersive theatre context where there is no separation between performer and audience and the actors are not 'on stage' in the same sense. Actors are not being viewed remotely or from a single dominant direction, but rather being engaged from multiple directions simultaneously by audience members who are inhabiting the same environment. This shift of audience member from viewer to experiencer in 'immersive theatre' allows for more subtle and intimate exchanges to take place and crucially foregrounds the importance of the phenomenal, embodied experience of the audience member precisely because of their live, proxemic relationship to the actor(s). However the subtleties of the invitation, so critical to the success of participatory work of this kind, and articulated clearly by performance scholars such as White (2013), are also absent from this study.

It is the vividness of the embodied experience of the participant that lies at the heart of the immersive 'experience machine' and relates directly to the notion of the 'unique power' of these theatrical encounters (Machon 2013). Consequently when this relationship is translated from actor/audience to actor/360-degree camera, new creative options arise for those engaged in designing audience experiences for digital content. However, it is important to note that the proxemic relationship in the filmed world is always mediated through the lens and cannot retain exactly the same power or impact as the close proximity of another human body in the live theatre encounter. Current technology does not allow us a full haptic experience, senses of taste and smell are absent while of course there is also no possibility of interaction or direct address. There is however room for the creative use of proxemic relationships as Pope et al. suggest: "For the first time, 360-degree filming and VR make it possible to harness the power of spatial relationships and configurations for recorded media. Rather than manipulating space in a fixed frame, such as close-ups and wide shots, actors can manipulate spatial relationships between one another in a way that is familiar in theatre and in everyday life." (p. 4470)

3.2 Experimenting with Camera Positions in 360-Degree Video

In *Estate 360°* we experimented not only with manipulating relationships between actors, but in scenes that emerged from our live performance and designed as one-to-one encounters, we specifically experimented with a number of different proxemic relationships between performers and the camera. This seems to be the key to a new 'power of spatial relationships' in 360-degree filming.

In one scene ('Bride Dancing') a young woman in a wedding dress dances around the camera, placing the viewer at the very centre of the scene. Although she doesn't speak, the experience we are offered appears to mirror the giddiness and turmoil of her personal situation – which has been suggested in previous encounters with her. In this scene in the ballroom, the experiencer using the HMD needs to continually turn if they wish to keep the bride in sight – but may choose to stay facing in one direction and allow her to continually enter, move through and disappear from their field of vision. In this way the spatial design of the scene allows the experiencer a degree of autonomy – some of which might alter the overall impact and intention of the original scene. This degree of choice – of where to look and where to move (using the virtual buttons) is in marked contrast to the conventional theatre experience where the audience might be bounded by their seats and distance from the stage. The 360-degree experience offers autonomy for the experiencer to design their own personal version of the performance knowing that when the performers address the camera (either directly or indirectly) they are still cast as central to the overall performance.

In another interior scene in *Estate 360°* set in the anthropologist's study-bedroom, we asked the performer to replicate the intensity of his one-to-one interaction with audience members in *ESTATE* by performing part of his scene very close to the camera. Despite the distortion caused by his extreme proximity to the lens, this sudden shift creates a startling and slightly sinister effect when experienced in the HMD which equates to the feelings of claustrophobia that were achieved in the original live performance. For a scene in the kitchen we chose to lower the height of the tripod so that the scene was experienced close to the floor, at the same level as the child who was taking refuge under a sink. Similarly in an earlier scene set beside the sea, the height of the camera was altered to match the eye-level of an audience member who would be sat in an adjacent chair. This scene works particularly well when wearing the HMD if the experiencer is also sat down.

3.3   Post-production Dramaturgy

In making one-to-one work of this nature, the designed spatial relationships are not created by one person (the director) alone, but rather through a series of complex interactions between bodies, objects and the space itself in which the expertise of the actor and the scenographer are also paramount. In translating this experience to 360-degree video the nature of the experience is also predicated on a series of technical and production decisions including; the selection and editing of the video, the stitching of the shots to create the illusion of 360-degree view, the application of sound editing skills and the insertion of interactive buttons. What is fundamental in this post-production process is also the key decisions taken about what scenes might be included and in which order. The number of scenes and their locations made this element a complex task. Some scenes were cut as they didn't translate well to 360-video or had sound recording issues that interfered with the sense of immersion within the world of the drama. Potential pathways were tested with the aim of allowing an almost total freedom of movement between scenes, and to wander through the landscape, but the strange geography of the houses and the use of rooms on different floors of the buildings meant that the 360-degree experience was ultimately confusing. Guided by the expertise of Kim Grinfeder, a balance needed to be struck between the choices offered to the participant and a reasonably logical pathway through the fragments of scenes that might offer a satisfying rather than ultimately frustrating experience. The particular time constraints of the original filming also resulted in a number of issues that came to prominence in the post-production period. With the advantage of hindsight, the creative team wished that instead of using an extant theatrical performance, that we could make a work using similar techniques specifically for 360-degree interactive video.

4 Making Space Speak – Interim Conclusions

The nature and power of the space as experienced in 360-degree video is a key element that is deliberately neutralised in Pope et al's study. Conducting their experiments within a black-box laboratory environment enabled the focus to be specifically on the nature of the proxemic relationships between actors and how this might convey meaning in HMD 360-degree and VR worlds. What is denied in this scenario however is the power of the space itself to make meaning. Ingold drawing on Bollnow asserts that "Every space has its own atmospheric character that impinges on us and takes hold of our feelings" (2012:79). This is particularly evident in immersive theatre practice, whether created in designed space within black-box theatre environments or in site-responsive or site-specific practice.

In *Estate 360°* the location was always going to be a key component of the experience – especially as the dramatic material had originated from a deep engagement with the site. In the filmed content, just as in the live performance, the materiality of the real world both demands attention and contributes to the meaning and resonance of each scene. The environment is the first thing that participants are aware of as they put on the HMD and are transported to this sub-tropical landscape. This can at first be disorienting. One respondent remarked:

"At the theatre there is some kind of performative airlock that holds you as an audience member in between states, (overture, announcement about phones...) closing one door behind you before opening the way to the unknown. In this 3D situation I am catapulted into the scene. I am reminded of Viola's words that open *Twelfth Night* [I, ii] –'What country, friends, is this?' as she drags herself ashore on the island." (Andrews 2018). Questions relating to notions of immersion and presence pervade analyses of digital media experiences as Biggin outlines below, and this is useful to consider in relation to this participant response. The analogy with the disorientation of Shakespeare's heroine arriving in a strange land and of feeling 'catapulted into the scene' suggests more than simply presence: "*Presence* is relatively easy to achieve in VR/immersive theatre: the player/spectator is surrounded by the environment as soon as the technology is enabled/they enter the space. Immersive *experience* is harder to achieve, and trickier to define. A feeling of "being there" of "feeling/reacting as if you are there," is characteristic of being highly immersed in a computer game: as the player is physically distant from the screen such responses indicate high levels of engagement" (Biggin 2017: 22-3 italics in original).

At about halfway through the *Estate 360°* journey, the experiencer finds themselves on a verandah amidst 13 empty rocking chairs which are all moving in ghostly fashion. Slowly they come to a stop. The scene, reminiscent of a computer game environment such as *Myst*, without human performer or spoken word seems to be the single most affective moment in the 360-video and one that of course could not have been achieved in the live performance. This points towards the potential to explore further sceno-graphic moments using the combination of theatrical and filmic techniques – in a further scene the two techniques come together in post-production where a performer is made to vanish into thin air as she speaks the word "disappear". These scenes fore-ground the necessity in the 360-degree experience of allowing time for the participant just to enjoy being immersed in each space thereby allowing both the space and the objects within the spaces to make meaning.

The importance of the scenographic elements; the actors, their costumes and the material objects within the world, the sound and the quality of light cannot be underestimated in their significant and inter-linked contribution to the audience experience of the digital world. While we cannot (yet) get close to the feelings of proximity and the full-bodied sensory experience of actually being on that site, in that space and with that actor, the advent of the 360-degree camera enables a fuller com-plete visual experience that is analogous to being in the real world. In prioritising the visual it encourages participants to look in perhaps a more active way than they might when stood in the actual spaces of performance. Joslin McKinney's analysis about how we see scenography in the theatre can also be helpfully applied to the experience of the 360-degree video: "Looking in the theatre is not a purely visual experience. To look at scenography is to apprehend not only illustrations or depictions, but to notice the composition and orchestration of materials and feel the way they work on us at a bodily level. This is a way of knowing and a kind of action because it connects us to our own experience of the world, our memories and imaginations and our experiential under-standings of daily life." (2018, p. 115)

Might the 360-degree video experience ask us to not only look but also to feel in a more active way that is not only a primarily visual one? Might this offer an experience where the digital world might be touched through the eyes? Laura Marks's formulation of haptic visuality (2000, 2002) perhaps offer one such approach in relation to understanding the potential experience of new digital media – since it offers a way of knowing that calls into play multiple senses but does not depend on the literal presence of those senses. Touching with the eyes opens the possibilities for new ways of understanding this medium and future dramatic possibilities in relation to multiple senses, affect and embodiment.

In practical terms, it is not therefore only the proxemic relationships that might be established between performer and audience, (in the live performance) or between actor and camera (in the 360-degree film experience) that are critical in making work of this nature, but rather the way in which the whole environment is organised to be expe-rienced. This requires a design process in which the scenographer needs to play a central role –and a process that is more akin to the iterative stages of design for user experience rather than more traditional methods of design for the theatre stage. Moving well beyond the creation of decorative backdrops in the theatre, this expanded role of scenography places the experience of the audience at its heart and should recognise the haptic potential of the new digital worlds experienced through the HMD and 360-degree and VR technologies.

References

ESTATE – site-specific, relational performance 19–22 April 2017. http://www.deeringestate.org/estate-site-specific-plays/. Accessed 20 Sept 2018

Estate 360° interactive video (2018) Homepage. https://interactive.miami.edu/estate/. Accessed 20 Sept 2018

Palmer, S.: A place to play - experimentation and interactions between technology and performance. In: Oddey, A., White, C. (eds.) The Potentials of Spaces: The Theory and Practice of Scenography and Performance, pp. 105–118. Intellect, Bristol (2006)

Palmer, S., Popat, S.: Dancing in the Streets: the sensuous manifold as a concept for designing experience. Int. J. Performance Art and Digital Media 2(3), 297–314 (2007). https://doi.org/10.1386/padm.2.3.297_1, http://eprints.whiterose.ac.uk/76894/. Accessed 20 Sept 2018

Bayliss, A., Palmer, S., Hales, D., Sheridan, J.G.: (Re)searching through play: play as a framework and methodology for collaborative design processes. Int. J. Arts Technol. 2.1–2:521 (2009). https://doi.org/10.1504/IJART.2009.024054, http://eprints.whiterose.ac.uk/79204/. Accessed 20 Sept 2018

Aronson, A.: Foreword. In: McKinney, Palmer (eds.) Scenography Expanded: an introduction to Contemporary Performance Design, London, Bloomsbury Methuen, pp. xiii–xvi (2017)

Alston, A.: Beyond Immersive Theatre: Aesthetics. Politics and Productive Participation. Palgrave Macmillan, London (2016)

Myst. (designed by Miller, R & Miller, R), Brøderbund (1993)

Klich, R.E.: Playing a punchdrunk game: immersive theatre and videogames. In: Frieze, J. (ed.) Framing Immersive Theatre: The Politics and Pragmatics of Participatory Performance, pp. 221–228. Palgrave Macmillan, Basingstoke (2015)

Biggin, R.: Immersive Theatre and Audience Experience: Space. Game and Story in the Work of Punchdrunk, Palgrave Macmillan, London (2017)

Pope, V., Dawes, R., Schweiger, F., Sheikh, A.: The geometry of storytelling: theatrical use of space for 360-degree videos and virtual reality. In: Proceedings of the 2017 CHI Conference on Human Factors in Computing Systems Denver, Colorado, USA, 06–11 May 2017, pp. 4468–4478. ACM, New York (2017)

Machon, J.: Immersive Theatres: Intimacy and Immediacy in Contemporary Performance. Palgrave Macmillan, Basingstoke (2013)

White, G.: Audience Participation in Theatre: Aesthetics of the Invitation. Palgrave Macmillan, Basingstoke (2013)

Ingold, T.: The Atmosphere. Chiasmi International 14(2012), 75–87 (2012). https://doi.org/10.5840/chiasmi20121410

Andrews, A.: Private e-mail correspondence with author 3/7/2018

McKinney, J.: Seeing Scenography: scopic regimes and the body of the spectator. In: Aronson, A. (ed.) The Routledge Companion to Scenography, pp. 102–118. Routledge, London (2018)

Marks, L.U.: The Skin of Film: Intercultural Cinema, Embodiment, and the Senses. Duke University Press, Durham (2000)

Marks, L.U.: Touch: Sensuous Theory and Multisensory Media. University of Minnesota Press, Minneapolis (2002)

From Literary Novel to Radio Drama to VR Project

The thousand autumns of Jacob de Zoet

Mirjam Vosmeer$^{(\boxtimes)}$, Alyea Sandovar, and Ben Schouten

Lectoraat Play & Civic Media, Amsterdam University of Applied Sciences,
Postbus 1025, 1000 BA Amsterdam, The Netherlands
{m.s.vosmeer,b.a.m.schouten}@hva.nl,
alyea@tinthue.com

Abstract. For this study we investigated if and how the merging of VR with radio drama can provide general insights into storytelling for VR. In order to present the student project *The thousand autumns of Jacob de Zoet* as a case study, we discuss environmental storytelling, and storytelling in relation to VR and radioplay. We conclude that the traditional *lean back* medium that is radio drama may benefit from the *lean in* quality of VR and we discuss a number of strong concepts that can be explored in order to gain further knowledge about storytelling for VR.

Keywords: Virtual reality · Radio drama · Environmental storytelling
Design research · Reflective design

1 Introduction

Developments in the field of virtual reality (VR) are often discussed in the light of technological progress, improvements in the usability of system hardware, or practical purposes such as data visualization, therapeutical tools or commercial applications [1]. Reflections on the specific narrative possibilities of this particular medium, however, are less common. Yet, in order to establish VR as a viable new carrier for interactive digital storytelling, it makes sense to keep exploring its possibilities for narrative transportation as well.

Researchers from different backgrounds have already tackled a number of practical issues that VR raises when it comes to storytelling, and insights have been shared regarding, for instance, guiding the user's attention in a desired direction [2–6], the use of audio-feedback and voice-over [7, 8] or the optimal techniques for scene transition within VR experiences [9, 10]. But what makes good VR storytelling - or what makes VR storytelling good? While filmmakers and theatre directors are still divided about the ultimate storytelling possibilities of VR [11, 12], academic researchers have started to investigate how insights and techniques that are borrowed from more traditional media, may also be used for VR [13]. In this light, we present our own research, which focuses on whether the 'historical phenomenon' that is radio drama [14] may provide insights into storytelling for VR.

© Springer Nature Switzerland AG 2018
R. Rouse et al. (Eds.): ICIDS 2018, LNCS 11318, pp. 392–400, 2018.
https://doi.org/10.1007/978-3-030-04028-4_46

Our current investigation starts with a student project that was carried out in the spring of 2018, for which the student developers were challenged with quite an extraordinary assignment. This assignment was proposed to them by a Dutch broadcasting company in collaboration with our VR research team and it implied the creation of a unique VR experience that would accompany a new literary radioplay. At first glance, the merging of VR and radio seems far-fetched, as the two media do not have much in common. However, a fact that has since long been stated about radio is that it is the most effective medium when it comes to stimulating the imagination [15]. And while VR has lots of intriguing qualities, encouraging users to be imaginative does not necessarily seem to be one of them. Users can be overwhelmed, impressed, or even experience 'awe' [16], but they are seldom triggered to use their imagination in order to fill in the gaps in a narrative. Good storytelling, however, benefits from some kind of imaginative engagement. For our current study we have therefore set out to investigate if and how the merging with radio drama can provide general insights into storytelling for VR. While the outcome of our investigation is not to be evaluated as a full prototype, we intend to share the insights on VR storytelling that this project provided, thus ultimately contributing to the field of interactive digital narrative.

2   The thousand autumns of Jacob de Zoet

The student project that inspired our current investigation into VR storytelling was based on a radio drama that was produced by De Hoorspelfabriek (The Radioplay Factory), commissioned by Dutch broadcasting company AVROTROS [17]. The radioplay itself was based upon the novel The thousand autumns of Jacob de Zoet, first published in 2010, by British author David Mitchell [18]. This historical novel is set during the Dutch trading concession with Japan in the late 18th century. The novel tells the story of the Dutch trader Jacob de Zoet who is stationed at the Dutch East India Company trading post Deshima in the harbor of Nagasaki. The storyline further develops around the conflicts between the Dutch and the English who aim to overtake Deshima and Jacob's love for a Japanese midwife named Orito Aibagawa.

For broadcasting company AVROTROS the goal for this assignment was twofold: on one hand the organization seeks to connect to the newest developments in media, and on the other hand it is looking for news ways to attract younger audiences. Adding VR to radio drama seemed like an interesting way to draw attention to the latter. Before elaborating further on the merging of radio drama and VR within this particular project, we will provide some background into storytelling for the separate media and discuss the concepts of environmental storytelling and generative design.

3   Storytelling and VR

In VR, the user can become engaged with the story in a way that is not entirely active, as in playing a videogame, nor fully passive, as in watching a movie or listening to radio drama. While the term 'lean back' is used for media that allows the user to sit back, relax, and receive information in a passive manner, the term 'lean forward' is used for media in which the user can interact and control the flow of information [19]. To differentiate the engagement styles that VR offers, Vosmeer and Schouten [20] have proposed the use of the term *lean in* for VR, referring to the viewer's agency in directing her gaze towards the information she wants to consider and become emotionally engaged in. In this paragraph we discuss how interactivity, presence and user engagement for lean in media may be connected.

Scholars in the field of interactive storytelling have often focused on the relative freedom the user may have in choosing alternative outcomes for stories [21]. However, offering choices for alternative routes within a VR experience also means that producers are faced with the immense task to pre-produce a multitude of different outcomes. Most users will thereby experience just one single outcome, and possibly miss out on other outcomes that would have been just as interesting. Tanenbaum [22] has pointed out that interactivity does not necessarily has to imply offering the user the ability to directly affect the plot of the story. But when users feel that they have some kind of agency, they do tend to enjoy an experience more [23]. This connects to Gennette thoughts on the function of interactivity: it should serve the narrative by focusing the viewer's attention on the story rather than on the process of storytelling [24].

The concept of *presence* is considered useful in the evaluation of VR as a whole. Following Ryan, presence is usually defined as the 'sense of being there' [25] and it is differentiated from immersion by defining immersion as an objective criterion that refers to the medium itself, while presence is a characteristic of the user experience. Of course, presence and immersion have been discussed extensively long before VR was developed, often in connection to involvement, engagement and transportation theory. Green and Brock have proposed transportation theory as a lens for understanding the concept of media enjoyment [26]. The theory suggests that enjoyment can benefit from the experience of being immersed in a narrative world, as well as from the consequences of that immersion.

The last concept that is important to present in the current context is that of environmental storytelling. The concept of narrative environments refers to how a space is organized and designed to tell a the story and how textures, music, and staging come together to reinforce a story. The concept was used by Jenkins [27] and others [28, 29] in discussion of video games and has been recently included in VR [30].

4   Radioplay and Storytelling

When discussing the format of radio drama, the first and foremost example that comes to mind is *War of the Worlds*, that was broadcast in 1938 and allegedly caused mass panic, when hundreds of its listeners flooded into the streets in fear of the actual alien invasion that the story foretold [31]. To this day, the case of *War of the Worlds* is a favorite example used in communication science courses to illustrate the impact that mass media can have on their audiences.

No less than seventy years have passed between the broadcast of *War of the Worlds* in 1938 and that of *The thousand autumns of Jacob de Zoet* in 2018. It is far beyond the scope of this paper to give an overview of how the medium evolved and manifested itself through the years, or to list all the topics that have been covered in academic publications such as the *Journal of Radio and Audio Media* [32] (formerly known as the *Journal of Radio Studies*). For our current paper we have selected a small number of studies that connected to the main objective of this paper.

The format of radio drama was central to radio's 'golden age', from the 1930s to the 1950s, but today it is mostly regarded as a historical phenomenon [14]. However, Bottomley points out how the current popularity of podcasts that focus on fictional narratives can almost be considered a revival of this almost forgotten medium. The author explains how the affordable digital production tools and the inexpensive distribution of podcasts over the internet are factors that contribute to this growing interest.

Good [33] reports on an often neglected phenomenon of early radio history, known as 'illustrated radio', that has in its design and intentions some striking parallels with the VR project that is the focus of this paper. Illustrated radio is the term that was used for a range of experiments that were undertaken between the 1920s and 1940s in which broadcasts were enhanced with visual materials. Good describes for instance how radio travelogue lectures were supplemented with newspaper images or how school lessons were delivered over the airwaves into classrooms and illustrated with lantern slides.

Rodero states that radio can be considered the most effective medium when it comes to stimulating the imagination and how its potential to do this stems from the very feature it does not possess: images [15]. The author presents a study in which she compares two kinds of presentation structures in a fictional radio story to determine the extent to which the imagination is aroused. These two basic styles of composition refer to presentation and dramatisation, which comes down the traditional divide between telling and showing of Aristotle, as Rodero points out.

5 Generative Design as a Research Approach

There is a growing body of literature within the Human Computer Interaction field [34–36] that provides opportunities for constructing knowledge that is not empirical in nature. From the larger field of design theory, we can assert that knowledge about design can either be generative (idea-centered) or evaluative (synthesis-focused) [37]. Generative centered design refers to the development of new ideas whereas evaluative design refers to the synthesizing of a direction for further development work. Particularly relevant to our research is Höök and Löwgren's proposal of *strong concepts* [34]. Strong concepts are design elements that can be taken from a particular digital or interactive design, to be used by designers in other applications. The concept of three in a row that exists in tic-tac-toe, for example, is an element that has been extracted to other games including various board games and a range of digital games such as *Candy Crush* [38]. The aim of our current project was to focus on the *strong concepts* that emerged during the design process, rather than on the final prototype.

In addition to being a conceptual process, design can be considered as a thought process, because it lives in the mind of the designer [39]. To support critical reflection throughout the design process, the student designers were asked over a six week period to complete weekly diaries with open ended questions as prompts, participated in reflection interviews with the design researcher and discussed findings in meetings with the project coach. Through these practices, students were to frame the design experience, including determining the problem, noting the problem's features, exacting a structure upon the situation, and finally making decisions to solve the problem [40].

6   Design Research: Merging Radio Drama with VR

For the current project, two short scenes were chosen from the audio files, lasting about ten minutes in total, which would form the basis of the VR experience. In the first fragment protagonist Jacob de Zoet is involved in a correspondence with Penhaligon, the commander of the English fleet, who plans to overtake the valuable trading post Deshima by force. In the audio narration Jacob and Penhaligon can both be heard reading the letters that they write to each other. In the second fragment the voice of Penhaligon is heard, encouraging his crew just before the English attack of Deshima. During the design process of the project a number of strong environmental storytelling concepts were identified. In this section, we present each concept and include the frames or problems that required solving, the design decisions (frame features), as well as the design (frame) solutions.

6.1   Environmental Storytelling Through Interaction

As the radio drama audio that was used as the base for this project was lineair - and was meant to remain so - changing the narrative structure, for instance to create a branching storyline, was not an option.

Frame 1. To heighten the user's sense of agency and presence, which interactive possibilities can be explored?

Frame 1 Solution. Two interactive storytelling elements were embedded in the experience. In the first scene, the user sees the two characters (Jacob and Penhaligon) in front of her, while pieces of paper float gently through the air. Focusing her attention on the papers triggers little images to pop up, such as a ship, a temple or a Japanese woman. The second solution for interaction was added by giving the user some agency over the timing of the scene: by moving her attention away from a floating paper she would stop the audio. The narration from the radio drama would continue when the user again focused on another floating paper or on the characters themselves.

6.2   Environmental Storytelling Through Mood and Emotion

Frame 2. The tension between Jacob and Penhaligon needed to be represented within the experience. How should the characters be designed and staged to define their hostility?

Frame 2 Solution. The characters in the scene are placed with their backs against each other. The design team chose to draw Penhaligon upright, standing and wearing his uniform to demonstrate his prestige and stature. Jacob on the other hand was designed sitting and in everyday clothing to give the user the feeling that he was a humble man.

Frame 3. In the second fragment of the radio drama, Penhaligon is encouraging his crew to attack. For this scene, the student team wanted to design a space without interactive possibilities, but to explore other ways to visually support the mood and emotions of the audio narrative.

Frame 3 Solution. The environmental design solution was to create an 'open' ship suggesting that the experience occurred on a ship, though the vessel itself is not present. Instead, it is symbolized by elements such as barrels, wooden floorboards and floating windows. In the middle of the scene Penhaligon can be seen, standing in front of his crew who appear to be ready for a fight, with their fists rising in the air. The scene is coloured with dark red and purple hues that set an ominous dark mood and visual elements such as a blazing sun and the firing cannons. A Japanese symbol and a Dutch flag remind the user again of the location of the action and the overall storyline.

6.3 Environmental Storytelling Through Sound

Music and sounds can contribute greatly to environmental storytelling experiences [23, 25]. While the audio of the radio drama formed the leading narrative within this project, the students explored the possibility of adding background music and sounds to the VR experience.

Frame 4. In the fragments of the radio drama that were chosen, it is not clear that the story is taking place in Deshima. How could music or sounds support the imagined location of Japan? How could sounds support a story segment?

Frame 4 Solution. In the first scene, traditional Shamisen music was added that provided an immediate Japanese atmosphere. In the second scene, sounds were added, such as the sound of the cannons that are fired at the Dutch. The sounds were meant to set an ominous mood and create the tension of an upcoming battle.

7 Conclusion and Discussion

The mixed media project *The thousand autumns of Jacob de Zoet* was an experiment to merge VR with the 'forgotten' medium of radio drama; intending to explore new insights into the practice of storytelling for VR. Adding images to radio broadcasts, to illustrate and further explain the content, is not new, as Good reported [33]. Therefore, we want to first speculate what VR could add to radio play. It could be argued that in modern life, listeners are often surrounded by visual stimuli from other media such as mobile phones, tablets and computers, which can make it difficult to focus on a radio broadcast. Keeping an audience member 'captive' in a VR surrounding, could help to focus her attention on the story. It could be an option for broadcasting companies to attract the attention of new and younger audiences by providing VR experiences with their radio drama productions. Producers of podcasts may also benefit from this strategy. Of course, these assumptions need further explorative research before any factual statements can be formulated.

An important insight gained during the design process is that environmental storytelling provides useful ways to add emotional content to radio drama. By using the environment to visualize small themes of the story, the designer can add to the mood of the narrative without interfering with the main storyline. The use of Japanese music served the same purpose. Because the interactive elements don't inform the user about the plot, but only reinforce the mood and atmosphere of the scene, they serve the narrative by focusing the viewer's attention on the story, as asserted by Genette [24].

Within the current project, interactivity was used in two different ways. Firstly, the user was given some agency over the timing of the scene by focusing her attention on visual elements in the environment and thereby restarting the paused narration. Secondly, the user was given agency over the visual environment as she could make little images pop up by focusing her attention on elements in her surrounding. Both types of interaction may function to increase the enjoyment of the experience (Fendt, Harrison, Ware, Cardona-Rivera and Roberts, 2012).

Transportation theory suggests that enjoyment can benefit from the experience of being immersed in a narrative world, as well as from the consequences of that immersion. For merged VR-radioplay productions such as *The thousand autumns of Jacob de Zoet*, we therefore hypothesize that the transportational qualities can benefit from adding mood enhancing visuals, atmospheric music and interactive elements. In this sense, the traditional *lean back* medium that is radio drama may benefit from the *lean in* quality of VR.

Acknowledgements. This research project is funded by SiA RAAK – Nationaal Regieorgaan Praktijkgericht Onderzoek. Special thanks to the student team consisting of Rowenna Roelofsen and Dionne Dol for creating the VR experience. We also want to thank AVROTROS and De Hoorspelfabriek for their cooperation.

References

1. Berntsen, K., Palacios, R.C., Herranz, E.: Virtual reality and its uses: a systematic literature review. In: Proceedings of the Fourth International Conference on Technological Ecosystems for Enhancing Multiculturality, pp. 435–439. ACM (2016)
2. Dwight, L.: These VR Film Tips Show How To Direct Audience Attention (2016). http://uploadvr.com/vr-film-tips-guiding-attention. Accessed 25 July 2018
3. Sheikh, A., Brown, A., Watson, Z., Evans, M.: Directing attention in 360-degree video. In: Proceedings of IBC 2016, p. 29 (2016)
4. Danieau, F., Antoine, G., Renaud, D.: Attention guidance for immersive video content in head-mounted displays. In: 2017 IEEE Virtual Reality (VR), pp. 205–206. IEEE (2017)
5. Grogorick, S., Stengel, M., Eisemann, E., Magnor, M.: Subtle gaze guidance for immersive environments. In: Proceedings of the ACM Symposium on Applied Perception, p. 4. ACM (2017)
6. Nielsen, L., et al.: Missing the point: an exploration of how to guide users' attention during cinematic virtual reality. In: Proceedings of the 22nd ACM Conference on Virtual Reality Software and Technology, pp. 229–232. ACM (2016)

7. Vosmeer, M., Roth, C., Schouten, B.: Interaction in surround video: the effect of auditory feedback on enjoyment. In: Schoenau-Fog, H., Bruni, L.E., Louchart, S., Baceviciute, S. (eds.) ICIDS 2015. LNCS, vol. 9445, pp. 202–210. Springer, Cham (2015). https://doi.org/10.1007/978-3-319-27036-4_19

8. Vosmeer, M., Roth, C., Koenitz, H.: Who are you? Voice-over perspective in surround video. In: Nunes, N., Oakley, I., Nisi, V. (eds.) ICIDS 2017. LNCS, vol. 10690, pp. 221–232. Springer, Cham (2017). https://doi.org/10.1007/978-3-319-71027-3_18

9. Men, L., Bryan-Kinns, N., Hassard, A.S., Ma, Z.: The impact of transitions on user experience in virtual reality. In: Proceedings of IEEE Virtual Reality, pp. 285–286 (2017)

10. Moghadam, K.R., Ragan, E.D.: Towards understanding scene transition techniques in immersive 360. In: Virtual Reality (VR), pp. 375–376. IEEE (2017)

11. Bishop, T.: Filmmaker Steven Soderbergh: Virtual Reality is never going to work for real movies (2017). https://www.geekwire.com/2017/filmmaker-steven-soderbergh-virtual-reality-never-going-work-real-movies/. Accessed 25 July 2018

12. Vosmeer, M., Schouten, B.: Project Orpheus. A research study into 360 cinematic VR. In: Proceedings of the 2017 ACM International Conference on Interactive Experiences for TV and Online Video, pp. 85–90 (2017)

13. Kjær, T., Lillelund, C.B., Moth-Poulsen, M., Nilsson, N.C., Nordahl, R., Serafin, S.: Can you cut it?: An exploration of the effects of editing in cinematic virtual reality. Paper presented at the Proceedings of the 23rd ACM Symposium on Virtual Reality Software and Technology, p. 4 (2017)

14. Bottomley, A.J.: Podcasting, welcome to night vale, and the revival of radio drama. J. Radio Audio Media 22(2), 179–189 (2015)

15. Rodero, E.: Stimulating the imagination in a radio story: the role of presentation structure and the degree of involvement of the listener. J. Radio Audio Media 19(1), 45–60 (2012)

16. Chirico, A., Yaden, D.B., Riva, G., Gaggioli, A.: The potential of virtual reality for the investigation of awe. Frontiers Psychol. 7, 1766 (2016)

17. AVROTROS. https://www.avrotros.nl/. Accessed 25 July 2018

18. Mitchell, D.: The thousand autumns of Jacob de Zoet. Sceptre, London (2010)

19. Katz, H.: The Media Handbook: A Complete Guide to Advertising Media Selection, Planning, Research, and Buying. Routledge, London (2010)

20. Vosmeer, M., Schouten, B.: Interactive cinema: engagement and interaction. In: Mitchell, A., Fernández-Vara, C., Thue, D. (eds.) ICIDS 2014. LNCS, vol. 8832, pp. 140–147. Springer, Cham (2014). https://doi.org/10.1007/978-3-319-12337-0_14

21. Stern, A.: Embracing the combinatorial explosion: a brief prescription for interactive story R&D. In: Spierling, U., Szilas, N. (eds.) ICIDS 2008. LNCS, vol. 5334, pp. 1–5. Springer, Heidelberg (2008). https://doi.org/10.1007/978-3-540-89454-4_1

22. Tanenbaum, J.: Imagining new design spaces for interactive digital storytelling. In: Si, M., Thue, D., André, E., Lester, J.C., Tanenbaum, J., Zammitto, V. (eds.) ICIDS 2011. LNCS, vol. 7069, pp. 261–271. Springer, Heidelberg (2011). https://doi.org/10.1007/978-3-642-25289-1_28

23. Fendt, M.W., Harrison, B., Ware, S.G., Cardona-Rivera, R.E., Roberts, D.L.: Achieving the illusion of agency. In: Oyarzun, D., Peinado, F., Young, R.M., Elizalde, A., Méndez, G. (eds.) ICIDS 2012. LNCS, vol. 7648, pp. 114–125. Springer, Heidelberg (2012). https://doi.org/10.1007/978-3-642-34851-8_11

24. Genette, G.: Narrative Discourse. Cornell University Press, New York (1980)

25. Ryan, M.L.: Narrative as Virtual Reality 2: Revisiting Immersion and Interactivity in Literature and Electronic Media. JHU Press (2015)

26. Green, M.C., Brock, T.C.: In the mind's eye: transportation-imagery model of narrative persuasion (2002)

27. Jenkins, H.: Game design as narrative. Computer **44**, 53 (2004)
28. Pearce, C.: Narrative Environments. Space Time Play, pp. 200–205 (2007)
29. Carson, D.: Environmental Storytelling: Creating Immersive 3D Worlds Using Lessons Learned from the Theme Park industry (2000). https://www.gamasutra.com/view/feature/131594/environmental_storytelling_.php. Accessed 25 July 2018
30. Faita, C., et al.: The effect of emotional narrative virtual environments on user experience. In: De Paolis, L.T., Mongelli, A. (eds.) AVR 2016, Part I. LNCS, vol. 9768, pp. 120–132. Springer, Cham (2016). https://doi.org/10.1007/978-3-319-40621-3_8
31. Hayes, J., Battles, K., Hilton-Morrow, W., Rugg, A.: War of the Worlds to Social Media. Peter Lang Publishing, New York (2013)
32. McLennan, A.: Journal of radio and audio media. Taylor & Francis (2018)
33. Good, K.D.: Radio's forgotten visuals. J. Radio Audio Media **23**(2), 364–368 (2016)
34. Höök, K., Löwgren, J.: Strong concepts: Intermediate-level knowledge in interaction design research. ACM Trans. Comput. Hum. Interact. (TOCHI) **19**(3), 23 (2012)
35. Jonas, W.: Design research and its meaning to the methodological development of the discipline. In: Design Research Now, pp. 187–206 (2007)
36. Stolterman, E.: The nature of design practice and implications for interaction design research. Int. J. Des. **2**(1), 55–65 (2008)
37. Kolko, J.: Exposing the Magic of Design: A Practitioner's Guide to the Methods and Theory of Synthesis. Oxford University Press, Oxford (2010)
38. Candy Crush: Digital image. Candy Crush Saga (2012)
39. Löwgren, J., Stolterman, E.: Thoughtful Interaction Design. MIT Press, Cambridge (2004)
40. Schön, D.A.: The Reflective Practitioner: How Professionals Think in Action. Routledge, London (1987)

fanSHEN's *Looking for Love*: A Case Study in How Theatrical and Performative Practices Inform Interactive Digital Narratives

Daniel Barnard[✉]

London South Bank University, London, UK
barnard2@lsbu.ac.uk

Abstract. This paper explores how theatrical and performative practices inform interactive digital narratives. It does this through a case study of *Looking for Love*, a new piece by fanSHEN. The creative process used to create *Looking for Love* is analysed in terms of its roots in theatrical processes, particularly in terms of characterization, the relationship between structure and improvisation, dramatic arc and the role of the spectator.

Keywords: Interactive digital narratives · Interactive theatre
Performance · fanSHEN · Looking for Love · Joe McAlister

1 Introduction

This paper addresses the conference theme "Interactive Digital Narrative Practices" and particularly focuses around the question of how theatrical and performative practices inform interactive digital narratives and vice versa.

It explores this question through a case study of fanSHEN who began as a theatre company and now describe themselves as "a recovering theatre company, who now design and create audience-centric experiences which involve elements of performance, game and installation." [1] fanSHEN are part of a generation of artists who are doing what Giannachi and Benford describe as employing "digital technologies to create distinctive forms of interactive, distributed, and often deeply subjective theatrical performance." [2]

This paper explores how fanSHEN's theatrical and performative background is informing their creative process and how they are adapting this process to create work in this new art form. It draws on my own experience as a collaborator on this project and on interviews I held with fanSHEN's Creative Director Rachel Briscoe and with *Looking for Love*'s computational artist Joe McAlister in July 2018.

It is not new for theatrical methodologies to inform interactive fiction; the techniques of improvisational theatre in particular have deeply informed the work of Brian Magerko and others [3, 4]. Similarly, concepts from interactive fiction and games design have deeply informed how performance scholars think about participatory and immersive performance [5, 6]. This paper seeks to identify what might be unique in the creation and experience of *Looking for Love* and what applications it might have for future interactive fiction or research.

© Springer Nature Switzerland AG 2018
R. Rouse et al. (Eds.): ICIDS 2018, LNCS 11318, pp. 401–407, 2018.
https://doi.org/10.1007/978-3-030-04028-4_47

2   Context about fanSHEN

2.1   fanSHEN's Trajectory Towards Interactive Digital Performance

fanSHEN were formed in 2007. Their early productions were of contemporary plays performed in a fairly naturalistic style. Their knowledge of dramaturgy (the technique of dramatic composition) was nurtured through Creative Director Rachel Briscoe's participation in the young writers' programmes at the Royal Court and Soho theatres [7]. Their rehearsal process was deeply rooted in the Stanislavski System of Acting. Both of these methodologies continue to inform their work, including the creative development of *Looking for Love*.

Their work became increasingly interactive over a number of productions, first using analogue technologies to stimulate interaction and then digital ones (in productions such as *Invisible Treasure, Disaster Party* and *Out of* Sight). fanSHEN embarked on their first collaboration with computational artist Joe McAlister, *The Justice Syndicate* in 2017. In this piece, 12 co-located audience-participants take on the role of jurors considering a difficult case. Each participant has a tablet on which they receive evidence (in document form), watch videos of witness testimonies, receive prompts to debate the case with fellow jurors and vote. The software behind the piece uses machine learning to send tasks to individuals based on their voting pattern in order to attempt to sway them from their original position. It also uses the voting data and time spent looking at different documents to attempt to predict the final vote of each juror and the overall outcome.

2.2   Looking for Love: fanSHEN's First Piece of Interactive Fiction

Looking for Love is a collaboration between Rachel Briscoe (fanSHEN's Creative Director), computational artist Joe McAlister and me.

In *Looking for Love* the participant starts by creating a dating profile and answering a personality quiz on an explicitly fictionalised dating app. They are then matched with three characters and choose one that they wish to continue chatting with. They chat with this character over a period of three weeks, over which time the character gradually reveals more and more about themselves and their story while also attempting to gather information about the participant. As the piece progresses, the character (who is played by a chat bot – and the participant is made aware of this at the beginning) also tries to adapt themselves more and more to the tastes of the participant, attempting to become their ideal partner, with shared values, habits and preferences. After three weeks the participant and character arrange to meet in a café. When the participant arrives at the café they have an Augmented Reality experience in which they see an animation of the "date" as if from the position of a spectator. As the two animated characters talk, the participant sees the character's thoughts and realises how much the character knows about them. They are then invited to look round an exhibition about data privacy and are given guidance on how to protect their data.

Briscoe sees the piece and how fanSHEN have developed it as a logical continuation of fanSHEN's work in terms of how it places the audience at the centre of the artwork: "I think we have been working with a dramaturgy of interactivity for the last three years. So it's about creating a structure and a series of really clear invitations and I think that's going to be as important here."

3 Narrative Structures and Theatrical Elements in *Looking for Love*

3.1 Narrative Structures and Dramaturgies

A key respect in which *Looking for* Love departs from most interactive fiction is in the nature of the characters and the character development process. In the majority of interactive fiction, the characters that the reader/player encounters have a plot function and are often of necessity archetypal rather than complex as this helps the reader/player know how to interact with them. In *Looking for Love,* the player only interacts with one character throughout, enabling a greater level of complexity to emerge. Having established the basic shape of the piece, fanSHEN began the second week of development by creating a number of characters, in an approach analogous to the devising techniques of Mike Leigh and Mike Bradwell [8]. While each player only interacts with one character, a number of characters exist within the piece so that the date you are matched with has a background and personality that make them a believable dating partner for the player. The questions that we used to develop the characters spanned both serious personality-forming topics (defining childhood experience, thing I'm most ashamed of, proudest moment) to topics particularly relevant to this piece (brands I like, preferred source of news, celebrity I think I resemble) to bespoke questions that would contribute to building the characters' chat bots (phrases or words I use a lot, quality of punctuation and grammar). Inspired by fanSHEN's study of drama and acting techniques, particularly those of American acting teacher Susan Batson [9] each character was built with a surface persona, an underlying secret and a source of grief.

In all truly interactive performance and in much one-on-one performance there is a balance between structure (which Briscoe described in her interview with me as a series of 'really clear invitations") and improvisation, sections in which the participant responds to those invitations and the performer(s) (where they are present) reacts. What is original about *Looking for Love*, in the field of performance at any rate, is the way in which this improvisatory role is being adopted by a chat bot rather than by a human. As computational artist Joe McAlister put it in his interview with me: "we follow a loose narrative that allows the player to provide multiple forms of response via text, or image, which a bot subsequently analyses and responds to relevantly. Unlike other interactive fiction, the user is free to guide this conversation in any direction they wish, chatting with the bot in regards to any subject." The chat bot is built with the aim of maintaining the illusion of a consistent and three-dimensional character through particular uses of language, that differ for each character (for example use of capitalization, grammar, habitual words for "good" and "bad" and repeated characteristic phrases) and through programming that combines improvisatory chat bot activity trained with LSTM Recurrent Neural Networks with text scripted by humans. For example, near the beginning of the experience the character suggests that you ask each other questions about what is written in your dating profile. Whichever topic the player asks about, there is a keyword-generated human-scripted response. On specific days over the three-week experience, the character sends human-scripted accounts of things that have happened in their life or asks the player pre-programmed questions. In between these pre-programmed interactions, the bot is programmed to engage in free chat whenever the player contacts them; ending conversations when there are questions it cannot respond to in a way intended to seem natural. This model is intended to address for the purposes of this artwork what Michael Mateas and Andrew Stern describes as "the fundamental freedom between player freedom and story structure." [10]. In this sense, the piece is, arguably, an example of what Mateas calls Expressive AI:

Expressive AI is a new interdiscipline of AI-based cultural production combining art practice and AI research practice. Expressive AI changes the focus from an AI system as a thing in itself (presumably demonstrating some essential feature of intelligence) to the communication between author and audience. The technical practice of building the artifact becomes one of exploring which architectures and techniques best serve as an inscription device within which the authors can express their message [11].

Briscoe describes the narrative structure of *Looking for Love* as a "reverse branching narrative." In contrast to the classic model of interactive fiction, in which all players start in the same situation and then take a series of choices that take the story in different directions, *Looking for Love* begins with a broad choice of which character to talk to, with each character having their own tastes and preferred topics. Whatever choices the participant makes, however, they all lead to the encounter in the café in which the Augmented Reality animation reveals what it knows about the participant. Approximately two weeks in to the experience, the character will reveal the story of the death of their previous partner and discuss their grief about the topic. The identity of the partner, the story of how they died and the way in which the character deals with their grief varies from character to character, but the basic structure remains the same.

fanSHEN's structuring of the journey that the participant goes on in their dialogue with the character is influenced by dramatic structures such as Freytag's dramatic arc, consisting of exposition, rising action, climax, falling action, and dénouement [12]. As Briscoe commented "I think the biggest thing about traditional story is that it means you keep watching" This reflects the findings of Petrelli and Wright that readers of digital fiction still want the story to "pull them along." [13].

When I interviewed Joe McAlister I asked him in what way collaborating with theatre artists such as Rachel Briscoe and me seemed different to the process of collaborating with a fellow computational artist. He responded:

"Dan and Rachel bring extensive knowledge of how to create an engaging and emotional narrative, something that I believe to be key to creating a realistic and relatable AI character. They also bring an entirely different approach to building this piece, unlike the methodical technology-centric approach that I am accustomed to."

3.2 Personalization and Privacy

Looking for Love personalizes the participant's experience in various ways. The participant is matched with a character after taking a "personality quiz' so that they are already offered a character who matches some of their tastes and opinions. Based on the information gleaned from this quiz, the character is already adapted to suit the participant; they prefer cats to dogs or cycling to driving if you do, or vice versa. In ensuing interactions, the character asks you to suggest a song for them to listen to and a few days later sends a similar song. They ask about your favourite films and then later use gifs from them. The programme scans the participant's social media and then sends them news stories with a similar political perspective. The purpose of this is both to explore how much we are drawn to people with similar tastes and opinions as ourselves but also to reveal to participants the price of personalization in terms of the volume of private information that we leak. In the final augmented reality section this data is revealed to the participant in manner designed to jolt them into a realization about how much information they leak online.

3.3   The Role of the Participant/Spectator

For the first three weeks of the piece until the Augmented Reality section in the café, the participant is one of two protagonists in the action, together with the character they are interacting with. The Augmented Reality section is an abrupt stylistic shift but also an abrupt shift in the role of the audience member, from active participant to that of a spectator, watching the action unfold before them. This shift in the role of the audience member is intended to help give them critical distance and invite them to reflect on how much information they have given away about themselves in an echo of the "attitude of criticism" that Brecht aimed sometimes to create for his audiences, in part through the use of the Verfremdungseffekt [14].

3.4   *Looking for Love* as Immersive or One-on-One Performance

In many respects, Looking for Love can be read as a continuation of the trend for "one on one" theatre and performance. According to Adam Alston, "one-on-one theatre is usually designed to be experienced by individual audience members in isolation from anyone other than a performer, or performers… One-on-one theatre tends to be participatory and may invite audiences to perform tasks, or interact with something or someone" [15]. What *Looking for Love* shares with one-on-one theatre is the level of intimacy that fanSHEN are aiming for between the participant and the character. The key difference is that, whereas in one-on-one theatre, the participant and performer(s) are co-located, in *Looking for Love* the participant and character and not co-located and instead the communication is mediated via a mobile phone. This raises questions over whether *Looking for Love* might be described as "immersive." According to Calleja, immersion can refer to a range of experiences including "general engagement, perceptions of realism, addiction, suspension of disbelief and identification with games characters." [16]. While *Looking for Love* might achieve absorption, the suspension of disbelief (participants can simultaneously know the character is a bot and treat it like a human being) and identification with the character, it does not seem to fit theatrical definitions of immersive:

"immersive theatre establishes a special kind of presence – visceral in every respect, being both embodied and noetic. In the realm of theatre, it can be understood that this feeling of "being there" is a fact; the audience-participant *is actually there*, physically inhabiting the fantasy world created." [17]

However, the "actually there" of online dating is wherever your phone is; it is an online rather than a physical space. According to Briscoe, she is interested in whether this permits a greater level of intimacy and emotional risk. In a blog she wrote:

"In research for a current project, I had a number of conversations about online dating. People said they were bolder, revealed more and took more risks while chatting online than they would have done face-to-face; research around computer-mediated communication would confirm this, and that it has to do with not getting verbal or visual feedback from the person you're talking to (so you're less likely to feel disapproved of). But one person also said something very interesting: that we tend, in general, to conflate emotional and physical safety when actually they're very different. When messaging from her house, where she was surrounded by all her stuff, warm, in comfy clothes etc., she felt physically safe – and this allowed her to take more emotional risks and reveal more." [18]

What may be lost in this process is the visceral, embodied experience made possible in co-located one-on-one or immersive performance. Does this potential lack of visceral embodiment mean that the level of intimacy and emotional risk in *Looking for Love* is less than in co-located one-on-one performance or is it merely different? In her analysis of Blast Theory's *Karen*, which is also experienced entirely via a phone and in which the participant interacts with a fictional life coach, Maria Chatzichristodoulou argues that the intimacy is, if anything, more intense:

"My relationship with Karen becomes increasingly complex and challenging, forcing me to ask myself questions about some uncomfortable matters." [19]

4   Conclusion

Looking for Love I, s arguably, a unique combination of digital performance and interactive fiction. In its creation of an intimate dialogue between a participant and character and its combination of structure and improvisation, it has similarities to one-on-one performance with the key differences that the character and participant are not co-located and the character is a chat bot rather than a human performers. It has some parallels with pieces like Blast Theory's *Karen* but whereas *Karen* gives the participant a limited range of choices, *Looking for Love* uses chat bot technologies to enable much more improvisation and machine learning to enable a higher level of personalization. It differs from much interactive fiction in the use of a complex character, created using theatrical character creation processes. The particular mix of chat bot improvisation and human-scripted text is unusual. The piece is currently in development; there is the potential for valuable future research into how well these elements function in terms of the participant's experience; how well they achieve Mateas' vision of "expressive AI" and what adjustments need to be made in terms of how they could function better.

References

1. fanSHEN About Page. https://www.fanshen.org.uk/about1/
2. Benford, S., Giannachi, G.: Performing Mixed Reality. The MIT Press, Chigago (2011)
3. deLeon, C., Dohogne, P., Magerko, B.: Employing fuzzy concept for digital improvisational theatre. In: 7th AAAI Conference on Artificial Intelligence and Interactive Digital Entertainment. AAAI Press, Menlo Park, California (2011)
4. Fuller, D., Magerko, B.: Shared mental models in improvisational performance. In: Proceedings of the Intelligent Narrative Technologies III Workshop on - INT3 2010 (2010). https://doi.org/10.1145/1822309.1822324
5. Swift, E.: What do audiences do? negotiating the possible worlds of participatory theatre. J. Contemp. Drama English, **4**(1), 134–149. De Gruyter, Berlin (2016). https://doi.org/10.1515/jcde-2016-0011
6. Machon, J.: Immersive theatres: intimacy and immediacy in contemporary performance. Palgrave Mamillan (Basingstoke) (2013)
7. fanSHEN About page. https://www.fanshen.org.uk/rachel-briscoe
8. Bradwell, M.: Inventing the Truth: Devising and Directing for the Theatre. Nick Hern Books, London (2012)
9. Batson, S.: Truth: Personas, Needs, and Flaws in the Art of Building Actors and Creating Characters. Webster/Stone, New York (2014)
10. Mateas, M., Stern, A.: Façade: an experiment in building a fully-realized interactive drama. In: Game Developers Conference, San Francisco (2003)
11. Mateas, M.: Expressive AI: A Hybrid Art and Science Practice. Art Gallery Siggraph, New Orleans (2000)
12. Freytag, G.: Technique of the Drama: An Exposition of Dramatic Composition and Art. S.C Griggs & Company, Chicago (1896)
13. Petrelli, D., Wright, H.: On the writing, reading and publishing of digital stories. Libr. Rev. **58**(7), 509–526. Emerald Insight, Bingley (2009). https://doi.org/10.1108/00242530910978208
14. Brecht, B.: Brecht on Theatre. Methuen, London (1978)
15. Alston, A.: Reflections on Intimacy and Narcissm in Ontroerend Goed's Personal Trilogy. Performing Ethos, pp. 107–119. Intellect Journals, Bristol (2012)
16. Calleja, G.: In-Game - From Immersion to Incorporation. MIT Press, London and Cambridge, MA (2011)
17. Machon, J.: Immersive theatres: intimacy and immediacy in contemporary performance. Palgrave Mamillan, Basingstoke (2013)
18. Briscoe, R.: fanSHEN blog. https://www.fanshen.org.uk/blog/2017/3/2/on-hospitality
19. Chatzichristodoulou, M.: Karen by blast theory: leaking privacy. In: Broadhurst, S., Price S.: Digital Bodies. Palgrave Macmillan, Basingstoke (2017)

Vox Populi

Sytze Schalk[(⊠)]

HKU University of the Arts Utrecht,
Nieuwekade 1, 3511 RV Utrecht, The Netherlands
sytze.schalk@gmail.com

Abstract. The Vox Populi demo is a prototype for an interactive narrative design which functions as a playful simulation of the creation of media narratives. The prototype is part of the European 'Borderline Offensive' project and the Professorship Interactive Narrative Design at the HKU University of the Arts Utrecht.

Keywords: Interactive narrative design · Theatre game · Media narratives
Representation of refugees

1 Introduction

The theatre game 'Vox Populi' is being developed as part of the European Borderline Offensive [1] project, an initiative which proposes using humor as a tool for tackling the subject of the refugee crisis in Europe. The project will be developed over the course of 2018–2019, perform at several European venues in 2019 and finally, be part of a conference in Göteborg in 2020 [2].

In addition to this, 'Vox Populi' is also the first case study in my doctoral research for which I will look at how existing models and techniques of interactive narrative and gamification can be applied within a performative framework to represent new forms of narrative (and thematical) complexity, and what the effects are of applying interactive narrative design techniques and models within a performative framework on the dramatic structure and the story experience by the audience. As part of my PhD research, I will set up user studies for new performances within the ongoing 'Shatterland' [3] transmedia storyworld. The first of those is 'Vox Populi', a new card-based interactive theatre game which explores the mechanics of media narratives and representations of the European refugee crisis. I will start the first prototyping phase this summer as part of the 'Borderline Offensive' project and would like to present and test a further developed prototype (between 30 and 40 min in length) at the ICIDS Conference. The aim of the demo is not only to test out the workings of the interactive narrative design for players, but also to reflect on the relation between the game mechanics and its moral implications. This is why I am interested in reflection and discussion about the ways interactive narrative design can lay bare the mechanics of power and how it would be possible to prevent presenting the mechanisms of harmful media narratives and opinions as something attractive or admirable.

R. Rouse et al. (Eds.): ICIDS 2018, LNCS 11318, pp. 408–411, 2018.
https://doi.org/10.1007/978-3-030-04028-4_48

2   Contents of the Project

'Vox Populi' is a theatre game about politics, public opinion and the power of media. In a combination between an analogue card game, digital technology and theatre performance the audience takes on the role of spin doctors for a presidential candidate in Lida, a country in the fictional storyworld of 'Shatterland'. They have only one goal: to win the elections at all costs. They will do this by using the media to manipulate the narrative around an incident involving a refugee and influence Lidanian voters.

Thematically and visually, the storyworld of Shatterland draws upon the fractured and complex history, present and future of the European continent. Its architecture is based on European cities such as Prague and Budapest. Its stories explore themes of xenophobia, social justice and how to remain empathetic in a volatile world. The transmedial setup allows for an intricate web of stories which are all interconnected but can be experienced and understood on their own.

Within the narrative frame of Vox Populi, the first free elections in Lida are coming up, after the people have gotten rid of the royal family who ruled the country for centuries. There is one topic that is keeping the country in its grip: a short while ago a large group of refugees have arrived in Lida. They are coming from the nearby Islands and have fled their homes after their lands have become unlivable because of drought and climate change. The refugees now live in makeshift camps at the edge of the capital and are viewed with suspicion by the Lidanians. The country is itself suffering from a shortage of food and jobs, and some people are worried that the refugees, with their 'different' habits and faith, form a threat to the Lidanian way of life.

Making matters worse is that here has been an incident in the build-up to the election involving a young refugee and a Lidanian family. Details are scarce, but according to first reports there has been a violent robbery during which the daughter of the family was severely wounded. It is yet to be seen if these reports are accurate, but every politician who wants to have any chance of winning the election will have to use the story for his or her own benefit and present a vision for the future of the refugees in the country for voters. Luckily for them, they're not on their own: each politician has access to a team of spindoctors who are experts in playing the media and presenting their candidate in the best possible way.

In Vox Populi players take on the role of these spindoctors, in teams of 5 spin-doctors per candidate. In the four weeks leading up to the election they will do everything to put their presidential candidate in the spotlight and keep him or her there. The game consists of four rounds and each round takes up one week in the run-up to the elections. Each round brings more information about what happened between the refugee and the family. A lot of these 'facts' are incomplete however, or can be explained in multiple ways. It is up to the spindoctors to interpret the events and convert them to an effective 'frame' which will sway the mood of voters. They do this by broadcasting theories, (half-) truths and slogans through different media channels. The spindoctors can encourage their candidate to conduct a newspaper interview for instance, or let him or her repeat certain conspiracy theories during a speech on a village square. The spindoctors who succeed in letting their candidate present the most coherent story of the events - whatever that story might be - will exert the most influence on the public and take a head start in the polls. But the relationship between politicians and the people works both ways: the mood of the Vox Populi determines which sources and interpretations about the incident will come available to the spin-doctors in later rounds. In this way, politicians, media and citizens cast a spell on each other and create a vicious circle together in which the reporting around the incident becomes more and more extreme in the build-up to the elections and takes on a life on its own.

This process of framing is presented in the form of a card game. The game is supported by a software package which serves as a tool for keeping the score and displays a never-ending stream of thoughts and opinions from the 'regular' people of Lida. Additionally, two actors act as game leaders. They will also show the consequences of the political battle on the Lidanian society in theatrical scenes in between rounds. In this scenes they take on different roles, from concerned citizens who are trying to help the refugees and business men who are looking for ways to benefit from the crisis, to the people who are the accidental main characters of the story: the refugee and the family. The choices made by the players during the game will not only determine who ultimately becomes the new president of Lida, but also shape the lives of all people who were involved in the incident, after the initial flurry of attention has subsided and the media have moved on to the next story.

3 Project Aims

As a researcher, artist and a (local) politician I often feel deeply conflicted about stories. When I look at the news or listen to a politician speaking to a crowd, I recognize the same techniques I use when I'm writing: the inciting incident, the use of conflict to create tension, a battle of wills and the inevitable climax. The use of these techniques is not a coincidence: they are age-old and proven methods to grip the attention and imagination of your audience. But stories are never neutral, they always have a moral and political dimension. All stories – even fictional ones – are not complete representations but selections of the reality they exist in, neatly structured to invoke emotions and convey certain (implicit) messages.

I feel this is especially true in 'stories' created around the topics of migration and refugees. Here, human lives are all too easily turned into polished narratives, experiences of suffering are turned into iconic images on our smartphones, and people desperately seeking safety are portrayed as antagonists, a faceless horde of 'Others'. In the ongoing debate regarding refugees and migrants in Europe, I feel there is relatively little attention being paid to the devices we use to conduct our 'conversation' and the underlying mechanics of the media we consume.

With Vox Populi, I want to make the invisible visible and make the complexity of our reality easier to understand. For me, the medium of interactive theater, in this case a combination between theatre performance, card game and storied software, is ideally suited for this, because it turns this difficult and invisible 'media machine' into something you can actually experience as an audience, instead of yet another story that you only passively consume. It is a way to represent the complexity of our modern reality and make abstract systems tangible for an audience. As a player in Vox Populi, you will not only see the consequences of your actions played out in real-time, but you also become responsible for the lives of the characters represented within the game. And because theatre is a medium that is collective by nature, it also fosters discussion, reflection, and the exchange of ideas and opinions during and after the experience.

4   Current State

The project of Vox Populi is in itself a spiritual sequel of sorts to 'Kaptka' [4], another card-based theatre game around storytelling I created two years ago. By placing the experience within a fictional storyworld, I can create a playful 'magic circle', as defined by historian Huizinga [5]. In the context of the Vox Populi project, the card game becomes essentially a 'safe' performative space which makes it easier to discuss and reflect upon the themes represented in the game.

At the same time however, I am well aware of the ethical challenges that will come into play with this idea. As a player, you will basically step into the shoes of an antagonist, a 'villain' of some sorts, and while that can be fun in and of itself, this also runs the risk of legitimizing the very people and institutions the theatre game is criticizing and satirizing. In other words: a joke only works as a joke when it is perceived as such. This is why I want to be very careful to not to turn these media narratives and opinions in something admirable or to turn the voiceless into figures of fun.

Creating something that is once subversive and unifying, both satirical and empathetic will be a great challenge, which for me is one of the big reasons why I would like to present and discuss the project at ICIDS. At the moment the project is in its early days of development. There is a working paper prototype with a first version of the game rules, dramatic scenes and visual design document. As part of my ongoing PhD-research I will iterate on this prototype with playtests in the coming months during several conferences and a follow-up artistic residency in Kosice, Slovakia, where the original concept has also been conceived. During this period, we also want to lay the foundation of the software for the game, although we purposefully want to keep its design and function open for the time being, so we can incorporate feedback and outcomes of playtests and talks into its design.

References

1. Borderline Offensive: About & Partners (2018). http://www.borderlineoffensive.eu/about/. Accessed 27 July 2018
2. Borderline Offensive: Call for Artists: More Info & Details (2018). http://www. borderlineoffensive.eu/call-for-artists-more-info-details/. Accessed 27 July 2018
3. Shatterland: De Wentel (2015). http://dewentel.nl/
4. Gameplay Video Kapta (2015). https://www.youtube.com/watch?v=gXkBgOuuidQ
5. Huizinga, J.: Homo Ludens: A Study of the Play-Element in Culture. The Beacon Press, Boston (1955)

Generative and Assistive Tools and Techniques

Automatic Detection of Conflicts in Complex Narrative Structures

Nicolas Szilas[(⊠)], Sergio Estupiñán, and Urs Richle

TECFA, FPSE, University of Geneva, 1211 Geneva 4, Switzerland
{Nicolas.Szilas,Sergio.Estupinan,Urs.Richle}@unige.ch

Abstract. The central notion of conflict in drama is well-acknowledged but not properly formalized. Computational models of conflict tend to target one specific type of conflict and consequently lose the global point of view on the story. Using a model of dramatic structure, this article specifies a number of conflict types within a unified model and proposes an algorithm to automatically extract all conflicts within a narrative structure. The algorithm is then tested on a storyworld that shows as many as 31 coexisting conflicts. Finally, a cluster analysis on these conflicts is performed, showing that in the considered case, conflicts can be reduced to three main "conflict groups."

Keywords: Interactive narrative · Computational models of narrative
Conflict · Rules

1 Dramatic Conflict: A Protelform Concept

In dramaturgy and screenwriting handbooks, *conflict*—or an analogous term—is often considered as the core of drama: "Any dramatic situation stems from a conflict between two main directions of effort"[1] ([14], p. 200), "Conflict is at the core of any dramatic work"(See footnote 1) ([9], p. 32), "All drama is conflict" ([6], p. 24), "Conflict is the basis of drama" ([16], p. 125), "Conflict is the heartbeat of all writing" ([5], p. 178), "A story without a struggle can never be a dramatic story" ([23], p. 143), and so forth. However, what is meant behind the term *conflict* often varies, and despite the common usage of the term, no agreed definition has emerged. Conflict is not just an opposition or contrast of elements (e.g., John is rich and strong, while Mark is poor and weak), but it is related to core actions in the story (e.g., both John and Mark want to marry Elisa). Conflict is usually discussed as a phenomenon occurring at the story or fabula level, contrary to other narrative effects (such as surprise) that may occur at both story and discourse levels.

In addition to definitions, many different characterizations and classifications of conflict have been proposed. First, a distinction between external and internal conflicts is often acknowledged: the former type occurs between a character's goals and resistance from the environment; the latter type occurs within a character and involves his or her internal needs (e.g., [12]). Second, within external conflicts, one can distinguish conflicts with the physical environment (further decomposed into obstacles and

---

[1] Our translation.

© Springer Nature Switzerland AG 2018
R. Rouse et al. (Eds.): ICIDS 2018, LNCS 11318, pp. 415–427, 2018.
https://doi.org/10.1007/978-3-030-04028-4_49

complications in [23]) from conflicts between characters (counter intention in [23], p. 146; conflict or opposition with an opponent in [22], p. 94). Third, conflict has been related to the moral values of characters and to the ethical dimension of the story as a whole [22]. The notion of conflict extends beyond drama and applies to narrative in general. For example, the six-actant model [7] contains a subject and an opponent. The paradox model proposed by Nichols [13] concerns narrative in general. The early myth model proposed by Levi Strauss is fundamentally based on a set of contradictions [10] (the conflict in this theory has not been attached to specific story elements).

A first observation following this overview is the wide variety of terminology that covers either different names of the conflict concept or specific cases of conflict—for example, *obstacle, complication, struggle, dilemma, paradox, opposition*, and *contradiction*. A second observation is the full heterogeneity of theories and classifications regarding conflict. Conflict thus appears as a proteiform concept that is not well-defined, raising the question of whether this concept should be used at all for formal and computational models of narrative and drama.

However, the notion of conflict is so central that it cannot be ignored, and several interactive digital storytelling systems have implemented various models of conflict. We have summarized the computational models of conflict in Table 1, matching each model with its narratological counterpart.

Each computational approach tends to focus on one aspect of conflict. For example, models of moral conflicts [2, 18] cover internal moral conflicts, not intercharacter conflicts. Conversely, Ware and Young's planning-based model of conflict considers conflicts between plans and therefore cannot account for conflicts between achievement goals and moral goals or values. GADIN [1] is one of the most complete models of conflict (as dilemma), but it covers only situations in which a social relationship is at stake (friends and enemies), putting aside internal conflicts. Conversely, the dilemma generation model [3] does not deal easily with intercharacter conflicts. The paradox-based model [19] focuses on internal conflict in general.

Ultimately, the variety of conflict-based computational models reflects the broadness and fuzziness of the original concept of conflict. To fully embrace the concept of conflict without reducing it to one specific expression, this article adopts an existing structural model of dramatic situation [21] and attempts to demonstrate that this model can accurately cover the variety of conflicts found in literature and computer implementations. In the next section, after the model's main principles are summarized, each type of conflict it can cover is systematically defined and characterized. In the process, the model is extended with new types of structural elements. In Sect. 3, the model is implemented, along with an algorithm that extracts existing conflicts from a given narrative structure. Section 4 provides a practical illustration of the algorithm on one story. The practical results of this experiment draw new lines of investigation regarding groups of conflicts to deal with the complexity that characterizes authentic storyworlds.

Table 1. Various types of conflicts and their computational models

Conflict in narrative theories	Conflict in computational model
Internal moral conflict [12]	IDtension: goals, tasks, and values [18] Conflict of goals and values [2] Dilemma generation models [3, 8] Moral dilemmas [15]
Inner (nonmoral) conflict [12]	Conflict within one character's plans [24]
External conflict: obstacle [9, 23]	IDtension: obstacle [18] Plan failure [4]
External conflict: personal conflicts [12], counter intention [23], conflict with antagonist [5], intercharacter conflict [22, 23]	Conflict between two characters' plans [24]
External conflict: social dilemma	GADIN: betrayal, sacrifice, greater good, take down, favor [1] Generation of dilemma [3]
Paradox [13]	Dramatic situations [19]

2   Conflicts and Their Modelling

2.1   A Unified Model of Conflict

We based this research on a model of a dramatic situation that was successfully used to manually analyze stories [21]. This model is based on goal-task structures that describe dramatic situations in terms of a relational network that consists of six types of *nodes*: goals, tasks, obstacles, side-effect, characters, and character sets. These elements are connected via different types of weighted and oriented *relations*. For example, the fact that a task enables a goal to be reached is represented by a *reaching* relation from the task to the goal, with weight "1." A given arrangement of nodes and relations creates a *situation*, formally described as a well-formed[2] and oriented graph. A situation may contain a *dramatic cycle*, which is a pattern that corresponds to conflicts. It is formally defined as follows:

- A dramatic cycle is a subgraph of a situation graph that forms a cycle, regardless of the relation's direction.
- Within a dramatic cycle, two nodes named the *start node* and the *end node* are such as there are two distinct paths from the start node to the end node, with strengths of opposite signs. The *strength* of a path is defined as the product of the weights of all relations it contains.

---

[2] Each relation needs to connect to nodes of the type specified for this type of relation.

This formal characterization of conflict expresses the fact that an element in the story has contradictory consequences. Figure 1a provides a generic example of a dramatic cycle with generic elements. In this example, a character may perform a task that, on the one hand, reaches his or her goal and, on the other hand, threatens another of his or her goals (via a side effect). Figure 1b provides a specific example that instantiates the generic example. Many other specific examples can be found elsewhere in literature [20, 21]. A key feature of this model is that it does not specify the type of start and end nodes in the dramatic cycle.

From a global perspective, one can analyze the model according to three levels:

- The metamodel: it encompasses the notions of nodes and relations. At this level, the general notion of conflict is defined as a dramatic cycle.
- The narrative model: it specifies a given set of node types and relation types.
- The story model: given a certain narrative model, it describes one specific story or storyworld.

In this article, while keeping the metamodel unchanged, we introduce new types of relations, thereby extending the narrative model to cover more cases of conflicts.

2.2   Exercises in Conflict Type

Let us now consider different topologies of dramatic cycles that correspond to different types of conflicts.

The paradox: the end node is a goal. If, in a dramatic cycle, the two opposite paths converge toward a goal, it means that the start node (typically a task) both leads to the achievement of the goal and prevents this achievement. This situation is frequent in narratives and has been described in detail by Nichols [13].

The internal conflict: the end node is a character and connected via two satisfying relations. If two paths of opposite signs lead to the same character via two different goals, on one hand a beneficial goal is achieved but, on the other hand, another beneficial goal is impaired. This corresponds to an internal conflict [9]. If one goal is an achievement goal and the other is a moral goal, then we have a moral dilemma or conflict [2, 18].

The intercharacter (social) conflict: the end node is a set and connected via two belonging relations. In this case, a task in the structure satisfies one character but not another character. Because the two characters belong to the same set (one can always define a general set of all characters), a conflict arises at the level of the social group (the set). Depending on the type of belonging relation, several subtypes of conflicts may occur; for example, if both characters are friends or brothers, this constitutes a stronger conflict than if the characters are just unrelated human beings. The strength of a conflict may be modeled by changing the weight of the relation (this possibility is not explored further in this article). Depending on which character has the possibility to act on the structure, the conflict can be either a betrayal (the character can act positively for himself or herself but negatively for the other) or a sacrifice (the character can act negatively for himself or herself but positively for the other), according to the wording of the GADIN system [1].

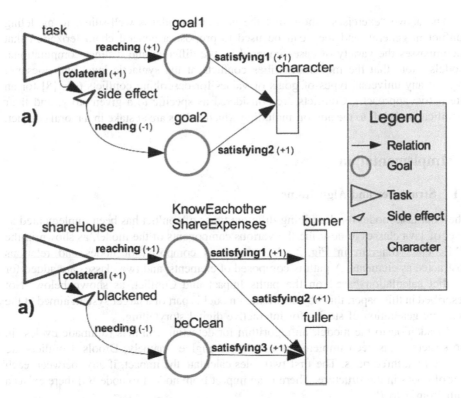

Fig. 1. An example of a dramatic cycle with the generic model (a) and a corresponding specific example (b), describing the Aesop fable "The Charcoal-Burner & the Fuller" (see text).

The internalized social conflict: the end node is a character, and one incoming relation is a mattering relation. Formally speaking, when a social conflict (see above) arises, the protagonists themselves do not really care about the conflict. The social conflict is processed only at the global level of the story; it is understood by the viewer but not empathetically through the characters. In this article, we introduce a new relation in the narrative model—the "mattering" relation—from a set to a character. This means not only that the character belongs to a group but also that it matters to him or her. In that case, a harmful event to the group is harmful to the character as well.

The authoritative conflict: the end node is a character, and one incoming relation is a domination relation. The above belonging relation enables a friendship to be modeled as a reciprocal relation that corresponds to the internalized social conflict. But in other cases, the conflict is between a character's goal and another character's goal, and the latter character is dominant. For example, a character may do something that is good on a personal level but bad for his or her boss, which creates conflict. Therefore, we introduce in this article a new relation called the *domination* relation, from the dominant to the dominated, which enables a conflict to be modeled on the basis of personal interest and social obligation.

The above "exercises" show that the goal-task model is well-suited to modeling conflict in general, and they can be used to propose a general characterization that encompasses the variety of cases covered by the different and distinct computational models. Note that the model describes conflicts at the syntactic level and does not suggest any universal types of goals or values for describing conflicts (see [8] for an alternative approach). Conflicts are considered as specific to a given story, and their specification is left to the author, including which values are at stake in a moral conflict.

3 Implementation

3.1 Structures and Algorithms

The goal-task model for describing different types of conflict has been implemented as a set of Java classes to describe the various components of the model, as shown in the UML class diagram in Fig. 2. A structure is composed of nodes and relations abstracted as elements. A path is composed of elements, and two classes are added for conflict calculation based on the paths Impact and Conflict, as shown below. Not described in this paper, this object-oriented model is part of a larger system aimed at the dynamic generation of stories for interactive digital storytelling.

In addition to the model, an algorithm for detecting conflicts (dramatic cycles) in the structure has been implemented in a rule engine—namely, Drools. Conflicts are detected via three rules. The first two rules calculate the impact, if any, between each pair of nodes in the structure. There is an impact from node A to node B if there exists a path from A to B.

The first rule initializes the impact by stating that if node A is connected to node B via relation r, then A impacts B:

```
rule "impacts initialization"
when
        $A: Node()
        $B: Node()
        $r: Relation( source==$A , target==$B )
        not Impacts( source==$A, target==$B )
    then
        insert( new Impacts( $A , $r , $B , $r.getWeight() ) );
    end
```

The first part of the rule, the left-hand side, defines the triggering condition. In the above case, it means that if there exists a node (assigned to A), if there exists a node (assigned to B), if there exists a relation between these nodes (assigned to r), and if there exist no impacts between these two nodes, then one should insert an impact between these nodes.

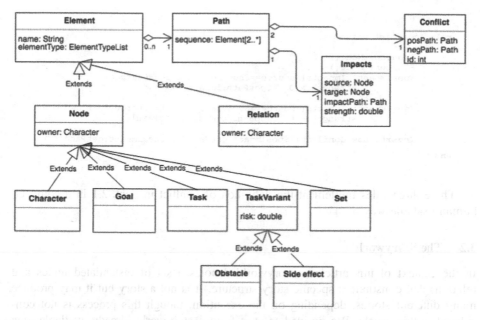

Fig. 2. UML class diagram of the narrative model. The lower left part describes the elements in the structures, while the three other classes are used to reason about conflicts (see text).

The second rule propagates the impact by applying a transitivity rule. if A impacts B and B impacts C, then A impacts C:

```
rule "impacts propagation"
    when
        $A: Node()
        $B: Node()
        $C: Node()
        $impAB: Impacts( source==$A , target==$B , $strengthAB:strength ,
                    $pathAB:ImpactPath )
        $impBC: Impacts( source==$B , target==$C , $strengthBC:strength ,
                    $pathBC:ImpactPath , $pathBC.disjoint($pathAB) )
        not Impacts( source == $A , target == $nB , ImpactPath.identical( new
                    Path( $pathAB , $pathBC ) ) )
    then
        Path $pathAC = new Path( $imp12.getImpactPath() , $imp23.getImpactPath() );
        Insert( new Impacts( $A , $C , $path , $impAB.getStrength() *
                    $impBC.getStrength() ) );
end
```

An additional condition was added to the transitivity: the second path should not contain an element in the first one, except the one that connects them. It prevents obtaining paths that repeat some edges (in graph theory terms, the positive and negative paths in a dramatic cycle are *trails*).

Finally, the third rule calculates the conflicts by identifying two nodes where there are two ways in which the first one impacts the second one, and these two paths are of opposite strength.

```
rule "conflict detection"
    when
        $source: Node()
        $target: Node()
        $posImpact: Impacts( source==$source , target==$target ,
                    strength > 0 , $posPath:impactPath)

        $negImpact: Impacts( source==$source , target==$target ,
                    strength < 0 , !$path2.crosses($posPath) )
    Then
        Insert( new Conflict( $posImpact.getPath(), $negImpact.getPath() );
end
```

These three rules implement the definition of conflict in Sect. 2.1 in a compact, human-readable way.

3.2   The Storyworld

In the context of this article, a storyworld denotes a set of instantiated nodes and relations that constitute a specific story structure. It is not a story but it may produce many different stories, depending on the execution, though this process is not considered in this article. We decided to start from a storyworld already available, one designed for a narrative engine under development. From a methodological point of view, the key point in this study is that this storyworld has a size sufficient to exhibit an authentic application of the conflict-detection algorithm, in contrast to a "toy problem," for which a small number of solutions are already known.

The storyworld was written in collaboration with a professional author; it is depicted in Fig. 3 and may be summarized as follows:

Frank has just moved into his new apartment. He has invited Julia for the evening. Julia is a gothic girl, and she sings in a gothic band. Frank is in love with her, but Julia does not know it yet. He has the plan to declare his love to her this evening, because the day after, Julia is leaving for three months for a concert tour. But this same evening, Frank's parents, Paul and Martina, have got tickets for the opera. They come to Frank's apartment and bring his little sister, Lili. They want him to take care of Lili during the opera, which spoils the romantic meeting with Julia. In addition, Frank's mother has a problem with Julia's style and would not leave her daughter with her during the evening. Frank may therefore want to introduce Julia better to her mother. The complicated situation may lead Julia to decide to leave the apartment. But Lili could also want to play karaoke with her or go to the circus with her father.

This storyworld contains 30 nodes and 42 relations. It is obviously complex to read in Fig. 3, but we estimate that its execution via a proper narrative engine would enable approximately 15–20 min of gameplay, which would be comparable with *Façade* [11] or *Nothing for Dinner* [25]. When this scenario was designed, three dramatic cycles were intentionally introduced:

- On one hand, if Frank takes care of Lili, he will please his father; on the other hand, he will not have privacy with Julia.   (C1)

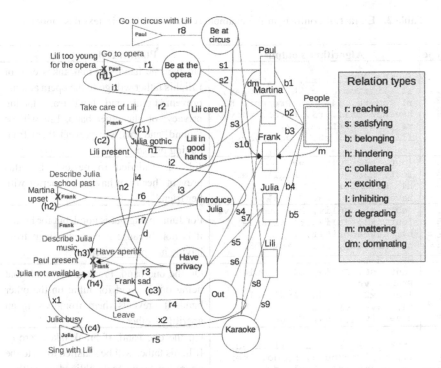

Fig. 3. Graphical representation of the narrative structure used for experimentation (see Fig. 1 for legend; red crosses are obstacles, and double rectangles are character sets). When an obstacle is placed on a task, it represents, in a compact way, a hindering link from the obstacle to the task —the relation is mentioned in parenthesis. Similarly, side effects (blue triangles) are represented directly on the task, and the collateral relation name is mentioned in parentheses. (Color figure online)

- On one hand, if Frank takes care of Lili, Martina will be happy to go to the opera, but she is unsatisfied with the idea of leaving her daughter with Julia.   (C2)
- On one hand, Julia is happy to sing karaoke with Lili, but on the other hand, this will prevent her from having privacy with Frank.   (C3)

Nothing was known regarding the number of additional dramatic cycles that may be present in the structure.

3.3   Results

The execution of the above algorithm on the structure depicted in Fig. 3 generated 31 conflicts. Among these 31 conflicts, we found 16 intercharacter conflicts, 7 internalized social conflicts, 1 authoritative conflict, 3 both internalized social and authoritative conflicts, 3 internal conflicts, and 1 paradox. For each example, we manually produced a text description of the conflict. We observed that each of the 31 conflicts made sense, though some of them might seem slightly far-fetched. Table 2 shows one example of each conflict category, with a hand-written, plain-text explanation of the conflict.

Table 2. Extract of conflicts in the example scenario, with plain-text descriptions

Type	Algorithm's output	Plain-text description
Paradox	`[takeCareLili, r2, liliCared, i1, liliTooYoung, h, goToOpera, r1, opera, i4, paulPresent, h3, haveAperitif, r3, havePrivacy]` **vs** `[takeCareLili, c2, liliPresent, n2, havePrivacy]`	On the one hand, if Frank takes care of Lili, his father will go to the opera and not prevent Frank and Julia from having privacy; on the other hand, Lili will be around, and this will prevent them from having privacy.
Internal	`[out, s6, Julia]` **vs** `[out, x2, juliaNotAvailable, h4, haveAperitif, r3, havePrivacy, s5, Julia]`	Julia is satisfied to be out, but this prevents her from having an aperitif with her friend.
Interchara cter	`[out, s6, Julia, b4, people]` **vs** `[out, x2, juliaNotAvailable, h4, haveAperitif, r3, havePrivacy, s4, Frank, b3, people]`	For Julia, being out is good, but for Frank, it is not, because it prevents them from having an aperitif together.
Internalized social	`[out, s6, Julia, b4, people, m, Frank]` **vs** `[out, x2, juliaNotAvailable, h4, haveAperitif, r3, havePrivacy, s4, Frank]`	On the one hand, Frank understands that being out is good for Julia; on the other hand, it prevents them from having an aperitif together.
Authoritative	`[takeCareLili, r2, liliCared, i1, liliTooYoung, h, goToOpera, r1, opera, s1, Paul, dm1, Frank]` **vs** `[takeCareLili, c2, liliPresent, n2, havePrivacy, s4, Frank]`	On the one hand, if Frank takes care of Lili, his father will be satisfied to go to the opera, so Frank feels obliged to do that. On the other hand, this would prevent him from having a private aperitif with Julia, because they will have to take care of his sister, Lili.

These results show that the number of conflicts formally found in the storyworld is much higher than the number of conflicts initially conceived by the creators of the story (see the three conflicts in Sect. 3.2). This main finding is discussed in the next section. In addition, the results show a high discrepancy in the number of conflicts in each category, and the intercharacter conflict is the most represented.

3.4   Discussion

The formalization of conflict as dramatic cycles has shown that a storyworld, even not a very elaborate one such as that represented in Fig. 3, exhibits many conflicts. Each of these conflicts makes sense in the narrative context, and most of them were discovered by the automatic analyses, as they were not designed a priori. This contrasts with the classical view in dramaturgy (the current inspiration of most screenwriting practices), which considers one or a few central dramatic situations that drive the plot [9, 14, 17]. According to the present study, drama is rather made of a constellation of specific and interwoven conflicting situations, which results in one or a few emerging global conflicts. This sheds a new light on the nature of drama that needs to be understood in terms of a complex system of conflicts.

More precisely, one individual conflict is often derived into several other related conflicts. For example, take the second conflict in Table 2, in which Julia is conflicted because she wants not only to leave because of Martina's attitude but also to have a drink with her friend. This is related to the third conflict in Table 2, in which Frank and Julia are conflicted about this same action. If one considers the authored conflict presented above (C1) and the 31 conflicts, several appear related to it; for example, there is a similar conflict with Julia (she, too, wants privacy), the internalization of the conflict within Frank (via the mattering relation), and the similar conflict motivated by the father's authority.

4   Further Analyses of the Results

These observations suggest that behind the diversity of conflicts, a few of the main conflicts may be extracted in order to conciliate with the general idea that a story should be built around a few main core ideas. Therefore, we statistically processed the 31 found conflicts to determine if it was possible to group them automatically into a small number of meaningful clusters.

To numerically process the conflicts, the first step was to define a distance measurement between two conflicts. This distance was defined as the average of the distance between two positive paths and two negative paths:

$$dist(C_1, C_2) = \frac{1}{2}[\Delta(C_1.posPath, C_2.posPath) + \Delta(C_1.negPath, C_2.negPath)]$$

Next, the distance Δ between two paths was calculated as the distance between the two sets of elements in each path, which could be simply calculated as the size of the symmetric difference[3] between the two sets.

Once the distance measurement was defined, we could establish a similarity matrix that gathered the distances of each pair of conflicts. Next, we applied the gap statistic method with the k-mean clustering algorithm to obtain automatically the optimal number of clusters. The 31 conflicts could be grouped into three clusters. Finally, we applied the partition around medoids (PAM) algorithm to our dataset, producing the three clusters represented in Fig. 4: the first one, in red, gathered 14 conflicts around Frank having privacy with Julia; the second one, in green, concerned Martina and her issue with Julia's style (7 conflicts); the third, in blue, one concerned consequences of taking care of Lili (10 conflicts).

In Fig. 4, one can see that the clusters group similar conflicts, meaning that the storyworld displayed in Fig. 3 can be expressed by taking only a few of its 31 conflicts —for example, one per cluster. In addition, one may notice that some conflicts are very similar (some dots are almost superimposed in Fig. 4), while others in the same cluster are different (e.g., see cluster 20 in blue).

---

[3] The symmetric difference between two sets is the union of the two sets, without the intersection.

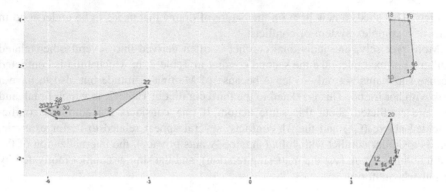

Fig. 4. Cluster plot with three clusters grouping the 21 detected conflicts. (Color figure online)

5 Conclusion and Future Applications

Conflict is an umbrella term but fundamental to understanding the story dynamics in drama. In this article, based on a general computational model of conflict, a theoretical categorization of conflict types was proposed. Next, this approach was empirically tested on a formally described storyworld of average complexity. The main result was that there was not one or two conflicts in a story but a constellation of conflicts; this result shows the complexity behind any nonelementary story. By applying a statistical analysis of extracted conflicts, we could also extract a small number of clusters, showing that behind the diversity of conflicts, main topics could be extracted.

In addition to the theoretical contribution of this work, there are several ways the proposed algorithm could support story generation. First, in case the narrative engine requires the author to enter the conflicts by hand, the automatic extraction of conflicts could help the author to define which ones should be expressed during the dynamic unfolding of the story. The clustering might help the author to pick conflicts that are different from each other. Second, a more sophisticated narrative engine could drive the story according to all conflicts present in a structure, not only the ones identified by the author. Given the number of conflicts, this approach may greatly increase the variability of the generated stories. Finally, it would be possible to use natural-language generation techniques to produce a text description of conflicts, which could then feed the generated story itself, with a character or a narrator explicitly referring to a dramatic conflict.

Acknowledgements. This research has been supported by the Swiss National Science Foundation under grant No. 159605 (Fine-grained Evaluation of the Interactive Narrative Experience).

References

1. Barber, H., Kudenko, D.: Dynamic generation of dilemma-based interactive narratives. In: Proceedings of Third Conference on Artificial Intelligence and Interactive Digital Entertainment – AIIDE, pp. 2–7. AAAI Press, Menlo Park (2007)
2. Battaglino, C., Damiano, R., Torino, U.: A character model with moral emotions: preliminary evaluation. In: Finlayson, M.A., Meister, J.C., Bruneau, E.G. (eds.) 5th Workshop on Computational Models of Narrative (CMN 2014), pp. 24–41. OASICS (2014)
3. Benabbou, A., Lourdeaux, D., Lenne, D.: Dynamic generation of dilemmas in virtual learning environments for non-technical skills training. In: Wang, Y., Howard, N., Widrow, B., Plataniotis, Y., Zadeh, L.A. (eds.) IEEE 15th International Conference on Cognitive Informatics & Cognitive Computing (ICCI*CC), pp. 231–234. IEEE (2016)
4. Cavazza, M., Charles, F., Mead, S.J.: Generation of humorous situations in cartoons through plan-based formalisations. In: Nijholt, A., Stock, O., Dix, A., Morkes, J. (eds.) ACM CHI-2003 Workshop: Humor Modeling in the Interface. University of Twente, Twente (2003)
5. Egri, L.: The Art of Dramatic Writing. Simon & Shuster, New York (1946)
6. Field, S.: Screenplay – The Foundations of Screenwriting. Dell Publishing, New York (1984)
7. Greimas, A.J.: Sémantique structurale. Presses universitaires de France, Paris (1966)
8. Harmon, S.: An expressive dilemma generation model for players and artificial agents. In: The Twelfth AAAI Conference on Artificial Intelligence and Interactive Digital Entertainment (AIIDE-2016), pp. 176–182 (2016)
9. Lavandier, Y.: La dramaturgie. Le clown et l'enfant, Cergy, France (1997)
10. Lévi-Strauss, C.: Anthropologie Structurale. Plon, Paris (1958)
11. Mateas, M., Stern, A.: Façade. http://games.softpedia.com/get/Freeware-Games/Facade.shtml
12. McKee, R.: Story: Substance, Structure, Style, and the Principles of Screenwriting. Harper Collins, New York (1997)
13. Nichols, B.: Ideology and the image. Indiana University Press, Bloomington (1981)
14. Polti, G.: Les trente-six situations dramatiques. Mercure de France, Paris (1903)
15. Saillenfest, A.: Modélisation Cognitive de la Pertinence Narrative en vue de l'Évaluation et de la Génération de Récits. Télécom ParisTech (2015)
16. Seger, L.: Making a Good Script Great. Samuel French Trade, Hollywood (1989)
17. Souriau, E.: Les deux cent mille Situations dramatiques. Flammarion, Paris (1950)
18. Szilas, N.: A computational model of an intelligent narrator for interactive narratives. Appl. Artif. Intell. **21**(8), 753–801 (2007)
19. Szilas, N.: Modeling and representing dramatic situations as paradoxical structures. Digit. Scholarsh. Humanit. **32**, 2 (2017)
20. Szilas, N.: Structural Analysis of the Aesop's Fables. http://tecfalabs.unige.ch/mediawiki-narrative/index.php/Aesop's_Fables
21. Szilas, N., Estupiñán, S., Richle, U.: Qualifying and quantifying interestingness in dramatic situations. In: Nack, F., Gordon, A.S. (eds.) ICIDS 2016. LNCS, vol. 10045, pp. 336–347. Springer, Cham (2016). https://doi.org/10.1007/978-3-319-48279-8_30
22. Truby, J.: Anatomy of Story. Faber and Faber, New York (2007)
23. Vale, E.: The Technique of Screenplay Writing. Grosset & Dunlap, New York (1973)
24. Ware, S.G., Young, R.M.: CPOCL: a narrative planner supporting conflict. In: Proceedings of the Seventh AAAI Conference on Artificial Intelligence and Interactive Digital Entertainment, pp. 97–102. AAAI Press, Palo Alto (2011)
25. Nothing For Dinner. http://nothingfordinner.org

Narrative Improvisation: Simulating Game Master Choices

Jonathan Strugnell[(✉)], Marsha Berry, Fabio Zambetta,
and Stefan Greuter

RMIT University, Melbourne, Australia
jonathan_str@yahoo.com

Abstract. Any computer game with a strong story has difficulty balancing the tension between narrative and agency. Strong narrative usually results in weak agency, and strong agency can weaken narrative structure. Narrative improvisation, adapting the story based on player reactions, is a difficult task for a game designer. Narrative improvisation, however, is regularly practised by the human game masters (GMs) of tabletop roleplaying games. As the first stage of building a game master agent (GMA), this paper examines the moment in which GMs decide if and how to alter their storyline due to player action. GMs were interviewed to discover their reactions when players make unexpected choices. Ten themes emerged from analysis of the interviews, we examined these themes to determine the thought processes that took place in the GMs' minds, and we represented the processes as flow charts. These decision charts are a first step in the construction of a GMA that could assist in the development of more responsive interactive narrative in computer games.

Keywords: Agency · Emergent narrative · Game master agent (GMA)
Interactive narrative · Narrative generation · Roleplaying game (RPG)

1 Introduction

When creating stories for computer games, designers must make the choice between favouring narrative and favouring agency. Balancing story progression and narrative is difficult because they are often at odds [20]. Narrative, for our purposes, means the art and science of telling a story; it includes construction of the plot around a main conflict, development of characters that make a meaningful contribution to the story, and the use of an appropriate structure. Agency, in game design terms, is the level of control players feel while they are in the game world, and the degree to which they consider their choices have a real impact on it [14, 15, 22].

Writers can craft structured stories that players can inhabit; branching storylines that players can choose between; and open worlds full of elements that players can use to create their own stories. However, each of these narrative techniques has trade-offs. The first technique leaves players with limited agency within the game world. The second results in the players having some agency, but their choices are limited and must be foreseen by the writer. The third provides strong agency, with players able to make their own story from game elements, but is unlikely to result in the type of pleasing story arc that could be constructed by a writer [16].

2 Background and Related Work

Many researchers have pursued the dream of a storytelling engine which can adjust to match player input, thus achieving both agency and narrative.

2.1 Attempts to Achieve Narrative Generation

Researchers have proposed a range of methods including grammar-driven models such as those of Vladimir Propp [18] and Alfred Correira, some of which can backtrack if the story encounters a conflict [23]. There are simulative algorithms like Klein's Automatic Novel Writer [8] with instruction packages for specific situations, and problem-solving algorithms such as TALE-SPIN [12] in which characters have knowledge lists and goals which update the story as characters try to fulfil them.

Another model is object-oriented narrative, in which the game world is composed of characters, locations, items, and actions, each of which has functions, conditions, reactions, and plot elements. When the player interacts with the objects, they construct their own narrative. In Façade, 'the... performance of the characters... are written as a vast collection of *behaviours*, which are short reactive procedures representing numerous goals and sub-goals for the characters' [11].

Narrative can be generated from the point of view of characters within the story. The Merchant of Venice Interactive Narrative [17] uses Shakespeare's play to create different stories for each character. Antonio might be a carefree risk taker who borrows money from Shylock with no thought for the consequences, or he might borrow the money because he is a loyal friend. Shylock might be a patient victim who extends a favour to Antonio, or he might be intent on revenge.

A narrative engine like UNIVERSE [23] picks a goal, selects a plot point from its library, executes it, and repeats for each sub-goal until it finds the most effective, and the generation system KIIDS [6] can store new plot points for later use. The BRUTUS [2] model builds narrative around a theme, setting up a betrayer, a betrayed, character goals, locations, and an action of treachery. Characters from the database are assigned these roles, and their attributes are used to determine the reasons for the betrayal.

Stories can also be seen as a constellation of possible worlds. There is the factual world of the story, as well as 'knowledge worlds, hypothetical worlds, intention worlds, wish worlds, worlds of moral values, obligation worlds and alternate universes' [23]. There are also overlapping worlds of knowledge, obligations, wishes, and fantasies for each character. Curveship [13] is an example of this model.

Narrative mediation 'gives a centralized author agent control of character actions. The system generates a linear narrative representing the ideal story to tell the user and then considers all the ways that the interactive user can interact with the world and with the other characters' [21]. It keeps the players following the story, and intervenes when they interfere with it [7], 'surreptitiously replacing a user action with a similar action, or failure mode, with different effects' [21].

A drama manager or story director builds a narrative arc around game events [4] and can treat characters as both autonomous entities and elements of the story [9]. A drama manager tracks player actions and relates them to a plot graph, testing for viability. It is 'an intelligent, omniscient, and disembodied agent that monitors the virtual world and intervenes to drive the narrative forward' [10] using beats (key story points that can be ordered to assemble a narrative) and schemas (structures and databases of character goals, knowledge, and actions) to make the tale progress. 'If schemas fail then that schema is revoked and the director searches for a new schema that better suits current status in the drama.' [1].

All these systems struggle to balance agency and narrative. Altering the story when a player makes a choice that conflicts with it, which we will call narrative improvisation, is currently only resolved successfully by human storytellers.

2.2   Roleplaying Games

There is already a game category that practises narrative improvisation: tabletop roleplaying games (RPGs) such as the well-known Dungeons & Dragons [5]. In RPGs, game masters (GMs) are the moderators and storytellers of the gaming experience. It is their task to describe the world that the players encounter and to arbitrate the players' actions within that world. RPGs are successful realisations of narrative improvisation because the GM can invent additional information when necessary. Greg Costikyan, designer of Paranoia, Toon, and Star Wars: The Roleplaying Game says: 'Only [in] the... game style, tabletop, do we escape the demands of linearity – and we do so, ultimately, only by relying on the creativity of a live gamemaster' [3].

Experienced GMs frequently encounter situations when players change the planned narrative by their actions or by their focus of interest. In a roleplaying game, GMs improvise and adapt their stories at a moment's notice, creating new characters, character arcs, and plot arcs on the fly. 'The Game Master (GM) is a special kind of player; he is the "interactive storyteller". He designs all the elements of the story and he manages all the possible events that can occur in its development, improvising the dialogue contributions of non-player characters, resolving players actions, etc.' [16]. 'The gamemaster provides the world and the story, as well as controlling any character not controlled specifically by players' [4]. He 'acts as a storyteller for the other players guiding them through an interactive drama, an adventure world full of monsters and NPCs played by the GM' [1]. GMs are 'in charge of keeping the narrative flowing, providing dynamic feedback to the actions of the player avatars, using e.g. on-the-fly updates...The GM is in these situations responsible for providing plot hooks and combines these as the play progresses' [24].

Elements of RPGs have been present in computer games since the dawn of the medium, and researchers have studied RPGs for clues about how to improve interactive narratives. However, one area that has received little attention is the thought process GMs engage in when players make unexpected choices. How and why do GMs adapt their story in response to player input? We will use the answer to this question to inform the development of a Game Master Agent (GMA) which could achieve a significant level of narrative improvisation.

3 Game Master Agent

A human GM acts in the same way as a drama manager, controlling narrative pace and direction, providing beats that fit along a plot graph, and fitting player actions to the story. But GMs also react to player input, profile players, and ensure that players drive the narrative. This paper is concerned with creating an agent to perform a specific subset of gamemaster functions – deciding when and how to alter a story.

3.1 Phases

The development of the GMA will be in four phases, of which this paper is the first. **Phase One** involves graphing when an existing storyline needs to be changed due to player desires and actions. What are the triggers for GMs deciding to change a story? What signals do players give that show they are engaged or not engaged with the current plot? How does a GM determine what story elements the player is interested in? **Phase Two** will be the development of a GMA narrative improvisation system in a game engine. The GMA, which will run alongside another systems (such as a drama manager) will monitor player choices and make the decision when to adapt or change the storyline. It will make minor changes and signal when it is necessary to invent new plots, but will not yet create them. **Phase Three** will involve graphing how new plots are generated, and **Phase Four** will be the inclusion of new plot generation into the narrative improvisation engine.

3.2 Interviews

Some GMs craft layers of arcing and overarching plotlines in advance, and some create elements that can be woven together as the players interact with them. But all GMs will prepare some level of narrative and anticipate how the players might move through it. They will create certain clues, elements, and sources of information to guide players that we will refer to as plot hooks. GM expectations of player choices will sometimes not be met, and the actions of the players may disrupt a planned plotline. To investigate how GMs are able to achieve narrative improvisation, we conducted a series of semi-structured interviews with GMs who have been running roleplaying games for at least five years, with a minimum average of ten gaming sessions per year. The RPGs include tabletop roleplaying games, live action roleplaying (LARP) games, and RPGs conducted online with the participants in different locations. We sought qualitative data about: the reasons why changes happen; how GMs choose whether to change the story; the GMs' thought processes when they change the story; how GMs get player feedback; and how GMs structure their stories, as well as general advice for interactive storytelling. We believed this would give us a starting point for exploring GM decisions. The interviews were conducted on Skype, Hangout, or telephone, and were recorded using XSplit [25] software.

3.3   Thematic Analysis

We elected to use the technique of thematic analysis (finding patterns in data and distilling key concepts) to study GMs responses. Conversation and discourse analysis (studying the structure of speech) might have yielded information about GM norms and relationships with the players, but was less relevant to GM choices. Using grounded theory (which minimises interpretation) was considered but our questions might have biased the results. We deemed thematic analysis to be most appropriate.

We transcribed the interviews with NVivo [19] data analysis software and looked through the responses, picking out keywords, phrases, and ideas that were repeated by the GMs. We then divided this feedback into broad categories. Four areas emerged: reasons why story changes become necessary; how players demonstrate interest in game elements; methods GMs use to decide new storylines; and recommendations for world building and crafting emergent storytelling;

The third and fourth categories relate to how GMs create new stories, and this data will be used in **Phase Three** of building the GMC. The first and second categories relate to **Phase One**. We examined these concepts and reorganised them, conflating similar ideas into common themes. A concept was deemed worthy of being included as a theme if it was reported by more than one GM.

4   Findings

Ten themes emerged from the first phase, each of which a reason for GMs to consider changing the story. We created flow charts for each of these themes.

4.1   Reasons Why Story Changes Become Necessary

According to the GMs interviewed, changes may be made to a storyline when players do the following (in order from most common to least common):

1. Miss plot hooks (clues the GM provides to lead players further into the story);
2. Forget details of plot hooks;
3. Misinterpret plot hooks;
4. Concentrate on side plots (sub-plots not directly connected with the main plot);
5. Exaggerate background elements (unimportant people, places, and objects);
6. Succeed too early in 'solving the problem';
7. Show they prefer a change of tone (feeling and style of play);
8. Show inattention to the plot;
9. Show lessened engagement with the plot; and
10. Show intense personal interest in a story element.

4.2   Decision Flow Charts

In consultation with the GMs, we laid out the decision-making process for each of these reasons as a set of icons, graphing the mental processes that a GM went through.

Players Wandering Aimlessly. When the players are not following the provided plot hook and seem to be aimless, there are four likely reasons: *Forget Details, Miss Plot Hook, Inattention to Plot,* or *Lessened Engagement.* If the players are attempting to engage with elements of the provided plot hook but not following them successfully, they may have forgotten some of the key information (*Forget Details*). If the players are engaging with elements in the world and seem to be trying to follow the story but ignore the plot hook, they may have been distracted and missed the hook (*Miss Plot Hook*). Alternatively, the players may not be attending to the story at all, but are still showing interest in the environment and the characters (*Inattention to Plot*). In the last case most GMs will probably allow the players to move at their own pace, and explore the world at their leisure. But at some point the GM will have to decide when to remind the players of the story, especially if there is a time limit built into it.

GMs respond to these three situations in a similar manner. The GM reaches a choice point, having to decide whether to reintroduce the plot hook. If other hooks exist that could lead the players to the same conclusions, the GM can choose to wait. Perhaps the players will follow one of the other hooks, or perhaps at a later date they will remember this clue and follow it. The danger here is that the players may mistake or forget the other clues as well. If there are no other plot hooks available, the GM may need to direct the players back to the clue and perhaps give a stronger hint that it is important. The GM can remind the players of the information they discovered earlier, or can create a new method for imparting that information, which might involve creating a new clue, character, or other delivery mechanism. GMs state that it is simple to reintroduce missed plot hooks, but warn that there is a danger in doing this too often. If the players realise they are being led to the solution, they will lose much of their sense of achievement and will not feel they have earned their victory. The GM must choose whether to keep dangling new hooks in front of the players from time to time, or letting them roam freely.

If the players are not following the plot hook and are also not giving attention to the environment and characters, then they may have lost interest in the story and will need to be re-engaged (*Lessened Engagement*). This lessened engagement could be for several reasons, and may not relate to the nature of the story. The players might be hungry or tired, or there might be distracting events occurring in the real world. Alternatively, they may not be connecting with events or themes of the story. For whatever reason, they are losing interest in the game events. Again, GMs have reached a choice point. They could call a halt to the game for a while. But if not, do they force player attention to the plot in some way, or do they throw in a new situation to energise the players? Ideally the new situation relates to the plot and can guide players back into the story while energising them, but if that is difficult to do, GMs can use an unrelated scene. Often GMs will have a few stock elements to use in situations such as this – set action pieces like a bar fight or a ninja attack which can occur if player energy is low. Once the players have been livened up, the GM will wait to see if they now follow the plot hooks (Fig. 1).

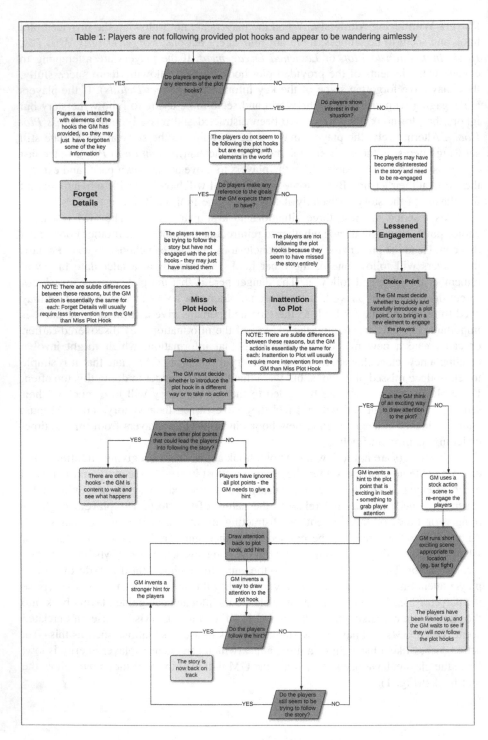

Fig. 1. Players wandering aimlessly

Players Pursuing Unrelated Goals. When players are actively pursuing goals that are unrelated to plot hooks, there are usually four reasons: *Concentrate on Side Plot, Misinterpret Plot Hook, Exaggerate Background Elements,* or *Personal Interest.*

If the players are ignoring a plot hook for the main story but are following hooks that relate to a side plot, then they may have a stronger interest in that sub-plot or think that it is the main plot (*Concentrate on Side Plot*). The GM will need to decide whether the side plot can be made to play a larger part in the main story. If not, the GM can use the side plot as the main narrative, abandoning the original idea or relegating it to a side plot, or can try to draw attention back to the main plot in the same manner as with *Forget Details, Miss Plot Hook,* and *Inattention to Plot.*

If the players seem to be actively pursuing a different goal but are still asking questions about the main story idea, they may think small elements of the plot are more important than the GM intended them to be (*Exaggerate Background Elements*) or they may have misunderstood a plot point and interpreted it as meaning something else (*Misinterpret Plot Hook*). Either way, the players now have a theory of their own. Players sometimes imagine that background elements or characters are more important than they are, and investigate them under the assumption that they are integral to the story. The GM intended these elements to be window dressing, but for some reason the players have fixated on them and spend time investigating them and speculating about them. The players now expect them to be part of the story. At this point the GM must decide whether the elements are interesting enough to be added into the existing narrative. The GM might need to flesh out characters that originally had a one-line description and incorporate them into the plot, or find a way for an object that caught the players' eyes to be linked to the unfolding drama. If the players' object of interest does not fit within the story, the GM must decide whether to disabuse them and guide them back to the plot, or to change the story completely to accommodate it. If players misinterpret a plot hook and invent their own theory, the GM may decide the players are not wrong at all, and change what the hooks meant, since the players will never know this was not the intention all along.

Sometimes players do not follow the main story because they are interested in specific elements of the world. An element resonates with them personally and holds greater appeal than important narrative elements. The GM is unlikely to anticipate this beforehand, since it is personal to the players. The GM needs to decide what further interactions with this element will look like, and what mechanics are involved. The choice point is whether to include the expanded element in the story or whether to recreate the story around it. Alternatively, does the GM allow the players to have fun with this experience but then create consequences for neglecting the main plot? Personal interest can be disruptive to multiplayer gaming, since it may only relate to one or two of the players. If they are the ones driving the story along because of this interest, the GM needs to monitor the engagement of the remaining players (Fig. 2).

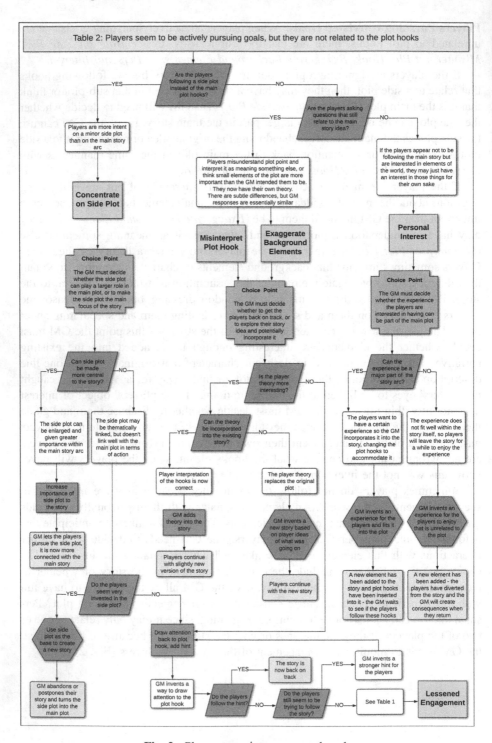

Fig. 2. Players pursuing unexpected goals

Players Being Too Successful. Though skill or luck, players may solve a problem faster than the GM expected, for example they might quickly kill off an enemy who was intended to be the main adversary for the whole adventure. The most common way to resolve this is to introduce a new layer on top of the solved problem – a hidden influence that has been acting behind the scenes. In the example above, the dead enemy is found to be the disciple of a greater villain who has now been revealed. GMs suggest that this can be done quite seamlessly, feels believable to the players, and is ultimately satisfying as part of a greater narrative. The choice point is whether to stop the story earlier than anticipated and begin another one, or to extend this story by introducing a further layer (Fig. 3).

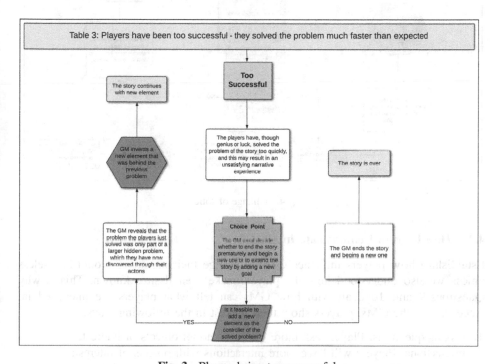

Fig. 3. Players being too successful

Change of Tone. Sometimes the tone of the game can change, and players are now enjoying a different style or genre, to which the original plot is no longer appropriate. If the GM decides to return to the original style of play, they must use language that stresses the intended tone, hoping to influence the players to return to the former style. If the players seem to be enjoying the new tone too much to change back, the GM must either change the language and action of the current story to match the new tone, or to invent a new story that suits the new tone better. One GM described a game which was designed as a mystery, an investigative thriller. The players did not seem interested in this, but reacted well when they needed to sneak into a guarded location. Responding to this, the GM made the game much more action-orientated with shootouts, heists, and chases (Fig. 4).

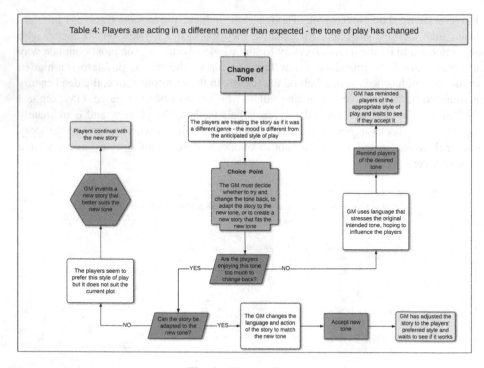

Fig. 4. Change of tone

4.3 How Players Demonstrate Interest

Establishing how players influence GMs to change their narratives would be useless unless we also understood how the players make their desires known. This is why Questions 9 and 10 dealt with how GMs can tell what players are interested in. According to the GMs, players show their interest in the following ways:

1. Asking questions. Players ask more questions about objects of interest;
2. Interactions. Players will have more interactions with objects of interest;
3. Discussion. Players will talk about in-game events between sessions;
4. Showing emotion. Players will show stronger emotion when they are engaged;
5. Body language. Players will show interest or lack of interest non-verbally;
6. Keeping playing. If players are enjoying themselves, they will play longer; and
7. Revisiting. Players will voluntarily choose to revisit areas or NPCs.

Some responses were deemed to be out of the scope of this study. Although it is possible for a computer to read non-verbal signals or tones of voice with facial motion capture and voice analysis, this is not our research focus.

5 Discussion and Implications

Our results suggest that this approach to designing a game master agent is promising, and points the way to further research and to the construction of such an agent.

5.1   Results of the Study

Having established ten reasons why story changes may become necessary (4.1) and seven ways in which players demonstrate interest in game elements (4.3), we created flow charts representing GM decision options for each of these reasons (Appendix 1). These flow charts were tested by consulting them during roleplaying game sessions and using them as a basis for the GMs deciding when to adjust the story. GMs reported that the charts were successful indicators of when and how a narrative could be altered due to player actions.

5.2   Implications of the Study

The GM decision charts demonstrate how a GMA can be designed from first principles. The flow charts, although simple at this point, are fair representations of how GMs make decisions about changing the narrative. If consulted while a roleplaying game is being run, the charts are capable of interpreting player choices, differentiating between them, and suggesting a solution. Together with the data about how players show their interest, the flow charts can be used to make these decisions. When a player is not following plot hooks, consulting the charts will find a possible reason for that behaviour, and guide the response of the GM. This will vary from adding an element to the story or reminding players of a plot hook, to making the decision to create new plot hooks or new plots if that would better satisfy perceived player needs. This evidence suggests that the flow charts are a good basis for creating a GMA.

5.3   Further Research

Phase Two of our research will use the flow charts to create a GMA in a game engine that will act as GM, prepared to adapt at any time. The action and themes of the story must change to suit player choices, and the experience must be structured in a dramatically-satisfying manner. We will create a scenario and the system will use the data from the GM interviews to make choices based on player actions and reactions. We will then conduct testing to determine how successfully the flow charts are being implemented. Players will play through the scenario with their experience managed by either the GMA or by a human GM. If conducted online, the players need not know which. The players will be asked to rate their experience during the game, and how satisfied they felt in the story that unfolded. If player satisfaction with the narrative generation system even approaches their satisfaction with a GM-controlled narrative, then the experiment will be deemed successful. **Phase Three** will be to analyse GM strategies for story creation and world building, and to graph how new plots can be created by the GMA. **Phase Four** will be to incorporate this data into the narrative improvisation system. Once again, this will be tested to determine whether the GMA can deliver players a similarly satisfying narrative to that provided by a human GM. We believe that the game master agent, and the results from this research, will make a meaningful contribution to the development of narrative improvisation.

References

1. Arinbjarnar, M., Kudenko, D.: Directed emergent drama vs. pen & paper role-playing game. In: AISB 2009 Symposium: AI & Games, Edinburgh UK (2009)
2. David, F., Bringsjord, S.: Artificial Intelligence and Literary Creativity: Inside the Mind of Brutus, A Storytelling Machine. Psychology Press, Bloomberg (1999)
3. Costikyan, G.: Games, storytelling, and breaking the string. In: Second Person: Roleplaying and Story in Games and Interactive Media. MIT Press, Cambridge (2007)
4. Flowers, A., Magerko, B., Gervás, P.: Gamemasters and interactive story: a categorization of storytelling techniques in live roleplaying. In: FuturePlay, London, Ontario, Canada (2006)
5. Gygax, G., Arneson, D.: Dungeons and Dragons. Tactical Studies Rules, Lake Geneva (1974)
6. Jaya, A., Uma, G.V.: A knowledge based study on automatic story generation system. Int. J. Comput. Intell. Res. **5**, 271 (2009)
7. Kim, S., Moon, S., Han, S., Chang, J.: Programming the story: interactive storytelling system. Informatica **35**, 221–229 (2011)
8. Klein, S., et al.: Automatic novel writing: a status report. In: International Conference on Computers in the Humanities, Minneapolis (1973)
9. Koenitz, K., Ferri, G., Haahr, M., Sezen, D., Sezen, T.: Interactive Digital Narrative: History, Theory and Practice. New York, Routledge (2015)
10. Martin, L.J., Harrison, B., Riedl, M.O.: Improvisational computational storytelling in open worlds. In: Nack, F., Gordon, A.S. (eds.) ICIDS 2016. LNCS, vol. 10045, pp. 73–84. Springer, Cham (2016). https://doi.org/10.1007/978-3-319-48279-8_7
11. Mateas, M., Stern, A.: Writing façade: a case study in procedural authorship. In: Second Person: Roleplaying and Story in Games and Interactive Media. The MIT Press, Cambridge (2007)
12. Meehan, J.: TALE-SPIN, an interactive program that writes stories. In: Proceedings of the Fifth International Joint Conference on Artificial Intelligence (1977)
13. Montford, N.: Curveship: Interactive Fiction + Interactive Narrating (2011)
14. Murray, J.: Hamlet on the Holodeck: the Future of Narrative in Cyberspace. MIT Press, Cambridge (1997)
15. Peinado, F., Gervás, P.: Automatic direction of interactive storytelling: formalizing the game master paradigm. In: Cavazza, M., Donikian, S. (eds.) ICVS 2007. LNCS, vol. 4871, pp. 196–201. Springer, Heidelberg (2007). https://doi.org/10.1007/978-3-540-77039-8_18
16. Peinado, F., Gervás, P.: Transferring game mastering laws to interactive digital storytelling. In: Göbel, S., et al. (eds.) TIDSE 2004. LNCS, vol. 3105, pp. 48–54. Springer, Heidelberg (2004). https://doi.org/10.1007/978-3-540-27797-2_7
17. Porteous, J., Cavazza, M., Charles, F.: Narrative generation through characters' point of view. In: 9th International Conference on Autonomous Agents and Multiagent Systems, Toronto, Canada (2010)
18. Propp, V.: Morphology of the Folktale. University of Texas Press, Austin (1968)
19. Richards, T.: NVivo. In: QSR International, p Software for analysing from qualitative and mixed-methods data
20. Riedl, M.O., Bulitko, V.: Interactive narrative: an intelligent systems approach. AI Mag. **34**(1), 67 (2013)
21. Riedl, M.O., Young, R.M.: Interactive narrative: from linear story generation to branching story graphs. IEEE Comput. Graph. Appl. **26**(3) 23–31 (2006)

22. Ryan, J.O., Mateas, M., Wardrip-Fruin, N.: Open design challenges for interactive emergent narrative. In: Schoenau-Fog, H., Bruni, L.E., Louchart, S., Baceviciute, S. (eds.) ICIDS 2015. LNCS, vol. 9445, pp. 14–26. Springer, Cham (2015). https://doi.org/10.1007/978-3-319-27036-4_2
23. Ryan, M.: Possible Worlds, Artificial Intelligence, and Narrative Theory. Indiana University Press, Bloomington & Indianapolis (1991)
24. Tychsen, A., Hitchens, M., Brolund, T., et al.: The game master. In: The Second Australasian Conference on Interactive Entertainment, pp. 215–222. Creativity & Cognition Studios Press, Sydney (2005)
25. Xsplit: XSplit Broadcaster. In: SplitmediaLabs, p Live streaming and recording software (2012)

Communicating Assertiveness in Robotic Storytellers

Raul Paradeda[1,2]([✉]), Maria José Ferreira[1,3], Carlos Martinho[1], and Ana Paiva[1]

[1] INESC-ID and Instituto Superior Técnico, University of Lisbon, Lisbon, Portugal
{raul.paradeda,maria.jose.ferreira}@tecnico.ulisboa.pt,
{carlos.martinho,ana.paiva}@gaips.inesc-id.pt
[2] State University of Rio Grande do Norte, Natal, Brazil
[3] Madeira Interactive Technologies Institute, Madeira, Portugal

Abstract. Social robots have been used to perform the role of story-tellers in areas like education and pediatric rehabilitation. With the use of this technology, it is possible to setup different voices, simulate emotional states and even personalities for the same robot. However, finding the best setting that might define a trait for a storyteller robot, is not an easy task. What elements should be manipulated? Should it have a personality? If yes, which one? In this work, we try to answer these questions by studying several setups that will allow us to create an assertive social robot to act as a storyteller. We evaluate the assertiveness impression by manipulating three robot characteristics: posture, pitch, and speech rate. A within-subject study was conducted with 37 participants watching eight videos in which a social robot tells a short story. In each video, the robot presents a different setup, and the participant reports the level of assertiveness of that robot. We found a significant difference between the setups of pitch and posture as well as an acceptable assertive robot's configuration using a combination of those three characteristics.

Keywords: Storytelling · Social robots · Assertiveness

1 Introduction

Emotions and voice changes are well-known characteristics that storytellers apply while telling stories to give a pleasant experience to the listeners. Changes in speech can be used to create the character's personality and emotional state [15], and appropriate voice manipulations can even give the illusion of more than one character, and depending on the narrative, create an exciting and engaging atmosphere. We all know that a monotonous voice in a storyteller can lead to audience disengagement whereas speech modulations can boost engagement, motivation, pleasure and immersion on the plot. A storyteller establishes the mood of the story flow. Further, through his/her expression and posture, a storyteller can convey enjoyment [22], happiness, hope, sadness, and many other feelings. A storyteller's facial expressions and posture, can enrich and colour the

© Springer Nature Switzerland AG 2018
R. Rouse et al. (Eds.): ICIDS 2018, LNCS 11318, pp. 442–452, 2018.
https://doi.org/10.1007/978-3-030-04028-4_51

ambience of each scene. For example, in a joyful scene, a storyteller can express happiness through the voice, expressions, etc [10].

As the field of social robotics develops, robots are now sufficiently developed to act as storytellers. Storyteller robots have been employed in learning environments [8], pediatric rehabilitation [21], persuasion [13] and games [5]. Yet, to build a robot (or agent) that acts as a storyteller, its voice features, combined with its expressions are crucial as they can help mitigate the uncanny valley problem [12] and generate engaging experiences.

In this paper we will consider that a robotic storyteller should exhibit a posture and voice in a way that is believable and simultaneously engaging for an audience. To achieve one needs to simulate specific human like characteristics, in particular personalities and traits. For example, by exhibiting personality traits, such as extroverted, introvert, assertive, among others, gives a consistency to the robots' behaviour that will make it more believable and engaging. In particular, through the capability of expressing emotions and beliefs in direct, honest and appropriate ways, we can convey an assertive personality type [2,11,14].

In this study we show how to use verbal and non-verbal cues in a social robot that convey assertiveness in order to, in future studies, influence a user interacting with a storyteller robot [19]. Persuasion strategies to implement into the storyteller robot is the assertive personality and thus boost the effects of persuasion and engagement in a story told by a social robot. To do this we parameterised a set of features in a robots storyteller and created videos of the robot telling a story. We evaluated the videos and the results have shown that there is a significant difference in the perception of assertiveness when features like voice and posture are changed.

2 Related Work

Different features can characterise voice, researchers have considered that pitch, timbre, volume and speech rate are the most relevant ones. Pitch is related to the rate of vibration of the vocal cords. As the number of vibrations per seconds increases, the pitch increases as well, and the voice would sound higher [16].

In the work of Page and Balloun [18], the participants perceived the speaker as most aggressive and lacking in self-assurance when speaking in a high voice volume. They heard audio recorded voices in either a low, moderate or high voice volume. In another work [7], the authors found evidence that subjects are recognised as assertive when they spoke louder. The conclusions were taken from the feedback of participants that measured the assertiveness from tapes where subjects answer trivia questions. Furthermore, the perception of emotions in dialogues can be affected by the speaking rate. In Devillers and Vasilescu [4], from the analysis of recorded audios, the participants judged that a faster speech rate is characteristic of irritation and satisfaction. The voice manipulations reported provide us indications that it might be possible to create different voice perceptions regarding the speaker's personality and emotional state.

Voice manipulation has been investigated in different ways, and most researchers resort to specific software to perform this manipulation. For example, in [9] and [24] PRAAT software was the selection of researchers to analyse voice features. In our work, we try to examine if using just the available resources of a standard computer it can achieve reliable results in a more natural/human voice. To do so, we focused our attention on a Text-to-Speech (TTS) from Windows and then examine which Speech Synthesis Markup Language (SSML) features could manipulate prosody.

From the human-robot interaction in a narrative scenario having the robot acting as the storyteller, it is possible to produce some benefits [17]. For example, in the work of Plaisant et al. [21], the authors developed a robot to act in a storytelling scenario with children in rehabilitation. The children could teach the robot to act out emotions like sad, happy and excited. In that study, the emotional expressions performed by the robot regarding the story flow aid to improve children interest as well as support the rehabilitation experience.

Striepe and Lugrin [26], compared the effects of emotions and non-verbal behaviours using an emotional social robot storyteller. The authors reported that the emotional robot could transport the participants equally well as the traditional audiobook. Besides, they advised that the use of social robots performing the role of storytellers needs to be linked with the display of emotions and non-verbal behaviours.

In general, storytelling is all about sharing stories, and the way we choose to tell them makes them more or less remarkable. In spite of the fact that people anthropomorphise technology [23] would a robot storyteller makes us have the same type of experience as we have with a human storyteller? Given this state of the art, in this paper we explore the assumption that through the manipulation of different features in a robot it is possible to create different perceptions regarding the storyteller's personality traits (e.g. assertiveness) and emotional state. As such, we test this assumption by creating different robotic storytellers, varying such features and comparing how they are perceived by users.

3   Research Methods

This paper presents a quantitative study conducted to find evidence that may provide a better robot configuration to convey assertiveness as it acts as a storyteller. To address it we recorded a social robot telling a short story with different setups. Then, participants filled in a questionnaire stating how much assertive s/he considered the robot in each configuration. The surveys and videos were run online via Google Forms. The study tested the following hypotheses:

- H1: Specific vocal manipulations can influence the perception of assertiveness in a social storyteller robot.
- H2: A fast speech rate of a storyteller robot can increase a person's understanding of assertiveness on the robot.
- H3: The posture of a social storyteller robot can induce a person's perception of assertiveness of the robot.
- H4: The use of vocal manipulations combined with posture boosts the perception of assertiveness in a social storyteller robot.

3.1 The Narrative

A short story named *"The Wise Rabbit"*[1] was narrated by the robot for one minute and ten seconds. In some parts of the story, depending on the narrative flow, the robot exhibited facial expressions, such as Joy and Anger.

As mentioned, the robot was programmed to tell the story by the manipulation of pitch and speech rate, since they are some aspects of voice that can indicate personality [1].

3.2 Materials

The EMYS robot was chosen to be the storyteller mainly because of its capability of exhibiting recognisable emotions through facial expressions (Fig. 1(a to g)). In each setting, the manipulated parameters in the robot's voice were pitch (with values x-low, default and x-high) and speech rate (values set as medium and +20%)[2]. The rate values were defined based on preliminary tests, where the rate faster than +20% speech understanding could be affected. Also, the robot's posture settings were changed to: (1) neutral, (2) pride and (3) shame. The neutral posture exhibits the robot with head and eyebrows in a levelled position. Differently, the pride posture (Fig. 1(h)) the robot presents the head in a higher place, and the eyebrows are more open than in the neutral pose. In the shame posture (Fig. 1(i)), the robot's head is tilted down, and the eyebrows are almost closed. Videos were recorded with the robot in each of those setups.

Fig. 1. Facial expression performed by EMYS robot (a to g) [6] and Postures pride (h) and shame (i).

---

[1] The Wise Rabbit. Born 1980, M, from Islamabad, Pakistan. https://www.storystar. com/story/11499/talha/fiction/drama-interest-2.

[2] Pitch and speech rate values were chosen from the prosody elements. https://www. w3.org/TR/speech-synthesis/#S3.2.4.

3.3 Questionnaire

A questionnaire, with ten questions [3], was used to measure the level of assertiveness. The questions measured how a person sees her/himself regarding some statements. Each statement is divided into positive and negative keys. The positive ones are: *Take charge; Try to lead others; Can talk others into doing things; Seek to influence others; Take control of things.* The negatives are *Wait for others to lead the way; Keep in the background; Have little to say; Don't like to draw attention to myself; Hold back my opinions.* The participant informed how much s/he agrees with each statement using a 5-point Likert scale (1 - strongly disagree, 5 - strongly agree). Furthermore, we also inquired about the level of assertiveness in the different possible names given to the robot (Emys, Glin and none of those).

3.4 Procedure

As participants start the experiment they provide some personal data, like gender and age, and then answer a set of questions measuring his/her assertiveness. Then, participants are asked to choose from two different names (Emys and Glin) pointing which one seems to be more assertive. Participants also inform if they ever interacted with the robot used in the study. Finally, a set of eight videos (presented in pairs) measuring a specific setup is shown to the participant. Videos were pairwise because we seek to identify which value of each setting influence more the perception of assertiveness individually.

In this way, each participant is going to view four comparisons each of which contains two videos. Each video presents the same assertiveness questionnaire that the user filled in with his data, but now regarding the storyteller robot's performance. Moreover, it was asked which emotion the participant perceived in the video from the options: joy, surprise, sadness, anger and none. As already discussed, the eight videos have a different robot's setting; the first six settings can be seen in Table 1.

Table 1. Robot's setting for each video.

Comparison	Video	Pitch	Rate	Posture
C1	V1	x-low	Medium	Neutral
	V2	x-high		
C2	V3	Default	Medium	Neutral
	V4		+20%	
C3	V5	Default	Medium	Pride
	V6			Shame

In Table 2, the last two configurations for the robot's settings are presented. These two setups were intended to represent what we believe to be a more assertive robot and a less assertive robot (V7 and V8 respectively). Those configurations were obtained according to our literature research and our perception when testing each feature in the robot before the participants' tests.

Table 2. Robot's setting to our predefined assertive and non-assertive configuration.

Comparison	Video	Pitch	Rate	Posture
C4	V7	x-low	+20%	Pride
	V8	x-high	Medium	Shame

Besides, to avoid the tiredness of evaluation, the comparisons were randomised at every ten participants employing a Latin square design. For example, the first ten participants watched the videos in the comparisons order C1-C2-C3-C4; then, the next order is C4-C3-C2-C1, and so on.

4 Results

To perform the statistical analysis of the data we used the SPSS software, and p-values of 0.05 or less as being considered significant. The analysis covers demographic information to statistical analysis of parametric and non-parametric data. Further, to measure the perception of the assertiveness trait from the answers of each video, it was calculated the average of all positive statements.

4.1 Demographic

Considering the described scenario, the questionnaires with the videos were available online for 15 days, and a total of 37 people answered it. Table 3 presents information about participants gender, age and if they ever interacted or not with the EMYS robot.

Table 3. Statistics of the participants.

Gender	Age Avg (Std.)	Quantity	Interacted EMYS	Not Interacted EMYS
Female	$34_{(11.75)}$	26	8	18
Male	$29.7_{(3.25)}$	11	1	10
Total	$32.7_{(10.19)}$	37	9	28

4.2 Assertiveness of Name

We questioned participants about which name seemed to be more assertive between three options Emys, Glin or none of them. Based on the results, 18 people recognised the Emys name as more confident, while 13 thought that Glin was more assertive and six none of them.

4.3   Normality Test

To assess the normality of our data, we first perform a normality test using the Shapiro-Wilk test. The results reveal that for video 6 (V6) and video 8 (V8) the data significantly deviate from a normal distribution with $p = 0.005$ and $p = 0.008$ respectively. For all the other videos the data presented a normal distribution.

4.4   Significant Difference

After the normality test, we ran a paired t-test to see if there were significant differences between the pitch, V1 (Pitch-Low) and V2 (Pitch-High) and the rate, V3 (Rate-Medium) and V4 (Rate + 20%). We found out that Pitch-Low and Pitch-High scores were not correlated ($r = 0.290$, $p = 0.081$), but the scores for Rate-Medium and Rate + 20% were weakly and positively correlated ($r = 0.365$, $p = 0.026$). On the opposite, the paired sample test reveals that there was a significant average difference between Pitch-Low and Pitch-High ($t_{36} = 2.343$, $p = 0.025$) but not for Rate-Medium and Rate + 20%.

For the non-parametric data, the posture, V5 (Posture-Pride) and V6 (Posture-Shame), we applied the Wilcoxon Signed Rank Test. The test indicated that there was a statistical difference between the postures, $Z = -2.534$, $p = 0.011$. Regarding our predefined configurations for assertiveness (V7) and non-assertiveness (V8), we applied a Wilcoxon Signed Rank Test. Statistical differences were detected among the two predefined configurations, $Z = -3.305$, $p = 0.001$.

To understand what was the impact that the dimensions pitch and posture had over the predefined configuration for assertiveness (V7) an ANOVA with repeated measures (Pitch-Low, Posture-Pride and V7, designated as behaviour) were considered. The Mauchly's Test of Sphericity indicated that the assumption of sphericity was not violated, $X^2(2) = 0.089$, $p = 0.956$. Having this in mind, the tests of within-subjects effects revealed that the mean scores for behaviour were statistically significant different $F(2,72) = 4.066$, $p = 0.021$. Since we wanted to understand where those differences occur, we analysed the post hoc test using the Bonferroni correction. The differences detected revealed that there were only significant differences in our configuration of assertiveness and the Posture-Pride ($p = 0.027$; $\eta^2 = 0.101$). This value of η means that 10% of the difference in the perception of assertiveness, the predefined configuration explained it, indicating a difference between our configuration and pride posture. The result can indicate that when we combine the pitch with value x-Low and the posture pride, we have a higher perception of assertiveness.

To know whichever is the influence of the dimensions pitch and posture had over the predefined configuration for non-assertiveness (V8) we ran the Friedman Test for Pitch-High, Posture-Shame and V8. The results revealed that there is no significant differences between them with $p > 0.05$.

In summary, the results reveal the perception that participants had over the video comparisons made regarding their assertiveness for the pitch, rate, posture and the predefined configurations. For two of the individual comparisons, pitch and posture, there were significant differences. Regarding the two predefined configurations for assertiveness and non-assertiveness, they were also considered statistically different. The results report that the posture pride has an impact on the predefined configuration of assertiveness when comparing both.

5 Discussion and Future Work

Comparing the robot settings with the respective value, we found that there is a significant difference in the perception of assertiveness. This difference occurred when comparing two values in pitch and posture dimensions, making them essential dimensions to not ignore when conveying assertiveness. In those cases, the manipulation between the pitch values x-low and x-high lead people to feel that the x-low value fitted more an assertive robot. This fact can be noticed by the mean of the assertiveness questionnaire for each pitch video, see Fig. 2 columns Pitch Low and Pitch High the mean and standard deviations. This perception can be justified by some studies that show that people tend to respond better to speakers with a lower pitch [25]. In this sense, our first hypothesis was validated, as the voice manipulation influenced the perception of assertiveness in a social storyteller robot by the participants.

A similar effect happened in the videos where the posture is assessed. The pride posture is distinguished as more assertive than a shame posture. The mean of pride posture video is higher than the shame posture video, see Fig. 2 columns Posture Pride and Posture Shame. The shame posture can be characterised as more non-assertive mainly because it is a posture where the robot is gazing less at the person, as the robot's head is most of the time tilt down. The pride posture, on the contrary, had the robot's gaze directed most of the time at the participant. In this sense, the eye contact is an essential factor to identify and be more assertive [20]. Further, the third hypothesis was also validated, once the robot's posture gives the perception of assertiveness in the participants.

		Pitch Low	Pitch High	Rate Medium	Rate + 20%	Posture Pride	Posture Shame	Assertive	Non-Assertive
N	Valid	37	37	37	37	37	37	37	37
	Missing	0	0	0	0	0	0	0	0
Mean		3.0000	2.5135	2.8919	2.7243	2.8162	2.3081	3.3622	2.3622
Median		3.0000	2.6000	3.0000	2.8000	3.0000	2.0000	3.4000	2.0000
Std. Deviation		.98658	1.12501	1.05892	1.10589	.93853	1.18565	1.06023	1.14002

Fig. 2. Descriptive statistics about all eight videos rated by participants.

However, the speed at which the robot tells the story did not create the perception of assertiveness. The videos where the robot tells the story at a medium rate and with +20% did not obtain significance difference. A possible justification of this might be due the +20% value not being enough to perceive the differences between each storytelling rate. Another argument is that this factor might not be perceived individually, it might need to be measured in consonance with others features. In this case, our second hypothesis could not be considered valid. It is necessary to perform more studies to investigate the effect of this setting using a different range of values. In fact, our results also show that the speed rate did not seem to influence the perception of assertiveness. However, we measured the robot telling the story +20% faster than a medium rate. In the future, it would be desirable to investigate the influence of a faster or a slower rate in storytelling by a robot.

However, the most significant difference happens in the case of the storytelling while performing the predefined configurations. This effect could be due to the combination of the robot's features to simulate an assertive and non-assertive behaviour. Based on the results, our last hypothesis was validated, the combination of vocal manipulations and posture can boost the perception of assertiveness in a social storyteller robot.

Finally, based on the results, we believe that it is possible to find a suitable setting for a social robot to play the role of a storyteller with assertiveness trait. We evaluate only three features in a universe of characteristics that can be measured. In fact, our study contributes with a valid configuration to use in scenarios where the assertiveness trait is important in a storyteller robot. With the increased use of social robots in storytelling scenarios and the fact that the robots configurations are dependent on several factors, such as the embodiment, more research is required to determine a suitable general configuration for assertiveness. The assertiveness trait is indeed considered essential in many contexts, such as for example in leadership roles, and giving orders. Because of that, we intend to use those configurations in a future scenario where it can be explored together with persuasion.

Acknowledgments. We would like to thank the National Council for Scientific and Technological Development (CNPq) program Science without border: 201833/2014-0 - Brazil and Agência Regional para o Desenvolvimento e Tecnologia (ARDITI) - M1420-09-5369-000001, for PhD grants to first and second authors respectively. This work was also supported by Fundação para a Ciência e a Tecnologia: (FCT) - UID/CEC/50021/2013 and the project AMIGOS:PTDC/EEISII/7174/2014.

References

1. Apple, W., Streeter, L.A., Krauss, R.M.: Effects of pitch and speech rate on personal attributions. J. Pers. Soc. Psychol. **37**(5), 715 (1979)
2. Bradley, J.H., Hebert, F.J.: The effect of personality type on team performance. J. Manag. Dev. **16**(5), 337–353 (1997). https://doi.org/10.1108/02621719710174525. https://www.emeraldinsight.com/doi/10.1108/02621719710174525
3. Costa, P.T., McCrae, R.R.: Revised NEO personality inventory (NEO PI-R) and NEP five-factor inventory (NEO-FFI): professional manual. Psychological Assessment Resources Lutz, FL (1992)

4. Devillers, L., Vasilescu, I.: Prosodic cues for emotion characterization in real-life spoken dialogs. In: Eighth European Conference on Speech Communication and Technology (2003)
5. Figueiredo, R., Brisson, A., Aylett, R., Paiva, A.: Emergent stories facilitated. In: Spierling, U., Szilas, N. (eds.) ICIDS 2008. LNCS, vol. 5334, pp. 218–229. Springer, Heidelberg (2008). https://doi.org/10.1007/978-3-540-89454-4_29
6. Kędzierski, J., Muszyński, R., Zoll, C., Oleksy, A., Frontkiewicz, M.: Emys-emotive head of a social robot. Int. J. Soc. Robot. **5**(2), 237–249 (2013)
7. Kimble, C.E., Seidel, S.D.: Vocal signs of confidence. J. Nonverbal Behav. **15**(2), 99–105 (1991)
8. Kory, J.J.M.: Storytelling with robots: effects of robot language level on children's language learning. Ph.D. thesis, Massachusetts Institute of Technology (2014)
9. Lubold, N., Pon-Barry, H., Walker, E.: Naturalness and rapport in a pitch adaptive learning companion. In: 2015 IEEE Workshop on Automatic Speech Recognition and Understanding (ASRU), pp. 103–110. IEEE, December 2015. https://doi.org/10.1109/ASRU.2015.7404781
10. Martinez, L., Falvello, V.B., Aviezer, H., Todorov, A.: Contributions of facial expressions and body language to the rapid perception of dynamic emotions. Cogn. Emot. **30**(5), 939–952 (2016)
11. Moon, Y., Nass, C.: How real are computer personalities? Commun. Res. **23**(6), 651–674 (1996). https://doi.org/10.1177/009365096023006002. http://journals.sagepub.com/doi/10.1177/009365096023006002
12. Mori, M., MacDorman, K.F., Kageki, N.: The uncanny valley [from the field]. IEEE Robot. Autom. Mag. **19**(2), 98–100 (2012). https://doi.org/10.1109/MRA.2012.2192811
13. Mutlu, B., Forlizzi, J., Hodgins, J.: A storytelling robot: modeling and evaluation of human-like gaze behavior. In: 2006 6th IEEE-RAS International Conference on Humanoid Robots, pp. 518–523. IEEE (2006)
14. Nass, C., Moon, Y., Fogg, B.J., Reeves, B., Dryer, C.: Can computer personalities be human personalities? In: Conference Companion on Human Factors in Computing Systems - CHI 1995, pp. 228–229. ACM Press, New York (1995). https://doi.org/10.1145/223355.223538. http://portal.acm.org/citation.cfm?doid=223355.223538
15. Niculescu, A., van Dijk, B., Nijholt, A., See, S.L.: The influence of voice pitch on the evaluation of a social robot receptionist. In: 2011 International Conference on User Science and Engineering (i-USEr), pp. 18–23, November 2011. https://doi.org/10.1109/iUSEr.2011.6150529
16. Niculescu, A., Van Dijk, B., Nijholt, A., See, S.L.: The influence of voice pitch on the evaluation of a social robot receptionist. In: 2011 International Conference on User Science and Engineering (i-USEr), pp. 18–23. IEEE (2011)
17. Ozaeta, L., Graña, M.: On intelligent systems for storytelling. In: Graña, M., et al. (eds.) SOCO'18-CISIS'18-ICEUTE'18 2018. AISC, vol. 771, pp. 571–578. Springer, Cham (2019). https://doi.org/10.1007/978-3-319-94120-2_56
18. Page, R.A., Balloun, J.L.: The effect of voice volume on the perception of personality. J. Soc. Psychol. **105**(1), 65–72 (1978)
19. Paradeda, R.B., Martinho, C., Paiva, A.: Persuasion based on personality traits: using a social robot as storyteller. In: Proceedings of the Companion of the 2017 ACM/IEEE International Conference on Human-Robot Interaction, pp. 367–368, HRI 2017. ACM, New York (2017). https://doi.org/10.1145/3029798.3034824. http://doi.acm.org/10.1145/3029798.3034824

20. Paterson, R.: The Assertiveness Workbook: How to Express Your Ideas and Stand Up for Yourself at Work and in Relationships. New Harbinger Publications, Oakland (2000)
21. Plaisant, C., et al.: A storytelling robot for pediatric rehabilitation. In: Proceedings of the Fourth International ACM Conference on Assistive Technologies, pp. 50–55. ACM (2000)
22. Ramirez, M.A.: Interactive storytelling in the library. (Chophayom J.) **27**, 87–94 (2016)
23. Reeves, B., Nass, C.I.: The Media Equation: How People Treat Computers, Television, and New Media Like Real People and Places. Cambridge University Press, New York (1996)
24. Rodero, E.: Intonation and emotion: influence of pitch levels and contour type on creating emotions. J. Voice **25**, e25–e34 (2011). https://doi.org/10.1016/j.jvoice.2010.02.002
25. Sprole, S.: 5 principles of Speaking With More Assertiveness - Accent Artisan. http://accentartisan.com/article/assertiveness/
26. Striepe, H., Lugrin, B.: There once was a robot storyteller: measuring the effects of emotion and non-verbal behaviour. In: Kheddar, A., et al. (eds.) ICSR 2017. LNCS, vol. 10652, pp. 126–136. Springer, Cham (2017). https://doi.org/10.1007/978-3-319-70022-9_13

Automatic Plot Generation Framework for Scenario Creation

Yoji Kawano[1]([⊠]), Eichi Takaya[1]([⊠]), Kazuki Yamanobe[2]([⊠]),
and Satoshi Kurihara[1]([⊠])

[1] Keio University, Yokohama, Japan
{yojimax822,etakaya,satoshi}@keio.jp
[2] EdgeWORKS Inc., Yokohama, Japan
yamanobe@edge-works.co.jp

Abstract. Recently, the need for scenarios is increasing due to the increasing number of large-scale games, and the development of an automatic plot generation framework is needed to reduce a scenario writer's workload. In previous studies, the main focus was to output the complete scenario from scratch. However, there is a problem in that the story does not have a degree of freedom and loses diversity, which is needed to avoid the breakdown of a story. In this study, we aim to generate stories with a high degree of freedom without any breakdown. We regard a story as a hierarchical structure and use a structural theory method to gradually generate the scenario. We performed an evaluation experiment where we generated the plot, which is the first stage of scenario generation, automatically using the thirteen-phase theory, which is a type of scenario structure. The results of the evaluation demonstrate that it was possible to automatically generate something close to a plot created by a scenario writer.

Keywords: Artificial intelligence · Automatic story generation
Hierarchical structure of stories

1 Introduction

For large-scale games, equally large-scale scenarios are necessary. Such games require a scenario equivalent to a ten-hour movie. From the viewpoint of reducing the burden of the scenario writers, it is considered necessary to develop a system that automatically generates a scenario. Therefore, we aim to develop a system that automatically generates scenarios for writers. We conducted experiments and evaluations to automatically generate what is described as the outline of a story called the plot. To generate a plot, we use a thirteen-phase structure [1] that is an extension of the typical three-act structure [2]. Narrative breakage can be prevented by utilizing this structure. In addition, since this configuration is merely a structure and has no relation with the story of the scenario, it is possible to generate a highly flexible scenario. The plots generated automatically by the system were evaluated by professional scenario writers who write animation and game scenarios.

© Springer Nature Switzerland AG 2018
R. Rouse et al. (Eds.): ICIDS 2018, LNCS 11318, pp. 453–461, 2018.
https://doi.org/10.1007/978-3-030-04028-4_52

2   Related Work

Various studies on the automatic generation of stories have been conducted. One area of study is in "interactive drama" in which readers relate to the story world and the story changes. In "interactive drama," stories are generated using plot graph structures. The Oz project [3], Facade system [4], PaSSAGE [5], Interactive Drama Architecture (IDA) system [6], and Experience Managers (EM) [7] use this type of structure. Parts of the story are created beforehand and connected to become a graph structure. The parts that the reader chooses and the behavior of the characters appearing in the story are also prepared beforehand. Choices made in these parts by the reader or the character cause interaction, creating variation in the story. A drawback of a system using the plot graph structure is the lack of extensibility and versatility. The parts of the story must be predefined and created, requiring a lot of preparations. There are some approaches to these preparations that exploit crowdsourcing [8–10] and that extract story information from wikipedia [11]. Also, since the story is based on a plot graph, it becomes a story line that traces a specific route. Examples of story generation systems that do not use a plot graph include the non-linear interactive storytelling game engine (NoLIST) [12], which uses a Bayesian network, and the open ended Proppian interactive adaptive tale engine (OPIATE) [13], which uses a planning method to generate a story based on Propp's narrative structure systems also cannot generate various stories. For all these systems, since the target is a reader, the story generated needs to be perfect, which causes the story generated to lose diversity. In this study, we attempt to solve this problem by generating a scenario hierarchically to create scenarios with diversity. Also, the targets of our system are scenario writers. Although there are studies on the scenario creation support tool for scenario writers [14,15], we aim to generate a plot automatically.

3   Proposal Technique

To automatically generate a story, we regard a story as a hierarchical structure. First, we generate the causal relationship, which is the basic structure of the story. Second, we generate the hierarchical structure of the story, which is based on the three-act structure. Furthermore, we add detailed information to the story and generate the completed scenario. In this study, we generate a plot, which is the first stage of scenario generation. We utilize a thirteen-phase structure, which is one of the scenario structures, to generate plots automatically. The thirteen-phase structure is the theoretical structure of a story advocated by Kaneko Mitsuru. This theory is an unfoldment structure of a story based on a wide variety of scenario analyses that are based on the 31 functions in Vladimir Propp's "Structure of fairytales" [16]. This is an expansion of the three-act structure, enabling scenario generation by using an engineering method. Since this theory is merely a structure and has no relation with the story line of the scenario, it is possible to generate a scenario with a high degree of freedom. In the three-act structure, the story of the scenario is divided into three stages of setup (act 1), confrontation (act 2), and resolution (act 3), but in the thirteen-phase structure, the acts are divided into three, seven, and three parts, respectively (Fig. 1). We generate a plot and plot configuration file on the basis of the thirteen-phase structure. The content of the plot describes each element of the story and is divided into 13 parts. Each element is a part where the story is unfolded and contains details of the story. The input data of our system to generate the plot consists of loglines. The contents of the setting file are "age," "place," "background," "synopsis outline," "who is," "why," "what to do," "main character," and "theme" of the story. The plot generation system is roughly composed of the following six stages.

1. creation of a scenario plot database
2. extraction of story information from loglines
3. generation of thirteen-phase structure skeleton
4. generation of main character
5. elimination of contradictions
6. generation of setting file

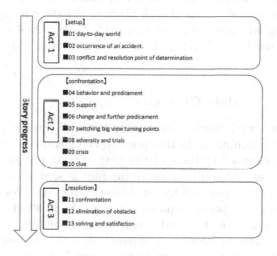

Fig. 1. Thirteen-phase structure

3.1   Creation of a Scenario Plot Database

We create a scenario plot database for plot generation. In the database, 94 plot samples created by professional scenario writers were used. These samples are based on the thirteen-phase structure. Each element of a plot is regarded as one block. In each block, tags related to "contents of setting file," "genre," "era," "place," and "thirteen-phase structure's roles" are inserted. A morphological analysis is performed to extract only nouns and verbs from the sentences in the database. Each plot sample in the database is allocated to a genre category. The number of samples for the genres Science Fiction (SF), Sports, Family, and Love are 27, 23, 24, and 20, respectively.

3.2   Extraction of Story Information by Input from Loglines

To generate a plot from a logline, it is necessary to extract story information such as "what kind of character," "what kind of place," and "what to do" from the logline. It is difficult to extract these from normal text. Therefore, in this study, we selected preset items from created loglines and extracted the information.

3.3   Generation of Thirteen-Phase Structure Skeleton

A plot based on the thirteen-phase structure is configured. From the input logline, "triggering event," "era," "genre," "ending," and "life and death of the main character" are extracted as story information conditions and used for plot generation. In the scenario plot database, a block unit that matches the extracted conditions is selected. If there are multiple sentences that fit the conditions, they are selected at random. The priority of block selection is in the order of "thirteen-phase structure's roles of each block in the story is matched," "age of the logline is matched," and "genre is matched." As described above, we arrange the sentences on the basis of the thirteen-phase structure and create a skeleton of the plot.

3.4   Generation of Main Character

If the main character's behavior is consistent, overall consistency in a scenario can be secured at a minimum. In this process, the inconsistency of an action of the main character caused by the skeleton generation of the plot is corrected. In the previous process, the composition of the plot is sentence-based, the action of the main character is changed by word-base correction. From the skeleton of the plot generated in the previous process, a sentence, in which a main character performs an action, is extracted, and a morphological analysis is performed. The words obtained by the analysis are compared with the scenario plot database, and words that does not matched in "genre," "era," or "role on the story" are replaced with matching words in the database.

3.5   Elimination of Contradictions

In this process, we eliminate contradictions in the story such as characters who have not appeared so far or have died that appear suddenly in the plot. If such a character occurs in the plot, it is replaced with another character. Alternatively, the description is deleted.

3.6   Generation of Setting File

To supplement the contents of the plot, a "setting file" in which the story setting is written is generated. We extract information on "era," "place," and "main character" from the logline and output it as a setting file. The contents of the outline are also extracted from the logline and added to the setting file.

4   Evaluation Experiment

A plot generation experiment using our method was conducted. We generated plots and setting files and asked professional scenario writers to answer a questionnaire.

4.1   Evaluation Experiment Setting

In this experiment, three plots were generated with the proposed method for verification and evaluation. The setting of the logline for generating the plot is as follows.

- Age of main character: 16
- Occupation: student
- Trigger event: meet unexpected people
- Stage: the world
- Era: the future
- Genre: SF
- Ending: the main character succeeds in eliminating obstacles
- Main character's life or death: life

Evaluation experiments were carried out using three plots generated under these conditions. Evaluators were 17 professional scenario writers. We prepared two plots created by a scenario writer, including three automatically generated ones for a total of five plots, as the evaluation targets. All plots were based on the premise that it was created by a scenario writer, and we performed questionnaire evaluations, hiding the fact that 3/5 of the plots were automatically generated. The questionnaire was prepared on the basis of the analysis items of the scenario used by a script doctor (Table 1).

Each question item was scored by using a five-stage evaluation (1: lowest, 5: highest). The plots to be evaluated were named A, B, C, D, and E. A and B were created by the scenario writer, with the remainder being automatically generated by the proposed method. At the end of the questionnaire, we asked the evaluators to select two plots they believed to the generated plots.

Table 1. Questionnaire items

Number	Question item
Q1	Do you think the story is consistent?
Q2	Was the story easy to read?
Q3	Is the theme of the story clearly implied?
Q4	Is the motif of the story clearly implied?
Q5	Do you feel a originality in the idea?
Q6	Do you feel the reality of the story?
Q7	Is there a catharsis in the story?
Q8	Do you agree with the ending of the story?
Q9	Is the character of the story attractive?
Q10	Is the amount of content in the story appropriate?

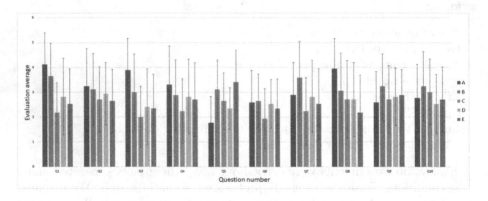

Fig. 2. Questionnaire results (average & standard deviation)

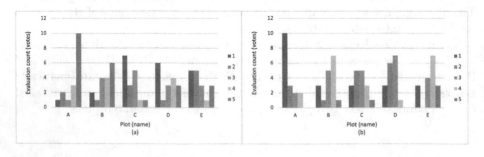

Fig. 3. Q1 result (a) & Q5 result (b)

- Plot D (An excerpt of only the plot sentences)
  1. "A" makes a date with "B".
  2. "A" notices that there is a discrepancy between the record of "A"'s memory chip and his own memory.
  3. "A" decides to stop the robot running away to protect the city.
  4. "A" repeated trial and error to cook space food to be more delicious.
  5. "A" will discover the fountain. "A" is impressed by the taste of the water.
  6. "A" invades the laboratory with the help of "E". "A" and "E" repair the robot control system of the laboratory to stop the robot running away in the city. The city robot returns to normal. The robot in the city resumes running away.
  7. "A" thinks about the reason why the robot in the city is running away. "A" notices that "D" is the cause of the robot in the city running away.
  8. "A" thinks to stop "D" by turning off its power. "A" and "E" look for devices to turn off the power while avoiding attacks from the city robots.
  9. "A" confronts "D" to stop the huge weapons. However, "A" can not defeat "D". "A" huge weapon finishes powering up. The laboratories of "A" lose the fight.
  10. "A" reads a book that "E" gave to distract his sorrow. "A" can laugh for the first time after the death of "E" because of that book.
  11. "A" will continue walking with painful feet.
  12. "A" knocks down "D".
  13. "A" returns to the Earth.

- Plot E (An excerpt of only the plot sentences)
  1. "A" is surfing the net as usual.
  2. "A" is transported to an unknown place due to a teleport accident.
  3. "A" loses a robot ride to someone other than "B". "A" swears vengeance on "C".
  4. "A" consults with "B". "B" says that "A" is a mistake to remember.
  5. "A" encounters a traffic accident. "B" saves "A"'s life with "B"'s ability.
  6. "A" gets the cooperation of "B". "A" will proceed with excavation and research to promote cooking to be more appealing to people.
  7. "A" finds that the supplement maker and the government have joined hands and lost their cooking by excavation.
  8. "A" gets an opportunity to act as a cook for "C" to get the confirmation of the wonder of the dish.
  9. "A" and "B" go fight with "C".
  10. "A" loses foods and falls into a dilemma. "B" finds mushrooms growing accidentally from behind the house. "A" notices that the mushrooms are food.
  11. "A" will continue walking with painful feet.
  12. "A" and "B" annihilate cosmic creature.
  13. "A" goes back to my dream chasing days and feeling that the job of my dreams is difficult.

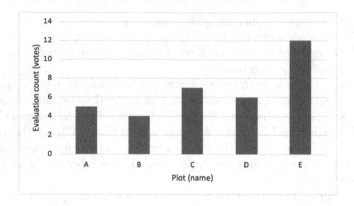

Fig. 4. Result of evaluators assumption of generated plots

4.2 Experimental Result

The evaluated results for the automatically generated plots are lower than those created by the scenario writer (Fig. 2). In particular, regarding the consistency of the story, the automatically generated plots were significantly lower in the evaluation result (Fig. 3(a)). However, in terms of originality of the story, the automatically generated plots marked higher (Fig. 3(b)). Plot E, where the evaluation of the consistency of the story was low, achieved the highest score. From this, the consistency and originality of the story seem to be closely related. The best evaluation among the automatically generated plots was Plot D. It was evaluated as having a relatively consistent story. All of the plots were evaluated as being automatically generated at least once (Fig. 4). In this experiment, it can be seen that there is a difference in quality depending on the plot. However, the results show that it is also possible to automatically generate something close to a plot created by a scenario writer.

5   Conclusion and Future Works

In this study, we developed a system for automatically generating plots and conducted an evaluation experiment. From the evaluation results, it can be said that the proposed method was able to achieve results. However, there is concern that if we reduce the contradictions of the plot and increase the consistency of the story, we can only generate stylized scenarios. The challenge is the automation of creating a scenario plot database that a scenario writer creates, and system improvements to reduce contradictions in the story. Achieving a balance between originality and consistency is required in the creation of stories. For future work, we would like to automatically generate plots other than those in the SF genre, and we want to raise the story hierarchy and generate a more complicated story than the plot.

References

1. Kaneko, M.: Golden Law of Scenario Writing: Making Content Interesting. Born Digital (2011)
2. Field, S.: Screenplay: The Foundations of Screenwriting. Delta Book (1979)
3. Bates, J.: Virtual reality, art, and entertainment. Presence Teleoperators Virtual Environ. 1(1), 133–138 (1992)
4. Mateas, M., Stern, A.: Facade: an experiment in building a fully-realized interactive drama. In: Game Developers Conference, Game Design Track (2003)
5. Thue, D., Bulitko, V., Spetch, M., Wasylishen, E.: Interactive storytelling: a player modelling approach. In: AIIDE 2007, Stanford, California (2007)
6. Magerko, B.: Player modeling in the interactive drama architecture, Ph.D. dissertation, The Department of Computer Science and Engineering, University of Michigan (2006)
7. Amos-Binks, A., Potts, C., Michael Young, R.: Planning graphs for efficient generation of desirable narrative trajectories. In: The AIIDE-2017 Workshop on Intelligent Narrative Technologies (2017)
8. Guzdial, M., Harrison, B., Li, B., Riedl, M.O.: Crowdsourcing open interactive narrative. In: FDG 2015 (2015)
9. Li, B., Lee-Urban, S., Johnston, G., Riedl, M.O.: Story generation with crowdsourced plot graphs. In: AAAI 2013 (2013)
10. Feng, D., Carstensdottir, E., Carnicke, S.M., El-Nasr, M.S., Marsella, S.: An active analysis and crowd sourced approach to social training. In: Nack, F., Gordon, A.S. (eds.) ICIDS 2016. LNCS, vol. 10045, pp. 156–167. Springer, Cham (2016). https://doi.org/10.1007/978-3-319-48279-8_14
11. Martin, L.J., et al.: Event representations for automated story generation with deep neural nets. In: Proceedings of the Thirty-Second AAAI Conference on Artificial Intelligence (2017)
12. Bangsø, O., Jensen, O.G., Jensen, F.V., Andersen, P.B., Kocka, T.: Non-linear interactive storytelling using object-oriented Bayesian networks. In: Proceedings of the International Conference on Computer Games: Artificial Intelligence, Design and Education (2004)
13. Fairclough, C.: Story games and the OPIATE system, Ph.D. dissertation, University of Dublin - Trinity College (2004)
14. Kawagoe, S., Ueno, M., Isahara, H.: A study on the efficiency of creating stories by the use of templates. In: 2nd International Conference on Advanced Informatics: Concepts, Theory and Applications (ICAICTA). IEEE (2015)
15. Katsui, T., Ueno, M., Isahara, H.: A creation support system to manage the story structure based on template sets and graph. In: The 31st Annual Conference of the Japanese Society for Artificial Intelligence (2017)
16. Propp, V.: Morphology of the Folktale, Leningrad (1928)

Towards Generating Stylistic Dialogues for Narratives Using Data-Driven Approaches

Weilai Xu[(✉)], Charlie Hargood, Wen Tang, and Fred Charles

Faculty of Science and Technology, Creative Technology Department,
Bournemouth University, Poole BH12 5BB, UK
{wxu,chargood,wtang,fcharles}@bournemouth.ac.uk

Abstract. Recently, there has been a renewed interest in generating dialogues for narratives. Within narrative dialogues, their structure and content are essential, though *style* holds an important role as a mean to express narrative dialogue through telling stories. Most existing approaches of narrative dialogue generation tend to leverage handcrafted rules and linguistic-level styles, which lead to limitations in their expressivity and issues with scalability. We aim to investigate the potential of generating more stylistic dialogues within the context of narratives. To reach this, we propose a new approach and demonstrate its feasibility through the support of deep learning. We also describe this approach using examples, where story-level features are analysed and modelled based on a classification of characters and genres.

Keywords: Dialogue generation · Interactive narratives
Dialogue style · Neural networks

1 Introduction

Stories can be represented through plot structures [20,21,24], and are often equated to a sequence of narrative actions [22], normally represented as objects, subjects, actions and other features. Narrative actions can be presented through discourse in different ways: visual [14], audio, and linguistic [10].

Dialogue plays an essential role in narratives, by which the story or plot can be conveyed, and characters are able to express their intentions, emotions, and personalities. In recent years, dialogue generation has become ever more popular as evidenced through an increase in research in natural language generation (NLG) [4,7,9,26]. However, most of these works concentrate on task-oriented dialogue generation and "chit-chat" conversations, along with only few works specifically undertaken within the context of interactive narratives.

Style is a crucial part of narrative dialogue, responsible for telling stories vividly and lively. Lin and Walker [14] point out that many linguistic styles can be designed to express dramatic characters in dialogue from television. Existing

© Springer Nature Switzerland AG 2018
R. Rouse et al. (Eds.): ICIDS 2018, LNCS 11318, pp. 462–472, 2018.
https://doi.org/10.1007/978-3-030-04028-4_53

research mostly relies on predefined hand-crafted rules or plans [2,5] to generate dialogue in narratives. These approaches are supposed to generate grammatically correct dialogues with the empirical knowledge, but in the meantime, they suffer from several limitations: a lack of style, difficulty to scale-up, and often a very onerous manual labour.

In dialogue generation, styles are usually described using linguistic features (e.g. sentence length, number of nouns/verbs) [14,30] or speaker profile features (e.g. age, occupation) [12]. To some extent, these features can represent the dialogue content style by changing the expression of the utterances (e.g. using interjections). While in narratives, those types of stylistic dialogues do not have a strong relationship with the storyline (i.e. the story plot has little effect on the dialogue generation). Here, we propose to introduce different characters' relationship types and genres as a measure of variability in dialogue generation.

In this paper, we propose a data-driven approach to generate story-level stylistic dialogues for narratives. To address these challenges, we investigate the potential of using neural networks to generate dialogues from input based on narrative actions, by analysing the story-level features which are able to provide dialogue styles with different aspects. Fortunately, the progressive development of neural network models [12,16,28] for dialogue generation provides the mechanism, which is a solid foundation to implement this theoretical approach through building this dialogue generator and incorporating the vectorised story-level features as dialogue styles.

2   Related Work

As we are working on generating stylistic dialogues for narratives using data-driven approaches, we concentrate on four relevant fields of prior work.

Narrative Representations. In narrative research, narrative action is strongly related to natural language generation because it provides all main semantic elements in a story through abstract representation. Previous research proposed different formalisms for the representation of narrative actions. Pichotta and Mooney [18] developed a 5-tuple event representation of (v, e_s, e_o, e_p, p), where v is the verb, p is a preposition, and e_s, e_o, and e_p are nouns representing the subject, direction object, and prepositional object, respectively. Chambers and Jurafsky [6] proposed unsupervised induction of similar schemata called narrative event chains which are centred around the protagonist. These narrative chains are related to structured sequences of participants and events called scripts [25].

NLG in Interactive Narratives. Storytelling through NLG is an important part in our work since the story should be represented in comprehensible natural language. Cavazza and Charles [5] generated natural dialogue through semantic templates using predetermined modalities of expression, which can be regarded as a rule-based strategy. Other systems using plan-based strategies can develop a plan composed of a series of (dialogue) actions, to reach goals in hierarchical tasks [2]. Bowden et al. [3] present algorithms for generating dialogues by converting a deep representation made by annotating and processing a story semantically [8,23].

Neural Networks and Dialogue Generation. Progressively, with the development of these data-driven methods, several approaches to dialogue systems and dialogue generation are inclined to apply different types of neural networks, e.g. Recurrent Neural Networks (RNN). Currently, many works [16,28,32] build dialogue systems using data-driven methods to provide an automated generation process. The Seq2Seq [28] model, an encoder-decoder RNN model for generating sequences of unfixed length, is well-suited for generating utterances. The efficiency of this model is improved with the assistance of both Long Short Term Memory (LSTM) [11] and Attention Mechanism [1]. LSTM is an RNN model for solving long term dependencies problem (i.e. it is capable of using context to improve language coherence) and Attention improves the decoding precision by increasing weight for information of interest. Martin et al. [16] present two Seq2Seq models for generating event representations and sentences. In our work, we aim to find the relationship between narrative actions and utterances and use their relation to generate dialogue. Both of these can be regarded as word sequences and processed by Seq2Seq with LSTM and Attention rationally following certain aspects (e.g. grammar accuracy, content diversity, context coherence).

Style Representation. Beyond the challenge of dialogue generation within a story context, the style of the dialogue (i.e. the ways to present the variant dialogues), is another key aspect this research focuses on. Walker et al. [29, 30] focus on generalizing character style from films on the basis of qualitative statistical analysis. Li et al. [12] created two persona-based models by generating different word embeddings for different speakers and addressees. Some works on narrative generation have strategies based on characters point of view (PoV) [20] and relationship between characters [21], which could be means to specify styles for dialogue generation.

3   Proposed Approach

In this section, we introduce our proposed approach for dialogue generation in narratives.

A story consists in a sequence of narrative actions, which are the backbone of the whole storyline. As dialogue is a recognised manifestation of narrative discourse, it is therefore reasonable for us to hypothesise that the narrative actions representation can be leveraged for the purpose of generating narrative dialogue efficiently.

Currently, narrative generation is a more mature field than narrative dialogue generation. Martin et al. [16] postulate that narrative actions and natural language can be equated to each other. They define a story as a sequence of

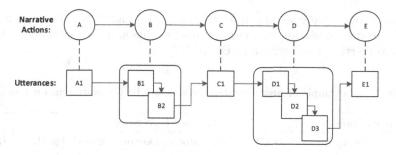

Fig. 1. The dialogue generation model.

events. Each event is formalised as a 4-tuple event representation (s, v, o, m), where v is a verb, s and o are the subject and object of the verb, and m indexes a modifier, which can be any other grammatical parts in a sentence besides the above three. They use an event representation to generate the next event representation which is followed by a conversion from this generated event representation to a natural language sentence. Inspired by this approach of story representation, we present our new approach for narrative dialogue generation.

3.1 Dialogue Generation Model

In Fig. 1, we present a dialogue generation model based on a sequence of narrative actions, which are generated by a plan-based narrative system (similar to [20, 21]). These pre-generated narrative actions are displayed as circles in Fig. 1. Each narrative action can be represented as one or several utterances (displayed as small squares in Fig. 1). For example, utterances $A1$, $C1$, and $E1$ represent narrative actions A, C, and E respectively. An utterance pair, $B1$ and $B2$ represent the narrative action B. Also, $D1$, $D2$, and $D3$ represent narrative action D jointly.

Each narrative action is supposed to be translated into one or multiple utterances as illustrated in Fig. 1 shown through a pre-trained Seq2Seq based neural network. Along with narrative actions, other necessary elements of the dialogue such as who is the "doer" (subject) and who is the "doee" (object), often referred to as characters. Besides, where the dialogue happens (location) is also considered. All these elements can be extracted from story plot (e.g. film descriptions) according to [27] and are able to provide dialogue styles, described in the next section.

In this generation process, the context coherence between each turn within the dialogue is an important issue. Some open-domain dialogue systems [13, 31] tackle coherence issues by discovering more relations between turn-pairs. In our model, the generated utterances should follow the direction of the narrative actions because the content of the story is represented by these utterances. Therefore, the coherence we consider here is between generated utterances and their corresponding narrative actions. An evaluation process must be undertaken after every utterance generation. Martin et al. [16] has shown that it is feasible to evaluate the correlation between the story events and the matching sentences using two metrics: Perplexity and BLEU [17].

Table 1. An example of how narrative actions can be translated into utterances.

Narrative actions	Utterance turn pairs
(*Offer-To-Repay-Loan*, *A D C*)	D: Antonio, Do you acknowledge the contract?
	A: Yes, I do
	D: Then you have to pay the money according to the contract and law
(*Show-Contempt-For*, *S D C*)	S: Oh, wise young judge, I honour you!
	D: Shylock, they're offering you three times the money you lent
	S: No, I made an oath in heaven. I urge you to deliver your verdict. I'm sticking to the contract
(*Call-For-Judgement*, *S D C*)	D: A pound of this merchant's flesh is yours. The court awards it and the law authorizes it
	S: What a righteous judge!
	D: But this contract doesn't give you any blood
(*Release-From-Forfeit*, *S D C*)	S: So give me my money and let me go
	D: The verdict is your penalty has been released
(*Receive-Verdict-Of-Court*, *S D C*)	D: Are you satisfied, Shylock?
	S: I'm satisfied

3.2   Example

Here we describe our dialogue generation model with an example displayed as Table 1. These five sequential narrative actions shown here are collected from [19], adapted from a well-known play of William Shakespeare, *Merchant of Venice*. The acronyms in narrative actions represent the names of the main characters and the locations of the scene. For the characters' name, A, D, and S indicates Antonio, the Duke of Venice, and Shylock respectively. The selected plots all occur at the court, which is indicated by C. As we can see in the table, a narrative action usually tends to be represented with more than one utterance, but normally no more than three utterances. If so, that narrative action should be split into some sub-narrative-actions, assuming the representation can be more precise with smaller granularity.

Table 2. Dialogue styles in different genres of film scripts.

Genre	Dialogue script pieces
Romance	Ilsa: Hello, Sam
	Sam: Hello, Miss Ilsa. I never expected to see you again
	Violet: Good afternoon, Mr. Bailey
	George: Hello, Violet. Hey, you look good. That's some dress you got on there
Western	Ringo: Well hello, Sherm
	Mcmasters: You wanted to talk?
	Ringo: Yeah, kinda, wanted to see if you'd join back up with us
	Woman: Hello?
	Chigurh: Is Llewelyn there?
	Woman: Llewelyn?! No, he ain't
Crime	Senator: Hi, Ace
	Ace: Hello, Senator
	Senator: Hey, I need a room. Need a room
	Nick: Hello... Send him up
	Nora: Who's that?
	Nick: Macaulay

4 Stylistic Dialogue Modelling

In this section, we introduce our thoughts on adding story-level styles in dialogues during the dialogue generation process.

Many other works that address the issues of stylistic dialogues focus more prominently on linguistic features (e.g. sentence length, number of nouns/verbs) [30] or speaker profile features (e.g. age, gender, and occupation) [12]. We aim to rely on the potential that the story-level features are able to affect dialogue style.

4.1 Genre Diversity

Table 2 shows film script pieces grouped in different genres, which are collected from Cornell Movie-Dialogs Corpus[1]. We select 6 pieces of script representing *greeting* in 3 different genres: romance, western, and crime. It is easy to observe that within each genre, dialogues are expressed through differing styles, often reflected in their linguistic aspects. For example, in the western genre, there exist informal spoken expressions (e.g. kinda, ain't). However, in our work, we are looking for a relation between story-level style and the genres. For example, we can see in the table that in western and crime genres, characters tend to

---

[1] https://www.cs.cornell.edu/~cristian/Cornell_Movie-Dialogs_Corpus.html.

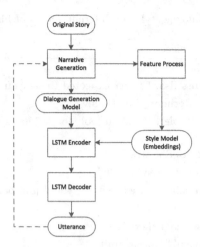

Fig. 2. Overview of the framework for our proposed approach.

come straight to the point for propelling the storyline when they start a dialogue with greetings (fast-paced). However, for the romance genre, characters are more likely to use witticisms to exaggerate the atmosphere of the scenes or make the audience more engaged (slow-paced). We aim to focus on the relations between genre and story-level style in dialogues, and analyse and quantify these relations.

4.2   Characters

For the purpose of characters, we put emphasis on the relationship between characters who participate in the dialogue exchange, which is different from previous literature that focus on the profile of interlocutors. In a story, a character normally plays a similar role across the narrative though will see an evolution in the relationship with other the characters. Porteous et al. [21] have presented a mechanism for narrative generation, which demonstrated that changes in the relationships between characters in a social network can yield significant qualitative difference in narratives of some genres of drama (e.g. medical drama). This approach can also be used for providing styles in dialogue generation. We are supporting our generation of different utterances on the basis of the different character relationships defined as part of a same narrative action.

5   Neural Network Framework Design

Here, we describe our neural network framework as illustrated in Fig. 2. We designed our dialogue generation framework based on Seq2Seq [28] with Attention mechanism [1], and on LSTM [11] for the encoder and decoder.

First, in the left principal stream, the original story will be preprocessed using a plan-based narrative engine, producing the sequence of relevant narrative actions through narrative generation. The generated narrative actions is used as the input into a LSTM encoder which is pre-trained using parallel narrative action/utterance corpora. After this stage, the learnt style embeddings will be incorporated with the LSTM encoder and the corresponding narrative actions, as the right branch stream shown. The LSTM decoder will receive the result from the encoder and generate the final utterance as the output.

Dialogue Generation. There are two potential ways to generate dialogue with narrative actions. The first is dialogue generation within each narrative action. This way, each narrative action is the input to be used for the neural network, and the output is one or multiple utterances. The other is to consider the dialogue generation process over the whole pre-generated story. An initial utterance is generated by the first narrative action, and the following utterances are iteratively generated based on the last generated utterance through evaluation. Either way, the story coherence is managed through the narrative generation process itself. If using the second one, the evaluation of whether the generated utterance is matching the narrative action is essential. Therefore, we choose the first mechanism to generate utterance through translating the narrative action.

Style Embeddings. Style embeddings is an independent model which is incorporated as part of the main pipeline. Several prior dialogue works use embedding to improve the word-level embeddings using multiple dimensions vectors to represent word distribution and cluster semantically similar words into near spaces, which can be visualised as a two-dimensional space projected from the high-dimension vectors.

Here, it is achievable to create sentence-level embeddings for representing each style aspect we mentioned before (e.g. genre, character). Lin et al. [15] use a two-dimensional matrix to represent the embeddings instead of a vector, with each row of the matrix corresponding to a different part of the sentence. For instance, the genre embedding can be created by promoting a supervised learning problem. Given a film script corpus, of which each utterance can be categorised into single or multiple genres, the genre embedding is being created by encoding utterances into matrices, since utterances with same genre(s) have similar encoding. This embedding can be viewed as a map containing the relations between genres and parts of the utterances. With this kind of embedding, we can add similar expressions through matching genres to our dialogue generation process.

6   Conclusion

In this paper, we have investigated the potential to integrate a data-driven approach within dialogue generation in narratives and have reasoned its feasibility theoretically and technically. We described a new model for dialogue generation based on the relations between utterances and narrative actions. We also introduced our style model in terms of story-level features, such as genre and character.

Our approach uses LSTM-based recurrent neural networks to generate dialogues, which will be derived from the given storyline. Although we have been working under the assumption of the complete knowledge of the narrative, within an *interactive* narrative paradigm, the narrative generation process must follows authorial control, which will also have to be managed for the purpose of dialogue generation. We may have to evaluate any potential remediation which will need to occur between the dialogue and the narrative generated interactively.

Our approach could be used in interactive computer games or interactive narratives. Normally, authors will create the necessary content components (e.g. characters, locations), where our approach can generate dialogues based upon those storylines and provide different styles learned from pre-existing corpora for providing more compelling and as such engaging dialogues.

References

1. Bahdanau, D., Cho, K., Bengio, Y.: Neural machine translation by jointly learning to align and translate (2014). arXiv preprint: arXiv:1409.0473
2. Bohus, D., Rudnicky, A.I.: Ravenclaw: dialog management using hierarchical task decomposition and an expectation agenda. In: Eighth European Conference on Speech Communication and Technology (2003)
3. Bowden, K.K., Lin, G.I., Reed, L.I., Fox Tree, J.E., Walker, M.A.: M2D: monolog to dialog generation for conversational story telling. In: Nack, F., Gordon, A.S. (eds.) ICIDS 2016. LNCS, vol. 10045, pp. 12–24. Springer, Cham (2016). https://doi.org/10.1007/978-3-319-48279-8_2
4. Burgan, D.: Dialogue systems and dialogue management. Technical report, DST Group Edinburgh Edinburgh SA Australia (2016)
5. Cavazza, M., Charles, F.: Dialogue generation in character-based interactive storytelling. In: Proceedings of the First AAAI Conference on Artificial Intelligence and Interactive Digital Entertainment, pp. 21–26. AAAI Press (2005)
6. Chambers, N., Jurafsky, D.: Unsupervised learning of narrative event chains. In: Proceedings of ACL 2008: HLT, pp. 789–797 (2008)
7. Chen, H., Liu, X., Yin, D., Tang, J.: A survey on dialogue systems: recent advances and new frontiers. ACM SIGKDD Explor. Newsl. **19**(2), 25–35 (2017)
8. Elson, D.K., McKeown, K.R.: A tool for deep semantic encoding of narrative texts. In: Proceedings of the ACL-IJCNLP 2009 Software Demonstrations, pp. 9–12. Association for Computational Linguistics (2009)
9. Gatt, A., Krahmer, E.: Survey of the state of the art in natural language generation: core tasks, applications and evaluation. J. Artif. Intell. Res. **61**, 65–170 (2018)
10. Gervás, P., Díaz-Agudo, B., Peinado, F., Hervás, R.: Story plot generation based on CBR. In: Macintosh, A., Ellis, R., Allen, T. (eds.) SGAI 2004, pp. 33–46. Springer, London (2005). https://doi.org/10.1007/1-84628-103-2_3
11. Hochreiter, S., Schmidhuber, J.: Long short-term memory. Neural Comput. **9**(8), 1735–1780 (1997)
12. Li, J., Galley, M., Brockett, C., Spithourakis, G., Gao, J., Dolan, B.: A persona-based neural conversation model. In: Proceedings of the 54th Annual Meeting of the Association for Computational Linguistics. Long Papers, vol. 1, pp. 994–1003 (2016)

13. Li, J., Monroe, W., Ritter, A., Jurafsky, D., Galley, M., Gao, J.: Deep reinforcement learning for dialogue generation. In: Proceedings of the 2016 Conference on Empirical Methods in Natural Language Processing, pp. 1192–1202 (2016)
14. Lin, G., Walker, M.: Stylistic variation in television dialogue for natural language generation. In: Proceedings of the Workshop on Stylistic Variation, pp. 85–93 (2017)
15. Lin, Z., et al.: A structured self-attentive sentence embedding (2017)
16. Martin, L., et al.: Event representations for automated story generation with deep neural nets. In: AAAI Conference on Artificial Intelligence (2018)
17. Papineni, K., Roukos, S., Ward, T., Zhu, W.J.: Bleu: a method for automatic evaluation of machine translation. In: Proceedings of the 40th Annual Meeting on Association for Computational Linguistics, pp. 311–318. Association for Computational Linguistics (2002)
18. Pichotta, K., Mooney, R.J.: Learning statistical scripts with LSTM recurrent neural networks. In: AAAI, pp. 2800–2806 (2016)
19. Porteous, J., Cavazza, M., Charles, F.: Applying planning to interactive storytelling: narrative control using state constraints. ACM Trans. Intell. Syst. Technol. (TIST) 1(2), 10 (2010)
20. Porteous, J., Cavazza, M., Charles, F.: Narrative generation through characters' point of view. In: Proceedings of the 9th International Conference on Autonomous Agents and Multiagent Systems, vol. 1, pp. 1297–1304. International Foundation for Autonomous Agents and Multiagent Systems (2010)
21. Porteous, J., Charles, F., Cavazza, M.: Networking: using character relationships for interactive narrative generation. In: Proceedings of the 2013 International Conference on Autonomous Agents and Multi-agent Systems, pp. 595–602. International Foundation for Autonomous Agents and Multiagent Systems (2013)
22. Riedl, M.O., Young, R.M.: Narrative planning: balancing plot and character. J. Artif. Intell. Res. 39, 217–268 (2010)
23. Rishes, E., Lukin, S.M., Elson, D.K., Walker, M.A.: Generating different story tellings from semantic representations of narrative. In: Koenitz, H., Sezen, T.I., Ferri, G., Haahr, M., Sezen, D., Ç atak, G. (eds.) ICIDS 2013. LNCS, vol. 8230, pp. 192–204. Springer, Cham (2013). https://doi.org/10.1007/978-3-319-02756-2_24
24. Rowe, J.P., Ha, E.Y., Lester, J.C.: Archetype-driven character dialogue generation for interactive narrative. In: Prendinger, H., Lester, J., Ishizuka, M. (eds.) IVA 2008. LNCS (LNAI), vol. 5208, pp. 45–58. Springer, Heidelberg (2008). https://doi.org/10.1007/978-3-540-85483-8_5
25. Schank, R.C., Abelson, R.P.: Scripts, plans, goals, and understanding: an inquiry into human knowledge structures (1977)
26. Serban, I.V., Lowe, R., Henderson, P., Charlin, L., Pineau, J.: A survey of available corpora for building data-driven dialogue systems (2015). arXiv preprint: arXiv:1512.05742
27. Tozzo, A., Jovanovic, D., Amer, M.: Neural event extraction from movies description. In: Proceedings of the First Workshop on Storytelling, pp. 60–66 (2018)
28. Vinyals, O., Le, Q.: A neural conversational model (2015). arXiv preprint: arXiv:1506.05869
29. Walker, M., Lin, G., Sawyer, J.: An annotated corpus of film dialogue for learning and characterizing character style. In: Proceedings of the Eighth International Conference on Language Resources and Evaluation (LREC 2012) (2012)

30. Walker, M.A., Grant, R., Sawyer, J., Lin, G.I., Wardrip-Fruin, N., Buell, M.: Perceived or not perceived: film character models for expressive NLG. In: Si, M., Thue, D., André, E., Lester, J.C., Tanenbaum, J., Zammitto, V. (eds.) ICIDS 2011. LNCS, vol. 7069, pp. 109–121. Springer, Heidelberg (2011). https://doi.org/10.1007/978-3-642-25289-1_12

31. Wen, T., et al.: A network-based end-to-end trainable task-oriented dialogue system. In: Proceedings of the 15th Conference of the European Chapter of the Association for Computational Linguistics, EACL 2017, vol. 1, pp. 438–449 (2017)

32. Wen, T.H., Gasic, M., Mrkšić, N., Su, P.H., Vandyke, D., Young, S.: Semantically conditioned LSTM-based natural language generation for spoken dialogue systems. In: Proceedings of the 2015 Conference on Empirical Methods in Natural Language Processing, pp. 1711–1721 (2015)

Expressive Range Analysis of a Possible Worlds Driven Emergent Narrative System

Ben Kybartas[1](✉), Clark Verbrugge[1], and Jonathan Lessard[2]

[1] McGill University, Montreal, Canada
ben.kybartas@mail.mcgill.ca, clump@cs.mcgill.ca
[2] Concordia University, Montreal, Canada
jonathan.lessard@concordia.ca

Abstract. Analyzing the potential and affordances of emergent narrative systems is an ongoing challenge, especially in novel or experimental systems. In this poster we explore the use of expressive range analysis (ERA) [1] to analyze an emergent system based upon the possible worlds model of Ryan [2]. We introduce the system and the properties of conflict that can be identified in a given work made in the system. The ERA analysis is performed by treating an emergent system as an exploration of a conflict space through actions. This paper serves as a foundation for deeper exploration of possible worlds narrative systems and quantifiable means for understanding them.

Keywords: Emergent narrative · Possible worlds
Expressive range analysis

1 Introduction

Emergent, or simulationist, narratives are an approach to interactive storytelling that often eschews the concept of fixed linear plots, in favour of exploring the potential of character-driven simulation [3,4]. A concern in many such systems is understanding the ability of the system itself to express certain narrative properties, and also how to evaluate the possible narratives of a given work designed in the system. Often, evaluation is done through user studies or the analysis of specific playthroughs [3], however deeper, player-agnostic and formal means of analyzing such systems remains interesting challenge. In this paper we analyze an emergent narrative system based upon the possible worlds (PW) model of Ryan [2] using expressive range analysis [1]. The system is described in a previous work [5], and models characters as having a set of desires treated as possible worlds of the current state of the actual world in the system. To analyze this system, we re-frame it as a set of generative methods for creating *conflicts*, using Ryan's definition of conflict as conflicting values between possible worlds. This allows us to use expressive range analysis to see the *space* of possible

© Springer Nature Switzerland AG 2018
R. Rouse et al. (Eds.): ICIDS 2018, LNCS 11318, pp. 473–477, 2018.
https://doi.org/10.1007/978-3-030-04028-4_54

conflicts given by an initial configuration of the system, as well as how these conflicts may be realized through the available *actions* which may be taken in the system. Although preliminary, the aim of this work is dual purpose, both to analyze a given work made in the system, but also in more deeply understanding Ryan's original model and perspectives on conflict and narrative.

2   Possible Worlds Model

Our system implements Ryan's concept of *wish worlds* and *conflict*. Essentially, in the system each character has a set of *wish worlds*, which are the ideal states of the *actual world* according to some theme (e.g. politics, religion, personal desires, etc.). The goal of each character is to make changes to the actual world through actions so that all the propositions in their wish worlds are true. However, this is impossible, as each character has different desires and even their internal desires may conflict. The resulting narrative then, emerges out of the character's attempts to achieve their goal, and the resulting conflicts that emerge both internally and between characters provides the main conflicts. The system is described in the previous work [5], but in essence our system consists of a set of *characters* and an *actual world*, with each character having a set of desired *worldviews* and a set of *actions* they can take. Both the actual world and each desired worldviews are a vector of values (in this case boolean) that show the state of each possible *proposition* in the world. Notably a character may not care about the state of a proposition in a given worldview, indicated by $\perp$. Each desired worldview is labelled with a specific *theme*, and each character has one desired worldview per theme. A *conflict* is any proposition for which two worlds hold a different value. For example, if two characters disagree on a given proposition for a worldview, then this is identified as an *interpersonal conflict*. An *internal conflict* occurs when a character has two worldviews that conflict (e.g. their religious beliefs conflict with their political beliefs). Lastly, the *actual*

Themes = {*Hunger, Pride*}   Actual World = $\langle T, F, F \rangle$
Propositions = {*Has cheese (Raven), Has cheese (Fox), Showing off (Raven)*}
Actions = {*Take Cheese, Sing*}

Action	Precondition	Postcondition
Take Cheese	$\langle F, F, \perp \rangle$	$\langle \perp, T, \perp \rangle$
Sing	$\langle \perp, \perp, \perp \rangle$	$\langle F, \perp, T \rangle$

Characters = {*Fox, Raven*}

Character	Actions	Worldviews	
		Hunger	Pride
Fox	{*Take Cheese*}	$\langle \perp, T, \perp \rangle$	$\langle \perp, \perp, \perp \rangle$
Raven	{*Sing*}	$\langle T, \perp, \perp \rangle$	$\langle \perp, \perp, T \rangle$

Fig. 1. The components of the narrative system for modelling the "Fox and the Raven" fable.

conflict is the number of propositions where a worldview's values differs from that of the actual world. This is in essence the Manhattan distance between the actual world and a given worldview, and we say the *distance* between any two worlds is number of propositions for which each world has differing values. In Fig. 1, a formal model of the Aesop's fable of the "Fox and the Raven" is shown, with two characters, the Fox and the Raven, two themes of the story, Pride and Hunger, as well as a set of actions.

3   Analysis

In this section we explore the potential space of conflicts afforded to us by the system with the "Fox and Raven" model using expressive range analysis. As stated previously, the core of the system surrounds each character's attempts to align all their worldviews with the actual world, however this overarching goal is impossible due to the constraints of actions and the interpersonal and internal conflict. What is then interesting to understand is precisely how each component affects this overarching goal and, in essence, the shape they form. Any action taken in the actual world will affect the actual conflict of each worldview, and we can thus treat any action as a change in distance for all possible worlds in the system. To create a conflict space, for each set of worldviews, the system iterates over all possible states of the actual world, and at each point plots the actual conflict for each worldview giving the expressive range of what areas of conflict we can explore in this given work. In each figure, arrows show directions we can move in the space given some action, i.e. if this action is taken, then the two points mark the new actual conflict for both worldviews at the new actual world. For simplicity, we do not mark any action that keeps both worlds at the same distance. In this sense, the actions show the possible paths through the conflict space and any point that does not have at least one arrow entering it is considered "inaccessible" unless it is the start position. Since the overarching goal is for all worlds to have an actual conflict of zero, we can say that for the internal space, both characters want to reach point $(0, 0)$, and for interpersonal space, they care more about reaching a position where their own conflict is 0. If the 0 position does not exist, or is inaccessible, then we are in a state where that particular conflict can never be resolved.

For the "Fox and Raven" work, there are four two-dimensional conflict spaces, the internal conflict space of the fox and raven, and the interpersonal conflict space for hunger and pride. Figure 2 shows each conflict space. In the case of the Fox and Raven, we can see that the fox's internal conflict (Fig. 2a) and the pride interpersonal conflict (Fig. 2d) may be resolved. Essentially, the fox need only take the cheese to be fully satisfied, and the raven singing fulfills pride. This is sensical, since the fox has no particular care about pride, nor the raven singing, so neither direction creates any conflict. The main source of conflict, however is hunger (Fig. 2b) and the raven (Fig. 2c). Focusing first on hunger, we start in a state where the raven is fully satisfied, and the fox is conflicted in terms of not having cheese. There are, however, two actions which can resolve the fox's

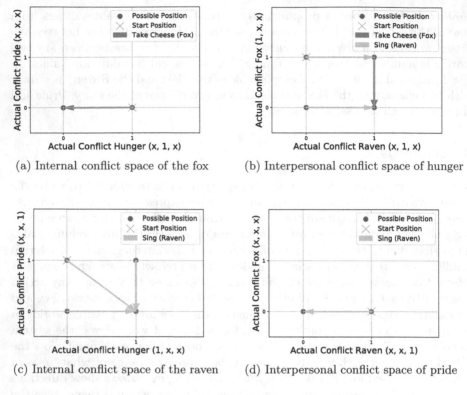

(a) Internal conflict space of the fox

(b) Interpersonal conflict space of hunger

(c) Internal conflict space of the raven

(d) Interpersonal conflict space of pride

Fig. 2. Interpersonal and internal potential conflict in the "Fox and Raven".

hunger, which is the raven singing followed by the fox taking the cheese. The (0, 0) point is inaccessible, thus we see that the interpersonal hunger conflict cannot be resolved. Similarly for the Raven, the optimal point is never accessible, with the only possible action being one that conflicts the hunger. Interestingly, a state where the fox and raven both have cheese and the raven is singing is ideal for both characters, however there is no set of actions that can make that actual world possible.

4   Conclusion

Possible worlds afford a number of possibilities for emergent narrative. In this paper, we used Ryan's work on possible worlds as an inspiration for an emergent narrative system and used Ryan's concepts of conflict to be able to quantify conflict in the system. We used this quantification in tandem with expressive range analysis to explore how conflict may be treated as an abstract space that is explored through actions. In an attempt to model a short fable, we showed some of the complexities of the conflict space, and we propose that expressive range analysis may be used even at the authoring level. Future work aims to further extend this analysis, ideally to the creation of an authoring tool that can assist in the production and understanding of larger works, as well as visualizing how new extensions to the system affords new manipulation of the conflict space.

References

1. Smith, G., Whitehead, J.: Analyzing the expressive range of a level generator. In: Proceedings of the 2010 Workshop on Procedural Content Generation in Games. ACM (2010)
2. Ryan, M.L.: The modal structure of narrative universes. In: Possible Worlds, Artificial Intelligence, and Narrative Theory, pp. 109–123. Indiana University Press, Bloomington (1991)
3. McCoy, J., Treanor, M., Samuel, B., Reed, A., Mateas, M., Wardrip-Fruin, N.: Social story worlds with comme il faut. IEEE Trans. Comput. Intell. AI Games 6(2), 97–112 (2014)
4. Evans, R., Short, E.: Versu—a simulationist storytelling system. IEEE Trans. Comput. Intell. AI Games 6(2), 113–130 (2014)
5. Kybartas, B., Verbrugge, C., Lessard, J.: Subject and subjectivity: a conversational game using possible worlds. In: Nunes, N., Oakley, I., Nisi, V. (eds.) ICIDS 2017. LNCS, vol. 10690, pp. 332–335. Springer, Cham (2017). https://doi.org/10.1007/978-3-319-71027-3_37

Playing Story Creation Games
with Logical Abduction

Andrew S. Gordon[1]([⊠]) and Ulrike Spierling[2]

[1] University of Southern California, Los Angeles, CA, USA
gordon@ict.usc.edu
[2] Hochschule RheinMain, University of Applied Sciences, Wiesbaden, Germany
ulrike.spierling@hs-rm.de

Abstract. Story Creation Games, such as Rory's Story Cubes and the Tell Tale card game, require players to invent creative and coherent narratives from a set of unconnected elements assembled by random chance, e.g., the throw of a die or the draw of a card. We model this human ability as a process of logical abduction, where the reasoning task is to identify a set of assumptions about a fictional world that logically entail the elements depicted on the dice or on the cards. We demonstrate the feasibility of this approach by hand-authoring a knowledge base of axioms that is sufficient to generate eight creative narratives each related to three Tell Tale cards, depicting a baseball player, a heart, and a train.

Keywords: Story creation games · Commonsense knowledge
Logical abduction

1 Introduction

Story Creation Games, such as Rory's Story Cubes and the Tell Tale card game, require players to invent creative and coherent narratives from a set of unconnected elements assembled by random chance, e.g., the throw of a die or the draw of a card. Often producing comical and entertaining storylines, these games also demonstrate the remarkable human capacity for sense-making, where one's knowledge and experience is used to explain the co-occurrence of novel combinations of observations.

We hypothesize that this sense-making capacity can be modeled algorithmically as a process of logical abduction. As first described by the philosopher Charles Pierce (1839–1914), logical abduction is a reasoning process, distinct from deduction or induction, that searches for assumptions that, if they were indeed true, would logically entail a set of observations given a knowledge base of logical axioms. Although abduction is not a sound reasoning mechanism, it is a natural fit for tasks where the goal is to find some set of unobserved states or events that would account for those that are observed, e.g., diagnostic tasks. In story creation games like Rory's Story Cubes and the Tell Tale card game,

© Springer Nature Switzerland AG 2018
R. Rouse et al. (Eds.): ICIDS 2018, LNCS 11318, pp. 478–482, 2018.
https://doi.org/10.1007/978-3-030-04028-4_55

Fig. 1. Images of a baseball player, a heart, and a train, as depicted on Tell Tale cards

the dice and cards are the observations, and the proof structure of the entailing assumptions provides a narrative solution.

To explore this approach to creative story generation, we attempted to use an existing abductive reasoning engine to output representations that corresponded to stories produced by human players of story creation games. We began by asking friends, family, and colleagues to produce fictional situations that included each of the elements depicted on three cards from the Tell Tale card game[1], as shown in Fig. 1. We selected eight of these solutions as targets to reproduce via logical abduction:

1. Once there was a boy playing baseball, and when it was his turn at bat, his heart was beating like a train in anticipation of the pitch.
2. Once there was a boy playing baseball, and when it was his turn at bat, his heart was beating like a train from the physical activity of the sport.
3. A professional baseball player commutes to the practice field by train, and eventually falls in love with the conductor who he sees each time.
4. If you love sports, you must train.
5. I missed the baseball game because the train was late and this broke my heart.
6. The life story of this devotional local baseball club member is not complete without mentioning that his death was caused by a heart disease that he developed over many years while having to practice close to train tracks, where he was constantly exposed to diesel exhausts containing nitrogen dioxide.
7. Once there was a train who loved watching baseball. It was always late when passing fields on game days.
8. A boy had his birthday party on a train and hit a heart-shaped piñata with a bat.

As a software engine for logical abduction, we utilized `EtcAbductionPy`[2], an open-source implementation of Etcetera Abduction [1] for knowledge bases expressed as definite clauses in first-order logic. For each of the eight stories,

---

[1] http://blueorangegames.com.
[2] https://github.com/asgordon/EtcAbductionPy.

we hand-authored a set of axioms (definite clauses) such that the top-ranked solution found using `EtcAbductionPy` mirrored our own conceptualization of its narrative structure. Although other researchers have shown that natural language representations can be generated from solutions of this sort [2], we made no attempts to generate natural language in our current research.

2 Example: Heart Beating Like a Train

To generate an abductive solution that approximated the first interpretation in the list above, we devised a set of axioms (definite clauses) such that each of the three cards could be logically entailed by an overlapping set of narrative assumptions. In these axioms, the cards themselves were represented as distinct predicates without arguments, while the narrative entities that explained them were encoded as predicates with variables representing events and states, as in the following examples:

$$at\_bat'(e, b) \land etc1(0.1, e, b) \rightarrow card\_baseball \tag{1}$$

$$etc2(0.1, e, b) \rightarrow at\_bat'(e, b) \tag{2}$$

Here, the predicate at_bat' represents the event e of a baseball player b being the batter at a moment in a baseball game. In the second of these axioms, this event is itself explained by an etcetera literal, i.e., an assumption that reifies the prior probability of the event. Defeasibly, the batter might experience performance anxiety during such an event, which would defeasibly lead them to have a racing heart, which explains the observed heart card, encoded in the following three axioms:

$$at\_bat'(e1, b) \land etc3(0.1, e1, e, b) \rightarrow performance\_anxiety'(e, b) \tag{3}$$

$$performance\_anxiety'(e1, p) \land etc4(0.1, e1, p, e, h) \rightarrow racing\_heart'(e, h) \tag{4}$$

$$racing\_heart'(e1, h) \land etc5(0.1, e1, h) \rightarrow card\_heart \tag{5}$$

Defeasibly, the event of a racing heart might be metaphorically like a train, and this metaphor itself explains the observation of the train card, encoded as follows:

$$racing\_heart'(e1, p) \land etc6(0.1, e, e1, p) \rightarrow like\_a\_train'(e, e1) \tag{6}$$

$$like\_a\_train'(e1, e2) \land etc7(0.1, e1, e2) \rightarrow card\_train \tag{7}$$

Given these seven axioms, `etcAbductionPy` finds solutions by backward-chaining from the three observations (the three cards), unifying antecedent literals wherever possible, until all assumptions are expressed as etcetera literals. Variables remaining in these literals are replaced with Skolem constants that instantiate events, objects, states, and characters in the imagined narrative. When using `etcAbductionPy`, a proof of the observables can be obtained by forward-chaining from any set of identified assumptions. Here, forward-chaining from these Skolemized assumptions using these seven axioms deductively entails the three observed cards.

Figure 2 is a graphical representation of this proof structure for our first story, as produced by etcAbductionPy. Here the heart and the train cards have a racing heart as a common factor, while the baseball player card and this racing heart have a common factor of a baseball player at bat.

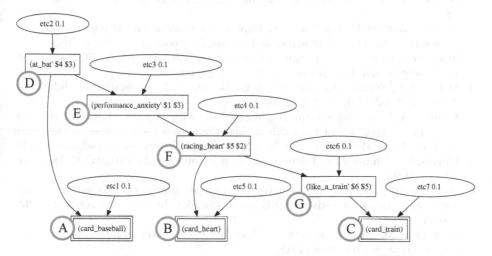

Fig. 2. Abductive proof representing the three cards (A, B, C), the inferred narrative (D, E, F, G), and seven assumptions (ovals) of prior and conditional probabilities.

In all, we authored 72 axioms (definite clauses) to reproduce the narrative structures in the eight stories of our analysis. The main finding of our analysis was that it was, indeed, possible for us to generate formal approximations of our own informal understandings of these eight stories using abductive reasoning. While the software itself was often cumbersome and the notation of axioms was prone to authoring errors, we found that the reasoning procedure of logical abduction was a natural fit for the algorithmic generation of creative storylines. Creative story generation can be modeled as a process of logical abduction, and in this respect shares much in common with the generation of causal explanations of observable evidence and in the interpretation of natural language discourse [3], and other interpretation tasks [4].

We contrast this approach with those proposed in related work on story generation [5,6], particularly with recent work on narrative text generation using neural networks [7–10]. Our analysis, where the three input cards generate extremely different yet coherent stories, highlights the combinatorial nature of the task as a search for coherent combination of associations among the input observations—and encourages future neural network approaches to incorporate analogous mechanisms in their architectures.

Acknowledgements. This research was supported by the Office of Naval Research, grant N00014-16-1-2435.

References

1. Gordon, A.S.: Commonsense interpretation of triangle behavior. In: Thirtieth AAAI Conference on Artificial Intelligence, 3719–3725. AAAI Press, Palo Alto (2016)
2. Ahn, E., Morbini, F., Gordon, A.S.: Improving fluency in narrative text generation with grammatical transformations and probabilistic parsing. In: Proceedings of the 9th International Natural Language Generation Conference, pp. 70–73. Association for Computational Linguistics, Stroudsburg, September 2016
3. Hobbs, J.R., Stickel, M.E., Appelt, D.E., Martin, P.: Interpretation as abduction. Artif. Intell. **63**(1–2), 69–142 (1993)
4. Gordon, A.S.: Solving interpretation problems with etcetera abduction (invited talk). In: Proceedings of the Fifth Annual Conference on Advances in Cognitive Systems, 12–14 May 2017, Troy, New York. Cognitive Systems Foundation (2017)
5. Gervás, P.: Computational approaches to storytelling and creativity. AI Mag. **30**, 49–62 (2009)
6. Kybartas, B., Bidarra, R.: A survey on story generation techniques for authoring computational narratives. IEEE Trans. Comput. Intell. AI Games **9**, 239–253 (2017)
7. Roemmele, M.: Neural Networks for Narrative Continuation. Ph.D. thesis, University of Southern California (2018)
8. Clark, E., Ross, A.S., Tan, C., Ji, Y., Smith, N.A.: Creative writing with a machine in the loop: case studies on slogans and stories. In: Proceedings of the 23rd International Conference on Intelligent User Interfaces. Association for Computing Machinery, New York (2018)
9. Peng, N., Ghazvininejad, M., May, J., Knight, K.: Towards controllable story generation. In: Proceedings of the First Workshop on Storytelling at NAACL HLT 2018. Association for Computational Linguistics, Stroudsburg (2018)
10. Gonzalez-Rico, D., Fuentes-Pineda, G.: Contextualize, show and tell: a neural visual storyteller. In: Proceedings of the First Workshop on Storytelling at NAACL HLT 2018. Association for Computational Linguistics, Stroudsburg (2018)

Apply Storytelling Techniques for Describing Time-Series Data

Zev Battad[✉] and Mei Si

Rensselaer Polytechnic Institute, Troy, NY 12180, USA
battadz@rpi.edu

Abstract. Narrative and storytelling have played an important role in communication. In this work, we demonstrate that the techniques of storytelling, and in particular raising attention to abnormality, can be used to add interestingness and memorability to descriptions of time-series data. A computational system has been developed for automatically generating descriptions for data graphs. The system identifies visual patterns in the graph, and treats the graph's deviations from corresponding ideal patterns as abnormal events. It then uses storytelling templates to generate a graph description with the abnormal events highlighted.

Keywords: Narrative · Graph description
Natural language generation

1 Introduction

Narrative has traditionally acted as an engaging and memorable way of communicating information. This is especially relevant in the current day, where machines must communicate large amounts of data and information to people through such applications as interactive data analysis [2,9,15] and interactive museum exhibits [7,10,14]. We believe that interactive information systems can benefit from an automated method of describing data sets that helps humans distinguish and remember them.

In this work, we investigate the use of one key storytelling technique: drawing audience's attention to abnormality. Rubin noted that oral storytellers often embellish parts of traditional story templates to make otherwise formulaic retellings more interesting and memorable [16]. In an experimental setting, Trabasso & Broek found that subjects were most likely to recall events which perturbed the sequence of events [17]. Similarly, Bower et al. found that actions which disrupted the familiar action sequence in a story were most likely to be remembered [4].

We explore the use of abnormality in narrative to enhance the interestingness and memorability of automatically-generated descriptions for time-series data. Key to the use of abnormality is a familiar basis which gets disrupted. We map this principle to having the system point out shapes that can be seen from

© Springer Nature Switzerland AG 2018
R. Rouse et al. (Eds.): ICIDS 2018, LNCS 11318, pp. 483–488, 2018.
https://doi.org/10.1007/978-3-030-04028-4_56

time-series scatter graphs and enabling the system to describe how the shapes it identifies are visually skewed. In the next sections, we present our algorithms and a preliminary evaluation.

2   Example Domain and Approach

We discuss and demonstrate our algorithm using freshwater data collected at Lake George, New York from 1980 through 2016 [5]. A typical variable contains 5000 values. Figure 2a shows an example scatter plot. The goal of the system is to generate a brief verbal or text description to accompany the display of data plots. We hope showing this description can make the user's data exploration process more interesting and more productive.

Our approach for automatically generating descriptions of time-series scatter graphs consists of four major steps, as shown in Fig. 1. First, **shape identification** identifies a set of shapes, S, that people can see in the scatter graph, P. Then, **abnormality identification** computes how visually skewed the shapes in S are and saves the abnormalities in a set, A. Third, based on S and A, the **topic selection** procedure selects a set of points to use in describing the graph. And finally, **text generation** creates the final text description, D.

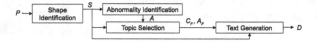

Fig. 1. System diagram.

Step 1: Shape Identification. To identify visual patterns in the data graph, we first create a piecewise linear approximation (PLA). Following Freeman's work, we define critical points for graph description as points where the PLA is non-differentiable [8], defining the sets of line-segments produced by a PLA. Figure 2b shows the PLA and critical points for Fig. 2a. Let C_g be the set of critical points for the graph. Each critical point, c_i, is marked as a peak or a trough. Let v_i be the marking of c_i, where $v_i = peak|trough$.

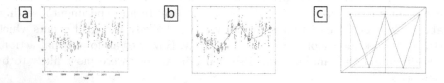

Fig. 2. Scatter graph for Calcium at Basin Bay (a), overlaid PLA lines and critical points circled (b), and shape with ideal symmetry and ratio (c).

The system identifies visible shapes from the PLA. Currently, we use four shape types that can dependably be extracted: letter 'W', letter 'V', and up/down trending lines. Each shape type, t_j, has a corresponding set of peaks and troughs, $U_j = u_{j,1}, ..., u_{j,q_j}$, of length q_j, where $u_{j,k} = peak|trough$. For any shape type t_j and sequence of critical points C_p of length q_j, if $v_i = u_{j,i}$ for each c_i in C_p, the shape type is considered a match. The resulting shape s_l has critical points $C_{s_l} = C_p$. Starting from the shape type t_j with the largest $|U_j|$, shape types are greedily matched to each concurrent subsequence of critical points, C_p, in C_g of length q_j for which no line segment defined by the points in C_p already appear in another shape's critical points. The set S contains all shapes created this way.

Step 2: Abnormality Identification. We examine shape skewedness from the perspectives of symmetry and ratio. As a significant determinant of human shape detection and preference, the symmetry constraint captures shape skewedness based on vertical mirror symmetry [3,11,12,19]. A symmetric shape can still appear too flat or too thin, calling for an independent measure of overall shape skewedness. The ratio constraint measures whether the shape's horizontal or vertical dimensions are too large or too small compared to one another. Given the importance, in human judgments of visual aesthetic quality, of relating object composition with bounding frames [1,13], the ratio of a shape's dimensions are judged against those of the graph as a whole.

For computing the symmetry property of a shape s, we define n as the number of critical points in s and $C_s = c_{s,0}, c_{s,1}, ..., c_{s,n-1}$ as the set of critical points, where each $c_{s,i} = (x_{s,i}, y_{s,i})$. The line of vertical mirror symmetry for s is then computed as $x_{sym} = x_{s,0} + \frac{(x_{s,n-1} - x_{s,0})}{2}$.

We define $c_{s,m}$ as the middle critical point of s, where $m = floor[\frac{n}{2}]$. For s to be ideally symmetric, $x_{s,m} = x_{sym}$ must be true within a certain threshold. If not, $c_{s,m}$ is part of a symmetry abnormality. Let $c_{s,j}$ denote the point symmetric to $c_{s,i}$, where $j = 2m - i$. For s to be symmetric, each pair of symmetric points must both be at the same y-value and be horizontally equidistant from the line of symmetry. Therefore, the following property must hold for each $c_{s,i}$ in C:

$$|x_{sym} - x_{s,i}| = |x_{sym} - x_{s,j}| \ AND \ y_{s,i} = y_{s,j} \qquad (1)$$

Any symmetric critical points $c_{s,i}, c_{s,j}$ for which property 1 does not hold, past a certain error threshold, are added as part of a symmetry abnormality.

For computing ratio, we define h_p and w_p as the height and width of the graph's vertical and horizontal axes, and h_s and w_s the height and width of an identified shape s. Note that h_s and w_s are measures of the visual space of the graph image itself, not the data's dimensions. If the shape is proportional to the overall graph, $\frac{h_p}{w_p} = \frac{h_s}{w_s}$ must be true, or within a certain threshold. Otherwise, the top and bottom-most, and left and right-most, critical points in s are treated as part of a ratio abnormality. Figure 2c shows an ideal shape.

Step 3: Topic Selection. Topic selection bounds the amount of information in the final description, allowing the system to keep its descriptions brief and engaging. Currently, we only consider the critical points and abnormalities generated in steps 1 and 2. Define $C_F \leftarrow \emptyset$ and $A_F \leftarrow \emptyset$ as the sets of critical points and abnormalities to keep as topics. To define the bounds of each shape, C_F initially contains the start and end critical points of each shape in S. Define a_k as the abnormality in A whose critical points, C_{a_k}, intersects with C_F the most. a_k with $max(|C_{a_k} \cap C_F|)$ in A is chosen. a_k is added to A_F, and each critical point in C_{a_k} is added to C_F. This is done iteratively until the total number of items in C_F and A_F reach the threshold for description size, e.g. 5.

Step 4: Story Generation. Generation of description text is accomplished using structural narrative templates. An example template is provided below. It is designed with an opening statement and a sequence of mini plots for each shape identified in the graph. We use abnormalities as the climax, inspired by Aristotle's three-act structure [6]. Though a Conclusion is not present, the Setup (shapes and critical points) and Confrontation (abnormalities) are in order.

 graph description $\rightarrow$ opener + shape s_1 + [transition + shape s_k]*
 shape s_i $\rightarrow$ identification + [critical points for s_i]* + [abnormalities for s_i]*

Example output (based on the graphs in Fig. 2): "The whole graph makes a 'w' shape up until 2015. You can see the start of the 'w' at 1995, and the low point before the middle at 2003. However, on the left side, the first leg's kind of stunted, and the whole shape looks too flat."

3   Evaluation and Discussion

We hypothesize that people are more likely to remember graphs paired with descriptions that emphasize abnormality. For testing this hypothesis, we asked subjects to study, and later identify, graphs under three conditions: without a description, paired with a description that did not include abnormality, and paired with a description including abnormality. We use recall to measure subjects' memory due to its use in gauging memory effects in storytelling [4,17,18].

 We used a between-group design. 90 subjects were recruited using Amazon's Mechanical Turk and randomly assigned to one of the conditions. Each subject was shown a series of five scatter graphs from the dataset, as in Fig. 2a. When description was included, it was shown as a text box right beneath the graph. Graphs were presented one at a time, in the same order for every subject. Then, the subjects were asked to examine five graph pairs, consisting of a graph seen previously and an unrelated graph, and were asked to identify the previously seen graph. The mean and standard deviation for the percent accuracy of recall of the no description, no abnormality, and with abnormality groups, respectively, are: 65.3 (20.1), 71.3 (16.3), 77.3 (14.6). One-way ANOVA shows a significant effect for conditions (p = 0.03). Post-hoc pairwise comparison reveals a significant difference between no-description and full-description groups (p = 0.01). Even though there is a trend of increased accuracy by adding descriptions and descriptions of abnormality to the graphs, the differences between the no-abnormality description condition and other two conditions do not reach a significant level.

We consider our hypothesis partially confirmed. The current experiment does not measure the subjects' experiences of how interesting the data exploration task is. A follow-up study exploring the relationship between the amount of interesting content in graph descriptions and subject memory of graphs may shed more light on the balance between information and interestingness.

Moving forward, we would like to implement this methodology of graph description in an interactive system, where automatically generated descriptions must be reactive to user exploration. The way in which abnormality is expressed can also be expanded upon. While shapes and their visual skewedness are used as sources of abnormality in this system, other features of numerical data, such as standard statistical measures or domain-specific formula, can also be explored.

References

1. Arnheim, R.: Art and visual perception. University of California Press (1974)
2. Bailey, T. Gatrell, A.: Interactive spatial data analysis. Longman Scientific & Technical Essex (1995)
3. Barlow, H.B., Reeves, B.C.: The versatility and absolute efficiency of detecting mirror symmetry in random dot displays. Vis. Res. **19**(7), 783–793 (1979)
4. Bower, G.H., Black, J.B., Turner, T.J.: Scripts in memory for text. Cogn. Psychol. **11**(2), 177–220 (1979)
5. Boylen, C., Eichler, L., Swinton, M., Nierzwicki-Bauer, S., Hannoun, I., Short, J.: The State of the Lake: Thirty Years of Water Quality Monitoring on Lake George (2014). https://fundforlakegeorge.org/StateoftheLake
6. Chatman, S.: Story and Discourse: Narrative Structure in Fiction and Film. Cornell University Press (1980)
7. Falk, J., Dierking, L.: The Museum Experience Revisited, 1st edn. Routledge, New York (2016)
8. Freeman, H.: Description via the use of critical points. Pattern Recognit. **10**, 159–166 (1978)
9. Heer, J., Shneiderman, B.: Interactive dynamics for visual analysis. Queue **10**(2), 30 (2012)
10. Hinrichs, U., Schmidt, H., Carpendale, S.: EMDialog: bringing information visualization into the museum. IEEE Trans. Vis. Comput. Graph. **14**(6), 1181–1188 (2008)
11. Lu, G., Zhang, D.: Review of shape representation and description techniques. Pattern Recognit. **37**, 1–19 (2004)
12. Machilsen, B., Pauwels, M., Wagemans, J.: The role of vertical mirror symmetry in visual shape detection. J. Vis. **9**(12), 11–11 (2009)
13. Palmer, S., Schloss, K., Sammartino, J.: Visual aesthetics and human preference. Annu. Rev. Psychol. **64**, 77–107 (2013)
14. Pallud, J.: Impact of interactive technologies on stimulating learning experiences in a museum. Inf. Manag. **54**(4), 465–478 (2017)
15. Robertson, N., et al.: DiscoverySpace: an interactive data analysis application. Genome Biol. **8**(1), R6 (2007)

16. Rubin, D.C.: Memory in oral traditions: The cognitive psychology of epic, ballads, and counting-out rhymes. Oxford University Press on Demand (1999)
17. Trabasso, T., Van Den Broek, P.: Causal thinking and the representation of narrative events. J. Mem. Lang. **24**(5), 612–630 (1985)
18. Thorndyke, P.W.: Cognitive structures in comprehension and memory of narrative discourse. Cogn. Psychol. **9**(1), 77–110 (1979)
19. Westphal-Fitch, G., Huber, L., Gomez, J.C., Fitch, W.T.: Production and perception rules underlying visual patterns: effects of symmetry and hierarchy. Phil. Trans. R. Soc. B **367**(1598), 2007–2022 (2012)

Would You Follow the Suggestions of a Storyteller Robot?

Raul Paradeda[1,2(✉)], Maria José Ferreira[1,3], Carlos Martinho[1], and Ana Paiva[1]

[1] INESC-ID and Instituto Superior Técnico, University of Lisbon, Lisbon, Portugal
{raul.paradeda,maria.jose.ferreira}@tecnico.ulisboa.pt,
{carlos.martinho,ana.paiva}@gaips.inesc-id.pt
[2] State University of Rio Grande do Norte, Natal, Brazil
[3] Madeira Interactive Technologies Institute, Madeira, Portugal

Abstract. This work describes a study in development that uses an autonomous social robot to act as storyteller and persuader in an interactive storytelling scenario. The robot employs techniques of persuasion to try to convince the audience to take a specific path in the story. The autonomous storyteller robot performs facial expression and head movements to express emotions regarding the story flow and the person's decisions. Through a pilot study with four participants, we were able to identify the improvements needed. The findings revealed that the robot could give better suggestions to try to persuade a person before s/he makes a final decision. At the same time, we believe that some interaction changes could potentially increase the motivation, interest and engagement of users in the task.

Keywords: Interactive storytelling · Social robotics · Persuasion

1 Introduction

The way that a story can be told has changed over time. In the old times, stories have been told as paintings on the walls while nowadays technological innovations provide the possibility of using creative resources to tell stories. For example, it may be possible to increase the motivation and interest of the audience via social robotics. Robots have been used for a wide range of purposes, such as education [5] and persuasion [7]. This happens because they are considered to be engaging and motivational. They also help encourage imagination, especially on children [1].

However, when there is interaction with social robots some ethical challenges and practical issues arise [10]. For example, in an interactive scenario where the robot acts as a persuasive agent storyteller, the person might not understand or trust in the persuasive cues given by the storyteller. So, some strategies can be applied to avoid those issues. For instance, trying to gain the robot trust through small talk [9], using gaze to the desired target [3] or even saying utterances in cues format [2].

R. Rouse et al. (Eds.): ICIDS 2018, LNCS 11318, pp. 489–493, 2018.
https://doi.org/10.1007/978-3-030-04028-4_57

Given these ideas, this work describes a study in progress that uses an autonomous social robot to act as storyteller and persuader in an interactive storytelling (IS) scenario. We aim with this study to evaluate how suggestive a social robot can be, as well as the efficacy of persuasion techniques as trust, gaze and utterance cues.

2   Materials and Methods

According to McWilliams [6] and the website Kidmunication[1], in the art of storytelling, facial expressions are essential features and have a greater impact when combined with voice. In fact, without facial expressions, a story becomes a flat and limp narration, instead of a magical and engaging tale. As a result, the teller would look just plain bored and disinterested. Considering the importance of facial expressions, we decided to use a robot that can perform those features, the EMYS robot. EMYS[2] is a robot only with a head that can represent emotions using facial expressions (Fig. 1).

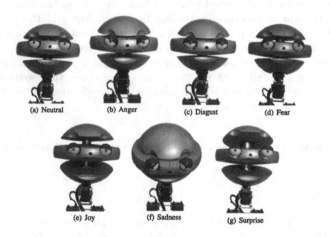

Fig. 1. Facial expressions performed by EMYS robot [4].

The story used in the scenario was written with the aid of a specialist in education. The story happens in the Middle Ages (or Medieval Period), the user performs the role of a country leader that received a threat from another country. Person's goal is to prevent her/his country from falling into the enemy hands. In this scenario, **immersion** is an important feature to make the participant feel like s/he is a part of the story. To captivate the person's attention and to

---

[1] Facial Expression and Masks in Storytelling — Kidmunication. Available at http:// kidmunication.com/telling-stories/story_telling_training/facial-expressions-and-masks-in-storytelling. Accessed on: 07/16/2018.

[2] EMYS. Available at https://emys.co/.

increase her/his immersion during the story flow, each scene includes a representative image of what is happening in the story and the robot tells the narrative regarding each scene. The screen disposition of the prototype developed in C# can be seen in Fig. 2.

As our scenario is an IS, each scene presents a Decision Point (DP) with two options that lead the listener to another path within the story (buttons left and right in Fig. 2). Depending on the decision made, the robot reacts positively or negatively, expressing joy or anger respectively. For each scene, the robot has its own desired option, and if the listener chooses the option according to the robot, it reacts positively, otherwise, negatively.

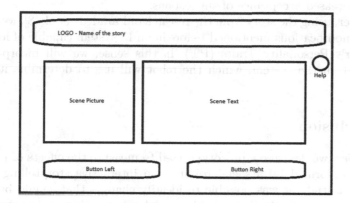

Fig. 2. Screen disposition of the prototype presented to participants.

Since we have chosen the EMYS robot, our first persuasion strategy to influence the listener consists of mainly non-verbal cues such as gaze, head movements, robot's facial expression (emotions) and embodiment. In sum, the robot performs gaze movements at the desired option in every DP, suggesting that the listener should choose that option.

3   Current Status and Future Directions

Using the scenario above, we performed a pilot study with four participants (two males; two females) to identify any possible gaps and improvements in the proposed methodology. We recognised that the system needs to improve the persuasion gaze methodology and the interaction with the robot.

The system interaction suffered changes, and now in this new version, the listener must inform the robot of his/her intention of choice. Then, the robot performs gaze movements towards his intended option. If the person's intended decision is different from the robot's suggestion, the robot will play an anger emotion expressing its discontent followed by an utterance cue, notifying the player that s/he will lose. Otherwise, the animation performed will be a joyful one, and the utterance cue will encourage the person to follow that path.

In future, our goal is to add to our current system a tool of suggestion in the form of utterance cues as well as a trust module. Mainly because, if the person does not trust in who is giving the advice, the reliability of the message transmitted is affected, making the person not be influenced to change their attitude, motivation and thoughts. With the trust module, the robot will try to increase the level of trust that a person can feel towards the robot. The work of Paradeda et al. [9] presents evidence that small talk can increase the trust felt during the experience. Following this line of work, we seek to implement small talk before the beginning of the story.We believe that a higher level of trust may result in increased acceptance of suggestions.

Moreover, using the story from the research of Paradeda et al. [8], we intend to apply the modifications mentioned before in an IS system capable of identifying the listener's Personality Traits (PT). In this sense, we will incorporate the person's PT in the system, which the robot will use to determine its desired option.

4   Conclusion

In this paper, we describe a prototype used to measure the effects of persuasion strategies performed by a social robot in an interactive storytelling scenario. From a pilot study, it was possible to identify changes that should be made in the persuasion approach. The use of a social robot acting as a storyteller can increase the motivation, interest and engagement in the task.

In sum, this work is aimed to identify better strategies for a social robot to perform suggestions or even persuade a person in a task that is necessary to make decisions. Moreover, we aim to highlight the powerful capabilities of social storytelling robots.

Acknowledgments. We would like to thank the National Council for Scientific and Technological Development (CNPq) program Science without Border: 201833/2014-0 - Brazil and Agência Regional para o Desenvolvimento e Tecnologia (ARDITI) - M1420-09-5369-000001, for PhD grants to first and second authors respectively. This work was also supported by Fundação para a Ciência e a Tecnologia: (FCT) - UID/CEC/50021/2013 and the project AMIGOS:PTDC/EEISII/7174/2014.

References

1. Chen, G.D., Nurkhamid, Wang, C.Y.: A survey on storytelling with robots. In: Chang, M., Hwang, W.Y., Chen, M.P., Müller, W. (eds.) Edutainment Technologies. Educational Games and Virtual Reality/Augmented Reality Applications. Edutainment 2011. LNCS, vol. 6872, pp. 450–456. Springer, Heidelberg (2011). https://doi.org/10.1007/978-3-642-23456-9_81
2. Figueiredo, R., Paiva, A.: Affecting choices in interactive storytelling. In: AAAI Fall Symposium: Computational Models of Narrative (2010)

3. Ham, J., Bokhorst, R., Cabibihan, J.: The influence of gazing and gestures of a storytelling robot on its persuasive power. In: International Conference on Social Robotics (2011)
4. Kedzierski, J., Muszyński, R., Zoll, C., Oleksy, A., Frontkiewicz, M.: Emys – emotive head of a social robot. Int. J. Soc. Rob. **5**(2), 237–249 (2013)
5. Kory, J.J.M.: Storytelling with robots: Effects of robot language level on children's language learning. Ph.D. thesis, Massachusetts Institute of Technology (2014)
6. McWilliams, B.: Effective storytelling-a manual for beginners. Accessed 8 Mar 2007 (1998)
7. Mutlu, B., Forlizzi, J., Hodgins, J.: A storytelling robot: modeling and evaluation of human-like gaze behavior. In: 2006 6th IEEE-RAS International Conference on Humanoid Robots, pp. 518–523. IEEE (2006)
8. Paradeda, R., Ferreira, M.J., Martinho, C., Paiva, A.: Using interactive storytelling to identify personality traits. In: Nunes, N., Oakley, I., Nisi, V. (eds.) ICIDS 2017. LNCS, vol. 10690, pp. 181–192. Springer, Cham (2017). https://doi.org/10.1007/978-3-319-71027-3_15
9. Paradeda, R.B., Hashemian, M., Rodrigues, R.A., Paiva, A.: How facial expressions and small talk may influence trust in a robot. In: Agah, A., Cabibihan, J.-J., Howard, A.M., Salichs, M.A., He, H. (eds.) ICSR 2016. LNCS (LNAI), vol. 9979, pp. 169–178. Springer, Cham (2016). https://doi.org/10.1007/978-3-319-47437-3_17
10. Salem, M., Lakatos, G., Amirabdollahian, F., Dautenhahn, K.: Towards safe and trustworthy social robots: ethical challenges and practical issues. Social Robotics. LNCS (LNAI), vol. 9388, pp. 584–593. Springer, Cham (2015). https://doi.org/10.1007/978-3-319-25554-5_58

A Character Focused Iterative Simulation Approach to Computational Storytelling

Leonid Berov[⊠]

University of Osnabrück, 49076 Osnabrück, Germany
lberov@uos.de

Abstract. My project aims at conceptualizing and implementing a computational storytelling system that derives creativity from an iterative cycle of simulation-based engagement and constraint-modifying reflection. It approaches this problem by first developing a computational model of stories that is grounded in narratological research, more specifically in mimetic, post-structuralist approaches centered around fictional characters. In the second stage, this narratological grounding will allow to measure and reason about the quality of a modeled story based on a formal notion called tellability. In the last stage, the parameter space that is set up by this representation can be explored in search for tellable stories, which are hypothesized to be of higher quality. Currently, the project is in the second stage.

1 Background

Storytelling research in the context of computational creativity is concerned with the study of algorithms that are capable of autonomously generating fictional narratives [9]. Usually, at least two components of a narrative are distinguished: A content plane, which is a causally ordered series of events, potentially happening in parallel at multiple locations (what is told); and an expression plane, which is the linear representation of events in a text, using stylistic devices like flashbacks, flash-forwards and point of view (how it is told) [11]. My work focuses only on generating the former (plot).

Another useful dichotomy is introduced by Currie [7], who distinguishes two perspectives on narratives: The *external perspectives* understands narratives as artefacts intentionally produced by an author to solve a set of narrative problems, while the *internal perspective* understands them as describing a (fictional) story world consisting of existents, events and dynamically changing according to fixed rules. I will adopt both views at different stages of my project.

2 Results: A Character Centered Plot Model

During the first stage of my project I performed a computational modeling of the internal perspective on plot, by employing Ryan's *possible-worlds framework* [13]. Her theory describes the emergence and the properties of plot, based on the goal-directed actions of fictional characters, which are structurally described by a set

© Springer Nature Switzerland AG 2018
R. Rouse et al. (Eds.): ICIDS 2018, LNCS 11318, pp. 494–497, 2018.
https://doi.org/10.1007/978-3-030-04028-4_58

of propositions capturing their interior state: beliefs, wishes, obligations and plans. This is beneficial, because it allows me an implementation using a Multi-Agent Simulation (MAS) approach [14] based on the Belief-Desire-Intention (BDI) framework [12], which is also built on a possible worlds semantics. This combination of narratological and computational approaches yields the interesting insight that Ryan's implied character model in itself is not enough to generate the differing choices of action performed by characters in existing narratives (for more details see: [4]).

I could resolve this problem by extending the model with Palmer's [10] analysis of characters as (paper-) beings endowed with fictional minds which, in many regards, function like real minds. This analysis points out the central role of personality and affect in characters' decision taking. Following it requires implementing these narrative phenomena in the BDI agent architecture, which I do based on a cognitively inspired simulation of affect and personality, as suggested by [2] as well as [8]. My system implements emotions (short-term affect) as affective appraisals of internal and external events. All active emotions are aggregated into a mood (long-term affect), which in turn influences decisions taken during the BDI reasoning cycle. An agent's mood always decays towards a default mood, which is computed based on it's personality traits, thus allowing to take into account both, stable action-dispositions as well as context, during decision taking. I demonstrate, that the resulting system is indeed capable of evoking in readers a perception of character-personality that is correlated with the one computationally modelled [6].

3   Current Status: Character-Based Tellability

Tellability is a measure that narratologists use to describe the internal quality of plot [1]. Following Ryan's theory [13], tellability depends highly on fictional character's embedded narratives. Embedded narratives capture characters' subjective experience of the unfolding plot, and are described by Palmer as "the whole of a character's mind in action" [10]. The architecture introduced above can be taken to simulate these minds and thus can serve as a basis for tellability analyses. Ryan suggests to perform such an analysis on the basis of a plot graph representation of embedded narratives. Such graphs can be used to identify functional plot units. She puts forward several principles—functional polyvalence, semantic opposition and symmetry—according to which plot units can interact in order to increase tellability. Currently, I am working on automatically identifying these principles in plot generation [5].

4   Next Steps: Iterative Simulation

Taking an external perspective, the introduced model is creating a narrative system whose properties are spanning a plot-space which can be explored in search of high tellability. The main parameters of such a system are the idiosyncrasies of the involved characters, the affordances of the story world and temporally distributable happenings[1]. In the terms of the implementation above, these can be understood as: the number of involved characters; their corresponding personality parameters as well as initial goals and beliefs; the possible actions and non-agentive existents implemented by the environment; as well as environment-events that are scheduled to be executed at a certain point of the simulation. I intend to implement an iterative process that involves setting up an environment with agents, executing a simulation, analyzing the emerging plot in terms of tellability, adjusting the described parameters and repeating until a plot with acceptable tellability is found.

5   Contribution

In conclusion, my doctoral project addresses the following underlying research questions: (1) How can plot generation be modeled computationally by taking an internal as well as an external narratological perspective, and what are the parameters that allow an interaction between these two perspectives. (2) Can an analytical narratological theory be operationalized using a generative, computational model, and what can such an approach contribute back to narrative theory.

My tentative answer to the first question is that a mimetic modelling of characters can be used to perform three distinct computational tasks that are involved in computational storytelling. It can, first, be employed to generate plot, which emerges from the interactions of characters and environment in a multi-agent simulation system. The resulting plot can, then, be submitted to an aesthetic analysis based on a set of formal properties of the included embedded narratives of the involved characters. Finally, a space of possible plots can be explored by automatically manipulating the acting characters by either: changing their personality, the events that happen to them, or their environment.

I suggest that this opens a way to resolve the *emergent narrative paradox* [3], which has been leveled as criticism against emergent storytelling systems. The paradox asks how plot, as an aesthetic organizational principle, can emerge from the unguided interactions of autonomous agents, which perform their action selection based on their internal states and reasoning processes. The repeated, incremental manipulation of characters, as suggested above, can be understood as high-level narrative organization with the goal of ensuring tellable stories while maintaining character autonomy.

In the context of interactive digital storytelling, my work addressed several relevant technical and theoretical issues: which narrative phenomena can be model to represent fictional characters; how emergent plot can be evaluated; and how autonomous agents can be steered to behave interestingly.

---

[1] Happenings are events that have patients but no agents, e.g. accidentental encounters or natural disasters. They are contrasted by actions: goal-directed events which necessarily have an agent [13].

The second question can be tentatively addressed by abducing from the insights gleaned by implementing Ryan's framework: computational models can help uncover the dynamic implications of the usually static, analytical models.

Acknowledgements. The author is grateful for support for this work provided by an Alexander von Humboldt Ph.D. fellowship.

References

1. Abbott, P.: Narrativity. In: Hühn, P., Meister, J.C., Pier, J., Schmid, W. (eds.) Handbook of Narratology. De Gruyter, Berlin (2014)
2. Alfonso, B., Vivancos, E., Botti, V.J.: An open architecture for affective traits in a BDI agent. In: Proceedings of the 6th International Conference on Evolutionary Computation Theory and Applications, Rome, Italy, pp. 320–325 (2014)
3. Aylett, R.: Emergent narrative, social immersion and "storification". In: Proceedings of the 1st International Workshop on Narrative and Interactive Learning Environments, pp. 35–44 (2000)
4. Berov, L.: Steering plot through personality and affect: an extended BDI model of fictional characters. In: Kern-Isberner, G., Fürnkranz, J., Thimm, M. (eds.) KI 2017. LNCS (LNAI), vol. 10505, pp. 293–299. Springer, Cham (2017). https://doi.org/10.1007/978-3-319-67190-1_23
5. Berov, L.: Towards a computational measure of plot tellability. In: Proceedings of the 10th International Workshop on Intelligent Narrative Technologies, pp. 169–175. AAAI Press, Snowbird, Utah (2017)
6. Berov, L., Kühnberger, K.U.: An evaluation of perceived personality in fictional characters generated by affective simulation. In: Proceedings of the Ninth International Conference on Computational Creativity, Salamanca, Spain (2018)
7. Currie, G.: Narratives and Narrators: A Philosophy of Stories. Oxford University Press, Oxford (2010)
8. Gebhard, P.: ALMA: a layered model of affect. In: Proceedings of the Fourth International Joint Conference on Autonomous Agents and Multiagent Systems, pp. 29–36. ACM (2005)
9. Gervás, P.: Computational approaches to storytelling and creativity. AI Mag. **30**(3), 49–62 (2009)
10. Palmer, A.: Fictional Minds. University of Nebraska Press, Lincoln (2004)
11. Prince, G.: A Dictionary of Narratology. University of Nebraska Press, Lincoln (2003)
12. Rao, A.S., Georgeff, M.P.: BDI agents: from theory to practice. In: Proceedings of the 1st International Conference of Multiagent Systems, pp. 312–319 (1995)
13. Ryan, M.L.: Possible Worlds, Artificial Intelligence, and Narrative Theory. Indiana University Press, Bloomington (1991)
14. Siebers, P.O., Aickelin, U.: Introduction to multi-agent simulation. arXiv preprint arXiv:0803.3905 (2008)

Development and Analysis of Authoring Systems

Contemporary Issues in Interactive Storytelling Authoring Systems

Daniel Green$^{(\boxtimes)}$, Charlie Hargood, and Fred Charles

Bournemouth University, Poole, UK
{dgreen,chargood,fcharles}@bournemouth.ac.uk

Abstract. Authoring tools for interactive narrative abstract underlying data models to allow authors to write creative works. Understanding how our program and interface design decisions alter the User Experience design could lead to more robust authoring experiences. We contribute a taxonomy of authoring tools with identified program and User Experience observations with discussion into their impact on the authoring experience as well as reflection on two detailed experiments. We then present our own authoring tool, Novella, and discuss how it has implemented the lessons learned from the analysis and how it approaches solving the identified challenges.

Keywords: Interactive narrative · Authoring tools · User experience

1 Introduction

The design of interactive narrative authoring tools is an emergent process from the underlying narrative data model that the tool supports. While this makes sense from a structural point of view it is possible that we are ignoring the User Experience (UX) impact of a variety of design decisions and interface paradigms. Without well-designed UX, accessibility is reduced and systems become restricted to users with the appropriate technical know-how, which can result in a frustrating user experience and can contribute to a reduced rate of adoption by interactive fiction communities. It is also possible that there may be repeated UI trends in the design of these authoring tools that may have an unforeseen impact on the resulting stories.

In this paper, we survey the current state of the art and present a categorized taxonomy of authoring tools for interactive fiction, a listing of what we believe to be the prominent challenges facing the interactive fiction authoring tools community accompanied by a more in-depth considering of two commonly used tools: Twine [11] and inklewriter [7]. We also present progress on our own authoring tool, Novella, which implements our previous model [20] and attempts to target some of these challenges. Our analysis focuses on authoring tools for structural and choice-based narratives rather than simulated or generative ones.

R. Rouse et al. (Eds.): ICIDS 2018, LNCS 11318, pp. 501–513, 2018.
https://doi.org/10.1007/978-3-030-04028-4_59

2   State of the Art

In our survey of the state of the art, we have considered 29 authoring tools. 14 were sourced from academically published research. 4 are developed and sold as commercial products. The remaining 11 come from other non-commercial, non-academic sources, such as open-source or otherwise free projects. We have found this distinction to be important, as the purpose of these tools differs based on their origin; commercial products are created with a different end-goal than academic systems, for instance, which can impact the focus and quality.

Delivery Methods and Interface Paradigms

These tools can be broadly categorized by their delivery methods (**Standalone**, **Web-based**, **Integrated**) and high-level interface design paradigms (**Form**, **Graph**, or **Text**-based).

Standalone tools offer a dedicated application which is independent from additional software other than the host platform. A drawback of such approaches is the difficulty of cross-platform support, although this is becoming less problematic. The Emo-Emma [15] authoring tool, for instance, provided a Windows binary, but does not support any other systems. Some standalone applications are able to export to generic or specific formats, which increases the usability of the tool. articy:draft [4], for example, can export to Unity [12] as well as providing an API for integration into arbitrary systems.

Web-based tools provide a browser-based solution which comes with the advantage of being mostly platform independent and easily accessible. Editors such as StoryPlaces and inklewriter present web interfaces for authoring, testing, and publishing of interactive fiction. Twine, which is based on web technologies, provides both a browser interface and a wrapped standalone multi-platform desktop application, which increases its accessibility and availability.

Integrated tools are built directly into host software such as game engines, having the advantage of being able to communicate directly with and be tailored to a given system. Fungus [5], for instance, is built as a Unity plugin, requiring no other software and being able to integrate directly with Unity's systems.

Table 1 presents an incomplete but representative taxonomy of authoring tools for interactive narrative classified by their method(s) of delivery.

Authoring tools can also be broadly grouped by the paradigms used in the interface with abstraction of data. It is to be noted that these paradigms are not mutually exclusive, and many tools make use of one or more in their design.

Form-based interface design is the most common interface paradigm by a large margin. These are atomic user interface controls that are often mapped closely or directly to a data model. For instance, a character editing interface using a form-based approach may contain text fields directly mapped the character's attributes. These kinds of fields are necessary in essentially any tool that requires data input. Their danger lies within misuse, as creating an interface purely of atomic controls can be difficult to maintain good UX, and can have little tangible benefit other than basic accessibility when it comes to abstraction of

Table 1. Authoring tools sorted by their method(s) of delivery.

Standalone	Integrated	Web
Academic		
ASAPS [24], DraMachina [16], Emo-Emma [15], FearNot! [25], GAIA [23], NM2 [31], PaSSAGE [30], Scenejo [19], StoryTec [17], SVC Editor [32], Virtual Human [18]	GHOST [21], Story World Builder [28]	StoryPlaces [22]
Commercial		
articy:draft 3 [4], HyperCard [1], Storyspace [2], Tinderbox [14]	None	None
Other		
Inform [6], Quest [8], Ren'Py [9], Squiffy [10], TADS [29], TextureWriter [26], Twine [11]	Fungus [5]	Genarrator [3], inklewriter [7], Playfic [13], Quest [8], Squiffy [10], Twine [11]

an underlying model for the layperson. The GAIA authoring tool [23] displayed in Fig. 1a demonstrates heavy use of a form-based editing approach.

Graph-based editors abstract the structure of data into visual graphs, the most common being a node-line graph. They may be for pure visualization purposes, such as in inklewriter, or as a core part of the actual editing experience, as in Twine. This abstraction of connected data into a more visual form provides a tangible benefit that is not possible with simpler form-based approaches. Figure 3b shows the Twine editor's graph view, which provides an overview of the story data and its connectedness in a node-line style editable interactive graph.

Text-based systems feature an augmented plain text editor as their core interface paradigm, providing additional features such as autocomplete, syntax highlighting, and other markup. This approach is commonly found partnered with a domain-specific, or other form of scripting language. For instance, the GUI application of Inform [6] is centered on a plain text editor with integration into the Inform language such as markup and simple debugging support. The Inform interface in Fig. 1b shows an augmented text-based implementation with full syntax highlighting based on the Inform language.

It is important to consider the way in which accessibility can be affected when choosing a delivery method. Standalone distributions, for instance, empower the possibility of native performance and can offer a homogenous experience within the host platform, but do so at the expense of difficulties encountered with cross-platform native development. Supporting only a single platform can reduce accessibility of a system. Web-based systems, on the other hand, have increased

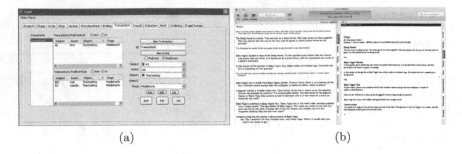

(a)   (b)

Fig. 1. GAIA (a) and Inform (b) using form-based and text-based designs.

accessibility due to their platform independence, although are faced with cross-browser complications and lesser performance. As technologies advance, however, cross-platform development difficulties and performance gaps, among other impediments, are shrinking, resulting in more freedom of choice with regards to delivery methods. Integrated solutions can tie closely into existing systems, but in doing so restrict themselves in scope.

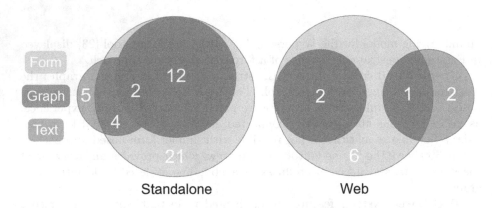

Fig. 2. Distribution of interface paradigms for Standalone and Web delivery methods. Integrated is not included as it has only 3 form and graphs, which both overlap.

Figure 2 shows Venn diagrams of the interface paradigms for standalone and web-based authoring tools. Each paradigm presents its own advantages and disadvantages to the authoring process. Using a given paradigm does not necessarily mean that the UX will be a certain way, as this is largely dependent upon the implementation. We can, however, conclude general observations of trends regarding accessibility when these paradigms are used. Based on our analysis, we found that text-based interfaces provide the most power to the user due to their exposing of a narrative grammar for authoring, but do so at the expense of usability. Authors must first learn the grammar and have little to no assistance beyond highlighting and documentation, which can make the authoring process tedious, especially for new or non-technical authors. On the other hand, we found that graph-based systems were the most accessible due to their prowess at data visualization, which is an ideal match for complex intertwining stories that are difficult to represent visually in text-based systems. This does come at the cost of losing some control that is provided by text-based systems due to the abstraction provided by graphs. Form-based approaches are variable, reliant on the visual presentation of the atomic controls. If well done, they can provide a good abstraction of the story data with reasonable levels of control, albeit less than a text-based approach. Caution must be taken when using form-based approaches to present meaningful data in a meaningful way, and to not overload authors with too much at once. This is evident by the number of systems, not only in interactive narrative, that appear to be designed by technical users for other technical or power users, rather than what the author really *needs* to see.

We summarize by concluding that these three paradigms (**Form**, **Graph**, or **Text**) play different roles in the design of interactive fiction authoring tools but that each has an impact on the UX - principally on *Accessibility* (the ease of use to construct a story), *Author Power* (the degree to which the author is able to express more detailed systems), and *Content Fidelity* (the accuracy with which the paradigm presents narrative structure or content specifics). Our survey already highlights potential trends in these design paradigms - **Graph** interfaces demonstrating a lower degree of *Author Power* than **Text** interfaces, but higher *Accessibility* - or **Graph** interfaces demonstrating good *Content Fidelity* at the structural level but potentially less at the specific content level than **Form** interfaces. A comprehensive review of the exact nature of the impact in these paradigms must form part of the future work in this area.

Availability

When evaluating the availability of an authoring tool, we looked at its presence online through official websites and third-party mentions (such as Redcap[1]), as well as the accessibility of both binaries and source code.

The availability and longevity of a tool directly affects its rate of adoption and its ability to be additionally developed or used otherwise for further research. Systems that have long become dormant, for instance, can become devalued relative to their initial contribution, and are unlikely to be adopted in the long term by interactive fiction authoring communities. Inform, for example, has been used and developed since 1993, but due to its online presence and community-driven development, remains a strong contender even today.

Online presence is an area that academic authoring tools struggle to maintain. Of the sampled tools, only six ever had a dedicated website, of which only four are functional today and are seldom updated. Temporary websites often result in unreachable links and are not a suitable substitute for a dedicated page where tools can be publicized. To illustrate, an article of Emo-Emma[2] provides links

---

[1] http://redcap.interactive-storytelling.de.

[2] http://redcap.interactive-storytelling.de/authoring-tools/emo-emma/.

to academic papers and binaries, but all links reside on a university staff page that no longer exists, making it difficult to source the original contribution.

Another related area that academic works struggle with is the distribution of binaries and source code. Some projects are understandably protected intellectually, but those that are not should attempt to share their work in order to best maximize its chance of adoption and provide an opportunity for further research to be conducted. Of the fourteen sampled tools, only five offered binaries at some point, with only *one* remaining available (StoryPlaces [22] which offers both the application and source code). Sometimes software is available upon request from the authors. StoryTec [17], for instance, used to provide a software request form, but has since removed it in 2015. The authors followed protocol outlined by ASAPS [24] website for requesting the software, but were unsuccessful in obtaining it. This highlights the need for care to be taken to ensure that if software is intended for public use, that it is made available, and remains easily available, otherwise any traction gained could be rapidly negated. The lack of availability of academic software also has serious research implications for this community, as it prevents the reproduction of any experimental results and hinders their study so that the community might incrementally improve and iterate on their work, or form a greater understanding of this area. While some conclusions can be drawn from documenting articles this is not a replacement for the software itself, and software availability and sustainability can be seen as a notable challenge for this community to overcome.

User Experience

In order to better understand the UX of select authoring tools, we participated in a reflective autoethnography by taking a story segment from Life is Strange[3] and recreating it using inklewriter and Twine. The chosen story segment[4] consisted of multiple choice discourse with some looping pathways and certain options becoming available only once set conditions were met (i.e. a given pathway node was experienced). We firstly familiarized ourselves with the tools by creating sample stories containing all of the features of our chosen story segment (i.e. how to branch, loop, present multiple choices, and lock choices until conditions are met). Each experiment was timed and narrated, and both audio and video were captured for further reflection on the authoring experience. Following the completion of the authoring process, UX laws and heuristics were applied, and any sources of usability frustration were noted. Each story was also tested to ensure accuracy, which is included in the recorded timing. To evaluate the UX of authoring systems, we applied a selection of heuristics as described by Nielsen [27], as well as the listing of the Laws of UX[5].

---

[3] Life Is Strange, Dontnod Entertainment, 2015.

[4] Section titled **Conversation with Juliet** from the game's script: http://life-is-strange.wikia.com/wiki/Episode_1:_Chrysalis_-_Script.

[5] https://lawsofux.com by Jon Yablonski. Many of the laws are grounded in research, and the few that are not are widely accepted heuristics.

inklewriter is a web-based authoring tool of interactive narrative shown in Fig. 3a. In the central pane, texts are displayed as detached segments, each of which can be edited inline. There is also a content browser for texts, and a static node-link graph view for better visualizing the flow of the story.

The *Doherty Threshold* states that system feedback should be $\leq$400 ms else user attention and productivity can suffer. However, the text segments in inklewriter animate before being presented, which takes around one second. While this may seem insignificant, if working on a large project that requires lots of navigation, the extra time can add up and reduce the overall authoring experience.

The *Law of Similarly* advises elements of differing functionality to be visually dissimilar, and those that are similar to be treated as related or as a group regardless of physical separation. In inklewriter, segments are accompanied by informative red italic text describing things such as the number of incoming or outgoing links. However, errors are also presented in the same visual style. Differentiating between information and errors can reduce potential confusion for users and help them focus on authoring rather than understanding the system.

Hick's Law suggests reducing complexity where possible, as the time it takes to make decisions or take actions is altered by the number and complexity of options available. In order to delete an unwanted segment, it must be first unlinked from surrounding segments, and then becomes detached. Then it must be located in the content explorer and manually removed. While this is likely by design in order to retain discarded texts, the complexity involved for the desired removal of such texts is high and could be reduced significantly. Keeping complexity low can aid UX and increase productivity.

Two of Nielsen's heuristics state that shortcuts should be included in order to satisfy experienced users, and that actions made should be easily reversible, or warned if they are not. inklewriter does not provide notable shortcuts and does not has the ability to undo changes beyond in text fields.

The total time spent authoring the story was 17 min 20 s. This is reasonable given the size of the story, but could have been improved, even if only a little, by the interface being less delayed.

Twine is a web and desktop authoring tool displayed in Fig. 3b. It uses a connected node graph for visualization and editing of the narrative texts. Content is edited through modal popups that fill the screen.

Jakob's Law specifies consistency in an array of manners, one of which is standardized and recognizable icons. While Twine's icons are largely consistent with those commonly used, its icon for 'find and replace' represents a list rather than something that would obviously indicate searching. Where possible, we should reuse common or recognizable adaptions of icons to reduce users having to guess functionality and to take advantage of already learned connections.

Miller's Law focuses on reducing cognitive load. Twine makes no major violations as such, but entering links, which is done manually, could be improved by providing autocomplete of existing nodes in order to reduce the number of items a user has to memorize at once and help mitigate errors.

The *Zeigarnik Effect* is about informing users of task progress. When a node in Twine defines a connection to another node that doesn't yet exist, it is replaced with a bold red **X**, indicating the incomplete state of the task. This could be improved, as regardless of the number of missing links, only one **X** is displayed. Showing multiple corresponding with the number of missing links would better implement this rule. Additionally, *Parkinson's Law* - the saving of time within a given task - could also be implemented here by allowing missing nodes to be created and linked by clicking the corresponding **X**.

The same two of Nielsen's heuristics that failed for inklewriter are likewise not implemented here. Accelerators are not provided beyond overriding a warning message when deleting nodes. Since Twine relies so heavily on a visual graph, it is ideal to include accelerators such as context menus to speed up development. Similarly, reversal of actions is not supported outside of modal content editing dialogs, which is scoped to the current modal session. After closing and reopening a modal dialog, the undo state resets, and requesting undo will delete all of the node's content. When implementing reversal of actions, we must ensure that they successfully return to a previous state.

The total time spent authoring the story was 20 min 48 s. This is significantly longer than inklewriter. It is likely that this is due to Twine requiring each node to have a unique name, and for the links to be manually typed using the exact names. Supporting autocomplete or adding an accelerator to create named nodes could potentially decrease the authoring time.

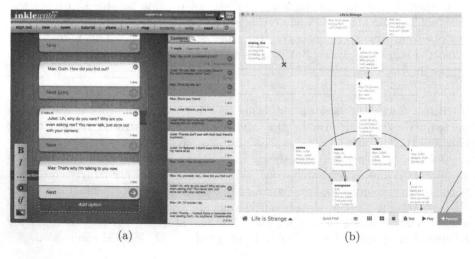

(a)   (b)

Fig. 3. A segment of Life is Strange written in (a) inklewriter and (b) Twine 2.

While the scope of our analysis is limited, we can still draw observations on the common problematic areas encountered. Authoring flow is an important concept and we must design our UX to minimize interruptions. In the case of Twine, having to manually open and rename each passage, and then remember the names to setup the links creates cognitive friction and can obstruct the authoring experience. With inklewriter, the delay for elements to enter the author's view, while less of a factor, can still contribute to slowing down the authoring process. We must consider our design decisions and prevent, or at least mitigate potential blocks in disrupting the authoring flow. Effective state communication ensures that the system and author are on the same page with regards to the story state; if there is a misunderstanding of state, it could leave the author guessing. Supporting the ability to undo and redo story state changes facilitates and encourages experimentation, which is important with creative works. Twine could better support experimentation if it better supported undoing, and had less faults when reverting textual content. In inklewriter, information and errors being conveyed in the same visual manner result in possible confusion for the author as to the current state of the story, making it difficult to differentiate mistakes from information. In a similar manner, we must strive to maintain the drafting process than an author expects by avoiding things that disrupt editing expectations. For instance, inklewriter's graph system at first appears as an alternative editing method, but is actually a static preview of the story state and connectedness.

3 Novella

We have taken the new game-centric model of interactive narrative from our previous work [20] and implemented it alongside an accompanying standalone authoring tool prototype. This model focuses on game specific narrative structure, but can readily represent traditional interactive fiction also. The authoring tool incorporates the UX lessons we have learned from this analysis, and represents a first prototype towards solving the challenges we have identified. Figure 4 demonstrates an example of the editing interface.

Our standalone tool primarily incorporates a graph-based paradigm, but also includes elements of both form and text-based solutions. The majority of the authoring is done through the central node-line graph. This was chosen as we felt that graphs provide the most accessible visualization of connectedness. Each node represents some form of narrative element from our model, such as describing discourse, providing context, and so on. Content of nodes is edited through detachable popover windows, reducing UI clutter. Variables and Entities are edited through separate interfaces accessible from the toolbar.

We should always strive to present our stories and their states as clearly as possible to reduce cognitive friction of authors and help them focus on writing rather than figuring out the system. Providing visual aids and reducing task complexity can contribute to maintaining author focus.

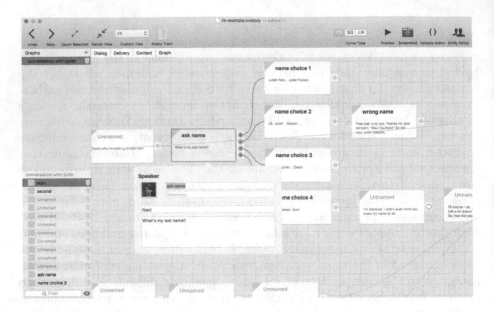

Fig. 4. Life is Strange story segment created in our own tool, Novella.

In Novella's graph system, each node has a distinctly colored flag in the top-left corner that represents the abstracted data from the internal model. For instance, dialog nodes are always colored teal, and delivery nodes orange (Fig. 5). These colors are used consistently throughout the interface which eases recognition at a glance of which kind of data is being handled thanks to the Law of Similarity. These flags follow the Serial Position Effect, where extremities are often more likely to be observed and remembered. Similarly, the green triangle in the top-right, representing that a given node is an entry point, likewise implements this law.

If nodes have outgoing links, we append a disconnected floating *pinboard* which appears grouped with the node due to the Law of Proximity (Fig. 5b). Pinboards contain pins representing each outgoing link. Pins are bordered to separate them from their neighbors, which is especially important for branch links, which have two pins (true/false). The pins and their curves are colored based on the type of node they connect to. This means that the type of node that follows can be rapidly identified at a glance based on the color of the pin and its curve. In dense graphs where curves are difficult to follow, this becomes especially useful. To further reduce complexity following curves in dense graphs, selecting a node will highlight all of its pins and curves to make them stand out from the rest of the graph. These efforts are to aid the author's identification of the story state.

It is also important to convey and highlight incomplete states to authors. In Novella, we use the Zeigarnik Effect to remind users of incomplete links without a destination by not coloring in the pins (Fig. 5c). As connected pins are filled and

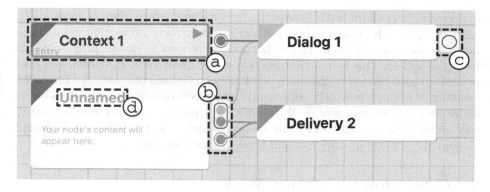

Fig. 5. Some Novella node UX features. (a) A selected node. (b) A pinboard of outgoing links. (c) An incomplete link. (d) An unnamed node.

brightly colored, those that are not filled in stand out. Similarly, we distinguish nodes that are not named with placeholder text that is lighter than the normal font to signal an incomplete state (Fig. 5d), although node names are optional in Novella.

Challenges

To ensure Novella's accessibility and longevity, the project's complete source code is available on GitHub[6]. Releases will be subsequently available, accompanying the source code as development continues.

Steps have been taken to reduce the interruption of authoring flow and to diminish UI clutter to ensure that writers can maintain focus on authoring rather than UI management without hindrance. Content for nodes is edited in popovers that can be temporarily opened and easily dismissed without using too much screen real-estate, which contributes to a reduction in UI clutter. Popovers can be optionally detached so that their presence is maintained if the author prefers. Animations in the interface, in particular with popovers, have been scoped to reasonable times as to not disrupt the authoring experience. Hiding the Story Preview, Variable Editor, and Entity Editor windows, which are lesser used than the primary graph editing interface, also helps to reduce UI clutter.

Communication of story state has been crafted to better inform the author in various ways, many of which we have discussed above. Additionally, Novella has a trashing feature akin to an operating system's recycle bin. Most content within the interface can be trashed before it is deleted. When items are trashed, they appear a color that is consistent with disabled UI elements, and most interactions are not available. This allows for visualization of removal without committing such changes instantly, and therefore the state communication must be clear.

The creative process an author takes is not linear; stories are not entered line-by-line without mistake and experimentation is integral to the authoring

---

[6] https://github.com/KasumiL5x/novella.

experience, especially with interactive storytelling where choices matter. To reduce cognitive friction and help authors maintain focus on writing, nodes need not be named as they do in Twine, but instead rely on unique identifiers hidden from the author. This means that nodes can be rapidly created, edited, and connected without having to manually book-keep the names of nodes. Additionally, undoing of actions is widely supported throughout our system, which helps to facilitate experimental works. Without such a feature, authors would have to rely on backups or even short-term memory, which would significantly limit and disrupt the authoring workflow and hinder experimenting.

4   Conclusion and Future Work

In this paper we have presented a categorized taxonomy of authoring tools for interactive narrative. We also identified methods of delivery as well as various interface design paradigms, and discussed the effect they have on the accessibility and UX of authoring tools. We then detailed at length challenges at the interactive fiction authoring tools research community faces, accompanied by an in-depth experiment. Concluding, we briefly presented our own authoring tool, Novella, and explained how the UX lessons we had learned were implemented in its interface design, and how it approaches the challenges we had identified.

In future work, we intend to further explore detailed analysis of the existing corpus of authoring tools to verify the observations made in this paper. Our own authoring tool will continue to be refined through further development and usability experiments.

References

1. HyperCard: Apple Computer, Inc. (1987)
2. Storyspace: Eastgate Systems, Inc. (1987)
3. Genarrator: Genarrator (2015). www.genarrator.org
4. articy:draft 3: articy Software GmbH & Co. KG (2017). www.nevigo.com
5. Fungus: Snozbot (2017). www.fungusgames.com
6. Inform 7: Community (2018). www.inform7.com
7. inklewriter: inkle Ltd. (2018). www.inklestudios.com
8. Quest: Community (2018). www.textadventures.co.uk
9. Ren'Py: Community (2018). www.renpy.org
10. Squiffy: Community (2018). www.textadventures.co.uk
11. Twine: Community (2018). www.twinery.org
12. Unity: Unity Technologies (2018). www.unity3d.com
13. Baio, A., McHatton, C.: Playfic (2018). www.playfic.com
14. Bernstein, M.: Collage, composites, construction. In: Proceedings of the Fourteenth ACM Conference on Hypertext and Hypermedia, pp. 122–123. ACM (2003)
15. Cavazza, M., Pizzi, D., Charles, F., Vogt, T., André, E.: Emotional input for character-based interactive storytelling. In: Proceedings of the 8th International Conference on Autonomous Agents and Multiagent Systems-Volume 1, pp. 313–320. International Foundation for Autonomous Agents and Multiagent Systems (2009)

16. Donikian, S., Portugal, J.-N.: Writing interactive fiction scenarii with DraMachina. In: Göbel, S., et al. (eds.) TIDSE 2004. LNCS, vol. 3105, pp. 101–112. Springer, Heidelberg (2004). https://doi.org/10.1007/978-3-540-27797-2_14
17. Göbel, S., Salvatore, L., Konrad, R.: StoryTec: a digital storytelling platform for the authoring and experiencing of interactive and non-linear stories. In: 2008 International Conference on Automated Solutions for Cross Media Content and Multi-Channel Distribution, pp. 103–110 (2008)
18. Göbel, S., Schneider, O., Iurgel, I., Feix, A., Knöpfle, C., Rettig, A.: Virtual human: storytelling and computer graphics for a virtual human platform. In: Göbel, S., et al. (eds.) TIDSE 2004. LNCS, vol. 3105, pp. 79–88. Springer, Heidelberg (2004). https://doi.org/10.1007/978-3-540-27797-2_11
19. Glock, F., et al.: "Office brawl": a conversational storytelling game and its creation process. In: Proceedings of the 8th International Conference on Advances in Computer Entertainment Technology, ACE 2011, pp. 88:1–88:2. ACM (2011)
20. Green, D., Hargood, C., Charles, F., Jones, A.: Novella: a proposition for game-based storytelling. In: Narrative and Hypertext 2018. ACM, July 2018
21. Guarneri, A., Ripamonti, L.A., Tissoni, F., Trubian, M., Maggiorini, D., Gadia, D.: GHOST: a GHOst STory-writer. In: Proceedings of the 12th Biannual Conference on Italian SIGCHI Chapter, CHItaly 2017, pp. 24:1–24:9. ACM (2017)
22. Hargood, C., Weal, M.J., Millard, D.E.: The storyplaces platform: building a web-based locative hypertext system. In: Proceedings of the 29th ACM Conference on Hypertext and Social Media, HT 2018. ACM (2018)
23. Kim, S., Moon, S., Han, S., Chan, J.: Programming the story: Interactive storytelling system. Informatica 35(2), 221–229 (2011)
24. Koenitz, H.: Extensible tools for practical experiments in IDN: the advanced stories authoring and presentation system. In: Si, M., Thue, D., André, E., Lester, J.C., Tanenbaum, J., Zammitto, V. (eds.) ICIDS 2011. LNCS, vol. 7069, pp. 79–84. Springer, Heidelberg (2011). https://doi.org/10.1007/978-3-642-25289-1_9
25. Kriegel, M., Aylett, R.: An authoring tool for an emergent narrative storytelling system. In: AAAI Fall, Symposium on Intelligent Narrative Technologies (2007)
26. Leinonen, J., Munroe, J.: TextureWriter (2018). www.texturewriter.com
27. Nielsen, J.: Enhancing the explanatory power of usability heuristics. In: Proceedings of the SIGCHI Conference on Human Factors in Computing Systems, CHI 1994, pp. 152–158. ACM (1994)
28. Poulakos, S., Kapadia, M., Schüpfer, A., Zünd, F., Sumner, R.W., Gross, M.: Towards an accessible interface for story world building. In: Eleventh Artificial Intelligence and Interactive Digital Entertainment Conference (2015)
29. Roberts, M.: TADS (2013). www.tads.org
30. Thue, D., Bulitko, V., Spetch, M., Wasylishen, E.: Interactive storytelling: a player modelling approach. In: Proceedings of the Third AAAI Conference on Artificial Intelligence and Interactive Digital Entertainment, AIIDE 2007, pp. 43–48. AAAI Press (2007)
31. Ursu, M.F., Cook, J.J., Zsombori, V., Kegel, I.: A genre-independent approach to producing interactive screen media narratives (2007)
32. Zünd, F., Poulakos, S., Kapadia, M., Sumner, R.W.: Story version control and graphical visualization for collaborative story authoring. In: Proceedings of the 14th European Conference on Visual Media Production, CVMP 2017, pp. 10:1–10:10. ACM (2017)

How Do Writing Tools Shape Interactive Stories?

Sofia Kitromili[⊠], James Jordan, and David E. Millard

University of Southampton, Southampton, UK
{skln15,jajl,dem}@soton.ac.uk

Abstract. Interactive Digital Storytelling is a diverse field, with a variety of different tools and platforms, many of them bespoke. Understanding how these tools effect the stories created using them would allow authors to better select tools for projects, and help developers understand the consequences of their design decisions. We present an initial exploration of this question, using a critical reflection method to analyze the process of adapting a story from StoryPlaces into both Twine and Inform 7. We report four significant differences that posed challenges for adaptation: support for rewinding and/or revisiting, the definition and description of locations, the way in which text is delivered to the reader, and how navigational cues are provided to help readers progress the story. Our observations show that tools impact the stories created using them in ways that are not obvious when working with one platform alone.

Keywords: Interactive storytelling · Writing tools · Interactive story authoring Hypertext fiction · Interactive fiction · Location aware narratives

1 Introduction

Digital interactive writing tools are systems used to author digital stories. The stories produced are interactive and typically non-linear. While there are a number of established systems, digital interactive storytelling is an experimental form, with a wide variety of different platforms and writing tools available. This raises an interesting question: *how does the design of writing tools impact the types of stories being written?* Researchers have studied the reading experiences and commented on improvements for interactive writing tools based on that experience [1, 2], but the authoring experience, and how it is mediated by tools, remains relatively unexplored [3].

This paper describes initial work to understand how different interactive writing platforms impact the authoring process, and ultimately shape the work of writers using those platforms. To approach this, we experimented with adapting an interactive story from one platform into two very different platforms. Our goal was to reflect on the way in which different tool affordances impacted the way in which the story was told. As such our methodology is one of critical reflection research [4] a reflexive qualitative approach that is strongly related to action research [4], and which produces insights into the researcher's own experience. The story we chose to adapt was *Fallen Branches* by Katie Lyons [5], a locative story set in Crystal Palace Park, and originally designed and deployed with the StoryPlaces platform [6]. In our work we adapted the story into Twine

© Springer Nature Switzerland AG 2018
R. Rouse et al. (Eds.): ICIDS 2018, LNCS 11318, pp. 514–522, 2018.
https://doi.org/10.1007/978-3-030-04028-4_60

[7] an open source hypertext fiction tool with a graphical authoring interface and no explicit modelling of location, and Inform 7 [8] an interactive fiction system that uses a natural language interface and has a virtual world model (similar to classical MUDs).

2 Background

While interactive fiction has its roots in non-digital experimental storytelling, the first digital stories to attract critical interest were those produced on the Storyspace platform [9], of which perhaps the best known is Michael Joyce's *afternoon, a story*. Storyspace represents the classical node-link model of hypertext, with hotspots appearing in the text that navigate the reader to another node. Storyspace stories can thus be represented as a network of nodes that can be analysed to reveal particular patterns of authorship [10]. The node-link model is only one example of how to create interactive narratives (albeit the dominant one). Bernstein calls the model 'calligraphic' as authors draw explicit navigational paths between nodes, and suggests that an alternative model might be 'sculptural' where all nodes are potentially linked, but rules and conditions sculpt away those links at runtime [10]. Sculptural hypertext systems include StoryPlaces, a locative hypertext system that includes location as one of the condition criteria [6] and StoryNexus by Failbetter Games (the engine behind *Fallen London*) where the approach is called Quality-Based [11]. Inform 7 also uses a world-model and rules to evaluate reader inputs, but is far more dynamic in nature than these other sculptural hypertext tools, producing an experience which is as game-like as it is hypertextual.

Spatial Hypertext is another alternative approach where text and structure are graphically manipulated into lists, groups and sets [12, 13]. Although rarely applied to narrative (with a proper spatial parser), spatial hypertext has influenced modern tools, such as StorySpace 3 and Twine, which embrace a graphical authoring paradigm.

The impact of different data models and tools on authoring is not well explored in the literature, perhaps because it is so difficult to separate the author experience, the requirements of a particular story, and the impact of the tool itself. For example, Hargood et al. attempted to investigate how a novel model called Fractal Hypertext might impact story choices and themes chosen by a set of authors, but concluded that poetics emerge gradually through use and that with novel models this is not mature enough to understand the relationships [14]. We are attempting to explore the same idea, and for this reason have chosen two established tools as target platforms for our work. StoryPlaces, our source platform, is locative and sculptural. While our target platforms are Twine, non-locative and calligraphic; and Inform 7, virtual locations and rules-based.

3 Methodology

Fallen Branches was first published on the StoryPlaces platform in 2017. As a short story of around ten thousand words it is of manageable size and complexity for our purposes.

Figure 1 shows the structure of *Fallen Branches*. It is composed of 11 chapters with each one containing non-consecutive located nodes. Each is part of one of three story threads; the main Fallen Branches thread, an account of a young woman called Sandy who is visiting Crystal Palace Park to meet with the museum curator and find out more about some family heirlooms; the Last Letter thread, a sequence of letters written between young lovers around the time of World War 1; and the Bones of Time, which recounts an episode in 1900 when two elephants escaped from the Crystal Palace. The reader moves through the park following Sandy, while the letters appear in the landscape around them. The tale of the elephants is effectively a sub-story that is available half-way around, and which temporarily switches the narration back to 1900.

We obtained the original JSON representation of Fallen Branches, and undertook an exercise to adapt it, firstly for Twine, and then for Inform 7. In both cases a structure model was created similar to the one in Fig. 1.

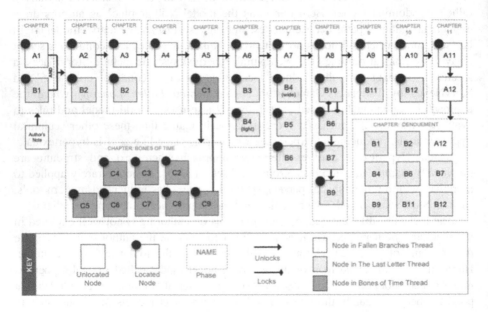

Fig. 1. Fallen Branches sculptural structure (taken from [5])

Throughout our adaptation process we met to brainstorm ideas and record our observations and decisions. Figure 2 shows the structure of the story in Twine. Passages in Twine are named after the titles of nodes in each chapter of Storyplaces, and links were created whenever navigation between those nodes was possible in the original story. As Twine contains no explicit representation of locations this does not appear in the Twine map, relying instead on the text to orientate the reader. It is interesting to note the complex relationships between the Bones of Time nodes (right and bottom) which exist because these can be visited in any order. In StoryPlaces sculptural system these are simple to model (there are no requirements so all are available throughout the sub-story until they are read) but in Twine's calligraphic system it results in a complex tangle of links [9].

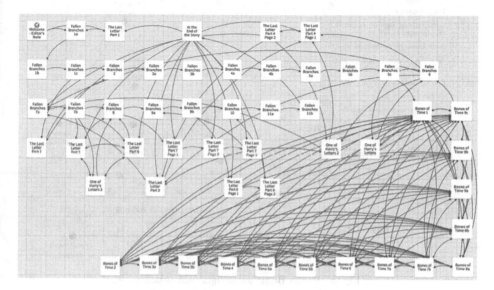

Fig. 2. Fallen Branches structure in Twine

With Inform 7 the process was quite different. In Inform 7 the process is to build a world model, which the reader can then explore (for example, using shortcuts such as 'N' to go north). The first step was to recreate the locations from Crystal Palace in as a series of rooms, with navigational routes between them that reflected their positions in the real world.

Figure 3 shows the navigational connections between locations authored as rooms in Inform 7. Inform 7 has another construct, Scenes, which are used to represent logical parts of a story that can be sequenced together (for example, acts of a story). In our adaptation, we translated the StoryPlaces chapters into scenes. This means that although the reader is free to move around the locations (as they are in StoryPlaces), the story itself plays out in a more sequential manner as dictated by where the scenes are set. Finally, Inform 7 has the notion of objects that exist within the story world and can be picked up and moved around. We used objects to represent the last letters, these are revealed and added to the users' inventory when first arriving in the correct room in the correct scene.

As described above Fallen Branches contains three story threads. The only path that readers must read to complete the story is the Fallen Branches thread. The rest are dependent on the path that the readers follow. The Last Letters are revealed and unlocked at specific locations as well as the Bones of Time sequence. If a letter is missed and the reader moves on, the letter cannot be discovered at a later point. If the Bones of Time story is activated, readers must complete reading all those events before

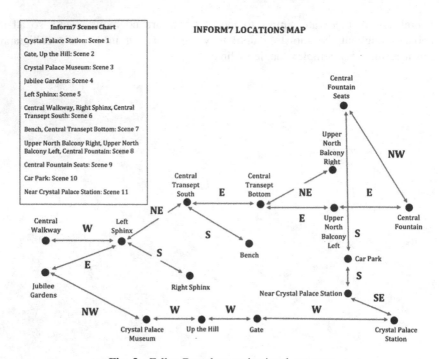

Fig. 3. Fallen Branches navigational structure

returning to the main story. The notion of this has been adapted while authoring the story in the other writing tools. In Twine all three threads have been implemented behind nodes which point to each other. In Inform 7 scenes where created to resemble chapters, rooms to resemble locations and items to resemble letters.

4   Analysis

During the adaptation process we observed how the tools impacted on the telling of the story. We were interested in cases where narrative design decisions made in Story-Places were difficult to replicate in the other models, and where the original author had made assumptions about how the story would be delivered that needed additional work to replicate or replace in the other tools. These points of tension are a good indicator of how the story has been shaped by the tool itself.

Observation 1: Rewinding and Revisiting: In StoryPlaces if the reader failed to read one of the Last Letter nodes then the letter would disappear from the map and the reader wouldn't be able to access it, even if they return to that location. Similarly, if the reader unlocks the first Bones of Time node the rest of the nodes disappear and do not reappear until the reader completes the sequence. We translated this logic to explicit links in Twine. Where a node was made available in Storyplaces a hyperlink was made available in Twine and when a node disappeared so did that hyperlink. However, Twine by default includes a back button in all the stories so that the reader can easily rewind to any state in the story and revisit missed nodes. Storyplaces allows these restrictions to give the reader momentum through the landscape, and prevent them doubling back, which is both time consuming and tiresome in real locations [5]. There are two functions here. Revisiting – meaning to return to a previous location and Rewinding – meaning to revert the story back to a previous state. Revisiting locations is possible in StoryPlaces, but rewinding nodes is not. Whereas Twine enables both revisiting and rewinding, and makes only a minor distinction between them (as nodes and locations are tied together). Similar to StoryPlaces, Inform 7 readers can navigate and revisit any location they want, but there is no way to take the narrative back to a previous state (as controlled via scenes), so revisiting is supported, but rewinding is not.

Observation 2: Definition and Description of Locations: All the locations mentioned in Fallen Branches are real places, identified via GPS coordinates and communicated to readers through a map interface. As a result, locations need to be defined, but not described, and there is no need to define the connections between them. Neither Twine nor Inform 7 use real world locations and therefore describing locations and connecting them together needs to be done manually. Inform 7 is based on a world model, and this can be done by using rooms and defining how they relate to one another. Twine has no location model at all, therefore locations need to be represented in the text of the nodes themselves (if at all). The text of Fallen Branches makes passing reference to specific locations (for example the museum) and in our judgement meant we did not need to add any additional location information. Should we have added additional text to describe locations and re-create the sense of place? The story clearly loses context as a result of not doing this, but there is no way of knowing what an author intended by placing a node in a location in the first place – or whether that intention is what readers took from the experience. If we made that obvious, either in Twine's text or Inform 7's location descriptions, we would be guessing at something that in a locative work is actually co-created by the reader and the real-world place.

Observation 3: Text Delivery: Text in Storyplaces is represented as pages tied to locations on the map, these are unlocked when a reader visits their location. The text can be of any form, and in Fallen Branches it appears as either a page describing the contemporary visit to the park, a page from an historical account of the elephant escape, or the text of a letter. This translates well into Twine, where individual nodes can also take different forms. However, text in Inform 7 is tied to the world model. For the reader to encounter the text, they must interact in some way with that model. For the visit story, and the elephant escape, we used the room description to convey the text. However, this does not work so well for the letters. To solve this, we added the letters to the world-model as objects. Rather than place them in the rooms to be discovered (which makes no narrative sense, as they are supposed to be in Sandy's possession from the beginning), we created them in particular rooms and automatically add them to Sandy's inventory at the appropriate room and scene in the story. A more radical adaptation of the story for Inform 7 would have taken this further, and taken more of the node content from the other threads and integrated that with the world model (for example, in descriptions of specific objects, or interactions with characters). But in doing so it would have fundamentally changed the way in which the story was experienced, and moved the authorial task towards a process akin to hiding treasure. The need to imaginatively integrate the text in this way is a significant difference between Inform 7 and Twine and StoryPlaces, and reflects Inform 7's game-like structure.

Observation 4: Navigational cues: When reading in Storyplaces the system shows locations on a map that when visited would unlock appropriate content to progress the story. The map therefore acts as a navigational cue. In theory readers can move anywhere, but the map shows which places they should visit next. In Twine the locations are tied to the nodes, it's impossible to move around locations without moving between story nodes, and therefore the only navigation that is possible are the links that progress the story. However, in Inform 7 the reader can still navigate around the defined locations, but there are no navigation cues to show which of those possibilities will progress the story. Writing in Storyplaces or Twine means that the author does not need to worry about these cues, whilst writing in Inform 7 means that they are important consideration and must be included in the story world somehow – otherwise how does the reader know what to do next? In our adaptation to solve this problem we used the Inform 7 description of rooms. When a reader visits a room a description of that room is displayed on the screen. That description is the text of the Fallen Branches story as it appears when activated in location. To enable cues, we added a check on the current scene, replacing or supplementing that text with an appropriate cue for the next scene. The presence of automatic cues in StoryPlaces and Twine is a major difference to Inform 7, where the author is responsible for making progress clear.

5   Conclusion

Understanding how tools influence interactive writing is a key challenge in the area of interactive digital storytelling. This potentially influences the choice of tools for particular projects, the design and development of new platforms, and critical analysis of interactive works. Developing an understanding is challenging, as authoring experience is subjective, and different creative projects have different requirements and therefore generate different frictions.

In this paper we have undertaken an initial exploration of the problem through critical reflection research. Our task was to adapt a story from one interactive form to two others, to reflect on that experience, and to use the process to identify differences between tools that might impact the ways in which an author chooses to tell a story. We have presented four differences that we observed between the tools in the experiment: support for rewinding and/or revisiting; the way in which locations are defined and described; the way in which text is delivered to the reader, and the way in which navigational cues are provided to the reader that help them to progress the story. Going in to the activity we expected StoryPlaces and Inform 7 to be closer in character, as both emphasize location, but our findings show a more complex picture. It is true that both StoryPlaces and Inform 7 do not allow rewinding, and decouple location from nodes, but in other ways they are more similar to Twine than each other. For example, Twine and Inform 7 are clear in how location is used and impacts story, whilst

StoryPlaces is more ambiguous – meaning the author has far less control. Twine and StoryPlaces also require less of the author in terms of providing navigational cues, and neither requires the author to consider text delivery, as both have a single mechanism for showing readers content. These last two characteristics could be said to separate the more traditional hypertext approach of StoryPlaces and Twine, from the environmental storytelling [15] aspects of Inform 7.

While this paper represents only initial work, it does demonstrate that differences in the impact of narrative models on the authoring task. These can begin to be identified, and their subsequent effect on the stories themselves explored. By testing a small sample of writing tools, we have discovered observations that work limited to one tool could not provide. One of the most valuable aspects of interactive digital narratives is the diversity of the form itself, represented by the different authoring tools and models in use, and we believe that efforts to develop theory around digital narratives and authorial practice can embrace this diversity and develop it as a strength.

References

1. Pope, J.: How do readers interact with hypertext fiction? An empirical study of readers' reactions to interactive narratives. Ph.D., Bournemouth University, Fern Barrow, Poole, Dorset, BH12 5BB, UK (2007)
2. Schneider, R.: Hypertext narrative and the reader: a view from cognitive theory. Eur. J. Engl. Stud. 9(2), 197–208 (2005)
3. Koenitz, H.: Three questions concerning authoring tools. In: Proceedings of the 10th International Conference on Interactive Digital Storytelling Workshops, Madeira, Portugal, p. 4 (2017)
4. Morley, C.: Critical reflection as a research methodology. In: Knowing Differently: Arts-Based and Collaborative Research Methods, pp. 265–280 (2008)
5. Packer, H.S., Hargood, C., Howard, Y., Papadopoulos, P., Millard, D.E.: Developing a writer's toolkit for interactive locative storytelling. In: Nunes, N., Oakley, I., Nisi, V. (eds.) ICIDS 2017. LNCS, vol. 10690, pp. 63–74. Springer, Cham (2017). https://doi.org/10.1007/978-3-319-71027-3_6
6. Hargood, C., Weal, M.J., Millard, D.E.: The StoryPlaces platform: building a web-based locative hypertext system. In: Proceedings of the 29th on Hypertext and Social Media, New York, NY, USA, pp. 128–135 (2018)
7. Twine/An open-source tool for telling interactive, nonlinear stories. http://twinery.org/. Accessed 03 May 2018
8. Inform. http://Inform7.com/. Accessed 03 May 2018
9. Bernstein, M.: Structural patterns and hypertext rhetoric. ACM Comput. Surv. 31(4es), 19 (1999)
10. Weal, M.J., Bernstein, M., Millard, D.: On Writing Sculptural Hypertext (2002)
11. Short, E.: Beyond branching: quality-based, salience-based, and waypoint narrative structures. In: Emily short's interactive storytelling, 12 April 2016
12. Marshall, C.C., Shipman, F.M.: Spatial hypertext: designing for change. Commun. ACM 38(8), 88–97 (1995)

13. Atzenbeck, C., Schedel, T., Tzagarakis, M., Roßner, D., Mages, L.: Revisiting hypertext infrastructure. In: Proceedings of the 28th ACM Conference on Hypertext and Social Media, New York, NY, USA, pp. 35–44 (2017)
14. Hargood, C., Davies, R., Millard, D., Taylor, M.R., Brooker, S.: Exploring (the poetics of) strange (and fractal) hypertexts. In: 23rd ACM Conference on Hypertext and Social Media (2012)
15. Jenkins, H.: Game design as narrative architecture. Computer **44**, 53 (2002)

A Framework for Classifying and Describing Authoring Tools for Interactive Digital Narrative

Yotam Shibolet[1], Noam Knoller[1] (ID), and Hartmut Koenitz[2]([⊠])

[1] Utrecht University, 3512 HE Utrecht, The Netherlands
y.shibolet@students.uu.nl, n.knoller@uu.nl
[2] HKU University of the Arts Utrecht, 3500 BM Utrecht, The Netherlands
hartmut.koenitz@hku.nl

Abstract. Authoring tools are a crucial component in the practice and research of interactive digital narrative design, yet no recent meta-analysis or mapping of such tools exists that would make it possible to comparatively study their defining qualities and characteristics and their effects on the artefacts produced with them. As a first step towards this goal, we created an online resource [1] in which we surveyed and classified over 300 tools. This paper lays out our proposed categorisation and description framework for IDN authoring tools. After exploring our definition of authoring tools and research methodology, we describe 9 categories and 38 descriptors for tool analysis and comparison. We conclude with a sample analysis of Twine [2].

Keywords: Authoring tools · Interactive digital narrative
Interactive narrative design · Interface · Twine

1 Introduction

Authoring tools, software that helps non-programmers create interactive digital narrative (IDN) artefacts, have accompanied the development of the field for at least three decades. Indeed, many researchers and practitioners saw the creation of their own tool as a necessary step to fulfil their specific vision for IDN. As Bolter noted, "in this field, everybody wants to have their own authoring tool" [3]. This practice has led to an abundance of tools, about which we actually know very little. To make sense of this abundance, a framework for surveying, categorising, comparing and analysing IDN authoring tools seems a long overdue, necessary effort to improve the discourse and move the field forward. In particular, it will enable scholars and practitioners to recognise specific features, compare different tools and identify areas needing further development. A classification framework will also increase the chances of interoperability between potentially complementary tools. On a more theoretical level, an enhanced understanding of the space of authoring tools will also facilitate an investigation of the relationship between tool and resulting artefact, itself an underdeveloped area in need of attention.

© Springer Nature Switzerland AG 2018
R. Rouse et al. (Eds.): ICIDS 2018, LNCS 11318, pp. 523–533, 2018.
https://doi.org/10.1007/978-3-030-04028-4_61

Our twofold aim with this paper is to lay the ground for a framework that could sustain both a categorised mapping of the authoring tools landscape, and a comparative analysis of tools. We approached this with a two-pronged effort:

Survey and Categorisation. Our work is a first attempt towards a comprehensive classification of authoring tools, based on an initial survey of over 300 specimens. In addition to tools developed by academics or artists with the specific intent of creating IDN artefacts, the survey covers many tools developed in industry, since these, too, are used (or can be used) for the creation of IDN works. While no comprehensive survey exists today, the real issue is not merely to account for the existing tools, but also to categorise them. We therefore offer a classification that enables sorting any given authoring tool into one of 9 categories. This division currently comprises of 183 specimens that fit our definition of IDN authoring tools (see next section) and keeps track of other tools and tool characteristics relevant to the field through 12 'sub-lists'. Ultimately, we hope to convert this overview into an online resource, with a tag-cloud structure, to enable advanced, multi-category search for tools.

Descriptive Framework for Comparison and Analysis. A list of 38 descriptors for tool analysis allows for a comparison of different tools from any of our categories. We hope this effort will enable scholars and practitioners to recognise specific features, compare different tools and identify areas needing further development.

2 Defining Authoring Tools

We define an IDN authoring tool pragmatically as digital software, which:

a. Is capable of functioning as an independent and comprehensive workspace (including an independent IDE (integrated development environment) and GUI (graphical user interface)), which allows a prospective author to create an interactive narrative work from start to finish.
b. Simplifies the authoring process: the design of the storyworld/protostory and\or of the end-user interaction model/protoprocess [4] is simplified and\or made more effective, so that the tools facilitate the IDN creative process better than a general-purpose programming language (or media processing tool) would. A 'better'\'simpler' IDN creative process could mean a workflow that is more directed and integrated, less time-consuming or one that demands fewer technical skills; improved accessibility and tangibility of design strategies and representation structures in the tool's UI, and/or improved narrative abstraction/conceptualization in the work environment, making these abstract structures and concepts ready-to-hand [5].
c. Is actively being used\was actively used in the past to create IDN products – focused on interactive narrative aspects – by a community of practice besides the tool's creator(s).

3 History and Past Work

The first software we are aware of that falls fully within our definition of an authoring tool is Donald Brown's *Eamon* (1979) [6], which included a creation kit for adventure games with combat mechanics. *The Adventure System* (1982) [7], a creation kit for Scott Adams format adventure games, is another early candidate. Sharples' thesis [8] from 1984 is one of the first academic texts that explicitly discusses authoring tools. It includes an interactive authoring tool in a dissertation on computer-use in creative writing and English teaching, though the distinction between interactive and non-interactive works authored through a computer remains rather blurred. Conklin's 1987 paper [9] includes an impressive overview of many or most hypertext authoring systems available at the time, but his survey does not focus on narrative hypertext and conflates problem exploration tools with IF tools. In a similarly broad framework, Theng's 1995 publication [10] discusses the significance of design and affordances of a hypertext authoring system, due to its influence on potential end products.

Bolter et al.'s 1987 [11] is likely the first text on authoring tools that focused specifically on the creative work of narrative authoring. Introducing *StorySpace*, it argues for the importance of structuring hypertext authoring of narrative work. Michael Mateas' "An Oz-centric review of interactive drama and believable agents" [12] may be the first overview that focuses exclusively on comparing the structure of interactive narrative systems (including both story generation tools and authoring tools).

Working at the time in Gloriana Davenport's Interactive Cinema group at MIT media lab, Kevin M Brooks' 1999 PhD dissertation [13] is probably the first large-scale academic project dedicated to the development both of an authoring tool for IDN (or in Brooks' terminology, "metalinear story"), and of a theoretical understanding of their fundamental importance to the creation of new kinds of digital works: "This thesis shows that in order to write a metalinear story, one must use a metalinear writing tool from the very beginning." [13, p. 59]. Brooks' PhD dissertation is arguably also the first academic publication to describe an authoring tool (his *Agent Stories*) in depth, and to view it as part of a broad field of new media, that isn't limited to its specific sub-genre (such as hypertext). Later papers [14–17] – focusing more often than not on presenting a newly developed tool - provide their own brief overviews of more or less closely-related previously-developed tools (a list of 14 tools in [18] presenting ASAPS seems to go the furthest). Since these early years, when the field was small enough to comprehensively review and analyse all known tools, we have not been able to locate in the literature a systematic overview study. Instead, more general discussions of authoring tools issues appear, for example, in [19, 20].

4 Listing and Classifying Authoring Tools

4.1 Categories

To compile the database, the we consulted several existing lists that were created within several communities of practice, both academic and non-academic, alongside any further tools our group members came across in the process. The two initial main sources used were:

- A list of 14 academically-developed tools referenced or included in many academic papers by members of the ICIDS community, originally compiled by Koenitz [18]. The same list has reoccurred in other IDN-related publications by Koenitz himself, David Thue and others.
- A list compiled by Deglaucy Jorge Teixeira, a researcher of interactive children's book with relevant industry experience in Brazil. Teixeira compiled a list of 39 authoring tools divided into 4 categories. As with all other mentioned lists, a fully referenced 'list of lists' is available online at the tools resource page [1].

Further lists we integrated originated from various sources such as NYU Game Center researcher Clara Fernández-Vara's 'Vagrant Cursor' WordPress page [21], StoryNexus' wiki domain [22], Interactive Fiction artist Emily Short's blog [23], a tool comparison excel sheet maintained by the IF community [24], and other similar web-sources.

At the time of writing, the full database includes a total of 183 tools (146 of which are 'alive') that fully meet all three criteria of our definition (over 100 tools surveyed were excluded since they did not meet the criteria). We believe our database includes the most central and noteworthy tools developed in both academic and non-academic contexts to date, alongside many other tools deemed relevant enough to note. A possible limitation is that we have only been able to look for tools that support English-language authoring, although the database does include some tools that were originally developed in Japanese, German and other languages, and adapted into an English version. A first selection criterion has been applied to the full database to distinguish between tools that are available and actively used at present day ('Alive'), and tools that no longer are ('In limbo'\'Dead'). 'Alive' tools were assigned a number, while noteworthy 'dead' or 'in limbo' tools are listed for each respective category without numbers.

We approached the task of classification from two directions: After integrating and meta-analysing the various lists, bottom up distinctions derived from an observation of the actual field of already existing authoring tools and the discourse surrounding them led us to classify the tools into nine top-level tool group categories. This primary level of classification is divided into two groups: Fully self-contained tools and Partially-generative and non-generative tools.

Fully Self-contained Tools. These are generative tools, whose end-products are entirely code based, meant to be played on a computer or console, ranging from text to real-time graphical rendering, and sorted into categories as follows:

Real-Time Graphical Rendering/Game-Creation Tools. These include: (I) Flexible game engines (e.g. Unity 3D [28]; Unreal [29]), (II) Genre-specific game makers (e.g. RPGMaker [30]; Adventuregamesstudios [31]), geared and templated towards the making of a particular category of narrative games. The genre-specific tools are generally more amateur-friendly.

Hybrid Text + Graphic Tools. These include (III) Visual novel authoring tools (e.g. Ren'Py [32]; Kirikiri [33]) and (IV) Other hybrid tools (e.g. ASAPS [18, 19, 34]; IDTension [35, 36], both from academics).

Interactive Fiction Tools. These include: (V) Hypertext tools (e.g. Twine [2]; StorySpace [37, 38]) – lexia-tree based structure, navigated by clicking portions of the text that function as link; (VI) Parser tools (e.g. Infrom 7 [39]; VaryTale [40]) - command-interface-based textual narratives [41]. Navigated by either an open-language command\dialogue board, such as in adventure games, or a system that facilitates a menu of commands through different, more approachable interfaces.

Generally, parser artefacts incline towards open navigation and are meant to feel like a world-generator, whereas hypertext is more like a choose-your-own-adventure book, often focused on narrative delivery and style rather than on proto-game-mechanics. This isn't an absolute distinction, however: game engines enable authoring via text, and many can produce text-based IDNs, and many IF engines afford real-time graphical rendering. Yet the primary ontology of the respective tools divides them, through their respective UIs, affordances and rhetoric, into either graphics or text. The hybrid list is composed of tools that highlight both textual and visual/pictorial representations as crucial elements, close to equally important in a typical resulting artefact.

Partially-Generative and Non-generative Tools. These tools support authoring with externally produced (e.g. recorded) assets: (VII) Interactive Video\documentary tools (e.g. Klynt [42]; Korsakow [43, 44]); (VIII) Augmented\mixed-reality tools (e.g. Aris [45]; StoryPlaces [46, 47]); (IX) VR\360 video tools (e.g. SceneVR [48]; VRDoodler\Haven [49]) – 'VR' is a hybrid category, as the concept is commonly used as a blanket term for both computer-generated, fully self-contained works typically developed through game engines, and 360 video works that import digital footage.

The strong differences in terms of design process and affordances between working with recorded or pre-rendered assets or real-world locations, on the one hand, and digitally generated storyworlds, on the other, justify our use of this difference as our primary classification. However, as the affordances for manipulation, integration and personalization of captured footage grows exponentially with technological developments, this division is increasingly not as distinct as it once was.

In addition to our main classification, other types and qualities of authoring tools were assessed during our bottom-up review process as relevant for further analysis. These groups, however, were not fit to form their own category. We thus have 12 additional sub-lists. 6 of them keep track of a certain purpose or quality of authoring tools, spanning both tools that were included in or excluded from our main overview: Academic tools (1); E-Learning Tools (2); Gestural Interface Tools (3); Interactive Journalism Tools (4); Mixed-Initiative authoring tools (5) and web portals for authoring (6). Other types of tools, excluded from the main lists were listed due to broader relevance to the field, for various reasons. These include: Prototypes\Under-development tools (7); Historical authoring tools (8); Middleware\interpreters (9); Story generation\procedural AI authoring tools (10); Tangible\material UI tools (11); and Writing aid\interactive tools for linear writing (12).

4.2 Descriptors

We further developed a system of 38 descriptors for the analysis and comparison of authoring tools, which attempts to describe which place a particular tool occupies on the widest definition available of the IDN expressive space. The underlying theoretical insights were gleaned primarily from two complementary theoretical models that strive to comprehensively describe the space of IDN/IDS: Koenitz's SPP model [11], which regards IDN as a system, and Knoller's userly text model [25–27], which regards IDS as interactive experience (see also a proposed synthesis of these two models in [4]). These insights were then crystallised into a list of descriptors describing what qualities of authoring tools are most pertinent and may be deducible via direct examination of tools themselves: their interface, design process, usage, etc.

Our approach to the analysis of tools has been strongly phenomenological: though some descriptors relate to a tool's structure and technical capabilities in isolation, our more complex categories relate to the authoring process itself as a *designed experience for experience design*. Owing to this approach, our focus is on analysing the authoring tools' affordances, rather than their functional potential, acknowledging, for example, that two tools that enable the same functionality (for example, designing timed events) can strongly differ in how salient this function is in their interface, and\or how simple it is to design and, thus, differ in the extent to which it should be a prevalent affordance.

The following Table 1 exemplifies our framework using the example of Twine, a popular hyperfiction authoring tool:

Table 1. Classification example: twine

Descriptor	Value
Name	Twine
Creator & affiliation	Chris Kilmas, American indie game designer
Year of release	2009 (Twine released 2014)
Category	Self-contained>IF>Hypertext
End-product media type(s)	Link-based interactive textual fiction
Main target audience	Amateur IF enthusiast, independent artists
Vitality	Alive
Number range of products made	1,000–10,000
Homepage	https://twinery.org/
Publishing portal link(s)\overview of products made	IFDB portal: goo.gl/So2WPp https://twinery.org/
Textual analysis sources	Porepentine manifesto: goo.gl/fU5smt Friedhoff, Jane. "Untangling Twine: A Platform Study." DiGRA Conference 2013
Sample end-product(s)	*Sacrilege* (Cara Ellison 2013): https://unwinnable.com/wp-content/uploads/2013/04/Sacrilege.html

(*continued*)

Table 1. (*continued*)

Descriptor	Value
Tutorial(s)	http://twinery.org/cookbook/ Tutorial playlist by Dan Cox: https://goo.gl/R1VZQf
Ownership type	Open-source; community-run
Latest stable release version	2.21 (January 2018)
Cost	Free
License type	GPL v3; Allows self-publishing
Programming language(s) written in	Javascript (V1 in Python)
Programming language employed in work-process	Twee; Harlowe\Sugarcube\Snowman
Role of coding in the creative process	Optional (basic branching story can be written without code, basic coding implementations are required for counters, conditionals, etc.)
Work platform(s)	Linux, Mac OS X, Windows, Web application
Import formats	Full HTML compatibility Twine1: Images: PNG, GIF JPEG, WebP, SVG Twine2: HTML only All media formats can be embedded into a Twine story via HTML but this is quite clumsy and requires some coding knowledge
Export formats	HTML
Interface screenshot(s)	
Main design window(s)	Basic lexia space page is Twine's only window
Primary Design Unit(s)	Passages – unified text lexia unit structure
Work-environment UI model	Lexia space
UI-modelling type & level of abstraction	High; Extendable objects (additional lexia are created by customising existing lexia)
Design interface intuitiveness	Very high
Initial learning curve complexity correlation	Very low
Advanced authoring complexity correlation	Medium
Degree of emphasis on narrative structuring	Medium
Prevalent narrative elements & concepts	Story progression\Events - choice based textual links between lexia Support for conditionals, counters, inventory, stats, RPG battles, randomisation

(*continued*)

Table 1. (*continued*)

Descriptor	Value
Prevalence of procedural elements	Supplementary-optional
Main available procedural authoring elements	Conditional linking (if-; else-if); Randomisers; counters (+procedural linking), 'combat' stats
Available end-product interaction model(s) & degree of flexibility	Point-and-click text; very low
End-product platform & control interface	PC (mouse), Smartphone (touchpad); no
Additional key interaction design affordances	None

Unfortunately, the scope of this paper does not allow for a nuanced explanation and discussion of our descriptors and the reasons for their inclusion. A more thorough presentation of the parameters, alongside a table comparing two additional central tools (Unity and ASAPS) to Twine, can be found on our online resource website [1].

5   Conclusion: Limitations and Future Work

Because our current list of descriptors traces the existing field of authoring tools, it isn't future proof, as it does not address what may be significant for the design of future authoring tools. We are particularly curious about tools that would model and connect the design of interfaces [50, 51, 54], interaction models and user experience [25, 52] with narrative design – particularly through embodied\gestural interfaces [26, 53]. These are accounted for in our models, as well as in IDN artefacts, but are at best implicit in IDN-specific authoring tools.

The full list, and even the list of active tools that fulfil all of the criteria, was too long to treat in equal and sufficient depth in a comprehensive meta-analysis. Therefore, we chose a set of 16 tools that we pragmatically deemed to be particularly interesting and relevant for further research on the topic. Our next planned step is to conduct comparative analysis of these tools through our framework. We further plan to integrate all tools, lists and sub-lists into a digital matrix, allowing prospective users to further explore these tools in a comparative context via, e.g. a tag cloud. This should further help uncover possible clusters and patterns within the data.

Our work can also serve to map the IDN field as a whole: its territories, borders and relevant qualities. We hope it will also evolve into a useful resource for prospective authors interested in interactive narrative and looking for the right tool to support them. However, the nature of this kind of pioneering effort is such that some aspects of our proposed framework might rightfully be criticised and omissions on our part are entirely likely. Consequently, we see our work as the start of a community resource that will improve over time, through further scholarly discourse.

To conclude, we invite the ICIDS community not only to keep track of this project and use its output, but also to collaborate, to get involved in improving the framework and, eventually, to submit tools and analyses.

References

1. IDN Authoring Tools Resource. interactivenarrativedesign.org/authoringtools/appendix.pdf. Accessed 25 July 2018
2. Twine. http://twinery.org/. Accessed 24 July 2018
3. Bolter, J.D.: Personal communication with Hartmut Koenitz
4. Koenitz, H., Dubbelman, T., Knoller, N., Roth, C.: An integrated and iterative research direction for interactive digital narrative. In: Nack, F., Gordon, Andrew S. (eds.) ICIDS 2016. LNCS, vol. 10045, pp. 51–60. Springer, Cham (2016). https://doi.org/10.1007/978-3-319-48279-8_5
5. Heidegger, M.: The question concerning technology. Technol. Values Essent. Read. **99**, 113 (1954)
6. Maher, J.: Eamon, part I, September 2011. https://www.filfre.net/2011/09/eamon-part-1/. Accessed 24 July 2018
7. Maher, J.: The Quill, July 2013. https://www.filfre.net/2013/07/the-quill/. Accessed 24 July 2018
8. Sharples, M.: Cognition, computers and creative writing. Diss. University of Edinburgh (1984)
9. Conklin, J.: Hypertext: an introduction and survey. Computer **20**(9), 17–41 (1987)
10. Theng, Y.L., Jones, M., Thimbleby, H.W.: Designer tools for hypertext authoring (1995)
11. Bolter, J.D., Joyce, M.: Hypertext and creative writing. In: Proceedings of the ACM Conference on Hypertext. ACM (1987)
12. Mateas, M.: An Oz-centric review of interactive drama and believable agents. In: Wooldridge, M.J., Veloso, M. (eds.) Artificial Intelligence Today. LNCS (LNAI), vol. 1600, pp. 297–328. Springer, Heidelberg (1999). https://doi.org/10.1007/3-540-48317-9_12
13. Brooks, K.M.: Metalinear cinematic narrative: theory, process, and tool. Diss. Massachusetts Institute of Technology (1999)
14. Magerko, B.: A comparative analysis of story representations for interactive narrative systems. In: AIIDE (2007)
15. Roberts, D.L., Isbell, C.L.: A survey and qualitative analysis of recent advances in drama management. Int. Trans. Syst. Sci. Appl. Spec. Issue Agent Based Syst. Hum. Learn. **4**(2), 61–75 (2008)
16. Arinbjarnar, M., Barber, H., Kudenko, D.: A critical review of interactive drama systems. In: AISB 2009 Symposium. AI & Games, Edinburgh (2009)
17. Riedl, M.O.: A comparison of interactive narrative system approaches using human improvisational actors. In: Proceedings of the Intelligent Narrative Technologies III Workshop. ACM (2010)
18. Koenitz, H.: Extensible tools for practical experiments in IDN: the advanced stories authoring and presentation system. In: Si, M., et al. (eds.) ICIDS 2011. LNCS, vol. 7069, pp. 79–84. Springer, Heidelberg (2011). https://doi.org/10.1007/978-3-642-25289-1_9
19. Koenitz, H., Chen, K.-J.: Genres, structures and strategies in interactive digital narratives – analyzing a body of works created in ASAPS. In: Oyarzun, D., Peinado, F., Young, R.M., Elizalde, A., Méndez, G. (eds.) ICIDS 2012. LNCS, vol. 7648, pp. 84–95. Springer, Heidelberg (2012). https://doi.org/10.1007/978-3-642-34851-8_8
20. Spierling, U., Weiß, S.A., Müller, W.: Towards accessible authoring tools for interactive storytelling. In: Göbel, S., Malkewitz, R., Iurgel, I. (eds.) TIDSE 2006. LNCS, vol. 4326, pp. 169–180. Springer, Heidelberg (2006). https://doi.org/10.1007/11944577_17

21. Fernandez-Vara, C.: Tools to Make Narrative Games. VagrantCursor, January 2018. https://vagrantcursor.wordpress.com/2018/01/02/tools-to-make-narrative-games/. Accessed 24 July 24 2018
22. StoryChoices (StoryNexus) Wiki. "Story Platforms". http://wiki.failbettergames.com/story-platforms. Accessed 24 July 2018
23. Short, E.: IF Tool Development in General. Emily Short's Interactive Storytelling, February 2017. https://emshort.blog/2017/02/21/if-tool-development-in-general/. Accessed July 24 2018
24. Another Interactive Fiction Engine List. https://docs.google.com/spreadsheets/d/1-B1yKIateTpwTdRNT9W_ZjDzC6XnFpHXrcZ4nr_x7LQ/edit#gid=0. Accessed 24 July 2018
25. Knoller, N.: The expressive space of IDS-as-art. In: Oyarzun, D., Peinado, F., Young, R.M., Elizalde, A., Méndez, G. (eds.) ICIDS 2012. LNCS, vol. 7648, pp. 30–41. Springer, Heidelberg (2012). https://doi.org/10.1007/978-3-642-34851-8_3
26. Knoller, N., Ben-Arie, U.: The holodeck is all around us—interface dispositifs in interactive digital storytelling. In: Koenitz, H., et al. (eds.) Interactive Digital Narrative - History, Theory and Practice, pp. 67-82. Routledge, New York (2015)
27. Knoller, N.: Complexity and the userly text. In: Grishakova, M., Poulaki, M. (eds.) Narrative Complexity - Cognition, Embodiment, Evolution. Nebraska University Press, Lincoln, Nebraska (2019, forthcoming)
28. Unity. https://unity3d.com/. Accessed 24 July 2018
29. Unreal Game Engine. https://www.unrealengine.com/en-US/what-is-unreal-engine-4. Accessed 24 July 2018
30. RPG Maker MV. http://www.rpgmakerweb.com/products/programs/rpg-maker-mv. Accessed 24 July 2018
31. Adventuregamesstudios. http://www.adventuregamestudio.co.uk/. Accessed 24 July 2018
32. Ren'Py. https://www.renpy.org/. Accessed 24 July 2018
33. Kirikiri, Z. https://github.com/krkrz/krkrz. Accessed 24 July 2018
34. ASAPS. http://advancedstories.net/. Accessed 24 July 2018
35. IDTension. http://redcap.interactive-storytelling.de/authoring-tools/idtension/. Accessed 24 July 2018
36. Szilas, N.: IDtension: a narrative engine for Interactive Drama. In: Proceedings of the Technologies for Interactive Digital Storytelling and Entertainment (TIDSE) Conference, vol. 3, no. 2 (2003)
37. StorySpace. http://www.eastgate.com/storyspace/. Accessed 24 July 2018
38. Bernstein, M.: Storyspace: Hypertext and the Process of Writing. In: Hypertext/Hypermedia Handbook. McGraw-Hill, Inc., Hightstown (1991)
39. Infrom7. http://inform7.com/. Accessed 24 July 2018
40. VaryTale. https://varytale.com/. Accessed 24 July 2018
41. Short, E.: So, Do We Need This Parser Thing Anyways?. Emily Short's Interactive Storytelling, June 2010. https://emshort.blog/2010/06/07/so-do-we-need-this-parser-thing-anyway/. Accessed 24 July 2018
42. Klynt. http://www.klynt.net/. Accessed 24 July 2018
43. Korsakow. http://korsakow.com/. Accessed 24 July 2018
44. Soar, M.: Making (with) the Korsakow system. In: New Documentary Ecologies, pp. 154–173. Palgrave Macmillan, London (2014)
45. ARis. https://fielddaylab.org/make/aris/. Accessed 24 July 2018
46. StoryPlaces. http://storyplaces.soton.ac.uk/. Accessed 24 July 2018
47. Millard, D.E., Hargood, C., Howard, Y., Packer, H.: The StoryPlaces Authoring Tool: pattern centric authoring. In: Authoring for Interactive Storytelling (2017)

48. SceneVR. https://scene.knightlab.com/. Accessed 24 July 2018
49. VRDoodler. http://vrdoodler.com/. Accessed 24 July 2018
50. Bizzocchi, J., Ben Lin, M.A., Tanenbaum, J.: Games, narrative and the design of interface. Int. J. Arts Technol. **4**(4), 460–479 (2011)
51. Dubbelman, T.: Narrative game mechanics. In: Nack, F., Gordon, Andrew S. (eds.) ICIDS 2016. LNCS, vol. 10045, pp. 39–50. Springer, Cham (2016). https://doi.org/10.1007/978-3-319-48279-8_4
52. Shibolet, Y.: Game Movement as Enactive Focalization. Press Start 4.2, pp. 51–71 (2018)
53. Kirsh, D.: Embodied cognition and the magical future of interaction design. ACM Trans. Comput. Hum. Interact. (TOCHI) **20**(1), 3 (2013)
54. Norman, D.A.: Natural user interfaces are not natural. Interactions **17**(3), 6–10 (2010)

StoryMINE: A System for Multiplayer Interactive Narrative Experiences

Callum Spawforth[✉], Nicholas Gibbins, and David E. Millard

University of Southampton, Southampton, UK
{cs14g13,nmg,dem}@soton.ac.uk

Abstract. Multiplayer Interactive Narrative Experiences (MINEs) are interactive authored narratives in which multiple players experience distinct narratives (multiplayer differentiability) and their actions influence the storylines of both themselves and others (inter-player agency). Little research has been done to explore the possibilities of this type of narrative, and no complete model nor system exists. In this paper we introduce a model for MINEs based on sculptural hypertext and describe its implementation in a prototype system: StoryMINE. Then using a number of working narrative scenarios we demonstrate that the model and system supports a variety of inter-player interactions. It is our hope that this system provides a platform for the creation and reading of MINEs, and that this in turn creates opportunities for further research into this novel form of digital storytelling.

Keywords: Sculptural hypertext · Narrative systems · Multi-player

1 Introduction

Interactive Narrative (IN) research has traditionally focused on singleplayer experiences, with little done to explore the potential of multiplayer story-telling [14]. Support for narratives where every player experiences a distinct narrative (multiplayer differentiability [14]) and each player has the ability to influence the narratives of other players (inter-player agency) is especially rare. We define the term Multiplayer Interactive Narrative Experiences (MINEs) as interactive authored narratives that demonstrate both multiplayer differentiability and inter-reader agency.

MINEs make new types of story possible. For example, consider a detective story in which the players experience the different narratives of a detective and a criminal. The clues available to the detective might be defined by the actions of the criminal, while the ultimate fate of the criminal might be decided by the effectiveness of the detective's investigation. Alternatively, consider the story of a player exploring a haunted house, where the player ultimately meets their demise. The nature of the next player's haunting could depend upon the decisions the previous player made when exploring the house. Here, the players take on

© Springer Nature Switzerland AG 2018
R. Rouse et al. (Eds.): ICIDS 2018, LNCS 11318, pp. 534–543, 2018.
https://doi.org/10.1007/978-3-030-04028-4_62

the role of the same character, but with a different story due to the actions of players in previous tellings.

Unfortunately little research exists that explores these ideas, frequently adopting a collaborative authoring or group-based perspective [4]. The result is a lack of models or systems with which to explore this space. While some attempts have been made to address this, they either lack sufficient detail to be implemented (for example, Riedl et al.'s MuSE [14]), or have implementations that are unclear and are now unobtainable (for example, Fairclough and Cunningham's case based story engine [3]). This is a clear barrier to further research.

In this paper, we present a narrative model based on sculptural hypertext [1] that enables the design of MINEs and a prototype system supporting this model, StoryMINE, to our knowledge the first of its type. We then present a scenario-based evaluation that demonstrates StoryMINE's support for all of the interaction types previously identified in non-narrative multi-player games [17].

2   Background

Few multiplayer IN systems exist, none of which completely support MINEs. The most relevant aspects of these systems are the extent to which the narrative is constrained by the author (known as authorial intent [15]), their support of multiplayer differentiability, and their level of inter-player agency.

Peinado and Gervas [4] adopt a generative approach, using case-based reasoning (CBR) to plan a sequences of scenes using Propp's Morphology of the Folk Tale [13]. However, the system treats the group of players as a single entity, resulting in a lack of *multiplayer differentiability*. Fairclough and Cunningham [3] also adopt a CBR based approach, using an experience manager [15] to generate an individual story for each player. However, the system treats *inter-player agency* as an emergent property. The efficacy of their system for multiplayer was never tested, and the system itself is now unavailable.

Manninen et al. [10] present an emergent [9] approach to multiplayer storytelling where the story arises from social conflict between players. The system assigns a role, task, objective, threat and item of knowledge to each player. Each of which brings them into conflict with other players. However, once these traits are assigned the system takes a hands-off approach, allowing the narrative to emerge from the conflict between players trying to achieve their goals.

Social Shark [1] represents one of few authored approaches to multiplayer interactive narrative. A collaborative system based on sculptural hypertext [1,7, 12], it represents fragments of the narrative as a deck of cards. Each card can be played when a set of card-specific constraints are satisfied. Each player has a hand of cards, taking it in turns to play cards and build the narrative. Unfortunately, this system does not offer *multiplayer differentiability* as the players share a common narrative. However, it is one of few highly authored examples.

The Multiplayer Storytelling Engine (MuSE) [14] also adopts an authored approach and closest to supporting what we define as MINEs. Based on Coloured

Petri Nets [8], it encodes scenes as places and players as tokens, while transitions encode the intended progression of players through the narrative. Notably, the system uses a partial-order planner to handle player actions which exceed the authored bounds of the story. Crucially, the model is designed to handle multiplayer differentiability, however it doesn't explicitly consider *inter-player agency*, instead supposing a shared virtual environment where players interact. Thus it only provides a broad description of the narrative (used for the planner), rather than a complete design.

In our own ICIDS 2017 paper, we previously considered the topic of multiplayer storytelling [17] and argued that it should be possible to translate the interaction characteristics of multi-player games to apply to multi-player narratives, and that these could be supported by a sculptural hypertext engine. It is this principle that underlies our work, and forms the basis of our evaluation.

3   Multiplayer Model and StoryMINE System

Our model for MINEs is based on sculptural hypertext. This is an approach to narrative based around rules and constraints, and has also been described as quality-based structure [16]. Traditional hypertext, described as calligraphic by Bernstein [1], consists of a graph of nodes connected by links explicitly added by an author. Sculptural hypertext [1,7,12] inverts this by making every node potentially accessible from every other node. Nodes are assigned a set of constraints that must be satisfied within the current story, in order for the node to be visitable. For example, a *"Free the prisoner"* node might only be available when the constraint *"Dragon has been dealt with"* is satisfied. To satisfy these conditions, each node is capable of making assertions about the story world when it is visited. This collection of assertions is known as the story state. In this case, visiting the nodes *"Slay the Dragon"* or *"Evade the Dragon"* would satisfy *"Dragon has been dealt with"*, and more complex structures are possible.

By default, sculptural hypertext assumes a single reader with their own instance of the story. But our multiplayer model extends this to support MINEs, adding mechanisms for inter-player agency and multiplayer differentiability. Inter-player agency is achieved by making multiple players share the same story instance and reading state. This enables the actions of any player to alter the shared state, changing the nodes available to other players.

However, in our earlier analysis of interaction in multiplayer games, the game Dark Souls demonstrated the interesting case where players exist within their own game world, but could trigger interactions that manifested in the game worlds of others. For example, a player might place a symbol on the ground that appears in the other worlds[1]. The game Moirai[2] also demonstrates this, with content generated by previous players appearing in the games of subsequent players. In sculptural hypertext, this cannot be accomplished by simply sharing a single story-world, as any changes will be localised to that world.

---

[1] http://darksouls.wikidot.com/orange-guidance-soapstone.

[2] https://kotaku.com/moirai-is-an-adventure-game-with-a-killer-twist-1795897859.

To resolve this, a new type of state is introduced that can be accessed from any instance of a given story. By modifying this state, other instances of the story can be influenced, allowing inter-player agency between any of the readers of a story - even if only a single role exists within the story.

The challenge with multiplayer differentiability in authored narrative is presenting different perspectives on the narrative to different players. In systems using virtual environments, this is achieved with locations [3, 10] or scenes [4, 14]. A similar form of narrative separation can't be used here as all state is shared, providing no strict division of the narrative space. To solve this, we introduce *roles*, unique identifiers defined by the author that are intended to represent a specific point of view. A role is assigned to each player, and an author can specify which parts of the story each role should experience using constraints.

Fig. 1. StoryMINE: Making a choice, reveals the text, and changes the available choices

The StoryMINE system (shown in Fig. 1 running one of the exemplars) is one possible implementation of this model. Rather than creating a sculptural hypertext engine from scratch, it extends the open-source StoryPlaces platform to support MINEs. StoryPlaces is a web-based platform for location-based narratives based on sculptural hypertext, although the use of location is not a requirement. A full description can be found in [6].

StoryMINE implements the model but it embeds the role selection mechanism into the story itself, providing nodes with the ability to set the a player's role upon reading. This allows the author the freedom to incorporate role selection into the narrative itself, and enables role changes as the story progresses.

Three key properties of sculptural hypertext were identified that are implicit for a single player hypertext, but needed to be explicitly supported for multiplayer StoryMINE. These are: atomicity, consistency and isolation, analogous the ACID properties of database transactions [5].

Atomicity states that visiting a node either succeeds or fails completely; it should be impossible for a reader to view the content of a node if all the actions for that node haven't successfully executed. *Consistency* states that synchronising state should always leave the hypertext in a valid state. In practice, this means that the system should never allow a node to be visited whose constraints are not satisfied. *Isolation* states that seemingly simultaneous node visits by multiple players should behave as if performed sequentially.

The full StoryMINE system is available as Open Source on GitHub[3].

4   Evaluation

We have performed a scenario-based evaluation of StoryMINE, considering each of the possible interaction characteristics from multi-player games [17]. We designed three brief exemplar narratives each featuring a subset of those characteristics and created them in StoryMINE, together they demonstrate the coverage of those characteristics by the system. These characteristics were:

Likelihood, the chance of an interaction occurring as the result of a given player action. **Interaction type**, describes whether an interaction merely provides additional information to the other player, or whether it has a mechanical effect. **Synchronicity**, whether an interaction requires the virtual presence of another player, typically because it is part of an action/response pair or sequence. **Awareness**, the extent to which a player knows they've been affected by another player's action. **Feedback**, the extent to which a player knows their action has affected another player. And **Identifiability**, whether a player knows the source or target of an interaction.

Table 1. Overview of the interaction characteristics demonstrated by the exemplars

	Exemplar 1	Exemplar 2	Exemplar 3
Likelihood	Guaranteed	Guaranteed	Possible
Type	Mechanical	Mechanical	Informational
Synchronicity	Sync.	Sync.	Async.
Awareness	Always	Always	Possible
Feedback	Always	Never	Possible
Initiator identifiable	Always	Possible	Always
Recipient identifiable	Always	Never	Possible

4.1   Exemplar Narrative Scenarios

The three exemplar scenarios are presented below. In each case the narrative scenario is described and a figure shows the implementation in StoryMINE. The figure consists of *nodes*, *locking relationships* and *unlocking relationships*. An *unlocking relationship* specifies that the destination node requires that the source node has been visited before it can be seen, while a *locking relationship* is where the destination node is unavailable if the source node has been visited.

Table 1 shows the mapping of characteristics to the three exemplars (Fig. 2).

---

[3] https://github.com/StoryMINE.

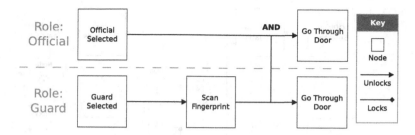

Fig. 2. Structure of Exemplar 1

Exemplar 1: The Secure Room. *A high-ranking* Official *is being escorted through a government facility by a* Guard. *Their destination is a locked metal door marked 'TOP SECRET'. In order to enter the room, the* Guard *must scan their fingerprint to unlock the door.*

Exemplar 1 demonstrates a guaranteed interaction, triggered by the guard scanning their fingerprint. As the *Official must* visit a node that is unlocked by the *Guard*, the *Official* will always experience the interaction.

This gating technique [7] can also be used to synchronise players that may be reading at different rates. Here, it forces a slow *Guard* to catch up to a quick-reading *Official* (which could be important if the following scene was synchronous). However, we imagine that overuse of this technique could lead to a poor experience if the narrative of one player is frequently blocked by the other.

Whether the players realise an interaction has occurred depends on the author. If the text makes it clear that another player was involved (such as through an extra-diegetic [11] message) it would be explicit awareness/feedback, if not then deductive. In a story with more roles the author could also use the text for identifiability, naming the Guard/Official, or could leave it ambiguous. In this case, as written, both players are *always* aware of the interaction and *always identifiable*.

Exemplar 2: The Meeting. *The* Official *and the* Guard *enter the 'TOP SECRET' room to find the other meeting attendees waiting around a large table that takes up the center of the room. As the* Official *goes to sit down, they knock some precariously perched files off of the table edge. The* Guard *has a short time to catch the files in order to avoid picking them up from the floor.*

Exemplar 2 demonstrates the second way that a narrative might contain synchronous interactions, using time sensitive nodes. When the *Official* knocks the files from the desk, a new node is opened up to the *Guard* for 5 s, allowing them to catch the files mid-air. With this mechanism, the time-limited node may expire before the player is able to view it due to them being too far behind in the narrative. This could be mitigated by frequent use of synchronisation mechanisms, such as the gating used in Exemplar 1.

The *Guard* will *always be aware* that the Official has knocked the files off of the table due to the content of the nodes. In contrast, the *Official* receives

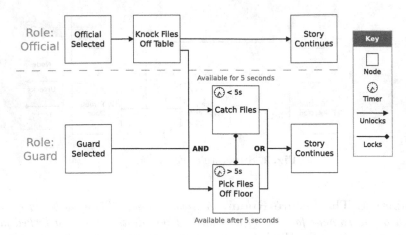

Fig. 3. Structure of Exemplar 2

feedback only if the story later refers to the guard catching or collecting the files. In the short exemplar shown this is omitted, so there is *never any feedback*. As a result, the guard is *never identifiable* (Figs. 3 and 4).

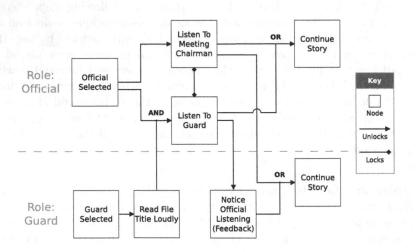

Fig. 4. Structure of Exemplar 3

Exemplar 3: The Important File. *Files in hand, the* Guard *places them back down on the table, reading out the title of the top file as they do so. The* Official *either listens to the chairman of the meeting talk, or listens to the guard, gaining the* Guard*'s attention if they do so. Having placed the files back on the table, the* Guard *goes and stands by the door.*

In Exemplar 3 the interaction triggered by the *Guard* reading the file causes the "Listen to Guard" node to appear for the *Official*. If the *Official* chooses to listen to the *Guard*, a new node is opened up for the *Guard* informing them of their impact on the *Official's* narrative. This provides *explicit feedback*. However, if the *Official* is presented with the choice and chooses not to listen to the *Guard* an interaction has still occurred, but the *Guard* won't receive any feedback.

This is also an informational interaction. For the *Official*, the narrative past this point isn't structurally impacted, however they may have been provided with information that could influence their decisions later.

5   Discussion and Conclusions

In this paper, we introduced the term MINEs as multiplayer authored interactive narratives that possess multi-player differentiability and inter-player agency. We briefly explored existing approaches to multiplayer interactive narrative before concluding that none offer full support for MINEs. Following this, we outlined a model and prototype system for MINEs based on sculptural hypertext and then demonstrated that the system supports the full variety of interaction types.

This system represents, to our knowledge, the first usable platform for MINEs, providing a basis for future work in multiplayer storytelling. By using a sculptural hypertext model, the system benefits from existing research into authoring [2] and a known ability to support a variety of interactive narratives.

Our model for MINEs makes no assumptions about how the narrative will be presented to the readers. Existing work [3,4,10,14] assumes a particular game-world through which narrative elements and interactions are presented. StoryMINE's requires no gameworld at all, and as the exemplars show can support players through an entirely text-based narrative experience.

However, as a consequence of needing to explicitly model individual interactions, there is likely to be an increase in authorial difficulty. Since each additional role requires interactions with each other role, there may be a non-linear increase in both quantity of content and structural complexity. This suggests a distinct challenge in scaling this system to a larger number of players.

Adding to the authoring challenges are concurrency problems such as starvation and deadlock - these are fully managed at the system layer, but can still appear in the narrative structure. For example, if gating is not employed, with one player able to finish before another, then the second player will be starved of agency over the first. However, if gating is employed there is the possibility of a deadlock, where the narrative cannot progress due to a lack of available nodes. Further work in MINE authoring will need to consider these challenges.

The provision of a model and a usable, open-source system enables the creation of publicly readable MINEs for the first time. This allows for research into the possibilities for multi-participant stories, particularly in terms of structure, poetics and authoring. For our future work we intend to develop and evaluate an extended MINE story, and it is our hope that the model, system, and examples will encourage further research into this novel area of digital storytelling.

References

1. Bernstein, M.: Card shark and thespis: exotic tools for hypertext narrative. In: Proceedings of the 12th ACM Conference on Hypertext and Hypermedia, HYPER-TEXT 2001, pp. 41–50. ACM, New York (2001). https://doi.org/10.1145/504216. 504233
2. Bernstein, M.: Storyspace 3. In: Proceedings of the 27th ACM Conference on Hypertext and Social Media, HT 2016, pp. 201–206. ACM, New York (2016). https://doi.org/10.1145/2914586.2914624
3. Fairclough, C., Cunningham, P.: A multiplayer case based story engine. Technical report, Trinity College Dublin, Department of Computer Science (2003). http://www.cs.tcd.ie/publications/tech-reports/reports.03/TCD-CS-2003-43.pdf
4. Peinado, F., Gervás, P.: Transferring game mastering laws to interactive digital storytelling. In: Göbel, S., et al. (eds.) TIDSE 2004. LNCS, vol. 3105, pp. 48–54. Springer, Heidelberg (2004). https://doi.org/10.1007/978-3-540-27797-2_7
5. Haerder, T., Reuter, A.: Principles of transaction-oriented database recovery. ACM Comput. Surv. **15**(4), 287–317 (1983). https://doi.org/10.1145/289.291. http://doi.acm.org/10.1145/289.291
6. Hargood, C., Weal, M., Millard, D.: The storyplaces platform: building a web-based locative hypertext system. In: Proceedings of ACM Hypertext 2018. ACM, April 2018. https://eprints.soton.ac.uk/421122/
7. Hargood, C., Weal, M.J., Millard, D.E.: Patterns of sculptural hypertext in location based narratives categories and subject descriptors. In: Proceedings of the 27th ACM Conference on Hypertext and Social Media, pp. 61–70 (2016)
8. Jensen, K.: Coloured Petri Nets: Basic Concepts, Analysis Methods and Practical Use. Monographs in Theoretical Computer Science. An EATCS Series, vol. 1, 2nd edn. Springer, Heidelberg (1996). https://doi.org/10.1007/978-3-662-03241-1. www.springer.com/gb/book/9783540609438
9. Louchart, S., Aylett, R.: Narrative theory and emergent interactive narrative. Int. J. Continuing Eng. Educ. Life Long Learn. **14**(6), 506–518 (2004). https://doi.org/10.1504/IJCEELL.2004.006017. http://www.inderscienceonline.com/doi/abs/10.1504/IJCEELL.2004.006017
10. Manninen, T., Vallius, L., Kujanpää, T.: Plot clusters – intertwined and re-playable storyline components in a multiplayer RPG. In: Göbel, S., Malkewitz, R., Iurgel, I. (eds.) TIDSE 2006. LNCS, vol. 4326, pp. 265–276. Springer, Heidelberg (2006). https://doi.org/10.1007/11944577_27
11. Mason, S.: On games and links: extending the vocabulary of agency and immersion in interactive narratives. In: Koenitz, H., Sezen, T.I., Ferri, G., Haahr, M., Sezen, D., Çatak, G. (eds.) ICIDS 2013. LNCS, vol. 8230, pp. 25–34. Springer, Cham (2013). https://doi.org/10.1007/978-3-319-02756-2_3
12. Millard, D.E., Hargood, C., Jewell, M.O., Weal, M.J.: Canyons, deltas and plains. In: Proceedings of the 24th ACM Conference on Hypertext and Social Media - HT 2013, pp. 109–118 (2013). https://doi.org/10.1145/2481492.2481504. http://dl.acm.org/citation.cfm?id=2481492.2481504
13. Propp, V.I.: Morphology of the Folktale, vol. 9. University of Texas Press, Austin (1968)
14. Riedl, M., Li, B., Ai, H., Ram, A.: Robust and authorable multiplayer storytelling experiences. In: AIIDE (2011)
15. Riedl, M.O., Bulitko, V.: Interactive narrative: an intelligent systems approach. AI Mag. **34**(1), 67 (2012). https://www.aaai.org/ojs/index.php/aimagazine/article/view/2449

16. Short, E.: Beyond Branching: Quality-Based, Salience-Based, and Waypoint Narrative Structures, April 2016. https://emshort.blog/2016/04/12/beyond-branching-quality-based-and-salience-based-narrative-structures/
17. Spawforth, C., Millard, D.E.: A framework for multi-participant narratives based on multiplayer game interactions. In: Interactive Storytelling: 10th International Conference, ICIDS 2017, Madeira, Portugal, 14–17 November 2017. Proceedings, September 2017

Authoring for Interactive Storytelling
When, Why, and Do We Actually Need Authoring Tools?

Alex Mitchell[1]([⊠]), Ulrike Spierling[2], Charlie Hargood[3], and David E. Millard[4]

[1] National University of Singapore, Singapore, Singapore
alexm@nus.edu.sg
[2] RheinMain University of Applied Sciences, Wiesbaden, Germany
ulrike.spierling@hs-rm.de
[3] Bournemouth University, Poole, England
chargood@bournemouth.ac.uk
[4] University of Southampton, Southampton, England
dem@ecs.soton.ac.uk

Abstract. One of the most significant challenges facing narrative systems research is the authoring of interactive stories, and the processes and technologies to support it. In this workshop we host a discussion and present new work in this space from researchers in creative and technical domains from both the Hypertext and Interactive Storytelling communities and explore the question: *When, why, and do we actually need authoring tools?*

Keywords: Interactive storytelling · Narrative systems
Authoring tools

1 Topic, Goals, and Outcomes

The authoring of interactive stories, and the processes and technology to support it, remains one of the most significant challenges facing narrative systems research. Attempts have been made within both academia and industry to create tools to support the authoring of interactive stories, but few, if any, of these tools have gained widespread acceptance. At the same time, many interesting works have been created either without any specialized authoring tools, or by using more general-purpose authoring tools such as *Unity* and *Twine*. This raises the question: *When, why, and do we actually need authoring tools?* Progressing from previous iterations of this workshop, and in response to discussions at last year's workshop, this year the workshop aims to answer this question.

This workshop brings together creatives, technologists, and associated researchers in a collective meeting to share research and advances in this space. Relevant work discussed at recent workshops has evoked a number of underlying questions: "What is a tool, anyway, in the context of authoring for interactive storytelling?" From visual editors to graphs or textual notations including scripting languages and story formalizations, tools can be considered very broadly as

© Springer Nature Switzerland AG 2018
R. Rouse et al. (Eds.): ICIDS 2018, LNCS 11318, pp. 544–547, 2018.
https://doi.org/10.1007/978-3-030-04028-4_63

any technology intended to assist interactive story creators. "What are the main merits of graphical or interactive tool creation?" In research projects, budget limitations often create a trade-off between sophisticated engine development vs. usable tools. While often the motivation for the latter is a greater accessibility, creative storytellers recently also criticized formal limitations of expressivity in specialized tools, a discrepancy that clearly needs to be addressed. "Are interactive storytelling tools necessarily specific to inherent interactive modalities?" Experimental paradigms of story creation for different settings, such as location-based, language-based or using virtual and augmented reality, add new dimensions for consideration beyond just character and conflict, including interaction design for end-users. "Can tools be door-openers for non-programmers to AI-based storytelling?" While easy-to-learn editors and tools often allowed for creating explicit storylines and simple branching interactivity, there is still very little reported experience with the successful implicit configuration of procedural content for stories. "Who are the future interactive storytellers and what are their talents?" All in all, due to the long-term nature of authoring projects, publications of fully evaluated principles and tools with different target groups (including insights on pitfalls and failures) are not as common as for example in the domain of E-Learning.

All of these questions relate to the basic assumptions underlying much existing research on authoring tools for interactive storytelling.

2   Format and Schedule

This workshop is a mixture of structured paper sessions and less structured "unconference" sessions. The purpose of these sessions is to gather community feedback on early progress, and stimulate discussion with new ideas in the area.

We do not necessarily expect reports on fully completed pieces of academic work - position and proposal papers are acceptable. The most important criteria is the work's relevance and interest to the wider interactive narrative research community, and its ability to stimulate useful discussion at the workshop. We do however appreciate and expect good scholarship and well founded ideas (even if the work itself is still clearly in progress). Justified opinions and visions as an answer to the workshop's title question are welcome.

Paper sessions provide an opportunity for researchers to share early or evaluated work on authoring tools and principles, and for sharing of early position papers on new ideas. In contrast, the "unconference" can be seen as: "a meeting for which the agenda is defined by the attendees at the start of the meeting". This format gives attendees an opportunity to launch more specific meetings and to use the workshop as a platform to host collaborations and conversations inspired by the earlier part of the workshop.

3   Organisation and Participants

3.1   Organisers

The workshop's organisers are academics from the wider interactive storytelling and narrative systems community. All have experience in running academic workshops (Hargood and Millard have run NHT since 2011 [2], and Mitchell and Spierling have separately or together run previous versions of ICIDS authoring workshops in 2008 [4], 2009 [5], 2010 [7], 2014 [6] and 2016 [1]). All the organisers jointly ran last year's ICIDS 2017 authoring workshop [3].

3.2   Participants

Workshop participants will come from the following groups:

- PhD Students and Early Career Researchers presenting their work on interactive digital narrative authoring
- Academics, Researchers, Writers, and members of the creative industries interested in interactive digital narrative authoring

We expect a maximum of 40 attendees, with a likely attendance of approximately 15–25. This is based on the organisers' experience of running similar workshops such as NHT and the earlier ICIDS workshops.

4   Contribution

Paper contributions by participants address or contribute to exploring the questions and issues mentioned above. Accepted papers will be published online, as in the previous year's workshop (see http://narrativeandplay.org/ais). A session at the workshop will be dedicated to collective discussion on the issues and positions presented beforehand. The outcomes of this discussion will be recorded and documented as a white paper after the workshop.

In summary, the workshop aims to:

- Create a meeting venue for active researchers in this area to come together and share their work,
- Foster a community around this work, as a step towards future collaboration, and provide a venue for publication of early work in this space, and
- Create a white paper summarizing the workshop discussion, and the main positions, regarding the need for and role of authoring tools.

References

1. Chen, F., Kampa, A., Mitchell, A., Spierling, U., Szilas, N., Wingate, S.: Exploring new approaches to narrative modelling and authoring. In: Nack, F., Gordon, A.S. (eds.) Interactive Storytelling, pp. 464–465. Springer, Cham (2016). https://doi.org/10.1007/978-3-319-48279-8
2. Hargood, C.: The Narrative and Hypertext Workshop Series and the Value of Workshops to Research Communities. SIGWEB Newsl. (Summer), pp. 2:1–2:6, September 2018. https://doi.org/10.1145/3266231.3266233
3. Hargood, C., Mitchell, A., Millard, D.E., Spierling, U.: Authoring for interactive storytelling workshop. In: Nunes, N., Oakley, I., Nisi, V. (eds.) ICIDS 2017. LNCS, vol. 10690, pp. 405–408. Springer, Cham (2017). https://doi.org/10.1007/978-3-319-71027-3_54
4. Spierling, U., Iurgel, I.: Workshop and panel: the authoring process in interactive storytelling. In: Spierling, U., Szilas, N. (eds.) ICIDS 2008. LNCS, vol. 5334, p. 331. Springer, Heidelberg (2008). https://doi.org/10.1007/978-3-540-89454-4_43
5. Spierling, U., Iurgel, I., Richle, U., Szilas, N.: Workshop on authoring methods and conception in interactive storytelling. In: Iurgel, I.A., Zagalo, N., Petta, P. (eds.) ICIDS 2009. LNCS, vol. 5915, pp. 356–357. Springer, Heidelberg (2009). https://doi.org/10.1007/978-3-642-10643-9_50
6. Spierling, U., Mitchell, A.: Story modeling and authoring. In: The Seventh International Conference on Interactive Digital Storytelling (ICIDS 2014), vol. 8832, pp. 262–263. Springer, Cham (2014). https://doi.org/10.1007/978-3-319-12337-0
7. Spierling, U., Szilas, N., Hoffmann, S., Richle, U.: Workshop: education in interactive digital storytelling. In: Aylett, R., Lim, M.Y., Louchart, S., Petta, P., Riedl, M. (eds.) ICIDS 2010. LNCS, vol. 6432, pp. 289–290. Springer, Heidelberg (2010). https://doi.org/10.1007/978-3-642-16638-9_45

Creating Interactive Adaptive Real Time Story Worlds

Henrik Schoenau-Fog[✉] and Bjarke Alexander Larsen

The Center for Applied Game Research (CEAGAR)
and Samsung Media Innovation Lab for Education (SMILE Lab),
Department of Architecture, Design and Media Technology,
Section of Medialogy, Aalborg University, Copenhagen, Denmark
hsf@create.aau.dk, mail@bjarke.it

Abstract. This workshop aims at exploring and addressing the challenges of creating interactive adaptive real-time story worlds. Participants will through various activities create their own concept of such experiences while investigating the potential of the field. The workshop will furthermore invite for international collaborations focusing of creating novel formats for interactive adaptive real-time digital storytelling.

Keywords: Interactive digital storytelling · Adaptive real-time story worlds
The narrative paradox · Storytelling · Real-time film- and animation production

1 Introduction and Topic

In recent years, the film- and TV industry has finally realized the potential for using the real-time capabilities of GPUs and game engines for creating content in the traditional linear formats, as productions can now be played back live and interactively directly in a game engine.

The technologies have for example recently been used in the production of animated TV series (e.g. 'Zafari' (Unreal Engine 2018)) and short films (e.g. 'Adam' episodes I-III in Unity 3D (Oats Studios 2018)).

With these powerful real-time production technologies, there is not only a potential to make linear productions more streamlined, creative and cheaper, but we can also utilise the exact same technologies (and content) for creating new forms of interactive narrative content. This obviously calls for the expansion of novel forms of interactive adaptive real-time story world experiences (Schoenau-Fog 2015).

In such experiences, the narrative understanding may emerge through the participant's/user's behaviour and individual actions in an interactive digital story world, where the experience is adapted to the user in real-time by using e.g.:

- Procedural/generative design (where the experience is created by the computer on-the-fly).
- Artificial Intelligence (AI - where virtual actors are interacting with the user).
- Machine learning (where the computer for example is used to create and orchestrate events and actions in a storyworld, based on user behaviour).

R. Rouse et al. (Eds.): ICIDS 2018, LNCS 11318, pp. 548–551, 2018.
https://doi.org/10.1007/978-3-030-04028-4_64

- Interactive characters recorded as performance avatars (virtual actors) and Real-Time Cinematography (E.g. Ninja Theory 2016).
- Knowledge about sustained user engagement in story worlds (e.g. Schoenau-Fog 2011)
- Game mechanics and narrative (Larsen and Schoenau-Fog 2016).

However, we believe that all this state-of-the-art technology is only a fraction of the equation. One of the challenges of creating these experiences is: How can the user's engagement in an interactive non-linear adaptive real-time free-roaming open story-world - e.g. as the one exemplified in Unity's 'Book of the Dead' project (Unity 2018) - be maintained by a 'story world builder' without the use of traditional linear dramaturgy and game mechanics?

In order to address such questions and to challenge traditional storytelling by developing truly novel interactive narrative formats beyond pre-determined branching structures, we need to create a fertile ground by launching an interdisciplinary community, where individuals, companies, and stakeholders with different backgrounds and skills meet. In such a collaboration, interactive storytelling scholars, film directors, programmers, game developers, 3D designers, sound engineers and other stakeholders are given the opportunity to experiment with the possibilities and address the challenges.

This workshop will be the one of the first steps in that direction

2 Purpose and Goals of the Workshop

The main purpose of the workshop is to address the grand challenges of creating engaging interactive adaptive real time story world experiences by exploring the field through conceptualization. In other words: How can we conceptualize experiences in interactive adaptive real-time story worlds, which are exploiting the latest real-time technologies, while making users want to continue, in purposeful, short intense experiences?

Furthermore, the goals are to advance knowledge, set a direction for future discoveries, to identify challenges, to initiate an international community and gather ideas about future collaborative activities.

3 Format

Participants will be introduced to the concept of Interactive Adaptive Real-Time Story Worlds (iARTs) and will explore the potential by creating their own concept of such experiences through a number of hands-on activities. These activities will contain the conceptualization of various story worlds through exercises concerned with lifeless worlds, interactive worlds, worlds with entities, engaging worlds and worlds driven by the latest technologies.

Participants will thus explore the field, share their knowledge, discuss and identify the challenges of the creation and implementation of iARTs and suggest future activities while discovering possible solutions of the challenges of creating these story worlds.

Potential participants are interactive digital storytelling scholars and practitioners, storytellers, film directors, VFX creators, game designers and -developers, programmers, asset creators, media companies etc.

4   Expected Outcome

The expected outcome of the workshop is that each participant will gain knowledge of creating a concept of an engaging Interactive Adaptive Real-Time Story World. The concepts may later be used as inspiration for multiple purposes, for example learning, communication, entertainment or simulation.

Participants will also meet like-minded scholars and practitioners with the potential of future international collaborations within this field. Furthermore, the community initiated at this workshop will be invited for future workshops, events and summits concerned with the VIZARTs project, funded by the Nordisk Film Foundation.

5   Conclusion

Ever since the early days of interactive digital storytelling, one of the ultimate goals and holy grails has been to create interactive adaptive real-time story worlds (e.g. The Holodeck (Murray, 2017) and interactive theatrical experiences (Laurel 2013)). In the last couple of years, a range of technological advances have been made, which may have potential to change the scene. This workshop will (probably) not solve all the problems of this endeavour – however, participants will together gather knowledge and address the challenges by exploring the potential that these new technologies and formats may give.

Acknowledgements. We would like to thank the Nordisk Film Foundation for supporting the VIZARTs project (VIsualiZation & Adaptive Real-Time Storytelling) and we are grateful for colleagues' and students' work on the project at Aalborg University. Finally, we would like to thank our partner, Samsung, who have provided equipment for many of the Interactive Digital Storytelling experiments conducted in the SMILE Lab.

References

Unreal Engine: Zafari. Tapping into Unreal Engine for Episodic Animation - Project Spotlight (2018). Video: https://www.youtube.com/watch?v=Mfqj3CFZyxU
Oats Studios/Unity: Project Adam (2018). Video: https://unity.com/madewith/adam

Schoenau-Fog, H.: Adaptive storyworlds - utilizing the space-time continuum in interactive digital storytelling. In: Schoenau-Fog, H., Bruni, L.E., Louchart, S., Baceviciute, S. (eds.) ICIDS 2015. LNCS, vol. 9445, pp. 58–65. Springer, Cham (2015). https://doi.org/10.1007/978-3-319-27036-4_6

Ninja Theory: Introducing Realtime Cinematography in Hellblade (2016). Video: https://www.youtube.com/watch?v=KeNXEjNkEs0

Schoenau-Fog, H.: Hooked! – evaluating engagement as continuation desire in interactive narratives. In: Si, M., Thue, D., André, E., Lester, J.C., Tanenbaum, J., Zammitto, V. (eds.) ICIDS 2011. LNCS, vol. 7069, pp. 219–230. Springer, Heidelberg (2011). https://doi.org/10.1007/978-3-642-25289-1_24

Larsen, B.A., Schoenau-Fog, H.: The narrative quality of game mechanics. In: Nack, F., Gordon, A.S. (eds.) ICIDS 2016. LNCS, vol. 10045, pp. 61–72. Springer, Cham (2016). https://doi.org/10.1007/978-3-319-48279-8_6

Unity: 'Book of the Dead' (2018). Video: https://unity3d.com/book-of-the-dead

Murray, J.H.: Hamlet on the Holodeck: The Future of Narrative in Cyberspace. MIT press, Cambridge (2017)

Laurel, B.: Computers as Theatre. Addison-Wesley, Upper Saddle River (2013)

Card-Based Methods in Interactive Narrative Prototyping

Hartmut Koenitz[1], Teun Dubbelman[1](✉), Noam Knoller[1],
Christian Roth[1], Mads Haahr[2], Digdem Sezen[3],
and Tonguc Ibrahim Sezen[4]

[1] Professorship Interactive Narrative Design, HKU University of the Arts
Utrecht, Nieuwekade 1, Postbox 1520, 3500 BM Utrecht, Netherlands
{Hartmut.koenitz,teun.dubbelman,noam.knoller,
christian.roth}@hku.nl
[2] School of Computer Science and Statistics, Trinity College, Dublin, Ireland
Mads.Haahr@cs.tcd.ie
[3] Faculty of Communications, Istanbul University, Kaptani Derya Ibrahim Pasa
Sk., 34452 Beyazit, Istanbul, Turkey
dsezen@istanbul.edu.tr
[4] Rhine-Waal University of Applied Sciences, Friedrich-Heinrich-Allee 25,
47475 Kamp-Lintfort, Germany
tongucibrahim.sezen@hochschule-rhein-waal.de

Abstract. Paper prototyping plays an important role in the creation of inter-active digital narratives (IDN). A structured prototyping approach can help improve the process of making IDNs. In particular, pre-made, specialized card designs can speed up the process considerably and also help in the transition to digital prototypes. In this workshop, we will introduce structured methods and use pre-made cards in successive rounds of working towards a detailed proto-type. Participant's feedback by means of questionnaires will also be used as a basis for future research.

Keywords: Interactive digital narrative · Interactive storytelling
Paper prototyping · Education · Pedagogy · Interactive narrative design

1 Introduction

Paper prototyping plays an important role in the creation of interactive digital narratives (IDN) (e.g. [1]). A structured prototyping approach can help improve the process of creating IDNs. In particular, pre-made, specialized card designs can speed up the process considerably and also help in the transition to digital prototypes. In this workshop, we will introduce structured methods and use pre-made cards in successive rounds of working towards a detailed prototype. We will also use this opportunity to evaluate different approaches through questionnaires and interviews.

R. Rouse et al. (Eds.): ICIDS 2018, LNCS 11318, pp. 552–555, 2018.
https://doi.org/10.1007/978-3-030-04028-4_65

2 Paper Prototyping

Paper-based approaches are often observed in the practice of interactive narrative design, for example in workshops [1] (see Fig. 1), but also in presentations at venues such as the Narrative Summit at the Games Developer Conference often show index cards or post-its on the wall of design companies and game studios.

Fig. 1. Paper-based prototyping at 2016 ACM TVX workshop [1]

2.1 Related Work

While the use of such paper-based methods is certainly methodological, it is striking how arbitrary its application in interactive narrative design appears. In contrast, specialized approaches towards card-based prototyping exist in game design [2–4] or for user interfaces [5]. Similarly, pre-made cards exist as tools to facilitate general design ideation [6]. In the case of creative writing, Storymatic's cards[1] are used by writers to generate story ideas through the combination of cards with the goal to create a non-interactive narrative.

Card games provide additional inspiration for paper-based prototyping. In the storytelling card game *Once Upon A Time* [7] players co-create a story using cards

---

[1] https://thestorymatic.com.

containing tropes from fairy tales. The goal for each player – as storyteller - is to lead their respective story to its ending without being replaced by other potential story-tellers. If a player mentions a trope on a card owned by another player, the other player can take over the story and move the plot in a new direction. Thus, players must recognize and use story tropes but also should be creative and try avoiding them. *Once Upon A Time* trope cards have been suggested as a writing aid for linear fiction [8] but the game mechanic can be seen inspirational for IDN creation. In particular, the spatial or thematic exploration points within the fictional world can be seen as precursors of interactive narrative branching points.

2.2   Interactive Narrative Prototyping

There is thus an opportunity for prototyping cards which are purpose-made for inter-active narratives. On this backdrop, we have developed several versions of paper

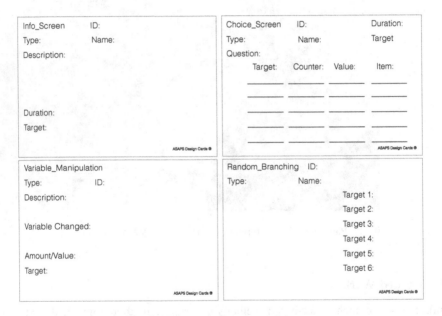

Fig. 2. Four cards from one of the sets.

design cards (see Fig. 2 for an example) and will use this material for the workshop.

For example, the cards in Fig. 1 represent beats – narrative units – in the IDN system ASAPS [9]. They are an intermediate step between free-form cards and using the actual program and while they can be used for general purpose they are especially designed to enable rapid prototyping for a particular platform.

3 Workshop Format

The half-day workshop kicks off with an introduction to the topic. A Research-through-Workshop (RtW) approach (thematic introductions, brief directed discussions, collaborative sketching and reasoned comparisons), developed in the organizers' previous workshops, will be employed to produce insights through collective brainstorming at the conference and online. The process places emphasis on informal discussion, is programmatically open-ended, and will produce raw data, which will be accessible to the research community through a public website.

The workshop is designed for up to 20 participants. After a short introduction, participants will be divided into groups. They will start with the same material to develop an interactive narrative prototype, but use different sets of prototyping cards in iterative steps. At the end of the workshop, the results will be compared and evaluated. This data is intended to generate insights for education and future research.

4 Call for Participation

We invite participants to our half-day workshop on paper-based prototyping for interactive digital narratives. Participants will learn how to apply a structured approach to prototyping, using purpose-made cards. In the process of developing a prototype, participants will get to know several card-based formats and through their feedback will help us to improve the card sets. The call for the workshop will be posted at http://interactivenarrativedesign.org/icids2018ws/. Results will also be shared at this location.

References

1. Koenitz, H.: Design strategies for interactive digital narratives. Presented at the Proceedings of the ACM International Conference on Interactive Experiences for TV and Online Video, New York, NY, USA (2016)
2. Fullerton, T., Swain, C., Hoffman, S.S.: Game Design Workshop. Morgan Kaufmann, Burlington (2008)
3. Design Tool: Exertion Cards. http://exertiongameslab.org/projects/design-tools-exertion-cards
4. Sezen, T.I.: Analog prototyping for digital game design. In: Lee, N. (ed.) Encyclopedia of Computer Graphics and Games, pp. 1–3. Springer, Cham (2018). https://doi.org/10.1007/978-3-319-08234-9
5. Snyder, C.: Paper Prototyping. Morgan Kaufmann, Burlington (2003)
6. Golembewski, M., Selby, M.: Ideation decks: a card-based design ideation tool. Presented at the Proceedings of the 8th ACM Conference on Designing Interactive Systems (2010)
7. Lambert, R., Rilstone, A., Wallis, J.: Once Upon a Time (1994)
8. Olmstead, K.: Once Upon a Time Writer's Handbook (2013)
9. Koenitz, H., Chen, K.-J.: Genres, structures and strategies in interactive digital narratives – analyzing a body of works created in ASAPS. In: Oyarzun, D., Peinado, F., Young, R.M., Elizalde, A., Méndez, G. (eds.) ICIDS 2012. LNCS, vol. 7648, pp. 84–95. Springer, Heidelberg (2012). https://doi.org/10.1007/978-3-642-34851-8_8

Novella: An Authoring Tool for Interactive Storytelling in Games

Daniel Green[✉]

Bournemouth University, Poole, UK
dgreen@bournemouth.ac.uk

Abstract. This research focuses on authoring tools and narrative models for interactive storytelling, in particular for video games. Specifically, it looks at developing a genre-independent model of interactive narrative for games, implementing such a model into an authoring tool, and identifying the impact of various interface paradigms on the authoring experience and resulting narratives.

Keywords: Hypertext · Narrative modeling · Interactive narrative
Authoring tools · User experience

1 Overview and Research Questions

This research is being conducted at Bournemouth University as part of a PhD focusing on authoring tools for digital storytelling. It is a combination of narrative theory meshed with authoring tool development and experimentation. I am currently around ten months into the degree as of this submission, and when the conference runs, 14 months.

We are trying to answer how interactive narrative can be modelled in a genre-agnostic way such that it is suitable for structural analysis and development. We are also exploring how a developed model can be implemented in an effective author-friendly tool. Additionally, we are investigating the poetic impact that varying types of interface paradigms have on the authoring experience and the resulting narrative as to better understand the effects of design decisions.

While this project is looking at interactive narrative on the whole, there is a special interest in the domain of video game narrative in particular. The outcomes of this PhD are expected to be a new model of interactive narrative that is able to capture the nuances of storytelling in video games, a well-refined authoring tool implementing such a model, as well as an understanding of the impact that various interface paradigms have on the authoring experience and resulting narratives.

2 Narrative Model

We have developed a narrative model that targets video game stories. Our initial research [5] had us explore existing models of interactive narrative, both game-specific and not. The observations made in this analysis provided us with a clear

R. Rouse et al. (Eds.): ICIDS 2018, LNCS 11318, pp. 556–559, 2018.
https://doi.org/10.1007/978-3-030-04028-4_66

understanding of previous approaches and techniques. As part of the analysis, we had applied various models to narratively simple[1] and comparatively complex[2] games to see which areas were able to be represented and which faced difficulties. The most influential in our analysis were a couple of Proppian variations [3,4], Aarseth's model [1], the CANVAS project [6], and Bernstein's hypertext patterns [2]. These observations of technique and gaps were crucial in the design of our model, as well as much experience playing games to identify areas of narrative that may be difficult to capture.

Our model's primary contribution was in the representation of narrative elements within video games that can be discovered, observed, or experienced – *Discoverable Narrative*. For example, item descriptions, collectable letters, findable books, mechanics as metaphor, and so on. Our solution consisted of a four-dimensional matrix that when combined could represent these abstract narrative elements. Figure 1 explains the different elements of the matrix. We plan to refine and update the model to better define it in terms of data. It has been implemented in its current form as the base for our own authoring tool.

Tangibility	Tangible	Intangible
	Text attached to an in-game object.	Text **not** attached to an in-game object.
Functionality	Narrative	Mechanical
	Primary purpose is for narrative.	Primary purpose is **not** for narrative.
Clarity	Explicit	Implicit
	Clearly and well defined.	Abstract and interpretative.
Delivery	Active	Passive
	Requires interaction to be consumed.	Is observed or experienced regardless of direct interaction.

Fig. 1. Discoverable narrative matrix of our model.

3 Authoring Tool

We have began development on our own authoring tool which contains an implementation of our model at its foundations. The tool will continue development, especially as usability and impact experiments take place. Regardless of being a working prototype, the developmental level is already quite mature. Its interface can be seen in Fig. 2.

Prior to development of this authoring interface, we undertook a detailed study of HCI and UX principles to better create an informed design. Notable sources include Nielsen's Usability Heuristics [7] and the Laws of UX[3]. Our tool has a large focus on UX design. The principles and techniques learned during

---

[1] Portal, Valve Corporation, 2007.

[2] The Stanley Parable, Galactic Cafe, 2013.

[3] https://lawsofux.com by Jon Yablonski. Many of the laws are grounded in research, and the few that are not are widely accepted heuristics.

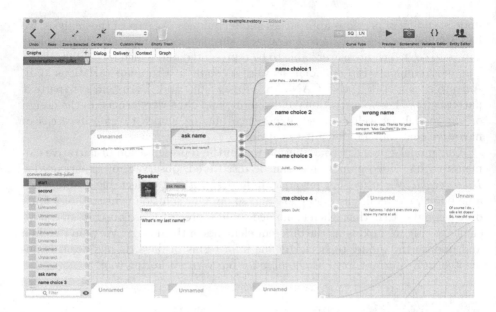

Fig. 2. The main interface of the authoring tool.

reading and a meta-analysis of existing tools have been largely implemented in our tool's UI design and authoring flow.

We opted for a node-based graph for story visualization and editing as our analysis showed it to be an efficient and reliable method, as well as the most prominent in existing tools, when displaying interconnected data. Much thought has gone into UX and interface design, mostly for the graph, to help reduce cognitive friction for authors using the system. For instance, the distinct coloring of node types, highlighting paths of selected nodes, and so on. We have also tried to reduce UI clutter where possible to further mitigate cognitive friction. For example, the content of our nodes are edited through non-modal popup dialogs that can be easily raised and dismissed, and optionally converted to floating windows. Similarly, features that are less commonly used than the main graph, such as variable editors, entity editors, and story previewing, are hidden in the toolbar until requested by the author.

We have developed this authoring tool as we would like to explore UX flows and designs that are not present in existing systems. We also plan to run experiments comparing the impact on the authoring experience of other UX approaches compared to our own.

4   Next Steps

We intend to continue refining our narrative model to better define video game narrative. This is a continual process, although we would like to largely finalize the model by next year.

Development of the tool will likewise continue until ready for experimentation. We plan for initial usability experiments experiments to run shortly that will allow us to refine the UX and interface design based on expert user feedback.

To better understand the impact on authoring of existing systems, we intend to run multiple experiments pinpointing specific areas of the authoring experience (primarily surrounding UX and interface presentation in order to discover the impact they have). These studies are still being designed. These experiments would also include our own system as to compare the impact of our own designs relative to existing works.

References

1. Aarseth, E.: A narrative theory of games. In: Proceedings of FDG 2012, pp. 129–133. ACM (2012)
2. Bernstein, M.: Patterns of hypertext. In: Proceedings of HT 1998, pp. 21–29. ACM (1998)
3. Bostan, B., Turan, O.: Deconstructing game stories with propp's morphology. System **17**, 18 (2017)
4. Brusentsev, A., Hitchens, M., Richards, D.: An investigation of Vladimir Propp's 31 functions and 8 broad character types and how they apply to the analysis of video games. In: Proceedings of IE 2012. pp. 2:1–2:10. ACM (2012)
5. Green, D., Hargood, C., Charles, F., Jones, A.: Novella: a proposition for game-based storytelling. In: Narrative and Hypertext 2018. ACM, July 2018
6. Kapadia, M., Frey, S., Shoulson, A., Sumner, R.W., Gross, M.: CANVAS: computer-assisted narrative animation synthesis. In: Proceedings of SCA 2016, pp. 199–209. Eurographics Association (2016)
7. Nielsen, J.: Enhancing the explanatory power of usability heuristics. In: Proceedings of the SIGCHI Conference on Human Factors in Computing Systems, CHI 1994, pp. 152–158. ACM (1994)

Impacts in Culture and Society

Spatial Participation Gap: Towards a Conceptual Perspective on Locative Storytelling Creation

Cláudia Silva(✉) [ID]

Madeira Interactive Technologies Institute, Funchal, Madeira Islands, Portugal
claudia.silva@m-iti.org

Abstract. This article draws on a historical need to use locative media to understand information in order to offer a critical conceptual perspective on those who do not have the means to create locative storytelling as a result of what is called participation gap. By drawing on two case studies with ethnographical data, one in Austin, Texas, US, and another in Monmouth, Wales, UK, I discuss the use of mobile interfaces such as QRcodes and the creation of location-based storytelling. Finally, the article introduces the notion of 'spatial participation gap', which is the unequal access to spaces and hybrid spaces.

Keywords: Hybrid space · Locative media · Locative storytelling
QRcodes · Underserved communities · Spatial segregation · Participation gap

1 Introduction

Interactive digital storytelling (IDS) is an interdisciplinary field that extends traditional storytelling through digital media. As Sizemore et al. [34] have noted, most research endeavors in IDS have focused on fictional storytelling. In this paper, I concentrate on the discussion of examples of non-fictional locative stories and locative technologies that enable interactivity and are anchored in physical places as well as the virtual. Packer et al. [27] describe locative stories as, "narratives read on mobile devices where the reader interacts with the story by physically moving between locations." For the purpose of this article, locative stories are defined as those created based on places and which are digitally or physically attached to them via technologies such as RFID, NFC, QRcodes, AR.

Farman [7] argues that people have attempted to attach stories to places for as long as tales have existed. He draws on McCullough [21] who has described two kinds of site-specific stories: durable inscriptions – such as those carved into stone or into the side of a building – and ephemeral inscriptions like graffiti, banners, and billboards. In addition, Farman [7] examines how these two forms of site-specific storytelling – named "urban markup" by McCullough – demonstrate the power dynamics and hierarchies involved in who is allowed to tell the story of a space. Those with economic wealth tend to be the ones who are able to place durable inscriptions throughout a city,

© Springer Nature Switzerland AG 2018
R. Rouse et al. (Eds.): ICIDS 2018, LNCS 11318, pp. 563–576, 2018.
https://doi.org/10.1007/978-3-030-04028-4_67

while graffiti, a sort of ephemeral locative media, tends to be created by those without power. Farman's viewpoint led me to consider the divide between those disadvantaged groups in current times who do not have the conditions and/or means to produce locative storytelling and therefore display stories in hybrid spaces, by merging physical and virtual places [3, 11]. To lay the foundations of my argument, I first turn to historical evidence about our fundamental need to use geographical tools to understand information. Attempting to avoid technological determinism, the goal of this approach is to critically argue that locative stories are not necessarily an outcome of GPS-enabled devices or other locative technologies. In this sense, I suggest elsewhere [32] that the fundamental notion of using maps to understand information, or to display storytelling, existed before the conceptualization of media, as some scholars presently understand it.

Actual maps functioned as a graphical supplement to newspapers, which readers could use to tie the stories and happenings to the locations where they occurred [32]. This argument is based on the work of the French scholar Jean Pierre Vittu [19, 39] who presented that, without the ability to consult maps [39], readers from the late 17th and early 18th centuries perceived news as a maze. Maps could be sold in the form of a bound atlas or as individual pages. Usually, readers could buy maps from newspaper vendors, or find them hanging at the front of bookstores specializing in geographical texts alongside the clock tower in Paris [Quai de l'Horloge]. The practice of using maps to understand information, local and foreign continued across centuries, as can be seen in the image from the 20th century, below.

On the image below (Fig. 1), a man climbs a ladder to update a map. A crowd of people waits for him to finish in order to learn the latest events of the First World War. According to the website "Paris en Images," from which this photograph was taken, the newspaper *Excelsior* gave this map to Parisians in late August, 1917 precisely so they could have a better understanding of the latest events of the war by visualizing them on the map. If we think of how digital maps are becoming handy today, due to their integration into smartphones, these images become much more powerful for their historical weight, and for their depiction of the eagerness to understand events and localize them in the world. Research in the 1980's provides evidence that maps enhance the comprehension of a story [10] or of news reports [22]. The relevance of maps for understanding information is also supported by more recent and seminal work on locative media by Gordon and de Souza e Silva [14], and others [24–26]. The rationale of this article relies on this historical hint that there was perhaps an ancient need to use locative media.

This paper proposes a critical debate about several local, under-served, communities that face what is called by Jenkins in media studies, *participation gap* [17], in the making of locative and mobile content. This includes geo-tagged content, locative storytelling or, more broadly, contributions to participatory media enabled by digital media. The main goal of this article is to challenge the assumption that anyone can be a content creator in the context of locative storytelling, as there are a multitude of socio-economic and socio-political constraints in play.

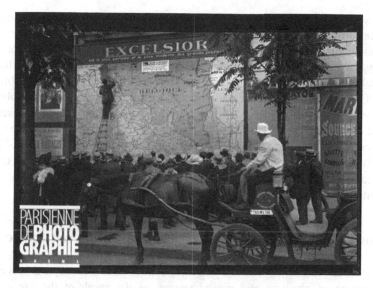

Fig. 1. Map in Paris. Source: parisenimages.fr

Jenkins [17] defines participation gap as "the unequal access to the opportunities, experiences, skills, and knowledge that will prepare youth for full participation in the world of tomorrow". In their book on locative media, Gordon and de Souza e Silva [14] draw on Jenkins [16], reflecting on the notion that it is not just a matter of simply having the technology but, rather, knowing what to do with it. Past research has shown that due to the widespread adoption of Internet-enabled mobile devices, digital divides based on access are no longer as significant as they once were [38]. What may constitute a challenge for under-served communities is having the knowledge and skills to take advantage of location-based services in order to augment experiences of place [12].

It is also relevant to note that, despite the participatory features of digital media communications platforms, participation gaps have not been eradicated [40]. With this in mind, Shaw and Hargittai [31] conceptualized online participation using the metaphor of a pipeline "to represent a sequence of stages through which an individual must pass in order to become more actively engaged in knowledge consumption and production activities through digital media". Based on this metaphor, the authors [31] suggest that "first, a user must have heard of a site to be able to contribute to it. Second, a user must have visited the site to participate in it. Third, a user must understand that it is possible to make contributions to the site in order to add content."

The authors continue to say that only once these conditions are met can a user participate in a site. Finally, Shaw and Hargittai [31] explain that this model describes a general sequence applicable to diverse contexts of online engagement, such as discussion threads on major news media sites like *The Guardian* or *Slate*, social media platforms like Facebook or Instagram, as well as sites dedicated to particular engagement activities such as support groups or learning. In their findings, the authors suggest that the "intermediate stages" matter and "that reducing gaps at these intermediate stages of the participation pipeline would make more equitable participation patterns possible".

As it will be explained throughout this paper, particularly in the section "From cyberspace to hybrid space and splintered space", we should engage with an in-depth understanding of sociopolitical context in the design of authoring tools for locative storytelling by addressing communities facing spatial segregation, or knowledge and skill gaps. With this research context in mind, and drawing on theories of mobile media [4, 7, 8, 41] studies, the concept of hybrid space [3, 11] generated by mobile technologies, and participation gap [5, 30, 38, 40], I draw on ethnographical observations conducted in Austin, Texas, US (case 1), and in Monmouth, Wales, UK (case 2). The data was collected in the context of doctoral studies by the author, between 2012 and 2014. Although the cases are very distinct, both cases involve the use of QRcodes, approached herein as locative media technologies, bridging the physical and virtual world thereby creating hybrid space.

2   From Cyberspace to Hybrid Space and Splintered Space

Hybrid space, as Adriana de Souza e Silva [3] defines it, is a conceptual space created by the merging of physical and digital spaces, as the result of the use of mobile technologies as social devices. She proposes the concept of hybrid space because, as she argues, cyberspace is no longer an appropriate term to describe the changes of socialization brought about by utilizing smartphones in the urban space. As she explains, "the concept of cyberspace applied to the Internet was responsible first for our view of physical and digital as disconnected spaces, second for our emphasis on the nodes of the networks instead is its spatial structure, and finally for the utopian view of the future in which social spaces would emerge mostly online". Smartphones disrupt this idea as they bring Internet connection into physical spaces.

De Souza e Silva [3] explains the need for a different perspective: "the concept of hybrid spaces arises to supply a gap opened when the Internet became mobile and when communities previously formed in cyberspace could be found in urban (hybrid) spaces". An interesting aspect of the concept of hybrid space is that, rather than thinking about immersion (e.g. the feeling of entering the Internet, or being in cyberspace), users may be more concerned about how their smartphones assist them in physical space and in places through location awareness by accessing historical information, locative storytelling, etc.

Unlike those [13, 28, 29] who argue that mobile phones detach people from physical and public spaces, de Souza e Silva [3] posits that, "in the hybrid-space logic, cell phones do not take users out of physical space".

In his 2015 book, the locative media scholar Jordan Frith [12], explains that the concept of hybrid space is useful for understanding the social impacts of smartphones as locative media [12]. When examining the future of locative media, Frith [12] presents the correlation between the increasing adoption of locative media and digital inequality as an area of concern for future research in locative media. Rather than use demographic numbers (which populations own smartphones and which do not), Frith [12] discusses how hybrid spaces may raise new issues of access and digital literacy.

This author [11] claims the hybrid spaces are not determined by technology and technological production, but are the outcome of social interactions and social production, although the author recognizes that, without access to the relevant technologies, there is no access to hybrid space. Extending the concept of hybrid space, Frith [11] proposes the concept of "splintered space," which is a combination of the concepts of "differential mobility" and the "digital divide".

"Differential mobility" refers to how people move through space (e.g. cities) and how mobility is a resource distributed unequally among social groups. Frith [11] points out the difference between someone driving a car to work with someone taking a city bus and argues the difference between these two types of mobility is the qualitative nature of mobility and how much control individuals have over their experiences while mobile. The term "splintered space" was derived from the book *Splintered Urbanism* by Graham and Marvin [15], which refers to the many ways the infrastructure of urban areas splinters access to services and mobility (paid fast-lanes, privatized skywalks, restricted access to places). For Frith [11], a new form of splintered urbanism is the "divide between those who have access to hybrid spaces and those who do not".

3 Case Study 1: Austin, Texas

The city of Austin, Texas, is considered a *Technopolis,* or technology-centered city economy, where technological skills and access are even more highly required for one to succeed in the labor market and education, and where the techno-field has been expanded to include almost everyone [35]. At the same time, Austin is one the most economically segregated metropolises in the US, according to [9]. For this case study, I draw on data collected in the context of locative media training in Southeast Austin, where the population is predominantly low-income Latino immigrants of Mexican descent and remains informally segregated living in run down neighborhoods.

This case study was carried out in 2013 within the scope of 45 days in a bilingual (Spanish and English) community computer training program provided by the non profit organization River City Youth Foundation (RCYF) [33]. For first task of the locative media training, the participants were invited to think of a meaningful location in their neighborhood. After choosing that location, participants had to take a photo of the location, or use one they already had. Then, they were asked to write a story about the place they had chosen, which could be based on personal memory, recent historical events, or current facts. As a final task, they had to upload the photo's location and geotag their story on the map of Austin via an already existing website, Historypin. Five women and two men, ranging in age from 34 to 64, were able to finish their locative stories and were interviewed afterwards.

Regarding the mobile and locative part of the training, participants were introduced to tablets and smartphones as tools to enhance everyday life. In order to do that, the researcher showed examples of mobile applications such as Camscanner, HeartBeat Instant Rate, and QRcodes readers, which would enable them to use their camera phone to do things beyond taking pictures. They were also introduced to how "location" is used in applications, such as Foursquare, Trulia, UrbanSpoon, Yelp, iJobs, Poetika, among others. Possible drawbacks of location sharing, such as stalking, unsolicited advertising, tracking, and surveillance were also discussed. Afterwards, the researcher introduced the concept of locative stories to the participants by sharing with them her own story channel on a content driven location-based application and website [33].

The study generated nine location-based stories that were digitally overlaid on the Austin map via the website/mobile application Historypin and published there on a page created for this project, entitled "Mapping Austin Memories[1]". Almost all the stories were written on a laptop computer at the organization, even though the participants used their own smartphones to take pictures. All the stories were written in the first person and included memories of moving to the United States and adapting to Austin, opinions about a dual language program school, experiences of facing a tragic flood, the experience of leading a community project to turn a park into a soccer field, and of computer learning at the organization, where the study was conducted.

I will provide reflections on their process of creating locative stories, and the sociotechnical limitations of authoring locative systems related to the hybrid space for this type of socio-demographic group living in segregated areas. Returning to the concept of splintered urbanism, a particular example I want to discuss is the case of Gisela (pseudonym), a Mexican immigrant, aged 39, who had been living in Austin for six years at the time of the study and moved around the city by bus. She wrote her story about the house where she was living, and the struggles about moving to an unfamiliar place. She begins her story: *"When you are taking the decision of moving to a new city, where you do not have any family or you do not know a lot of people, is important to have at least someone to help you to settle down"* (see Fig. 2).

Fig. 2. Screenshot of the locative story produced by a local resident in Austin, Texas, and geotagged through Historypin in the channel "Mapping Austin Memories"

---

[1] See at https://www.historypin.org/en/person/47908.

The processes involved in creating her locative story provide an interesting case. Throughout the locative media training, I attempted to convey the concept of places having hidden stories and encouraged participants to look around to find meaningful places they wanted to write about. Following this instruction, Gisela first wanted to write about a place close to her house, which looked like for her a new school. She gave up on that location because, as she said in her interview, she could not find any information online about the place, or through the people who were working there. Throughout the training, Gisela struggled to find a place that was meaningful for her and eventually chose perhaps the most intimate one: her house. That led me to ask her how she learned about places.

She replied that she uses her smartphone to learn directions if she has an appointment. As she said "*checo en el mapa y ubico la dirección y lo pongo en lo mapa, y miro al capital metro*" or ("*I check the map, I search for a location, and use the capital metro*"). Gisela mentioned that after learning about QRcodes in the locative media training, she downloaded a QRcode reader application to learn about the bus schedule, facilitated by a public transportation company in Austin, Capital Metro. During the locative media training, several participants said they did not know what QRcodes were. When asked if she used her smartphone to explore new and unknown places, Gisela said no. It is interesting to note that she looked only for places she needed to go to meet her immediate needs. In her words: "*No tengo necesidade de ir a lugares que no conozco.*" ("*I have no need to go to places that I do not know*"). "*Conozco muchos lugares en Dove Springs pero no hay esta conexión*" or ("*I know many places in Dove Springs - the neighborhood where she lives- but there is no connection with them*"). Arguably, there are many reasons for this limited exploration of place, such as motivation, subjectivity, or simply the comfort of being close to home but other possible factors could be presented, such as differential mobility.

This is more easily understood if we consider the struggles and financial distress that low-income immigrants may well face. Due to several socioeconomic as well as psychological factors, lower income immigrants often have far less time to explore leisure activities and places in a serendipitous way (a concept that some consider key for locative storytelling). Several participants in this study said they wrote the first story of their lives during the locative media training. A 64 year-old woman who had been living in Austin for 20 years, said she never thought she would be able to write a story. She wrote two short pieces - one about a community project she was involved in, and another about a devastating flood that swept through the community in 2013 and caused the death of five people.

Gisela's story potentially illustrates the relevance of investing in training to foster use of existing and future authoring tools related to locative storytelling. Designers of authoring tools, and locative writers for IDS, should perhaps take into account that not all people move around places equally, and so social, economic, and digital barriers to the design of tools, or creation of place-based stories, could be a consideration. This concern with locations has been addressed by [27], whose study advises locative content writers pay attention to certain locations that are difficult to reach (e.g., steep hill or steps, or other difficult to access locations). This current paper brings to the discussion a different aspect concerning location in locative content creation; that is a sociopolitical one that addresses the limitations some people face due to informal segregation.

Regarding the relevance of locations for locative storytelling tools and locative writers, it is important to stress that, as Frith [11] articulates, experiencing mobility in a qualitatively different way may affect how people perceive places and, specifically, hybrid spaces. These issues of space become even more prevalent when talking about a segregated space because there are interrelated issues that complicate the splintered space. Firstly, segregated spaces typically deal with a lack of digital information or digital locative storytelling (e.g., geotagged stories), as the inhabitants often do not have the skills and knowledge to author their own digital storytelling. Secondly, when location information regarding the segregated space is available, an outsider has often produced it (such as professional writers or content producers, or students, etc.); Inhabitants of that segregated space *a priori* might not have the knowledge and skills to access it.

That said, I would suggest that *spatial segregation may contribute to the advancement of another sort of segregation, a kind that goes beyond the physical space, which also encompasses the virtual world: the so-called hybrid space, understood as the merging of virtual and physicals spaces.* One could challenge this rationale by claiming that, with the diffusion of social networking websites and mobile apps, people are able to extend their social ties and social capital [6]. However, if the majority of inhabitants of segregated spaces are excluded from hybrid space, they are less likely to expand their social networks through digital channels, or even in the physical space, as they also often face mobility inequality. Additionally, as Straubhaar et al. [35] found in Austin, Texas, digital exclusion still tends to follow the historical lines of racial segregation. That said, as well as perpetuating the vicious circle of poverty [36, 37], spatial segregation widens the participation gap, cements media illiteracy, lessens geographical and cultural literacy, and creates (locative) media and storytelling deserts.

4   Case Study 2: Monmouthpedia, Wales

The town of Monmouth, in Wales, is 2 miles from the border with England, and has a population of 10,508 inhabitants. It became the first location-based Wikipedia town by attempting to tag all notable places, people, and flora through the technology of QRpedia (Fig. 3), specific QRcodes that allow the display of Wikipedia entries in the user's own language. Locals and tourists with smartphones were invited to scan QRpedias at points of interest and have information about the landmark sent to their smartphones. It is worth noting that, while QRpedias may not be considered IDS per se, when embedded in the physicality of places and making a bridge between the physical and the virtual, QRpedias can provide narrative material to users to build stories as they walk and experience the city and use digital media at the same time, commensurate with the psycho-geography movement [2].

Drawing on Lynch [20], who described traveling through a city as a narrative experience, Monmouthpedia itself may perhaps be considered a narrative experience. One could also suggest that QRpedia is part of a larger phenomena of digital storytelling, just as Alexander [1], when discussing what constitutes digital storytelling, says that Wikipedia entries could be part of a potential digital storytelling of the Obama campaign (2008 US president campaign), along with social media components. Although this discussion of what may be considered an interactive narrative or digital storytelling is a complex and uncertain one, it is still important to expand it, echoing the ideas explored by Nack and Waern [23], between locative practices and the idea of space as inherently narrative.

The potential for the locative and interactive dimensions of Monmouthpedia are also expressed in the fact that the articles have coordinates (geotags) to allow a virtual tour of the town using Wikipedia's mobile apps (or the Wikipedia layer on Google Streetview) and are available via augmented reality software, including Layar. I conducted ethnographic observations in Monmouth and had several interactions with residents and with the chair of Wikimedia UK, Roger Bamkin. The first resident with whom I interacted was the receptionist of the hotel where I was staying, a young woman in her twenties. I told her why I had come to Monmouth by explaining that I was conducting research about Monmouthpedia. Politely enough, the receptionist paid attention to what I was saying, but she had no idea what I was talking about. She was not aware of the deployment of QRpedias in historical buildings and commercial stores in town, including the hotel where she was working. She explained that she was not a local and had moved to the town recently.

Fig. 3. Example of QRpedia (within the red circle) stuck in a historical building in Monmouth, Wales. (Color figure online)

Fig. 4. Several banners promoting Monmouthpedia as "local knowledge with global reach" were spread throughout this Welsh town in 2012.

The second interaction was with a sales assistant, in a store, also a woman in her twenties. Unlike the hotel receptionist, she had heard of Monmouthpedia, but she had never accessed it because she did not have a smartphone to scan the codes. The store was located in the main road of the downtown, where there are Cafés, restaurants and all sort of stores. On this street, the majority of stores had blue stickers of small QRpedias on their show windows, though many of them were not easily visible.

I talked also to two employees of a drug store with a blue sticker of QRpedias. While one had no idea about the codes, the other had tried it and could see some value in it. During one week of observations and informal conversations with residents in Monmouth, I observed that some locals I talked to did not have a smartphone. Some locals did not have even a mobile phone. A middle-aged woman said to me: "the mobile phone is the most unsocial thing I have seen…" Another woman said she was not interested in QRpedias because she was a local and knew everything about local places. Monmouthpedia presents itself as a great case study, firstly because it is a kind of physical laboratory, in which Wikipedia entries are not created by the dispersed community of Wikipedia collaborators, but by those resident in the locality and the holders of local knowledge.

I observed during the ethnographic visit, and after conducting informal interviews with local residents in 2012, that several residents were not aware of Monmouthpedia, and were not scanning the QRcodes or even producing content about their own locality. Although the technology was made pervasive and ubiquitous, many in the local community seemed not to be endowed with the knowledge, skills, or technology access to use it, despite Monmouth being a relatively wealthy, small town.

This lack of interest in the QRpedias may be because locals possibly regarded them as something for tourists and outsiders. Perhaps by assuming themselves to be familiar with their local environment, there was a low, or even non-existent motivation, to use the system or to pay it any attention.

What I found most interesting in my ethnographical observations in Monmouth-pedia was the contradiction between its design goal and what was actually happening in regards to the role of local participation in the creation of content for the QRpedias. Some of the content creators – promoted as creators of local knowledge (see Fig. 4) for Monmouthpedia - were outsiders, as they were not physically present in Monmouth (Bamkin, 2012, August 12, Telephone Interview). Roger Bamkin (2012, Skype Interview) gave the example of a North-American woman (Wikipedian collaborator) who wrote several articles about Monmouth from Chicago. In his words: "In just a day she wrote an article of 4000–5000 words with 10–15 references all well linked with images and maps." Bamkin was struck by the fact that that woman was motivated to write so many articles, which were supposed to be written with a basis on local knowledge, without being physically present there.

This gap between local knowledge and not being physically present in the locality led me to think that, although the materiality of content is expressed through the QRpedia integrated in buildings, the production of local storytelling is dislocated from its local context elsewhere in the world (the impact of the global village). Instead of increasing local community, Monmouthpedia might contribute to the development of a new kind of imagined community not linked to geography, but to a global community of Wikipedian collaborators.

What is relevant for the IDS community, especially for non-fictional locative narratives, is who will produce the stories strongly anchored in places, if locals don't find the motivation to do so? Will places gain a different personality if outsiders write about them and leave their literary digital footprint behind?

Another interesting aspect of Monmouthpedia is access. How should locative/geolocalized stories be displayed in physical space in a way that not only tourists become interested in them? QRpedia had international recognition, at least in the popular press, but less so in local terms in terms of local awareness. I wonder, however, if those codes could allow local residents to add their personal stories about certain places, would that make the Wikipedia articles more appealing and so more often scanned?

5 The Spatial Participation Gap in Locative Storytelling

Based on the observations of the two case studies above, this paper suggests that some members of under-served and disadvantaged communities, and living in segregated spaces, like Gisela, or like those inhabiting small towns such as Monmouth, may encounter the participation gap not only in the making of media content, and locative storytelling, but also in the exploration of locative technologies such as QRcodes, or the hybrid space. The reasons for the two different case studies are different and various. The case of Gisela represents different potential struggles, intersected as financial distress, language barriers, digital access, age, and also gender issues and immigration status. The case of Monmouthpedia, however, is related to HCI issues, such as the usability of QRcodes embedded in the physical place, as well as cultural constraints related to the lack of smartphone use by the elder inhabitants in a small town with a relatively high level of tourism.

This participation gap, associated with locative media and the hybrid space, generates what I call here, spatial participation gap. "Spatial Participation Gap" (hence, SPG) may be defined as the unequal access to hybrid spaces and the inability, due to lack of knowledge or skills (Case 1), or cultural constraints (Case 2) to take advantage of, and benefit from, the hybrid space. By highlighting this, I do not to intend to imply that all people need to be in the so-called hybrid space. Rather, the proposal of this framework aims to engage the community of programmers of authoring tools, researchers, and content creators in IDS, with a greater critical understanding of how storytelling and mobile/locative technologies are intertwined with sociopolitical issues as well as geographical, cultural and digital literacies.

I would also encourage designers to take into account local communities, whether under-served for social and political reasons as in the case 1, or those who live in small towns, as in the case 2. The concept of SPG is necessary as it builds upon on the previous three concepts of participation gap, splintered space, and hybrid space. The framework may be useful for the creation of mobile narratives, locatives and AR, and IDS, as a whole.

In Case 1, low-income immigrants often lack social, cultural and techno capital to take advantages of even simple basic benefits of being in the hybrid space (e.g., taking a Uber, using apps such as camscanner). This becomes even more difficult with IDS apps or authoring tools (even the simple ones such as Historypin) that they are not often exposed to. In the case of Monmouth's inhabitants, although they might have the means to use the technology, they may well not see a need to do so. In this sense, it becomes crucial to include different socio-demographic groups in user tests of authoring tools. Quite often, tools are evaluated by tech savvy students [e.g., 18].

SPG may provide a framework for authoring tools designers to add some level of social complexity into their user tests. In this sense, SPG may be a useful concept to help explain the limitations of the digital divide (the gap between those who do have access to technology and those who don't), as well as using splintered space and hybrid space to explain the complexities of place and space in the context of digital media.

SPG is intended to address the issues of merging the physical and virtual, as well as inequalities in terms of mobility (splintered space). As mentioned previously, Frith [11] presents the correlation between the increasing adoption of locative media and digital inequality as an issue for future research into locative media. Rather than use demographic numbers (which populations own smartphones and which do not), Frith [11] discusses how hybrid spaces may raise new concerns around access and digital literacy.

By drawing on these, the term SPG seeks to represent the cause and effects of not having access to the hybrid space generated by locative media, and its erosive effects on the participation on the creation of locative storytelling by groups of people with different social identities. The SPG proposes stages, inspired by the pipeline metaphor [31], that individuals should pass in order to produce widely locative storytelling. I summarize these stages as follows:

- First, individuals should be able to explore the physical world as freely as possible in order to have the opportunity to choose locations about which to write locative stories as suggested by Packer et al. [27]. This is a complex task, as there are several factors as discussed throughout this paper that prevent individuals from exploring the physical world: lack of motivation, financial limitations, or perhaps even subjectivity (what places and locale one choose to geotag or geolocate may also indicate a form of SPG, like in the case of the woman from Chicago). In this sense, IDS scholarship may further explore how the subjectivity of individuals, who are afar, play a role in the creation of locative storytelling where they are not located. How does it affect the programming of authoring tools?
- Second, individuals should have awareness of locative apps that allow them to create and access content on the spot, or to be able to access spatial information. Here, programmers and researchers in IDS may consider including under-served communities in the creating of authoring tools through HCI methods such as participatory design.
- Third, individuals should have the digital skills to produce locative content. While this third stage encompasses several sociopolitical dimensions, the usefulness of this notion of the SPG may be relevant for designers of authoring tools in the sense that may assist them in regard to the design of mobile interfaces, as the SPG adds the spatial level to the debate of participation gaps [5, 30, 38, 40].

In conclusion, this article aims to provide a critical view of the participation gap related to the creation of locative stories and the design of authoring tools for storytelling regarding the hybrid space (including issues of the physical space as well as virtual space). In this sense, it is important to note that SPG is a gap that exists in today's digital society, but one may well argue that this concept has perhaps always existed. Mobile and digital technologies may have exacerbated this, and may well deepen the gap in the future. Further research may analyze the interrelated factors that compose the SPG by including under-served communities in the design of authoring tools for locative storytelling and understanding further gaps related to the use and creation of spatial content, such as locative storytelling.

References

1. Alexander, B.: The New Digital Storytelling: Creating Narratives with New Media–Revised and Updated Edition. ABC-CLIO (2017)
2. DeBord, G.E.: Introduction to a critique of urban geography, Les Lèvres Nues #6 (1955). http://library.nothingness.org/articles/SI/en/display/2 Accessed 19 Sept 2018
3. de Souza e Silva, A.: From cyber to hybrid mobile technologies as interfaces of hybrid spaces. Space Cult. **9**(3), 261–278 (2006)
4. de Souza e Silva, A., Frith, J.: Mobile Interfaces in Public Spaces: Location Privacy, Control and Urban Sociability. Routledge, New York (2012)
5. DiMaggio, P., Hargittai, E., Celeste, C., Shafer, S.: Digital inequality. In: Social Inequality: From Unequal Access to Differentiated Use, pp. 355–400 (2004)
6. Ellison, N.B., Steinfield, C., Lampe, C.: The benefits of Facebook "friends:" Social capital and college students' use of online social network sites. J. Comput. Mediat. Commun. **12**(4), 1143–1168 (2007)
7. Farman, J.: Mobile Interface: Embodied Space and Locative Media. Routledge, New York (2012)
8. Farman, J.: Storytelling with mobile media: exploring the intersection of site-specificity, content, and materiality. Routledge Companion Mob. Media, 528–537 (2014)
9. Florida, R., Mellander, C.: Segregated city: the geography of economic segregation in America's metros (2015)
10. Freundschuh, S.M., Sharma, M.: Spatial image schemata, locative terms, and geographic spaces in children's narrative: fostering spatial skills in children. Cartographica **32**(2), 38 (1995)
11. Frith, J.: Splintered space: hybrid spaces and differential mobility. Mobilities **7**(1), 131–149 (2012)
12. Frith, J.: Smartphones as Locative Media. DMS–Digital Media and Society, New York (2015)
13. Gergen, K.J.: The challenged of absent presence. In: Perpetual Contact: Mobile Communication, Private Talk, Public Performance, p. 227 (2002)
14. Gordon, E., de Souza e Silva, A.: Net Locality: Why Location Matters in a Networked World. Willey- Black Well, MA (2011)
15. Graham, S., Marvin, S.: Splintering Urbanism: Networked Infrastructures, Technological Mobilities and the Urban Condition. Psychology Press (2001)
16. Jenkins, H.: Convergence Culture: Where Old and New Media Collide. NYU press, New York (2006)
17. Jenkins, H.: Confronting the Challenges of Participatory Culture: Media Education for the 21st Century. MIT Press, Cambridge (2009)
18. Kampa, A.: Authoring concepts and tools for interactive digital storytelling in the field of mobile augmented reality. In: Nunes, N., Oakley, I., Nisi, V. (eds.) ICIDS 2017. LNCS, vol. 10690, pp. 372–375. Springer, Cham (2017). https://doi.org/10.1007/978-3-319-71027-3_46
19. Kenny, N.: The Uses of Curiosity in Early Modern France and Germany. Oxford University Press, Oxford (2004). 484p.
20. Lynch, K.: The Image of the City, vol. 11. MIT press, Cambridge (1960)

21. McCullough, M.: Epigraphy and public library. In: Aurigi, A., De Cindio, F. (eds.) Augmented Urban Spaces: Articulating the Physical and Eletronic City, pp. 61–72. Ashgate, Burlington (2008)

22. Monmonier, M.: Maps with the News: The Development of American Journalistic Cartography. University of Chicago Press, Chicago (1989)

23. Nack, F., Waern, A.: Mobile digital interactive storytelling—a winding path. New Rev. Hypermedia Multimed. **18**(1–2), 3–9 (2012)

24. Nisi, V., Oakley, I., Haahr, M.: Inner city locative media: design and experience of a location-aware mobile narrative for the dublin liberties neighborhood. In: Intelligent Agent, vol. 6, no. 2, August, 2006

25. Nisi, V., Haahr, M.: Weird view: interactive multilinear narratives and real-life community stories. Crossings **2**, 27 (2006)

26. Nisi, V., Oakley, I., Haahr, M.: Location-aware multimedia stories: turning spaces into places. Universidade Católica Portuguesa, pp. 72–93 (2008)

27. Packer, H.S., Hargood, C., Howard, Y., Papadopoulos, P., Millard, D.E.: Developing a writer's toolkit for interactive locative storytelling. In: Nunes, N., Oakley, I., Nisi, V. (eds.) ICIDS 2017. LNCS, vol. 10690, pp. 63–74. Springer, Cham (2017)

28. Plant, S.: On the mobile: The effects of mobile telephones on social and individual life (2001).   http://www.ingedewaard.net/papers/mobile/2003_SadiePlant_OnTheMobile_EffectsOfMobilePhonesOneSocialAndIndividualLife.pdf

29. Puro, J.P.: Finland: a mobile culture. In: Katz, J., Aakhus, M. (eds.) Perpetual Contact: Mobile Communication, Private Talk, Public Performance, pp. 19–29. Cambridge University Press, Cambridge (2002)

30. Schradie, J.: The digital production gap: the digital divide and Web 2.0 collide. Poetics **39** (2), 145–168 (2011)

31. Shaw, A., Hargittai, E.: The pipeline of online participation inequalities: the case of wikipedia editing. J. Commun. **68**(1), 143–168 (2018)

32. Silva, C.: Back to the future of news: looking at locative media principles in the pre-news era. #ISOJ (2014)

33. Silva, C., Nisi, V., Straubhaar, J.D.: Share yourself first: exploring strategies for the creation of locative content for and by low-literacy communities. In: Proceedings of the 8th International Conference on Communities and Technologies (C&T 2017), 10 pages. ACM (2017).   https://doi.org/10.1145/3083671.308369

34. Sizemore, J.H., Zhu, J.: Interactive non-fiction: towards a new approach for storytelling in digital journalism. In: Si, M., Thue, D., André, E., Lester, J.C., Tanenbaum, J., Zammitto, V. (eds.) ICIDS 2011. LNCS, vol. 7069, pp. 313–316. Springer, Heidelberg (2011)

35. Straubhaar, J., Spence, J., Tufekci, Z., Lentz, R.G. (eds.): Inequity in the technopolis: Race, class, gender, and the digital divide in Austin. University of Texas Press, Austin (2012)

36. Tammaru, T., Marcińczak, S., Van Ham, M., Musterd, S.: East Meets West: New Perspectives on Socio-economic Segregation in European Capital Cities (2015)

37. van Ham, M., Tammaru, T.: New perspectives on ethnic segregation over time and space. A domains approach. Urban Geogr. **37**, 953–962 (2016)

38. Vickery, J.R.: The role of after-school digital media clubs in closing participation gaps and expanding social networks. Equity Excel. Educ. **47**(1), 78–95 (2014)

39. Vittu, J.P.: "Le peuple est fort curieux de nouvelles"?: l'information périodique dans la France des années 1690. Studies on Voltaire and the eighteenth century, vol. 320, pp. 105–144. The Voltaire Foundation, Oxford (1994)

40. Watkins, C.S.: Digital divide: navigating the digital edge. Int. J. Learn. Media, 1–12 (2011)

41. Wilken, R., Goggin, G.: Mobile Technology and Place. Routledge, New York (2012)

Toward an Ethics of Interactive Storytelling at Dark Tourism Sites in Virtual Reality

Joshua A. Fisher[✉] and Sara Schoemann

Georgia Institute of Technology, Digital Media Program,
Tech Square Research Building, 85 5th St NW, Atlanta, GA, USA
{jadlerfisher, sschoemann3}@gatech.edu

Abstract. A number of VR storytelling experiences transport their users to representations of real world sites in which there has been death, pain, suffering, and tragedy. Much of the current scholarship regarding these VR experiences grapples with their technical success or failure. Less explored are the philosophical and ethical implications of transporting users to such dark sites. In an effort to fill in a knowledge gap, research from the field of dark tourism studies will be used to inform how VR stories might morally construct their representations. For over two decades, the field of dark tourism has grappled with the ethical planning, managing, and facilitating of tours at sites where atrocities, crimes, disaster, tragedy, and death have occurred. Dark tourism tour guides, interactive storytellers in their own right, have negotiated these dark narratives for centuries. This paper proposes that visits to dark tourism sites in VR should not just parallel current models of dark tourism but utilize the affordances of the medium to facilitate new opportunities for ethical compassion and understanding in the mediation of mortality. A foundational step toward an ethics for these kinds of dark VR experiences is put forward for future discussion.

Keywords: Dark tourism · Virtual reality · Ethics · Design

1 Introduction

A number of existing Virtual Reality (VR) experiences take place at historical sites where pain, suffering, atrocity, disaster, and death have occurred. Their intentions—to educate, to encourage empathy and compassion, and to build community—are worthy of praise [1–3]. However, the broader ethical and social implications of these VR experiences have received limited critical attention [2]. The consumption of enhanced spectacles of historical pain, violence, and death afforded by VR experiences require an ethical evaluation if they are to be morally designed and developed.

To develop such an evaluation, this paper relies upon existing dark tourism scholarship. This relatively new sub-field of tourism studies addresses visits to sites somehow related to death, suffering, atrocity, tragedy or crime. The sites of dark tourism range from cemeteries and museums to the favelas of Brazil, low-lying areas in New Orleans after Katrina, and former Nazi concentration camps. The field has been grappling with the social implications and ethical issues of developing and visiting these dark sites for two decades.

R. Rouse et al. (Eds.): ICIDS 2018, LNCS 11318, pp. 577–590, 2018.
https://doi.org/10.1007/978-3-030-04028-4_68

At first consideration, the connection between tourism and interactive storytelling seems tenuous. However, the two disciplines have been connected ever since MIT's Aspen Movie Map from 1981 [4]. In this foundational interactive hypermedia experience, users were able to navigate through the city and change the seasons at will. Each user was able to enjoy an experience of Aspen that was uniquely their own, created by their navigational choices. Further, tourism as a field is quite focused on narrative in their practice. Tourist experiences can be viewed as, "value-laden, emotion-conferring collective narrative constructions that are associated with and enacted in a particular place" [5]. Additionally, the connection between tourism and digital storytelling has been advocated by scholars in recent years [6–8]. It is clear that tourism studies believe that interactive digital storytelling can be a venue for integrating and exploring multiple perspectives and historical experiences at sites. These experiences are sites for moral deliberation and education for a group of users.

VR documentarians and experience designers taken with this affordance construct their stories around actual places. Producers such as Chris Milk, Nonny de la Peña, Gabo Arora, and Ari Palitz construct their experiences as journeys to said places. The headset is rhetorically invoked as a liminal device that transports users to a different time and place. Such rhetoric has also been adopted by the tourism industry for their own non-narrative VR experience as well. This paper accepts VR's rhetoric of telepresence, the idea that VR experiences might be considered journeys to the actual places represented. Subsequently, in this paper, dark VR experiences connected to real-world sites will be aligned with ethical deliberations within dark tourism studies to derive some foundational design ethics for storytelling.

Note that tourism itself can be a problematic practice [9]. Patterns of inequality, consumption, colonialism, structural injustice, and unwelcome gazing come together in an unpleasant knot. When digital destinations are the sites of historical pain, tourists confront and consume the spectacle of death as it is mediated. Given the centuries long practice of visiting dark sites, this recreational practice will continue in other media forms. By the end of this paper, we hope that an understanding of how VR might be used to ethically create and facilitate these narrative experiences will be established.

1.1 Existing Scholarship on VR Experiences of Dark Sites

Existing scholarship regarding dark VR experiences in relation to their sites focus on technical viability. A theme that runs through much of the scholarship is that the sheer authenticity of a VR representation, and how closely it parallels the site in physical reality, fundamentally justifies the existence of the user experience at the VR dark site. In an interview with *Wired*, the producers of the *Last Goodbye*, a 360 VR experience of the Majdanek concentration camp said the following:

> Making the recreation accurate to a pixel-by-pixel level was absolutely integral. Hol -ocaust deniers, Smith notes, often point to small details as proof that something was falsified, and the very point of *Last Goodbye* was its authenticity [...] "We didn't want to do anything in modeling or CG terms that seemed fake in any way." [...] It was a tough process, but the result feels as real as anything in VR can right now [10].

While the act of documentation in the wake of atrocity has a strong historical precedent[1], and the appeal of achieving a factually accurate representation in the face of Holocaust deniers is understandable, the developers' assertion that the results "feels as real as anything in VR can right now" fails to address the underlying question of why the deliberate realism of VR is the appropriate medium for experiencing this site of historical horror.

In another article on VR journalism, Nonny de la Peña explains that the entire motivation behind her use of this medium is its capacity for capturing the authentic on-location. In *Daniel's Story*, a young gay man named Daniel comes out to his homophobic family in their living room. The confrontation quickly turns violent and Daniel is forced to leave his home.

> We used videogrammetry to create holograms of Daniel and his peers and recreate the event using video captured by Daniel at the time. It was a challenging and emotionally raw experience because we were asking Daniel to recount the brutal attack [...] so that we could reenact the event with motion capture and stay as true to the actual experience as possible. Having his words as a guidepost is a really important part of our process to instill the experience with integrity and authenticity [11].

De la Peña also invokes a rhetoric of forensic accuracy as innately valuable. In turn, she conflates the proposed integrity of the piece with its supposed accuracy. While this equivocation, based in photography's myth of scientific inscription, is presented straightforwardly, it begs the question of whether the ends, in the case of a disturbing virtual experience, are substantive enough to justify realism's use for representing violence. Given the emotional trauma that a user may experience as a result of de la Peña's portrayal of Daniel's attack, or as a result of a VR story at any dark tourism site, it seems more justification is needed than the appeal of fine details and high-resolution textures.

While realism is a natural impulse, what's at stake in this discussion is not only the perception of these sanctified and commemorated sites of humanity's dark heritage, but how users of VR respond to them. As stated, the goals of these experiences are ostensibly pedagogical, heritage-based, empathy-seeking, and restorative [9]. These all align with the intentions of dark tourism. In a study in the *Annals of Tourism Research* on visitors' reactions to holocaust memorials, one thousand individuals were asked to classify their emotional responses to these dark heritage sites [12]. The researchers grouped the most common feelings, "afraid, awe, compassion, contempt, despair, disgust, fascination, fear, gratitude, hope, pride, sadness, and shame" into three categories: misery, sympathy, and positivity [12]. Feelings of misery and guilt sanitized the violence at the site, as people wanted to distance themselves from the tragedy. Feelings of sympathy and positivity encouraged altruistic action. This might include donations to the local community and site caretakers or through volunteering [13]. The ethical discussion and observations in this paper are meant to help future developers and documentarians create ethical dark VR experiences that result in altruistic action. After all, when a user departs an experience, the goals embedded by a designer can have

---

[1] Consider the U.S. Government's preservation of a reported 40,000 linear feet of bureaucratic documentation of the Holocaust generated by the German government [36].

consequences in someone's lived reality. These outcomes (misery or positivity and sympathy) can be used to evaluate the ethics of design choices. With this in mind, the overriding opinion of this paper is that causing pain and misery alone must be avoided at all costs.

2 Dark Tourism

Dark tourism is a contested field of study [9]. Not only is its terminology diverse and problematic, but its very existence has been questioned [9, 14]. Its critical engagement is controversial and addresses sensitive subjects. The field's infancy and interdisciplinary nature perhaps make it easy for more established fields to dismiss it. However, to address a pattern of VR experiences, we use the concept of dark tourism as a way to describe storytelling experiences at sites of historical or ongoing death, suffering, atrocity, tragedy, or crime [9]. The ethical discussions are meant to be kept within the scope of these kinds of experiences in VR.

Visits to these sites also enable visitors to reflect upon mortality, which fundamentally differentiates these sites from other heritage experiences [9, 15]. Visits to dark sites may involve reflecting on the motives of oppressors, the suffering of victims, and/or the legacy of survivors. In a secular western world that sensationalizes death in mass media but also largely hides the day to day experience of mortality within a medical context, dark sites have become a venue for engaging with themes of death and mortality through the past deaths of others [15]. How a visitor interprets a dark VR experience is mediated by a number of variables. They arrive at the site with their own conceptions of death, their anxiety regarding their own death, a socio-cultural understanding of death, and their personal narrative [15]. Additionally, a visitor may or may not have a direct connection to what they are visiting [16]. Each of these factors stand to influence a user's experience.

Consider contemporary sites of atrocity in which survivors and oppressors may both be physically present on a tour. Each one of them has a unique perspective and story regarding the site. Designing a tour that provides each with a just experience that is ethically and intellectually satisfying is a challenge. Existing non-VR solutions, which include market segmentation and the development of "heritage force fields" are unproductive [9]. The latter results in fewer participants, nominally the historical powerbrokers and stakeholders of heritage sites, engaged in the development of the site and how it is perceived [16]. An unfortunate result may be national amnesia, the intentional sanitizing and censoring of a trauma to make it more palatable for a mainstream audience [9]. To derive more productive methods for VR, each site requires a unique approach to its management, facilitation, and design.

3 Dark Tourism Sites in VR

It has been proposed that there are three different kinds of dark tourism based on their proximity to the location of suffering: dark, darker, and darkest [17]. The closer the sites is to the original trauma, in regards to both time and space, the darker it is.

A fourth shade of dark tourism, dystopian tourism, has been proposed as an experience that allows one to simulate a historical reconstruction of death, pain, or suffering. This dystopian tourism recognizes a claimed "innate violence in humanity" and its relation to our sense of justice and morality [18]. The embodied and acted through process of violence and oppression at a dystopian site has been claimed to bring an individual closer to the "real." The real in this instance being an uncensored version of a violent death [18]. In this manner, it is claimed that dystopian tourism allows a secular, ostensibly western society to confront the taboo "inassimilable, ugliness, brutality, and excessive negativity" of reality [18].

Just like augmented reality (AR) or mixed reality (MR) examples, VR experiences may be situated in places ranging from on-location at a dark site to in a museum or a user's living room. Dark tourism research doesn't address this potential parallel of simultaneous real and virtual experiences as a possibility. To move the discussion forward for media studies, it helps to consider these experiences as varying shades of darkness as stated by Strange and Kempa [19]. However, for VR, these shades are also layered simultaneously in both lived reality and virtuality. The lightest of such experiences would be in the user's home, within the room they feel the most comfortable. The most dystopian would be on site, re-enacting or living through, a simulation of a contemporary violence being perpetrated as it occurs. These shades are layered atop one another. The first layer of mediation is the VR experience, the darkness of its shade; the second, is where the user is located, whether they are at home or at the dark site itself. These shades work commutatively and layer atop one another with ethical implications. A VR experience of a historical murder experienced in the quiet of one's own home versus at the physical site of the perpetrated violence itself has different moral stakes. To clarify these ramifications, the next section addresses four shades of dark VR experiences.

3.1 Dark Sites in VR

Dark sites are those that take place in a museum or at an offsite memorial. They are removed by both time and space from the original physical site of violence or atrocity. Non-VR experiences include the Holocaust Museum in Washington D.C. and the Center for Civil and Human Rights in Atlanta. The key difference between these experiences and darker tourism is that the latter takes place at the actual physical site.

Dark sites are constructed within and by institutions. They are assumed to have ethically developed scaffolding for the emotional wellbeing of visitors. This pedagogical infrastructure is meant to support each individual's journey through the site as they grapple with their own narrative and mortality. In VR, this kind of facilitation can mediate experiences of darker shades, helping visitors cope with traumatic experiences. For example, docents were on hand at the Sundance Film Festival during Nonny de la Peña's exhibition of KIYA, a VR documentary of a domestic violence incident that results in a death [20].

Dark sites in VR may be recreations of museum tours [21] and interactive exhibits [22]. What unites these experiences beyond representing atrocity is their pedagogical and cultural intentions. They seek to use the affordances of VR, as well as its rhetoric of telepresence, to enhance the visitor experience. Quite often this enhancement relies upon representational strategies of hypermediation. This may involve the remediation of archival material, including photographs and letters into VR so that the user can interact with them. These experiences could be part of larger deliberations and discussions regarding national and community identity. Conversely, there is also the risk that they might be used to encourage national amnesia, the intentional censoring of a nation-state's painful and conflicted past [16]. For example, the Martin Luther King, Jr. holiday, a celebration of the civil rights movement, ignores King's radical actions for the urban poor in Chicago and Mississippi in 1966. The holiday frames King within, "[…] the relatively safe categories of 'civil rights leader,' 'great orator,' harmless dreamer of black and white children on the hillside" [23]. King's moral fight for the nation's poor, black and white and others, is forgotten: diminished by the symbolic power and popularity of his iconic "I Have a Dream" speech. This amnesia only harms the United States. It contains MLK's legacy within the politically safe frame of "great orator" and ignores his crucial fight against economic inequality [23].

3.2   Darker Sites in VR

Darker tourism sites may make up or be part of a historical physical location of pain, suffering, and death. The sites range from the somber or less distressing, such as cemeteries; to in the extreme, potentially disturbing sites such as concentration camps and mass gravesites. Though these sites are darker, they are still historical in nature. Darker sites do not encompass journeys to sites where death and violence is ongoing. A dark tourist comes as close to the scene of death and violence without interacting directly with it. The claim made by dark tourism scholars is that the physical immediacy to the site itself encourages empathy. Like appeals to the inherent value of forensic realism in VR experiences, such a claim requires further study and has already been critiqued for VR [2, 24].

In VR, a darker experience might be the tour of a Nazi concentration camp [3], the scene of a massacre [1], or a visit to ruins associated with death [25]. This is not a complete list. What differentiates these kinds of experiences from darker kinds is their temporality and lack of user agency. These VR experiences focus on a visit to a historical dark site or its reconstruction. They do not give users the experience of contemporaneous death and violence. Further, they do not allow (or demand) that visitors directly simulate or engage with the site. Users are taken through a haunted house on a track, a la Janet Murray's amusement park fun house metaphor [26].

This distinction is of an ethical importance. Take again *The Last Goodbye*, the VR film by Gabo Arora and Ari Palitz. It commemorates the story of Holocaust survivor Pinchas Gutter. The experience takes users to the site where Pinchas survived, Majdanek Concentration Camp. This is an exploration of a historical site by a survivor. In the room-scale version, when the user is taken to the concentration camp's gas chambers and ovens, the camera stops just outside the door and does not enter [27]. This creative choice was made for ethical reasons [27]. The producers felt that forcing a user to enter a gas chamber would too closely parallel the original horrific act [27]. A user experiencing *The Last Goodbye* is not forced to experience a recreation of the suffering and death of others. However, it is still on display for purposes of reflection. Evidence is instead presented that death and violence have taken place. This historical trauma is allowed to reverberate into our present. It is not recreated or re-simulated for the user. Not only does this respect the legacy of survivors, but it respects the autonomy of users. Allowing them to determine their own engagement with death is of ethical importance.

3.3 Darkest Sites in VR

Darkest sites are those at which suffering, death, destruction, disaster, and pain are still occurring. William F.S. Miles envisioned these experiences as live tours of "active detention camps, killing fields, death rows, and execution chambers" through telepresence [17]. Although such visits seemed unimaginable and dangerous to scholars of dark tourism studies, VR is making such experiences possible through actual telepresence and through its rhetorical invocation. For a darkest tourism experience, the line between virtuality and reality is problematically blurred. Kate Nash has addressed this in her recent discussion on the moral affordances of VR for mediated witnessing [2]. She recognizes that the medium provides an opportunity to imagine a distant other and to embody another [2]. This could be a survivor or oppressor that the user embodies. This distance between the user and physical reality can create, "an improper distance in which the experience of 'being in' VR, a narcissistic reflection on one's own experience, becomes the foundation for moral response" [2]. The site becomes less about what others are suffering, and more about the user's reflection on their own experience. The result is an almost instantaneous commodification and consumption of the death, suffering, and pain of others.

Consider the backlash against Facebook and the American Red Cross when Mark Zuckerberg and his Head of Social VR conversed with one another as virtual talking heads suspended over 360 footage of the flooded streets of Puerto Rico after hurricanes Maria and Irma [28]. Their reaction was seen as blasé by some, and the perceived lack of respect for survivors and those who were lost offended others. Not only was death commodified by Facebook, it was used to promote and elevate a hardware platform (the Oculus Rift) as a tool for empathy. The irony is tragic. The immediate corporate commodification of pain trespassed many ethical boundaries. Indeed, perhaps it was the temporal immediacy of the moment that made the exploitation even more heinous. Other examples, experiences that take place in the recent past and rely on a rhetoric of telepresence, are not met with such moral disgust. Chris Milk and his production house take visitors to some of our recent past's darkest sites, including refugee camps and demolished towns in Ukraine. Yet, these experiences are not abhorrent to most users.

We can draw a crucial ethical distinction between Zuckerberg's problematic virtual engagement with suffering and pain in the present and Chris Milk's 360 documentaries chronicling our recent tragic past. It's a distinction that provides at least two conditions for the creation of these kinds of VR experiences. First, that the dark event has passed and that no one's present suffering might be commodified. Second, that the designers, developers, and organizations create or facilitate an experience that takes care to not make light of survivors' pain or desecrate the sanctity of lost lives. While these requirements may seem obvious (and they should be), it's important recognize that traditional darker tourism and darker VR experiences invariably differ. While physical visits to darker tourism sites are likely to have guides or other guests that chide joking children and other disrespectful visitors, VR experiences offer no guarantee that users will engage respectfully. Authorship decisions must be made responsibly if they are to facilitate a respectful and ethical engagement with the darkest sites.

3.4 Dystopian Sites in VR

While the darkest tourism experiences involve the curious gazing and consumption of pain, death, and calamity, dystopian experiences go one step further. Dystopian tourism involves the simulation or re-enactment of the violent or tragic act(s). Examples from non-VR include Charles Manson's Helter Skelter tour and The London Dungeon Experience [18]. Both events seek to immerse the user in sites of death and destruction by giving them the opportunity to act out moments of pain and suffering as both victims and perpetrators. While these are entertainment events that no doubt trade in the shock value of their content, they also ultimately provide the visitor an opportunity to confront the horror experienced by the victim in an attempt to better understand a moral trespass. It's a confrontation with profoundly disturbing historical realities, and to make the experience tolerable to participants requires care, scaffolding, and transparency. To endeavor to expose participants to depictions of violence without attending to the ethics of care needed to support their productive engagement is to risk recreating trauma and creating vicarious trauma.

Take a forthcoming VR experience, one that recreates the 1999 massacre at Columbine High School in Colorado. Its purported goal is to develop empathy for victims of gun violence and to promote gun control in the U.S. [29]. The experience, called *HERO*, begins when the first pipe-bomb goes off in the school [29]. Users then have to navigate the school with the unstated goal of getting as many students to safety as possible. The creator of the experience, Brooks Browne, was a friend of the two shooters who survived due to a warning he received from them before the attack. Now as an adult grappling with the trauma of having survived the massacre, he hopes his VR experience causes an emotional shock to his users. Though his goal is for users to then experience empathy and behave altruistically afterward, his method and VR design is a perverse reflection of his morally complex relationship to the original event and its perpetrators.

Research suggests that trauma does not lead to positive behavior change but desensitization—it is an obstacle to empathy [12]. Trauma does not allow an individual to reify, sanctify, or commemorate a dark site; it only facilitates a confrontation with pain [30]. In turn, the more immediate trauma desensitizes the historical pain. In VR, this occurs through the commodification of the tragedy as an experience to be visited and embodied. In test runs of *HERO*, multiple users asked to be pulled out of the experience with tears streaming down their faces. Browne sees this as success. It is the position of this paper that it is not. Sympathy and positivity can be achieved through dystopian VR sites, but they require a benevolent and ethical approach.

Browne recognizes that users are themselves within the VR space and hopes they will make choices that align with their ethics within that situation. His presumption is that by providing users with agency in a dystopian space that they will act morally or ethically. That users will, without question, find ways to remove as many students before they become victims. This is a naïve belief. How users behave within these VR experiences can only be suggested. Some users may choose to do nothing and watch intelligent agents representing students perish. This is how easily *HERO*'s experience becomes anything but heroic. It highlights the ethical stakes of dramatic agency in these dystopian VR experiences but fails to guide the experience towards one that is ethical and ultimately redeeming.

Unlike the three previous shades of dark tourism, interactivity is at the core of VR dystopian tourism and requires special attention. In a dystopian scenario, a user may be acutely aware of their own morals and mortality. It is in these moments that the choices they make, the effect of their dramatic agency, has an ethical consequence. As an interactive storyteller, the ethical consequences of choices in these VR experiences must be transparent. If a user does not have a clear understanding of why a particular action may be unethical, a VR experience may enforce a behavior in a way that is immoral. Further, if a user enacts an unethical choice in ignorance, it may lead to misery and guilt about the act, which can in turn shut them off from experiencing compassion.

When putting the user through the motions of a historical atrocity, each interaction must be transparent in its ethical consequence. It must be made contextual and explained. Steps should be taken to support the user's autonomy in making their choice, whether they're the oppressor or survivor in the experience. Ensuring they are well informed is one way to encourage critical reflection on their actions. Even if budgets or capabilities keep a production studio from developing an ethical response to each interaction, an effort should be made to design scenarios in which user interaction is directed to the most ethical choice. This is critical for VR experiences that engage with morally complex topics or historical evil. If it is the intention of a VR designer to educate the user by having them embody a historical oppressor, then directing the user toward the most ethical choice creates a moral tension between the embodied role and the user's own ethics. It is within this negotiation that a user in a VR dystopian experience might be afforded the opportunity to act ethically in an immoral situation.

Lastly, these sites of interaction can become a site where users explore the morality of other cultures. For example, this paper has been written from the authors' perspectives which are ostensibly western, feminist, and pluralist. This has led us to develop a particular kind of design ethics, as discussed later in this paper, that is steeped in this perspective. One might consider creating experiences that afford users the opportunity to explore different ethical codes based on alternative cultural expectations. This might happen when a user is engaging in a particular ethical choice. They could inform how one might view the action in one culture versus another. Pedagogical in nature, such a practice may provide users with a more comprehensive understanding of morality.

3.5   The Absent Aura of Dark Sites in VR

Before moving on, the absent aura of dark sites in VR requires attention. There have been discussions about the utility of aura at dark sites for an MR experience [31], but scholarship hasn't addressed it in VR. Aura, an ambiguous term popularized by Walter Benjamin, is used by the scholar to describe the inherent uniqueness of a moment captured through the act of painting [32]. Each painting contains a unique aura that can be felt by the viewer and is formed by the materiality of canvas and paints, the time painting takes, the space it captures, and the labor of the artist. Benjamin contends that the aura dissipates when paintings are mechanically mass produced as images [32]. There's been some disagreement about this [33].

However, it is the position of this paper that historical events contain a particular aura attached not just to its spatial and temporal aspects, but the choreography of human, natural and technological actions as well [32–34]. Sites of mass murder and death contain a dark aura; a dark underbelly of realism [18]. VR developers and designers invoke the rhetoric of this aura when they impress upon users that they're actually at the sites being simulated. When Milk impresses upon us that we're sitting with refugees he is invoking an auratic rhetoric [35]. How this aura is felt may impact how a user perceives the experience. In VR, a user's perception of a place's aura is mediated by strategies of transparency and hypermediation [33]. Transparency enhances aura by removing the interface of VR. Certainly, the darker tourism trips to concentration camps and other sites rely on transparency to enhance the aura for the user. Hypermediation on the other hand, calls into question the VR dark site by emphasizing the mediated nature of what the user is experiencing.

A "hands off" approach is suggested by the dark tourism scholarship in regards to maintaining the aura of sites and experiences. We believe that this echoes Benjamin's assertion. As Eli Weisel has stated, sometimes using the minimal amount of words to describe the trauma can achieve the maximum effect [36]. There is a great concern that too much commercialization of the site will lead to its trivialization. This turns the experience into a direct act of consumption hastened by commodification. In VR, the use of hypermediation strategies may result in billboards, games, offensive content or even advertisements. These will alter the perceived aura of the site, perhaps belittling it.

What's at stake is missing the aspect of the site that makes it important to humanity's dark heritage to begin with. Take this anecdote told by Abba Kovner, a survivor of the holocaust encountering a scale model of Treblinka by another survivor at an Israeli Kibbutz. When evaluating the replica, Kovner was asked what was missing from the perfect to-scale recreation of the camp's architecture, of which he explained "the horror was missing" [36]. Kovner's story highlights two aspects for us. First, how critical the strategies of visual representation and interaction are to maintain the aura of a site in VR experiences; and second, that the manner in which they're utilized has ethical consequences. Creators of interactive digital stories in VR must be mindful of these aspects when choosing and constructing the settings for their dark experiences.

4   Foundational Ethics for VR Experiences at Dark Sites

This paper has engaged in a strictly evaluative study of contemporary VR experiences involving dark tourism sites. Since tourism is a form of storytelling tied to place, a VR tourist experience is a form of interactive storytelling. The shades that we have outlined highlight two core principles that we want to draw attention to. Specifically, that the goal for realism and authenticity does not alone justify putting the user through a traumatic experience. Second, a scaffolding of care and support is needed to mediate the experience of users if they are to have a meaningful encounter with depictions of historical atrocities, death, suffering, poverty, and pain. To achieve these core principles, we have highlighted some tactics for achieving an emotionally and intellectually fulfilling experience. However, these tactics have been derived from the existing material, some of which is problematic, and it is our hope that these suggestions will be seen as foundations for future study.

1. Don't cause misery. If the goal of the VR experience is to educate, encourage cultural awareness, and restorative justice than an encounter that deliberately causes only misery will hamper a user's ability to access compassion and enact real world altruism.
2. If a user has dramatic agency, care must be taken to support their emotional wellbeing. However, achieving only an emotional response on the part of the user results in a narrow moral response. To afford a broader reflection, all interactions, especially those that simulate the perpetuation of historical violence, should be constructed with sensitivity to the user's moral agency and autonomy. It would be unjust to simulate problematic behavior without informing a user of the moral consequences of their choices.
3. Violence for the sake of spectacle is not constructive for pedagogical or altruistic purposes in VR. Sometimes the most ethical choice is to let the historical act of violence speak for itself and to not recreate it.
4. VR experiences should not commodify existent dark events. No one's immediate suffering should be commodified through VR without their consent. Further, designers, developers, and organizations should not create or facilitate experiences that make light of survivors' pain or desecrate lost lives for commercial purposes.
5. Achieving a complete understanding of these traumatic experiences through the pursuit of perfect recreation is an idealistic myth. It will never be satisfied by more data, archival material, or immersive reproductions. The march of time and the mediation of place in VR will forever hold the user at a distance from the lived historical experience. The rhetoric of telepresence needlessly obfuscates this reality.

It needs to be mentioned that these ethics are based on the primarily western values embodied by the authors. We would note that the fungibility of interactive digital storytelling allows VR experience designers to explore alternative moral viewpoints. The five guidelines we've put forward may, for example, just inform one of many moral lenses. Dystopian VR experiences may afford the greatest opportunity to explore multiple moral codes through dramatic agency and sites of ethical interaction.

5   Conclusion

Our natural inclination to learn and plumb our dark heritage will be satiated by the burgeoning VR industry in new ways. The unique affordances of emerging media are a means to this end. This paper has suggested that the manner in which designers and storytellers use these affordances has immediate ethical consequences. Admittedly, what has been suggested is purely foundational. It's a groundwork for future discussions in the interactive storytelling community about how to construct experiences that use these sites as settings. Future work might evaluate how dark VR experiences produce altruistic behavior in lived reality. Additionally, how narrative can be used to support these goals requires evaluation. We expect that different structures provide emotional support and care in unique ways, but also have a myriad of ethical consequences. As the number of dark VR experiences increases these questions will be all the more important to address. The ethical and philosophical impact of the mediation of mortality in VR is still a mystery, one that's both exciting and problematic. It is our hope that this paper encourages others to engage in this area of study.

References

1. The Chicago History Museum: CHICAGO ØØ| The St. Valentine's Day Massacre, Virtual Reality Experience. In: YouTube. https://www.youtube.com/watch?v=rWeBOEIG4Yw. Accessed 12 Feb 2017
2. Nash, K.: Virtual reality witness: exploring the ethics of mediated presence. Stud. Doc. Film (2017)
3. Kaelber, L.: A memorial as virtual traumascape: darkest tourism in 3D and cyber-space to the gas chambers of Auschwitz. e-Rev. Tour. Res. 5(2), 24–33 (2007)
4. MIT Media Lab Speech Interface Group: Aspen Interactive Movie Map. In: YouTube. https://www.youtube.com/watch?v=Hf6LkqgXPMU
5. Chronis, A.: Between place and story: gettysburg as tourism imaginary. Ann. Tour. Res. 39 (4), 1797–1816 (2012)
6. Ferreiraa, S., Pimenta Alvesa, A., Quico, C.: Location based transmedia storytelling: enhancing the tourism experience. Inf. Commun. Technol. Tour. 4, 4 (2014)
7. Choi, S.: A study on effect of tourism storytelling of tourism destination brand value and tourist behavioral intentions. Indian J. Sci. Technol. 9(46), 1–6 (2016)
8. Qiongli, W.: Commercialization of digital storytelling: an integrated approach for cultural tourism, the Beijing olympics and wireless VAS. Int. J. Cult. Stud. 9(3), 383–394 (2006)
9. Light, D.: Progress in dark tourism and thanatourism research: an uneasy relationship with heritage tourism. Tour. Manag. 61, 275–301 (2017)
10. Watercutter, A.: The Incredible, Urgent Power of Remembering the Holocaust in VR. In: Wired. https://www.wired.com/2017/04/vr-holocaust-history-preservation/. Accessed 20 Apr 2017
11. Goldman, N.: Nonny De La Peña: Pioneering VR and Immersive Journalism. In: The Magazine of the Visual Effects Society. http://vfxvoice.com/nonny-de-la-pena-pioneering-vr-and-immersive-journalism/. Accessed 3 Apr 2018
12. Nawijn, J., Isaac, R., Liempt, A., Gridnevskiy, K.: Emotion clusters for concentration camp memorials. Ann. Tour. Res. 61, 213–267 (2016)
13. Pezzullo, P.: "This is the only tour that sells": tourism, disaster, and national identity in New Orleans. J. Tour. Cult. Chang. 7(2), 99–114 (2009)
14. Seaton, A.: Thanatourism and its discontents: an appraisal of a decade's work with some future issues and directions. In: Jamal, T., Robinson, M. (eds.) The Sage Handbook of Tourism Studies. Sage, London (2009)
15. Stone, P.: Dark tourism and significant other death. Towards a model of mortality mediation. Ann. Tour. Res. 39(3), 1565–1587 (2012)
16. Stone, P., Sharpley, R.: Consuming dark tourism: a Thanatological perspective. Ann. Tour. Res. 35(2), 574–595 (2008)
17. Miles, W.: Auschwitz: museum interpretation and darker tourism. Ann. Tour. Res. 29(4), 1175–1178 (2002)

18. Podoshen, J., Venkatesh, V., Wallin, J., Andrzejewski, S., Jin, Z.: Dystopian dark tourism: an exploratory examination. Tour. Manag. **51**, 316–328 (2015)

19. Strange, C., Kempa, M.: Shades of dark tourism: Alcatraz and Robben Island. Ann. Tour. Res. **30**(2), 386–405 (2003)

20. Robertson, A.: Virtual reality pioneer Nonny de la Peña charts the future of VR journalism. In: The Verge. https://www.theverge.com/2016/1/25/10826384/sundance-2016-nonny-de-la-pena-virtual-reality-interview. Accessed 25 Jan 2016

21. Holocaust Memorial Center: Virtual tour. In: Holocaust Memorial Center Zekelman Family Campus. https://www.holocaustcenter.org/virtual-tour. Accessed 2013

22. Ma, M., Coward, S., Walker, C.: Question-answering virtual humans based on pre-recorded testimonies for holocaust education. In: Ma, M., Oikonomou, A. (eds.) Serious Games and Edutainment Applications, pp. 391–409. Springer, Cham (2017). https://doi.org/10.1007/978-3-319-51645-5_18

23. Harding, V.: Beyond Amnesia: Martin Luther King, Jr., and the future of America. J. Am. Hist. **74**(2), 468–476 (1987)

24. Fisher, J.A.: Empathic actualities: toward a taxonomy of empathy in virtual reality. In: Nunes, N., Oakley, I., Nisi, V. (eds.) ICIDS 2017. LNCS, vol. 10690, pp. 233–244. Springer, Cham (2017). https://doi.org/10.1007/978-3-319-71027-3_19

25. Bentley, M.: Immersive ruin: chernobyl and virtual decay. In: Lyons, S. (ed.) Ruin Porn and the Obsession with Decay, pp. 181–200. Springer, Cham (2018). https://doi.org/10.1007/978-3-319-93390-0_10

26. Murray, J.: Hamlet on the Holodeck. MIT Press, Boston (2017)

27. Alexander, N.: How Virtual Reality is Reinventing Holocaust Remembrance. In: Haaretz. https://www.haaretz.com/jewish/holocaust-remembrance-day/.premium-how-virtual-reality-is-reinventing-holocaust-remembrance-1.5464154. Accessed 25 Apr 2017

28. Barron, L.: Mark Zuckerberg Apologizes For Facebook's Puerto Rico Virtual Reality 'Tour'. In: Fortune. http://fortune.com/2017/10/10/mark-zuckerberg-puert-rico-vr-apology/. Accessed 11 Oct 2017

29. Farrell, J.: A Columbine massacre survivor uses virtual reality to create empathy for tragedy. In: Silicon Angle. https://siliconangle.com/blog/2018/01/25/columbine-school-massacre-survivor-hopes-create-empathy-giving-users-experience-intense-virtual-reality-trauma/. Accessed 25 Jan 2018

30. Foote, K.: Heritage tourism, the geography of memory, and the politics of place in Southeastern Colorado. In: The Southeast Colorado heritage tourism project report, Wash Park Media, Denver (2009)

31. Dow, S., Lee, J., Oezbek, C., MacIntyre, B., Bolter, J., Gandy, M.: Exploring spatial narratives and mixed reality experiences in Oakland Cemetery. In: Valencia (2005)

32. Benjamin, W.: The Work of Art in the Age of Mechanical Reproduction. Illuminations (1935)

33. Bolter, J., MacIntyre, B., Gandy, M., Schweitzer, P.: New media and the permanent crisis of aura. Converg. Int. J. Res. New Media Technol. **1**, 21–39 (2006)

34. Benjamin, W.: What is epic theater? In: Illuminations, pp. 147–153 (1968)

35. Milk, C.: How virtual reality can create the ultimate empathy machine. In: TED.com. https://www.ted.com/talks/chris_milk_how_virtual_reality_can_create_the_ultimate_empathy_machine. Accessed 2015

36. Hilberg, R.: I was not there. In: Writing and the Holocaust, pp. 17–26. Holms & Meier, New York (1988)

37. de la Pena, N., et al.: Immersive journalism: immersive virtual reality for the first-person experience of news. Presence **19**(4), 291–301 (2010)

38. de la Peña, N.: Nonny de la Peña on Empathy in VR. In: Voices of VR. http://voicesofvr.com/298-nonny-de-la-pena-on-empathy-in-vr/. Accessed 2016
39. Boyles, F.: Andersonville: a site steeped in controversy. In: Ashworth, G., Hartmann, R. (eds.) Horror and Human Tragedy Revisited: The Management of Sites of Atrocities for Tourism. Cognizant Communication Corporation, New York (2005)
40. Osbaldiston, N., Petray, T.: The role of horror and dread in the sacred experience. Tour. Stud. **11**(2), 175–190 (2011)
41. Outterson, K., Selinger, E., Whyte, K.: Poverty tourism, justice, and policy. Public Integr. **14**(1), 39–50 (2011)
42. Jafarinaimi, N., Nathan, L., Hargraves, I.: Values as hypotheses: design, inquiry, and the service of values. Des. Issues **31**(4), 91–104 (2015)
43. Sather-Wagstaff, J.: Heritage that Hurts: Tourists in the Memoryscapes of September 11. Routledge, New York (2016)
44. Nash, K., Corner, J.: Strategic impact documentary: contexts of production and social intervention. Eur. J. Commun. **31**(3), 227–242 (2016)

Interactive Digital Narratives (IDN) for Change

Educational Approaches and Challenges in a Project Focused on Migration

Teun Dubbelman[⊠], Christian Roth, and Hartmut Koenitz

Professorship Interactive Narrative Design, HKU University of the Arts Utrecht,
Nieuwekade 1, 3511 RV Utrecht, The Netherlands
{teun.dubbelman, christian.roth,
hartmut.koenitz}@hku.nl

Abstract. This paper shares the results of an interactive digital narrative (IDN) project, conducted at HKU University of the Arts Utrecht. We consider the potential of 'IDN for change', before we describe the project, the underlying design approach and the educational approaches. A particular focus of this paper is on pedagogical considerations. We describe the educational challenges we have encountered during the project as well as the pedagogical interventions we have implemented to counter these difficulties. On this basis, we discuss a more general perspective on the state and issues in IDN-focused pedagogy.

Keywords: Interactive digital narratives (IDN) for change · IDN design
Education · Pedagogy · Migration · IDN and society

1 Introduction

Interactive Digital Narrative (IDN) is often discussed in the context of entertainment, yet, more serious applications, in line with 'serious games' are equally possible and have actually been a staple of the form at least since Glorianna Davenport's early interactive documentaries on the changing cityscape of New Orleans in the 1980s [1]. In fact, IDN in this regard holds several particular advantages over fixed narratives when it comes to representations of complex and controversial topics, due to its procedural, participatory and encyclopaedic nature [2]. The latter affordance allows for encyclopaedic depth of information that can be presented, while the former two in concert empower the interactor to make her own decisions and experience the consequences of particular choices. The educational aspect of IDNs is further supported by the ability to replay, the potential to revisit earlier decisions and explore a topic from additional perspectives and thus allows for insights that cannot be offered by linear and static representations.

Migration is a complex topic that warrants such a treatment of complex representation – and we might even argue that the topic requires it. This foundational understanding of 'serious IDNs' is the basis for the migration-focused project discussed

© Springer Nature Switzerland AG 2018
R. Rouse et al. (Eds.): ICIDS 2018, LNCS 11318, pp. 591–602, 2018.
https://doi.org/10.1007/978-3-030-04028-4_69

in this paper. Indeed, a recent study finds interactive narrative to be effective in reducing prejudices against, and increasing support for, migrants: "participants who experienced *Migrate* [the IDN used in the study] subsequently reported more positive affect toward Mexicans living in the United States" [3].

2   The Project: IDN with a Purpose

This paper shares the results of an IDN project, conducted by a group of students, researchers and teachers from HKU University of the Arts Utrecht. Specifically, the paper describes our overall approach towards interactive narrative design, the educational challenges we have encountered during the project as well as the pedagogical interventions we have implemented to counter these difficulties.

In this particular project, we wanted to create a 'purposeful' interactive digital narrative; an IDN with potential societal value. We chose to focus on the critical topic of migration. We gave a team of four students the assignment to develop an interactive narrative that could show the complexity behind the integration and socialization of migrants in Dutch society. The students worked fulltime on the project for one semester, and were given some freedom to choose specificities, such as target group, platform and overall goal.

In the role of interactive narrative designers, students chose to develop an IDN experience for Dutch adolescents in the 18–25 age group, to be played on smart phones. Its main purpose was raising awareness; by playing the IDN, the target group should become more aware of the difficulties that migrants face when trying to integrate in Dutch society. During the semester, the students had regular sessions with teachers and researchers to collaboratively work on the project and overcome conceptual, designerly and technical challenges.

This paper in particular focuses on the educational challenges we have encountered in supervising this project, and we share relevant pedagogical interventions we have implemented. Consequently, we will not describe in detail the design of the various prototypes, nor the design process.

3   Approaches Towards Teaching IDN Design

Janet Murray is one of the first and few scholars who has written about the pedagogy of IDN design in 1995. In a chapter called 'The pedagogy of cyberfiction: teaching a course on reading and writing interactive narrative' [4], Murray describes a course she has taught at the Massachusetts Institute of Technology (MIT) in the beginning of the 1990s. Emphasizing the pioneering aspect of this course, she writes: "I set out in this course to help establish the conventions and building blocks of an art form that is only emerging" [4]. In this chapter, Murray explains her approach to training students in what she calls the art of "cyberfiction", more widely known as interactive literature. In the same period, Martin Rieser gave a keynote at ISEA, titled 'Interactive narrative: educating the authors' [5]. Here, Rieser highlights the need for artistic, cross-disciplinary IDN design education. He writes: "Only through the open minded commitment of artists, writers and programmers who are prepared to explore the full expressive potential of the medium can we even begin to see a meaningful artform emerge" [5]. Rieser sees interactive digital narrative, with Murray, as a potential new artform. This artform can only blossom if practitioners are well-trained. To this end, several educational obstacles need to be cleared. Rieser and Murray both point towards the problematic legacy of established media and dominant, normative forms of linear narrative representation, particularly in terms of conceptual creative thinking. Rieser describes the need for practitioners to abandon the traditional notion of authorial control; unlike established media, interactive digital narratives hand over a considerable degree of control to users/interactors. Similarly, Murray advocates the importance of procedural thinking for IDN practitioners, as an unconventional, multilinear way of envisioning narrative structures. Additionally, both scholars express concern about the lack of adequate authoring tools, acclaimed examples and established design conventions.

Unfortunately, as we will demonstrate, many of the challenges identified by Murray and Rieser are still persistent today, as research efforts have been focused mostly on technical and conceptual approaches and less on education. Although solutions might exist, these are not widely known, since relatively little knowledge on IDN pedagogy has been shared and distributed since Murray's and Rieser's observations [6].

Indeed, Hartmut Koenitz in 2014 identifies the lack of "attention [..] paid to the creative process of actually creating IDN experiences" [7] as one of five areas in need of scholarly attention in the field. In the context of discussing authoring tools, he states "Educating others in the use of the tools [...] was not an area of focus for most projects" and points to Spierling and Szilas's discussion [8] in the framework of the European research project IRIS [9] as one of the few exceptions. Koenitz' 2015 paper [10] offers some insights from his own teaching practice, but is focused on describing a generalized design process and design principles in contrast to earlier case studies [11–13]. Finally, we like to acknowledge promising educational approaches in the ongoing work of Daiute, [14, 15] that has not yet reached final conclusions.

Consequently, with this paper, we hope to spark new academic interest in the topic of IDN pedagogy and take a first step in sharing useful pedagogical approaches.

4 Challenges and Approaches

Before discussing the educational challenges and pedagogical approaches, let us first establish the project's context. The project was part of a bachelor degree program in Creative Media and Game Technologies, at HKU University of the Arts Utrecht. Consequently, the learning experience of the students was built on established educational practices from the transdisciplinary field of Creative Technology. Amongst others, it included project-based learning [16], design thinking [17], learning by doing [18], 21st century skill development [19], T-shaped education [20], flipping the classroom [21] and blended learning [22]. Consequently, the educational challenges we have encountered in the project were partly general in nature. That is, some aspects were not specific to IDN design education, but concerned more general problems, often encountered in the educational practices mentioned above. These challenges included topics like poor project planning, unforeseen team dynamics, inadequate topic research, limited access to the target group or insufficient development capacity. For this paper, we focus solely on those challenges that are specific to interactive narrative design and to the subject of migration.

In this respect, the challenges we have encountered can be divided into three categories: conceptual, designerly and technical.

4.1 Conceptual Challenge

As mentioned, the main goal of the project was to develop a purposeful IDN experience for Dutch adolescents. By playing the IDN, the target group should become more aware of the difficulties that migrants face when trying to integrate in Dutch society. For us, it was important that the IDN did not convey the story of one particular migrant, but embraced the possibilities of interactivity by allowing users to play around with different perspectives, creating their own, personal story and opinion about this complex topic and thus making use of the specific affordances of IDN for the representation of complex topics, mentioned in the introduction of this paper.

For the students, however, this approach proved to be a considerable conceptual hurdle. In particular, they found it difficult to create a concept that included multiple perspectives, and that incorporated the real-time exploration of these perspectives, through meaningful interactions. Instead, they kept coming back to a fixed, linear story of one particular migrant.

In our experience, many students, also in the courses we teach, have a tendency to tell relatively static stories, that is, students find it extremely difficult to approach narrative from a different angle than the dominant model of linear storytelling. Even students with training in game design succumb to the authorial reflex of 'telling stories' (versus offering opportunities for interaction within a narrative space) when asked to design an interactive narrative. Instead of the usual prototyping and playtesting, they start making scripts, storyboards and world-building bibles. User-interaction is integrated at some point, later in the design process, becoming a nice add-on at best, but not the experiential core it should be. The challenge for us as teachers is therefore to help these students with rethinking their concept of what a narrative could be, and show them that many of the tools and methods they have learned for building interactive experiences (mainly games) are also applicable to interactive narrative design.

The best way to do this is to help them rethink their role as author. Many scholars have searched for alternative terms to describe the IDN practitioner. For example, Mark Stephen Meadows proposes to think of the IDN designer as an architect:

> In most cases, it should be considered that the goal of an interactive narrative is not to author the narrative, but to provide a context and an environment in which the narrative can be discovered or built by the readers of the story. In this way, designers and authors of interactive narrative are far more like architects than they are like writers [23].

Echoing the words of Meadows, Henry Jenkins prefers the term "narrative architect" when describing designers of narrative games: "it makes sense to think of game designers less as storytellers than as narrative architects" [24]. According to Jenkins, game designers do not tell stories, but design "spaces ripe with narrative possibility" [24]. Following Jenkins, Michael Nitsche elaborates on the notion of narrative architects by including the user, since (s)he can be allowed to construct parts of the narrative [25]. In a similar fashion, Murray [2] emphasizes the need for a "cyberbard" or "cyberdramatist" – a Homer or Shakespeare of the post-print age – to create narrative systems, allowing interactors to perform a role, and in doing so, to actively create belief. Koenitz explicitly positions the cyberbard as a "system designer" emphasizing the difference to traditional authorship with the motto: 'I will sit back and watch with amazement what the audience will do with it' [10]. Koenitz et al. [26] further define this argument by foregrounding the systemic aspects of IDN creation. They described the IDN creator as having the ability to design an IDN system in such a way that meaningful narratives emerge in the imagination of users when they interact with the system [26]. Following cognitive narratologists such as Ryan [27], Bordwell [28] and Herman [29], narratives are understood here as being mental constructs, triggered in response to the user's interaction with the system, which is seen as the equivalent of the narratological category of 'text'.

It is important to confront students with these different understandings of the IDN practitioner, and the implication it has for the practice of IDN design. On a pragmatic level, however, telling the students is not enough. We experienced that the best way to help them 'unlearn' the notion of conventional storytelling is to deprive them of the time to envision a story in any detail, and invite them early on in the project to imagine user interactions instead. In one of the first weeks of the project, we organized a workshop, in which students presented some of their initial concepts. These concepts were tested and elaborated upon by making and playing several physical prototypes. Because physical prototypes foreground user interactions (i.e. they need to be playable) students were forced early on in the process to think and act as designers of user interactions, instead of storytellers.

This does not mean that the authored stories they came up with were useless. On the contrary, they contained interesting themes and directions. We helped the students with deconstructing their stories into essential components (characters, character actions, character motives, setting, etc.). Then, we explored if and how these components could be translated into the components of an interactive system (users, user actions, user goals, user spaces, etc.). For example, we asked whether the actions of the main character could be turned into interesting narrative game mechanics [30]. Does the story setting afford interesting user actions? Can we change the events in the story so that their order of appearance becomes more flexible or even irrelevant?

We have noticed that doing this exercise with students helps them in changing their conceptual model; their way of looking at the practice of interactive narrative design and their role as interactive narrative designer.

4.2 Designerly Challenge

The students in the project were given a complex design assignment. We asked them to design an interactive narrative, for migrants, using new technologies, with the purpose of creating societal impact. After the first student presentation, in which they shared their initial ideas, it became clear to us that this assignment was particularly difficult for them.

The first idea was called 'perspective puzzler', a game in the spirit of games like *Super Paper Mario* [31] or *Perspective* [32]. The player would solve spatial puzzles by changing the game camera's perspective, for example between 2D and 3D. The game would demonstrate, in an abstract manner, the value of switching perspectives when trying to understand and solve societal issues.

The second idea was called 'metal migrant', a 3D robot brawler, similar to a game like *Transformers: Devastation* [33]. The player would control a robot in a foreign land, fighting off waves of enemies. In the beginning, the player-character was not accepted by the country's inhabitants, but as (s)he slayed more enemies, acceptance grew. The idea was to communicate the message of 'migrants only find acceptance when they work hard'.

The third idea was called 'employment agency simulator', a game in the spirit of *The Sims* [34]. In this game, the user would play a migrant, trying to get a job. The simulation game should confront the user with the prejudices and difficulties that migrants face when applying for job vacancies.

Although these ideas contain some interesting directions, they all suffer from the same problem – they take their gameplay ideas from existing games. In our experience, students with a background in game development often have the tendencies to blindly copy the gameplay from existing games when developing applied (serious) narrative games. They only change the narrative context in order to include the game's societal purpose. Indeed, this tendency is not confined to students, but it is a well-known phenomenon in the development of applied games in general. This phenomenon is commonly named 'chocolate covered broccoli'. Games with this issue "fail to align the learning outcomes with the game mechanics, instead forcing learning into a game, or game mechanics into a learning activity" [35]. An often mentioned example is the game *Food Force* [36], an educational game published by the United Nations World Food Program (WFP). The game tries to educate players on famine. In certain levels, the player controls a helicopter, dropping food packages. The gameplay is highly reminiscent of games like *Urban Strike* [37]. Although the player drops packages instead of explosives, the gameplay of *Food Force* still revolves around precision aiming and spatial navigation, and essentially fails to educate on the topic of food scarcity.

By borrowing mechanics of existing games, the student's initial ideas all ran the risk of becoming chocolate covered broccoli. By copying proven mechanics, these narrative games might have been fun to play, but it was unclear how the mechanics could create the desired awareness. The intended migrant narratives were put on top of the gameplay, rather forcefully (and were also relatively static, pre-authored). Ideally, the mechanics themselves express the desired narratives, showing the complexity behind integrating in Dutch society.

To alleviate this issue, we focused our energy on helping the students find mechanics that aligned with the narrative context. In other words, we searched for fitting narrative game mechanics, understood here as follows: "narrative game mechanics invite agents, including the player, to perform actions that support the construction of engaging stories and fictional worlds in the embodied mind of the player" [30]. We did this first by showing the students example games that successfully integrated gameplay and narrative, amongst others, *Karen* [38], *Bury me, my Love* [39] and *Florence* [40]. We discussed together in length how these interactive narratives used interaction to convey their message. Secondly, we organized several paper prototyping and play testing sessions. By inviting students to build interesting, novel interactions, and testing if these interactions conveyed the intended narratives, the team succeeded in the end in developing a promising design.

Although it is not our intention to discuss the final design in full detail, we do want to share some of its core design elements. The final prototype, named RSVP, revolves around the idea of planning an intercultural party with friends and colleagues, and the challenges that this task presents from the perspective of a Muslim migrant in the Netherlands.

This interactive narrative offers the player meaningful interaction possibilities on two levels: chat interface and environment of the apartment. Within a simulated smart phone chat function (Fig. 1), the player discusses the party preparation with friends, family, colleagues and a work supervisor – each having his or her own preferences, requirements and demands, and different and potentially clashing cultural backgrounds. The player then has to find a balance between adapting to the culture and associated expectations of the friends and colleagues, who are used to the consumption of alcoholic beverages and pork meat products during festive activities, and the culture of religious friends, who are most likely offended by these. Other areas of conflict are the party's theme, music and dress code.

Given the player's knowledge of the guests' cultural sensitivities (gained during chat conversations), the player weighs options and makes decisions. Now, it is time to put decisions into action by placing party props, decoration, food and drinks into the virtual apartment (Fig. 2). The player is able to see the decorated apartment by tilting his or her phone, which tells the app to switch from the simulated chat to the inside of the virtual AR apartment. Once back in the apartment environment, the player can look around by moving their physical smartphone.

Once everything is prepared, the party starts and plays out based on the reactions of the guests. After the party, the player finds out how the guests liked the party by seeing their comments in the chat. Comments and reactions vary from being happy, grateful, blaming the player for a ruined evening or, in some instances, being so upset that they block the player.

4.3   Technical Challenge

The main technical challenge was in a lack of flexible, tailored authoring tools that would allow for the implementation of AR features (looking around in the apartment by moving the smartphone, switching to the chat interface by lowering the device). This required the design and building of a custom made tool, which translated into a large amount of time and energy. Students built their own tool that enabled the integration of a branching narrative created with Twine into Unity. This concept makes IDN design more accessible: using the simple interface of Twine, even non-programmers can easily make editorial changes to the text of the chat conversations, thus improving the writing and flow.

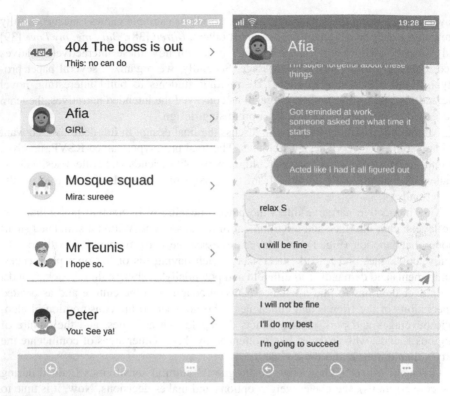

Fig. 1. Screenshots of the chat simulation in RSVP, chat selection (left) and interaction options with a chat partner (right).

Another challenge lies in the lack of support for art work from the self-made text-based authoring tool. The team had no visual artist, which affected the creation of a convincing representation of an apartment more than the representation of the chat module. Consequently, character images are simple placeholders in the current prototype. The lack of a dedicated visual artist was compensated by the decision to go for a more simplistic, comical 2D look. Instead of rendering a 3D environment for the apartment that would require 3D models of every object, the team implemented a 360 view of a panoramic 2D image. While our student team overcame this limitation by deciding for a simpler art style, future teams need to be more balanced, including a dedicated visual artist and writer.

Fig. 2. Screenshot of the apartment in RSVP, objects can be placed here.

5 Discussion

Our intention for the current project was the creation of a 'serious IDN', focused on the topic of migration with the potential to positively affect attitudes towards this subject. Irrespective of considerable obstacles, the resulting prototype supports this goal in two ways and can thus be considered a success. Parrot and Carpentier identify the adoption of another person's role as a first step towards a changed understanding: "the sheer action of digitally adopting another person's perspective in an interactive narrative may itself nurture positive attitudes concerning the character and issues related to the character" [3]. This aspect is covered by the final prototype as it puts the interactor in the role of a migrant encountering the difficult task of organizing a multicultural party that attending guests would enjoy.

In addition, we see potential for the use of this interactive narrative experience as a discussion-starter for workshops on the topic of migration, especially in the context of the challenging relationship between diversity and integration. Living in an alien culture, deprived from familiarity, can lead to a culture shock and a crisis of personality or identity. This potential crisis is often intensified by the pressure for cultural adaption and integration [41]. Our project can help raise awareness of this issue, especially in the target group of Dutch youths.

In continuing the project, we will take the lessons learned in the first iteration on board. In particular, we will focus even more on the aspect of 'unlearning' the dominant model of linear storytelling and instead facilitate a perspective on narrative game mechanics as a concrete practice of IDN design. In addition, we see a need for stronger guidance and therefore will not conduct the project again as student-led, but re-organize it as a virtual game studio with teachers in leading positions: studio head, narrative lead, programming lead, sound lead, user research lead etc.

Finally, we will apply Phoebe Senger's method of "Reflective design" [42] to integrate migrants themselves in the design process. This method provides the means to turn project clients into contributors, which we feel is an essential aspect of our undertaking.

6 Conclusion

Our project applies the potential of serious applications for interactive narratives, as 'IDNs for change,' in an educational setting. The resulting prototype RSVP uses the activity of planning an intercultural party as a metaphor for challenges that arise when humans coming from different cultural backgrounds aim to find common ground between diverse habits and belief systems. Experiencing perspective change is a crucial ingredient for better understanding and communication between migrants and locals. In order to further improve this aspect, future iterations of the project will emphasize the inclusion of all target-groups during the design phase to create an authentic, meaningful and, in the best case, positively transformative experience.

From a research perspective, the project exposes a lack of accessible pedagogical resources to teach IDN design in the struggle to keep the participating students from falling into the trap of linear storytelling methods on the one hand and simple game mechanics with a thin layer of 'narrative sugar coating' on the other side. We are still in the situation where successful narrative game design/IDN design depends too much on the expertise of a particular teacher/mentor. The creation of accessible pedagogical resources for IDN design is therefore a challenge that the community needs to address with increased research and sharing of existing resources. That this need was already identified by Murray and Rieser in the 1990s should make clear that it is high time to finally do something about it.

Acknowledgements. We would like to thank the following students and teachers for participating in the project: Timothy Schelhaas, Ruben Bimmel, Davey Verhoef, Ermis Chalkiadakis, Sytze Schalk, Roger Lenoir, Ruben Abels and Valentijn Muijrers.

References

1. Davenport, G.: New Orleans in transition, 1983–1986: the interactive delivery of a cinematic case study. In: Presented at The International Congress for Design Planning and Theory, Education Group Conference, Boston, MA (1987)
2. Murray, J.H.: Hamlet on the Holodeck: The Future of Narrative in Cyberspace. Free Press, New York (1997)
3. Parrott, S., Carpentier, F.R.D., Northup, C.T.: A test of interactive narrative as a tool against prejudice. Howard J. Commun. **28**, 1–16 (2017)
4. Murray, J.H.: The pedagogy of cyberfiction: teaching a course on reading and writing interactive narrative. In: Barrett, E., Redmond, M. (eds.) Contextual Media: Multimedia and Interpretation, pp. 129–162. MIT Press, Cambridge (1995)
5. Rieser, M.: Interactive narrative: educating the authors. In: Presented at the Seventh International Symposium on Electronic Art 1996, Rotterdam (1996)

6. Spierling, U., Szilas, N., Hoffmann, S., Richle, U.: Workshop: education in interactive digital storytelling. In: Aylett, R., Lim, M.Y., Louchart, S., Petta, P., Riedl, M. (eds.) ICIDS 2010. LNCS, vol. 6432, pp. 289–290. Springer, Heidelberg (2010). https://doi.org/10.1007/978-3-642-16638-9_45

7. Koenitz, H.: Five theses for interactive digital narrative. In: Mitchell, A., Fernández-Vara, C., Thue, D. (eds.) ICIDS 2014. LNCS, vol. 8832, pp. 134–139. Springer, Cham (2014). https://doi.org/10.1007/978-3-319-12337-0_13

8. Spierling, U., Szilas, N.: Authoring issues beyond tools. In: Iurgel, I.A., Zagalo, N., Petta, P. (eds.) ICIDS 2009. LNCS, vol. 5915, pp. 50–61. Springer, Heidelberg (2009). https://doi.org/10.1007/978-3-642-10643-9_9

9. Cavazza, M., et al.: The IRIS network of excellence: integrating research in interactive storytelling. In: Spierling, U., Szilas, N. (eds.) ICIDS 2008. LNCS, vol. 5334, pp. 14–19. Springer, Heidelberg (2008). https://doi.org/10.1007/978-3-540-89454-4_3

10. Koenitz, H.: Design approaches for interactive digital narrative. In: Schoenau-Fog, H., Bruni, L.E., Louchart, S., Baceviciute, S. (eds.) ICIDS 2015. LNCS, vol. 9445, pp. 50–57. Springer, Cham (2015). https://doi.org/10.1007/978-3-319-27036-4_5

11. Strohecker, C.: A case study in interactive narrative design. In: Proceedings of the 2nd Conference on Designing Interactive Systems Processes, Practices, Methods, and Techniques, pp. 377–380. ACM, New York (1997)

12. Bizzocchi, J., Woodbury, R.F.: A case study in the design of interactive narrative: the subversion of the interface. Simul. Gaming **34**, 550–568 (2003)

13. Mateas, M., Stern, A.: Procedural authorship: a case-study of the interactive drama Façade. In: Proceedings of the Digital Arts and Culture, DAC 2005 (2005)

14. Daiute, C., Koenitz, H.: What is shared? - a pedagogical perspective on interactive digital narrative and literary narrative. In: Nack, F., Gordon, A.S. (eds.) ICIDS 2016. LNCS, vol. 10045, pp. 407–410. Springer, Cham (2016). https://doi.org/10.1007/978-3-319-48279-8_37

15. Daiute, C., Duncan, R.O.: Interactive imagining in interactive digital narrative. In: Nunes, N., Oakley, I., Nisi, V. (eds.) ICIDS 2017. LNCS, vol. 10690, pp. 282–285. Springer, Cham (2017). https://doi.org/10.1007/978-3-319-71027-3_26

16. Chu, S.K.W., Reynolds, R.B., Tavares, N.J., Notari, M., Lee, C.W.Y.: 21st Century Skills Development Through Inquiry-Based Learning. Springer, Singapore (2017). https://doi.org/10.1007/978-981-10-2481-8

17. Brown, T.: Change by Design. HarperCollins, New York (2009)

18. Aldrich, C.: Learning by Doing: A Comprehensive Guide to Simulations, Computer Games, and Pedagogy in e-Learning and Other Educational Experiences. Pfeiffer, San Francisco (2005)

19. Beetham, H., Sharpe, R. (eds.): Rethinking Pedagogy for a Digital Age: Designing for 21st Century Learning. Routledge, New York (2013)

20. Lou, Y., Ma, J.: A 3D "T-shaped" design education framework. In: Bast, G., Carayannis, E. G., Campbell, D.F.J. (eds.) Arts, Research, Innovation and Society. ARIS, pp. 123–136. Springer, Cham (2015). https://doi.org/10.1007/978-3-319-09909-5_7

21. Santos Green, L., Banas, J.R., Perkins, R.A. (eds.): The Flipped College Classroom. Springer, Cham (2017). https://doi.org/10.1007/978-3-319-41855-1

22. Zurita, G., Hasbun, B., Baloian, N., Jerez, O.: A blended learning environment for enhancing meaningful learning using 21st century skills. In: Chen, G., Kumar, V., Kinshuk, Huang, R., Kong, S.C. (eds.) Emerging Issues in Smart Learning. LNET, pp. 1–8. Springer, Heidelberg (2015). https://doi.org/10.1007/978-3-662-44188-6_1

23. Meadows, M.S.: Pause & Effect. New Riders Press, Indianapolis (2003)

24. Jenkins, H.: Game design as narrative architecture. In: Wardrip-Fruin, N., Harrigan, P. (eds.) First Person: New Media as Story, Performance, and Game, pp. 118–130. MIT Press, Cambridge (2004)
25. Nitsche, M.: Video Game Spaces. MIT Press, Cambridge (2008)
26. Koenitz, H., Dubbelman, T., Knoller, N., Roth, C.: An Integrated and Iterative Research Direction for Interactive Digital Narrative. In: Nack, F., Gordon, A.S. (eds.) ICIDS 2016. LNCS, vol. 10045, pp. 51–60. Springer, Cham (2016). https://doi.org/10.1007/978-3-319-48279-8_5
27. Ryan, M.-L., Ruppert, J., Bernet, J.W.: Narrative Across Media. University of Nebraska Press, Lincoln (2004)
28. Bordwell, D.: Poetics of Cinema. Routledge, New York (2007)
29. Herman, D.: Story Logic. University of Nebraska Press, Lincoln (2002)
30. Dubbelman, T.: Narrative Game Mechanics. In: Nack, F., Gordon, A.S. (eds.) ICIDS 2016. LNCS, vol. 10045, pp. 39–50. Springer, Cham (2016). https://doi.org/10.1007/978-3-319-48279-8_4
31. Nintendo: Super Paper Mario (2007)
32. DigiPen Institute of Technology: Perspective (2012)
33. Platinum Games: Transformers: Devastation (2015)
34. Maxis: The Sims (2000)
35. Moseley, A., Whitton, N. (eds.): New Traditional Games for Learning. Routledge, New York (2014)
36. United Nations World Food Program: Food Force (2005)
37. THQ Inc.: Urban Strike, (1995)
38. Blast Theory: Karen (2014)
39. The Pixel Hunt, Figs: Bury me, my Love (2017)
40. Mountains: Florence (2018)
41. Castles, S.: Migration. Citizenship and Identity. Edward Elgar Publishing, Northampton (2017)
42. Sengers, P., Boehner, K., David, S., Kaye, J.: Reflective design. In: Presented at the 4th Decennial Conference on Critical Computing: Between Sense and Sensibility (2005)

Applying Interactive Storytelling in Cultural Heritage: Opportunities, Challenges and Lessons Learned

Akrivi Katifori[1,2]([✉]), Manos Karvounis[1,2], Vassilis Kourtis[1,2],
Sara Perry[3], Maria Roussou[1,2], and Yannis Ioanidis[1,2]

[1] ATHENA Research Center,
Artemidos 6 & Epidavrou, 15125 Maroussi, Greece
[2] Department of Informatics and Telecommunications,
National and Kapodistrian University of Athens,
Panepistimioupolis, Ilissia, Greece
{vivi,manosk,vkourtis,mroussou,yannis}@di.uoa.gr
[3] Department of Archaeology, University of York, York, UK
sara.perry@york.ac.uk

Abstract. Digital storytelling in cultural heritage contexts has been recognized as a direction that cultural heritage institutions, including museums and historical sites, need to invest in to attract and engage their audiences. The term "interactive storytelling" is often used to characterize existing digital applications, whether these incorporate narrative structures or not. However, is "interactive storytelling" with its strict definition actually strongly present as an art form within the domain of cultural heritage, especially for on-site mobile experiences? In this work, we report on our experience and lessons learnt during our efforts to apply the genre of interactive storytelling in the heritage sector with the aim to more effectively support both authors and users of mobile interactive storytelling apps.

Keywords: Interactive storytelling · Authoring · Branching narratives · Cultural heritage

1 Introduction

Digital storytelling in cultural heritage contexts has been universally recognized as a direction that cultural heritage institutions, including museums and historical sites, need to invest in to attract and engage their audiences (Pujol et al. 2013; Twiss-Garrity et al. 2008). An increasing number of cultural institutions around the world use mobile guides which employ narratives of different forms to enhance the visitor experience. The definition of "digital storytelling" in cultural heritage contexts has, in this sense, been "overextended" to include a variety of multimedia apps including guides offering purely informational content. These storytelling apps are often characterized as "interactive" when in fact they simply offer options that allow the users to control their navigation around the site and to select informational content.

© Springer Nature Switzerland AG 2018
R. Rouse et al. (Eds.): ICIDS 2018, LNCS 11318, pp. 603–612, 2018.
https://doi.org/10.1007/978-3-030-04028-4_70

So is "interactive storytelling" actually strongly present as an art form within the domain of cultural heritage? Considering the simple definition of interactive storytelling as an experience in which the user can influence the story and its characters, and reach different outcomes according to her actions, there are in actuality very few interactive storytelling mobile experiences that have been applied in the heritage domain for on-site visits. In the case of virtual, off-site experiences, there have been efforts to introduce the genre in interactive television productions (Meadows et al. 2009).

In this work we aim to explore the specific challenges arising from applying the interactive storytelling concept in cultural heritage. We focus on mobile experiences, addressed to visitors that are present at a cultural site, rather than those accessing a reconstruction of an archaeological site or a virtual museum from a remote location. We report on our experience and lessons learnt during our efforts to apply the interactive storytelling genre in the heritage sector with the aim to more effectively support both the authors and users of mobile interactive storytelling apps.

Section 2 briefly presents the background of these efforts; Sect. 3 the specifics of the authoring workflow; Sect. 4 reports on the identified challenges and lessons learnt; and Sect. 5 presents our conclusions.

2 Background

To design augmented guidebooks (Poole 2017), museums often employ specialized staff and external creative experts. Yet the design and production of appropriate content for meaningful mobile interactive storytelling experiences remains a challenge. The field lacks robust and established practices as well as standard authoring workflows. This lack of standard methodologies, guidelines, and appropriate authoring tools specifically designed to support cultural institutions in developing mobile interactive storytelling experiences has been an impediment to the integration of interactive storytelling in museum practices and cultural heritage in general.

The CHESS project (CHESS project; Katifori et al. 2014; Roussou and Katifori 2018) explored different aspects of digital interactive and personalized storytelling with the objective of enhancing the visitor experience on-site. The project produced branching narratives which interweaved informational content with storytelling elements combined in a coherent plot via a graph based authoring tool (Vayanou et al. 2014).

The project EMOTIVE[1] (Emotive virtual cultural experiences through personalized storytelling), building upon the CHESS methodologies and tools, is a Research and Innovation (RIA) action, that aims to research, design, develop and evaluate methods for creating narratives and experiences based on the power of 'emotive storytelling'. Through collaboration with a variety of cultural sites, both projects have fostered continuous experimentation with the interactive storytelling genre in different institutions and the evaluation of produced stories with different audiences. This work has led to the identification of the basic elements of a preliminary conceptual framework (Perry et al. 2017; EMOTIVE Conceptual Framework and Guide report) and the development

---

[1] https://www.emotiveproject.eu.

and testing of story prototyping tools for the authors of storytelling experiences for cultural heritage.

3   The Need for an Effective Authoring Workflow

The production of digital storytelling experiences for cultural heritage is a result of collaboration in multidisciplinary teams, involving experts from different domains, including the cultural and creative industry (Roussou et al. 2015). These may include a wide range of roles, in some cases with one individual representing multiple areas of expertise:

- Domain experts. These include museum curators and experts in museum content and topics (archaeologists, historians, art history experts, etc.). They provide the interpretation material on which the storytelling experiences are based.
- Exhibition designers. They are responsible for the set-up of the museum exhibitions and the material that is made available to the public in relation to them. They provide a view of what the visitors need, in terms of common questions, interests and approaches that work, or not, in the Gallery or Site.
- Storytellers. They provide the plot of the story and author its textual parts.
- Digital asset designers. They are in charge of digital asset creation and the combination of such assets into interactive activities, composing thus the complete storytelling experience.

In less complex productions, involving proven and widely accepted methodologies and technologies, such as the making of audio guides or multimedia productions for a museum website, the conceptual and technological aspect is considered a "given" and the team can focus mostly on content design with specific guidelines. Even in these cases, emotional engagement with the content is not the subject of much discussion, and most of the evaluations that exist for audio guides focus on functionality, not on the experience or true engagement with the narrative.

However, even in such cases where clear guidelines and technological solutions are available, this process is not always straightforward or smooth. Cultural site experts include scientists who have a deep research interest and understanding of the exhibited content, whether objects or the cultural space itself. When asked to deliver "meaningful", "interesting" or "engaging" content it can be very challenging for them to choose the most appropriate content for their intended "consumers", the visitors, without projecting on them their own needs, interests and concepts for what would be an ideal experience. An "interesting" piece of information of a particular archaeological site for an archaeologist may be completely irrelevant or uninterpretable to the uninformed visitor and vice versa. This issue has also been noted in different heritage related media, including videogames (Copplestone 2017). In these cases, it may become a significant challenge to leverage the objectives of the site experts for the delivery of particular content with the actual needs of their intended audiences.

In fields like interactive storytelling, which arguably are still in an experimental stage, the process can become even more complicated. On one hand, cultural site experts may have no clear concept of what the resulting product, the produced digital experience, will be. On the other hand, the interaction design and computer experts could bring ideas and proposals that may not yet be tested or fully accepted by the domain experts. However, the most important goal remains the same for cultural institutions: to bridge the gap between the domain experts, their research and inter-pretations, and the visitors, their interests, preferences and needs.

4 Authoring Challenges

As discussed in the previous section, digital mobile storytelling experience (co)creation is not without challenges. On the one hand, the re-definition of the museum's internal organization or workflow, which now has to open to vertical but also external exchanges, i.e. with professionals from outside the institution. On the other hand, pure academic skills are no longer enough; authors need to have an interdisciplinary background or at least some familiarity with new methodologies (e.g., visitor-centred design, less academic and more emotionally-evocative interactive storytelling tech-niques) and tools (e.g., authoring and publishing software).

Additionally, interactive storytelling as a tool to enhance the on-site visitor expe-rience presents a specific set of challenges that are not so prominent in other domains. This section discusses the most critical of these challenges.

4.1 Establishing a Common Vision

The first step towards bringing an interactive storytelling experience into a cultural institution is establishing a common vision between the domain experts and the creative industries involved in the production of the envisioned experience. Museums are often perceived as guardians of our historical memories and as such may be reluctant to experiment with the presentation of the factual evidence in order to facilitate more engaging storytelling experiences. Even the inclusion of fictional characters, especially in main roles in a story, can become a major challenge, and authors can be asked to make compromises so that the characters they design can be approved by the domain experts. As Staiff (2014, 104) comments, this often leads to 'flat' and poorly developed characters.

This constant controversy between "facts" and "fiction" is one of the main chal-lenges for the full introduction of interactive storytelling in cultural heritage digital experiences. It can only be resolved through the establishment of an authoring work-flow that promotes communication between all involved experts and that sets the vision for – as well as measures for navigating and critically understanding – the creative license deployed in the storyline.

4.2 Understanding Interactive Storytelling

Creating a quality experience requires a deep understanding of the concept of inter-active storytelling and the best practices of its application in cultural heritage. At the moment there are very few, if any, experts in storytelling for heritage who can claim expertise in this art form, applied in real world contexts, beyond particular specialty research themes. All authors should be made aware through an appropriately presented conceptual framework of the characteristics, challenges and limitations of the mobile interactive storytelling approach and establish early on their objective, taking into account the institutional needs and budget.

A relevant, overlooked issue in the domain of heritage is that of genres and their relation to offering personalized content to the users. The entire movie, book and videogame industries are built around genres and services like Netflix have minute data on people's specific genre interests that allow them to develop niche shows perfectly tailored to their audiences (Madrigal 2014). And this isn't at all reflected in the museums sector, where in most cases a "one experience fits all" approach is applied.

4.3   A Strong Need for Guidelines and Tools

An interactive storytelling approach for story design and implementation in cultural contexts requires specific and detailed guidelines for each step of the authoring process, starting from the collection of the interpretation material to staging of the story in the physical space to the creation of assets and the compilation of the end experience.

All involved experts need to be trained not only in the use of possible authoring tools, but also in the overall authoring methodology—even in the simple notion of the need for interaction in the plot level and branching narratives. This may be especially true for cultural heritage professionals who are less familiar with the affordances of digital tools (interaction, non-linearity), and hence might require some initial guidance to assimilate them in their interpretative practices.

Concrete guidelines, in different forms for different uses, should be available to support ideation, design and development. Building upon the need for specific guidelines, tools are needed to support and automate the story creation process each step of the way, providing a direct means to structure the interpretation material, guide the interactive story design and ensure an implementation that will adhere to the given guidelines and protect the authors from repeating common mistakes.

4.4   Defining Personas

Museum experts who have been exposed to the use of personas (Roussou et al. 2013) during the design process have insisted on their strong presence throughout the development process. They consider them very convenient not only as design tools, but also to convey easily the idea that a particular image, narrative style, subject, character, or story part may be interesting for one visitor category but irrelevant to another. Thus, personas feature among the design tools available to the author when compiling a story. They can be used to "tag" particular story elements and assets such as images, videos and other material. These persona tags are translated into user characteristics to be later matched with user profiles and possibly used to personalize the visitor experience by recommending specific storytelling experiences.

However, in the heritage or museum context, it is relatively rare for a visitor to present themselves at a site alone; guests tend, instead, to visit as a part of a family, friendship, or wider tourist party. With this in mind, we feel that it would be important to develop storytelling applications and experiences for groups of people, and not only individuals.

While the literature on group personas is thin, Kuniavsky (2004) is among the few to discuss such multi-individual personas, specifically in relation to theme parks. He proposes that descriptions and outlines of group personas should perhaps be less pointed and focused than individual personas. Instead, needs and goals must be shared across the group, demanding prioritization and compromise between the various players. Our work so far, following up to this approach shows promising results in the use of group personas to support the design of storytelling experiences for heritage.

4.5   Stories Should be About People, not Exhibits

Amongst the primary objectives of a cultural institution is to promote visitor engagement and connection with the site exhibits and artefacts on display and the site itself. This need influences decisions on story concept and plot and dictates the presence of these objects, directly or indirectly, in the story. However, as Crawford (2005, 17) suggests, "Stories are about people, not things" and the attempt to create storytelling where the objects themselves are the main objective and the plot and characters are built around them results in experiences that are bound to leave the visitor feeling that something is missing, that "the experience is not a story" (Roussou and Katifori 2018).

As a result, in the cultural heritage domain the creation of engaging storytelling is a challenge. Stories, especially interactive ones, to be engaging and truly moving, cannot only revolve around objects. Crawford (2005, 20) suggests that they should concern choices that characters make, either dramatically salient ones or less obvious ones that establish character.

4.6   Staging the Experience

When designing an interactive storytelling experience for an on-site visit to a cultural site, the space or "stage" of the experience is an important factor to be taken into account, just as with the site's exhibits and artifacts. This need is more pronounced if the site itself is of historical interest and not just a building that houses important artifacts.

To design a story that incorporates the site itself and effectively balances the story parts with visitors' movements, it is paramount that staging, i.e., the development of the story in the exhibition space or the cultural site, is taken into account during the authoring workflow.

Yet, staging can be done in different ways. As shown in several creative authoring workshops (Roussou et al. 2015), no matter the author's familiarity with the gallery or the quality of available gallery maps, storytelling is improved by testing on-site or with an appropriate simulation tool at hand. In the cases where the participants did not spend time early on in the gallery/site, the produced stories had issues with visitor navigation and positioning in relation to the exhibits and hotspots on site; although the plot might be engaging, they needed tweaking to be more effective in relation to the gallery's or site's spatial arrangement.

As discussed in Sect. 4.6, along with the importance placed on objects and exhibits, the fact that space is also crucial in cultural heritage is a disrupting factor to storytelling. Either because it is the historical monument itself we need to focus on - or simply the need to navigate and guide the user in the real physical space of a museum or site – these staging-related issues complicate immersion in the story.

A more difficult issue to tackle, however, is the possible discontinuity between the actual physical space the visitor is experiencing the story in and the stage of the story itself. Even if the story is taking place in a specific historical monument where the visitor is present, if there is a difference in the time period, the user has to reconcile this past-present temporal disconnect via the storytelling, a fact which could impact negatively on the whole experience.

In the context of our work in EMOTIVE, we have developed experiences which are set in the present, exploring concepts and ideas that were manifest in the past, but through a contemporary lens (Perry et al. 2019). In this sense, the visitor is using their own experiences to help make sense of the past, not inhabiting the bodies of past people as though we can completely understand what they were doing and thinking in pre-modern times. Rather, visitors in the present are guided through a story in the present that makes them think about how people in the past might have navigated and negotiated the same issues. There is no disconnect, then, and the only staging-related issues that are left to manage are those common to any sites; and places like Disney have arguably written the textbooks on how to handle these matters in exceptional fashion, completely immersing visitors from the moment they approach the car park. Disney might be the extreme example, but there are many lessons to be learned that can apply at more modest levels.

4.7 Designing for Meaningful Interaction

One of the constant user evaluation results from storytelling experiences created during and after the CHESS project was the need for "more interaction". Interviewed visitors who tried the interactive storytelling experiences felt for some reason that they were not "interactive" enough. When prompted further they explained that this comment does not mean they would like to "interact more with the mobile screen or the application, on the contrary". They focused this need for "interactivity" on two main points:

- Interacting with the exhibits: Several users felt that complex exhibits (e.g. scientific instruments) would be better showcased through an interactive activity explaining their different parts and their use, if such an activity could fit in the overall story concept.
- Interacting with the story plot: As already mentioned, although the stories featured several branching and decision points, most users felt that they were too guided and too "linear". They felt that they had no actual control on the plot itself, on how the story unfolds. Although they were given initially a role in the story and a task, there were no crucial decision points that could potentially change the outcome of the story. Branches revolved around information content that the visitors could access or the path they could follow on-site. Their role in the story was in reality that of a spectator, an "invisible" and transparent character that follows the main character

with no possibility to actually interact with him or her in a meaningful way. Some visitors, especially with more pronounced gaming backgrounds, felt restricted by this. As Crawford (2005) explains, story "richness depends on the functional significance of each choice and the perceived completeness of choices offered".

4.8 Screen vs. Space

All storytelling approaches applied so far showed the need for the capacity of digital storytelling to link not only exhibits under different discourses, but also existing digital and analogue assets, which can be "recycled" into engaging narrations. This is important given the fact that digital productions still constitute a major economic and personal effort for museums and cultural institutions in general.

However, it is also important, as Crawford (2005) suggests, especially in the field of cultural heritage, to keep in mind that "spectacle does not make stories and visual thinking should not dominate storytelling" (pp. 22–23). As previously mentioned, the objective is to enhance the visit on-site, not replace it. The absorbing power of the screen has been proven to sometimes distract the visitors from focusing their attention on the exhibits themselves. Leveraging this delicate balance between the physical world and the creative story world, and ensuring that interactive storytelling augments rather than competes with the exhibition is possibly amongst the most difficult challenges to tackle in cultural heritage settings.

5   Conclusions

It becomes prominent that, while very little work has been done to introduce interactive narrative in the context of cultural heritage, there are indications that this aspect could effectively improve digital storytelling experiences, making them more engaging for the visitors. Visitors seemed to request "more interaction", which seemed to translate to more control over the story plot. However, applying interactive storytelling in cultural heritage is not a straightforward endeavour. In this article we have tried to summarize the main challenges faced when introducing interactive storytelling in on-site mobile cultural heritage experiences.

Focusing on the authoring process, we presented eight challenges that we need to overcome every time we create this type of experience:

- A common vision has to be established in order to avoid conflicts between the various experts taking part in the process
- There needs to be a good understanding of what an interactive narrative is and what are the opportunities, challenges and limitations that it could bring in the process
- Authors need to follow concrete guidelines and learn how to use new types of authoring tools
- Group personas need to be defined in order to target group visits, which are much more common than individual ones but often overlooked by technology experts.

- The stories created should be about people and not objects, regardless of whether these people are invented characters, historical persons, or even the visitors themselves
- Experiences need to be carefully staged in the physical space in order to help the narrative unfold and create a connection between past and present
- Interactivity should be meaningful to the visitor and focused on the visitor-exhibit interaction as well as the interaction with the story plot
- A delicate balance between the physical world and the story world is needed to avoid having visitors absorbed by their mobile's screen.

Based on these findings we focus our future work on providing concrete and detailed guidelines that will help experts from various fields collaborate for the common goal of creating meaningful interactive storytelling on-site experiences in cultural heritage contexts.

Additionally, we will be offering a set of software tools that are designed with these guidelines in mind and will support the overall creation process and the collaboration among the different authoring roles, namely the Domain experts, Exhibition designers, Storytellers and Digital asset designers.

References

Kuniavsky, M.: Extending a Technique: Group Personas (2004). http://boxesandarrows.com/extending-a-technique-group-personas/. Accessed 7 Feb 2017

Twiss-Garrity, B.A., Fisher, M., Sastre, A.: The art of storytelling: enriching art museum exhibits and education through visitor narratives. In: Trant, J., Bearman, D. (eds.) Museums and the Web 2008. Archives & Museum Informatics, Montreal (2008)

Pujol, L., Roussou, M., Poulou, S., Balet, O., Vayanou, M., Ioannidis, Y.: Personalizing interactive digital storytelling in archaeological museums: the CHESS project. In: Earl, G., et al. (eds.) Archaeology in the Digital Era. Papers from the 40th Annual Conference of Computer Applications and Quantitative Methods in Archaeology (CAA). Southampton, UK, 26–29 March 2012. Amsterdam University Press (2013)

Perry, S., Roussou, M., Economou, M., Young, H., Pujol, L.: Moving beyond the virtual museum: engaging visitors emotionally. In: Proceedings of the 23rd International Conference on Virtual Systems and Multimedia -VSMM 2017. IEEE, Dublin (2017)

The CHESS project. http://www.chessexperience.eu/

The EMOTIVE Project. https://www.emotiveproject.eu/

Perry, S., Roussou, M., Mirashrafi, S., et al.: Shared digital experiences supporting collaborative meaning-making at heritage sites. In: Lewi, H., Smith, W., Cooke, S., vom Lehn, D. (eds.) The Routledge International Handbook of New Digital Practices in Galleries, Libraries, Archives, Museums and Heritage Sites. Routledge International Handbook. Routledge, In Press

Crawford, C.: On interactive storytelling. New Riders, Berkeley (2005)

Roussou, M., Pujol, L., Katifori, A., Chrysanthi, A., Perry, S., Vayanou, M.: The museum as digital storyteller: collaborative participatory creation of interactive digital experiences. In: Museums and the Web 2015, MW2015 (2015). http://mw2015.museumsandtheweb.com/paper/the-museum-as-digital-storyteller-collaborative-participatory-creation-of-interactive-digital-experiences/. Accessed 28 Sept 2015, Published 31 January 2015

Katifori, A., et al.: CHESS: personalized storytelling experiences in museums. In: Mitchell, A., Fernández-Vara, C., Thue, D. (eds.) ICIDS 2014. LNCS, vol. 8832, pp. 232–235. Springer, Cham (2014). https://doi.org/10.1007/978-3-319-12337-0_28

Roussou, M., Katifori, A.: Flow, staging, wayfinding, personalization: evaluating user experience with mobile museum narratives. Multimodal Technol. Interact. 2(2), 32 (2018). http://www.mdpi.com/2414-4088/2/2/32/pdf

Vayanou, M., et al.: Authoring personalized interactive museum stories. In: Mitchell, A., Fernández-Vara, C., Thue, D. (eds.) ICIDS 2014. LNCS, vol. 8832, pp. 37–48. Springer, Cham (2014). https://doi.org/10.1007/978-3-319-12337-0_4

Roussou, M., Katifori, A., Pujol, L., Vayanou, M., Rennick-Egglestone, S.J.: A life of their own: museum visitor personas penetrating the design lifecycle of a mobile experience. In: ACM SIGCHI Conference on Human Factors in Computing Systems (CHI, Paris, France, 27 April–2 May 2013, pp. 547–552 (2013). https://doi.org/10.1145/2468356.2468453. ISBN 9781450319522

EMOTIVE Deliverable 5.1 EMOTIVE Conceptual Framework and Guide. https://emotiveproject.eu/cms/wp-content/uploads/2017/11/EMOTIVE_D5.1_ConceptualFrame-Guide_v1.0.pdf. Accessed 11 July 2018

Copplestone, T.J.: But that's not accurate: the differing perceptions of accuracy in cultural-heritage videogames between creators, consumers and critics. Rethink. Hist. 21(3), 415–438 (2017)

Staiff, R.: Re-imagining Heritage Interpretation: Enchanting the Past-Future, 202 p. Ashgate, Farnham. (2014). ISBN: 978-1-4094-5550-9 (hbk), ISBN: 978-1-4724-0735-1 (ePUB)

Poole, S.: Ghosts in the Garden: locative gameplay and historical interpretation from below. Int. J. Herit. Stud. 24(3), 300–314 (2017). https://doi.org/10.1080/13527258.2017.1347887

Madrigal, A.C.: How Netflix Reverse Engineered Hollywood. The Atlantic (2014). https://www.theatlantic.com/technology/archive/2014/01/how-netflix-reverse-engineered-hollywood/282679/

Meadows, D., Kidd, J.: 'Capture Wales': the BBC digital storytelling project. In: Hartley, J., McWilliam, K. (eds.) Story Circle: Digital Storytelling Around the World, pp. 91–117. Wiley-Blackwell, Chichester (2009)

From Co-Curation to Co-Creation: Users as Collective Authors of Archive-Based Cultural Heritage Narratives

Fabian Mohr[(✉)], Soenke Zehle, and Michael Schmitz

Experimental Media Lab, Academy of Fine Arts Saar,
Keplerstr. 3-5, 66117 Saarbruecken, Germany
{f.mohr,s.zehle,m.schmitz}@xmlab.org

Abstract. To deepen the engagement of exhibition visitors with cultural heritage, we develop an interactive design approach to storytelling in which users can act both as co-curators and co-authors through a multitouch interface.

Keywords: Cross-generational user involvement
Public prototyping · Co-creation · Cultural heritage
Virtual museums and curatorial practices

1 Introduction

Multitouch interfaces are a key element of the interaction design in Resonanzen, a collaborative cultural heritage research project aiming to build an interactive archive and exhibition of French post-war architecture in the Franco-German border region [12]. Its title ("Resonances: The Long Waves of Utopia") is inspired by one of the signature buildings explored in the course of the research process, the now-defunct long-wave radio station of the French private broadcasting service Europe 1 built in the 1950s whose coverage reached across Western Europe, the Mediterranean, and Northern Africa [13]. This focus on broadcasting technology acknowledges the central role of communication architectures in the exploration of cultural heritage and frames an interaction design process that aims to make this cultural heritage tangible. Interactive experiences have been deployed and explored under various lenses, particularly in cultural heritage settings [9]. Multi-user tabletop installations in particular have been examined to identify how interactivity can enhance information visualization [4,8], visitor engagement [5,6] and what impact the design of the user interface on aesthetic and informative qualities may have [1–3,7]. It has been shown that such installations have the potential to be inspiring and evocative, fostering collaboration and social engagement [2,3]. But it is essential to design the interface carefully, to let it disperse and allow meaningful interaction with the actual contents [1,3]. Our approach to use a multitouch interface to involve users in the curatorial process of categorising and exploring archived data is an effort to connect elements of

© Springer Nature Switzerland AG 2018
R. Rouse et al. (Eds.): ICIDS 2018, LNCS 11318, pp. 613–620, 2018.
https://doi.org/10.1007/978-3-030-04028-4_71

interactive documentaries, the digitalisation of cultural data (as well as ways to display and use them in new and innovative ways) and user-driven design methods. In our first testing period, we encourage users to immerse themselves in a vast, deeply linked and comprehensively tagged pool of items on post-war architecture and their creators, effectively letting them curate their experience and own narrative of their journey through a multifaceted topic in a time and location charged with social, economic and political tension. The qualitative feedback well receive will be used to strengthen and reiterate both the interface and the way users can create their own narratives and share them with other visitors.

2   Technology

2.1   User Interface Design

The User Interface follows a minimalist, content-focused approach. A large map builds the foundation of our experience, with new windows created upon most interactions. The intuitive touch-actions (moving, scaling, rotating etc.) prevent this from becoming overwhelming, while encouraging users to share windows and newly found data with each other (Fig. 1).

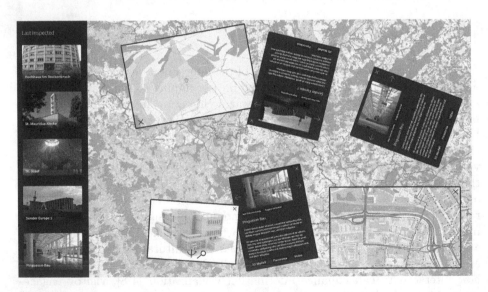

Fig. 1. A mockup for the UI design. A history stack on the left, broad map with detailed maps and object information on top of it. Single elements are capable of common touch-interactions (moving, rotating, zooming etc.)

2.2 User Experience Flow

A big, custom-drawn map is the entry point of our interface. It's a geographically non-accurate map, featuring markers of the architecture and objects of the exhibition which are located all across the Franco-German border region. By touching an area and/or object of interest, a new window opens for the user, depicting a geographically accurate map of the touched point and its surrounding area. Here again are markers for the architecture. Touching one of the markers opens another window on top of the map, and this window shows information about the selected building/architectural object. We display a big, non-uniform variety of data for each building, depending on the amount of material available for the object in question. The material is primarily images, but also a text-based description with accompanying metadata like year of building, the architect and other available media. Other media includes 3D-models, 360 panoramic images and videos. They can be looked at and interacted with depending on their format, meaning users can look around in 360 degree material, rotate and zoom in on 3D-files and watch videos. Each of those special media types open in their own respective window, ready to be shared with other users. By touching tags and architects, the user can navigate between similar buildings and other works of the same person, creating their own individual route through the cultural objects, learning about their historic context and the persons behind them. The ability of the multitouch table allows a multitude of users to interact with our interface simultaneously and encourages intuitive sharing of their findings, telling each other about the things they learned and hopefully discussing their different takes on the different aspects of the buildings.

2.3 Technical Implementation

Media We Need to Consider. Before we could decide on a structural approach for our implementation, we had to define all the different types of media our interface should be able to handle. Our main medium are images, but we also have to support text, tags, geo coordinates, videos, dates, 3d files and models, CAD files, ground plans and 360 panoramas and videos. The tagging and categorisation is a big part and important part for this, because our approach, to let the user decide on what tags and information they continue their journey through the post-war architecture, relied on having a lot of accurate, precise tags for each building, ranging from the architect and type of building (eg. church, school, government buildings) to their respective locations, cost and enthusiasm among the general population they received.

The Medium. Our interfaces leverages the possibilities of a 65 inch multitouch table. It supports up to 50 concurrent touches and enables users to use intuitive gestures and mechanics to freely move through the displayed content. The big size allows multiple users to operate the interface without getting in each others ways.

Backend. The backend we developed allows for easy uploading and managing of objects, their media and relationship with architects and other objects. It is built with Spring Boot[1], an opinionated take on the Spring framework[2]. Spring Boot enables us to rapidly iterate the backend as new needs develop, allowing us to stay agile with new types of media and their requirements.

We also use different services like Cloudinary[3], automatically optimizing the images we receive from our partners, increasing the performance and efficiency of our interface and application as a whole.

Frontend. Our frontend is browser-based and uses non-proprietary, open source software wherever possible. Our browser-based approach allows us to run it on any pc with a web-browser (or even as a cross-platform, standalone application if combined with a wrapper like Electron[4]. It is built on the popular React-library, an open-source, high-performance JavaScript library with a small footprint. We also use a healthy range of plugins to support our different types of media, such as:

Leaflet.[5] This open-source JavaScript library runs the foundation of our interface: The different maps we display. Leaflet allows us to create maps with custom coordinate systems, images and markers. With its highly customisable set of features and open-source nature, Leaflet is a perfect fit for our project.

Panellum.[6] "A Lightweight Panorama Viewer for the Web". Another open-source library. This library enables us to display 360 material like images, videos and even virtual tours of our objects. Users can touch to zoom, pan and rotate images with native, intuitive controls.

three.js.[7] For our 3D models and CAD files, we use three.js, an open-source library for abstracting WebGL, shaders and other 3D specific nuts and bolts into JavaScript. It allows us to serve the 3D and CAD files with great performance and controls, enabling the user to rotate, zoom and switch between models and plans on the fly.

Putting it all Together. In the end, our frontend needs to communicate with our backend. In our pilot project, this happens by running a local webserver (the backend) on our PC. This is the same PC that runs the multitouch interface, so the data from backend is supplied from the same PC running the frontend, which means virtually no latency and a very high performance of both loading and displaying interface and requested data. However, our web-based approach allows us to outsource the backend to a server/infrastructure of our choosing, which would then enable us to run the same (or an expanded and/or more intricately linked) interface from multiple machines.

---

[1] https://spring.io/projects/spring-boot.
[2] https://spring.io/.
[3] https://cloudinary.com/.
[4] https://electronjs.org/.
[5] https://leafletjs.com/.
[6] https://pannellum.org/.
[7] https://threejs.org.

2.4   Iterative Approach Based on Qualitative Feedback

The main focus of our research is the development of an cross-generational approach to co-authored storytelling that is workable in a "live" exhibition. Building on previous archive-based exhibition projects [14,16], our goal is to generate visual stories to deepen engagement with cultural heritage items whose historical significance is much better understood through user-driven contextualization.

The involvement of users in a a co-creative interface design process usually ends prior to its deployment in an exhibition process. In our case, we aim to involve users in an iterative design process throughout the exhibition since such a real-life experience offers a much more comprehensive co-creation setting than an isolated workshop. However, this requires adjustments to conventional user testing methods. We will begin by designing a workshop series that combines guided exhibition visits with on-site documentation by users of their broader museum experience to better understand how use of the archive station is framed (and affected by) the awareness of other exhibition modules and the overall interaction design of the exhibition space.

3   Perspectives

3.1   End of Project

While the exhibition ends in 2018, its archival components are mobile and can easily be integrated into other exhibition contexts. We will explore the possibility of involving users in other sites (and countries) in a follow-up process that allows us to iterate our co-creation approach to interface design.

3.2   Vision

While our work on the project in context with the exhibition nears completion, we already have both tangible and more distant goals and possibilities in mind. For one goal, we want to strengthen the storytelling aspect, the user as co-author and co-creator, even further.

User-Driven Memory Mapping. One approach is a form of "memory mapping". We track and save the way users engage with the cultural heritage data, linking subjective individual memories with the"objective" meaning of said data, effectively translating memory maps into contextual metadata. A key concern for this would be a simple yet effective component for our multitouch interface, enabling simple export of data. Connecting this with an already established software and/or API (eg. digiCult[8] would omit the need of backend functionality that rivals or duplicates already existing features of collections management software.

---

[8] https://www.digicult-verbund.de/.

Expansion by Contextualisation. The way our users interact and share their "findings" and contextualise them lends itself very well to crowd-source otherwise invisible connections between different cultural heritage data. This would allow cultural heritage collection platforms like europeana[9] to increase their impact, not by (as usually assumed and realized) the amount of data available but by using the individual contextualisation and connections users can supply, effectively turning users into active co-creators of cultural heritage archive infrastructures. This could strengthen the impact of such platforms by a large margin, because as seen in our first tests in previous exhibitions users are far more likely to engage with cultural heritage if they have a chance to build their own narrative and explore archival content on their own terms instead of being exposed to it by narration or reading alone.

The Future of Our Interface. The technical implementation of our interface allows for very flexible outputs. This means we are by no means limited to the multitouch interface, which would rather serve as (one) interaction point for our users. Content could then be mapped to different outputs, such as displays, audio speakers or even transmedia installations. We also have the option to develop a plugin for exporting collected user data into a machine readable format, eg. for feeding it back into other collection management platforms like digiCULT [19] or Europeana. The flexible output could also be used to further enable users to share their narrative and take on the available data with other visitors, saving it for review or displaying it prominently in the exhibition. This would build on previous iterations where we created a multi-touch interface to show user-generated playlists in a museum [15]. We also have the possibility to build on the "user as co-curator" perspective by letting users save content interesting to them and then generating a summary of their findings and experience, creating an individually tailored exhibition experience. Every user would therefore experience the exhibition based on their own interests and receives a responsive narrative, their own "passage through the archive". This would encourage aesthetic education, an important aspect of working in the field of cultural impact.

Our Vision for Cultural Heritage. Our goal is not to "school" people with the past, but providing them with a window into history and our rich cultural heritage. We believe it is important to accessibly archive cultural heritage and knowledge, because we do not know what will be of interest and importance to people looking back onto culture in ten, a hundred or even a thousand years, both as individuals and society as a whole. Our focus on greater user involvement on curatorial processes reflects a broader trend across the cultural heritage field [18]. We also strongly support open data approaches in cultural heritage and hope to share archival content with as few restrictions for reuse as possible [17]. Our multitouch concept offers an open, expandable approach how to create an interface for a huge, diverse amount of data for users who can use this interface to find and facilitate information from this set of data relevant to them, enabling them to create their own, individual connections and approaches to a cultural heritage we share as society.

---

[9] https://www.europeana.eu/portal/.

References

1. Hornecker, E.: I don't understand it either, but it is cool-visitor interactions with a multi-touch table in a museum. In: 2008 3rd IEEE International Workshop on Horizontal Interactive Human Computer Systems, TABLETOP 2008. IEEE (2008)
2. Ciocca, G., Olivo, P., Schettini, R.: Browsing museum image collections on a multi-touch table. Inf. Syst. **37**(2), 169–182 (2012)
3. Correia, N., Mota, T., Nóbrega, R., Silva, L., Almeida, A.: A multi-touch tabletop for robust multimedia interaction in museums. In: ACM International Conference on Interactive Tabletops and Surfaces (ITS 2010), pp. 117–120. ACM, New York (2010). https://doi.org/10.1145/1936652.1936674
4. Lee, B., et al.: Beyond mouse and keyboard: expanding design considerations for information visualization interactions. IEEE Trans. Vis. Comput. Graph. **18**(12), 2689–2698 (2012)
5. Horn, M., et al.: Of BATs and APEs: an interactive tabletop game for natural history museums. In: Proceedings of the SIGCHI Conference on Human Factors in Computing Systems (CHI 2012), pp. 2059–2068. ACM, New York (2012). https://doi.org/10.1145/2207676.2208355
6. Block, F., et al.: Fluid grouping: quantifying group engagement around interactive tabletop exhibits in the wild. In: Proceedings of the 33rd Annual ACM Conference on Human Factors in Computing Systems (CHI 2015), pp. 867–876. ACM, New York (2015). https://doi.org/10.1145/2702123.2702231
7. Creed, C., Sivell, J., Sear, J.: Multi-touch tables for exploring heritage content in public spaces. In: Ch'ng, E., Gaffney, V., Chapman, H. (eds.) Visual Heritage in the Digital Age. SSCC, pp. 67–90. Springer, London (2013). https://doi.org/10.1007/978-1-4471-5535-5_5
8. Dumas, B., Moerman, B., Trullemans, S., Signer, B.: ArtVis: combining advanced visualisation and tangible interaction for the exploration, analysis and browsing of digital artwork collections. In: Proceedings of the 2014 International Working Conference on Advanced Visual Interfaces (AVI 2014), pp. 65–72. ACM, New York (2014). https://doi.org/10.1145/2598153.2598159
9. Koutsabasis, P.: Empirical evaluations of interactive systems in cultural heritage: a review. Int. J. Comput. Methods Heritage Sci. (IJCMHS) **1**(1), 100–122 (2017)
10. Staedel Museum Digitorials. http://www.staedelmuseum.de/de/angebote/digitorial. Accessed 15 July 2018
11. Europeana Collections. https://www.europeana.eu. Accessed 25 July 2018
12. Resonanzen: Die langen Wellen der Utopie. http://resonanzen.eu/. Accessed 25 July 2018
13. Fickers, A.: Die Anfnge des kommerziellen Rundfunks im Saarland. Die Geschichte der Saarlndischen Fernseh AG (Tele Saar und Europe No. 1). In: Zimmermann, C. et al. (eds.) Medienlandschaft Saar. Von 1945 bis in die Gegenwart. Bd. 1 Medien zwischen Demokratisierung und Kontrolle (1945–55), pp. 241–308. DeGruyter, Mnchen (2010)
14. Zehle, S., Elburn, H.; Kaiser, C. Paehler, S.: Archive interfaces: toward the user as co-curator. In: Krueger, A., Gehring, S. (eds.) Proceedings of the 4th International Symposium on Pervasive Displays, PerDis 2015, pp. 277–78. ACM, New York (2015)
15. Zehle, S., Elburn, H., Kaiser, C.: Common gestures: visual design for a collaborative archive interface. In: Krueger, A., Gehring, S. (eds.) Proceedings of the 4th International Symposium on Pervasive Displays, PerDis 2015, pp. 263–264. ACM, New York (2015)

16. Scheffer, B., Stenzer, C., Weibel, P., Zehle, S. (eds.): Typemotion: Type as Image in Motion, pp. 46–54. Hatje Cantz, Ostfildern (2015)
17. Schmidt, A.: MKG Collection Online: the potential of open museum collections. Hamburger J. fr Kulturanthropologie (HJK) **7**, 25–39 (2018). https://journals.sub.uni-hamburg.de/hjk/article/view/1191. Accessed 15 July 2018
18. Landes, L.: Gemeinsam kuratieren auf DDBstudio, der virtuellen Ausstellungsplatform der DDB. 7. Internationale Konferenz "Zugang gestalten! Mehr Verantwortung fr das kulturelle Erbe" unter Schirmherrschaft der Deutschen UNESCO-Kommission e.V. - ein Beitrag zum Europischen Kulturerbejahr 2018 SHARING HERITAGE (18–20 Oktober 2017). https://irights.info/artikel/zusammenarbeit-in-museen-archiven-bibliotheken-die-konferenz-zugang-gestalten-zum-nachsehen/28829. Accessed 15 July 2018
19. Meifort C.; Schill B.; Vitzthum A.; Wuensche R.: Neues zu digiCULT: Entwicklungen und Infrastruktur, digiCULT Verbundkonferenz, 10 July 2017. http://www.digicult-verbund.de/vortraege/2017/2017_verbundkonf_20170710_dcTeam.pdf. Accessed 15 July 2018

Interactive Digital Storytelling and Self-expression in the Context of Young Male Migrants

Carolina Beniamina Rutta[1,2](✉), Gianluca Schiavo[1],
and Massimo Zancanaro[1]

[1] Fondazione Bruno Kessler, Trento, Italy
{rutta,gschiavo,zancana}@fbk.eu
[2] Università degli studi di Trento, Trento, Italy

Abstract. This paper describes *Communics,* a digital tool aimed at producing interactive digital storytelling in form of comics to facilitate self-expression. In particular, we investigated how *Communics* can support young male migrants to reflect on situations involving discrimination by elaborating digital narratives in counterstory. In this first stage, we built a set of graphical and textual content to be included in the software involving NGO operators and young migrants providing the users with elements to compose the visual story. Furthermore, we initially assessed the narrative approach. General considerations on this process and implications for the future user study are presented.

Keywords: Interactive digital storytelling · Migrants · Digital comic
Counterstory

1 Introduction

During the last years, the number of migrants, mostly from Sub-Saharan countries, increased dramatically in Europe [1]. Most of them, when arriving in the new country, experience situations in which they are stereotyped due to mainly cultural differences [2]. Often, they do not have ways to reflect and cope with these experiences. In this prospect, it might be helpful to provide them with a supportive system for self-expression on situations involving discriminations, needed for their inclusion and integration path.

We aim to provide a contribution in this direction exploring how a specific digital tool for interactive digital storytelling, *Communics,* can support young migrants in producing comics for self-expression on discrimination and in elaborating counterstories. In the paper, we present a first phase of this project, in which textual and graphical content to be included in *Communics* were collaboratively prepared with a group of young male migrants and NGO operators, and the narrative approach was assessed.

© Springer Nature Switzerland AG 2018
R. Rouse et al. (Eds.): ICIDS 2018, LNCS 11318, pp. 621–626, 2018.
https://doi.org/10.1007/978-3-030-04028-4_72

2   Related Work

Digital storytelling for self-expression were already applied in different studies in diverse contexts of use and populations. For example, in the field of health and wellbeing, digital storytelling has been used for helping patients coping with their illnesses [3, 4]. In the educational field, it has been used for different purposes such us supporting the exploration of identity and communication issues [5] and discovering more about professional identity [6]. Furthermore, interactive digital storytelling has been used to support language learning [7] and to motivate students to learn computer programming [8]. The medium of comics has been demonstrated to be useful in several contexts [14–17]. In our work, we propose a tool for interactive digital storytelling with the aim to support young migrants in producing comics for self-expression and elaboration of master narratives in counterstories in situations involving discriminations. In particular, we considered the concepts of master narrative and counterstories as guiding approach. Master narratives are stories that exercise a captive force over a minority group [10, 11], in this case young migrants, damaging their identity; while counterstories are narratives that resist an oppressive identity and attempt to replace the master narrative, providing a different perspective on the story [9].

3   *Communics*: A Digital Tool for Interactive Storytelling

Communics is a digital tool aimed at supporting the interactive production of storytelling in the form of comics [12, 13] combining both graphical and textual elements (Fig. 1). The users produce digital narratives by choosing backgrounds and using characters, objects and emoticons from a library. The participants can add the textual material freely and several pre-defined expressions are also available in the library to overcome the "blank page syndrome" (in which an author finds difficulties to come up with ideas to produce a story) as well as to facilitate the development of counterstories.

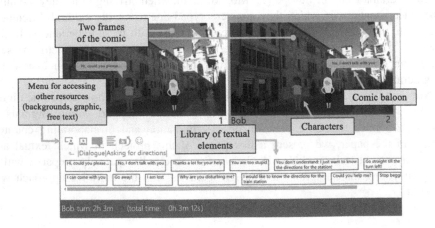

Fig. 1. The *Communics* interface

3.1   Content Creation and Pilot Study

The preparation of the library is a crucial part of an intervention because participants have to find enough material to express their point of view and to elaborate an interactive narrative. At the same time, the amount of material should not be too large because of the risk of precluding the possibility of navigating and understanding it.

In this study, the content creation process started with three focus groups: two involving 9 NGO operators (respectively 4 and 5 people) and one involving 6 young male migrants. The NGO operators, aged between 30 and 54, worked at a migrant reception center in Trento that receives migrants upon their arrival in Italy for a 12-months period. The migrants were all males aged between 19 and 32 living in the same center. They came from Sub-Saharan Africa countries, namely Cameroon, Guinea, Niger and Nigeria. Four of them spoke English and two French as primary language, while all of them have a good understanding of Italian. In these focus groups, participants were asked to discuss situations of discrimination or prejudice targeting the migrant community.

Three general situations involving discrimination were identified in the focus groups as the most common ones among the migrants in the area.

- A first situation concerns when migrants approach a local person with the intent of asking for directions or information: usually they are ignored, or they immediately receive a negative answer, such as "*I don't carry cash*" (assuming that they are begging) or "*go away*".
- A second situation represents migrant stereotypes as thieves: for example, when a police officer stops a migrant riding a bike asking if he had stolen the bike.
- A third situation regards migrants stereotyped as unclean and as a threat to public decorum. The example reported is the one representing a migrant blamed for some garbage on the ground.

Based on these situations, we built an initial set of materials (images for backgrounds and objects and characters as well as pre-defined textual expressions) for the use in *Communics*.

Following these focus groups, other 12 young male migrants were invited to try out the system. They were recruited in the same center of the previous group. They were between 19 and 30 years old, and they came from Cameroon, Ghana, Guinea, Mali, Niger, Nigeria, Senegal and Sierra Leone.

They were involved individually in producing a story regarding stereotyped episodes on migrants, starting from the graphical and textual material and provided in the tool. This pilot study was mainly aimed at assessing the content included in the tool and the narrative approach outlined above. Here, we briefly present the main issues and the strengths of the system identified from the participants' feedback:

Non-familiarity with Visual Stories. One of the issue that emerged is that several migrants were not very familiar with the comics' medium.

Starting Elements. Participants found difficulties in starting a story from a blank interface ("blank page syndrome"). Even if they could browse the graphical and the textual elements, they express the need of an incipit to start the story.

Backgrounds. Participants appreciated finding in the library photos of the city in which they live. Familiar backgrounds helped them recalling their experiences and, consequently, they felt more engaged in the storytelling.

Pre-defined Language Sentences. The textual material were considered useful as it gave ideas about the development of the stories to the users.

Emoticons. Participants were familiar with emoticons and considered them useful in expressing the feeling of the characters in the story.

Characters. Migrants expressed their willingness to have more types of characters (we provided in the library a black man, a black woman, a white man and a white woman) to choose the ones that most represent themselves.

General Considerations on Usability. In general, participants understood quite well how to use the interface despite their lack of familiarity with the use of keyboard and mouse (although they all are proficient smartphone users).

Challenging in the Fieldwork. As noticed in other similar studies on the development of digital solutions targeting migrants (for example, [18–23]), we faced some challenges in working with this community of users. Some issues arose because of the need by the NGO operators to mediate the relation between the researchers and the migrants. Although they helped in facilitating contacts and trust, the overall interaction was sometime less smooth because of this indirectness. For example, it happened frequently that participants arrived late because they were not informed in time about the interview's place or did not know about the meeting object. Another problematic aspect was related to the establishment and maintenance of trust among the migrants' participants and the researchers. In this respect, the presence of the NGO operators was very useful but the participants needed to be continuously reassured about the project's objectives and scopes because they fear that the material could be used to question their right to stay in the country.

4   Lessons Learned

This paper describes the preliminary activities aimed at using a digital tool for interactive storytelling, *Communics,* to support production of visual stories for self-expression in situations involving discrimination within migrant community.

Specifically, we involved migrants and NGO operators to prepare the content library, needed for the user to elaborate an interactive narratives, and we piloted the tool for further studies.

The lessons learned in this initial phase included the need of tuning the intervention approach by using incipits to facilitate the starting of the storytelling but also the questioning of some of our assumptions like the simplicity of comics as a medium and the familiarity with computers. Furthermore, we learnt not to underestimate the need to establish and maintain a robust trust relation between researchers and migrants before conducting a larger intervention. Still, we collected initial evidences that the approach proposed by *Communics* is appreciated and it may well support the elaboration of counterstories.

References

1. UNHCR, with 1 human in every 113 affected, forced displacement hits record high. http://www.unhcr.org/afr/news/press/2016/6/5763ace54/1-human-113-affected-forced-displacement-hits-record-high.html. Accessed 25 June 2018
2. Rapport, N.: Migrant selves and stereotypes: personal context in a postmodern world. In: Mapping the Subject: Geographies of Cultural Transformation, pp. 267–282 (1995)
3. Bers, M.U., Gonzalez-Heydrich, J., DeMaso, D.R.: Identity construction environments: supporting a virtual therapeutic community of pediatric patients undergoing dialysis. In: Proceedings of the SIGCHI Conference on Human Factors in Computing Systems, pp. 380–387. ACM (2018)
4. Mamykina, L., Miller, A.D., Mynatt, E.D., Greenblatt, D.: Constructing identities through storytelling in diabetes management. In: Proceedings of the SIGCHI Conference on Human Factors in Computing Systems, pp. 1203–1212. ACM (2010)
5. Umaschi, M.: SAGE storytellers: learning about identity, language and technology. In: Proceedings of the 1996 International Conference on Learning Sciences, pp. 526–531. International Society of Learning Science (1996)
6. Marín, V.I., Tur, G., Challinor, J.: An interdisciplinary approach to the development of professional identity through digital storytelling in health and social care and teacher education. Soc. Work Educ. **37**(3), 396–412 (2018)
7. Müller, W., Iurgel, I., Otero, N., Massler, U.: Teaching english as a second language utilizing authoring tools for interactive digital storytelling. In: Aylett, R., Lim, M.Y., Louchart, S., Petta, P., Riedl, M. (eds.) ICIDS 2010. LNCS, vol. 6432, pp. 222–227. Springer, Heidelberg (2010). https://doi.org/10.1007/978-3-642-16638-9_28
8. Kelleher, C.: Supporting storytelling in a programming environment for middle school children. In: Iurgel, Ido A., Zagalo, N., Petta, P. (eds.) ICIDS 2009. LNCS, vol. 5915, pp. 1–4. Springer, Heidelberg (2009). https://doi.org/10.1007/978-3-642-10643-9_1
9. Lindemann Nelson, H.: Damaged Identities, Narrative Repair, Cornell University Press (2001)
10. Hammack, P.L.: Narrative and the cultural psychology of identity. Pers. Soc. Psychol. Rev. **12**(3), 222–247 (2008)
11. McLean, K.C., Syed, M.: Personal, master, and alternative narratives: an integrative framework for understanding identity development in context. Hum. Develop. **58**(6), 318–349 (2015)
12. Mencarini, E., Schiavo, G., Cappelletti, A., Stock, O., Zancanaro, M.: Formative evaluation of a constrained composition approach for storytelling. In: Proceedings of the 8th Nordic Conference on Human-Computer Interaction: Fun, Fast, Foundational, pp. 987–990. ACM (2014)
13. Mencarini, E., Schiavo, G., Cappelletti, A., Stock, O., Zancanaro, M.: Assessing a collaborative application for comic strips composition. In: Abascal, J., Barbosa, S., Fetter, M., Gross, T., Palanque, P., Winckler, M. (eds.) INTERACT 2015. LNCS, vol. 9297, pp. 73–80. Springer, Cham (2015). https://doi.org/10.1007/978-3-319-22668-2_6
14. Andrews, D., Baber, C.: Visualizing interactive narratives: employing a branching comic to tell a story and show its readings. In: Proceedings of the SIGCHI Conference on Human Factors in Computing Systems, pp. 1895–1904. ACM (2014)
15. Herbst, P., Chazan, D., Chen, C.L., Chieu, V.M., Weiss, M.: Using comics-based representations of teaching, and technology, to bring practice to teacher education courses. ZDM **43**(1), 91–103 (2011)

16. McNicol, S.: The potential of educational comics as a health information medium. Health Inf. Libr. J. **34**(1), 20–31 (2017)
17. Czerwiec, M.K., Huang, M.N.: Hospice comics: representations of patient and family experience of illness and death in graphic novels. J. Med. Humanit. **38**(2), 95–111 (2017)
18. Fisher, K.E., Bishop, A.P., Magassa, L., Fawcett, P.: Action! co-designing interactive technology with immigrant teens. In: Proceedings of the 2014 Conference on Interaction Design and Children, pp. 345–348. ACM (2014)
19. Fisher, K.E., Yefimova, K., Yafi, E.: "Future's Butterflies:" co-designing ICT wayfaring technology with refugee syrian youth. In: Proceedings of the 15th International Conference on Interaction Design and Children, pp. 25–36. ACM (2016)
20. Bishop, A.P., Fisher, E.K.: Using ICT design to learn about immigrant teens from Myanmar. In: Proceedings of the Seventh International Conference on Information and Communication Technologies and Development, p. 56. ACM (2015)
21. Weibert, A., Wulf, V.: "All of a sudden, we had this dialogue…:" intercultural computer clubs' contribution to sustainable integration. In: Proceedings of the 3rd International Conference on Intercultural Collaboration, pp. 93–102. ACM(2010)
22. Bobeth, J., Schreitter, S., Schmehl, S., Deutsch, S., Tscheligi, M.: User-centered design between cultures: designing for and with immigrants. In: Kotzé, P., Marsden, G., Lindgaard, G., Wesson, J., Winckler, M. (eds.) INTERACT 2013. LNCS, vol. 8120, pp. 713–720. Springer, Heidelberg (2013). https://doi.org/10.1007/978-3-642-40498-6_65
23. Duarde, A.M.B., Brendel, N., Degbelo, A., Kray, C.: Participatory design and participatory research: an HCI case study with young forced migrants. ACM Trans. Comput. Hum. Interact. (TOCHI) **25**(1), 3 (2018)

A Top-Down Narrative Design Approach for Networked Cultural Institutions

Tonguc Ibrahim Sezen[1]([⊠]), Ido Iurgel[1], Nicolas Fischöder[1],
René Bakker[2], Koen van Turnhout[2], and Digdem Sezen[3]

[1] Rhine-Waal University of Applied Sciences,
Friedrich-Heinrich-Allee 25, 47475 Kamp-Lintfort, Germany
{tongucibrahim.sezen,ido.iurgel,
nicolas.fischoeder}@hochschule-rhein-waal.de
[2] Hogeschool van Arnhem en Nijmegen, Ruitenberglaan 26,
6826CC Arnhem, The Netherlands
{Rene.Bakker,Koen.vanTurnhout}@han.nl
[3] Istanbul Universitesi, İletişim Fakültesi, Kaptanı Derya İbrahim
Paşa Sokak Beyazıt Fatih, 34116 İstanbul, Turkey
dsezen@istanbul.edu.tr

Abstract. In 2020 the RheijnLand.Xperiences project will connect 8 museums along the Dutch-German border by a network using a story-driven application for mobile devices for an audience between the ages of 14 and 22. While the project foresees the design of individually tailored experiences for each museum, an overarching narrative and experience structure is also required to establish connections between the museums. This structure relies heavily on the concepts of interactive digital storytelling and is required to compensate the environmental and thematic diversity of each museum while also enriching the overall experience of visiting multiple museums in the network. In this regard in this poster, we summarize our approach and core elements of the "universal" narrative and experience design.

Keywords: Continuation network · Narrative design · Secondary world
Museum

1 Introduction

The RheijnLand.Xperiences (RLX) project aims to create a "continuation network" between eight museums in the Rhine-Waal region of Germany and the Netherlands by employing junctures build through "interactive digital storytelling" (IDS) [1]. A modular and flexible framework for narrative and experience design is planned to manage the cross-organizational museum visits. Methodologically the team followed a double top-down and bottom-up strategy to answer the local needs and expectations of each museum while also building a sustainable network and a continuous universal experience. This poster summarizes the core elements of the top-down "universal" design which main goal is to establish a continuous and sustainable narrative design model for the eight museums participating in the project.

© Springer Nature Switzerland AG 2018
R. Rouse et al. (Eds.): ICIDS 2018, LNCS 11318, pp. 627–632, 2018.
https://doi.org/10.1007/978-3-030-04028-4_73

2   State of the Art

Over the years mobile digital technologies have been used to enhance museum visit experiences trough storytelling and games [2–6]. Most of such projects cover only one museum or cultural institution, and cross-institutional projects are comparatively rare. The digital storytelling project The Tales of Things which collected local stories about exhibition objects using a standardized model, had run at several U.K. museums but did not connect them directly [7]. Aiming the entire museum sector, the CHESS project conducted extensive research in the application of mobile technologies and storytelling; and two prototypes were tested [8]. While using the same technical aspects and design paradigms, both prototypes may be considered independent from each other thematically and narratively. The formulation of a narrative umbrella over individual cultural institutions can be achieved through the formation of a secondary fictional world. According to Wolf, the subcreation of a secondary world combines existing concepts of the Primary World, in which we live in, with inventions that replace or reset them; i.e., the "overlaid world" of Spider-Man's New York [9].

3   Narrative Design

The current iteration of the secondary world of RLX-app story invites the users to become an apprentice of a trader, Sophia, who deals with emotions, memories, and ideas surrounding the art pieces and historical artifacts in RLX museums. Sophia lives in a realm which is invisible and inaccessible without the use of the RLX-app. This core fictional logic not only connects the museums – there must be trade between them - but also allows any individual stories due to its connection to each museum's collection – the emotions, ideas, and memories emerge from the artifacts in the collections.

The character of Sophia, the Trader, is functionally similar to the alien smuggler of earlier iterations [1] but is inspired by the Glückel of Hameln; a 17th-century businesswoman who had visited the Rhine-Waal region and head kept diaries about it [10]. Each location features non-player characters called "museum mascots" who embody the characteristics of each museum and act as story companions throughout the visit. In term of enhancing a museum visit by adding distinct personal voices, museum mascots carry a resemblance to the fictional storyteller companions used by Nationalmuseum Stockholm and Universeum SDC Gothenburg, who add new perspectives to the visitors' experience of a museum through their personal stories [11]. Museum mascots were created in collaboration with the museum curators following a series of interviews and workshops. There are also other characters in the overarching story who were inspired by historical and mythical figures of the Rhine-Waal region, such as the legendary Geldern Dragon or the 16th-century Dutch field marshal Maarten van Rossum.

3.1 Story Modules

The current narrative and experience design of the RLX-app can be described as a combination of an episodic and linear "universal story module" (USM) with interchanging "local story modules" (LSM), and unique "local experience modules" (LXM) which also use standardized "interaction modules" (IM) within different contexts. The USM is an overall linear episodic story which flow does not impose a specific museum-visit order to the visitors. While each episode is self-contained, together they also form an overarching story which not only connects the museums within a larger narrative but also can be divided into 3 acts in which the role of the visitor changes over time thus offers a transforming narrative experience instead of a repetitive "museum of the week" structure. Throughout these acts, Sophia and the user shift from traders into smugglers, from smugglers to rebels, and finally from companions to adversaries.

Any RLX museum visited by the first time RLX-app user automatically becomes the first museum, and thus the setting for the first episode of the USM. Each continuing visit to a new RLX museum activates a new episode and the story concludes at the end of the 8th museum visit, or the 8th episode of the USM. Throughout the experience, the USM acts as what Ryan [12] calls a "vector-based narrative" preserving linearity of temporal sequence and causal structure. Each USM episode is divided into an introduction, conclusion, and a small number of conversation scenes which are separated by LSMs and LXMs. These LSMs and LXMs form the interchanging and branching sections of the narrative vector. In other words, combined with the LSM and LXMs the USM build up a "foldback story" structure [13] similar to the ones found in contemporary episodic adventure games [14].

LSMs are local stories tied directly to individual museums and thus reflect their characteristics, unique features, historical backgrounds, etc. Each LSM has multiple versions parallel to USM episodes. Based on which order a museum is visited USM episodes and LSM variations get paired and create a continuing story. If a museum X is visited by a user as the 3rd museum of the USM she experiences USM episode 3 and the episode 3 variant of the LSM of this museum. These pairings change the narrative framing of LXMs which are unique for each museum (see Fig. 1).

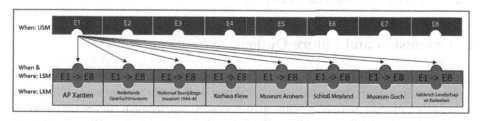

Fig. 1. USM and corresponding LSMs frame LXMs build individually for each museum.

3.2   Experience Modules

LXMs are interactive experiences individually tailored for each museum. As interactive and playful components they take various forms, and their purpose is to offer visitors new perspectives to the RLX museums. While each museum offers a fixed number of LXMs their narrative framing gets changed by LSMs; i.e., a culture caching activity gets framed as a rescue or a hunt.

LXMs can be divided into two main categories, app-based offerings, and tangible offerings. App-based offerings are shaped by the environmental features and limitations of the museums listed above. To provide a streamlined production process and keep the technical requirements in line with the technical specifications of average mobile devices on which the users will experience the RLX-app with, several IMs were created.

IMs can be described as standardized mini-games which can be used within different contexts through replacement of assets or slightly re-contextualizing of their interaction processes. In other words, an LXM is a specific combination of an object or location in an RLX museum with an IM. At the current stage IMs developed by the RLX-team can be divided into 3 technical categories; iBeacon-based IMs, computer vision-based IMs, and screen-based IMs. In line with their underlying technologies, the IMs under the first category provide area-based AR interactions. IMs under the second category are used to create object-based AR interactions. Screen-based IMs, on the other hand, encourage visitors to gather information, which they are asked to use as input for screen-based puzzles or riddles. Throughout the RLX museums these IMs are distributed in accordance of the thematic and environmental factors; i.e., computer-vision based IMs were not used if the exhibition design of a museum created an environment filled with highly reflective surfaces or a museum relies heavily on temporary exhibitions.

In contrast to app-based offerings, tangible offerings are unique interactive physical constructs which themselves take the form of an exhibition piece within an RLX museum. Tangible offerings are planned to be experienced independently from the RLX-app but at the same time will provide an input material at the end of each experience to be used with the RLX-app; i.e., a kiosk combining multisensory elements with digital components revels at the end of its usage a marker which will be used as an input for a computer vision-based IM.

4   Conclusion and Future Outlook

In the present poster, an overall narrative design approach for an inter-institutional application has been presented. The modular and flexible framework allows the inclusion of diverse museums with environmental and thematic differences into an ongoing shared experience while maintaining their own identity. We consider the creation of small branches or switchable mobile blocks within the internal structures of the LSMs. This is not only a concern regarding the agency-level of the individual users but also based on user scenarios where multiple users, such as a group of students, may use the RLX-app simultaneously. The development of a digital prototype of the overarching narrative design in articy:draft 3 [15] is still in continuing. In line with our double top-down and bottom-up design and development strategy in addition to the USM we have also focused on LSM and LXM combinations. Following several workshops and interviews with museum curators, and two prototypes were created for Museum Kurhaus Kleve, and Archäologischer Park Xanten which are under evaluation. In addition, several IMs were prototyped in Unity [16] and tested on mobile devices independent from the museums. Testing and evaluation of the established framework and early prototypes will provide us with a solid base to build an appealing and successful product.

References

1. Kahl, T., Iurgel, I., Zimmer, F., Bakker, R., van Turnhout, K.: RheijnLand.Xperiences – a storytelling framework for cross-museum experiences. In: Nunes, N., Oakley, I., Nisi, V. (eds.) ICIDS 2017. LNCS, vol. 10690, pp. 3–11. Springer, Cham (2017). https://doi.org/10.1007/978-3-319-71027-3_1

2. Springer, J., Borst Brazas, J., Kajder, S.: Digital storytelling at the national gallery of art. In: Bearman, D., Trant, J. (eds.) Museums and the Web. Archives & Museums Informatics, Arlington (2004)

3. Rossi, C., Carnall, M., Hudson-Smith, A., Warwick, C., Terras, M., Gray, S.: Enhancing museum narratives. In: Farman, J. (ed.) The Mobile Story, pp. 400–411. Routledge, New York (2014)

4. Beale, K.: Museums at Play: Games, Interaction and Learning. Museums Etc, Edinburgh (2011)

5. Radeta, M., Cesario, V., Matos, S., Nisi, V.: Gaming versus storytelling: understanding children's interactive experiences in a museum setting. In: Nunes, N., Oakley, I., Nisi, V. (eds.) ICIDS 2017. LNCS, vol. 10690, pp. 163–178. Springer, Cham (2017). https://doi.org/10.1007/978-3-319-71027-3_14

6. Spierling, U., Winzer, P., Massarczyk, E.: Experiencing the presence of historical stories with location-based augmented reality. In: Nunes, N., Oakley, I., Nisi, V. (eds.) ICIDS 2017. LNCS, vol. 10690, pp. 49–62. Springer, Cham (2017). https://doi.org/10.1007/978-3-319-71027-3_5

7. Merritt, E.E., Katz, M.P.: TrendsWatch 2013. American Alliance of Museums, Arlington (2013)

8. Katifori, A., et al.: CHESS: personalized storytelling experiences in museums. In: Mitchell, A., Fernández-Vara, C., Thue, D. (eds.) ICIDS 2014. LNCS, vol. 8832, pp. 232–235. Springer, Cham (2014). https://doi.org/10.1007/978-3-319-12337-0_28

9. Wold, M.J.P.: Building Imaginary Worlds: The Theory and History of Subcreation. Routledge, New York (2012)

10. Turniansky, C.: Glueckel of Hameln. https://jwa.org/encyclopedia/article/glueckel-of-hameln. Accessed 13 July 2018

11. Gottlieb, I.: Interactive adventures. In: Tallon, L., Walker, K. (eds.) Digital Technologies and The Museum Experience: Handheld Guides and Other Media, pp. 167–178. AltaMira Press, Plymouth (2008)

12. Ryan, M.L.: Narrative as Virtual Reality 2: Revisiting Immersion and Interactivity in Literature and Electronic Media. Johns Hopkins University Press, Baltimore (2015)

13. Adams, E.: Fundamentals of Game Design, 3rd edn. New Riders, San Francisco (2014)
14. Mitchell, A.: Reflective rereading and the simcity effect in interactive stories. In: Schoenau-Fog, H., Bruni, L.E., Louchart, S., Baceviciute, S. (eds.) ICIDS 2015. LNCS, vol. 9445, pp. 27–39. Springer, Cham (2015). https://doi.org/10.1007/978-3-319-27036-4_3
15. Articy:draft 3. https://www.nevigo.com/en/articydraft/overview/
16. Unity. http://unity3d.com

Digital Storytelling and Phrasal Verbs in L2 Acquisition: Teaching Phraseology Through Technology

Annalisa Raffone[✉]

L'Orientale University of Naples, 80121 Naples, NA, Italy
annalisa.raffone14@gmail.com, araffone@unior.it

Abstract. This paper discusses the use of Digital Storytelling (DST) as an innovative educational approach in teaching and learning English as a second language. Specifically, it deals with English phraseology, focusing on the teaching and learning of Multi-word expressions, in particular Phrasal Verbs (PVs), usually a challenging feature for Italian learners of English, who find them hard to understand and memorize.

Motivated by Constructivist principles, Technological Pedagogical Content Knowledge (TPCK) Theory, the Narrative paradigm, The Cognitive Theory of Multimedia Learning and also growing developments in neuroscience and neuropsychology, this paper argues that, by combining the visual and the verbal, DST has the potential to make students better process, understand, and recall even difficult instructional content. Finally, it presents preliminary results of a first exploratory implementation of DST in an L2 secondary classroom of Italian learners of English. They show that DST could be a meaningful technology tool to enhance students' critical thinking, motivation and collaboration.

This paper also aims to shed new light on educational strategies in the context of Second Language Acquisition (SLA).

Keywords: Digital Storytelling · Phraseology · Second Language Acquisition

1 Introduction

A critical aspect of Second Language Acquisition (SLA) is the mastery of vocabulary which is crucial in a foreign language environment because it represents the fundamental factor that helps people communicate in another language.

Mastering vocabulary is a process made up of not only words but also a larger set that includes their meaning, orthography, pronunciation, context, and conjugation. Therefore, recent linguistic research [10] has underlined the key role played by vocabulary in SLA and its constructive impact on the learners' ability to build up their own language proficiency as a whole.

A challenging aspect of SLA are *multi-word expressions* (MWEs), units that include routine formulas, discourse organizers, idioms, proverbs, phrasal verbs, prepositional phrases, compounds and collocations, that are considered as «one of the hallmarks of native-speaker competence» [6]. Nevertheless, it has been noted [8] that

R. Rouse et al. (Eds.): ICIDS 2018, LNCS 11318, pp. 633–637, 2018.
https://doi.org/10.1007/978-3-030-04028-4_74

even advanced L2 learners usually lack the phraseological richness typical of native-speaker discourse, mostly replaced by more generic and unspecific single words.

In the context of English language instruction, one of the most challenging aspects of language learning seems to be the English phrasal verbs (PVs) [5].

Motivated by the importance of MWEs in SLA, this paper aims to propose Digital Storytelling (DST) as an innovative meaningful approach in teaching and learning phraseological units. In particular, it focuses on the teaching and learning of PVs by Italian learners of English.

2   DST as an Innovative Approach in Phraseological Units Learning

Several researches [13] have shown that DST has a higher impact than traditional storytelling because, due to the fact that it combines traditional storytelling with digital multimedia (e.g. images, video, music, voice-over), it enables teachers to work on even difficult topics by simultaneously maintaining students' attention while increasing their critical thinking.

Indeed, DST seems to be an appealing approach in L2 classroom because, as *digital natives* [12] are heavy users of new technologies, the mixing of the visual (images, videos, photos) and the verbal (words, music, voice-over) makes them able to memorize and recall the information released by the digital story easily and precisely.

In this way, digital stories function as «anticipatory set or *hook* to capture the attention of students and increase their interest in exploring new ideas» [13].

Having said that, this paper presents a preliminary experiment to introduce – by means of a digital story – Italian secondary school students with some of the most common English PVs in order to make their comprehension and assimilation more affordable, interactive, dynamic and significant.

3   Theoretical Framework

Educational uses of DST are supported by a series of paradigms: 1. *Technological Pedagogical Content Knowledge (TPCK) Theory* which emphasizes the role of the teacher in knowing how to perfectly integrate technology into the classroom [13]; 2. *Social Constructivism*, that highlights the role of an authentic learning environment in helping students construct their own knowledge [3]; 3. The *Narrative paradigm* that assumes that all forms of communication can be seen as stories, perceived as interpretations of aspects of the real world [1]; 4. *Cognitive Theory of Multimedia Learning* [9] according to which when narration is enhanced by visual elements, such as images, photos, music and video, it becomes even more powerful: in fact, while being entertained by digital content, students learn from and through stories by enhancing their communication skills, critical thinking and motivation; 5. *Neuroscience and neuropsychology* [11] that state that stories play a fundamental role in memory formation: in the context of SLA, several studies [18] have shown that, especially at the early stage of language acquisition, academic achievement is strictly related to the act of repeating.

In effect, as Schank explains, telling and listening to stories can shape our mind and highly influence early learning [14]. This means that the meaning and the amusing content of a digital story, together with the incessant recall of words and phrases both make lexicon easier for students to remember and also strengthen their memory while enhancing their cognitive development.

4 Challenges in MWEs and PVs Acquisition by L2 Learners

As researchers affirm [17], one of the greater problems of L2 learners of MWEs lies in their failure to pick up the MWEs they encounter and add them to their repertoire: according to Wray, Sharwood-Smith [15] and Van Patten [16] this happens because language users usually process the content of messages and not the linguistic packaging of the content. Consequently, as Garcia and Skehan [4] claim, non-native speakers, unlike native-speakers – who use conventional expressions to convey meaning –, tend to rely on rules to formulate their sentences instead of using MWEs. In addition, even when they recognize MWEs, learners generally fail or simply fear to reproduce MWEs and replace them with single-words: this happens because MWEs are frequently longer – and so more challenging to recall – than single-words that are, on the contrary, considered easier to use. According to Laufer [7] and Dagut [2], learners enact the "avoidance strategy" mentioned above especially with specific MWEs, namely idioms (when they do not understand their meaning) and PVs (in the case of L2 MWEs absent from the learners' L1).

PVs are recognized as a typical challenging feature of the English language because: 1. as for Italian learners of English, PVs are not a common feature of their native language. Actually, PVs do exist in Italian – they are called *verbi sintagmatici* – but they are mainly used in spoken language and are often related to specific linguistic varieties; 2. there is a great amount of PVs in English: this means that a single PV can be followed by different particles and, according to the particle, it will completely change its meaning, and even the particles can take different meanings; 3. some combinations have more than one meaning and, consequently, the learner does not know how to recognize which meaning is used; 4. PVs are very idiomatic, namely that it is not possible to define the meaning of the PV according to the meaning of the particle.

5 A Preliminary Study on Teaching PVs Through DST and Future Research

A first preliminary experiment on teaching phraseology through DST was conducted in April 2018: two classes, respectively composed by 14 and 21 students between the ages of 10–11 years old of an Italian secondary school in Naples – were introduced to this innovative learning approach.

The purpose of the study was to understand if DST could be an effective instructional tool in SLA and, in particular, in teaching English phraseology.

The focus of the preliminary experiment were English PVs related to daily routine actions.

First, a grammar pre-test was conducted to figure out students' level of knowledge of the most common PVs. Their results were, in general, below the passing grade. After the test, the students were introduced to a digital story called *A day in my life* developed by the author. The story is about an 11-year-old boy called Luke who struggles with learning and remembering PVs because there are too many of them and he often forgets their meanings. The character was chosen in order to establish a mental connection with the students to make them able to experience the story narrated and identify themselves with the character and his learning struggles. Moreover, Luke "interacts" with the students by talking to them and explaining his troubles. After having mentioned all his problems with PVs, Luke explains how he managed to understand, learn and use the PVs to the students: the key is to connect PVs to his routine actions. Therefore, by explaining his routine actions from the morning to the evening, Luke uses and repeats several PVs. At the end of the story, Luke helps the students to repeat all the PVs previously mentioned and asks them to develop their own digital stories on their daily routine.

The digital story was shown to the students twice. Then, they were given a grammar post-test based on the PVs they had previously encountered in the digital story and they were asked to work in groups. The results were encouraging: both the two classes shared a new level of knowledge of daily-routine PVs because, almost the 70% of the total number of students were able to recognize and understand their meanings. Moreover, a final questionnaire was conducted to check students' opinion about this new way of teaching and learning and to figure out what they had actually learned. They reported that they had enjoyed the learning process because they felt part of it, they shared Luke's feelings and were able to recognize and comprehend the PVs due to the visual representations. Actually, during the DST process, students appeared to be completely absorbed by the story, the music and the situation and they maintained their attention all the time. Moreover, working in groups served to foster their motivation and collaboration: students helped each other showing a low level of competition.

The results of this preliminary study make a point in favor of the possibility to effectively implement DST in the classroom and, especially, in L2 classroom. However, they are not sufficient to claim the potential of this new pedagogical tool and further experiments need to be carried out to assess the effective power of DST in the curriculum and, in particular, in teaching and learning English as a second language, together with its possible effects on cognitive development, students' motivation and collaboration.

This preliminary study aims to represent only a first step towards the implementation of DST in the classroom but, due to the satisfactory exploratory results gained, it attempts to shed new light on instructional strategies in the context of SLA.

References

1. Bruner, J.S.: Actual Minds, Possible Worlds. Harvard University Press, Cambridge (1986)
2. Dagut, M., Laufer, B.: Avoidance of phrasal verbs – a case for contrastive analysis. Stud. Second Lang. Acquisition **7**(01), 73 (1985)

3. Fosnot, C.T.: Constructivism: Theory, Perspectives, and Practice, 2nd edn. Teachers College Press, New York (2005)
4. Garcia, P., Skehan, P.: A cognitive approach to language learning. TESOL Q. **33**(4), 769 (1999). https://doi.org/10.2307/3587891
5. Gardner, D., Davies, M.: Pointing out frequent phrasal verbs: a corpus-based analysis. TESOL Q. **41**(2), 339–359 (2007). https://doi.org/10.1002/j.1545-7249.2007.tb00062.x
6. Hoang, H., Boers, F.: Re-telling a story in a second language: how well do adult learners mine an input text for multi word expressions? Stud. Second Lang. Learn. Teach. **6**(3), 513–535 (2016). https://doi.org/10.14746/ssllt.2016.6.3.7
7. Laufer, B.: The lexical plight in second language reading: words you don't know, words you think you know, and words you can't guess. In: Second Language Vocabulary Acquisition, pp. 20–34 (1997)
8. Li, J., Schmitt, N.: The development of collocation use in academic text by advanced L2 learners: a multiple case-study approach. In: Wood, D. (eds.) Perspectives on Formulaic Language: Acquisition and Communication, pp. 23–46. Continuum, London (2010)
9. Mayer, R.E.: A cognitive theory of multimedia learning. In: Mayer, R.E. (eds.) Multimedia Learning, pp. 41–62 (2012)
10. Meara, P.: The rediscovery of vocabulary. Second Lang. Res. **18**(4), 393–407 (2002)
11. Milner, B., Squire, L.R., Kandel, E.R.: Cognitive neuroscience and the study of memory. Neuron **20**, 445–468 (1998)
12. Prensky, M.: Digital natives, digital immigrants Part 1. On the Horizon **9**(5), 1–6 (2001)
13. Robin, B.R.: Digital storytelling: a powerful technology tool for the 21st century classroom. Theory Into Practice **47**(3), 220–228 (2008)
14. Schank, R.C.: Tell Me A Story: Narrative and Intelligence. Northwestern Univ. Press, Evanston (2000)
15. Smith, M.S.: Input enhancement in instructed SLA. Stud. Second Lang.e Acquisit. **15**(02), 165 (1993)
16. Van Patten, B.: Processing Instruction Theory, Research and Commentary. Routledge, New York (2015)
17. Wray, A.: Formulaic Language and Lexicon. Cambridge University Press, Cambridge (2005)
18. Yang, Y.C., Wu, W.I.: Digital storytelling for enhancing student academic achievement, critical thinking, and learning motivation: a year-long experimental study. Comput. Educ. **59**, 339–352 (2012)

Designing Learning Experiences for Interactive Digital Narrative Literacy: A New Paradigm

Emily Bell, Emily Coolidge Toker[(✉)], and Paul Hanna

Harvard University, Cambridge, MA 02138, USA
{emily_bell, phanna}@fas.harvard.edu,
emily_coolidgetoker@harvard.edu

Abstract. Leveraging librarians' expertise in the design and support of literacy programs, this workshop will provide a forum for educators and practitioners to critically examine the nature and role of interactive digital narrative literacy. Workshop participants will collaborate in the development of a framework of interactive digital narrative literacy competencies through critical examination of representative case studies.

Keywords: Digital narrative literacy · Interactive digital narratives
Media literacy · Critical information consumption

1 Workshop Description

1.1 Topic

All mediums of content delivery require of its users a particular set of skills necessary for comprehension, judgment, appropriate integration, and creative reproduction. The degree to which a medium could be considered 'fixed' has traditionally been the first consideration in considering material presented in it: the fixity of the printed word, and its primacy as a medium for the transmission of information, has for centuries determined the nature of narrative literacy. However, as interactive and immersive narratives are increasingly, and seamlessly, incorporated into our daily experiences, we often miss that moment of critical awareness formerly framed by opening a book. Identifying an authorial presence and remaining mindful of that positionality in today's interactive digital narratives is more difficult, and requires a more robust set of skills.

As librarians working with undergraduate and graduate students in the context of information (including digital) literacy, we see repeated patterns of digital natives who have reached adulthood having developed a facility with diverse content platforms, yet exhibit a certain lack of critical understanding necessary for the appraisal of the digital artifacts with which they interact. These artifacts, which range from commercial promotions to Pulitzer Prize-winning articles, from Google tools to games, or, increasingly, an amalgam of these and other formats, are less tolerant of passive users, even in immersive environments. In many cases, effective participation in an interactive digital narrative requires both increased self-awareness on the part of the user, and the tools necessary to develop informed critical awareness of the artifact(s) with which they interact. Platforms like ARIS (Augmented Reality and Interactive Storytelling) [1] are

R. Rouse et al. (Eds.): ICIDS 2018, LNCS 11318, pp. 638–641, 2018.
https://doi.org/10.1007/978-3-030-04028-4_75

democratizing authorship in ways that further emphasize the need for a deeper understanding of the relationship(s) between authorship and agency in interactive digital narratives.

Groups like Voyage Virtual use collaborative VR experiences to produce "powerful virtual media and marketing material" for large corporate clients, while another group, also called Voyage, creates collaborative, classroom-scale VR experiences designed to supplement the curriculum [2, 3]. At MIT, a team called Resonant Games has "identified the levers that impact user acquisition, revenue and retention" in support of platform agnostic multiplayer games [4]. The same team has recently published a book presenting principles for designing games that "are embedded in a long-form experience of exploration, discovery, and collaboration that takes into consideration the learning environment" [5]. Other permutations of this include 360-video, MMORPGs and other video games, transmedia storyworlds, virtual exchange, constructionist innovations in the virtual world, and AR.

So much effort is deployed by the authors of interactive digital narratives to minimize their existence that users require significant training to effectively parse the authority and content of interactive digital narrative experiences. Interactive digital narrative literacy requires the development of an aesthetic understanding of the artifact, its primacy (or lack thereof), and its origins in a historical and cultural context as well as a critical appreciation of the ideological nuance undergirding the experience writ large. Such aliteracy has the potential to promote the development of critical citizens, while supporting global citizenry and the further democratization of knowledge production and dissemination.

Working together, librarians and practitioners can pool their expertise to establish a foundational understanding of the nature and role of interactive digital narrative literacy and how this literacy can be created. In this workshop, we will identify the skills needed to evaluate interactive digital narratives and use the information literacy pedagogy techniques to critically examine a series of narratives with a view towards developing a set of recommendations for fostering these skills in others.

1.2 Goals

- Determine major skill sets required for interactive digital narrative literacy;
- Suggest definitions of terminology, such as 'novice' and 'expert', in each major skill set;
- Examine ways of identifying the ideological underpinnings of an interactive digital narrative;
- Consider new relationship(s) between users and authorial power.

1.3 Proposed Schedule and Format

Short presentation from organizers on the following foundational questions:

(1) How to help people determine the source of content
(2) The differences between individual and company authorship and how these affect the user's experience of an interactive digital narrative

(3) The nature of authorial agency in interactive digital narratives and potential new relationship(s) with authorial power

(4) How to determine the ideological nature of the content and its consequences for the narrative and the user

Small group work (2–4 individuals) considering the foundational questions in light of a particular case study.

Each group is given 10–15 min to present on their case study; group discussion to follow.

1.4 Expected Outcomes

This workshop will provide an opportunity for practitioners and digital literacy instructors to come together and consider the nature and role of interactive digital narrative literacy and how this literacy can be created through case studies submitted by interested participants. Each case study will contribute to a discussion of authorial and participant agency, authorship and ideological underpinnings, and related questions about the skills required to navigate an audiovisual/narrative matrix.

Responses will be compiled and shared with participants with an eye towards developing a more comprehensive approach to interactive digital narrative literacy.

2 Draft of Call for Participation

Join your peers and colleagues to discuss the nature and role of interactive digital narrative literacy. Research Librarians Emily Bell and Emily Coolidge Toker will provide initial insights, informed by years of experience in digital and media literacy development in academic libraries, into existing literacy frameworks and the special considerations introduced by artifacts employing interactive digital narratives. Paul Hanna, a graphic novel author and illustrator as well as a librarian, will provide initial insights into the audiovisual/narrative matrix as a means of understanding the complex relationships between content and medium.

Participants are encouraged (but not required) to submit an example of an interactive digital narrative which will be considered for inclusion in the hands-on portion of the workshop. These case studies will be used to provide a focus for small group discussion.

Innovation is limited by an audience's capacity to engage at a critical level. Come help us lay a foundation for increased audience capacity to engage with complex media artifacts. Broaden your understanding of your users and help build a foundation for creating a responsible, critically-aware global audience.

Questions for Case Study Submissions
Participants will be asked to submit potential case studies for discussion dissection exemplification. Organizers will choose four or five to work with, based on the number of expected participants.

1. Title of project
2. Author of project
3. Please describe the project (<250 words)
4. Why did you choose this project as a case study for interactive digital narrative literacy? (<250 words)
5. URL or other access point.

References

1. ARIS games Homepage. https://fielddaylab.org/make/aris/. Accessed 6 Aug 2018
2. Voyage Virtual Homepage. https://www.voyagevirtualmedia.com/. Accessed 31 July 2018
3. Voyage Homepage. https://www.etc.cmu.edu/projects/voyage/. Accessed 31 July 2018
4. Resonant Games. http://resonantgames.com/index.html. Accessed 2 Aug 2018
5. Klopfer, E., Haas, J., Osterweil, S., Rosenheck, L.: Resonant Games, Design Principles for Learning Games that Connect Hearts, Minds, and the Everyday. PubPub (2018). Avail through open access. https://www.resonant.games/pub/resonantgames. Accessed 5 Aug 2018

Co-constructing Cultural Heritage Through a Web-Based Interactive Digital Narrative

Nicole Basaraba(✉) iD

Trinity College Dublin, Dublin, Ireland
nicole.basaraba@adaptcentre.ie

Abstract. Cultural heritage institutions (CHIs), educators, and the creative industries are increasingly using digital media to engage audiences in new ways such as through edutainment and gamification. The Internet and social media have increased access to information and public participation in digital narratives, and CHIs are beginning to increase their focus on storytelling. This PhD explores how digital media can be used not only to engage and educate, but to foster the co-construction of cultural heritage narratives. Two key challenges are which media and modalities can/should be used to create a purposeful non-fiction IDN and how can public participation be incorporated while avoiding the issue of ludonarrative dissonance. A transdisciplinary approach is used to develop creation and evaluation frameworks for non-fiction IDNs which will be tested on the use case of the UNESCO World Heritage Australia Convict Sites.

Keywords: Interactive digital narrative · Cultural heritage tourism Multimodality · Participatory culture · Shared heritage

1 Introduction

This research examines the potential of interactive digital narrative (IDN) as one way to address the real-world challenges of fostering shared cultural heritage, increasing public participation in narrative creation, and a lack of existing narratives for cultural heritage tourists. Many digital humanities scholars focus on the preservation of historical and cultural heritage through various large-scale digitisation projects, which are also made accessible to the public, such as the Europeana Collections [1], but often become underutilised post-completion. The popularity of travel writing/blogging, "quit-work-to-travel" campaigns, and the "bucket list" travel mentality has significantly increased the volume of online travel content because non-industry professionals of diverse demographics are participating in narrative creation through social media in addition to travel

This PhD research is supported by the ADAPT Centre and is supervised by Drs. Owen Conlan, Jennifer Edmond, and Peter Arnds of Trinity College Dublin, Ireland.

R. Rouse et al. (Eds.): ICIDS 2018, LNCS 11318, pp. 642–645, 2018.
https://doi.org/10.1007/978-3-030-04028-4_76

guide publishers, journalists and professional writers [2]. This cross-media content creates mass amounts of fragmented information that cultural heritage tourists need to hunt, gather, decipher and piece together. Cultural heritage tourism, a subcategory of tourism, involves traveling to a location for the sake of experiencing its history, landscape, and culture [3]. Cultural heritage tourists tend to seek local heritage through archaeological sites, historic landscapes, local architecture, museums, art expressions, traditions and practices of the past [4]. Recognising the shift towards digital culture, CHIs are digitising their materials, creating virtual tours, and personalised experiences for the public to see and experience history and culture [5]. However, heritage is socially constructed, and heritage meanings and values are not attached to artefacts, buildings, or sites nor are they frozen in time; they result from ongoing interactions of ordinary people in the lived world [6]. IDNs present an opportunity to tell complex narratives, increase interest in and respect of cultural heritage, create digital access where physical access cannot be granted, democratise heritage by creating opportunities for different or underrepresented social groups to be recognised and recorded, and allow for evolving interpretations and public contributions to cultural heritage narratives.

The social construction of cultural heritage through IDNs raises the key challenge of avoiding ludonarrative dissonance–the feeling of detachment game players experience when their actions do not coincide with the narrative/story because the ludic structure works in opposition to its narrative structure [7]. A cultural heritage IDN needs to balance user agency with authorial control to produce persuasive emergent narratives, but IDNs are a still-developing area of scholarly research and, as Mateas and Stern (2005) explain, "there exists no theoretical framework that allows one to formally define the problem and solution criteria" [8]. Based on analyses of different IDN formats in fiction, Koenitz et al. [9] proposed an IDN theory comprised of the system–digital artefact with all potential narratives, process–user's interaction with the system, and product–unique or emergent narrative created by each user. The main question this research addresses is: how can a transdisciplinary approach expand IDN theory into creation and evaluation frameworks for multimodal, participatory narratives in the non-fiction genre? The non-fiction genre of focus for this use case being cultural heritage.

2   Expanding IDN Theory for Non-fiction

This research has taken a transdisciplinary approach by borrowing and adapting concepts and "tools" from media studies, narratology, and human-computer interaction to develop a theoretical framework for creating non-fiction IDNs that is bottom-up and iterative (an outline of this framework is included in this issue of the ICIDS 2018 proceedings), and a systematic framework for evaluating whether the IDN has met the pre-established rhetorical goals. The aim is for these frameworks to be understandable and deployable by academics and non-academics (e.g., CHIs, creative industries). These two frameworks involved establishing a transdisciplinary IDN vocabulary and a digital rhetorical communication model the–"Creator-*Produser* Transaction Model" (as detailed in chapters two and three of the thesis).

The majority of narratologists and game studies scholars focus on the fiction genre, but this IDN application looks at its potential for creating engaging and persuasive non-fiction narratives. The UNESCO World Heritage Australian Convict Sites were selected as a use case because: they are recognised as culturally significant to the world rather than a single culture; their designation involves a rigorous selection process based on a set of 10 criteria [10]; cultural heritage tourism is an area with identified gaps in digital storytelling (e.g., creator aptitude, personalisation); and the amount of existing cultural data/content is substantial enough for a large-scale analysis. It is argued that one use case is sufficient to test whether the IDN creation and evaluation frameworks are useable tools and because the scale of developing a single IDN beta version is considerable within a PhD timeframe. The IDN will be created as a website rather than as a mobile application because websites are the medium of choice for many publishers of tourism content and CHIs, they are easily editable allowing for an iterative design process and further user participation, and it mitigates issues of requiring cellular data for user testing or the dangers and logistics of location-based content delivery. In future work, the IDN could be expanded into a full working version, which could incorporate more new media technologies (e.g. AR, location-based services, etc.) and expand into a transmedia narrative.

3   Proposed Methodology for Use Case Testing

The mixed methodology for this IDN use case will draw upon cultural analytics because it involves analysing historical artefacts, digital visual culture, professional culture, artefacts created by non-professionals, how people use social media, and how social phenomena arise from social networks [11]. Once quantitative/qualitative user modelling for cultural heritage tourists is completed, a multimodal discourse analysis (MDA) [12] will be conducted to identify whether the hypothesised gaps or differences between professionally-produced and user-generated heritage content about the UNESCO Australian Convict Sites exists. The results of the user modelling research and MDA will be applied in the proposed non-fiction IDN creation framework as developed for this research in order to create bottom-up IDN protostories. The protostories will then be evaluated for accuracy by experts (e.g., museum curators, historians) and any edits or modifications required will be made before a beta IDN is tested on users. The proposed IDN evaluation framework will provide qualitative feedback on a variety of user-experience related questions and help determine whether the rhetorical goals were achieved. The next steps are to carry out these methods and begin data collection to inform the creation of a cultural heritage IDN on the Australian Convict Sites.

References

1. Europeana Collections (2018). https://www.europeana.eu/portal/en
2. TBEX: The Future of Travel Media. http://tbexcon.com/about/
3. Ungvarsky, J.: Heritage Tourism. Salem Press Encyclopaedia (2017)
4. Timothy, D.J., Nyaupane, G.P.: Protecting the past: challenges and opportunities (2009). In: Cultural Heritage and Tourism in the Developing World, pp. 34–55. Routledge (2017)
5. Ardissono, L., Kuflik, T., Petrelli, D.: Personalization in cultural heritage: the road travelled and the one ahead. User Model. User-Adap. Inter. **22**(1–2), 73–99 (2012)
6. Byrne, D.: Heritage as social action. In: Fairclough, G., Harrison, R., Schonfield, J., Jameson, J.H. (eds.) The Heritage Reader. Routledge, London (2008)
7. Hocking, C.: Ludonarrative Dissonance in Bioshock. Click Nothing. 7 October 2007. http://clicknothing.typepad.com/click_nothing/2007/10/ludonarrative
8. Szilas, N.: Reconsidering the role of AI in interactive digital narrative. In: Koenitz, H., Ferri, G., Haahr, M., Sezen, D., Sezen, T.I. (eds.) Interactive Digital Narrative: History, Theory, and Practice, pp. 136–149. Routledge, London (2015)
9. Koenitz, H., Haahr, M., Ferri, G., Sezen, T.I.: First steps towards a unified theory for interactive digital narrative. In: Pan, Z., Cheok, A.D., Müller, W., Iurgel, I., Petta, P., Urban, B. (eds.) Transactions on Edutainment X. LNCS, vol. 7775, pp. 20–35. Springer, Heidelberg (2013). https://doi.org/10.1007/978-3-642-37919-2_2
10. UNESCO. United Nations Education, Scientific and Cultural Organization. http://whc.unesco.org/en/criteria/
11. Manovich, L.: The science of culture? Social computing, digital humanities and cultural analytics. J. Cult. Analytics **10**(22148/16), 004 (2016)
12. O'Halloran, K.L.: Multimodal analysis and digital technology. In: Interdisciplinary Perspectives on Multimodality: Theory and Practice, Proceedings of the Third International Conference on Multimodality, Palladino, Campobasso (2009)

Leveraging on Transmedia Entertainment Education to Augment Tourists' Awareness Towards Social Issues

Mara Dionisio[1,2(✉)], Valentina Nisi[1], and Nuno Correia[2]

[1] Madeira-ITI, University of Madeira, Campus da Penteada,
9020-105 Funchal, Portugal
{mara.dionisio,valentina.nisi}@m-iti.org
[2] Faculdade de Ciencias e Tecnologia da Universidade Nova de Lisboa,
Campus da Caparica, Lisbon, Portugal
nmc@fct.unl.pt

Abstract. Stories are increasingly becoming an important technique to engage, inspire and gather audiences online and offline. Interactive technologies provide the tools to empower audiences to participate in new interactive storytelling experiences applied to tourism. We envisage that in this context transmedia entertainment-education experiences combining a compelling story with engaging technologies can expose tourists towards local pressing issues and social good while providing them with a rich entertaining and educating experience. We describe the research approach that leads to design and implementation of a bespoke transmedia entertainment education experience: *Fragments of Laura*. The experience was designed to encourage visitors to learn about Madeira's rich natural heritage and develop knowledge and awareness about its history and biodiversity.

Keywords: Transmedia Storytelling · Entertainment Education
Mobile technologies · Tourism experience · Research through design

1 Motivation and Objectives

Tourism is an activity within reach of millions enabling the travel and hosting industry to flourish globally, and destinations need to be able to offer for new innovative and compelling experiences [1, 2]. This research proposes to study the fields of Entertainment Education (EE) and story-driven entertainment such as Transmedia Storytelling (TS) in order to explore how they can be at the service of the tourism industry.

The overall research aim is, to analyze how can TS and EE approaches be combined into a unified framework that make tourists aware of concerns present in the destination's social context. By using a research by designing approach [3] our objective is: (1) To design tourist experience by using TS and EE approaches that conveys a socially responsible message regarding tourist destination; (2) Identify how to integrate and adapt current strategies and metrics to evaluate the impact of the designed experience. (3) Comprehensively study the tourist experience while engaging with the designed experience in the real-world context.

© Springer Nature Switzerland AG 2018
R. Rouse et al. (Eds.): ICIDS 2018, LNCS 11318, pp. 646–651, 2018.
https://doi.org/10.1007/978-3-030-04028-4_77

2 Building Blocks of the Theoretical Framework

2.1 Tourism and the Tourist Experience

The attitudes of people towards tourism as an experience and what to expect from it are continuously changing [1, 2]. Right now many tourists are in the quest for the "authentic experience", which has been widely debated within scholar community [4–6]. This quest is connected to "the modern discourse of anti-tourism" [7], translating into the desire of travelers to go beyond superficial tourism experiences and connect to locals and local knowledge [8]. The use of digital technologies has fostered a transformation of tourists experiences and expectations towards more meaningful complex and authentic ones [9–15]. Furthermore, in response to the tourist's quest for "authenticity" [1, 5] there is a current trend of applications and services designed to foster the connection between tourists and locals [7] where locals are turned into guides, offering travel experiences.

2.2 Entertainment Education and Transmedia Storytelling

Entertainment-Education (EE) is the process of purposely designing and implementing a media message to both entertain and educate in order to increase audience members' knowledge about an educational issue [16]. There is an opportunity to enhance the ubiquitous nature of entertainment to educate people [17] a subject that could contribute to this is Transmedia Storytelling (TS). Jenkins [18] defined it as: "A transmedia story unfolds across multiple media platforms with each new text making a distinctive and valuable contribution to the whole." TS is becoming a popular genre and a populated playground for storytellers to act in and create world-changing experiences.

While EE programs have been following mostly a traditional media approach TS has been taking advantage of the power of ubiquitous technologies making today's urban spaces augmented with digital information. We envisage that EE and TS experiences can play a role in sensitizing tourists towards local issues while providing rich entertaining and educating experiences. PE and IEM are the first steps in laying common grounds for the TS field still they lack a systematic documentation and validation of projects following these models. Hence, the research conducted leads to the need of a creating an unified framework that lays grounds to guide the design of experiences that involve entertainment, interpretation, education, personal grown of tourists.

The term: Pervasive Entertainment (PE) emerge as: "Transmedia Storytelling evolved" [19]. According to Pratten, stories matter need to be told to the right people at the right time so that they can have an impact on their lives and on the lives of those around them. In 2014 Nedra Kline Weinreich presented a further evolution of Pratten's equation: the Immersive Engagement Model (IEM), see Fig. 3 [20], with the addition of a behavior change component. The IEM ultimate goal is to create an experience that leads the audience in taking some sort of action as a result of being engaged and motivated.

3   Research Questions

The overall research goal of this work is: To understand if **TS and EE** approaches when combined into a **unified framework** improve the tourists **awareness** of issues present in the **destination's context**. To achieve this and based on the state of the art this research proposes an adaptation of the Pratten/Weindrech models into a new unified framework, called Transmedia Entertainment Education Experience Framework, see Fig. 1. The framework differences are justified by the special target audience, tourists. People when traveling for leisure purposes search for specific experiences [21] therefore the framework takes this into account aligning its offer with the tourists needs and expectations. Finally, the experience should take into account and reflect the destination social context challenges in order to achieve awareness.

Transmedia Entertainment Education Framework

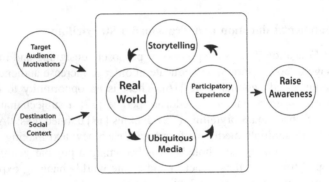

Fig. 1. Proposed framework for designing a transmedia entertainment education experience

The following research questions and objectives stimulate and underpin this enquiry:

RQ1 – What is the impact of a TEE Experience in the tourist experience?

RQ2 – Can a TEE Experience deliver a memorable tourist experience while raising awareness towards issues resent in the destination's context?

RQ3 – What current strategies and metrics can be adapted to evaluate a TEE tourist experience?

4   Case Study: Fragments of Laura a TEE Experience

A research prototype of a TEE experience was designed and implemented following the proposed framework, see Fig X called "Fragments of Laura" (FoL) it was shaped by Madeira's natural heritage - the Laurisilva Forest, which holds 'great importance for its biodiversity conservation' [22] that many tourists overlook. The design of FoL is currently composed by two interconnected components: mobile location-aware story and an online web platform. With mobile application, the goal is to engage the audience with its narrative, which invites the audience to embark on a quest to follow its heroine, Laura Silva with a unique talent and passion for taking care of nature. At the end of each plot point, an interview clip, synthesized from in-depth recorded conversations with local scientists and local knowledge holders, is proposed to the participant, who can choose to watch or save it for later viewing. The full version of the interviews is available in the web platform, which collects a variety of scientific facts about the island natural heritage, collected and edited as video clips and available online. The web platform is designed to deliver scientific and information while fostering a connection to the local community, creating empathy and respect regarding Madeiran heritage (Fig. 2).

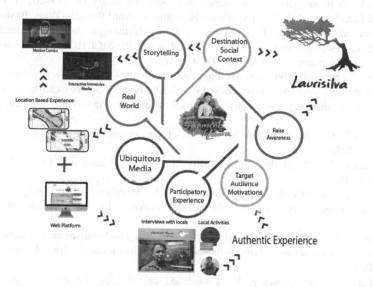

Fig. 2. FoL TEE experience components

4.1   Proposed Evaluation of TEEE Prototype

We plan to study the experience of at least 50 tourists interacting with the designed TEEE. Firstly, we'll conduct a pilot study to validate and refine the protocol. The protocol will involve a mixed method approach involving interviews, observation, pre and post-experience questionnaires that will address the role of the different TEE components contribution to the overall experience. Questionnaires that build upon current and established scales will be used such as:

Narrative Transportation Scale (NTS)
That Assess Participants' Ability to Be Transported into the Experience's Narrative [23].

Memorable Tourism Experience Scale

A reliable and valid instrument that touches upon ten experiential dimensions of the tourism experience: e.g. authentic local experiences; novel experiences; self-beneficial experiences; significant travel experiences; serendipitous and surprising experiences; fulfilment of personal travel interests and affective emotions [24].

AttrakDiffTM Questionnaire

That Can Assess FoL in Terms of the Overall User Experience [25].

References

1. Cohen, E.: A phenomenology of tourist experiences. Sociology **13**, 179–201 (1979)
2. Pine, B.J., Gilmore, J.H.: The Experience Economy. Harvard Business Press, Boston (2011)
3. Zimmerman, J., Forlizzi, J., Evenson, S.: Research through design as a method for interaction design research in HCI. In: Proceedings of the SIGCHI Conference on Human Factors in Computing Systems, pp. 493–502. ACM (2007)
4. Dennett, A., Song, H.: Why tourists thirst for authenticity – and how they can find it. http://theconversation.com/why-tourists-thirst-for-authenticity-and-how-they-can-find-it-68108
5. Wang, N.: Rethinking authenticity in tourism experience. Ann. Tour. Res. **26**, 349–370 (1999)
6. MacCannell, D.: The Tourist: A New Theory of the Leisure Class. University of California Press, Berkeley (1976)
7. van Nuenen, T.: The production of locality on peer-to-peer platforms. Cogent Soc. Sci. **2**, 1215780 (2016)
8. Paulauskaite, D., Powell, R., Coca-Stefaniak, J.A., Morrison, A.M.: Living like a local: authentic tourism experiences and the sharing economy. Int. J. Tour. Res. **19**, 619–628 (2017)
9. Buhalis, D., Law, R.: Progress in information technology and tourism management: 20 years on and 10 years after the Internet—the state of eTourism research. Tour. Manag. **29**, 609–623 (2008)
10. Prahalad, C.K., Ramaswamy, V.: Co-creation experiences: the next practice in value creation. J. Interact. Mark. **18**, 5–14 (2004)
11. Stamboulis, Y., Skayannis, P.: Innovation strategies and technology for experience-based tourism. Tour. Manag. **24**, 35–43 (2003)
12. Neuhofer, B., Buhalis, D., Ladkin, A.: Technology as a catalyst of change: enablers and barriers of the tourist experience and their consequences. In: Tussyadiah, I., Inversini, A. (eds.) Information and Communication Technologies in Tourism 2015, pp. 789–802. Springer, Cham (2015). https://doi.org/10.1007/978-3-319-14343-9_57
13. Neuhofer, B., Buhalis, D., Ladkin, A.: A typology of technology-enhanced tourism experiences. Int. J. Tour. Res. **16**, 340–350 (2014)
14. Tussyadiah, I.P.: Toward a theoretical foundation for experience design in tourism. J. Travel Res. **53**, 543–564 (2014)
15. Wang, D., Park, S., Fesenmaier, D.R.: The role of smartphones in mediating the touristic experience. J. Travel Res. **51**, 371–387 (2012)
16. Singhal, A., Rogers, E.M.: The entertainment-education strategy in communication campaigns. Public Commun. Campaigns **3**, 343–356 (2001)
17. Singhal, A., Rogers, E.: Entertainment-Education: A Communication Strategy for Social Change. Routledge, Abingdon (2012)

18. Jenkins, H.: Convergence Culture: Where Old and New Media Collide. New York University Press, New York (2006)
19. What is Pervasive Entertainment? – Transmedia Storyteller. http://www.tstoryteller.com/what-is-pervasive-entertainment
20. The Immersive Engagement Model: Transmedia Storytelling for Social Change. http://www.social-marketing.com/immersive-engagement.html
21. Pine, B.J., Gilmore, J.H.: The Experience Economy: Work is Theatre & Every Business a Stage. Harvard Business Press, Boston (1999)
22. Laurisilva of Madeira: World Heritage Centre. In: Periodic Report - Section II (2014)
23. Green, M.C., Brock, T.C.: The role of transportation in the persuasiveness of public narratives. J. Pers. Soc. Psychol. **79**, 701–721 (2000)
24. Chandralal, L., Valenzuela, F.-R.: Memorable Tourism Experiences: Scale Development. Contemp. Manag. Res. **11**, 291–310 (2015)
25. User Experience Questionnaire Handbook Version 2. https://www.researchgate.net/publication/303880829_User_Experience_Questionnaire_Handbook_Version_2

Folklore and Digital Media: Unpacking the Meaning of Place Through Digital Storytelling

Tanis Grandison^(✉) (ORCID)

Edinburgh Napier University, Edinburgh EH10 5DT, UK
t.grandison@napier.ac.uk

Abstract. This research investigates how digital folklore and digital media can be used as a method to unpack the meaning of place and to discover personal geographies of place. The research focuses on Wester Hailes, a deprived area to the West of Edinburgh. This research combines a critical heritage approach with psychogeography to elicit folklore from Wester Hailes school children. The paper argues that this inter-disciplinary approach affords children with competencies to create their own stories through physical computing and digital storytelling techniques.

Keywords: Psychogeography · Physical computing · Co-creation
Digital media · Critical heritage

1 Introduction and Background

1.1 Wester Hailes

Deemed as one of the most deprived areas of Scotland [1], Wester Hailes lies approximately 5.5 miles West of Edinburgh city-center. The area's reputation and folklore consistently revolve around the themes of crime, poverty, drug abuse and undesirable individuals [2]. The studies undertaken in this research are in collaboration with a local arts organization WHALE Arts, established in the area for over 25 years. WHALE Arts have recently recruited a new role, that of Creative Placemaker, a position that has been agreed for three years. The Creative Placemaker aims to develop digital technology as a key method in the Placemaking process. Reflecting on recent research with school children from the area, this research investigates how digital media and folklore can been used as a method for unpacking individual place-based meanings.

The research explores the ways in which the creation of digital folklore through participatory mapping exercises can lead to communities of practice [3]. Research suggests that collective emotion is fostered through a shared interest in both the medium and the stories involved in the co-creation of place [4].

© Springer Nature Switzerland AG 2018
R. Rouse et al. (Eds.): ICIDS 2018, LNCS 11318, pp. 652–656, 2018.
https://doi.org/10.1007/978-3-030-04028-4_78

1.2   Digital Folklore and Digital Media

Folklore consists of two main components. The Folk; defined as two or more people with a commonality. Lore, delineated into four broad categories of Things we (i) Say, (ii) Do, (iii) Make and (iv) Believe [5]. For something to be folklore it needs to be 'traditional'. In this context, this means that it needs to be passed on through time in some way, by methods such as sharing on social media [5]. In this way, we can understand folklore as *flow* rather content; this emphasis allows for an understanding of how flow might be transposed onto digital media. In the context of digital media, the flow of folklore is key because it affords individuals methods of appropriating place-based narratives in ways that are meaningful to them; thereby making folklore a "living category" [6]. This livedness is demonstrated through modifications and repetitions of a folk group [6].

1.3   Critical Heritage

Critical Heritage occupies a counter-position in relation to mainstream heritage and the tourism industry with which it is associated [7]. Critical Heritage can be understood as oppositional to Authorised Heritage Discourse (AHD) which constructs categories of value, systems of protection and cultural identity. AHD is also associated with an educational imperative whether through heritage sites, museums or digital resources. As the dominant heritage discourse in society AHD often leads to an authoritative singular 'expert' voice which can exclude narratives that do not align with wider issues of national identity and cultural institutions. AHD necessarily excludes more complex narratives that belong to minority groups whose histories are not formally recognised through funding or institutional systems [7]. Winter [8], argues that the critical element of Critical Heritage should go further to address social issues. He argues that we need to recognise the impact heritage can have on issues such as the socio-political and environment.

Digital media has created a shift from audiences as observers to creators and producers [9]. This shift is significant in the production and consumption of heritage. Gürel's [10] examination of Xerox folklore proposed that digital technology is no longer the medium used solely to consume folklore, instead it can also be used as a tool to produce new folklore. Using digital media to share their collective stories through interactive drawings on a co-created map, participants were able to articulate a counter heritage.

The evolving use of digital media within Critical Heritage affords numerous opportunities for exploring narratives, spaces and identity in a variety of ways. Collaborative Methods such as the co-creative mapping workshops undertook as part of this study afforded participants a platform to reveal the significance of local places. These methods facilitate a more plural approach to the identity of place wherein a poly vocal narrative of place opens up multiple identities and interactions [11] Modern practice employing Digital Media "do not obscure but bring to the fore the character of place as the very matrix out of which human significance and meaning arise" [12].

1.4   Gap in Knowledge

Critical Heritage has previously been informed by digital media, most notably The Center for Digital Storytelling [13]. However, there are opportunities to further understand the process of Critical Heritage, digital storytelling and meaningful geographies as a collaborative approach with community organisations and not as a means of eliciting creative storytelling.

2   Digi-Mapping Pilot Study

The Digi-Mapping project is a participatory design project that initially took place over six weeks in collaboration with Clovenstone Primary School, WHALE Arts and Dr. Tom Flint. The project uses mapping to elicit memories, feelings and stories (folklore) about the local area. This project is the first in a series of three similar projects being conducted with primary school children in Wester Hailes. Using various media such as audio recording, photography, drawing and storytelling. This project is in partnership with primary school children collaboratively creating a large interactive map using Bare Conductive 'Touch Boards' to tell their stories. The 'Touch Boards' have capacitive touch sensors that enable sound files to be triggered that are stored on a micro SD card. The 'Touch boards embedded circuitry lets participants play these sounds stored on the micro SD card using an attached speaker.

Part of this project took place outdoors in the form of a derive, a method of spatial enquiry rooted in psychogeography [14], which can broadly be defined as "the study of the precise laws and specific effects of the geographical environment, consciously organized or not, on the emotions and behavior of individuals" [14].

Using this method, the children recorded stories of importance to them, feelings and memories of places they had identified as meaningful (Fig. 1).

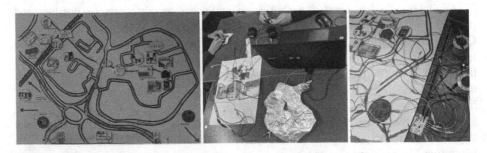

Fig. 1. Final map and development in workshops

2.1   Findings

From the first pilot study several observations have emerged, helping to shape the final empirical research approach.

Firstly, the workshop itself; (i) Children were engaged with digital media and can learn it in a relatively short period of time which is shaping the timeframe of the workshops. (ii) After demonstrating the 'Touch Boards' and conductive materials, creative enquiry quickly began with some of the pupils. They began testing as many metallic materials as they could find to see if they could be an audio trigger for their stories. Examples of this included paper clips, staples and even the zip on a jacket were tested for interactivity. (iii) Having conversations and encouraging participants to be creative with their storytelling helps the research to consider other creative methods of storytelling through folklore.

Secondly, some of the children that co-created the map were invited to demonstrate what they had learned at Edinburgh Mini Maker Faire 2018. It is unlikely that children from Wester Hailes would venture into the city to see the Mini Maker Faire, let alone take part. They were given a large map of Scotland and various sounds with the aim of demonstrating how to create interactive touch sounds. With very little support they took charge of their exhibit and were enthusiastic in helping others. In a short period of time, the children became confident computing demonstrators.

Lastly, from the evaluation of the workshop, children commented on how they found the experience; comments such as "made me want to learn science", "imaginative", "Phenomanal [sic] and Brilliant" and "extrordnery [sic] fun", and "hard but easy" showed that children engaged and enjoyed the workshop's and that the workshop's design appropriate, fun and learning is suited to the age range.

3 Next Steps

The next stages for this research project is to carry out the Digi-Mapping project in another two primary schools in the local area. From these studies, themes of meaning can begin to be identified of community attitudes to meaningful places.

Building on the workshop structure from the Digi-Mapping project and using similar methods, the next series of workshops will focus on memories, stories and feelings about the local community-built huts which were important places to the community in Wester Hails. Children will be tasked with finding out about these huts and imagining what they would be like today and in the future. They are to tell their stories using Augmented Reality authoring software and placing their stories onto one of the remaining huts in the local area. The cumulation of this research aims to propose a method and for unpacking meaning of places by using folklore, psychogeography and sharing stories through digital media tools.

References

1. SIMD. https://www.gov.scot/Topics/Statistics/SIMD. Accessed 5 July 2018
2. Anderson, S. et.al.: Cautionary Tales: Young People, Crime and Policing in Edinburgh, Avebury, UK (1994)
3. Wegner.   http://wenger-trayner.com/introduction-to-communities-of-practice/.   Accessed 1 July 2018

4. Combes, M.: Gilbert Simondon and the Philosophy of the Transindividual. MIT Press, Cambridge (2013)
5. McNeil, L.: Folklore Rules. Utah State University Press, Colorado (2013)
6. Krawczyk- Wasilewska, V.: Folklore in the Digital Age: Collected Essays. Łódź University Press, Krakow (2017)
7. Smith, L.: Uses of Heritage. Taylor & Francis, Oxon (2006)
8. Winter, T.: Clarifying the critical in critical heritage studies. Int. J. Herit. Stud. **19**(6), 532–545 (2012)
9. Lister, M., et al.: New Media: A Critical Introduction, 2nd edn. Routledge, Oxon (2009)
10. Gurel, P.: Folklore Matters: The Folklore Scholarship of Alan Dundes and the New American Studies [ebook]. http://columbia.edu/cu/cjas/print/folklore_matters.pdf. Accessed 4 July 2018 (n.d.)
11. Farman, J.: Mobile media stories and the process of designing contested landscapes. In: Papacharissi, Z. (ed.) A Networked Self and Platforms, Stories, Connections. Routledge, New York (2018)
12. Storycenter. https://www.storycenter.org/. Accessed 24 July 2018
13. Malpas, J.: New media, cultural heritage and the sense of place: mapping the conceptual ground. Int. J. Herit. Stud. **14**(3), 197–209 (2008)
14. Debord, G.: Introduction to a Critique of Urban Geography [ebook] (1955). http://www.praxis-epress.org/CGR/3-Debord.pdf. Accessed 1 July 2018

Interactive Comic-Based Digital Storytelling for Self-expression

Carolina Beniamina Rutta[1,2(✉)], Gianluca Schiavo[1], and Massimo Zancanaro[1]

[1] Fondazione Bruno Kessler, Trento, Italy
{rutta,gschiavo,zancana}@fbk.eu
[2] Università degli Studi di Trento, Trento, Italy

Abstract. The Ph.D. project explores how a digital tool for comic-based storytelling can support young migrants and teenagers in producing and elaborating narratives for self-expression in the form of counterstories. Migrants and teen-agers are two communities that have few outlets to express themselves when discriminant situations occur. On one hand, migrants who arrive in a host country often experience episodes in which they are stereotyped and discriminated, and not many supports assist them in reflecting on their condition. On the other hand, teenagers have few means to critically structure their reality prospective regarding discriminant situations. In this stage of the research project, we investigate how a digital system can support self-expression and counterstory elaboration, using comic-based storytelling and the use of predefined text and incipits to facilitate this process.

Keywords: Digital storytelling · Migrants · Teenagers · Stereotypes Counterstories

1 Introduction

Both young migrants and teenagers experience or witness discriminant situations related to cultural, sociological and historical dissimilarities among different communities. On one hand, migrants are often perceived as potential threat by the host society and they experience firsthand situations in which they are victims of stereotypes [21]. On the other hand, teenagers are inclined to perceive current phenomena through other sources (media, parents, friends or teachers), and they do not have outlet to build their personal perspective [1]. In this context, it might be useful to provide a tool that can assist the two communities to face with these situations.

The research project proposes interactive digital storytelling based on comics as supportive communication practice through which young migrants and teenagers can express themselves and reflect on discriminant situations. In particular, the approach is grounded on the philosophical framework of master narratives and counterstories [2]. Master narratives are stories that exercise a captive force over a powerless group damaged their identity, while counterstories

© Springer Nature Switzerland AG 2018
R. Rouse et al. (Eds.): ICIDS 2018, LNCS 11318, pp. 657–661, 2018.
https://doi.org/10.1007/978-3-030-04028-4_79

are defined as stories that resist an oppressive identity and attempt to replace the master narrative with one that commands respect. In this context, young migrants and teenagers, assimilating the dominant master narratives, do not practice their agency freely, limiting their reflection on the on stereotyped situations [2].

2   Storytelling and Counterstories

The master narrative and counterstory concepts were introduced in many studies to explain the elaboration processes through which powerless communities freely restore moral agency [3–7]. For example, Hanne Thommesen [3] examines the role of master narratives in self-narratives told by people with both mental health and drug problems. She highlights that the personal stories are infiltrated and dominated by master narratives about drug abuser. Hume [4] investigates the construction and impact of the master narrative on breast cancer patients, focusing on how their counterstories, which resist and replace the master narrative, reconstruct the powerless community identities, and restore moral agency. Espino [5] uncovers and contextualizes his own experience as a Mexican American Ph.D. can resist and reproduce power relations, racism, sexism, and classism through master narratives constructed by the dominant culture to justify low rates of Mexican American educational attainment. The process of elaborating the master narratives in counterstories was also used among seniors in the field of narrative gerontology study [6], among teenagers in a primary literacy classroom [7], among women, transsexual, and lesbian [2], focusing on how these communities resist oppressive discriminant condition.

In the literature, Digital Storytelling has been applied in different contexts as a means for self-expression, such in education [8–11], health [12,13], and social change [14]. In the same way, the power of comic for self-expression was studied in many works regarding the community of students [15,16], educators [17] and in health-focus project [19]. However, to our knowledge there are no studies that investigated the role that digital storytelling can have in supporting the elaboration of master narratives and counterstories.

3   Research Question

The research question addressed in the Ph.D. project is the following:

How does a digital tool can support young migrants and teenagers in producing storytelling for self-expression and for elaborating counterstories?

The research projects uses an existing tool, called *Communics* [18], to explore this research question. Specifically, *Communics* is based on the use of comics as a medium to create narrations, and pre-defined graphical and textual elements to support the elaboration of counterstories. On one hand, comic represents a complete medium for the self-expression, as a result of the combination of both graphical and textual elements, the logical structure, and the enjoyable aspect (see the literature above). On the other, pre-defined textual elements, included in a library, can facilitate to overcome the "blank page syndrome" (in which an author finds difficulties to come up with ideas to produce a story) and to provide help to create counterstories. Still, incipits were introduced in *Communics* to facilitate the start of the story.

4 Result: The Migrants' Community

The first target group of our research consists of young migrants. In order to build both graphical (backgrounds, objects, characters and emoticons) and textual pre-defined content to be included in *Communics*, we collected a number of discriminant situations against migrants' community, viewed as master narratives, interviewing 9 NGO professionals and 6 young migrants. Following this first phase, we involved 16 young migrants in elaborating digital narratives created with *Communics*, investigating the form, content and counterstory elements of the 32 (2 for each participant) narratives produced.

The empirical results show that, firstly, the use of pre-defined text facilitate the creative process for the self-expression and the overcoming of the "blank page syndrome", although the impact on the counterstories production has to be further investigated in future studies. Secondly, the comic medium was perceived as useful to produce storytelling. Thirdly, the incipit was considered functional to start the story-telling. In conclusion, comics, pre-defined libraries and incipit seem promising in supporting the young migrants in elaborating the plot of their narratives.

5 Future Plan: The Teenagers' Community

For the second phase, a longitudinal intervention will be planned in four high schools involving teenagers and their teachers in elaborating and reflecting on the conflict among migrants and local population. *Communics* will be used by small groups of students to elaborate master narratives and counterstories. With this intervention, we aim at assessing the opportunities and limitation of *Communics* in a more structured approach.

References

1. York, C., Scholl, R.M.: Youth antecedents to news media consumption: parent and youth newspaper use, news discussion, and long-term news behavior. Journal. Mass Commun. Q. **92**(3), 681–699 (2015)
2. Nelson, H.L.: Damaged Identities, Narrative Repair. Cornell University Press, Ithaca (2001)
3. Thommesen H.: Master narratives and narratives as told by people with mental health and drug problems. J. Comp. Soc. Work **5**(1) (2015)

4. Hume J. C.: Unthink pink: master narratives and counterstories of breast cancer. Electronic Theses and Dissertations, Paper 2659 (2017)
5. Espino M.M.: Master Narratives and Counter-Narratives: An Analysis of Mexican American Life Stories of Oppression and Resistance along the Journeys to the Doctorate. Ph.D. dissertation, Center for the Study of Higher Education, University of Arizona, (2008)
6. De Medeiros, K.: Narrative gerontology: countering the master narratives of aging. Narr. Works Issues Invest. Interv. **6**(1), 63–81 (2016)
7. Kelly, L.B.: Welcoming counterstory in the primary literacy classroom. J. Crit. Thought Prax. **6**(1), 4 (2017)
8. Umaschi M.: SAGE storytellers: learning about identity, language and technology. In: Proceedings of the 1996 International Conference on Learning Sciences, pp. 526–531 (1996)
9. Marn, V.I., Tur, G., Challinor, J.: An interdisciplinary approach to the development of professional identity through digital storytelling in health and social care and teacher education. Soc. Work Educ. **37**(3), 396–412 (2018)
10. Müller, W., Iurgel, I., Otero, N., Massler, U.: Teaching English as a second language utilizing authoring tools for interactive digital storytelling. In: Aylett, R., Lim, M.Y., Louchart, S., Petta, P., Riedl, M. (eds.) ICIDS 2010. LNCS, vol. 6432, pp. 222–227. Springer, Heidelberg (2010). https://doi.org/10.1007/978-3-642-16638-9_28
11. Kelleher, C.: Supporting storytelling in a programming environment for middle school children. In: Iurgel, I.A., Zagalo, N., Petta, P. (eds.) ICIDS 2009. LNCS, vol. 5915, pp. 1–4. Springer, Heidelberg (2009). https://doi.org/10.1007/978-3-642-10643-9_1
12. Bers, M.U., Gonzalez-Heydrich, J., DeMaso, D.R.: Identity construction environments: supporting a virtual therapeutic community of pediatric patients undergoing dialysis. In: Proceedings of the SIGCHI Conference on Human factors in Computing Systems, pp. 380–387 (2018)
13. Mamykina, L., Miller, A.D., Mynatt, E.D., Greenblatt, D.: Constructing identities through storytelling in diabetes management. In: Proceedings of the SIGCHI Conference on Human Factors in Computing Systems, pp. 1203–1212 (2010)
14. Dimond, P.J., Dye, M., LaRose, D., Bruckman, A.S.: Hollaback!: the role of collective storytelling online in a social movement organization. In: Proceedings of the 2013 Conference on Computer Supported Cooperative Work, pp. 477–490 (2013)
15. Andrews, D., Baber, C., Efremov, S., Komarov, M.: Creating and using interactive narratives: reading and writing branching comics. In: Proceedings of the SIGCHI Conference on Human Factors in Computing Systems, pp. 1703–1712 (2012)
16. Andrews, D., Baber, C.: Visualizing interactive narratives: employing a branching comic to tell a story and show its readings. In: Proceedings of the SIGCHI Conference on Human Factors in Computing Systems, pp. 1895–1904 (2014)
17. Herbst, P., Chazan, D., Chen, C.L., Chieu, V.M., Weiss, M.: Using comics-based representations of teaching, and technology, to bring practice to teacher education courses. ZDM **43**(1), 91–103 (2011)
18. Mencarini, E., Schiavo, G., Cappelletti, A., Stock, O., Zancanaro, M.: Assessing a collaborative application for comic strips composition. In: Abascal, J., Barbosa, S., Fetter, M., Gross, T., Palanque, P., Winckler, M. (eds.) INTERACT 2015. LNCS, vol. 9297, pp. 73–80. Springer, Cham (2015). https://doi.org/10.1007/978-3-319-22668-2_6
19. McNicol, S.: The potential of educational comics as a health information medium. Health Inf. Libr. J. **34**(1), 20–31 (2017)

20. Czerwiec, M.K., Huang, M.N.: Hospice comics: representations of patient and family experience of illness and death in graphic novels. J. Med. Humanit. **38**(2), 95–113 (2017)

21. Rapport, N.: Migrant selves and stereotypes: personal context in a postmodern world. In: Mapping the Subject: Geographies of Cultural Transformation, pp. 267–282 (1995)

Creating a Virtual Support Group in an Interactive Narrative: A Companionship Game for Cancer Patients

Alice Bowman[✉]

Abertay University, Bell Street, Dundee DD1 1HG, UK
1704646@abertay.ac.uk

Abstract. Over one in five cancer patients are affected by feelings of loneliness [1]. This paper proposes a text-based game aimed at affected cancer patients, in which the player develops relationships with non-player characters in the context of a fictitious cancer support group. This would be designed with the aim of alleviating patient loneliness and fostering a sense of companionship. This work is part of an interdisciplinary project led by Abertay University and partnered with Macmillan Cancer Support, exploring the ways in which interactive storytelling can be used to support cancer patients. The game's narrative and characters will be designed drawing on real patient experiences gathered in interviews. The game will go through several iterations of feedback and rewriting in response to focus groups held with patients and healthcare professionals.

1 Introduction

Cancer patients are often affected by feelings of loneliness and isolation. Macmillan Cancer Support published findings in 2014 that estimated more than one in five cancer patients (22%) experience loneliness [1]. These findings indicate that patients who have reported loneliness are three times more likely to struggle to follow their treatment plan than those who are not lonely. The research work described in this paper is part of an interdisciplinary project at Abertay University in partnership with Macmillan Cancer Support, the goal of which is to support cancer patients through interactive storytelling. The project detailed here aims to fulfil this goal through the development of a text-based game aimed at cancer patients affected by loneliness. The game's narrative will focus on developing positive relationships between the player and non-player characters in the context of a fictitious cancer support group, in order to establish a sense of companionship.

A. Bowman—I would like to thank Dr. Dayna Galloway, Prof. James Bown and Dr. Sonia Fizek for their guidance and feedback in writing this paper.

R. Rouse et al. (Eds.): ICIDS 2018, LNCS 11318, pp. 662–665, 2018.
https://doi.org/10.1007/978-3-030-04028-4_80

2   Research Questions

The overall project asks how interactive storytelling can be employed to support cancer patients. There are a multitude of problem areas in the lives of cancer patients that could be supported by digital tools, the problem areas of loneliness and isolation were chosen as the focus for this game for two reasons. Firstly, because of how widely reported these feelings are among cancer patients and the severity with which they can impact quality of life and prognosis [1]. Secondly, based on existing games and the relationships players are able to develop with characters [2], there is a strong case for hypothesising that a character focused text-game will be able to reduce loneliness and create feelings of support, and that such a game will be deliverable within the scope of this project.

The thesis being written parallel to the development of this game will not just focus on games for healthcare or games designed to combat loneliness. It will be centred around the question of how to create compelling, emotionally engaging game characters in a serious narrative context - with the proposed game being used as a case study. Within the bounds of this research a serious game narrative will refer to both serious games and other types of game in which the narrative features sensitive and/or mature themes. In Serious Games: Games That Educate, Train and Inform [3] serious games are defined as 'a game in which education (in its various forms) is the primary goal rather than entertainment.' The need for engaging and meaningful characters in this type of game arises from a necessity of the player being engaged and invested in the play experience in order for the game to achieve its goals.

3   Methodology

The first step in planning this project was assessing the user base in order to determine how a game would be able to provide support, and what issues to focus on. This was done through evaluation and thematic analysis of posts on cancer-related public Internet forums, patient blogs and video blogs, resources and information directed at patients, and various media aimed at cancer patients or telling the stories of cancer patients.

Based on this research user personas [4] were created. Patient statistics and the gathered materials on patient experiences were used together to design a sample of fictional cancer patients to represent the user base. Early design concepts for potential games were created in response to these personas, and ultimately a game to support lonely and isolated patients was chosen for development due to this preliminary research highlighting the prevalence and severity of these problems.

Semi-Structured interviews will be carried out with cancer patients, discussing their experiences since diagnosis. These interviews will be facilitated by Macmillan Cancer Support, and the information gathered here will be used to inform the narrative of the game. This will be done in order to gain a deeper understanding of patient lifestyle, and to give a clearer voice to the patients being represented in the game. In order for the game's fiction to be realistic and engaging patients must feel that the narrative is an accurate representation of their experiences.

With a design shaped by the data gathered in these interviews, the initial prototype of the game will be created using Twine 2 [5]. After the prototype is developed and playtested internally it will be presented to a focus group comprised of stakeholders with a background in healthcare. The purpose of this focus group will be to assess whether the game is at a stage to be used by patients, and to discuss any concerns the stakeholders raise. Patient wellbeing will remain the priority throughout the project, and so any concerns or criticism at this stage will be addressed in a new iteration of the game.

When the prototype is at a stage deemed suitable for patient playtesting another focus group will be created consisting of cancer patients. This group will be asked to complete a questionnaire assessing emotional state before and after playing the game, and will also be interviewed in order to gather feedback on the game. Patients will be asked to report back on playing the game over a period of two weeks, as well as giving feedback following a single play session. This data will be used as a preliminary indicator of the game's effectiveness, with patient feedback being incorporated into changes in the next iteration of the game.

Subject to positive indicators of the game's effectiveness the game will be launched on a wider scale. The game will be made available on iOS, android and the Internet. Data from these platforms will not be analysed beyond reference to player statistics due to the scale of the data. Parallel to this digital launch, the game will also be launched locally, with installations at community access points. Further evaluation of the game's effectiveness will be carried out in situ at these installations.

4   Prototype Design Outline

The thematic analysis carried out on Internet forum posts indicated that patients felt a deeper sense of support from others who had been through the same experiences and treatment, some writing that they felt only others who had been through these experiences could understand. The decision to set the game in the context of a support group was based off of this, the cast of non-player characters will be going through similar experiences to the player, this is intended to create a sense of empathy and camaraderie.

The dialogue options will be pre-defined rather than freeform text due to the scope of the project and limitations on resources. These dialogue options will branch the narrative, changing the response the player receives dependant on choice, the structure will then reconverge. Tracked variables will define different aspects of relationships between the player character and non-player characters, tracking their familiarity and dynamic, as well as accounting for the demonstrated personality of the player character. Passages of the game will vary depending of the state of certain variables.

The game will play in real time with game events following a pre-defined schedule, the player will receive notifications when a game event is playable or a non-player character tries to contact them. This aspect of the design draws inspiration from the Lifeline [6] series and Mystic Messenger [7]. Pacing the game in real time permits the game to be designed to fit with play patterns expected from the user persona, and will add a sense of realism to the game and interactions with non-player characters.

5   Next Steps

At the time of writing, patient interviews are scheduled to take place in September 2018. Once this data has been analysed writing for the prototype will begin. A working build of the prototype will be presented at the ICIDS 2018 Doctoral Consortium.

The version of the prototype will be a work in progress and writing for the initial iteration is scheduled to continue until February 2019. At this stage, feedback on the writing, branching structure and overall narrative of the design would be highly appreciated. The continued timescale of work on the prototype means that feedback and critique can be incorporated into later iterations.

Further steps on the project will include the cycle of playtesting, gathering feedback and iterating on the prototype, as detailed in the above methodology section. By working closely with cancer patients and healthcare professionals to hone the design, the project aims to deliver an interactive narrative that can quantifiably alleviate loneliness in cancer patients.

References

1. Macmillan: Lonely cancer patients three times more likely to struggle with treatment (2014). https://www.macmillan.org.uk/aboutus/news/latest_news/lonelycancerpatientsthreetimesmorelikelytostrugglewithtreatment.aspx. Accessed 18 July 2018
2. Waern, A.: I'm in love with someone that doesn't exist!! Bleed in the Context of a Computer Game'. Paper from the Nordic DiGRA Conference, Stockholm (2010). http://www.nordic-digra.org/nordicdigra2010_submission_18.pdf. Accessed 18 July 2018
3. Chen, S., Michael, D.: Serious Games: Games That Educate, Train and Inform. Course Technology PTR, Boston (2005)
4. Adlin, T., Pruitt, J.: The Persona Lifecycle: Keeping People in Mind Throughout Product Design. Morgan Kaufmann, Massachusetts (2005)
5. Klimas, C.: Twine 2 (Version 2.2.1) [Computer program] (2015). https://twinery.org/2/#!/stories. Accessed 20 July 2018
6. 3 Minute Games: Lifeline - iOS [Mobile game]. Big Fish Games (2015)
7. Cheritz: Mystic Messenger - iOS [Mobile game]. Cheritz Co., Ltd. (2016)

Author Index

Printed in the United States
By Bookmasters